The SABR
Baseball List & Record Book

Baseball's Most Fascinating Records
and Unusual Statistics

Edited by Lyle Spatz
Chairman, SABR Baseball Records Committee

SOCIETY FOR AMERICAN BASEBALL RESEARCH

SCRIBNER
New York London Toronto Sydney

SCRIBNER
A Division of Simon & Schuster, Inc.
1230 Avenue of the Americas
New York, NY 10020

First Scribner trade paperback edition March 2007

SCRIBNER and design are trademarks of Macmillan Library Reference USA, Inc.,
used under license by Simon & Schuster, the publisher of this work.

For information about special discounts for bulk purchases,
please contact Simon & Schuster Special Sales:
1-800-456-6798 or business@simonandschuster.com

Designed by Lisa Hochstein

Manufactured in the United States of America

1   3   5   7   9   10   8   6   4   2

Library of Congress Cataloging-in-Publication Data is available.

ISBN-13: 978-1-4165-3245-3
ISBN-10: 1-4165-3245-5

Contents

Introduction

THIS BOOK IS INTENDED TO FILL what we in SABR feel is a void in the reference publications that fans and media depend upon. It is not a record book in the sense that *The Sporting News Complete Baseball Record and Fact Book* and *The Elias Book of Baseball Records* are record books. And it is not an encyclopedia in the sense that *The ESPN Baseball Encyclopedia* or *Total Baseball* is. Nor is it in any way meant to compete with those most valuable resources. It is rather to supplement them, and the few overlaps that occur are minimal. So where TSN and Elias might show the record for "Most RBI in a Season by a Rookie," we have a list of every rookie who batted in at least 100 runs. And where *The Baseball Encyclopedia* shows the top 100 home run hitters, we might show the top 50 for right-handed batters, left-handed batters, and switch-hitters.

In addition to going deep into the leader lists, there will also be lists of things that fans and media people might wonder about, but would otherwise find difficult to locate. For instance, pitchers winning 20 games in a season they were traded, or the closest batting races ever, or every game-ending home run by a pitcher, or players who won a reverse Triple Crown (finishing last in their league in each of the Triple Crown categories). For a list to be included, it had to meet two requirements: (1) It it had to be technically correct, and (2) It it had to impart information that is interesting or meaningful.

The lists cover regular season play for the years 1876 to 2006. They include the National League, the American League, the American Association, the

Union Association, the Players League, and the Federal League. They do not include the National Association of 1871-1875, nor are there any lists devoted to the World Series or any other post-season achievements.

We like to think of baseball history as a seamless web, but in truth the first decade and a half or so after the formation of the National League in 1876 did not just differ from the modern game, but it differed by an order of magnitude. Obvious major differences included (for all or some of this period):

(1) Only rudimentary gloves

(2) Different number of balls for a walk

(3) No overhand pitching

(4) A shorter pitching distance

(5) One hurler pitching a majority of the team's innings

(6) Lack of an organized player procurement system

(7) Non-league teams jumping into (and often leaving) the league

For these reasons we decided to split many of the seasonal batting and pitching lists into pre- and post-1893 sections. We chose 1893, rather than 1900, as the dividing line because 1893 was the year the current pitching distance was established, and so for our purposes can be considered the beginning of the "modern" era. Additionally, splitting many of the lists into a before-1893 category and a since-1893 category, allows numerous pre-1893 era batters and pitchers, many of whom are not familiar to modern-day fans, to get the recognition they deserve. To make them more meaningful, given the tremendous changes in playing surfaces and gloves, among other variables, two seasonal fielding lists, those for worst fielding average and most errors by position, are limited to the years beginning with

1946. In general, fielding data has been the most difficult to collect and may contain some inconsistencies that at this point we are unable to resolve.

We used Pete Palmer and Gary Gillette's *ESPN Baseball Encyclopedia* as our final word on both statistics and as our style guide. All league and city abbreviations will be as they appear there. Same with players' names, with a few exceptions, some of which include a middle initial or a Sr. or Jr. to distinguish players with the same name. Thus we use Frank J. Thomas to identify the National League outfielder of the 1950s and 1960s, and Frank E. Thomas to identify the American League first baseman of the 1990s, currently still active.

Every list in this book was provided by and checked by a member of SABR's Baseball Records Committee. Some provided many lists, some a few, and some only one. The same occurred with the checking of lists: some checked many, some a few, and some only one. And some members both provided lists and checked others. I thank them all for their contributions. Apologizing in advance if I omit anyone, the contributors include: Mark Armour, Bill Carle, Steve Breen, Keith Carlson, Jim Charlton, Clem Comly, Bill Deane, Ted DiTullio, Jon Dunkel, Clay Eals, Sean Forman, Bill Gilbert, Steven Glassman, Tim Hannan, Dan Heisman, Jim Herdman, Gordon Hurlburt, Tom Kern, Jan Larson, Bob McConnell, Trent McCotter, Wayne McElreavey, Madison McEntire, Tom Meder, John O'Malley, Adam Palant, Doug Pappas, Brian Rash, John Rickert, Stephen Roney, Chuck Rosciam, Mitch Soivenski, David Smith, Jim Smith, Stew Thornley, Bob Tiemann, Stan Tyler, Walt Wilson, and Tom Zocco. Thanks also to those who sent me a single correction for a date, or a typo, or a transposed number they spotted in the preliminary tables.

Everett Cope and Dan Levitt deserve special mention for their numerous contributions, as does Records Committee vice-chairman Joe Dittmar, who checked every list in the book. I'd also like to thank Lisa Hochstein, Scott Flatow, and SABR Publications Director Jim Charlton. Lisa designed the tables, succeeding Glenn LeDoux and then Clay Eals; Scott did a general review, checking names and numbers for consistency; and Jim, in addition to contributing some lists and checking others, served as an advisor and sounding board throughout the whole process. Finally, many of the lists that appear here were provided by Pete Palmer and David Vincent. Without their help, cooperation, and generosity of spirit in sharing their knowledge, this book would not have been possible.

SABR membership is open to anyone with an interest in baseball history and/or statistics. Since you are reading this book, you qualify! Learn more about SABR at our website **www.sabr.org** or call **1-800-969-SABR** (7227) and ask that a brochure be mailed to you.

Lyle Spatz, Chairman
SABR Baseball Records Committee

ABBREVIATIONS

Leagues

AA	American Association (1882-1891)	NL	National League (1876-2006)
AL	American League (1901-2006)	PL	Players League (1890)
FL	Federal League (1914-1915)	UA	Union Association (1884)

Teams

ALT	Altoona	MIL	Milwaukee
ANA	Anaheim	MIN	Minnesota
ARI	Arizona	MON	Montreal
ATL	Atlanta	NEW	Newark
BAL	Baltimore	NY	New York
BOS	Boston	OAK	Oakland
BRO	Brooklyn	PHI	Philadelphia
BUF	Buffalo	PIT	Pittsburgh
CAL	California	PRO	Providence
CHI	Chicago	ROC	Rochester
CP	Chicago combined with Pittsburgh (UA 1884)	STL	St. Louis
		SD	San Diego
CIN	Cincinnati	SF	San Francisco
CLE	Cleveland	SEA	Seattle
COL	Columbus (AA 1883-84, 1889-91)	SYR	Syracuse
COL	Colorado (NL 1993-2006)	TB	Tampa Bay
DET	Detroit	TEX	Texas
FLA	Florida	TOL	Toledo
HAR	Hartford	TOR	Toronto
HOU	Houston	TRO	Troy
IND	Indianapolis	WAS	Washington
KC	Kansas City	WIL	Wilmington
LA	Los Angeles	WOR	Worcester
LOU	Louisville		

The SABR
Baseball List & Record Book

BATTING RECORDS

PHOTO: GEORGE BRACE

Batting Records

(001) Most Career Games Played

3562	Pete Rose	2709	Craig Biggio	2480	Nap Lajoie
3308	Carl Yastrzemski	2707	George Brett	2476	Max Carey
3298	Hank Aaron	2700	Graig Nettles	2472	Julio Franco
3081	Rickey Henderson	2687	Darrell Evans	2469	Rod Carew
3034	Ty Cobb	2683	Paul Molitor	2469	Vada Pinson
3026	Eddie Murray	2670	Rabbit Maranville	2466	Dave Parker
3026	Stan Musial	2649	Joe Morgan	2460	Fred McGriff
3001	Cal Ripken	2627	Andre Dawson	2456	Ted Simmons
2992	Willie Mays	2616	Lou Brock	2444	Bill Dahlen
2973	Dave Winfield	2606	Dwight Evans	2443	Omar Vizquel
2951	Rusty Staub	2599	Luis Aparicio	2442	Ron Fairly
2896	Brooks Robinson	2588	Willie McCovey	2440	Tony Gwynn
2860	Barry Bonds	2573	Ozzie Smith	2440	Wade Boggs
2856	Robin Yount	2549	Paul Waner	2436	Chili Davis
2834	Al Kaline	2540	Steve Finley	2435	Harmon Killebrew
2831	Rafael Palmeiro	2528	Ernie Banks	2433	Roberto Clemente
2830	Harold Baines	2517	Sam Crawford	2429	Willie Davis
2826	Eddie Collins	2517	Bill Buckner	2422	Luke Appling
2820	Reggie Jackson	2507	Gary Gaetti	2410	Zack Wheat
2808	Frank Robinson	2503	Babe Ruth	2409	Mickey Vernon
2794	Honus Wagner	2502	Tim Raines	2405	Buddy Bell
2789	Tris Speaker	2499	Carlton Fisk	2404	Mike Schmidt
2777	Tony Perez	2488	Dave Concepcion	2404	Sam Rice
2730	Mel Ott	2488	Billy Williams	2401	Mickey Mantle

(002) Most Career At-bats

14053	Pete Rose	10359	Craig Biggio	9589	Nap Lajoie
12364	Hank Aaron	10349	George Brett	9570	Sam Crawford
11988	Carl Yastrzemski	10332	Lou Brock	9538	Jake Beckley
11551	Cal Ripken	10230	Luis Aparicio	9507	Barry Bonds
11434	Ty Cobb	10195	Tris Speaker	9459	Paul Waner
11336	Eddie Murray	10116	Al Kaline	9456	Mel Ott
11008	Robin Yount	10078	Rabbit Maranville	9454	Roberto Clemente
11003	Dave Winfield	10006	Frank Robinson	9421	Ernie Banks
10972	Stan Musial	9949	Eddie Collins	9397	Bill Buckner
10961	Rickey Henderson	9927	Andre Dawson	9396	Ozzie Smith
10881	Willie Mays	9908	Harold Baines	9363	Max Carey
10835	Paul Molitor	9864	Reggie Jackson	9358	Dave Parker
10654	Brooks Robinson	9778	Tony Perez	9350	Billy Williams
10472	Rafael Palmeiro	9720	Rusty Staub	9315	Rod Carew
10439	Honus Wagner	9645	Vada Pinson	9303	Steve Finley

(003) Most Career At-bats by a Left-handed Batter

11988	Carl Yastrzemski	9538	Jake Beckley	9180	Wade Boggs
11434	Ty Cobb	9507	Barry Bonds	9174	Willie Davis
10972	Stan Musial	9459	Paul Waner	9140	Doc Cramer
10472	Rafael Palmeiro	9456	Mel Ott	9106	Zack Wheat
10349	George Brett	9397	Bill Buckner	9049	Al Oliver
10332	Lou Brock	9358	Dave Parker	8986	Graig Nettles
10195	Tris Speaker	9350	Billy Williams	8973	Darrell Evans
9949	Eddie Collins	9315	Rod Carew	8860	Charlie Gehringer
9908	Harold Baines	9303	Steve Finley	8785	Harry Hooper
9864	Reggie Jackson	9288	Tony Gwynn	8757	Fred McGriff
9720	Rusty Staub	9277	Joe Morgan	8731	Mickey Vernon
9645	Vada Pinson	9269	Sam Rice	8656	Goose Goslin
9570	Sam Crawford	9232	Nellie Fox		

(004) Most Career At-bats by a Right-handed Batter

12364	Hank Aaron	9927	Andre Dawson	8759	Al Simmons
11551	Cal Ripken	9778	Tony Perez	8756	Carlton Fisk
11008	Robin Yount	9589	Nap Lajoie	8723	Dave Concepcion
11003	Dave Winfield	9454	Roberto Clemente	8684	Bert Campaneris
10961	Rickey Henderson	9421	Ernie Banks	8618	Bobby Wallace
10881	Willie Mays	9104	Cap Anson	8587	Julio Franco
10835	Paul Molitor	9085	Lave Cross	8422	Joe Carter
10654	Brooks Robinson	9036	Bill Dahlen	8401	Sammy Sosa
10439	Honus Wagner	8996	Dwight Evans	8385	Ryne Sandberg
10359	Craig Biggio	8995	Buddy Bell	8352	Mike Schmidt
10230	Luis Aparicio	8951	Gary Gaetti	8304	Bid McPhee
10116	Al Kaline	8856	Luke Appling	8288	Alan Trammell
10078	Rabbit Maranville	8835	Steve Garvey	8275	Marquis Grissom
10006	Frank Robinson	8812	Tommy Corcoran	8225	Jim Rice

(005) Most Career At-bats by a Switch-hitter

14053	Pete Rose	8872	Tim Raines	7869	Bernie Williams
11336	Eddie Murray	8680	Ted Simmons	7731	Willie Wilson
9396	Ozzie Smith	8673	Chili Davis	7721	Garry Templeton
9363	Max Carey	8479	Red Schoendienst	7651	Don Kessinger
9112	Frankie Frisch	8418	Larry Bowa	7649	Willie McGee
9073	Roberto Alomar	8102	Mickey Mantle	7617	Tony Phillips
9045	George Davis	8044	Ruben Sierra	7588	Maury Wills
8966	Omar Vizquel	7911	Tony Fernandez		

If someone switch hit for most of his career, he is shown as a switch hitter on lists of career accomplishments.

(006) Most Career Plate Appearances

15890	Pete Rose	12037	Eddie Collins	11229	Rusty Staub
13992	Carl Yastrzemski	11988	Tris Speaker	11092	Harold Baines
13940	Hank Aaron	11949	Craig Biggio	10861	Tony Perez
13346	Rickey Henderson	11782	Brooks Robinson	10778	Ozzie Smith
13068	Ty Cobb	11748	Honus Wagner	10770	Max Carey
12883	Cal Ripken	11744	Frank Robinson	10769	Andre Dawson
12817	Eddie Murray	11625	George Brett	10762	Paul Waner
12712	Stan Musial	11597	Al Kaline	10740	Wade Boggs
12493	Willie Mays	11417	Reggie Jackson	10737	Darrell Evans
12358	Dave Winfield	11337	Mel Ott	10617	Babe Ruth
12249	Robin Yount	11329	Joe Morgan	10594	Sam Crawford
12167	Paul Molitor	11256	Rabbit Maranville	10569	Dwight Evans
12129	Barry Bonds	11240	Lou Brock	10550	Rod Carew
12046	Rafael Palmeiro	11230	Luis Aparicio	10519	Billy Williams

Plate Appearances=AB+BB+HBP+SF+SH+defensive interference.

(007) Most Career Plate Appearances by a Left-handed Batter

13992	Carl Yastrzemski	10762	Paul Waner	10232	Tony Gwynn
13068	Ty Cobb	10740	Wade Boggs	10226	Graig Nettles
12712	Stan Musial	10737	Darrell Evans	10184	Dave Parker
12129	Barry Bonds	10617	Babe Ruth	10174	Fred McGriff
12046	Rafael Palmeiro	10594	Sam Crawford	10101	Eddie Mathews
12037	Eddie Collins	10550	Rod Carew	10037	Bill Buckner
11988	Tris Speaker	10519	Billy Williams	9996	Zack Wheat
11625	George Brett	10504	Jake Beckley	9967	Lou Whitaker
11417	Reggie Jackson	10403	Vada Pinson	9933	Doc Cramer
11337	Mel Ott	10358	Steve Finley	9837	Fred Clarke
11329	Joe Morgan	10350	Nellie Fox	9834	Mickey Vernon
11240	Lou Brock	10246	Sam Rice	9822	Goose Goslin
11229	Rusty Staub	10244	Harry Hooper	9822	Willie Davis
11092	Harold Baines	10237	Charlie Gehringer		

(008) Most Career Plate Appearances by a Right-handed Batter

13940	Hank Aaron	11256	Rabbit Maranville	10009	Buddy Bell
13346	Rickey Henderson	11230	Luis Aparicio	9853	Carlton Fisk
12883	Cal Ripken	10861	Tony Perez	9831	Harmon Killebrew
12493	Willie Mays	10769	Andre Dawson	9817	Gary Gaetti
12358	Dave Winfield	10569	Dwight Evans	9742	Lave Cross
12249	Robin Yount	10460	Nap Lajoie	9670	Jimmie Foxx
12167	Paul Molitor	10405	Bill Dahlen	9640	Dave Concepcion
11949	Craig Biggio	10395	Ernie Banks	9625	Julio Franco
11782	Brooks Robinson	10243	Luke Appling	9625	Bert Campaneris
11748	Honus Wagner	10212	Roberto Clemente	9612	Bobby Wallace
11744	Frank Robinson	10123	Cap Anson	9560	Gary Sheffield
11597	Al Kaline	10062	Mike Schmidt	9515	Al Simmons

(009) Most Career Plate Appearances by a Switch-hitter

15890	Pete Rose	10178	George Davis	9109	Larry Bowa
12817	Eddie Murray	10100	Frankie Frisch	9053	Bernie Williams
10778	Ozzie Smith	9997	Chili Davis	8793	Tony Fernandez
10770	Max Carey	9909	Mickey Mantle	8782	Ruben Sierra
10400	Roberto Alomar	9685	Ted Simmons	8734	Donie Bush
10359	Tim Raines	9222	Red Schoendienst	8559	Ken Singleton
10207	Omar Vizquel	9110	Tony Phillips	8530	Don Kessinger

(010) Most Career Hits

4256	Pete Rose	3142	Robin Yount	2932	Willie Keeler
4189	Ty Cobb	3141	Tony Gwynn	2930	Rogers Hornsby
3771	Hank Aaron	3110	Dave Winfield	2930	Craig Biggio
3630	Stan Musial	3055	Rickey Henderson	2927	Al Simmons
3514	Tris Speaker	3053	Rod Carew	2884	Zack Wheat
3420	Honus Wagner	3023	Lou Brock	2880	Frankie Frisch
3419	Carl Yastrzemski	3020	Rafael Palmeiro	2876	Mel Ott
3319	Paul Molitor	3012	Cap Anson	2873	Babe Ruth
3315	Eddie Collins	3010	Wade Boggs	2866	Harold Baines
3283	Willie Mays	3007	Al Kaline	2850	Jesse Burkett
3255	Eddie Murray	3000	Roberto Clemente	2848	Brooks Robinson
3242	Nap Lajoie	2987	Sam Rice	2841	Barry Bonds
3184	Cal Ripken	2961	Sam Crawford	2839	Charlie Gehringer
3154	George Brett	2943	Frank Robinson	2812	George Sisler
3152	Paul Waner	2934	Jake Beckley		

(011) Most Career Hits by a Left-handed Batter

4189	Ty Cobb	2934	Jake Beckley	2712	Dave Parker
3630	Stan Musial	2884	Zack Wheat	2711	Billy Williams
3514	Tris Speaker	2876	Mel Ott	2705	Doc Cramer
3419	Carl Yastrzemski	2873	Babe Ruth	2678	Fred Clarke
3315	Eddie Collins	2866	Harold Baines	2663	Nellie Fox
3154	George Brett	2850	Jesse Burkett	2654	Ted Williams
3152	Paul Waner	2841	Barry Bonds	2584	Reggie Jackson
3141	Tony Gwynn	2839	Charlie Gehringer	2574	Richie Ashburn
3053	Rod Carew	2812	George Sisler	2561	Willie Davis
3023	Lou Brock	2757	Vada Pinson	2544	George Van Haltren
3020	Rafael Palmeiro	2743	Al Oliver	2531	Steve Finley
3010	Wade Boggs	2735	Goose Goslin	2524	Heinie Manush
2987	Sam Rice	2721	Lou Gehrig	2517	Joe Morgan
2961	Sam Crawford	2716	Rusty Staub		
2932	Willie Keeler	2715	Bill Buckner		

(012) Most Career Hits by a Right-handed Batter

3771	Hank Aaron	2930	Rogers Hornsby	2597	Ed Delahanty
3420	Honus Wagner	2930	Craig Biggio	2583	Ernie Banks
3319	Paul Molitor	2927	Al Simmons	2566	Julio Franco
3283	Willie Mays	2848	Brooks Robinson	2514	Buddy Bell
3242	Nap Lajoie	2774	Andre Dawson	2513	Jimmy Ryan
3184	Cal Ripken	2749	Luke Appling	2471	Joe Medwick
3142	Robin Yount	2732	Tony Perez	2461	Bill Dahlen
3110	Dave Winfield	2677	Luis Aparicio	2452	Jim Rice
3055	Rickey Henderson	2660	Harry Heilmann	2446	Dwight Evans
3012	Cap Anson	2651	Lave Cross	2416	Pie Traynor
3007	Al Kaline	2646	Jimmie Foxx	2405	Stuffy McInnis
3000	Roberto Clemente	2605	Rabbit Maranville		
2943	Frank Robinson	2599	Steve Garvey		

(013) Most Career Hits by a Switch-hitter

4256	Pete Rose	2460	Ozzie Smith	2152	Ruben Sierra
3255	Eddie Murray	2449	Red Schoendienst	2134	Maury Wills
2880	Frankie Frisch	2415	Mickey Mantle	2096	Garry Templeton
2724	Roberto Alomar	2380	Chili Davis	2029	Ken Singleton
2665	Max Carey	2336	Bernie Williams	2023	Tony Phillips
2665	George Davis	2276	Tony Fernandez	2020	Reggie Smith
2605	Tim Raines	2254	Willie McGee	2010	Bobby Bonilla
2472	Ted Simmons	2207	Willie Wilson	2004	Dave Bancroft
2472	Omar Vizquel	2191	Larry Bowa		

(014) More Career Games Played than Plate Appearances by Non-pitchers, since 1900 (min. 100 G)

	YEARS	GAMES	PA
Matt Alexander	1973-1981	374	195
Charles Gipson	1998-2005	373	358
Glen Barker	1999-2001	235	197
Jack Reed	1961-1963	222	144
Allan Lewis	1967-1970, 72-73	156	31
Ross Moschitto	1965, 1967	110	39
Herb Washington	1974-1975	105	0

(015) Players with 3,000 Hits

			PITCHER					
Cap Anson	NL	CHI	Dad Clarke	LOU	Sep	19	1897	
Honus Wagner	NL	PIT	Erskine Mayer	PHI	Jun	9	1914	
Nap Lajoie	AL	CLE	Marty McHale	NY	Sep	27	1914	1G
Ty Cobb	AL	DET	Elmer Myers	BOS	Aug	19	1921	
Tris Speaker	AL	CLE	Tom Zachary	WAS	May	17	1925	
Eddie Collins	AL	CHI	Rip Collins	DET	Jun	3	1925	
Paul Waner	NL	BOS	Rip Sewell	PIT	Jun	19	1942	
Stan Musial	NL	STL	Moe Drabowsky	CHI	May	13	1958	
Hank Aaron	NL	ATL	Wayne Simpson	CIN	May	17	1970	
Willie Mays	NL	SF	Mike Wegener	MON	Jul	18	1970	
Roberto Clemente	NL	PIT	Jon Matlack	NY	Sep	30	1972	
Al Kaline	AL	DET	Dave McNally	BAL	Sep	24	1974	
Pete Rose	NL	PHI	Steve Rogers	MON	May	5	1978	
Lou Brock	NL	STL	Dennis Lamp	CHI	Aug	13	1979	
Carl Yastrzemski	AL	BOS	Jim Beattie	NY	Sep	12	1979	
Rod Carew	AL	CAL	Frank Viola	MIN	Aug	4	1985	
Robin Yount	AL	MIL	Jose Mesa	CLE	Sep	9	1992	
George Brett	AL	KC	Tim Fortugno	CAL	Sep	30	1992	
Dave Winfield	AL	MIN	Dennis Eckersley	OAK	Sep	16	1993	
Eddie Murray	AL	CLE	Mike Trombley	MIN	Jun	30	1995	
Paul Molitor	AL	MIN	Jose Rosado	KC	Sep	16	1996	
Tony Gwynn	NL	SD	Dan Smith	MON	Aug	6	1999	
Wade Boggs	AL	TB	Chris Haney	CLE	Aug	7	1999	Home run
Cal Ripken	AL	BAL	Hector Carrasco	MIN	Apr	15	2000	
Rickey Henderson	NL	SD	John Thomson	COL	Oct	7	2001	
Rafael Palmeiro	AL	BAL	Joel Pineiro	SEA	Jul	15	2005	

(016) Youngest Players to Reach 1,000 Hits

YRS-MO-DAYS		DATE OF BIRTH	DATE OF HIT
24-4-25	Ty Cobb	Dec 18, 1886	May 13, 1911
24-5-2	Mel Ott	Mar 2, 1909	Aug 4, 1933
24-7-23	Al Kaline	Dec 19, 1934	Aug 11, 1959
24-8-10	Freddie Lindstrom	Nov 21, 1905	Jul 31, 1930
24-9-23	Buddy Lewis	Aug 10, 1916	Jun 2, 1941
24-11-0	Robin Yount	Sep 16, 1955	Aug 16, 1980

(017) Youngest Players to Reach 2,000 Hits

YRS-MO-DAYS		DATE OF BIRTH	DATE OF HIT
29-6-2	Ty Cobb	Dec 18, 1886	Jun 20, 1916
30-1-27	Rogers Hornsby	Apr 27, 1896	Jun 23, 1926
30-3-20	Mel Ott	Mar 2, 1909	Jun 22, 1939
30-5-7	Hank Aaron	Feb 5, 1934	Jul 12, 1964
30-9-19	Joe Medwick	Nov 24, 1911	Sep 12, 1942
30-10-4	Jimmie Foxx	Oct 22, 1907	Aug 26, 1938
30-11-21	Robin Yount	Sep 16, 1955	Sep 6, 1986
30-11-24	Alex Rodriguez	Jul 27, 1975	Jul 21, 2006

(018) Most Career Singles

3215	Pete Rose	2253	Stan Musial	2108	Luis Aparicio
3053	Ty Cobb	2253	Wade Boggs	2106	Cal Ripken
2643	Eddie Collins	2247	Lou Brock	2104	Zack Wheat
2513	Willie Keeler	2243	Paul Waner	2097	Sam Crawford
2424	Honus Wagner	2182	Rickey Henderson	2056	Lave Cross
2404	Rod Carew	2182	Robin Yount	2035	George Brett
2383	Tris Speaker	2171	Frankie Frisch	2035	Al Kaline
2378	Tony Gwynn	2163	Doc Cramer	2033	Lloyd Waner
2366	Paul Molitor	2162	Luke Appling	2030	Brooks Robinson
2340	Nap Lajoie	2161	Nellie Fox	2030	Fred Clarke
2294	Hank Aaron	2156	Eddie Murray	2028	George Van Haltren
2273	Jesse Burkett	2154	Roberto Clemente	2020	Rabbit Maranville
2271	Sam Rice	2130	Jake Beckley	2017	Max Carey
2262	Cap Anson	2121	George Sisler	2017	Dave Winfield
2262	Carl Yastrzemski	2119	Richie Ashburn		

GEORGE BRACE

Hank Aaron

9

(019) Most Career Singles by a Left-handed Batter

3053	Ty Cobb	2130	Jake Beckley	1889	Vada Pinson
2643	Eddie Collins	2121	George Sisler	1878	Rusty Staub
2513	Willie Keeler	2119	Richie Ashburn	1862	Fred Tenney
2404	Rod Carew	2104	Zack Wheat	1855	Jake Daubert
2383	Tris Speaker	2097	Sam Crawford	1846	Willie Davis
2378	Tony Gwynn	2035	George Brett	1842	Harry Hooper
2273	Jesse Burkett	2033	Lloyd Waner	1828	Rafael Palmeiro
2271	Sam Rice	2030	Fred Clarke	1814	Goose Goslin
2262	Carl Yastrzemski	2028	George Van Haltren	1805	Mel Ott
2253	Wade Boggs	1994	Bill Buckner	1787	Edd Roush
2253	Stan Musial	1957	Patsy Donovan	1787	Billy Hamilton
2247	Lou Brock	1945	Harold Baines	1772	Dave Parker
2243	Paul Waner	1935	Charlie Gehringer	1763	Heinie Manush
2163	Doc Cramer	1918	Al Oliver	1763	Billy Williams
2161	Nellie Fox	1913	Brett Butler	1754	John Ward

(020) Most Career Singles by a Right-handed Batter

2424	Honus Wagner	2020	Rabbit Maranville	1787	Jimmy Ryan
2366	Paul Molitor	2017	Dave Winfield	1784	Harry Heilmann
2340	Nap Lajoie	1972	Stuffy McInnis	1778	Tommy Corcoran
2294	Hank Aaron	1960	Willie Mays	1775	Willie Randolph
2262	Cap Anson	1960	Craig Biggio	1771	Bert Campaneris
2182	Robin Yount	1936	Julio Franco	1769	Tony Perez
2182	Rickey Henderson	1932	Al Simmons	1757	Frank Robinson
2162	Luke Appling	1919	Rogers Hornsby	1743	Hugh Duffy
2154	Roberto Clemente	1844	Steve Garvey	1741	Bobby Wallace
2108	Luis Aparicio	1832	Buddy Bell	1735	Andre Dawson
2106	Cal Ripken	1823	Pie Traynor	1730	Billy Herman
2056	Lave Cross	1801	Bill Dahlen	1713	Alan Trammell
2035	Al Kaline	1788	Ed Delahanty	1713	Bid McPhee
2030	Brooks Robinson	1788	Dave Concepcion	1708	Jim O'Rourke

(021) Most Career Singles by a Switch-hitter

3215	Pete Rose	1676	Tony Fernandez	1341	Alfredo Griffin
2171	Frankie Frisch	1634	Kid Gleason	1341	John Anderson
2156	Eddie Murray	1591	Garry Templeton	1317	Claude Ritchey
2017	Max Carey	1583	Don Kessinger	1292	Roy White
1976	George Davis	1576	Chili Davis	1286	Reggie Smith
1961	Ozzie Smith	1575	Dave Bancroft	1277	Devon White
1933	Omar Vizquel	1545	Bernie Williams	1269	Miller Huggins
1930	Roberto Alomar	1535	Donie Bush	1268	Dave Philley
1892	Tim Raines	1515	Tommy Tucker	1254	Bobby Bonilla
1866	Maury Wills	1463	Mickey Mantle	1247	Mark McLemore
1860	Red Schoendienst	1453	Tony Phillips	1224	Lu Blue
1815	Larry Bowa	1449	Jim Gilliam	1223	Luis Castillo
1738	Willie Wilson	1441	Ken Singleton	1210	Ray Durham
1731	Willie McGee	1362	Terry Pendleton		
1694	Ted Simmons	1359	Ruben Sierra		

(022) Most Career Doubles

792	Tris Speaker	583	Robin Yount	526	Dave Parker
746	Pete Rose	578	Wade Boggs	525	Ted Williams
725	Stan Musial	574	Charlie Gehringer	523	Willie Mays
724	Ty Cobb	560	Eddie Murray	522	Ed Delahanty
665	George Brett	547	Luis Gonzalez	515	Joe Cronin
657	Nap Lajoie	543	Tony Gwynn	514	Edgar Martinez
646	Carl Yastrzemski	542	Harry Heilmann	511	Mark Grace
643	Honus Wagner	541	Rogers Hornsby	510	Rickey Henderson
637	Craig Biggio	540	Joe Medwick	506	Babe Ruth
624	Hank Aaron	540	Dave Winfield	505	Tony Perez
605	Paul Molitor	539	Al Simmons	504	Roberto Alomar
605	Paul Waner	534	Lou Gehrig	503	Andre Dawson
603	Cal Ripken	529	Cap Anson	501	Jeff Kent
587	Barry Bonds	529	Al Oliver	500	Goose Goslin
585	Rafael Palmeiro	528	Frank Robinson	500	John Olerud

(023) Most Career Doubles by a Left-handed Batter

792	Tris Speaker	529	Al Oliver	488	Mel Ott
725	Stan Musial	526	Dave Parker	486	Lou Brock
724	Ty Cobb	525	Ted Williams	485	Vada Pinson
665	George Brett	511	Mark Grace	476	Zack Wheat
646	Carl Yastrzemski	506	Babe Ruth	473	Jake Beckley
605	Paul Waner	500	Goose Goslin	471	Larry Walker
587	Barry Bonds	500	John Olerud	465	Jim Bottomley
585	Rafael Palmeiro	499	Rusty Staub	463	Reggie Jackson
578	Wade Boggs	498	Bill Buckner	460	Dan Brouthers
574	Charlie Gehringer	498	Sam Rice	458	Sam Crawford
547	Luis Gonzalez	491	Heinie Manush	451	Paul O'Neill
543	Tony Gwynn	490	Mickey Vernon		
534	Lou Gehrig	488	Harold Baines		

(024) Most Career Doubles by a Right-handed Batter

657	Nap Lajoie	515	Joe Cronin	451	Jimmy Ryan
643	Honus Wagner	514	Edgar Martinez	444	Andres Galarraga
637	Craig Biggio	510	Rickey Henderson	444	George H. Burns
624	Hank Aaron	505	Tony Perez	443	Gary Gaetti
605	Paul Molitor	503	Andre Dawson	442	Dick Bartell
603	Cal Ripken	501	Jeff Kent	441	Barry Larkin
583	Robin Yount	498	Al Kaline	440	Roberto Clemente
542	Harry Heilmann	488	Jeff Bagwell	440	Steve Garvey
541	Rogers Hornsby	486	Billy Herman	440	Luke Appling
540	Joe Medwick	484	Hal McRae	436	Cesar Cedeno
540	Dave Winfield	483	Dwight Evans	432	Joe Carter
539	Al Simmons	482	Brooks Robinson	432	Tim Wallach
529	Cap Anson	473	Ivan Rodriguez	425	Sherry Magee
528	Frank Robinson	458	Jimmie Foxx	425	Buddy Bell
523	Willie Mays	458	Frank E. Thomas		
522	Ed Delahanty	453	Jimmy Dykes		

(025) Most Career Doubles by a Switch-hitter

746	Pete Rose	453	George Davis	424	Chili Davis
560	Eddie Murray	449	Bernie Williams	419	Max Carey
504	Roberto Alomar	430	Tim Raines	414	Tony Fernandez
483	Ted Simmons	428	Ruben Sierra	408	Bobby Bonilla
466	Frankie Frisch	427	Red Schoendienst	402	Ozzie Smith

(026) Most Career Triples

309	Sam Crawford	182	Jesse Burkett	165	Jake Daubert
295	Ty Cobb	182	Edd Roush	164	Pie Traynor
252	Honus Wagner	182	Ed Konetchy	164	George Sisler
244	Jake Beckley	178	Buck Ewing	164	Elmer Flick
233	Roger Connor	177	Stan Musial	163	Bill Dahlen
222	Tris Speaker	177	Rabbit Maranville	163	George Davis
220	Fred Clarke	174	Harry Stovey	163	Nap Lajoie
205	Dan Brouthers	173	Goose Goslin	163	Lou Gehrig
194	Joe Kelley	172	Zack Wheat	162	Mike Tiernan
191	Paul Waner	172	Tommy Leach	161	George Van Haltren
189	Bid McPhee	169	Rogers Hornsby	161	Sam Thompson
187	Eddie Collins	168	Joe Jackson	160	Harry Hooper
186	Ed Delahanty	166	Roberto Clemente	160	Heinie Manush
184	Sam Rice	166	Sherry Magee		

COURTESY OF THE HOUSTON ASTROS

Craig Biggio

(027) Most Career Triples by a Left-handed Batter

309	Sam Crawford	177	Stan Musial	160	Heinie Manush
295	Ty Cobb	173	Goose Goslin	159	Joe Judge
244	Jake Beckley	172	Zack Wheat	154	Earle Combs
233	Roger Connor	168	Joe Jackson	151	Jim Bottomley
222	Tris Speaker	165	Jake Daubert	148	Enos Slaughter
220	Fred Clarke	164	George Sisler	148	Wally Pipp
205	Dan Brouthers	164	Elmer Flick	147	Bobby Veach
191	Paul Waner	163	Lou Gehrig	146	Charlie Gehringer
187	Eddie Collins	162	Mike Tiernan	145	Willie Keeler
184	Sam Rice	161	George Van Haltren	141	Lou Brock
182	Jesse Burkett	161	Sam Thompson		
182	Edd Roush	160	Harry Hooper		

(028) Most Career Triples by a Right-handed Batter

252	Honus Wagner	164	Pie Traynor	140	Willie Mays
194	Joe Kelley	163	Nap Lajoie	139	John Reilly
189	Bid McPhee	163	Bill Dahlen	139	Jimmy Williams
186	Ed Delahanty	158	Ed McKean	136	Lave Cross
182	Ed Konetchy	157	Kiki Cuyler	133	Shano Collins
178	Buck Ewing	157	Jimmy Ryan	132	Jim O'Rourke
177	Rabbit Maranville	155	Tommy Corcoran	131	Joe DiMaggio
174	Harry Stovey	151	Harry Heilmann	129	Oyster Burns
172	Tommy Leach	149	Al Simmons	126	Hardy Richardson
169	Rogers Hornsby	149	Kip Selbach	126	Robin Yount
166	Roberto Clemente	145	Harry Davis	125	Jimmie Foxx
166	Sherry Magee	143	Bobby Wallace		

(029) Most Career Triples by a Switch-hitter

163	George Davis	103	Tom Daly	81	Kid Gleason
159	Max Carey	100	Dan McGann	80	Roberto Alomar
147	Willie Wilson	99	Larry Bowa	80	Don Kessinger
138	Frankie Frisch	94	Willie McGee	79	Frank Shugart
135	Pete Rose	92	Tony Fernandez	78	Red Schoendienst
124	John Anderson	92	Walt Wilmot	78	Alfredo Griffin
123	Duke Farrell	90	Wally Schang	77	Dave Bancroft
113	Tim Raines	89	Vince Coleman	76	Tom McCreery
109	Lu Blue	87	Candy LaChance	76	Jimmy Austin
106	Garry Templeton	85	Tommy Tucker	75	Billy Rogell

(030) Highest Career Batting Average (min. 1,500 hits)

.366	Ty Cobb	.338	Jesse Burkett	.326	Hugh Duffy
.358	Rogers Hornsby	.338	Tony Gwynn	.325	Jimmie Foxx
.356	Joe Jackson	.338	Nap Lajoie	.325	Earle Combs
.346	Ed Delahanty	.336	Riggs Stephenson	.325	Joe DiMaggio
.345	Tris Speaker	.334	Al Simmons	.325	Vladimir Guerrero
.344	Ted Williams	.333	Todd Helton	.324	Babe Herman
.344	Billy Hamilton	.333	Paul Waner	.324	Joe Medwick
.342	Dan Brouthers	.333	Eddie Collins	.323	Edd Roush
.342	Babe Ruth	.331	Cap Anson	.322	Sam Rice
.342	Harry Heilmann	.331	Stan Musial	.321	Kiki Cuyler
.341	Pete Browning	.331	Sam Thompson	.320	Charlie Gehringer
.341	Willie Keeler	.330	Heinie Manush	.320	Chuck Klein
.341	Bill Terry	.328	Wade Boggs	.320	Pie Traynor
.340	George Sisler	.328	Rod Carew	.320	Mickey Cochrane
.340	Lou Gehrig	.328	Honus Wagner		

(031) Highest Career Batting Average by a Left-handed Batter (min. 1,500 hits)

.366	Ty Cobb	.331	Stan Musial	.316	Roger Connor
.356	Joe Jackson	.331	Sam Thompson	.316	Lloyd Waner
.345	Tris Speaker	.330	Heinie Manush	.316	Goose Goslin
.344	Ted Williams	.328	Wade Boggs	.316	George Van Haltren
.344	Billy Hamilton	.328	Rod Carew	.314	Cecil Travis
.342	Dan Brouthers	.325	Earle Combs	.313	Larry Walker
.342	Babe Ruth	.324	Babe Herman	.313	Jack Fournier
.341	Willie Keeler	.323	Edd Roush	.313	Elmer Flick
.341	Bill Terry	.322	Sam Rice	.313	Bill Dickey
.340	George Sisler	.320	Charlie Gehringer	.312	Johnny Mize
.340	Lou Gehrig	.320	Chuck Klein	.312	Joe Sewell
.338	Jesse Burkett	.320	Mickey Cochrane	.312	Fred Clarke
.338	Tony Gwynn	.319	Ken Williams	.311	Ginger Beaumont
.333	Todd Helton	.318	Earl Averill	.311	Mike Tiernan
.333	Paul Waner	.318	Arky Vaughan	.310	Bobby Veach
.333	Eddie Collins	.317	Zack Wheat	.310	Jim Bottomley

(032) Highest Career Batting Average by a Right-handed Batter (min. 1,500 hits)

.358	Rogers Hornsby	.320	Pie Traynor	.310	Jim O'Rourke
.346	Ed Delahanty	.318	Kirby Puckett	.309	Mike Piazza
.342	Harry Heilmann	.317	Roberto Clemente	.309	Bob Meusel
.341	Pete Browning	.317	Joe Kelley	.308	King Kelly
.338	Nap Lajoie	.317	Derek Jeter	.308	Jimmy Ryan
.336	Riggs Stephenson	.314	Manny Ramirez	.308	Stuffy McInnis
.334	Al Simmons	.313	Hank Greenberg	.307	Joe Vosmik
.331	Cap Anson	.312	Edgar Martinez	.307	George H. Burns
.328	Honus Wagner	.312	Hughie Jennings	.306	George Kell
.326	Hugh Duffy	.311	Bing Miller	.306	Paul Molitor
.325	Jimmie Foxx	.311	Freddie Lindstrom	.306	Ernie Lombardi
.325	Joe DiMaggio	.311	Jackie Robinson	.305	Frank E. Thomas
.325	Vladimir Guerrero	.311	Baby Doll Jacobson	.305	Alex Rodriguez
.324	Joe Medwick	.310	Irish Meusel	.305	Hank Aaron
.321	Kiki Cuyler	.310	Luke Appling	.305	Bill Madlock

(033) Highest Career Batting Average by a Switch-hitter (min. 1,500 hits)

.316	Frankie Frisch	.291	Carlos Baerga	.287	Reggie Smith
.304	Chipper Jones	.290	Tommy Tucker	.287	Eddie Murray
.303	Pete Rose	.290	John Anderson	.285	Willie Wilson
.300	Roberto Alomar	.290	Johnny Ray	.285	Ted Simmons
.298	Mickey Mantle	.289	Red Schoendienst	.285	Max Carey
.297	Bernie Williams	.289	Gregg Jefferies	.284	Wally Schang
.295	Willie McGee	.288	Tony Fernandez	.282	Ken Singleton
.295	George Davis	.287	Augie Galan	.281	Maury Wills
.294	Tim Raines	.287	Lu Blue	.281	Ray Durham

(034) Highest Career On Base Percentage (min. 5,000 PA)

.482	Ted Williams	.415	Jesse Burkett	.402	Lu Blue
.474	Babe Ruth	.414	Mel Ott	.402	Chipper Jones
.455	Billy Hamilton	.413	Roy Thomas	.401	Rickey Henderson
.447	Lou Gehrig	.413	Jason Giambi	.400	Larry Walker
.443	Barry Bonds	.412	Hank Greenberg	.399	Ross Youngs
.434	Rogers Hornsby	.412	Bobby Abreu	.399	Luke Appling
.433	Ty Cobb	.411	Ed Delahanty	.398	Gary Sheffield
.430	Todd Helton	.411	Manny Ramirez	.398	John Olerud
.428	Tris Speaker	.410	Harry Heilmann	.398	Elmer Valo
.428	Jimmie Foxx	.410	Eddie Stanky	.398	Elmer Smith
.424	Frank E. Thomas	.409	Jackie Robinson	.398	Joe DiMaggio
.424	Eddie Collins	.409	Jim Thome	.398	Ralph Kiner
.423	Max Bishop	.408	Brian Giles	.397	Earle Combs
.423	Dan Brouthers	.408	Jeff Bagwell	.397	Roger Connor
.423	Joe Jackson	.407	Denny Lyons	.397	Johnny Mize
.421	Mickey Mantle	.407	Riggs Stephenson	.396	Richie Ashburn
.419	Mickey Cochrane	.406	Arky Vaughan	.396	Mike Hargrove
.418	Edgar Martinez	.404	Charlie Gehringer	.396	Cap Anson
.417	Stan Musial	.404	Paul Waner	.395	Earl Averill
.416	Cupid Childs	.403	Pete Browning	.395	Hack Wilson
.415	Wade Boggs	.402	Joe Kelley		

(035) Highest Career On Base Percentage by a Left-handed Batter (min. 5,000 PA)

.482	Ted Williams	.415	Jesse Burkett	.397	Roger Connor
.474	Babe Ruth	.414	Mel Ott	.397	Johnny Mize
.455	Billy Hamilton	.413	Roy Thomas	.396	Richie Ashburn
.447	Lou Gehrig	.413	Jason Giambi	.396	Mike Hargrove
.443	Barry Bonds	.412	Bobby Abreu	.395	Earl Averill
.433	Ty Cobb	.409	Jim Thome	.394	Stan Hack
.430	Todd Helton	.408	Brian Giles	.394	Johnny Pesky
.428	Tris Speaker	.406	Arky Vaughan	.393	Rod Carew
.424	Eddie Collins	.404	Charlie Gehringer	.393	Ken Williams
.423	Max Bishop	.404	Paul Waner	.393	Bill Terry
.423	Dan Brouthers	.400	Larry Walker	.392	Jack Fournier
.423	Joe Jackson	.399	Ross Youngs	.392	George Grantham
.419	Mickey Cochrane	.398	John Olerud	.392	Joe Morgan
.417	Stan Musial	.398	Elmer Valo	.392	Mike Tiernan
.416	Cupid Childs	.398	Elmer Smith	.391	Joe Sewell
.415	Wade Boggs	.397	Earle Combs	.390	Carlos Delgado

(036) Highest Career On Base Percentage by a Right-handed Batter (min. 5,000 PA)

.434	Rogers Hornsby	.398	Gary Sheffield	.386	Roger Bresnahan
.428	Jimmie Foxx	.398	Joe DiMaggio	.386	Kiki Cuyler
.424	Frank E. Thomas	.398	Ralph Kiner	.386	Hugh Duffy
.418	Edgar Martinez	.396	Cap Anson	.386	Alex Rodriguez
.412	Hank Greenberg	.395	Hack Wilson	.385	Tim Salmon
.411	Ed Delahanty	.394	Mark McGwire	.384	Willie Mays
.411	Manny Ramirez	.394	Eddie Yost	.383	Ben Chapman
.410	Harry Heilmann	.393	Bob L. Johnson	.383	Earl Sheely
.410	Eddie Stanky	.391	Honus Wagner	.383	Dom DiMaggio
.409	Jackie Robinson	.391	Hughie Jennings	.381	Jason Kendall
.408	Jeff Bagwell	.390	Vladimir Guerrero	.380	Lou Boudreau
.407	Denny Lyons	.390	Harland Clift	.380	Nap Lajoie
.407	Riggs Stephenson	.390	Joe Cronin	.380	Henry Larkin
.403	Pete Browning	.389	Minnie Minoso	.380	Tony Lazzeri
.402	Joe Kelley	.389	Frank Robinson	.380	Mike Schmidt
.401	Rickey Henderson	.388	Gene Tenace	.380	Al Simmons
.399	Luke Appling	.388	Derek Jeter		

(037) Highest Career On Base Percentage by a Switch-hitter (min. 5,000 PA)

.421	Mickey Mantle	.366	Reggie Smith	.355	Dave Bancroft
.402	Lu Blue	.364	Dan McGann	.354	Bill Doran
.402	Chipper Jones	.364	Tommy Tucker	.354	Ray Durham
.393	Wally Schang	.362	Don Buford	.353	Bob Bescher
.390	Augie Galan	.362	George Davis	.351	Billy Rogell
.388	Ken Singleton	.361	Max Carey	.351	Walt Weiss
.385	Tim Raines	.361	Tom Daly	.349	Mark McLemore
.382	Miller Huggins	.360	Jose Offerman	.349	Jerry Mumphrey
.381	Bernie Williams	.360	Chili Davis	.348	Claude Ritchey
.375	Jorge Posada	.360	Jim Gilliam	.348	Ted Simmons
.375	Pete Rose	.360	Roy White	.347	Ken Caminiti
.374	Tony Phillips	.359	Eddie Murray	.347	Tony Fernandez
.371	Roberto Alomar	.359	David Segui	.347	Tom Herr
.369	Frankie Frisch	.358	Bobby Bonilla	.345	Stan Javier
.369	Mickey Tettleton	.356	Donie Bush	.345	Roy Smalley Jr.

(038) Highest Career Slugging Average (min. 5,000 PA)

.690	Babe Ruth	.562	Johnny Mize	.537	Sammy Sosa
.634	Ted Williams	.561	Juan Gonzalez	.537	Frank Robinson
.632	Lou Gehrig	.559	Stan Musial	.535	Al Simmons
.609	Jimmie Foxx	.558	Carlos Delgado	.534	Earl Averill
.608	Barry Bonds	.557	Ken Griffey Jr.	.534	Dick Allen
.605	Hank Greenberg	.557	Willie Mays	.533	Mel Ott
.600	Manny Ramirez	.557	Mickey Mantle	.532	Babe Herman
.593	Todd Helton	.555	Hank Aaron	.530	Ken Williams
.588	Mark McGwire	.551	Mike Piazza	.529	Willie Stargell
.583	Vladimir Guerrero	.548	Ralph Kiner	.527	Mike Schmidt
.579	Joe DiMaggio	.545	Hack Wilson	.526	Chick Hafey
.577	Rogers Hornsby	.543	Chuck Klein	.525	Brian Giles
.573	Alex Rodriguez	.542	Chipper Jones	.525	Gary Sheffield
.566	Frank E. Thomas	.541	Jason Giambi	.523	Mo Vaughn
.565	Larry Walker	.540	Duke Snider	.522	Hal Trosky
.565	Jim Thome	.540	Jeff Bagwell	.522	Wally Berger
.564	Albert Belle	.539	Jim Edmonds	.520	Harry Heilmann

(039) Highest Career Slugging Average by a Left-handed Batter (min. 5,000 PA)

.690	Babe Ruth	.532	Babe Herman	.505	Darryl Strawberry
.634	Ted Williams	.530	Ken Williams	.505	Sam Thompson
.632	Lou Gehrig	.529	Willie Stargell	.500	Tris Speaker
.608	Barry Bonds	.525	Brian Giles	.500	David Justice
.593	Todd Helton	.523	Mo Vaughn	.500	Jim Bottomley
.565	Larry Walker	.522	Hal Trosky	.500	Goose Goslin
.565	Jim Thome	.519	Dan Brouthers	.499	Shawn Green
.562	Johnny Mize	.517	Joe Jackson	.498	Ted Kluszewski
.559	Stan Musial	.515	Rafael Palmeiro	.497	Will Clark
.558	Carlos Delgado	.515	Willie McCovey	.494	Cliff Floyd
.557	Ken Griffey Jr.	.512	Ty Cobb	.492	Billy Williams
.543	Chuck Klein	.509	Eddie Mathews	.492	Dolph Camilli
.541	Jason Giambi	.509	Fred McGriff	.491	Tommy Henrich
.540	Duke Snider	.509	Jeff Heath	.490	Larry Doby
.539	Jim Edmonds	.507	Bobby Abreu	.490	Reggie Jackson
.534	Earl Averill	.507	Ryan Klesko		
.533	Mel Ott	.506	Bill Terry		

(040) Highest Career Slugging Average by a Right-handed Batter (min. 5,000 PA)

.609	Jimmie Foxx	.535	Al Simmons	.500	Ernie Banks
.605	Hank Greenberg	.534	Dick Allen	.499	Orlando Cepeda
.600	Manny Ramirez	.527	Mike Schmidt	.499	Dante Bichette
.588	Mark McGwire	.526	Chick Hafey	.499	Andres Galarraga
.583	Vladimir Guerrero	.525	Gary Sheffield	.499	Frank Howard
.579	Joe DiMaggio	.522	Wally Berger	.498	Tim Salmon
.577	Rogers Hornsby	.520	Harry Heilmann	.497	Bob Meusel
.573	Alex Rodriguez	.516	Moises Alou	.496	Hank Sauer
.566	Frank E. Thomas	.515	Edgar Martinez	.496	Danny Tartabull
.564	Albert Belle	.515	Jose Canseco	.494	Jay Buhner
.561	Juan Gonzalez	.515	Scott Rolen	.491	Javy Lopez
.557	Willie Mays	.510	Ellis Burks	.489	Gabby Hartnett
.555	Hank Aaron	.509	Harmon Killebrew	.489	Matt Williams
.551	Mike Piazza	.506	Bob L. Johnson	.489	Rocky Colavito
.548	Ralph Kiner	.505	Ed Delahanty	.487	Reggie Sanders
.545	Hack Wilson	.505	Joe Medwick	.487	Ivan Rodriguez
.540	Jeff Bagwell	.505	Andruw Jones	.487	Gil Hodges
.537	Sammy Sosa	.504	Jeff Kent	.485	Raul Mondesi
.537	Frank Robinson	.502	Jim Rice	.485	Joe Adcock

(041) Highest Career Slugging Average by a Switch-hitter (min. 5,000 PA)

.557	Mickey Mantle	.451	Chili Davis	.443	Ray Durham
.542	Chipper Jones	.450	Ruben Sierra	.437	Ted Simmons
.489	Reggie Smith	.450	Jose Valentin	.436	Ken Singleton
.477	Bernie Williams	.449	Mickey Tettleton	.432	Frankie Frisch
.476	Eddie Murray	.447	Ken Caminiti	.425	Tim Raines
.472	Bobby Bonilla	.446	Howard Johnson	.423	Carlos Baerga
.472	Jorge Posada	.443	Roberto Alomar	.421	Gregg Jefferies
.462	Carl Everett	.443	David Segui		

(042) Highest Career On Base Percentage plus Slugging Average (min. 5,000 PA)

1.164	Babe Ruth	.958	Alex Rodriguez	.929	Earl Averill
1.116	Ted Williams	.954	Jason Giambi	.929	Hank Aaron
1.079	Lou Gehrig	.948	Carlos Delgado	.928	Tris Speaker
1.051	Barry Bonds	.948	Jeff Bagwell	.926	Frank Robinson
1.037	Jimmie Foxx	.947	Mel Ott	.923	Gary Sheffield
1.023	Todd Helton	.946	Ralph Kiner	.923	Ken Williams
1.017	Hank Greenberg	.945	Ty Cobb	.922	Chuck Klein
1.011	Rogers Hornsby	.943	Chipper Jones	.921	Jim Edmonds
1.011	Manny Ramirez	.942	Dan Brouthers	.920	Duke Snider
.990	Frank E. Thomas	.941	Willie Mays	.919	Bobby Abreu
.982	Mark McGwire	.940	Joe Jackson	.916	Ed Delahanty
.978	Mickey Mantle	.940	Hack Wilson	.915	Babe Herman
.977	Joe DiMaggio	.933	Brian Giles	.915	Al Simmons
.976	Stan Musial	.933	Albert Belle	.912	Dick Allen
.974	Jim Thome	.933	Edgar Martinez	.907	Mike Schmidt
.972	Vladimir Guerrero	.931	Ken Griffey Jr.	.906	Mo Vaughn
.965	Larry Walker	.931	Mike Piazza	.904	Juan Gonzalez
.959	Johnny Mize	.930	Harry Heilmann		

(043) Highest Career On Base Percentage plus Slugging Average by a Left-handed Batter (min. 5,000 PA)

1.164	Babe Ruth	.931	Ken Griffey Jr.	.887	Billy Hamilton
1.116	Ted Williams	.929	Earl Averill	.887	Goose Goslin
1.079	Lou Gehrig	.928	Tris Speaker	.886	Rafael Palmeiro
1.051	Barry Bonds	.923	Ken Williams	.886	Fred McGriff
1.023	Todd Helton	.922	Chuck Klein	.885	Eddie Mathews
.976	Stan Musial	.921	Jim Edmonds	.884	Charlie Gehringer
.974	Jim Thome	.920	Duke Snider	.883	Roger Connor
.965	Larry Walker	.919	Bobby Abreu	.881	Will Clark
.959	Johnny Mize	.915	Babe Herman	.880	Dolph Camilli
.954	Jason Giambi	.906	Mo Vaughn	.879	Jeff Heath
.948	Carlos Delgado	.899	Bill Terry	.878	David Justice
.947	Mel Ott	.897	Mickey Cochrane	.878	Ryan Klesko
.945	Ty Cobb	.893	Hal Trosky	.877	Paul Waner
.942	Dan Brouthers	.889	Willie McCovey	.876	Larry Doby
.940	Joe Jackson	.889	Willie Stargell	.875	Jack Fournier
.933	Brian Giles	.889	Sam Thompson	.873	Tommy Henrich

(044) Highest Career On Base Percentage plus Slugging Average by a Right-handed Batter (min. 5,000 PA)

1.037	Jimmie Foxx	.926	Frank Robinson	.870	Pete Browning
1.017	Hank Greenberg	.923	Gary Sheffield	.868	Jose Canseco
1.011	Rogers Hornsby	.916	Ed Delahanty	.867	Joe Medwick
1.011	Manny Ramirez	.915	Al Simmons	.864	Danny Tartabull
.990	Frank E. Thomas	.912	Dick Allen	.860	Kiki Cuyler
.982	Mark McGwire	.907	Mike Schmidt	.860	Jeff Kent
.977	Joe DiMaggio	.904	Juan Gonzalez	.859	Gabby Hartnett
.972	Vladimir Guerrero	.899	Bob L. Johnson	.858	Honus Wagner
.958	Alex Rodriguez	.898	Chick Hafey	.858	Joe Cronin
.948	Jeff Bagwell	.890	Scott Rolen	.856	Al Kaline
.946	Ralph Kiner	.885	Harmon Killebrew	.855	Jack Clark
.941	Willie Mays	.884	Tim Salmon	.854	Jim Rice
.940	Hack Wilson	.884	Moises Alou	.853	Joe Kelley
.933	Albert Belle	.883	Jackie Robinson	.853	Bob Meusel
.933	Edgar Martinez	.882	Sammy Sosa	.853	Jay Buhner
.931	Mike Piazza	.881	Wally Berger	.851	Frank Howard
.930	Harry Heilmann	.880	Riggs Stephenson	.850	Pedro Guerrero
.929	Hank Aaron	.873	Ellis Burks		

(045) Highest Career On Base Percentage plus Slugging Average by a Switch-hitter (min. 5,000 PA)

.978	Mickey Mantle	.802	Carl Everett	.747	Max Carey
.943	Chipper Jones	.801	Frankie Frisch	.747	Tom Daly
.858	Bernie Williams	.797	Ray Durham	.746	Tony Fernandez
.855	Reggie Smith	.794	Ken Caminiti	.745	Dan McGann
.847	Jorge Posada	.794	Wally Schang	.745	Jerry Mumphrey
.835	Eddie Murray	.786	Howard Johnson	.741	Don Buford
.830	Bobby Bonilla	.785	Ted Simmons	.740	Roy Smalley Jr.
.824	Ken Singleton	.784	Pete Rose	.739	Ken Henderson
.818	Mickey Tettleton	.772	Jose Valentin	.738	Devon White
.814	Roberto Alomar	.767	George Davis	.737	Tommy Tucker
.811	Chili Davis	.765	Ruben Sierra	.734	Kevin Bass
.810	Tim Raines	.765	Gregg Jefferies	.734	John Anderson
.809	Augie Galan	.764	Roy White	.733	Jose Offerman
.803	Lu Blue	.763	Tony Phillips		
.802	David Segui	.755	Carlos Baerga		

(046) Lowest Career Batting Average (min. 1,000 AB)

.170	Bill Bergen	.208	Bill Holbert	.213	Dick Tracewski
.175	Ray Oyler	.208	Tom Prince	.213	Billy Sullivan Sr.
.189	Charlie Bastian	.209	Tom Needham	.213	Jerry Kindall
.193	Mike Ryan	.210	Steve Jeltz	.214	Jeff Torborg
.203	Jim Mason	.210	Luis Gomez	.214	Doc Bushong
.204	Sam Agnew	.211	Davy Force	.214	Dave Duncan
.207	John P. Henry	.212	Dave Nicholson	.214	Lena Blackburne
.207	Barney Gilligan	.212	Rusty Torres	.215	Mario Mendoza
.208	Gabby Street	.213	Red Kleinow	.215	George Creamer
.208	Jackie Hernandez	.213	Mick Kelleher	.215	Bobby Wine

(047) Lowest Career Batting Average (min. 2,500 AB)

.170	Bill Bergen	.221	Ron Karkovice	.226	Charley O'Leary
.211	Davy Force	.221	Lou Criger	.227	Joe Gerhardt
.213	Billy Sullivan Sr.	.222	Pop Smith	.227	Dick Schofield
.214	Dave Duncan	.222	Johnnie LeMaster	.227	Roy Smalley
.215	Bobby Wine	.223	Art Whitney	.228	Mark Belanger
.217	Dal Maxvill	.224	George Strickland	.228	Hal Lanier
.218	George McBride	.224	Ed Brinkman	.228	Steve Yeager
.219	Malachi Kittridge	.225	Gorman Thomas	.228	Jim Hegan
.220	Rob Deer	.225	Paul Casanova	.228	Kevin Elster
.220	Lee Tannehill	.225	Buck Martinez	.228	Frank Hankinson

(048) Lowest Career Batting Average (min. 5,000 AB)

.218	George McBride	.242	Greg Vaughn	.247	Leo Durocher
.224	Ed Brinkman	.242	Freddie Patek	.247	Darrell Porter
.228	Mark Belanger	.242	Zoilo Versalles	.247	Dick McAuliffe
.230	Mickey Doolan	.243	Roy McMillan	.248	Mickey Stanley
.234	Monte Cross	.243	Germany Smith	.248	Graig Nettles
.236	Dave Kingman	.244	Deron Johnson	.248	Darrell Evans
.237	Aurelio Rodriguez	.245	Tom Brunansky	.248	Jim Sundberg
.238	Eddie Miller	.245	Frankie Crosetti	.248	Ken McMullen
.239	Eddie Joost	.246	Chris Speier	.248	Wid Conroy
.242	Clete Boyer	.246	Jimmy Austin	.249	Alfredo Griffin

(049) Lowest Career Batting Average by a Pitcher (min. 200 AB)

.029	Ron Herbel	.085	Hank Aguirre	.094	Pedro Martinez
.057	Don Carmen	.085	Roger Craig	.094	Tommie Sisk
.058	Mark Clark	.086	Bill Stoneman	.094	Wally Bunker
.066	Dean Chance	.086	Bob Kuzava	.095	Matt Clement
.066	Aaron Harang	.086	Dave Wickersham	.095	Miguel Batista
.071	Doug Davis	.086	Ike Delock	.095	Bob Hendley
.075	Clem Labine	.088	Dick Ellsworth	.095	Charles Hudson
.077	Dick Drago	.088	Hoyt Wilhelm	.095	Gary Gentry
.077	Ryan Dempster	.088	Jim Deshaies	.096	Rollie Sheldon
.078	Bill Hands	.089	Bob Buhl	.097	George A. Smith
.078	Mike Bielecki	.089	George Brunet	.097	John Montefusco
.078	Ben Sheets	.090	Sterling Hitchcock	.097	Sandy Koufax
.079	Lee Stange	.091	Jim Hannan	.097	Scott Sanderson
.081	Bruce Ruffin	.091	Johnny Broaca	.098	Al Benton
.083	Jeff Fassero	.091	Jose DeLeon	.098	Cannonball Titcomb
.083	Karl Drews	.092	Ron Kline	.098	Clay Kirby
.084	Ed Rakow	.092	Vicente Padilla	.099	Carl Willey
.084	Wilbur Wood	.093	Dustin Hermanson		
.085	Al Leiter	.093	John Burkett		

(050) Most Career RBI

2297	Hank Aaron	1812	Frank Robinson	1579	Frank E. Thomas
2213	Babe Ruth	1733	Honus Wagner	1578	Jake Beckley
1995	Lou Gehrig	1702	Reggie Jackson	1575	Sammy Sosa
1951	Stan Musial	1695	Cal Ripken	1555	Willie McCovey
1938	Ty Cobb	1652	Tony Perez	1550	Fred McGriff
1930	Barry Bonds	1636	Ernie Banks	1540	Willie Stargell
1922	Jimmie Foxx	1628	Harold Baines	1539	Harry Heilmann
1917	Eddie Murray	1609	Goose Goslin	1537	Joe DiMaggio
1903	Willie Mays	1608	Ken Griffey Jr.	1529	Tris Speaker
1880	Cap Anson	1599	Nap Lajoie	1529	Jeff Bagwell
1860	Mel Ott	1595	Mike Schmidt	1525	Sam Crawford
1844	Carl Yastrzemski	1595	George Brett	1516	Manny Ramirez
1839	Ted Williams	1591	Andre Dawson	1509	Mickey Mantle
1835	Rafael Palmeiro	1584	Harmon Killebrew	1501	Gary Sheffield
1833	Dave Winfield	1584	Rogers Hornsby		
1827	Al Simmons	1583	Al Kaline		

(051) Most Career RBI by a Left-handed Batter

2213	Babe Ruth	1540	Willie Stargell	1311	Mickey Vernon
1995	Lou Gehrig	1529	Tris Speaker	1311	Larry Walker
1951	Stan Musial	1525	Sam Crawford	1309	Paul Waner
1938	Ty Cobb	1493	Dave Parker	1305	Sam Thompson
1930	Barry Bonds	1475	Billy Williams	1304	Enos Slaughter
1860	Mel Ott	1466	Rusty Staub	1302	Jim Thome
1844	Carl Yastrzemski	1453	Eddie Mathews	1300	Eddie Collins
1839	Ted Williams	1430	Yogi Berra	1296	Dan Brouthers
1835	Rafael Palmeiro	1427	Charlie Gehringer	1287	Carlos Delgado
1702	Reggie Jackson	1422	Jim Bottomley	1271	Tino Martinez
1628	Harold Baines	1354	Darrell Evans	1269	Paul O'Neill
1609	Goose Goslin	1337	Johnny Mize	1248	Zack Wheat
1608	Ken Griffey Jr.	1333	Duke Snider	1230	John Olerud
1595	George Brett	1326	Al Oliver	1209	Bill Dickey
1578	Jake Beckley	1324	Luis Gonzalez	1208	Bill Buckner
1555	Willie McCovey	1323	Roger Connor	1205	Will Clark
1550	Fred McGriff	1314	Graig Nettles	1201	Chuck Klein

(052) Most Career RBI by a Right-handed Batter

2297	Hank Aaron	1575	Sammy Sosa	1378	Lave Cross
1922	Jimmie Foxx	1539	Harry Heilmann	1376	Johnny Bench
1903	Willie Mays	1537	Joe DiMaggio	1365	Orlando Cepeda
1880	Cap Anson	1529	Jeff Bagwell	1357	Brooks Robinson
1833	Dave Winfield	1516	Manny Ramirez	1347	Alex Rodriguez
1827	Al Simmons	1501	Gary Sheffield	1341	Gary Gaetti
1812	Frank Robinson	1466	Ed Delahanty	1331	Ron Santo
1733	Honus Wagner	1451	Jim Rice	1330	Carlton Fisk
1695	Cal Ripken	1445	Joe Carter	1308	Steve Garvey
1652	Tony Perez	1425	Andres Galarraga	1307	Paul Molitor
1636	Ernie Banks	1424	Joe Cronin	1305	Roberto Clemente
1599	Nap Lajoie	1414	Mark McGwire	1302	Hugh Duffy
1595	Mike Schmidt	1407	Jose Canseco	1291	Mike Piazza
1591	Andre Dawson	1406	Robin Yount	1284	Del Ennis
1584	Harmon Killebrew	1404	Juan Gonzalez	1283	Bob L. Johnson
1584	Rogers Hornsby	1384	Dwight Evans	1276	Hank Greenberg
1583	Al Kaline	1383	Joe Medwick	1276	Don Baylor
1579	Frank E. Thomas	1380	Jeff Kent		

(053) Most Career RBI by a Switch-hitter

1917	Eddie Murray	1257	Bernie Williams	983	Ken Caminiti
1509	Mickey Mantle	1244	Frankie Frisch	980	Tim Raines
1440	George Davis	1197	Chipper Jones	978	John Anderson
1389	Ted Simmons	1173	Bobby Bonilla	946	Terry Pendleton
1372	Chili Davis	1134	Roberto Alomar	916	Duke Farrell
1322	Ruben Sierra	1092	Reggie Smith		
1314	Pete Rose	1065	Ken Singleton		

(054) Most Career Runs

2295	Rickey Henderson	1776	Craig Biggio	1632	Robin Yount
2246	Ty Cobb	1774	Charlie Gehringer	1627	Eddie Murray
2174	Hank Aaron	1751	Jimmie Foxx	1627	Paul Waner
2174	Babe Ruth	1739	Honus Wagner	1622	Al Kaline
2165	Pete Rose	1722	Cap Anson	1622	Fred Clarke
2152	Barry Bonds	1720	Jesse Burkett	1620	Roger Connor
2062	Willie Mays	1719	Willie Keeler	1610	Lou Brock
1949	Stan Musial	1697	Billy Hamilton	1602	Jake Beckley
1888	Lou Gehrig	1684	Bid McPhee	1600	Ed Delahanty
1882	Tris Speaker	1677	Mickey Mantle	1590	Bill Dahlen
1859	Mel Ott	1669	Dave Winfield	1583	George Brett
1829	Frank Robinson	1663	Rafael Palmeiro	1579	Rogers Hornsby
1821	Eddie Collins	1650	Joe Morgan	1571	Tim Raines
1816	Carl Yastrzemski	1647	Cal Ripken	1554	Hugh Duffy
1798	Ted Williams	1643	Jimmy Ryan	1551	Reggie Jackson
1782	Paul Molitor	1642	George Van Haltren		

Roberto Clemente

GEORGE BRACE

(055) Most Career Runs by a Left-handed Batter

2246	Ty Cobb	1622	Fred Clarke	1424	Rod Carew
2174	Babe Ruth	1620	Roger Connor	1410	Billy Williams
2152	Barry Bonds	1610	Lou Brock	1410	John Ward
1949	Stan Musial	1602	Jake Beckley	1406	Mike Griffin
1888	Lou Gehrig	1583	George Brett	1391	Sam Crawford
1882	Tris Speaker	1551	Reggie Jackson	1386	Lou Whitaker
1859	Mel Ott	1523	Dan Brouthers	1383	Tony Gwynn
1821	Eddie Collins	1523	Tom Brown	1366	Vada Pinson
1816	Carl Yastrzemski	1514	Sam Rice	1359	Brett Butler
1798	Ted Williams	1513	Wade Boggs	1357	Doc Cramer
1774	Charlie Gehringer	1509	Eddie Mathews	1355	Larry Walker
1720	Jesse Burkett	1483	Goose Goslin	1349	Fred McGriff
1719	Willie Keeler	1467	Ken Griffey Jr.	1344	Darrell Evans
1697	Billy Hamilton	1456	Herman Long	1327	George Gore
1663	Rafael Palmeiro	1442	Kenny Lofton	1322	Richie Ashburn
1650	Joe Morgan	1434	Steve Finley	1321	Patsy Donovan
1642	George Van Haltren	1429	Harry Hooper		
1627	Paul Waner	1429	Dummy Hoy		

(056) Most Career Runs by a Right-handed Batter

2295	Rickey Henderson	1554	Hugh Duffy	1355	Tommy Leach
2174	Hank Aaron	1517	Jeff Bagwell	1338	Pee Wee Reese
2062	Willie Mays	1507	Al Simmons	1338	Lave Cross
1829	Frank Robinson	1506	Mike Schmidt	1335	Luis Aparicio
1782	Paul Molitor	1504	Nap Lajoie	1329	Barry Larkin
1776	Craig Biggio	1492	Harry Stovey	1319	Luke Appling
1751	Jimmie Foxx	1481	Arlie Latham	1318	Ryne Sandberg
1739	Honus Wagner	1470	Dwight Evans	1305	Kiki Cuyler
1722	Cap Anson	1446	Jim O'Rourke	1305	Ernie Banks
1684	Bid McPhee	1433	Gary Sheffield	1291	Harry Heilmann
1669	Dave Winfield	1422	Sammy Sosa	1283	Harmon Killebrew
1647	Cal Ripken	1421	Joe Kelley	1277	Julio Franco
1643	Jimmy Ryan	1416	Roberto Clemente	1277	Derek Jeter
1632	Robin Yount	1404	Frank E. Thomas	1276	Carlton Fisk
1622	Al Kaline	1390	Joe DiMaggio	1272	Tony Perez
1600	Ed Delahanty	1373	Andre Dawson	1258	Bobby Bonds
1590	Bill Dahlen	1358	Alex Rodriguez	1258	Manny Ramirez
1579	Rogers Hornsby	1357	King Kelly	1255	Rabbit Maranville

(057) Most Career Runs by a Switch-hitter

2165	Pete Rose	1280	Donie Bush	1084	Bobby Bonilla
1677	Mickey Mantle	1257	Ozzie Smith	1084	Tommy Tucker
1627	Eddie Murray	1240	Chili Davis	1084	Ruben Sierra
1571	Tim Raines	1223	Red Schoendienst	1074	Ted Simmons
1545	Max Carey	1188	Chipper Jones	1067	Maury Wills
1545	George Davis	1169	Willie Wilson	1057	Tony Fernandez
1532	Frankie Frisch	1163	Jim Gilliam	1048	Dave Bancroft
1508	Roberto Alomar	1151	Lu Blue	1025	Tom Daly
1366	Bernie Williams	1129	Ray Durham	1022	Kid Gleason
1300	Tony Phillips	1125	Devon White	1010	Willie McGee
1283	Omar Vizquel	1123	Reggie Smith	1004	Augie Galan

(058) Most Career Extra Base Hits

1477	Hank Aaron	1075	Reggie Jackson	956	Frank E. Thomas
1398	Barry Bonds	1071	Mel Ott	953	Paul Molitor
1377	Stan Musial	1048	Ken Griffey Jr.	953	Willie Stargell
1356	Babe Ruth	1041	Pete Rose	952	Mickey Mantle
1323	Willie Mays	1039	Andre Dawson	948	Billy Williams
1192	Rafael Palmeiro	1015	Mike Schmidt	943	Luis Gonzalez
1190	Lou Gehrig	1011	Rogers Hornsby	941	Dwight Evans
1186	Frank Robinson	1009	Ernie Banks	940	Dave Parker
1157	Carl Yastrzemski	996	Honus Wagner	938	Eddie Mathews
1136	Ty Cobb	995	Al Simmons	924	Manny Ramirez
1131	Tris Speaker	987	Sammy Sosa	921	Harold Baines
1119	George Brett	972	Al Kaline	921	Goose Goslin
1117	Jimmie Foxx	970	Craig Biggio	920	Willie McCovey
1117	Ted Williams	969	Jeff Bagwell	916	Larry Walker
1099	Eddie Murray	963	Tony Perez	909	Paul Waner
1093	Dave Winfield	960	Robin Yount	904	Charlie Gehringer
1078	Cal Ripken	958	Fred McGriff		

(059) Most Career Extra Base Hits by a Left-handed Batter

1398	Barry Bonds	958	Fred McGriff	868	Vada Pinson
1377	Stan Musial	953	Willie Stargell	864	Sam Crawford
1356	Babe Ruth	948	Billy Williams	850	Duke Snider
1192	Rafael Palmeiro	943	Luis Gonzalez	846	Jim Thome
1190	Lou Gehrig	940	Dave Parker	838	Rusty Staub
1157	Carl Yastrzemski	938	Eddie Mathews	837	Carlos Delgado
1136	Ty Cobb	921	Harold Baines	835	Jim Bottomley
1131	Tris Speaker	921	Goose Goslin	825	Al Oliver
1119	George Brett	920	Willie McCovey	813	Joe Morgan
1117	Ted Williams	916	Larry Walker	812	Roger Connor
1075	Reggie Jackson	909	Paul Waner	809	Johnny Mize
1071	Mel Ott	904	Charlie Gehringer	804	Jake Beckley
1048	Ken Griffey Jr.	873	Steve Finley		

(060) Most Career Extra Base Hits by a Right-handed Batter

1477	Hank Aaron	963	Tony Perez	854	Alex Rodriguez
1323	Willie Mays	960	Robin Yount	847	Juan Gonzalez
1186	Frank Robinson	956	Frank E. Thomas	846	Roberto Clemente
1117	Jimmie Foxx	953	Paul Molitor	844	Carlton Fisk
1093	Dave Winfield	941	Dwight Evans	842	Gary Gaetti
1078	Cal Ripken	924	Manny Ramirez	841	Mark McGwire
1039	Andre Dawson	902	Nap Lajoie	838	Edgar Martinez
1015	Mike Schmidt	897	Gary Sheffield	834	Jim Rice
1011	Rogers Hornsby	891	Jeff Kent	823	Orlando Cepeda
1009	Ernie Banks	887	Harmon Killebrew	818	Brooks Robinson
996	Honus Wagner	881	Joe Carter	817	Ellis Burks
995	Al Simmons	881	Joe DiMaggio	816	Jose Canseco
987	Sammy Sosa	876	Harry Heilmann	809	Ed Delahanty
972	Al Kaline	875	Andres Galarraga	803	Joe Cronin
970	Craig Biggio	873	Rickey Henderson		
969	Jeff Bagwell	858	Joe Medwick		

(061) Most Career Extra Base Hits by a Switch-hitter

1099	Eddie Murray	778	Ted Simmons	657	Devon White
1041	Pete Rose	770	Chipper Jones	648	Max Carey
952	Mickey Mantle	756	Bobby Bonilla	636	Ray Durham
804	Chili Davis	734	Reggie Smith	604	Ken Caminiti
794	Roberto Alomar	713	Tim Raines	600	Tony Fernandez
793	Ruben Sierra	709	Frankie Frisch		
791	Bernie Williams	689	George Davis		

(062) Most Career Total Bases

6856	Hank Aaron	5044	George Brett	4599	Billy Williams
6134	Stan Musial	5041	Mel Ott	4588	Rickey Henderson
6066	Willie Mays	4956	Jimmie Foxx	4532	Tony Perez
5854	Ty Cobb	4884	Ted Williams	4514	Craig Biggio
5793	Babe Ruth	4870	Honus Wagner	4511	Mickey Mantle
5784	Barry Bonds	4854	Paul Molitor	4511	Sammy Sosa
5752	Pete Rose	4852	Al Kaline	4492	Roberto Clemente
5539	Carl Yastrzemski	4834	Reggie Jackson	4478	Paul Waner
5397	Eddie Murray	4787	Andre Dawson	4471	Nap Lajoie
5388	Rafael Palmeiro	4730	Robin Yount	4458	Fred McGriff
5373	Frank Robinson	4712	Rogers Hornsby	4405	Dave Parker
5221	Dave Winfield	4706	Ernie Banks	4404	Mike Schmidt
5168	Cal Ripken	4685	Al Simmons	4349	Eddie Mathews
5101	Tris Speaker	4622	Ken Griffey Jr.	4328	Sam Crawford
5060	Lou Gehrig	4604	Harold Baines	4325	Goose Goslin

(063) Most Career Total Bases by a Left-handed Batter

6134	Stan Musial	4478	Paul Waner	4134	Steve Finley
5854	Ty Cobb	4458	Fred McGriff	4100	Zack Wheat
5793	Babe Ruth	4405	Dave Parker	4083	Al Oliver
5784	Barry Bonds	4349	Eddie Mathews	4064	Wade Boggs
5539	Carl Yastrzemski	4328	Sam Crawford	4043	Luis Gonzalez
5388	Rafael Palmeiro	4325	Goose Goslin	3998	Rod Carew
5101	Tris Speaker	4268	Eddie Collins	3962	Joe Morgan
5060	Lou Gehrig	4264	Vada Pinson	3955	Sam Rice
5044	George Brett	4259	Tony Gwynn	3904	Larry Walker
5041	Mel Ott	4257	Charlie Gehringer	3871	George Sisler
4884	Ted Williams	4238	Lou Brock	3866	Darrell Evans
4834	Reggie Jackson	4219	Willie McCovey	3865	Duke Snider
4622	Ken Griffey Jr.	4190	Willie Stargell	3833	Bill Buckner
4604	Harold Baines	4185	Rusty Staub		
4599	Billy Williams	4156	Jake Beckley		

(064) Most Career Total Bases by a Right-handed Batter

6856	Hank Aaron	4514	Craig Biggio	3959	Orlando Cepeda
6066	Willie Mays	4511	Sammy Sosa	3948	Joe DiMaggio
5373	Frank Robinson	4492	Roberto Clemente	3946	Manny Ramirez
5221	Dave Winfield	4471	Nap Lajoie	3941	Steve Garvey
5168	Cal Ripken	4404	Mike Schmidt	3910	Joe Carter
4956	Jimmie Foxx	4270	Brooks Robinson	3881	Gary Gaetti
4870	Honus Wagner	4230	Dwight Evans	3875	Alex Rodriguez
4854	Paul Molitor	4221	Gary Sheffield	3852	Joe Medwick
4852	Al Kaline	4213	Jeff Bagwell	3815	Jeff Kent
4787	Andre Dawson	4203	Frank E. Thomas	3794	Ed Delahanty
4730	Robin Yount	4143	Harmon Killebrew	3787	Ryne Sandberg
4712	Rogers Hornsby	4129	Jim Rice	3779	Ron Santo
4706	Ernie Banks	4080	Cap Anson	3742	Ivan Rodriguez
4685	Al Simmons	4053	Harry Heilmann	3733	Dale Murphy
4588	Rickey Henderson	4038	Andres Galarraga	3718	Edgar Martinez
4532	Tony Perez	3999	Carlton Fisk		

(065) Most Career Total Bases by a Switch-hitter

5752	Pete Rose	3458	Chipper Jones	2905	Willie Wilson
5397	Eddie Murray	3439	Reggie Smith	2847	Garry Templeton
4511	Mickey Mantle	3401	Bobby Bonilla	2809	Ken Caminiti
4018	Roberto Alomar	3284	Red Schoendienst	2751	Terry Pendleton
3937	Frankie Frisch	3225	Omar Vizquel	2696	Larry Bowa
3914	Chili Davis	3156	Tony Fernandez	2685	Roy White
3793	Ted Simmons	3134	Ken Singleton	2574	Dave Bancroft
3771	Tim Raines	3084	Ozzie Smith	2569	John Anderson
3756	Bernie Williams	3078	Devon White	2530	Jim Gilliam
3663	George Davis	3029	Willie McGee	2513	Maury Wills
3616	Ruben Sierra	2963	Tony Phillips		
3612	Max Carey	2909	Ray Durham		

(066) Longest Gap between 100-RBI Seasons

YEARS					RBI					RBI	
14	Harold Baines	1985	AL	CHI	113		1999	AL	BAL-CLE	103	BAL (81); CLE (22)
13	Willie Horton	1966	AL	DET	100		1979	AL	SEA	106	
10	Ken Keltner	1938	AL	CLE	113		1948	AL	CLE	119	1945 in the military
9	Sam Crawford	1901	NL	CIN	104		1910	AL	DET	120	
8	Lou Boudreau	1940	AL	CLE	101		1948	AL	CLE	106	1942-44 and most of 1945 in the military
8	Sam Chapman	1941	AL	PHI	106		1949	AL	PHI	108	
8	Ted Simmons	1975	NL	STL	100		1983	AL	MIL	108	
8	Carlton Fisk	1977	AL	BOS	102		1985	AL	CHI	107	
8	Eddie Murray	1985	AL	BAL	124		1993	NL	NY	100	
7	Lave Cross	1895	NL	PHI	101		1902	AL	PHI	108	
7	Frankie Frisch	1923	NL	NY	111		1930	NL	STL	114	
7	Al Kaline	1956	AL	DET	128		1963	AL	DET	101	
7	Jim Wynn	1967	NL	HOU	107		1974	NL	LA	108	
7	Dave Parker	1978	NL	PIT	117		1985	NL	CIN	125	
7	Jose Canseco	1991	AL	OAK	122		1998	AL	TOR	107	
7	Will Clark	1991	NL	SF	116		1998	AL	TEX	102	

(067) Retired Players with Fewest Career RBI that Had a 100-RBI Season

CAREER RBI		BEST RBI SEASON				
170	Ray Pepper	101	AL	STL	1934	
225	Bill Brubaker	102	NL	PIT	1936	
249	Buster Adams	109	NL	PHI-STL	1945	PHI (8); STL (101)
272	Luis Olmo	110	NL	BRO	1945	
282	Jim Greengrass	100	NL	CIN	1953	
286	Austin McHenry	102	NL	STL	1921	
289	Johnny Rizzo	111	NL	PIT	1938	
292	Phil Plantier	100	NL	SD	1993	
301	Dick Dietz	107	NL	SF	1970	
303	Maurice Van Robays	116	NL	PIT	1940	
313	Smead Jolley	114	AL	CHI	1930	Two 100-RBI seasons
329	Ray Sanders	102	NL	STL	1944	
333	Earl Webb	103	AL	BOS	1931	
339	Fernando Tatis	107	NL	STL	1999	
340	Luke Easter	107	AL	CLE	1950	Two 100-RBI seasons
356	Joe Hauser	115	AL	PHI	1924	
374	Bob Cerv	104	AL	KC	1958	
381	Harry Simpson	105	AL	KC	1956	
382	Geronimo Berroa	106	AL	OAK	1996	
389	Sam Leslie	102	NL	BRO	1934	
389	Bill John Sweeney	100	NL	BOS	1912	
391	Del Bissonette	113	NL	BRO	1930	Two 100-RBI seasons
397	Butch Hobson	112	AL	BOS	1977	

(068) Most Career RBI without a 100-RBI Season

CAREER RBI		BEST RBI SEASON				
1314	Pete Rose	82	NL	CIN	1969	
1300	Eddie Collins	86	AL	CHI	1924	
1178	Julio Franco	98	AL	CHI	1994	Strike-shortened season
1146	Mark Grace	98	NL	CHI	1993	
1125	Craig Biggio	88	NL	HOU	1998	
1115	Rickey Henderson	74	AL	OAK	1986	
1084	Lou Whitaker	85	AL	DET	1989	
1078	Sam Rice	87	AL	WAS	1925	
1078	Charlie Grimm	99	NL	PIT	1923	
1077	Jose Cruz Sr.	95	NL	HOU	1984	
1073	Brian Downing	95	AL	CAL	1986	
1071	Jimmy Dykes	90	AL	PHI	1932	
1053	Willie Davis	93	NL	LA	1970	
1044	Ron Fairly	77	NL	LA	1963	
1043	Bobby Murcer	96	AL	NY	1972	
1034	Joe Judge	93	AL	WAS	1928	
1014	Wade Boggs	89	AL	BOS	1987	
1013	Dusty Baker	99	NL	ATL	1973	
1007	Amos Otis	96	AL	KC	1978	
992	Ed Konetchy	93	FL	PIT	1915	
990	Ernie Lombardi	95	NL	CIN	1938	
981	Edd Roush	90	NL	CIN	1920	
980	Tim Raines	71	NL	MON	1983	
978	Gary Matthews Sr.	90	NL	ATL	1979	
972	Chris Chambliss	96	AL	NY	1976	
972	Reggie Sanders	99	NL	CIN	1995	
967	Marquis Grissom	95	NL	MON	1993	
960	Barry Larkin	89	NL	CIN	1996	
950	Dave Concepcion	84	NL	CIN	1979	

(069) Players with 500 RBI in Two Different Leagues

TOTAL RBI		AL RBI	NL RBI
1833	Dave Winfield	1207	626
1812	Frank Robinson	744	1068
1550	Fred McGriff	664	886
1244	Lee May	507	737
1206	Ellis Burks	655	551
1092	Reggie Smith	536	556

(070) Most Career RBI without ever Leading League

1903	Willie Mays	1466	Rusty Staub	1331	Ron Santo
1835	Rafael Palmeiro	1453	Eddie Mathews	1330	Carlton Fisk
1695	Cal Ripken	1430	Yogi Berra	1324	Luis Gonzalez
1652	Tony Perez	1427	Charlie Gehringer	1314	Graig Nettles
1628	Harold Baines	1424	Joe Cronin	1314	Pete Rose
1595	George Brett	1406	Robin Yount	1311	Larry Walker
1583	Al Kaline	1389	Ted Simmons	1311	Mickey Vernon
1579	Frank E. Thomas	1384	Dwight Evans	1308	Steve Garvey
1550	Fred McGriff	1380	Jeff Kent	1307	Paul Molitor
1539	Harry Heilmann	1372	Chili Davis	1305	Roberto Clemente
1501	Gary Sheffield	1354	Darrell Evans	1302	Jim Thome
1475	Billy Williams	1341	Gary Gaetti	1300	Eddie Collins

(071) Grounded into Most Career Double Plays

350	Cal Ripken	266	Dave Concepcion	234	Tony Pena
328	Hank Aaron	261	Ernie Lombardi	232	Chili Davis
323	Carl Yastrzemski	260	Tony Gwynn	232	John Olerud
319	Dave Winfield	256	Ron Santo	232	Rafael Palmeiro
316	Eddie Murray	255	Buddy Bell	229	Ernie Banks
315	Jim Rice	255	Ivan Rodriguez	227	Dwight Evans
310	Julio Franco	254	Al Oliver	226	Fred McGriff
298	Harold Baines	251	Willie Mays	224	Vinny Castilla
297	Brooks Robinson	251	Steve Garvey	223	Joe Adcock
297	Rusty Staub	248	Ken Singleton	223	Todd Zeile
287	Ted Simmons	247	Bill Buckner	223	Bernie Williams
284	Joe Torre	247	Pete Rose	221	Paul O'Neill
277	George Scott	243	Stan Musial	221	Jeff Bagwell
275	Roberto Clemente	243	Harmon Killebrew	220	Dick Groat
271	Al Kaline	236	Wade Boggs	220	Mike Piazza
269	Frank Robinson	236	Gary Gaetti		
268	Tony Perez	235	George Brett		

(072) Batters who Were the Hardest to Strike Out (min. 1,000 G)

AB PER K		AB PER K		AB PER K	
62.6	Joe Sewell	29.9	Don Mueller	24.9	Sparky Adams
44.9	Lloyd Waner	29.5	Billy Southworth	24.9	Lou Finney
42.7	Nellie Fox	28.9	Rip Radcliff	24.8	Deacon White
40.9	Tommy Holmes	28.3	Edd Roush	24.8	Jack Rowe
33.8	Andy High	27.2	Pie Traynor	24.6	Irish Meusel
33.7	Sam Rice	26.5	Doc Cramer	24.6	Ezra Sutton
33.5	Frankie Frisch	26.0	Carson Bigbee	24.5	Red Schoendienst
33.5	Dale Mitchell	25.5	Hank Severeid	24.5	Vic Power
31.5	Johnny Cooney	25.3	George Sisler	24.0	Arky Vaughan
30.3	Frank McCormick	25.2	Paul Waner		

Some, like Tris Speaker, are missing because we have incomplete data for strikeouts in some years.

(073) Batters who Were the Easiest to Strike Out (min. 1,000 G)

AB PER K		AB PER K		AB PER K	
2.75	Rob Deer	3.69	Cory Snyder	3.85	Charles Johnson
3.31	Pete Incaviglia	3.69	Preston Wilson	3.86	Jesse Barfield
3.32	Jose Hernandez	3.71	Ray Lankford	3.86	Reggie Sanders
3.36	Jim Thome	3.74	Richie Sexson	3.87	Mo Vaughn
3.49	Gorman Thomas	3.79	Gary Pettis	3.88	Mark McGwire
3.57	Jay Buhner	3.79	Nate Colbert	3.91	Jim Edmonds
3.59	Mickey Tettleton	3.80	Reggie Jackson	3.92	Cecil Fielder
3.63	Jose Canseco	3.80	Troy Glaus	3.94	John Vander Wal
3.64	Mike Cameron	3.81	Eric Davis	3.98	Geoff Jenkins
3.68	Dave Kingman	3.81	Todd Hundley	4.00	Lee Stevens
3.68	Danny Tartabull	3.82	Tony Clark		
3.68	Dean Palmer	3.83	Sammy Sosa		

(074) Most Career Batter Strikeouts

2597	Reggie Jackson	1698	Chili Davis	1527	Lance Parrish
2194	Sammy Sosa	1697	Dwight Evans	1526	Willie Mays
2003	Andres Galarraga	1694	Rickey Henderson	1526	Devon White
1942	Jose Canseco	1686	Dave Winfield	1516	Eddie Murray
1936	Willie Stargell	1641	Craig Biggio	1513	Rick Monday
1909	Jim Thome	1602	Gary Gaetti	1513	Greg Vaughn
1883	Mike Schmidt	1599	Reggie Sanders	1512	Jim Edmonds
1882	Fred McGriff	1596	Mark McGwire	1509	Andre Dawson
1867	Tony Perez	1570	Lee May	1499	Tony Phillips
1816	Dave Kingman	1558	Jeff Bagwell	1495	Greg Luzinski
1757	Bobby Bonds	1556	Dick Allen	1494	Ken Griffey Jr.
1748	Dale Murphy	1550	Ray Lankford	1487	Eddie Mathews
1730	Lou Brock	1550	Willie McCovey	1485	Barry Bonds
1710	Mickey Mantle	1537	Dave Parker	1483	Carlos Delgado
1699	Harmon Killebrew	1532	Frank Robinson	1460	Frank Howard

(075) Most Career Batter Strikeouts by a Left-handed Batter

2597	Reggie Jackson	1429	Mo Vaughn	1190	Will Clark
1936	Willie Stargell	1410	Darrell Evans	1181	Bobby Abreu
1909	Jim Thome	1393	Carl Yastrzemski	1179	Robin Ventura
1882	Fred McGriff	1376	Jeromy Burnitz	1166	Paul O'Neill
1730	Lou Brock	1352	Darryl Strawberry	1135	Lloyd Moseby
1550	Ray Lankford	1348	Rafael Palmeiro	1131	Jason Giambi
1550	Willie McCovey	1330	Babe Ruth	1119	Luis Gonzalez
1537	Dave Parker	1295	Steve Finley	1116	Fred Lynn
1513	Rick Monday	1285	Kirk Gibson	1099	Lou Whitaker
1512	Jim Edmonds	1266	Claudell Washington	1091	Norm Cash
1494	Ken Griffey Jr.	1253	Shawn Green	1069	Tino Martinez
1487	Eddie Mathews	1237	Duke Snider	1064	Johnny Callison
1485	Barry Bonds	1231	Larry Walker	1063	Andy Van Slyke
1483	Carlos Delgado	1209	Graig Nettles	1061	Delino Deshields
1441	Harold Baines	1196	Vada Pinson		

(076) Most Career Batter Strikeouts by a Right-handed Batter

2194	Sammy Sosa	1558	Jeff Bagwell	1411	Ron Gant
2003	Andres Galarraga	1556	Dick Allen	1409	Rob Deer
1942	Jose Canseco	1532	Frank Robinson	1409	Jeff Kent
1883	Mike Schmidt	1527	Lance Parrish	1406	Jay Buhner
1867	Tony Perez	1526	Willie Mays	1404	Alex Rodriguez
1816	Dave Kingman	1513	Greg Vaughn	1398	Eric Davis
1757	Bobby Bonds	1509	Andre Dawson	1391	Jose Hernandez
1748	Dale Murphy	1495	Greg Luzinski	1387	Joe Carter
1699	Harmon Killebrew	1460	Frank Howard	1386	Carlton Fisk
1697	Dwight Evans	1451	Manny Ramirez	1383	Hank Aaron
1694	Rickey Henderson	1443	Jay Bell	1369	Travis Fryman
1686	Dave Winfield	1442	Juan Samuel	1363	Matt Williams
1641	Craig Biggio	1441	Jack Clark	1362	Danny Tartabull
1602	Gary Gaetti	1427	Jim Wynn	1359	Larry Parrish
1599	Reggie Sanders	1423	Jim Rice	1350	Robin Yount
1596	Mark McGwire	1419	George Foster		
1570	Lee May	1418	George Scott		

(077) Most Career Batter Strikeouts by a Switch-hitter

1710	Mickey Mantle	1239	Ruben Sierra	1073	Jose Cruz Jr.
1698	Chili Davis	1238	Willie McGee	1054	Ray Durham
1526	Devon White	1212	Bernie Williams	1053	Howard Johnson
1516	Eddie Murray	1163	Ken Caminiti	1041	Jorge Posada
1499	Tony Phillips	1144	Willie Wilson	1021	Carl Everett
1307	Mickey Tettleton	1143	Pete Rose	1006	Chipper Jones
1266	Jose Valentin	1140	Roberto Alomar		
1246	Ken Singleton	1092	Garry Templeton		

(078) Most Career Hit by a Pitch

287	Hughie Jennings	141	Art Fletcher	114	Frankie Crosetti
282	Craig Biggio	140	Bill Dahlen	114	Bill Freehan
272	Tommy Tucker	139	Chuck Knoblauch	113	Jeff Kent
267	Don Baylor	138	Larry Walker	111	Andre Dawson
243	Ron Hunt	137	Frank Chance	111	Steve Evans
230	Dan McGann	134	Dummy Hoy	110	George H. Burns
209	Jason Kendall	134	Nap Lajoie	109	Sherry Magee
198	Frank Robinson	134	John McGraw	108	Bill Joyce
192	Minnie Minoso	132	Steve Brodie	108	Mo Vaughn
183	Jake Beckley	129	Brian Downing	107	Pete Rose
178	Andres Galarraga	129	Willie Keeler	107	Wally Schang
173	Curt Welch	128	Jeff Bagwell	107	Luis Gonzalez
165	Kid Elberfeld	127	Jason Giambi	106	Alex Rodriguez
157	Fernando Vina	125	Honus Wagner	105	Dan Brouthers
154	Brady Anderson	120	Buck Herzog	104	David Eckstein
154	Fred Clarke	120	Damion Easley	103	Barry Bonds
151	Chet Lemon	119	Gary Sheffield	103	Tris Speaker
149	Carlos Delgado	115	Jimmy Dykes	102	Orlando Cepeda
143	Carlton Fisk	115	Sherm Lollar	101	Henry Larkin
142	Nellie Fox	115	Derek Jeter		

(079) Most Career Batter Walks

2426	Barry Bonds	1499	Eddie Collins	1319	Tony Phillips
2190	Rickey Henderson	1464	Willie Mays	1317	Mark McGwire
2062	Babe Ruth	1452	Jimmie Foxx	1305	Fred McGriff
2021	Ted Williams	1444	Eddie Mathews	1302	Luke Appling
1865	Joe Morgan	1420	Frank Robinson	1293	Gary Sheffield
1845	Carl Yastrzemski	1412	Wade Boggs	1283	Edgar Martinez
1733	Mickey Mantle	1402	Hank Aaron	1277	Al Kaline
1708	Mel Ott	1401	Jeff Bagwell	1275	John Olerud
1614	Eddie Yost	1391	Dwight Evans	1263	Ken Singleton
1605	Darrell Evans	1381	Tris Speaker	1262	Jack Clark
1599	Stan Musial	1375	Reggie Jackson	1255	Rusty Staub
1566	Pete Rose	1364	Jim Thome	1249	Ty Cobb
1559	Harmon Killebrew	1353	Rafael Palmeiro	1243	Willie Randolph
1547	Frank E. Thomas	1345	Willie McCovey	1224	Jim Wynn
1508	Lou Gehrig	1333	Eddie Murray	1216	Dave Winfield
1507	Mike Schmidt	1330	Tim Raines	1210	Pee Wee Reese

Tony Oliva

(080) Most Career Batter Walks by a Left-handed Batter

2426	Barry Bonds	1305	Fred McGriff	1075	Robin Ventura
2062	Babe Ruth	1275	John Olerud	1075	Mark Grace
2021	Ted Williams	1255	Rusty Staub	1070	Keith Hernandez
1865	Joe Morgan	1249	Ty Cobb	1062	Harold Baines
1845	Carl Yastrzemski	1198	Richie Ashburn	1058	Luis Gonzalez
1708	Mel Ott	1197	Lou Whitaker	1052	Ron Fairly
1605	Darrell Evans	1189	Billy Hamilton	1045	Billy Williams
1599	Stan Musial	1186	Charlie Gehringer	1043	Norm Cash
1508	Lou Gehrig	1156	Max Bishop	1042	Roy Thomas
1499	Eddie Collins	1136	Harry Hooper	1029	Jesse Burkett
1444	Eddie Mathews	1135	Jimmy Sheckard	1018	Enos Slaughter
1412	Wade Boggs	1129	Brett Butler	1018	Rod Carew
1381	Tris Speaker	1096	George Brett	1006	Dummy Hoy
1375	Reggie Jackson	1092	Stan Hack	1003	Bobby Abreu
1364	Jim Thome	1091	Paul Waner	1002	Roger Connor
1353	Rafael Palmeiro	1088	Graig Nettles	1001	Boog Powell
1345	Willie McCovey	1077	Ken Griffey Jr.		

(081) Most Career Batter Walks by a Right-handed Batter

2190	Rickey Henderson	1262	Jack Clark	1054	Manny Ramirez
1614	Eddie Yost	1243	Willie Randolph	1043	Eddie Joost
1559	Harmon Killebrew	1224	Jim Wynn	1038	Rogers Hornsby
1547	Frank E. Thomas	1216	Dave Winfield	1031	Sal Bando
1507	Mike Schmidt	1210	Pee Wee Reese	1012	Ron Cey
1464	Willie Mays	1197	Brian Downing	1011	Ralph Kiner
1452	Jimmie Foxx	1153	Toby Harrah	996	Eddie Stanky
1420	Frank Robinson	1137	Craig Biggio	986	Dale Murphy
1402	Hank Aaron	1129	Cal Ripken	984	Gene Tenace
1401	Jeff Bagwell	1108	Ron Santo	982	Bid McPhee
1391	Dwight Evans	1094	Paul Molitor	967	Bob Elliott
1317	Mark McGwire	1087	Bobby Grich	966	Robin Yount
1302	Luke Appling	1075	Bob L. Johnson	963	Honus Wagner
1293	Gary Sheffield	1070	Harlond Clift	958	Jimmy Dykes
1283	Edgar Martinez	1064	Bill Dahlen	953	Cap Anson
1277	Al Kaline	1059	Joe Cronin	951	Rocky Colavito

(082) Most Career Batter Walks by a Switch-hitter

1733	Mickey Mantle	1070	Chipper Jones	897	Omar Vizquel
1566	Pete Rose	1069	Bernie Williams	890	Reggie Smith
1333	Eddie Murray	1040	Max Carey	875	Mark McLemore
1330	Tim Raines	1036	Jim Gilliam	874	George Davis
1319	Tony Phillips	1032	Roberto Alomar	855	Ted Simmons
1263	Ken Singleton	1003	Miller Huggins	853	Roy Cullenbine
1194	Chili Davis	979	Augie Galan	849	Wally Schang
1158	Donie Bush	949	Mickey Tettleton	827	Dave Bancroft
1092	Lu Blue	934	Roy White		
1072	Ozzie Smith	912	Bobby Bonilla		

(083) Most Career Batter Intentional Walks, since 1955

645	Barry Bonds	172	Dave Winfield	146	Mike Piazza
293	Hank Aaron	172	Rafael Palmeiro	146	Todd Helton
260	Willie McCovey	171	Fred McGriff	145	Luis Gonzalez
229	George Brett	170	Dave Parker	144	Rod Carew
227	Willie Stargell	167	Roberto Clemente	144	Garry Templeton
222	Eddie Murray	167	Pete Rose	144	Mo Vaughn
218	Frank Robinson	165	Frank E. Thomas	143	Andre Dawson
216	Ken Griffey Jr.	164	Reggie Jackson	142	Jose Cruz Sr.
203	Tony Gwynn	160	Harmon Killebrew	141	Darrell Evans
201	Mike Schmidt	159	Dale Murphy	140	Boog Powell
198	Ernie Banks	159	Carlos Delgado	139	Jim Thome
195	Vladimir Guerrero	157	John Olerud	138	Dick Allen
193	Rusty Staub	155	Will Clark	136	Don Mattingly
192	Willie Mays	155	Jeff Bagwell	135	Johnny Bench
190	Carl Yastrzemski	154	Orlando Cepeda	135	Frank Howard
188	Chili Davis	154	Manny Ramirez	132	Robin Ventura
188	Ted Simmons	151	Sammy Sosa	131	Al Kaline
187	Harold Baines	150	Mark McGwire	131	Tony Oliva
182	Billy Williams	150	Tony Perez	131	Darryl Strawberry
180	Wade Boggs	148	Tim Raines	130	Keith Hernandez

(084) Non-Pitchers with more Career Walks than Hits (min. 100 AB)

AT-BATS			GAMES	WALKS	HITS
727	Frank Fernandez	1967-72	285	164	145
607	Jim French	1965-71	234	121	119
500	Tony Smith	1907, 10-11	170	95	90
379	Marty Hopkins	1934-35	136	85	80
192	Glenn Gulliver	1982-83	73	46	39
186	Dick Smith	1951-55	70	30	25
164	Tom Burgess	1954, 62	104	39	28
145	Charlie Sands	1967, 71-75	93	36	31
125	Mike Jordan	1890	37	15	12
123	Bob Farley	1961-62	84	30	20
122	Jim McCauley	1884-86	39	24	23
122	John H. Riddle	1889-90	38	19	15
107	Scotty Barr	1908-09	41	14	12

(085) Most Career At-bats without a Hit by a Non-Pitcher

23	Larry Littleton	1981	14	Jim Riley	1921, 23	11	Ches Crist	1906	
23	Mike Potter	1976-77	13	Offa Neal	1905	11	Lyle Judy	1935	
18	Cy Wright	1916	13	Paul Dicken	1964, 66	11	Larry Eschen	1942	
16	Ramon Conde	1962	12	Red Gust	1911	11	Eddie Samcoff	1951	
15	Gus Creely	1890	12	Gil Britton	1913	11	Tom Wieghaus	1981, 83-84	
15	Dutch Lerchen	1910	12	Norm Glockson	1914	10	Ray Stoviak	1938	
15	Roy Luebbe	1925	12	Dave Coleman	1977	10	Neil Wilson	1960	
15	John O'Neill	1899, 1902	12	Sap Randall	1988	10	William Williams	1969	
15	Mike Gulan	1997, 2001	12	Ken Ramos	1997	10	Rich Puig	1974	
14	Ed Boyle	1896	11	Bill Clymer	1891	10	Tom Magrann	1989	
14	Josh Labandeira	2004	11	Jim A. McCormick	1892	10	Yohanny Valera	2000	

(086) Most Seasons Batting .300 or Better (min. 100 hits per season)

22	Ty Cobb	13	Roberto Clemente	11	Jimmy Ryan
18	Tris Speaker	13	Willie Keeler	11	Joe Kelley
17	Stan Musial	12	Dan Brouthers	11	Joe Medwick
16	Cap Anson	12	George Van Haltren	11	Patsy Donovan
16	Eddie Collins	12	Harry Heilmann	10	Bill Dickey
16	Tony Gwynn	12	Jake Beckley	10	Bill Terry
15	Honus Wagner	12	Lou Gehrig	10	Edgar Martinez
15	Pete Rose	12	Paul Molitor	10	Fred Clarke
15	Ted Williams	12	Sam Rice	10	Heinie Manush
14	Babe Ruth	12	Zack Wheat	10	Jake Daubert
14	Hank Aaron	11	Roger Connor	10	Jim O'Rourke
14	Nap Lajoie	11	Al Oliver	10	Dixie Walker
14	Rod Carew	11	Arky Vaughan	10	Ivan Rodriguez
14	Rogers Hornsby	11	Barry Bonds	10	Joe DiMaggio
14	Wade Boggs	11	Billy Hamilton	10	Mel Ott
13	Al Simmons	11	Ed Delahanty	10	Pie Traynor
13	Charlie Gehringer	11	Edd Roush	10	Sam Crawford
13	Frankie Frisch	11	George Brett	10	Stuffy McInnis
13	George Sisler	11	Goose Goslin	10	Willie Mays
13	Luke Appling	11	Jesse Burkett	10	Manny Ramirez
13	Paul Waner	11	Jimmie Foxx		

COURTESY OF THE COLORADO ROCKIES

Todd Helton

(087) Most Seasons with at least 100 Runs Scored

15	Hank Aaron	11	Jimmie Foxx	9	Dummy Hoy
13	Rickey Henderson	11	Alex Rodriguez	9	Paul Waner
13	Lou Gehrig	10	Bid McPhee	9	Ted Williams
12	Charlie Gehringer	10	Pete Rose	9	Jesse Burkett
12	Barry Bonds	10	Ed Delahanty	9	Harry Stovey
12	Willie Mays	10	Mike Griffin	9	Mickey Mantle
12	Babe Ruth	10	Sam Thompson	9	Arlie Latham
11	Stan Musial	10	Derek Jeter	9	Jeff Bagwell
11	Ty Cobb	9	Hugh Duffy	9	Earl Averill
11	Billy Hamilton	9	Frank E. Thomas	9	Johnny Damon
11	George Van Haltren	9	Mel Ott		

(088) Most Seasons with at least 100 RBI

13	Jimmie Foxx	9	Joe DiMaggio	8	Joe Cronin
13	Lou Gehrig	9	Mel Ott	8	Johnny Mize
13	Babe Ruth	9	Ted Williams	8	Juan Gonzalez
12	Barry Bonds	9	Mike Schmidt	8	Chipper Jones
12	Al Simmons	9	Albert Belle	8	Ken Griffey Jr.
11	Hank Aaron	9	Sammy Sosa	8	Dave Winfield
11	Goose Goslin	9	Honus Wagner	8	Harry Heilmann
11	Frank E. Thomas	9	Harmon Killebrew	8	Jeff Bagwell
11	Manny Ramirez	9	Jim Thome	8	Bob L. Johnson
10	Willie Mays	8	Cap Anson	8	Fred McGriff
10	Rafael Palmeiro	8	Ernie Banks	8	Jeff Kent
10	Joe Carter	8	Hugh Duffy	8	Carlos Delgado
10	Stan Musial	8	Jim Rice	8	Vladimir Guerrero
10	Alex Rodriguez	8	Sam Thompson	8	Gary Sheffield

(089) Most Seasons with at least 100 Hits

23	Pete Rose	19	Rickey Henderson	17	Zack Wheat
22	Carl Yastrzemski	19	Cal Ripken	17	Roger Connor
22	Ty Cobb	19	Robin Yount	17	Eddie Collins
21	Hank Aaron	18	Roberto Clemente	17	Wade Boggs
20	Eddie Murray	18	Al Kaline	17	Reggie Jackson
20	George Brett	18	Luis Aparicio	17	Rod Carew
19	Nap Lajoie	18	Frank Robinson	17	Ozzie Smith
19	Cap Anson	18	Stan Musial	17	Andre Dawson
19	Paul Molitor	18	Craig Biggio	17	George Davis
19	Tris Speaker	17	Barry Bonds	17	Mel Ott
19	Honus Wagner	17	Rafael Palmeiro	17	Jimmy Ryan
19	Willie Mays	17	Lou Brock	17	Harold Baines
19	Dave Winfield	17	Jake Beckley	17	Chili Davis

(090) Most Seasons with at least 150 Hits

18	Tris Speaker	13	Jesse Burkett	12	Billy Williams
18	Pete Rose	13	George Sisler	12	George Van Haltren
18	Ty Cobb	13	Sam Rice	12	Brett Butler
17	Hank Aaron	13	Nap Lajoie	12	Charlie Gehringer
16	Honus Wagner	13	Carl Yastrzemski	12	Patsy Donovan
15	Stan Musial	13	Willie Mays	12	Jake Beckley
15	Eddie Collins	13	Lou Brock	12	Doc Cramer
15	Cal Ripken	13	Harry Heilmann	12	Pie Traynor
14	Sam Crawford	13	Rafael Palmeiro	12	Al Simmons
14	Goose Goslin	13	Rod Carew	12	Roberto Alomar
14	Eddie Murray	13	Rogers Hornsby	12	Mel Ott
14	Tony Gwynn	13	Willie Keeler	12	Roberto Clemente
14	Paul Waner	13	Frankie Frisch	12	Nellie Fox
13	Lou Gehrig	13	Paul Molitor	12	Jeff Bagwell
13	Richie Ashburn	13	Craig Biggio	12	Jimmie Foxx

(091) Most Seasons with at least 200 Hits

10	Pete Rose	6	Al Simmons	4	Joe Medwick
9	Ty Cobb	6	Steve Garvey	4	Heinie Manush
8	Lou Gehrig	6	Ichiro Suzuki	4	Rod Carew
8	Paul Waner	5	Chuck Klein	4	Nap Lajoie
8	Willie Keeler	5	Kirby Puckett	4	Joe Jackson
7	Wade Boggs	5	Tony Gwynn	4	Lou Brock
7	Charlie Gehringer	5	Derek Jeter	4	Harry Heilmann
7	Rogers Hornsby	4	Ed Delahanty	4	Tris Speaker
6	George Sisler	4	Roberto Clemente	4	Lloyd Waner
6	Sam Rice	4	Jim Rice	4	Vladimir Guerrero
6	Jesse Burkett	4	Jack Tobin	4	Juan Pierre
6	Bill Terry	4	Vada Pinson	4	Michael Young
6	Stan Musial	4	Paul Molitor		

(092) Most Seasons with at least 100 Walks

13	Babe Ruth	8	Eddie Yost	7	Roy Thomas
13	Barry Bonds	8	Bobby Abreu	6	Ralph Kiner
11	Ted Williams	8	Max Bishop	6	Carl Yastrzemski
11	Lou Gehrig	7	Jason Giambi	6	Jim Wynn
10	Frank E. Thomas	7	Mike Schmidt	6	Eddie Stanky
10	Mel Ott	7	Jimmie Foxx	6	Gene Tenace
10	Mickey Mantle	7	Jeff Bagwell	6	Harlond Clift
9	Jim Thome	7	Harmon Killebrew	6	Eddie Joost
8	Joe Morgan	7	Rickey Henderson		

(093) Most Seasons with at least 100 Singles

21	Pete Rose	15	Tony Gwynn	14	Nap Lajoie
19	Ty Cobb	15	Eddie Murray	14	Max Carey
17	Honus Wagner	15	Paul Molitor	14	Richie Ashburn
16	Stan Musial	15	Rod Carew	14	Zack Wheat
16	Tris Speaker	14	Paul Waner	14	Hank Aaron
16	Eddie Collins	14	Luis Aparicio	14	Jesse Burkett
15	Lou Brock	14	George Davis	14	George Sisler
15	Sam Crawford	14	Carl Yastrzemski		
15	Luke Appling	14	Frankie Frisch		

(094) Most Seasons with at least 40 Doubles

10	Tris Speaker	5	Hank Greenberg	4	Joe Jackson
9	Stan Musial	5	Paul Waner	4	Billy Herman
8	Wade Boggs	5	Ed Delahanty	4	Roberto Alomar
8	Harry Heilmann	5	Joe Sewell	4	Lou Boudreau
7	Nap Lajoie	5	Bob Meusel	4	Ted Williams
7	Joe Medwick	5	Edgar Martinez	4	Ben Chapman
7	Pete Rose	5	Bobby Abreu	4	Rafael Palmeiro
7	Rogers Hornsby	4	George H. Burns	4	Garret Anderson
7	Lou Gehrig	4	Chuck Klein	4	Don Mattingly
7	Charlie Gehringer	4	Albert Pujols	4	Nomar Garciaparra
7	Craig Biggio	4	Larry Walker	4	Carlos Delgado
6	Joe Cronin	4	Ty Cobb	4	Luis Gonzalez
6	Heinie Manush	4	Jeff Kent	4	Orlando Cabrera
6	Todd Helton	4	Robin Yount		
5	George Brett	4	Al Simmons		

(095) Most Seasons with at least 10 Triples

17	Ty Cobb	11	Buck Ewing	10	Jesse Burkett
17	Sam Crawford	11	Roger Connor	10	Ed Konetchy
14	Fred Clarke	11	Pie Traynor	10	Elmer Flick
14	Jake Beckley	11	Edd Roush	10	Paul Waner
13	Tris Speaker	11	Zack Wheat	10	Sam Rice
13	Honus Wagner	10	Bid McPhee	10	Harry Stovey
12	Eddie Collins	10	Joe Kelley	10	Ed Delahanty
11	Mike Tiernan	10	Bobby Veach		
11	Dan Brouthers	10	Ed McKean		

(096) Most Seasons with at least 20 Triples

5	Sam Crawford	3	Sam Thompson	2	Perry Werden
4	Ty Cobb	3	Jimmy Williams	2	Mike Tiernan
3	Harry Stovey	3	Joe Jackson	2	Buck Freeman
3	Dan Brouthers	3	Earle Combs	2	Honus Wagner
3	Roger Connor	2	Dave Orr	2	Stan Musial

(097) Most Career Home Runs

755	Hank Aaron	511	Mel Ott	431	Cal Ripken
734	Barry Bonds	504	Eddie Murray	426	Billy Williams
714	Babe Ruth	493	Lou Gehrig	419	Mike Piazza
660	Willie Mays	493	Fred McGriff	414	Darrell Evans
588	Sammy Sosa	487	Frank E. Thomas	407	Carlos Delgado
586	Frank Robinson	475	Stan Musial	407	Duke Snider
583	Mark McGwire	475	Willie Stargell	399	Al Kaline
573	Harmon Killebrew	472	Jim Thome	399	Andres Galarraga
569	Rafael Palmeiro	470	Manny Ramirez	398	Dale Murphy
563	Reggie Jackson	465	Dave Winfield	396	Joe Carter
563	Ken Griffey Jr.	464	Alex Rodriguez	390	Graig Nettles
548	Mike Schmidt	462	Jose Canseco	389	Johnny Bench
536	Mickey Mantle	455	Gary Sheffield	385	Dwight Evans
534	Jimmie Foxx	452	Carl Yastrzemski	384	Harold Baines
521	Willie McCovey	449	Jeff Bagwell	383	Larry Walker
521	Ted Williams	442	Dave Kingman	382	Frank Howard
512	Ernie Banks	438	Andre Dawson	382	Jim Rice
512	Eddie Mathews	434	Juan Gonzalez	381	Albert Belle

(098) Most Career Home Runs by a Left-handed Batter

734	Barry Bonds	452	Carl Yastrzemski	339	Boog Powell
714	Babe Ruth	426	Billy Williams	339	Tino Martinez
569	Rafael Palmeiro	414	Darrell Evans	335	Darryl Strawberry
563	Reggie Jackson	407	Duke Snider	331	Luis Gonzalez
563	Ken Griffey Jr.	407	Carlos Delgado	328	Mo Vaughn
521	Willie McCovey	390	Graig Nettles	318	Shawn Green
521	Ted Williams	384	Harold Baines	317	George Brett
512	Eddie Mathews	383	Larry Walker	315	Jeromy Burnitz
511	Mel Ott	377	Norm Cash	306	Fred Lynn
493	Lou Gehrig	359	Johnny Mize	305	David Justice
493	Fred McGriff	358	Yogi Berra	303	Steve Finley
475	Stan Musial	350	Jason Giambi	300	Chuck Klein
475	Willie Stargell	350	Jim Edmonds		
472	Jim Thome	339	Dave Parker		

(099) Most Career Home Runs by a Right-handed Batter

755	Hank Aaron	434	Juan Gonzalez	369	Ralph Kiner
660	Willie Mays	431	Cal Ripken	361	Joe DiMaggio
588	Sammy Sosa	419	Mike Piazza	360	Gary Gaetti
586	Frank Robinson	399	Al Kaline	355	Greg Vaughn
583	Mark McGwire	399	Andres Galarraga	354	Lee May
573	Harmon Killebrew	398	Dale Murphy	352	Ellis Burks
548	Mike Schmidt	396	Joe Carter	351	Dick Allen
534	Jimmie Foxx	389	Johnny Bench	348	George Foster
512	Ernie Banks	385	Dwight Evans	345	Jeff Kent
487	Frank E. Thomas	382	Jim Rice	342	Ron Santo
470	Manny Ramirez	382	Frank Howard	342	Andruw Jones
465	Dave Winfield	381	Albert Belle	340	Jack Clark
464	Alex Rodriguez	379	Orlando Cepeda	338	Don Baylor
462	Jose Canseco	379	Tony Perez	338	Vladimir Guerrero
455	Gary Sheffield	378	Matt Williams	336	Joe Adcock
449	Jeff Bagwell	376	Carlton Fisk	332	Bobby Bonds
442	Dave Kingman	374	Rocky Colavito	331	Hank Greenberg
438	Andre Dawson	370	Gil Hodges		

(100) Most Career Home Runs by a Switch-hitter

536	Mickey Mantle	287	Bernie Williams	227	Tony Clark
504	Eddie Murray	248	Ted Simmons	225	Lance Berkman
357	Chipper Jones	246	Jose Valentin	210	Roberto Alomar
350	Chili Davis	246	Ken Singleton	208	Devon White
314	Reggie Smith	245	Mickey Tettleton	203	Carlos Beltran
306	Ruben Sierra	239	Ken Caminiti	202	Todd Hundley
287	Bobby Bonilla	228	Howard Johnson	202	Carl Everett

(101) Most Career Pinch-hit Home Runs

20	Cliff Johnson	12	Bob Cerv	10	Dave Clark
18	Jerry Lynch	12	Graig Nettles	10	Jim Dwyer
17	John Vander Wal	12	Craig Wilson	10	Mike Lum
16	Smoky Burgess	12	Jose Morales	10	Ken McMullen
16	Gates Brown	11	Jeff Burroughs	10	Don Mincher
16	Willie McCovey	11	Jay Johnstone	10	Wally Post
15	Dave Hansen	11	Candy Maldonado	10	Champ Summers
14	George Crowe	11	Fred Whitfield	10	Jerry Turner
13	Mark Sweeney	11	Cy Williams	10	Gus Zernial
13	Glenallen Hill	11	Orlando Merced		
12	Joe Adcock	10	Mark Carreon		

(102) Most Career Home Runs by a Pitcher

37	Wes Ferrell	20	Milt Pappas	15	Don Newcombe
35	Bob Lemon	19	Jack Harshman	15	Joe Nuxhall
35	Warren Spahn	18	Cy Young	15	Claude Passeau
34	Red Ruffing	16	Jim Kaat	15	Gary Peters
33	Earl Wilson	16	Schoolboy Rowe	15	Pedro Ramos
29	Don Drysdale	16	Jim Tobin	15	Hal Schumacher
24	John Clarkson	15	Johnny Antonelli	15	Rick Wise
24	Bob Gibson	15	Don Cardwell	15	Early Wynn
23	Walter Johnson	15	Dick Donovan	15	Mike Hampton
21	Jack Stivetts	15	Lefty Grove		
20	Dizzy Trout	15	Jouett Meekin		

All the career home runs by position are only those hit while the player was playing that position.

(103) Most Career Home Runs by a Catcher

396	Mike Piazza	243	Javy Lopez	193	Jorge Posada
351	Carlton Fisk	239	Roy Campanella	184	Bill Freehan
327	Johnny Bench	232	Gabby Hartnett	182	Ernie Lombardi
306	Yogi Berra	213	Benito Santiago	174	Del Crandall
299	Lance Parrish	200	Bill Dickey	167	Walker Cooper
298	Gary Carter	195	Ted Simmons	164	Darrell Porter
270	Ivan Rodriguez	193	Todd Hundley	164	Charles Johnson

(104) Most Career Home Runs by a First Baseman

566	Mark McGwire	409	Eddie Murray	310	Orlando Cepeda
493	Lou Gehrig	387	Andres Galarraga	310	Jim Thome
482	Jimmie Foxx	366	Norm Cash	292	Mo Vaughn
462	Fred McGriff	362	Carlos Delgado	285	Joe Adcock
446	Jeff Bagwell	350	Johnny Mize	285	Lee May
440	Rafael Palmeiro	335	Gil Hodges	283	Todd Helton
439	Willie McCovey	318	Tino Martinez	282	Eric Karros

(105) Most Career Home Runs by a Second Baseman

319	Jeff Kent	221	Bobby Doerr	156	Frank White
277	Ryne Sandberg	217	Craig Biggio	150	Tony Lazzeri
266	Joe Morgan	207	Roberto Alomar	137	Bill Mazeroski
265	Rogers Hornsby	195	Bobby Grich	125	Davey Lopes
251	Bret Boone	181	Charlie Gehringer	123	Damion Easley
246	Joe Gordon	169	Ray Durham	120	Juan Samuel
239	Lou Whitaker	157	Alfonso Soriano		

(106) Most Career Home Runs by a Third Baseman

509	Mike Schmidt	306	Vinny Castilla	243	Dean Palmer
486	Eddie Mathews	281	Chipper Jones	238	Troy Glaus
368	Graig Nettles	278	Robin Ventura	235	Sal Bando
359	Matt Williams	265	Brooks Robinson	233	Ken Caminiti
337	Ron Santo	260	Ken Boyer	232	Doug DeCinces
332	Gary Gaetti	252	Scott Rolen	206	Eric Chavez
312	Ron Cey	249	Tim Wallach		

(107) Most Career Home Runs by a Shortstop

345	Cal Ripken	183	Nomar Garciaparra	128	Alex S. Gonzalez
344	Alex Rodriguez	182	Derek Jeter	127	Rico Petrocelli
277	Ernie Banks	177	Alan Trammell	122	Pee Wee Reese
237	Miguel Tejada	156	Joe Cronin	122	Robin Yount
213	Vern Stephens	136	Rich Aurilia	121	Jay Bell
194	Barry Larkin	129	Eddie Joost	119	Shawon Dunston
192	Jose Valentin	128	Travis Jackson		

(108) Most Career Home Runs by a Left Fielder

698	Barry Bonds	286	Greg Vaughn	221	Gus Zernial
477	Ted Williams	283	Albert Belle	220	Ron Gant
334	Ralph Kiner	277	Carl Yastrzemski	219	Greg Luzinski
326	Luis Gonzalez	269	Jim Rice	218	Goose Goslin
313	Babe Ruth	268	Willie Stargell	216	Rickey Henderson
301	Billy Williams	233	Bob L. Johnson	213	Al Simmons
292	George Foster	223	Hank Sauer		

(109) Most Career Home Runs by a Center Fielder

640	Willie Mays	295	Steve Finley	202	Dale Murphy
540	Ken Griffey Jr.	266	Fred Lynn	200	Hack Wilson
431	Mickey Mantle	261	Bernie Williams	198	Gorman Thomas
356	Duke Snider	237	Larry Doby	197	Vada Pinson
344	Joe DiMaggio	227	Earl Averill	197	Carlos Beltran
335	Jim Edmonds	212	Marquis Grissom	191	Rick Monday
328	Andruw Jones	204	Jim Wynn		

(110) Most Career Home Runs by a Right Fielder

536	Sammy Sosa	320	Dwight Evans	268	Rocky Colavito
527	Hank Aaron	293	Jay Buhner	267	Bobby Bonds
433	Mel Ott	292	Al Kaline	264	Dave Parker
431	Reggie Jackson	285	Dave Winfield	261	Paul O'Neill
354	Babe Ruth	282	Darryl Strawberry	251	Jeromy Burnitz
338	Larry Walker	278	Frank Robinson	249	Tim Salmon
325	Vladimir Guerrero	270	Shawn Green		

(111) Most Career Home Runs by a Designated Hitter

243	Edgar Martinez	145	Hal McRae	102	Paul Molitor
236	Harold Baines	125	Brian Downing	101	Reggie Jackson
236	Frank E. Thomas	125	Andre Thornton	101	Dave Kingman
219	Don Baylor	115	Cliff Johnson	98	Cecil Fielder
207	Jose Canseco	107	Rafael Palmeiro	98	Jim Rice
200	Chili Davis	107	Travis Hafner	96	Willie Horton
192	David Ortiz	104	Juan Gonzalez	96	Ken Phelps

(112) Leadoff Home Runs in both Games of a Doubleheader

Harry Hooper	AL	BOS	May 30, 1913
Rickey Henderson	AL	OAK	Jul 5, 1993
Brady Anderson	AL	BAL	Aug 21, 1999

(113) Longest Time between Home Runs in a Park for a Batter

DAYS		PARK	CITY	FROM	TO
5824	Sammy Sosa	Fenway Park	BOS	Jun 21, 1989	Jun 1, 2005
5810	Luke Appling	Sportsman's Park III	STL	Jun 4, 1933	May 1, 1949
5520	Sam Rice	Shibe Park	PHI	May 5, 1919	Jun 15, 1934
5445	Early Wynn	Comiskey Park I	CHI	Jun 3, 1944	May 1, 1959
5401	Fred Clarke	West Side Park II	CHI	Jul 4, 1896	Apr 17, 1911
5367	Gary Sheffield	Network Associates Coliseum	OAK	Oct 1, 1988	Jun 12, 2003
5331	Jimmy Dykes	Griffith Stadium	WAS	Oct 2, 1921	May 7, 1936
5116	Pee Wee Reese	Wrigley Field	CHI	Aug 2, 1941	Aug 5, 1955
5095	Ralph Winegarner	Sportsman's Park III	STL	Aug 11, 1935	Jul 23, 1949
5075	Luke Appling	Fenway Park	BOS	Aug 26, 1932	Jul 19, 1946
5070	Gary Sheffield	Yankee Stadium	NY	Jun 28, 1990	May 15, 2004
5052	Buck Martinez	Memorial Stadium	BAL	Aug 5, 1969	Jun 5, 1983
5050	Ron Fairly	County Stadium	MIL	Jul 21, 1963	May 18, 1977
5007	Rafael Palmeiro	Wrigley Field	CHI	Oct 2, 1988	Jun 18, 2002

(114) Most Home Runs by a Batter in a Doubleheader

5	Stan Musial	NL	STL	May 2, 1954		4	Roger Maris	AL	NY	Jul 25, 1961
5	Nate Colbert	NL	SD	Aug 1, 1972		4	Rocky Colavito	AL	DET	Aug 27, 1961
4	Bobby Lowe	NL	BOS	May 30, 1894		4	Harmon Killebrew	AL	MIN	Sep 21, 1963
4	Earl Averill	AL	CLE	Sep 17, 1930		4	Leo Cardenas	NL	CIN	Jun 5, 1966
4	Jimmie Foxx	AL	PHI	Jul 2, 1933		4	Adolfo Phillips	NL	CHI	Jun 11, 1967
4	Jim Tabor	AL	BOS	Jul 4, 1939		4	Lee May	NL	CIN	Jul 15, 1969
4	Bill Nicholson	NL	CHI	Jul 23, 1944		4	Bobby Murcer	AL	NY	Jun 24, 1970
4	Ralph Kiner	NL	PIT	Sep 11, 1947		4	Rusty Staub	NL	MON	Aug 1, 1970
4	Pat Seerey	AL	CHI	Jul 18, 1948		4	Graig Nettles	AL	NY	Apr 14, 1974
4	Gus Zernial	AL	CHI	Oct 1, 1950		4	Otto Velez	AL	TOR	May 4, 1980
4	Wally Post	NL	CIN	Apr 29, 1956		4	Al Oliver	AL	TEX	Aug 17 1980
4	Bobby Thomson	NL	MIL	May 30, 1956		4	Jason Thompson	NL	PIT	Jun 26, 1984
4	Charlie Maxwell	AL	DET	May 3, 1959		4	Mark Whiten	NL	STL	Sep 7, 1993

(115) Teammates Hitting Home Runs Most Times in the Same Game

75	Hank Aaron	Eddie Mathews		46	Mark McGwire	Jose Canseco
73	Lou Gehrig	Babe Ruth		46	Jeff Bagwell	Craig Biggio
68	Willie Mays	Willie McCovey		46	Jim Edmonds	Albert Pujols
67	Gil Hodges	Duke Snider		44	Ken Griffey Jr.	Edgar Martinez
64	Ron Santo	Billy Williams		43	Ernie Banks	Ron Santo
61	Harmon Killebrew	Bob Allison		42	Manny Ramirez	David Ortiz
56	Eddie Mathews	Joe Adcock		42	Mickey Mantle	Roger Maris
56	Jim Rice	Dwight Evans		42	Harmon Killebrew	Tony Oliva
55	Mickey Mantle	Yogi Berra		42	Ernie Banks	Billy Williams
55	Chipper Jones	Andruw Jones		42	Frank E. Thomas	Robin Ventura
53	Ken Griffey Jr.	Jay Buhner		42	Rafael Palmeiro	Alex Rodriguez
50	Willie Mays	Orlando Cepeda		41	Johnny Bench	Tony Perez
48	Manny Ramirez	Jim Thome		40	Barry Bonds	Jeff Kent
47	Babe Ruth	Bob Meusel				

Babe Ruth

Lou Gehrig

GEORGE BRACE

GEORGE BRACE

(116) Players with 100+ Home Runs for Three Different Teams

Darrell Evans	ATL (NL) 131	SF (NL) 142	DET (AL) 141
Reggie Jackson	KC-OAK (AL) 269	NY (AL) 144	CAL (AL) 123
Alex Rodriguez	SEA (AL) 189	TEX (AL) 156	NY (AL) 119

(117) Most Career Game-ending Home Runs

12	Jimmie Foxx	12	Babe Ruth	10	Reggie Jackson
12	Mickey Mantle	11	Tony Perez	10	Mike Schmidt
12	Stan Musial	10	Dick Allen	10	Sammy Sosa
12	Frank Robinson	10	Harold Baines	10	Barry Bonds

(118) Best Career Strikeout to Home Run Ratio (Min. 250 HR)

RATIO		STRIKEOUTS	HR	RATIO		STRIKEOUTS	HR
1.02	Joe DiMaggio	369	361	1.83	Hank Aaron	1383	755
1.16	Yogi Berra	414	358	1.86	Babe Ruth	1330	714
1.31	Ted Kluszewski	365	279	1.99	Vladimir Guerrero	674	338
1.36	Ted Williams	709	521	2.03	Barry Bonds	1434	708
1.46	Johnny Mize	524	359	2.03	Ralph Kiner	749	369
1.47	Stan Musial	696	475	2.13	Gary Sheffield	971	455
1.58	Albert Pujols	394	250	2.26	Rogers Hornsby	679	301
1.60	Lou Gehrig	790	493	2.31	Willie Mays	1526	660
1.74	Chuck Klein	521	300	2.35	Rocky Colavito	880	374
1.75	Mel Ott	896	511	2.37	Rafael Palmeiro	1348	569
				2.40	Todd Helton	686	286

(119) Most Career Extra-inning Home Runs

22	Willie Mays	14	Hank Aaron	11	Harmon Killebrew
18	Jack Clark	13	Ted Williams	11	Stan Musial
16	Babe Ruth	12	Willie Stargell	11	Graig Nettles
16	Frank Robinson	12	Mark McGwire	11	Lance Parrish
14	Jimmie Foxx	12	Rafael Palmeiro		
14	Mickey Mantle	11	Barry Bonds		

(120) Most Career Grand Slams

23	Lou Gehrig	16	Hank Aaron	13	Albert Belle
20	Manny Ramirez	16	Dave Kingman	13	Joe DiMaggio
19	Eddie Murray	15	Ken Griffey Jr.	13	George Foster
18	Willie McCovey	14	Mike Piazza	13	Ralph Kiner
18	Robin Ventura	14	Gil Hodges	13	Jeff Kent
17	Jimmie Foxx	14	Mark McGwire	13	Alex Rodriguez
17	Ted Williams	14	Richie Sexson		
16	Babe Ruth	13	Harold Baines		

(121) Most Career Home Runs without ever Winning a Season Title

585	Rafael Palmeiro	449	Jeff Bagwell	399	Al Kaline
487	Frank E. Thomas	431	Cal Ripken	396	Joe Carter
475	Stan Musial	426	Billy Williams	384	Harold Baines
465	Dave Winfield	419	Mike Piazza		
455	Gary Sheffield	407	Carlos Delgado		

(122) Most Career Games with Multiple Home Runs

72	Babe Ruth	49	Mel Ott	43	Dave Kingman
69	Barry Bonds	49	Eddie Mathews	42	Ernie Banks
68	Sammy Sosa	48	Juan Gonzalez	42	Lou Gehrig
67	Mark McGwire	47	Manny Ramirez	42	Reggie Jackson
63	Willie Mays	46	Harmon Killebrew	40	Ralph Kiner
62	Hank Aaron	46	Mickey Mantle	40	Fred McGriff
55	Jimmie Foxx	44	Willie McCovey	40	Carlos Delgado
54	Frank Robinson	44	Mike Schmidt		
53	Ken Griffey Jr.	44	Alex Rodriguez		

(123) Most Career Games with Home Runs from Both Sides of the Plate

11	Eddie Murray	6	Jorge Posada	3	Ted Simmons
11	Chili Davis	5	Roberto Alomar	3	Dale Sveum
10	Ken Caminiti	5	Carl Everett	3	Mickey Tettleton
10	Mickey Mantle	5	Todd Hundley	3	Tom Tresh
9	Tony Clark	5	Chipper Jones	3	Devon White
8	Bernie Williams	5	Roy White	3	Geoff Blum
6	Bobby Bonilla	4	Jose Valentin	3	Carlos Guillen
6	Ruben Sierra	4	Carlos Beltran	3	Mark Teixeira
6	Reggie Smith	3	Kevin Bass		

(124) Most Career Leadoff Home Runs

81	Rickey Henderson	30	Tony Phillips	22	Shannon Stewart
50	Craig Biggio	28	Kenny Lofton	21	Johnny Damon
44	Brady Anderson	28	Davey Lopes	21	Ichiro Suzuki
35	Bobby Bonds	27	Eddie Yost	20	Felipe Alou
34	Ray Durham	25	Brian Downing	20	Barry Bonds
34	Devon White	24	Lou Brock	20	Lenny Dykstra
33	Paul Molitor	23	Tommy Harper	20	Jacque Jones
32	Alfonso Soriano	23	Lou Whitaker	20	Eric Young
31	Chuck Knoblauch	22	Jimmy Ryan		

(125) Most Career Inside the Park Home Runs

55	Jesse Burkett	43	Honus Wagner	31	Jake Daubert
52	Sam Crawford	40	Tris Speaker	31	Edd Roush
49	Ty Cobb	38	Jake Beckley		
49	Tommy Leach	33	Rogers Hornsby		

(126) Most Career Times Hitting a Home Run in a 1-0 Game

5   Ted Williams   Williams's only career IPHR
clinched the '46 pennant;
the 4th HR was #400

4   Bobby Bonds
4   Bobby Grich
4   Jim Wynn
4   Dwight Evans
3   Dolph Camilli
3   Andy Pafko
3   Willie Mays   Mays's 16th inning HR
on July 2, 1963 broke up duel
between Spahn and Marichal

3   Ken Boyer
3   Ernie Banks
3   Al Kaline

3   Frank Howard
3   Donn Clendenon
3   Gene Oliver
3   Harmon Killebrew
3   Willie Horton
3   Julian Javier
3   Joe Pepitone
3   Brooks Robinson
3   Dave Winfield
3   Jerry Morales
3   Dave Henderson
3   Orlando Merced
3   Gary Sheffield   Hit all three in 2001, a record
3   Bret Boone

GEORGE BRACE

Willie Mays

(127) Progression of Career Home Run Record

5	George Hall	1876		117	Harry Stovey	1891		470	Babe Ruth	1928
6	Charley Jones	1877		121	Harry Stovey	1892		516	Babe Ruth	1929
9	Charley Jones	1878		122	Harry Stovey	1893		565	Babe Ruth	1930
18	Charley Jones	1879		126	Roger Connor	1895		611	Babe Ruth	1931
23	Charley Jones	1880		137	Roger Connor	1896		652	Babe Ruth	1932
33	Charley Jones	1883		138	Roger Connor	1897		686	Babe Ruth	1933
40	Charley Jones	1884		162	Babe Ruth	1921		708	Babe Ruth	1934
50	Harry Stovey	1885		197	Babe Ruth	1922		714	Babe Ruth	1935
57	Harry Stovey	1886		238	Babe Ruth	1923		733	Hank Aaron	1974
65	Dan Brouthers	1887		284	Babe Ruth	1924		745	Hank Aaron	1975
74	Dan Brouthers	1888		309	Babe Ruth	1925		755	Hank Aaron	1976
89	Harry Stovey	1889		356	Babe Ruth	1926				
101	Harry Stovey	1890		416	Babe Ruth	1927				

(128) Most Seasons with a .300 Batting Average, 30 Home Runs, and 100 RBI

12	Babe Ruth	1920-21, 1923-24, 1926-33		6	Albert Pujols	2001-06
10	Lou Gehrig	1927, 1929-37		5	Hank Greenberg	1935, 1937-40
9	Jimmie Foxx	1929-30, 1932-36, 1938-39		5	Frank Robinson	1959, 1961-62, 1966, 1969
9	Barry Bonds	1990, 1992-93, 1996, 1998, 2000-02, 2004		5	Juan Gonzalez	1993, 1996, 1998-99, 2001
9	Manny Ramirez	1995-96, 1999-2004, 2006		5	Jeff Bagwell	1994, 1996, 1998-2000
8	Vladimir Guerrero	1998-2002, 2004-06		5	Chipper Jones	1996, 1998-2001
7	Joe DiMaggio	1937-41, 1948, 1950		5	Todd Helton	1999-2003
7	Ted Williams	1939, 1941-42, 1946-47, 1949, 1951		4	Hack Wilson	1927-30
7	Willie Mays	1954-55, 1959, 1961-63, 1965		4	Chuck Klein	1929-32
7	Hank Aaron	1957, 1959, 1961-63, 1967, 1971		4	Duke Snider	1950, 1953-55
7	Frank E. Thomas	1991, 1993-97, 2000		4	Ted Kluszewski	1953-56
6	Mel Ott	1929, 1932, 1934-36, 1938		4	Jim Rice	1977-79, 1983
6	Stan Musial	1948-49, 1951, 1953-55		4	Albert Belle	1994-96, 1998
6	Gary Sheffield	1992, 1996, 1999-2001, 2003		4	Larry Walker	1995, 1997, 1999, 2001
6	Mike Piazza	1993, 1996-2000		4	Jason Giambi	1999-2002
6	Alex Rodriguez	1996, 1998, 2000-02, 2005		4	Magglio Ordonez	1999-2002

(129) Batters with 300 Home Runs and a .300 Career Batting Average

	HR	BAV			HR	BAV			HR	BAV
Hank Aaron	755	.305		Stan Musial	475	.331		Vladimir Guerrero	338	.325
Babe Ruth	714	.342		Manny Ramirez	470	.314		Hank Greenberg	331	.313
Willie Mays	660	.302		Alex Rodriguez	464	.305		Moises Alou	319	.301
Jimmie Foxx	534	.325		Mike Piazza	419	.309		George Brett	317	.305
Ted Williams	521	.344		Larry Walker	383	.313		Edgar Martinez	309	.312
Mel Ott	511	.304		Joe DiMaggio	361	.325		Al Simmons	307	.304
Lou Gehrig	493	.340		Johnny Mize	359	.312		Rogers Hornsby	301	.358
Frank E. Thomas	487	.305		Chipper Jones	357	.304		Chuck Klein	300	.320

(130) Batters with 100 Career Triples and 200 Career Home Runs

	3B	HR		3B	HR		3B	HR
Stan Musial	177	475	Al Simmons	149	307	Vada Pinson	127	256
Goose Goslin	173	248	Willie Mays	140	660	Robin Yount	126	251
Rogers Hornsby	169	301	George Brett	137	317	Jimmie Foxx	125	534
Roberto Clemente	166	240	Babe Ruth	136	714	Steve Finley	124	303
Lou Gehrig	162	493	Joe DiMaggio	131	361	Paul Molitor	114	234
Jim Bottomley	151	219	Earl Averill	128	238	Joe Medwick	113	205

(131) Most Consecutive Games Played

2632	Cal Ripken	May 30, 1982 to Sep 19, 1998	798	Nellie Fox	Aug 7, 1955 to Sep 3, 1960
2130	Lou Gehrig	Jun 1, 1925 to Apr 30, 1939	745	Pete Rose	Sep 1, 1978 to Aug 23, 1983
1307	Deacon Scott	Jun 20, 1916 to May 5, 1925	740	Dale Murphy	Sep 26, 1981 to Jul 9, 1986
1207	Steve Garvey	Sep 3, 1975 to Jul 29 1983	730	Richie Ashburn	Jun 7, 1950 to Sep 26, 1954
1117	Billy Williams	Sep 22, 1963 to Sep 2, 1970	717	Ernie Banks	Aug 26, 1956 to Jun 22, 1961
1103	Joe Sewell	Sep 13, 1922 to Apr 30, 1930	678	Pete Rose	Sep 28, 1973 to May 7, 1978
1080	Miguel Tejada	Jun 2, 2000 to Oct 1, 2006	673	Earl Averill	Apr 14 1931 to Jun 25, 1935
		streak active through 2006	652	Frank McCormick	Apr 19, 1938 to May 24, 1942
895	Stan Musial	Apr 15, 1952 to Aug 22, 1957	648	Sandy Alomar Sr.	May 16, 1969 to May 20, 1973
829	Eddie Yost	Aug 30, 1949 to May 11, 1955	618	Eddie Brown	Jun 5, 1924 to Jun 7, 1928
822	Gus Suhr	Sep 11, 1931 to Jun 4, 1937			

(132) Most Consecutive Seasons with 60+ Home Runs

2	Mark McGwire	1998-1999
2	Sammy Sosa	1998-1999
1	Babe Ruth	1927
1	Roger Maris	1961
1	Sammy Sosa	2001
1	Barry Bonds	2001

(133) Most Consecutive Seasons with 50+ Home Runs

4	Mark McGwire	1996-1999
4	Sammy Sosa	1998-2001
2	Babe Ruth	1920-1921
2	Babe Ruth	1927-1928
2	Ken Griffey Jr.	1997-1998
2	Alex Rodriguez	2001-2002

(134) Most Consecutive Seasons with 40+ Home Runs

7	Babe Ruth	1926-1932		4	Albert Pujols	2003-2006
6	Sammy Sosa	1998-2003		3	Jimmie Foxx	1932-1934
6	Alex Rodriguez	1998-2003		3	Ted Kluszewski	1953-1955
5	Ralph Kiner	1947-1951		3	Eddie Mathews	1953-1955
5	Duke Snider	1953-1957		3	Frank Howard	1968-1970
5	Ken Griffey Jr.	1996-2000		3	Jay Buhner	1995-1997
5	Barry Bonds	2000-2004		3	Andres Galarraga	1996-1998
4	Ernie Banks	1957-1960		3	Juan Gonzalez	1996-1998
4	Harmon Killebrew	1961-1964		3	Vinny Castilla	1996-1998
4	Mark McGwire	1996-1999		3	David Ortiz	2004-2006
4	Jim Thome	2001-2004		3	Adam Dunn	2004-2006

(135) Most Consecutive Seasons with 30+ Home Runs

13	Barry Bonds	1992-2004		8	Albert Belle	1992-1999
12	Jimmie Foxx	1929-1940		8	Mike Piazza	1995-2002
10	Sammy Sosa	1995-2004		8	Jeff Bagwell	1996-2003
10	Carlos Delgado	1997-2006		7	Ralph Kiner	1947-1953
9	Lou Gehrig	1929-1937		7	Hank Aaron	1957-1963
9	Eddie Mathews	1953-1961		7	Fred McGriff	1988-1994
9	Mike Schmidt	1979-1987		6	Harmon Killebrew	1959-1964
9	Rafael Palmeiro	1995-2003		6	Willie Mays	1961-1966
9	Jim Thome	1996-2004		6	Willie McCovey	1965-1970
9	Manny Ramirez	1998-2006		6	Mark McGwire	1995-2000
9	Alex Rodriguez	1998-2006		6	Mo Vaughn	1995-2000
8	Babe Ruth	1926-1933		6	Todd Helton	1999-2004
8	Mickey Mantle	1955-1962		6	Albert Pujols	2001-2006

(136) Most Consecutive Seasons with 20+ Home Runs

20	Hank Aaron	1955-1974		13	Willie Stargell	1964-1976
16	Babe Ruth	1919-1934		13	Reggie Jackson	1968-1980
15	Willie Mays	1954-1968		12	Manny Ramirez	1995-2006
15	Barry Bonds	1990-2004		12	Lou Gehrig	1927-1938
14	Eddie Mathews	1952-1965		12	Jimmie Foxx	1956-1967
14	Mike Schmidt	1974-1987		12	Joe Carter	1986-1997
14	Rafael Palmeiro	1991-2004		12	Sammy Sosa	1993-2004
13	Billy Williams	1961-1973		12	Jeff Bagwell	1993-2004

(137) Most Consecutive Seasons with 10+ Home Runs

23	Hank Aaron	1954-1976		18	Mickey Mantle	1951-1968
20	Al Kaline	1955-1974		18	Willie Mays	1954-1971
20	Carl Yastrzemski	1961-1980		18	Willie Stargell	1963-1980
20	Reggie Jackson	1968-1987		18	Dwight Evans	1973-1990
20	Eddie Murray	1977-1996		18	Andre Dawson	1977-1994
20	Cal Ripken	1982-2001		18	Harold Baines	1980-1997
19	Frank Robinson	1956-1974		17	Babe Ruth	1918-1934
19	Darrell Evans	1971-1989		17	Ernie Banks	1954-1970
19	Barry Bonds	1986-2004		17	Willie McCovey	1959-1975
18	Mel Ott	1928-1945		17	Graig Nettles	1970-1986
18	Stan Musial	1946-1963		17	Fred McGriff	1987-2003

(138) Most Consecutive Seasons with a Home Run

25	Rickey Henderson	1979-2003		21	Eddie Murray	1977-1997
24	Ty Cobb	1905-1928		21	Harold Baines	1980-2000
23	Hank Aaron	1954-1976		21	Barry Bonds	1986-2006
23	Carl Yastrzemski	1961-1983		20	Honus Wagner	1897-1916
23	Rusty Staub	1963-1985		20	Mel Ott	1927-1946
23	Carlton Fisk	1971-1993		20	Willie Mays	1954-1973
22	Al Kaline	1953-1974		20	Bill Buckner	1971-1990
22	Brooks Robinson	1956-1977		20	Dwight Evans	1972-1991
22	Willie McCovey	1959-1980		20	Brian Downing	1973-1992
22	Tony Perez	1965-1986		20	George Brett	1974-1993
21	Babe Ruth	1915-1935		20	Robin Yount	1974-1993
21	Frank Robinson	1956-1976		20	Andre Dawson	1977-1996
21	Ron Fairly	1958-1978		20	Tony Gwynn	1982-2001
21	Reggie Jackson	1967-1987		20	Cal Ripken	1982-2001
21	Graig Nettles	1968-1988		20	Rafael Palmeiro	1986-2005

(139) Players who Retired with Fewer than 100 Career Home Runs but who Hit 30 in a Season

	CAREER HR	BEST SEASON			
Butch Hobson	98	30	AL	BOS	1977
Ival Goodman	95	30	NL	CIN	1938
Larry Sheets	94	31	AL	BAL	1987
Luke Easter	93	31	AL	CLE	1952
Phil Plantier	91	34	NL	SD	1993
Felix Mantilla	89	30	AL	BOS	1964
George Crowe	81	31	NL	CIN	1957
Rick Wilkins	81	30	NL	CHI	1993

(140) Players who Retired with Fewer than 200 Career Home Runs but who Hit 40 in a Season

	CAREER HR	BEST SEASON			
Al Rosen	192	43	AL	CLE	1953
Jim Gentile	179	46	AL	BAL	1961
Davey Johnson	136	43	NL	ATL	1973

(141) Players who Retired with Fewer than 300 Career Home Runs but who Hit 50 in a Season

	CAREER HR	BEST SEASON			
Roger Maris	275	61	AL	NY	1961
Hack Wilson	244	56	NL	CHI	1930
Brady Anderson	210	50	AL	BAL	1996

(142) Most Career Games with Three Home Runs

6 Johnny Mize	4 Barry Bonds	3 Eddie Murray
6 Sammy Sosa	4 Steve Finley	3 Mike Schmidt
5 Dave Kingman	3 Goose Goslin	3 Harold Baines
5 Joe Carter	3 Joe DiMaggio	3 Cecil Fielder
5 Mark McGwire	3 Ted Williams	3 Jeff Bagwell
5 Carlos Delgado	3 Rocky Colavito	3 Albert Belle
4 Lou Gehrig	3 Willie Mays	3 Juan Gonzalez
4 Ralph Kiner	3 Boog Powell	3 Larry Walker
4 Ernie Banks	3 Willie McCovey	3 Alex Rodriguez
4 Willie Stargell	3 Johnny Bench	3 Albert Pujols
4 Larry Parrish	3 Ben Oglivie	3 Aramis Ramirez

Yogi Berra

TRANSCENDENTAL GRAPHICS

(143) Most Career Home Runs without ever Hitting 20 in a Season

215	Ron Fairly	164	Claudell Washington
178	Tony Lazzeri	163	Bill Madlock
174	Bill Buckner	162	Keith Hernandez
173	Mark Grace	160	Pete Rose
170	Tim Raines	153	Dan Driessen
169	Enos Slaughter	151	Carney Lansford
165	Jose Cruz Sr.	150	Shawon Dunston

(144) Most Career Home Runs without ever Hitting 30 in a Season

399	Al Kaline	268	Joe Morgan
384	Harold Baines	267	George Hendrick
297	Rickey Henderson	260	Tim Wallach
281	Paul O'Neill	256	Vada Pinson
281	Craig Biggio	255	Kirk Gibson
275	Brian Downing	255	John Olerud
268	Brooks Robinson	251	Robin Yount

(145) Most Career Home Runs without ever Hitting 40 in a Season

504	Eddie Murray	385	Dwight Evans
493	Fred McGriff	384	Harold Baines
475	Stan Musial	376	Carlton Fisk
465	Dave Winfield	360	Gary Gaetti
431	Cal Ripken	358	Yogi Berra
399	Al Kaline	354	Lee May
396	Joe Carter	350	Chili Davis
389	Graig Nettles		

(146) Game-ending Home Runs in 1-0 Games

				INN.	PITCHER	TEAM	
Charley Radbourn	NL	PRO	Aug 17, 1882	18	Stump Wiedman	DET	Weidman and John Ward pitched CG Radbourn played OF this game
Mike Tiernan	NL	NY	May 12, 1890	13	Kid Nichols	BOS	
Charlie Bennett	NL	BOS	Aug 12, 1890	12	Phenomenal Smith	PHI	
Johnny Bates	NL	BOS	Jul 2, 1906	9	Togie Pittinger	PHI	
Claude Rossman	AL	DET	Sep 25, 1908	10	Biff Schlitzer	PHI	2G; Detroit's Ed Summers pitched two CG victories
Bill John Sweeney	NL	BOS	Jun 4, 1910	12	Mordecai Brown	CHI	
Jimmy Archer	NL	CHI	Aug 2, 1911	10	Nap Rucker	BKL	
Steve Evans	FL	BKL	Jul 13, 1914	12	Walt Dickson	PIT	Only one in Federal League history
Gee Walker	NL	CIN	Sep 26, 1943	9	Nate Andrews	BOS	2G
Frank McCormick	NL	CIN	Apr 26, 1944	13	Al Jurisch	STL	
Roy Cullenbine	AL	CLE	Aug 27, 1944	9	Johnny Humphries	CHI	2G
Roy Cullenbine	AL	DET	May 6, 1945	9	Tex Shirley	STL	2G
Eddie Mayo	AL	DET	Jul 27, 1945	9	Johnny Humphries	CHI	
Del Ennis	NL	PHI	Apr 14, 1949	9	Max Lanier	STL	
Del Rice	NL	STL	Apr 30, 1950	13	Johnny Schmitz	CHI	
Vic Wertz	AL	DET	May 15, 1952	9	Bob Porterfield	WAS	No-hitter by Virgil Trucks
Eddie Mathews	NL	BOS	Sep 14, 1952	9	Johnny Klippstein	CHI	1G
Bobby Thomson	NL	NY	Apr 30, 1953	9	Vern Bickford	MIL	
Dick Kokos	AL	STL	Sep 5, 1953	12	Ralph Branca	DET	
Harvey Kuenn	AL	DET	Jul 5, 1954	11	Don Mossi	CLE	2G
Hobie Landrith	NL	CIN	Jul 19, 1954	12	Al Corwin	NY	
Ted Kluszewski	NL	PIT	May 9, 1958	12	Robin Roberts	PHI	
Bill Virdon	NL	PIT	Sep 5, 1958	10	Carl Willey	MIL	
Tito Francona	AL	CLE	Aug 23, 1959	9	Tom Brewer	BOS	1G
Ernie Banks	NL	CHI	Aug 17, 1960	9	Don Drysdale	LA	
Bobby Smith	NL	PHI	Apr 23, 1961	9	Dick Ellsworth	CHI	1G
Ed Bouchee	NL	CHI	May 20, 1961	9	Larry Jackson	STL	Bouchee tied ML record with 22 chances at 1B
Tommy Davis	NL	LA	Jun 18, 1962	9	Bob Gibson	STL	Third time a Davis HR gave Sandy Koufax a 1-0 win
Willie Mays	NL	SF	Jul 2, 1963	16	Warren Spahn	MIL	Spahn and Juan Marichal pitched CG; Spahn's longest 1-0 game ended by a HR
Bob Bailey	NL	PIT	Apr 12, 1965	10	Juan Marichal	SF	Opening Day
Willie Mays	NL	SF	Aug 12, 1966	9	Mike Cuellar	HOU	
Tony Oliva	AL	MIN	Sep 25, 1966	9	Earl Wilson	DET	
Tom Haller	NL	SF	Sep 22, 1967	9	Al McBean	PIT	
Tony Horton	AL	CLE	Sep 28, 1967	12	Moe Drabowsky	BAL	
Joe Pepitone	AL	NY	May 18, 1969	9	Hoyt Wilhelm	CAL	2G
Tommie Agee	NL	NY	Aug 19, 1969	14	Juan Marichal	SF	

(146) *(continued)*

				INN.	PITCHER	TEAM	
Don Mincher	AL	OAK	Aug 2, 1970	9	Horacio Pina	WAS	2G
Jerry Grote	NL	NY	Apr 11, 1971	11	Wayne Granger	CIN	
Joe Pepitone	NL	CHI	Jun 8, 1971	12	Mudcat Grant	PIT	Pepitone first to do it in both leagues
Jim Wynn	NL	HOU	Jun 16, 1972	11	Dick Selma	PHI	
Dusty Baker	NL	ATL	Jun 28, 1974	10	Don Gullett	CIN	2G
Bobby Grich	AL	BAL	May 16, 1975	9	Frank Tanana	CAL	1G
Johnny Grubb	NL	SD	May 19, 1975	10	Jack Curtis	STL	
Dave Kingman	NL	NY	Jun 17, 1976	14	Charlie Hough	LA	
Bobby Murcer	NL	SF	Jul 16, 1976	9	Jim Kaat	PHI	
Larvell Blanks	AL	CLE	May 10, 1977	9	Jim Slaton	MIL	1G
Joe Rudi	AL	CAL	Apr 13, 1978	11	Tom Johnson	MIN	
Rick Bosetti	AL	TOR	Apr 17, 1980	9	Lary Sorensen	MIL	
George Hendrick	NL	STL	Jul 4, 1980	10	Kevin Saucier	PHI	
Dave Stapleton	AL	BOS	Jul 18, 1980	10	Roger Erickson	MIN	
Jim Dwyer	AL	BAL	Sep 23, 1981	9	Dan Petry	DET	
Bob E. Johnson	AL	TEX	Oct 3, 1981	9	Angel Moreno	CAL	
Glenn Davis	NL	HOU	Jul 22, 1986	10	Floyd Youmans	MON	
Alvin Davis	AL	SEA	Aug 15, 1986	9	Keith Atherton	MIN	
Vance Law	NL	MON	Sep 2, 1986	9	Bob Welch	LA	
Cory Snyder	AL	CLE	May 19, 1988	9	Bobby Thigpen	CHI	
Paul O'Neill	NL	CIN	May 18, 1990	9	Ken Dayley	STL	
Jim Eisenreich	AL	KC	Aug 14, 1990	9	Gary Mielke	TEX	
Steve Decker	NL	SF	Apr 21, 1991	9	Curt Schilling	HOU	
Delino DeShields	NL	MON	Apr 30, 1991	9	Mike Morgan	LA	
Tim Teufel	NL	SD	Sep 7, 1991	10	Chris Carpenter	STL	
Brian Harper	AL	MIN	Aug 26, 1992	9	John Kiely	DET	
Scott Brosius	AL	OAK	Jun 29, 1994	9	Chuck Finley	CAL	
Terry Pendleton	NL	FLA	Apr 6, 1996	10	Mark Dewey	SF	Pendleton only batter faced by Dewey
Gary Gaetti	NL	STL	Aug 7, 1996	9	Doug Bochtler	SD	
Jeromy Burnitz	AL	MIL	Jun 16, 1997	9	Alan Benes	STL	InterLeague game
Alex Gonzalez	NL	FLA	Sep 26, 1998	13	Ricky Bottalico	PHI	
Eric Karros	NL	LA	Sep 20, 2000	9	Byung-Hyun Kim	ARI	Karros only batter faced by Kim
Gary Sheffield	NL	LA	May 12, 2001	9	Matt Whiteside	ATL	
Ryan Klesko	NL	SD	Sep 2, 2001	13	Byung-Hyun Kim	ARI	Klesko only batter faced by Kim
Paul Lo Duca	NL	LA	Sep 27, 2002	10	Jeremy Fikac	SD	
Casey Blake	AL	CLE	May 28, 2004	9	Jim Mecir	OAK	
Ruben Sierra	AL	NY	Jul 22, 2004	9	Vinnie Chulk	TOR	
Russell Martin	NL	LA	Aug 13, 2006	10	Vinnie Chulk	SF	
Geoff Jenkins	NL	MIL	Sep 20, 2006	9	Tyler Johnson	STL	

(147) Ultimate Grand Slam Home Runs
(Coming when down by three runs in final at-bat)

				INN	PITCHER	TEAM	SCORE	
Roger Connor	NL	TRO	Sep 10, 1881	9	Lee Richmond	WOR	8-7	
Babe Ruth	AL	NY	Sep 24, 1925	10	Sarge Connally	CHI	6-5	
Sammy Byrd	NL	CIN	May 23, 1936	9	Cy Blanton	PIT	4-3	
Jack Phillips	NL	PIT	Jul 8, 1950	9	Harry Brecheen	STL	7-6	
Bobby Thomson	NL	NY	Jun 16, 1952	9	Willard Schmidt	STL	8-7	
Eddie Joost	AL	PHI	Jul 15, 1952	9	Satchel Paige	STL	7-6	
Del Crandall	NL	MIL	Sep 11, 1955	9	Herm Wehmeier	PHI	5-4	
Danny Kravitz	NL	PIT	May 11, 1956	9	Jack Meyer	PHI	6-5	
Roberto Clemente	NL	PIT	Jul 25, 1956	9	Jim Brosnan	CHI	9-8	
Ellis Burton	NL	CHI	Aug 31, 1963	9	Hal Woodeshick	HOU	6-5	
Tony Taylor	NL	PHI	Aug 2, 1970	9	Mike Davison	SF	7-6	
Carl Taylor	NL	STL	Aug 11, 1970	9	Ron Herbel	SD	11-10	
Ron Lolich	AL	CLE	Apr 22, 1973	11	Sonny Siebert	BOS	8-7	
Roger Freed	NL	STL	May 1, 1979	9	Joe Sambito	HOU	7-6	
Bo Diaz	NL	PHI	Apr 13, 1983	9	Neil Allen	NY	10-9	
Buddy Bell	AL	TEX	Aug 31, 1984	9	Pete Ladd	MIL	7-6	
Phil Bradley	AL	SEA	Apr 13, 1985	9	Ron Davis	MIN	8-7	
Dick Schofield Jr.	AL	CAL	Aug 29, 1986	9	Willie Hernandez	DET	13-12	
Alan Trammell	AL	DET	Jun 21, 1988	9	Cecilio Guante	NY	7-6	
Chris Hoiles	AL	BAL	May 17, 1996	9	Norm Charlton	SEA	14-13	
Brian Giles	NL	PIT	Jul 28, 2001	9	Billy Wagner	HOU	9-8	1G
Jason Giambi	AL	NY	May 17, 2002	14	Mike Trombley	MIN	13-12	
Adam Dunn	NL	CIN	Jun 30, 2006	9	Bob Wickman	CLE	9-8	

(148) Leadoff Home Runs that Won 1-0 Games

				PITCHER			
Hardy Richardson	NL	BOS	Sep 2, 1889	Henry Boyle	IND	2G	
Harry Lumley	NL	BRO	Apr 29, 1906	Bill Duggleby	PHI	First pitch	
Harry Hooper	AL	BOS	May 30, 1913	Walter Johnson	WAS	2G; also had leadoff HR in 1G	
Jim Kelly	FL	PIT	May 11, 1915	Fred Anderson	BUF	First pitch	
Heinie Groh	NL	CIN	Jun 17, 1916	Al Demaree	PHI		
Ira Flagstead	AL	BOS	May 28, 1924	Roy Meeker	PHI	2G	
Bobby Reeves	AL	BOS	Aug 17, 1929	Lefty Stewart	STL		
Len Koenecke	NL	BRO	Jun 7, 1934	George Darrow	PHI		
Pete Rose	NL	CIN	Sep 2, 1963	Jay Hook	NY	2G; First pitch	
John Briggs	NL	PHI	Jun 12, 1969	Bill Singer	LA	First HR of season	
Bobby Bonds	NL	SF	Apr 28, 1973	Reggie Cleveland	STL		
Wayne Garrett	NL	NY	Sep 7, 1973	Steve Renko	MON	1G	
Don Money	AL	MIL	Apr 26, 1976	Frank Tanana	CAL		
Terry Puhl	NL	HOU	May 20, 1979	Gaylord Perry	SD	1G	
Willie Wilson	AL	KC	Aug 25, 1979	Mike Torrez	BOS	Inside the park	
Denny Walling	NL	HOU	Apr 26, 1981	Mario Soto	CIN	First HR of season	
Darren Lewis	NL	SF	Aug 7, 1991	Charlie Leibrandt	ATL	First career HR	
Greg Briley	AL	SEA	Jun 19, 1992	Kevin Tapani	MIN		
Carlos Garcia	NL	PIT	Sep 14, 1993	Chris Hammond	FLA		
Kaz Matsui	NL	NY	May 12, 2004	Randy Johnson	ARI		

(149) Batters who Hit a Home Run on First Major League Pitch

Walter Mueller	NL	PIT	May 7, 1922		Junior Felix	AL	TOR	May 4, 1989	
Clise Dudley	NL	BRO	Apr 27, 1929		Jim Bullinger	NL	CHI	Jun 8, 1992	Pitcher
Eddie Morgan	NL	STL	Apr 14, 1936	Pinch hit	Jay Gainer	NL	COL	May 14, 1993	
Bill Lefebvre	AL	BOS	Jun 10, 1938		Esteban Yan	AL	TB	Jun 4, 2000	Pitcher
Clyde Vollmer	NL	CIN	May 31, 1942	2G	Chris Richard	NL	STL	Jul 17, 2000	
George Vico	AL	DET	Apr 20, 1948		Gene Stechschulte	NL	STL	Apr 17, 2001	Pitcher
Chuck Tanner	NL	MIL	Apr 12, 1955	Pinch hit	Marcus Thames	AL	NY	Jun 10, 2002	
Bert Campaneris	AL	KC	Jul 23, 1964		Kaz Matsui	NL	NY	Apr 6, 2004	
Brant Alyea	AL	WAS	Sep 12, 1965		Andy Phillips	AL	NY	Sep 26, 2004	
Don Rose	AL	CAL	May 24, 1972		Adam Wainwright	NL	STL	May 24, 2006	Pitcher
Al Woods	AL	TOR	Apr 7, 1977		Kevin Kouzmanoff	AL	CLE	Sep 2, 2006	Grand slam
Jay Bell	AL	CLE	Sep 29, 1986						

COURTESY OF THE HOUSTON ASTROS

Lance Berkman

(150) Batters Who Hit Two Grand Slams in the Same Game

Tony Lazzeri	AL	NY	May 24, 1936	15 TB; AL record 11 RBI
Jim Tabor	AL	BOS	Jul 4, 1939	2G
Rudy York	AL	BOS	Jul 27, 1946	
Jim Gentile	AL	BAL	May 9, 1961	Consecutive at bats
Tony Cloninger	NL	ATL	Jul 3, 1966	ML record 9 RBI for a pitcher
Jim Northrup	AL	DET	Jun 24, 1968	Struck out once with bases loaded
Frank Robinson	AL	BAL	Jun 26, 1970	
Robin Ventura	AL	CHI	Sep 4, 1995	Consecutive at bats
Chris Hoiles	AL	BAL	Aug 14, 1998	
Fernando Tatis	NL	STL	Apr 23, 1999	Same inning; ML record 8 RBI in an inning
Nomar Garciaparra	AL	BOS	May 10, 1999	Hit three HR in game
Bill Mueller	AL	BOS	Jul 29, 2003	Hit three HR in game

(151) Back to Back Home Runs by the Same Batters Twice in a Game

Paul Hines	Jerry Denny	NL	IND	Jun 14, 1889	
Goose Goslin	Joe Judge	AL	WAS	May 26, 1930	
Johnny Frederick	Babe Herman	NL	BRO	Jun 1, 1930	
Bill Terry	Mel Ott	NL	NY	Aug 13, 1932	
Rudy York	Hank Greenberg	AL	DET	May 25, 1938	
Joe DiMaggio	Charlie Keller	AL	NY	Jul 28, 1940	
Hank Greenberg	Bruce Campbell	AL	DET	May 6, 1941	
Toby Atwell	Jerry Lynch	NL	PIT	Apr 27, 1954	
Ernie Banks	Dee Fondy	NL	CHI	Apr 16, 1955	
Daryl Spencer	Wes Westrum	NL	NY	Jul 8, 1956	
Walt Bond	John Romano	AL	CLE	Sep 19, 1962	
Chuck Hinton	Rocky Colavito	AL	CLE	Jul 17, 1966	2G
Don Money	Greg Luzinski	NL	PHI	Oct 3, 1972	
Gary Sheffield	Fred McGriff	NL	SD	Aug 6, 1992	
Barry Bonds	Matt Williams	NL	SF	Aug 15, 1993	
Fred McGriff	David Justice	NL	ATL	Aug 25, 1993	
Mo Vaughn	Tim Naehring	AL	BOS	Apr 19, 1994	
Julio Franco	Robin Ventura	AL	CHI	Apr 24, 1994	
Ken Griffey Jr.	Edgar Martinez	AL	SEA	Apr 21, 1996	All off Erik Hanson
Javy Lopez	Andruw Jones	NL	ATL	Jun 13, 1998	
Mo Vaughn	Tim Salmon	AL	ANA	Apr 21, 2000	Troy Glaus also homered in both those innings. Only time three batters have homered twice in the same inning.
Raul Mondesi	Carlos Delgado	AL	TOR	Apr 20, 2001	
Richie Sexson	Jeromy Burnitz	NL	MIL	Sep 25, 2001	
Bret Boone	Mike Cameron	AL	SEA	May 2, 2002	Same inning
Jeromy Burnitz	Matt Holliday	NL	COL	May 18, 2004	
Craig Biggio	Lance Berkman	NL	HOU	Jul 25, 2005	

(152) Leadoff Home Runs by Both Teams in the Same Game

				SITE		
George Wood	DET	Abner Dalrymple	CHI	CHI	NL	May 29, 1884
Mike Griffin	BAL	Bug Holliday	CIN	CIN	AA	May 16, 1889
Curt Welch	BAL	Tom Brown	BOS	BOS	AA	Jun 25, 1891
Harry Hooper	BOS	Roger Peckinpaugh	NY	NY	AL	Jun 25, 1920
Sam Jethroe	BOS	Hank Schenz	PIT	PIT	NL	Jun 3, 1950
Eddie Yost	WAS	Hank Bauer	NY	NY	AL	Sep 3, 1955
Willie Randolph	NY	Al Bumbry	BAL	BAL	AL	Aug 15, 1980
Jimmy Ryan	CHI	Bug Holliday	CIN	CIN	NL	Sep 29, 1982
Butch Davis	KC	Rickey Henderson	OAK	OAK	AL	Oct 2, 1983
Rickey Henderson	NY	Oddibe McDowell	TEX	TEX	AL	Jul 27, 1985
Eric Davis	CIN	Dan Gladden	SF	SF	NL	Oct 1, 1985
Curt Ford	STL	Jeff Stone	PHI	PHI	NL	Jun 20, 1986
Chuck Knoblauch	MIN	Tony Phillips	DET	DET	AL	Jun 5, 1994
Bernard Gilkey	STL	Trenidad Hubbard	COL	COL	NL	Aug 25, 1995
Chuck Knoblauch	MIN	Tony Phillips	CAL	CAL	AL	Sep 8, 1995
Joey Cora	SEA	Randy Velarde	CAL	CAL	AL	Sep 25, 1996
Devon White	ARI	F. P. Santangelo	MON	MON	NL	May 1, 1998
Doug Glanville	PHI (NL)	Jose Offerman	BOS (AL)	BOS	AL	Jul 15, 1999
Brady Clark	CIN (NL)	Ray Durham	CHI (AL)	CHI	AL	Jun 13, 2001
Michael Young	TEX	Chuck Knoblauch	NY	NY	AL	Aug 1, 2001
Shannon Stewart	TOR (AL)	Brad Wilkerson	MON (NL)	MON	NL	Jun 16, 2002
Ichiro Suzuki	SEA	Randy Winn	TB	TB	AL	Jul 13, 2002
Jacque Jones	MIN	Ray Durham	OAK	OAK	AL	Aug 30, 2002
Shannon Stewart	MIN	David DeJesus	KC	KC	AL	Jul 16, 2004
Orlando Palmeiro	HOU	Felipe Lopez	CIN	CIN	NL	Jul 2, 2005
Kevin Youkilis	BOS (AL)	Hanley Ramirez	FLA (NL)	FLA	NL	Jul 2, 2006
Grady Sizemore	CLE	Luis Castillo	MIN	MIN	AL	Jul 16, 2006
Alfonso Soriano	WAS	Hanley Ramirez	FLA	FLA	NL	Jul 18, 2006
Brian Roberts	BAL	Johnny Damon	NY	NY	AL	Aug 17, 2006
David DeJesus	KC	Pablo Ozuna	CHI	CHI	AL	Aug 17, 2006

(153) Home Runs by the First Three Batters of a Game

Marvell Wynne	Tony Gwynn	John Kruk	NL	SD	Apr 13, 1987	Off Roger Mason; Giants win 13-6
Rafael Furcal	Mark DeRosa	Gary Sheffield	NL	ATL	May 28, 2003	Off Jeff Austin; Javy Lopez also homers in 1st inn.

(154) Home Runs by First Two Batters of a Game

Tom Brown	Bill Joyce	AA	BOS	Jun 25, 1891	
Jim McTamany	Henry Larkin	AA	PHI	Aug 21, 1891	
Josh Devore	Larry Doyle	NL	NY	Jul 13, 1911	Both inside the park
Roy Johnson	Rabbit Warstler	NL	BOS	Aug 6, 1937	
Boze Berger	Mike Kreevich	AL	CHI	Sep 2, 1937	
Barney McCosky	Earl Averill	AL	DET	Jun 22, 1939	
Pete Coscarart	Jim Russell	NL	PIT	Jul 6, 1945	
Grady Hatton	Bobby Adams	NL	CIN	Apr 19, 1952	
Hank Bauer	Andy Carey	AL	NY	Apr 27, 1955	
Whitey Lockman	Willie Kirkland	NL	SF	Jul 6, 1958	
Curt Flood	Gene Freese	NL	STL	Aug 17, 1958	
Bill Tuttle	Roger Maris	AL	KC	Sep 18, 1958	
Lenny Green	Vic Power	AL	MIN	May 10, 1962	
Chuck Hiller	Duke Snider	NL	SF	May 27, 1964	
Pete Rose	Bobby Tolan	NL	CIN	Apr 7, 1969	
Pete Rose	Bobby Tolan	NL	CIN	Aug 18, 1969	
Pete Rose	Bobby Tolan	NL	CIN	Jun 28, 1970	
Luis Aparicio	Reggie Smith	AL	BOS	May 1, 1971	
Graig Nettles	Vada Pinson	AL	CLE	Jun 19, 1971	
Rick Miller	Reggie Smith	AL	BOS	Jun 20, 1973	
Don Money	Darrell Porter	AL	MIL	Jul 29, 1975	
Rick Burleson	Fred Lynn	AL	BOS	Jun 17, 1977	
Omar Moreno	Johnny Ray	NL	PIT	Jul 5, 1982	
Rickey Henderson	Mike Davis	AL	OAK	Sep 9, 1983	
Darryl Motley	Pat Sheridan	AL	KC	May 3, 1984	
Juan Samuel	Von Hayes	NL	PHI	Jul 29, 1984	
Dwight Evans	Wade Boggs	AL	BOS	Sep 5, 1985	
Gary Redus	Juan Samuel	NL	PHI	Jul 7, 1986	
Kirby Puckett	Gary Gaetti	AL	MIN	Jul 18, 1986	
Lou Whitaker	Alan Trammell	AL	DET	Aug 5, 1986	2G
Kal Daniels	Tracy Jones	NL	CIN	Jun 20, 1987	
Ken Gerhart	Fred Lynn	AL	BAL	Jun 23, 1988	
Devon White	Roberto Alomar	AL	TOR	Aug 18, 1991	
Brady Anderson	Mike Devereaux	AL	BAL	Jul 9, 1992	
Rickey Henderson	Craig Paquette	AL	OAK	Jun 12, 1993	
Roberto Kelly	Jeff Blauser	NL	ATL	Jun 22, 1994	
Jacob Brumfield	Bret Boone	NL	CIN	Aug 3, 1994	
Brady Anderson	Kevin Bass	AL	BAL	Jun 8, 1995	
Troy O'Leary	John Valentin	AL	BOS	Jul 21, 1995	
Luis Gonzalez	Jose Hernandez	NL	CHI	Sep 27, 1995	
Lenny Dykstra	Mickey Morandini	NL	PHI	Apr 16, 1996	
Jeff Cirillo	Pat Listach	AL	MIL	Apr 25, 1996	
Eric Young	Ellis Burks	NL	COL	May 4, 1996	
Rex Hudler	Don Slaught	AL	CAL	May 21, 1996	
Thomas Howard	Hal Morris	NL	CIN	Sep 9, 1996	
Quinton McCracken	Wade Boggs	AL	TB	Jun 15, 1998	
Tom Goodwin	Mark McLemore	AL	TEX	May 7, 1999	
Brady Anderson	Mike Bordick	AL	BAL	Jun 12, 1999	
Chuck Knoblauch	Derek Jeter	AL	NY	Jul 30, 1999	
Eric Young	Ricky Gutierrez	NL	CHI	Apr 27, 2000	
Terrence Long	Randy Velarde	AL	OAK	May 16, 2000	
Ray Durham	Jose Valentin	AL	CHI	Jul 4, 2000	

(154) *(continued)*

Tom Goodwin	Mark Grudzielanek	NL	LA	Apr 5, 2001	
Rusty Greer	Randy Velarde	AL	TEX	Apr 13, 2001	
Jerry Hairston Jr.	Mike Bordick	AL	BAL	Jun 6, 2001	
Alex Ochoa	Barry Larkin	NL	CIN	Jun 26, 2001	
Ramon Santiago	Damion Easley	AL	DET	Jun 3, 2002	
Brad Wilkerson	Jose Vidro	NL	MON	Jun 16, 2002	
Chris Magruder	Omar Vizquel	AL	CLE	Jul 21, 2002	
Jacque Jones	Cristian Guzman	AL	MIN	Aug 19, 2002	
Ichiro Suzuki	Desi Relaford	AL	SEA	Sep 9, 2002	
Alfonso Soriano	Nick Johnson	AL	NY	Apr 6, 2003	
Alfonso Soriano	Derek Jeter	AL	NY	Jun 28, 2003	2G
Tony Womack	Reggie Sanders	NL	STL	Apr 16, 2004	
Jimmy Rollins	Placido Polanco	NL	PHI	Sep 9, 2004	
Omar Infante	Bobby Higginson	AL	DET	Sep 28, 2004	
Adam Everett	Craig Biggio	NL	HOU	May 20, 2005	
Derek Jeter	Robinson Cano	AL	NY	Sep 23, 2005	
Craig Biggio	Mike Lamb	NL	HOU	Jun 9, 2006	
Alex Rios	Frank Catalanotto	AL	TOR	Jun 14, 2006	
Ichiro Suzuki	Chris Snelling	AL	SEA	Aug 29, 2006	

Rabbit Maranville

(155) Game-ending Extra-inning Home Runs (16th inning or later)

INN.				OPP.		
25	Harold Baines	AL	CHI	MIL	May 9, 1984	Game began on May 8
22	Pedro Munoz	AL	MIN	CLE	Sep 1, 1993	Game began on Aug 31
21	Dick Allen	AL	CHI	CLE	May 27, 1973	Game began on May 26
19	Willie Kirkland	AL	CLE	WAS	Jun 14, 1963	Also HR in 11th inn.
19	Andy Etchebarren	AL	BAL	WAS	Jun 4, 1967	
19	Joe Rudi	AL	OAK	CHI	Aug 11, 1972	Game began on Aug 10
19	Mike Cameron	AL	SEA	BOS	Aug 1, 2000	
18	Charley Radbourn	NL	PRO	DET	Aug 17, 1882	Final score, 1-0
18	Claudell Washington	AL	NY	DET	Sep 11, 1988	
18	Jeff King	NL	PIT	CHI	Aug 6, 1989	
18	Shea Hillenbrand	AL	BOS	DET	Jun 5, 2001	
18	Alfonso Soriano	AL	TEX	SEA	Jun 24, 2004	
17	Mule Haas	AL	PHI	CLE	Aug 22, 1928	
17	Del Ennis	NL	PHI	BOS	Sep 6, 1952	1G
17	Jim Finigan	AL	KC	WAS	May 23, 1956	
17	Roy Sievers	AL	WAS	DET	Aug 3, 1957	
17	Earl Torgeson	AL	CHI	BAL	Jun 4, 1959	
17	Roberto Clemente	NL	PIT	SD	Jul 15, 1971	
17	Dave May	AL	MIL	CLE	May 15, 1973	
17	Lenny Randle	NL	NY	MON	Jul 9, 1977	
17	Dave Kingman	NL	NY	MON	Jun 10, 1983	
16	Max Bishop	AL	PHI	NY	Jun 1, 1932	1G
16	George Selkirk	AL	NY	CLE	Jun 7, 1936	
16	Clyde Vollmer	AL	BOS	CLE	Jul 28, 1951	
16	Wes Covington	NL	PHI	PIT	Sep 23, 1961	
16	Willie Mays	NL	SF	MIL	Jul 2, 1963	Ends 1-0 classic duel as Marichal defeats Spahn
16	Tim Harkness	NL	NY	MIL	Sep 1, 1963	
16	Jim Gosger	AL	BOS	NY	Jun 4, 1966	
16	Ken Berry	AL	CHI	CLE	Jul 25, 1967	1G
16	Joe Torre	NL	ATL	HOU	Aug 11, 1967	
16	Jim Northrup	AL	DET	CAL	Aug 1, 1971	
16	Bob Coluccio	AL	MIL	CLE	Apr 17, 1974	
16	Adrian Garrett	AL	CAL	CHI	Sep 22, 1975	Three-run pinch-hit HR
16	Lance Parrish	AL	DET	SEA	May 16, 1978	
16	George Brett	AL	KC	BAL	May 28, 1979	
16	Steve Garvey	NL	LA	SD	Sep 13, 1982	
16	Greg Pryor	AL	KC	CHI	Aug 26, 1984	
16	Mark Parent	NL	SD	LAN	Sep 28, 1988	
16	Greg Briley	AL	SEA	NY	May 5, 1991	
16	Jon Nunnally	AL	KC	DET	Jul 29, 1995	
16	Carlos Beltran	NL	NY	PHI	May 23, 2006	
16	Ramon Martinez	NL	LA	CIN	Aug 29, 2006	

(156) Home Runs by Brothers in the Same Game

Lloyd Waner	PIT	Paul Waner	PIT	NL	Sep 4, 1927	Both bounce HR
Lloyd Waner	PIT	Paul Waner	PIT	NL	Jun 9, 1929	
Rick Ferrell	BOS	Wes Ferrell	CLE	AL	Jul 19, 1933	Rick's HR off Wes
Al Cuccinello	NY	Tony Cuccinello	BRO	NL	Jul 5, 1935	
Lloyd Waner	PIT	Paul Waner	PIT	NL	Sep 15, 1938	Back to back
Joe DiMaggio	NY	Dom DiMaggio	BOS	AL	Jun 30, 1950	
Felipe Alou	SF	Matty Alou	SF	NL	May 15, 1961	
Hank Aaron	MIL	Tommie Aaron	MIL	NL	Jun 12, 1962	
Hank Aaron	MIL	Tommie Aaron	MIL	NL	Jul 12, 1962	
Hank Aaron	MIL	Tommie Aaron	MIL	NL	Aug 14, 1962	
Clete Boyer	NY	Ken Boyer	STL	WS	Oct 15, 1964	World Series game 7
Matty Alou	SF	Jesus Alou	SF	NL	Aug 12, 1965	1G
Billy Conigliaro	BOS	Tony Conigliaro	BOS	AL	Jul 4, 1970	
Billy Conigliaro	BOS	Tony Conigliaro	BOS	AL	Sep 19, 1970	2G
Graig Nettles	CLE	Jim Nettles	MIN	AL	Jun 11, 1972	
Graig Nettles	NY	Jim Nettles	DET	AL	Sep 14, 1974	
Hector Cruz	CHI	Jose Cruz Sr.	HOU	NL	May 4, 1981	
Cal Ripken	BAL	Billy Ripken	BAL	AL	Sep 15, 1990	
Cal Ripken	BAL	Billy Ripken	BAL	AL	May 28, 1996	Cal had 3 HR in game
Vladimir Guerrero	MON	Wilton Guerrero	MON	NL	Aug 15, 1998	
Bret Boone	ATL	Aaron Boone	CIN	NL	Sep 1, 1999	
Vladimir Guerrero	MON	Wilton Guerrero	MON	NL	Oct 2, 1999	
Jason Giambi	OAK	Jeremy Giambi	OAK	AL	May 8, 2000	
Bret Boone	SD	Aaron Boone	CIN	NL	May 11, 2000	
Vladimir Guerrero	MON	Wilton Guerrero	MON	NL	May 18, 2000	
Jason Giambi	OAK	Jeremy Giambi	OAK	AL	Sep 15, 2000	
Vladimir Guerrero	MON	Wilton Guerrero	MON	NL	Sep 18, 2000	Vladimir had 2 HR in game
Felipe Crespo	SF	Cesar Crespo	SD	NL	Jun 7, 2001	Felipe had 2 HR in game
Jason Giambi	OAK	Jeremy Giambi	OAK	AL	Jun 21, 2001	
Jason Giambi	OAK	Jeremy Giambi	OAK	AL	Aug 11, 2001	
Bengie Molina	LA	Jose Molina	LA	AL	Jul 31, 2005	

(157) Home Runs by Father and Son in the Same Game

FATHER			SON			
Ken Griffey Sr.	AL	SEA	Ken Griffey Jr.	AL	SEA	Sep 14, 1990 Back to back

(158) Four Home Runs in a Game

Bobby Lowe	NL	BOS	May 30, 1894	2G
Ed Delahanty	NL	PHI	Jul 13, 1896	In a losing effort
Lou Gehrig	AL	NY	Jun 3, 1932	
Chuck Klein	NL	PHI	Jul 10, 1936	10 inn.
Pat Seerey	AL	CHI	Jul 18, 1948	1G; 11 Inn.
Gil Hodges	NL	BRO	Aug 31, 1950	
Joe Adcock	NL	MIL	Jul 31, 1954	
Rocky Colavito	AL	CLE	Jun 10, 1959	Also a double; 18 total bases
Willie Mays	NL	SF	Apr 30, 1961	
Mike Schmidt	NL	PHI	Apr 17, 1976	10 Inn.
Bob Horner	NL	ATL	Jul 6, 1986	In a losing effort
Mark Whiten	NL	STL	Sep 7, 1993	2G
Mike Cameron	AL	SEA	May 2, 2002	
Shawn Green	NL	LA	May 23, 2002	Also a single and double; 19 total bases
Carlos Delgado	AL	TOR	Sep 25, 2003	

(159) Game-ending Home Runs by a Pitcher

				OPP.	INN.	
John Ward	NL	NY	May 2, 1883	BOS	9	
Jack Stivetts	AA	STL	Jun 10, 1890	TOL	9	
John Clarkson	NL	CLE	Sep 18, 1893	BOS	10	
Jouett Meekin	NL	NY	Sep 6, 1894	PIT	9	
Jack Powell	NL	STL	Aug 1, 1899	BOS	14	
John Malarkey	NL	BOS	Sep 11, 1902	STL	11	Only Major League HR
Chick Fraser	NL	PHI	Jun 16, 1903	NY	12	
Jack Quinn	FL	BAL	Apr 21, 1914	BRO	10	
Ferdie Schupp	NL	STL	Sep 11, 1919	BRO	9	Only Major League HR
Grover Alexander	NL	CHI	May 31, 1920	CIN	10	1G
Leon Cadore	NL	BRO	Aug 5, 1922	CIN	10	2G
Jack Bentley	NL	NY	Aug 29, 1925	STL	11	
Red Ruffing	AL	NY	Apr 14, 1933	BOS	9	
Wes Ferrell	AL	BOS	Aug 22, 1934	CHI	10	
Wes Ferrell	AL	BOS	Jul 22, 1935	STL	9	
Dizzy Dean	NL	STL	Aug 6, 1935	CIN	10	
Jack Wilson	AL	BOS	Sep 2, 1935	WAS	11	1G
Dizzy Trout	AL	DET	May 30, 1944	NY	9	1G
Jim Tobin	AL	DET	Aug 12, 1945	NY	11	
Claude Passeau	NL	CHI	Jun 7, 1946	BRO	9	
Kirby Higbe	NL	PIT	Sep 11, 1947	BOS	13	1G
Harry Gumbert	NL	CIN	Aug 23, 1948	PHI	10	Only hit of season
Kirby Higbe	NL	PIT	Aug 27, 1948	PHI	9	
Lou Sleater	AL	DET	May 30, 1957	KC	10	
Bob Grim	AL	NY	Sep 5, 1957	BOS	9	
Murry Dickson	AL	KC	May 26, 1958	BAL	10	
Glen Hobbie	NL	CHI	Aug 25, 1960	PIT	9	First Major League HR
Lindy McDaniel	NL	CHI	Jun 6, 1963	SF	10	
Juan Marichal	NL	SF	Sep 21, 1966	PIT	9	
Steve Hargan	AL	CLE	Jun 19, 1967	KC	9	
Jim Hardin	AL	BAL	May 10, 1969	KC	9	First Major League HR
Craig Lefferts	NL	SD	Apr 25, 1986	SF	12	First Major League HR

(160) Most Plate Appearances by One Player in a Nine-inning Game

8	Abner Dalrymple	NL	CHI	Jul, 24, 1882	
8	King Kelly	NL	CHI	Jul, 24, 1882	
8	Jim Whitney	NL	BOS	Jun 9, 1883	
8	Joe Hornung	NL	BOS	Jun 9, 1883	
8	Sam Wise	NL	BOS	Jun 9, 1883	
8	Ezra Sutton	NL	BOS	Jun 9, 1883	
8	Jim Whitney	NL	BOS	Jun 20, 1883	
8	Abner Dalrymple	NL	CHI	Jul 3, 1883	
8	George Gore	NL	CHI	Jul 3, 1883	
8	King Kelly	NL	CHI	Jul 3, 1883	
8	Jimmy Ryan	NL	CHI	Aug 25, 1891	
8	Arlie Latham	NL	CIN	Jun 18, 1893	
8	Bid McPhee	NL	CIN	Jun 18, 1893	
8	Piggy Ward	NL	CIN	Jun 18, 1893	
8	Jack Boyle	NL	PHIL	Aug 17, 1894	
8	Lave Cross	NL	PHIL	Aug 17, 1894	
8	Fred Tenney	NL	BOS	May 31, 1897	
8	Barry McCormick	NL	CHI	Jun 29, 1897	
8	Russell Wrightstone	NL	PHI	Aug 25, 1922	
8	Frank Parkinson	NL	PHI	Aug 25, 1922	
8	Taylor Douthit	NL	STL	Jul 6, 1929	1G
8	Andy High	NL	STL	Jul 6, 1929	1G
8	Clyde Vollmer	AL	BOS	Jun 8, 1950	
8	Darryl Hamilton	AL	MIL	Aug 28, 1992	
8	Mike Cameron	NL	CIN	May 19, 1999	

Fred Tenney

(161) Most Doubles in a Game

4	John O'Rourke	NL	BOS	Sep 15, 1880	
4	Abner Dalrymple	NL	CHI	Jul 3, 1883	
4	Cap Anson	NL	CHI	Jul 3, 1883	
4	Henry Larkin	AA	PHI	Jul 29, 1885	
4	Jocko Milligan	AA	PHI	May 2, 1886	8 Inn.
4	Tommy Tucker	NL	BOS	Jul 22, 1893	
4	Frank Bonner	NL	BAL	Aug 4, 1894	Consecutive
4	Joe Kelley	NL	BAL	Sep 3, 1894	Consecutive; 2G; 6 inn.
4	Ed Delahanty	NL	PHI	May 13, 1899	
4	Pop Dillon	AL	DET	Apr 25, 1901	
4	Sherry Magee	NL	PHI	Jun 17, 1914	10 Inn.; game-winning hit into bleachers scored as a double
4	Gavy Cravath	NL	PHI	Aug 8, 1915	
4	Denny Sothern	NL	PHI	Jun 6, 1930	
4	Paul Waner	NL	PIT	May 20, 1932	
4	Dick Bartell	NL	PHI	Apr 25, 1933	Consecutive
4	Ernie Lombardi	NL	CIN	May 8, 1935	Consecutive; 1G
4	Billy Werber	AL	BOS	Jul 17, 1935	Consecutive; 1G
4	Frankie Hayes	AL	PHI	Jul 25, 1936	
4	Joe Medwick	NL	STL	Aug 4, 1937	
4	Mike Kreevich	AL	CHI	Sep 4, 1937	Consecutive
4	Marv Owen	AL	CHI	Apr 23, 1939	
4	Billy Werber	NL	CIN	May 13, 1940	Consecutive; 14 inn.
4	Johnny Lindell	AL	NY	Aug 17, 1944	Consecutive
4	Lou Boudreau	AL	CLE	Jul 14, 1946	Consecutive; 1G
4	Willie Jones	NL	PHI	Apr 20, 1949	Consecutive
4	Al Zarilla	AL	BOS	Jun 8, 1950	
4	Jim Greengrass	NL	CIN	Apr 13, 1954	
4	Vic Wertz	AL	CLE	Sep 26, 1956	Consecutive
4	Charlie Lau	AL	BAL	Jul 13, 1962	
4	Billy Bruton	AL	DET	May 19, 1963	Consecutive
4	Billy Williams	NL	CHI	Apr 9, 1969	Consecutive
4	Orlando Cepeda	AL	BOS	Aug 8, 1973	
4	Jim Mason	AL	NY	Jul 8, 1974	
4	Dave Duncan	AL	BAL	Jun 30, 1975	Consecutive; 2G
4	Rick Miller	AL	BOS	May 11, 1981	
4	Rafael Ramirez	NL	ATL	May 21, 1986	13 inn.
4	Damaso Garcia	AL	TOR	Jun 27, 1986	
4	Kirby Puckett	AL	MIN	May 13, 1989	
4	Billy Hatcher	NL	CIN	Aug 21, 1990	
4	Jeff Bagwell	NL	HOU	Jun 14, 1996	
4	Sandy Alomar Jr.	AL	CLE	Jun 6, 1997	Consecutive
4	Albert Belle	AL	BAL	Aug 29, 1999	
4	Albert Belle	AL	BAL	Sep 23, 1999	
4	Johnny Damon	AL	KC	Jul 18, 2000	
4	Shannon Stewart	AL	TOR	Jul 18, 2000	
4	Marcus Giles	NL	ATL	Jul 27, 2003	Consecutive
4	Adam LaRoche	NL	ATL	May 15, 2004	
4	Tomas Perez	AL	TB	Jul 29, 2006	
4	Matt Murton	NL	CHI	Aug 3, 2006	2G

(162) Most Triples in a Game

4	George Strief	AA	PHI	Jun 25, 1885	Also a 2B
4	Bill Joyce	NL	NY	May 18, 1897	
3	George Hall	NL	PHI	Jun 14, 1876	Also a HR
3	Ezra Sutton	NL	PHI	Jun 14, 1876	
3	Buck Ewing	NL	NY	Jun 9, 1883	
3	Dave Rowe	UA	STL	Jun 24, 1884	
3	Charley Jones	AA	CIN	Jul 20, 1884	
3	Harry Stovey	AA	PHI	Aug 18, 1884	
3	Sadie Houck	AA	PHI	Aug 27, 1884	
3	King Kelly	NL	CHI	Sep 29, 1885	
3	Hardy Richardson	NL	DET	Sep 9, 1886	8 Inn.
3	Sam Thompson	NL	DET	May 13, 1887	
3	Marty Sullivan	NL	CHI	May 17, 1887	
3	Oyster Burns	AA	BAL	Jun 13, 1887	
3	Billy Hamilton	AA	KC	Jun 28, 1889	1G
3	Larry Twitchell	NL	CLE	Aug 15, 1889	Also a 2B and a HR
3	John Reilly	NL	CIN	Jun 14, 1890	
3	Bid McPhee	NL	CIN	Jun 28, 1890	
3	Sid Farrar	PL	PHI	Aug 28, 1890	
3	George Davis	NL	CLE	Apr 25, 1891	Also a HR; HR and 3B in 7th inn.
3	Tom Brown	AA	BOS	May 7, 1891	14 Inn.; all 3B in 9 inn.
3	Billy Hamilton	NL	PHI	Jul 14, 1891	
3	Harry Stovey	NL	BAL	Jul 21, 1892	
3	Jouett Meekin	NL	NY	Jul 4, 1894	1G
3	George Davis	NL	NY	Jul 14, 1894	
3	Bill Hassamaer	NL	WAS	Jul 25, 1894	2G
3	Hugh Duffy	NL	BOS	Sep 18, 1894	Also a 2B
3	Frank Shugart	NL	LOU	Jul 30, 1895	two 3B in 5th inn.
3	Bill Dahlen	NL	CHI	May 3, 1896	
3	Jake Beckley	NL	CIN	May 19, 1898	
3	Bill Dahlen	NL	CHI	Jun 6, 1898	
3	Elmer Flick	NL	PHI	Jun 20, 1898	
3	Ginger Beaumont	NL	PIT	Aug 9, 1899	Also a 2B
3	Harry Wolverton	NL	PHI	Jul 13, 1900	8 inn.
3	Jimmy Sheckard	NL	BRO	Apr 18, 1901	
3	Elmer Flick	AL	CLE	Jul 6, 1902	
3	Bill Bradley	AL	CLE	Jul 28, 1903	
3	Patsy Dougherty	AL	BOS	Sep 5, 1903	8 inn.
3	Mike Donlin	NL	CIN	Sep 22, 1903	2G; 7 inn.
3	Billy Lush	AL	DET	Sep 26, 1903	1G
3	Nap Lajoie	AL	CLE	Jul 13, 1904	
3	Miller Huggins	NL	CIN	Oct 8, 1904	2G
3	Dave Brain	NL	STL	May 29, 1905	
3	Dave Brain	NL	PIT	Aug 8, 1905	10 inn.; all 3B in 9 inn.
3	Pat Moran	NL	BOS	Aug 10, 1905	
3	Hal Chase	AL	NY	Aug 30, 1906	2G; 10 inn.; all 3B in 9 inn.; also a 2B
3	Chief Wilson	NL	PIT	Jul 24, 1911	
3	Joe Jackson	AL	CLE	Jun 30, 1912	2G
3	Gus Williams	AL	STL	Apr 24, 1913	
3	Jack Lewis	FL	PIT	May 7, 1914	
3	Fred Smith	FL	BUF	Apr 27, 1915	
3	Al Shaw	FL	KC	Jul 4, 1915	

(162) *(continued)*

3	Ross Youngs	NL	NY	May 11, 1920	
3	Joe Judge	AL	WAS	Aug 9, 1921	19 inn.; all 3B in 9 inn.
3	Ray Powell	NL	BOS	Sep 27, 1921	1G
3	Charlie Hollocher	NL	CHI	Aug 13, 1922	
3	Baby Doll Jacobson	AL	STL	Sep 9, 1922	
3	Jim Bottomley	NL	STL	May 15, 1923	
3	Jackie Tavener	AL	DET	Sep 12, 1925	1G; 13 inn.; all 3B in 9 inn.
3	Les Bell	NL	STL	Sep 22, 1926	Also a 2B
3	Jim Bottomley	NL	STL	Jun 21, 1927	
3	Earle Combs	AL	NY	Sep 22, 1927	
3	Lance Richbourg	NL	BOS	Jul 31, 1929	1G
3	Charlie Gehringer	AL	DET	Aug 5, 1929	
3	Joe Kuhel	AL	WAS	May 13, 1937	
3	Joe DiMaggio	AL	NY	Aug 27, 1938	1G
3	Ben Chapman	AL	CLE	Jul 3, 1939	
3	Carlos Bernier	NL	PIT	May 2, 1953	
3	Danny O'Connell	NL	MIL	Jun 13, 1956	
3	Roberto Clemente	NL	PIT	Sep 8, 1958	
3	Willie Mays	NL	SF	Sep 15, 1960	
3	Ernie Banks	NL	CHI	Jun 11, 1966	
3	Bert Campaneris	AL	KC	Aug 29, 1967	10 inn.; all 3B in 9 inn.
3	Al Bumbry	AL	BAL	Sep 22, 1973	
3	Ken Landreaux	AL	MIN	Jul 3, 1980	
3	Doug Flynn	NL	NY	Aug 5, 1980	11 inn. a 3B in 11th
3	Craig Reynolds	NL	HOU	May 16, 1981	
3	Shawon Dunston	NL	CHI	Jul 28, 1990	
3	Herm Winningham	NL	CIN	Aug 15, 1990	12 inn.
3	Lance Johnson	AL	CHI	Sep 23, 1995	
3	Rafael Furcal	NL	ATL	Apr 21, 2002	

(163) Most RBI in a Game, since 1893

12	Jim Bottomley	NL	STL	Sep 16, 1924	
12	Mark Whiten	NL	STL	Sep 7, 1993	2G
11	Tony Lazzeri	AL	NY	May 24, 1936	
11	Phil Weintraub	NL	NY	Apr 30, 1944	1G
10	Rudy York	AL	BOS	Jul 27, 1946	
10	Walker Cooper	NL	CIN	Jul 6, 1949	
10	Norm Zauchin	AL	BOS	May 27, 1955	
10	Reggie Jackson	AL	OAK	Jun 14, 1969	
10	Fred Lynn	AL	BOS	Jun 18, 1975	
10	Nomar Garciaparra	AL	BOS	May 10, 1999	
10	Alex Rodriguez	AL	NY	Apr 26, 2005	
9	Harry Staley	NL	BOS	Jun 1, 1893	
9	Heinie Zimmerman	NL	CHI	Jun 11, 1911	
9	Jimmie Foxx	AL	PHI	Aug 14, 1933	
9	Johnny Rizzo	NL	PIT	May 30, 1939	2G
9	Jim Tabor	AL	BOS	Jul 4, 1939	2G
9	Gil Hodges	NL	BRO	Aug 31, 1950	
9	Smoky Burgess	NL	CIN	Jul 29, 1955	
9	Jackie Jensen	AL	BOS	Aug 2, 1956	
9	Jim Gentile	AL	BAL	May 9, 1961	
9	Tony Cloninger	NL	ATL	Jul 3, 1966	Pitcher
9	Roy Howell	AL	TOR	Sep 10, 1977	
9	Eddie Murray	AL	BAL	Aug 26, 1985	
9	Chris James	AL	CLE	May 4, 1991	
9	Danny Tartabull	AL	NY	Sep 8, 1992	
9	Mike Greenwell	AL	BOS	Sep 2, 1996	
9	Ivan Rodriguez	AL	TEX	Apr 13, 1999	
9	Erubiel Durazo	NL	ARI	May 17, 2002	
9	Sammy Sosa	NL	CHI	Aug 10, 2002	
9	Bill Mueller	AL	BOS	Jul 29, 2003	
9	Vladimir Guerrero	AL	ANA	Jun 2, 2004	
9	James Loney	NL	LA	Sep 28, 2006	

(164) Most Total Bases in a Game

19	Shawn Green	NL	LA	May 23, 2002		16	Mark Whiten	NL	STL	Sep 7, 1993
18	Joe Adcock	NL	MIL	Jul 31, 1954						2G
17	Bobby Lowe	NL	BOS	May 30, 1894		16	Edgardo Alfonzo	NL	NY	Aug 30, 1999
17	Ed Delahanty	NL	PHI	Jul 13, 1896		16	Mike Cameron	AL	SEA	May 2, 2002
17	Gil Hodges	NL	Bro	Aug 31, 1950		16	Carlos Delgado	AL	TOR	Sep 25, 2003
17	Mike Schmidt	NL	PHI	Apr 17, 1976		15	Dan Brouthers	NL	DET	Sep 10, 1886
				10 inn.		15	George Kelly	NL	NY	Sep 17, 1923
16	Larry Twitchell	NL	Cle	Aug 15, 1889		15	Les Bell	NL	BOS	Jun 2, 1928
16	Ty Cobb	AL	Det	May 5, 1925		15	Tony Lazzeri	AL	NY	May 24, 1936
16	Lou Gehrig	AL	NY	Jun 3, 1932		15	Pat Seerey	AL	CLE	Jul 13, 1945
16	Jimmie Foxx	AL	PHI	Jul 10, 1932		15	Walker Cooper	NL	CIN	Jul 6, 1949
				18 inn.		15	Wes Westrum	NL	NY	Jun 24, 1950
16	Chuck Klein	NL	PHI	Jul 10, 1936		15	Bobby Avila	AL	CLE	Jun 20, 1951
				10 inn.		15	Willie Mays	NL	SF	May 13, 1958
16	Pat Seerey	AL	CHI	Jul 18, 1948		15	Willie Stargell	NL	PIT	May 22, 1968
				1G; 11 inn.		15	Davey Lopes	NL	LA	Aug 20, 1974
16	Rocky Colavito	AL	CLE	Jun 10, 1959		15	Dave Winfield	AL	CAL	Apr 13, 1991
16	Willie Mays	NL	SF	Apr 30, 1961		15	Dmitri Young	AL	DET	May 6, 2003
16	Fred Lynn	AL	BOS	Jun 18, 1975		15	Shea Hillenbrand	NL	ARI	Jul 7, 2003
16	Bob Horner	NL	ATL	Jul 6, 1986		15	Albert Pujols	NL	STL	Jul 20, 2004

(165) Leadoff Home Run in Most Consecutive Games

4	Brady Anderson	AL	BAL	Apr 18, 19, 20, 21, 1996	Orioles lose all 4 games
2	Abner Dalrymple	NL	CHI	Jun 27, 29, 1885	
2	Dick Johnston	NL	BOS	Sep 5, 7, 1888	
2	Jack Crooks	NL	STL	May 10, 11, 1892	
2	Sam Mertes	NL	CHI	Jun 8, 9, 1900	
2	Harry Hooper	AL	BOS	May 30 (1G), 30 (2G), 1913	2G homer off Walter Johnson in 1-0 game
2	Sherry Robertson	AL	WAS	Sep 17-18, 1946	
2	Carl Furillo	NL	BRO	Jul 12, 13, 1951	
2	Whitey Lockman	NL	NY	Jul 18, 19, 1953	
2	Hank Bauer	AL	NY	Sep 11, 12, 1956	
2	Hank Bauer	AL	NY	Aug 6, 7, 1957	
2	Denis Menke	NL	MIL	Jul 26, 27, 1964	
2	Tony Kubek	AL	NY	Sep 6, 7, 1964	
2	Felipe Alou	NL	MIL	Jul 26, 27, 1965	
2	Felipe Alou	NL	ATL	Aug 9, 10, 1966	
2	Dick McAuliffe	AL	DET	Apr 28, 29, 1969	
2	Bobby Bonds	NL	SF	Jun 5, 6, 1973	
2	Rick Monday	NL	CHI	Jun 25, 26, 1976	
2	Pete Rose	NL	CIN	Jul 25, 26, 1976	
2	Mike Hargrove	AL	TEX	Aug 13, 14, 1977	
2	Paul Molitor	AL	MIL	Jun 30, Jul 1, 1979	
2	Al Bumbry	AL	BAL	Aug 4, 5, 1982	
2	Lou Whitaker	AL	DET	May 6, 7, 1983	
2	Damaso Garcia	AL	TOR	Jun 1, 2, 1983	
2	Gary Redus	NL	CIN	Jul 1, 2, 1983	
2	Eddie Milner	NL	CIN	Jun 24, 25, 1984	
2	Oddibe McDowell	AL	TEX	Jul 27, 28, 1985	

(165) *(continued)*

2	Dan Gladden	NL	SF	Oct 1, 2, 1985	
2	Kirby Puckett	AL	MIN	May 2, 3, 1986	
2	Brian Downing	AL	CAL	Apr 14, 15, 1987	
2	Barry Bonds	NL	PIT	May 12, 13, 1988	
2	Randy Ready	NL	PHI	Jun 15, 16, 1989	
2	Rickey Henderson	AL	OAK	May 5, 6, 1990	
2	Ron Gant	NL	ATL	May 27, 28 1991	
2	Rickey Henderson	AL	OAK	Jul 5 (1G), 5 (2G), 1993	1st time in doubleheader since Hooper
2	Ray Lankford	NL	STL	May 1, 3, 1994	
2	Tony Tarasco	NL	MON	May 8, 9, 1995	
2	Rex Hudler	AL	CAL	May 20, 21, 1996	
2	Brian L. Hunter	NL	HOU	Aug 11, 12, 1996	
2	Chuck Knoblauch	AL	MIN	Sep 1, 2, 1996	
2	Kenny Lofton	NL	ATL	Aug 23, 24, 1997	
2	Denny Hocking	AL	MIN	Jul 17, 18, 1999	
2	Chuck Knoblauch	AL	NY	Jul 30, 31, 1999	
2	Brady Anderson	AL	BAL	Aug 21 (1G), 21 (2G), 1999	
2	Jose Cruz Jr.	AL	TOR	Apr 22, 23, 2000	
2	Rickey Henderson	AL	SEA	May 20, 21, 2000	1st AB as a Mariner
2	Ron Belliard	NL	MIL	Jun 17, 18, 2000	
2	Julio Lugo	NL	HOU	May 13, 14, 2001	
2	Craig Biggio	NL	HOU	Jun 21, 22, 2001	
2	Craig Biggio	NL	HOU	Aug 13, 14, 2001	
2	Derek Jeter	AL	NY	Aug 17, 18, 2001	
2	Jimmy Rollins	NL	PHI	May 16, 17, 2002	
2	Ramon Santiago	AL	DET	Jun 3, 4, 2002	
2	Melvin Mora	AL	BAL	Jun 28, 29, 2002	
2	Kenny Lofton	AL	CHI	Jul 18, 19, 2002	
2	Jacque Jones	AL	MIN	Aug 19, 20, 2002	
2	Kaz Matsui	NL	NY	May 22, 23, 2004	
2	Scott Podsednik	NL	MIL	Jun 1, 2, 2004	
2	Ichiro Suzuki	AL	SEA	Aug 15, 17, 2004	
2	Damian Jackson	NL	SD	Jun 26, 27, 2005	
2	David Dellucci	AL	TEX	Jun 30, Jul 1, 2005	
2	Jimmy Rollins	NL	PHI	Sep 25, 26, 2005	
2	Hanley Ramirez	NL	FLA	Jul 17, 18, 2006	

(166) Pinch-Hit Home Run as the Only Run of the Game

			PITCHER			
Bill Taylor	NL	NY	Gene Conley	MIL	Jun 10, 1954	10th inn. 1st ML HR
Candy Maldonado	NL	LA	Mark Davis	SF	Apr 13, 1985	
Travis Lee	AL	TB	Bob Wickman	CLE	Aug 14, 2005	

(167) Pinch-Hit Home Run in First Major League At-bat

			PITCHER				
Eddie Morgan	NL	STL	Lon Warneke	NL	CHI	Apr 14, 1936	Only Major League HR
Ace Parker	AL	PHI	Wes Ferrell	AL	BOS	Apr 30, 1937	
Les Layton	NL	NY	Johnny Schmitz	NL	CHI	May 21, 1948	
Ted Tappe	NL	CIN	Erv Palica	NL	BRO	Sep 14, 1950	
Chuck Tanner	NL	MIL	Gerry Staley	NL	CIN	Apr 12, 1955	
John Kennedy	AL	WAS	Dick Stigman	AL	MIN	Sep 5, 1962	
Gates Brown	AL	DET	Bob Heffner	AL	BOS	Jun 19, 1963	
Bill Roman	AL	DET	Jim Bouton	AL	NY	Sep 30, 1964	Only Major League HR
Brant Alyea	AL	WAS	Rudy May	AL	CAL	Sep 12, 1965	
Joe Keough	AL	OAK	Lindy McDaniel	AL	NY	Aug 7, 1968	2G
Al Woods	AL	TOR	Francisco Barrios	AL	CHI	Apr 7, 1977	
Garey Ingram	NL	LA	Mike Munoz	NL	COL	May 19, 1994	
Brad Fullmer	NL	MON	Bret Saberhagen	AL	BOS	Sep 2, 1997	
Marlon Anderson	NL	PHI	Mel Rojas	NL	NY	Sep 8, 1998	
Alex Cabrera	NL	ARI	Yorkis Perez	NL	HOU	Jun 26, 2000	
Keith McDonald	NL	STL	Andy Larkin	NL	CIN	Jul 4, 2000	
Gene Stechschulte	NL	STL	Armando Reynoso	NL	ARI	Apr 17, 2001	Only Major League HR
Dave Matranga	NL	HOU	Joaquin Benoit	AL	TEX	Jun 27, 2003	
Greg Dobbs	AL	SEA	Bob Wickman	AL	CLE	Sep 8, 2004	
Andy Phillips	AL	NY	Terry Adams	AL	BOS	Sep 26, 2004	
Mike Jacobs	NL	NY	Esteban Loaiza	NL	WAS	Aug 21, 2005	
Jeremy Hermida	NL	FLA	Al Reyes	NL	STL	Aug 31, 2005	
Charlton Jimerson	NL	HOU	Cole Hamels	NL	PHI	Sep 4, 2006	

(168) Hitting a Grand Slam in Two Consecutive Games

Jimmy Bannon	NL	BOS	Aug 6, 7, 1894
Jimmy Sheckard	NL	BRO	Sep 23, 24, 1901
Babe Ruth	AL	NY	Sep 27, 29, 1927
Babe Ruth	AL	NY	Aug 6, 7 (1G), 1929
Bill Dickey	AL	NY	Aug 3 (2G), 4, 1937
Jimmie Foxx	AL	BOS	May 20, 21, 1940
Jim Busby	AL	CLE	Jul 5, 6, 1956
Brooks Robinson	AL	BAL	May 6, 9, 1962
Phil Garner	NL	PIT	Sep 14, 15, 1978
Willie Aikens	AL	CAL	Jun 13, 14, 1979
Greg Luzinski	AL	CHI	Jun 8, 9, 1984
Rob Deer	AL	MIL	Aug 19. 20, 1987
Fred McGriff	NL	SD	Aug 13, 14, 1991
Mike Blowers	AL	SEA	May 16, 17, 1993
Dan Gladden	AL	DET	Aug 10, 11, 1993
Eric Davis	NL	CIN	May 4, 5, 1996
Mike Piazza	NL	LA	Apr 9, 10, 1998
Sammy Sosa	NL	CHI	Jul 27, 28, 1998
Ken Griffey Jr.	AL	SEA	Apr 29, 30, 1999
Robin Ventura	NL	NY	May 20 (1G), 20 (2G), 1999
Albert Belle	AL	BAL	Jun 14, 15, 2000
David Eckstein	AL	ANA	Apr 27, 28, 2002
Carlos Beltran	NL	NY	Jul 16, 18, 2006

(169) Two Extra-inning Home Runs by a Batter in a Game

Ralph Garr	NL	ATL	May 17, 1971	
Willie Kirkland	AL	CLE	Jun 14, 1963	2G
Art Shamsky	NL	CIN	Aug 12, 1966	
Vern Stephens	AL	STL	Sep 29, 1943	1G
Mike Young	AL	BAL	May 28, 1987	

(170) Three Home Runs in a Game by a Pitcher

			OPP.	
Guy Hecker	AA	LOU	BAL	Aug 15, 1886
Jim Tobin	NL	BOS	CHI	May 13, 1942

(171) Most Runs by a Player in a Game, before 1893

7	Guy Hecker	AA	LOU	Aug 15, 1886	2G, winning pitcher
6	Jim Whitney	NL	BOS	Jun 9, 1883	
6	John Reilly	AA	CIN	Sep 12, 1883	6 hits
6	Cap Anson	NL	CHI	Aug 24, 1886	
6	Mike Tiernan	NL	NY	Jun 15, 1887	
6	King Kelly	NL	BOS	Aug 27, 1887	Only game where 2 players each score 6 runs
6	Ezra Sutton	NL	BOS	Aug 27, 1887	Only game where 2 players each score 6 runs
6	Monk Cline	AA	KC	Sep 30, 1888	

George Brett

(172) Most Runs by a Player in a Game, since 1893

6	Jimmy Ryan	NL	CHI	Jul 25, 1894	
6	Bobby Lowe	NL	BOS	May 3, 1895	
6	Ginger Beaumont	NL	PIT	Jul 22, 1899	Hits
6	Mel Ott	NL	NY	Aug 4, 1934	2G
6	Mel Ott	NL	NY	Apr 30, 1944	1G; 5 walks and 2 singles
6	Johnny Pesky	AL	BOS	May 8, 1946	
6	Frank Torre	NL	MIL	Sep 2, 1957	1G
6	Spike Owen	AL	BOS	Aug 21, 1986	
6	Edgardo Alfonzo	NL	NY	Aug 30, 1999	
6	Shawn Green	NL	LA	May 23, 2002	4 HR; ML record 19 TB
6	Joe Randa	AL	KC	Sep 9, 2004	1G
5	Tommy Dowd	NL	STL	May 10, 1893	
5	Bill Hallman	NL	PHI	Aug 5, 1893	
5	Frank Shugart	NL	STL	Sep 30, 1893	2G
5	Herman Long	NL	BOS	May 30, 1894	1G; ML record 9 runs in a DH
5	Lou Bierbauer	NL	PIT	Jun 6, 1894	
5	Bill Dahlen	NL	CHI	Jul 5, 1894	
5	Jake Beckley	NL	PIT	Jul 10, 1894	
5	Farmer Vaughn	NL	CIN	Jul 28, 1894	
5	Jimmy Ryan	NL	CHI	Aug 1, 1894	
5	Walt Wilmot	NL	CHI	Aug 1, 1894	
5	Billy Hamilton	NL	PHI	Aug 8, 1894	
5	Joe Kelley	NL	BAL	Aug 10, 1894	
5	Ed Delahanty	NL	PHI	Aug 17, 1894	
5	Frank Connaughton	NL	BOS	Aug 21, 1894	2G; 6 inn.
5	Bill Dahlen	NL	CHI	Sep 20, 1894	
5	Cupid Childs	NL	CLE	Sep 27, 1894	
5	Herman Long	NL	BOS	May 3, 1895	
5	Arlie Latham	NL	CIN	May 17, 1895	
5	Bill Everitt	NL	CHI	May 20, 1895	
5	Hugh Duffy	NL	BOS	Jun 13, 1895	
5	Nig Cuppy	NL	CLE	Aug 9, 1895	Winning pitcher
5	Jesse Burkett	NL	CLE	Aug 24, 1895	
5	Willie Keeler	NL	BAL	Aug 24, 1895	
5	Willie Keeler	NL	BAL	Sep 14, 1895	
5	Jesse Burkett	NL	CLE	Sep 15, 1895	1G
5	Billy Hamilton	NL	PHI	Sep 30, 1895	10 inn.
5	Dan Brouthers	NL	PHI	Apr 23, 1896	
5	Mike Griffin	NL	BRO	May 20, 1896	
5	Dummy Hoy	NL	CIN	May 26, 1896	
5	Heinie Peitz	NL	CIN	Jun 29, 1896	
5	Cupid Childs	NL	CLE	Jul 1, 1896	
5	Joe Kelley	NL	BAL	Aug 8, 1896	
5	Jack Stivetts	NL	BOS	Sep 2, 1896	1G
5	Billy Hamilton	NL	BOS	Sep 3, 1896	1G
5	Fred Tenney	NL	BOS	Sep 3, 1896	1G
5	Hugh Duffy	NL	BOS	May 31, 1897	
5	Chick Stahl	NL	BOS	May 31, 1897	
5	Barry McCormick	NL	CHI	Jun 29, 1897	
5	Jimmy Ryan	NL	CHI	Jun 29, 1897	
5	Willie Keeler	NL	BAL	Jul 17, 1897	
5	Mike Griffin	NL	BRO	Aug 2, 1897	

(172) *(continued)*

5	Bill Lange	NL	CHI	Aug 4, 1897	
5	Tommy Corcoran	NL	CIN	Aug 4, 1897	1G
5	Willie Keeler	NL	BAL	Sep 3, 1897	
5	Joe Kelley	NL	BAL	Sep 3, 1897	
5	Bill Douglass	NL	PHI	Aug 22, 1898	
5	Fred Clarke	NL	LOU	Sep 21, 1898	
5	Roy Thomas	NL	PHI	Sep 5, 1899	
5	Kip Selbach	NL	CIN	Sep 5, 1899	1G
5	Charlie Hickman	NL	NY	Jun 9, 1901	Forfeit with 2 outs in 9th due to crowds on field
5	George Van Haltren	NL	NY	Jun 9, 1901	
5	Willie Keeler	NL	BRO	Jun 21, 1901	
5	Mike Donlin	AL	BAL	Jun 24, 1901	
5	Tom Daly	NL	BRO	Sep 23, 1901	
5	Willie Keeler	NL	BRO	Apr 24, 1902	Record 6th time scoring 5 runs
5	Herm McFarland	AL	BAL	Aug 25, 1902	
5	Harry Bay	AL	CLE	Sep 2, 1902	
5	Bill Bradley	AL	CLE	Sep 2, 1902	
5	Ginger Beaumont	AL	PIT	Jul 16, 1903	
5	Davy Jones	NL	CHI	May 3, 1904	
5	Jiggs Donahue	AL	CHI	Jun 27, 1904	
5	Bill Bradley	AL	CLE	Jul 13, 1904	
5	Cy Seymour	NL	CIN	Jul 23, 1904	2G
5	Miller Huggins	NL	CIN	Aug 5, 1905	
5	Dave Altizer	AL	WAS	Jul 2, 1906	2G; 7 inn.
5	Bob Ganley	AL	WAS	Jul 17, 1907	
5	Germany Schaefer	AL	DET	Jul 17, 1908	
5	Cy Seymour	NL	NY	Aug 11, 1909	
5	Jimmy Sheckard	NL	CHI	Jun 11, 1911	
5	Rollie Zeider	AL	CHI	Oct 8, 1911	
5	John Titus	NL	PHI	Jun 4, 1912	
5	Miller Huggins	NL	STL	Jul 6, 1912	
5	Beals Becker	NL	CIN	May 15, 1913	
5	Max Carey	NL	PIT	Jul 25, 1913	No hits in game; 4 stolen bases
5	Jimmy Walsh	AL	PHI	Sep 23, 1913	
5	Max Carey	NL	PIT	Sep 3, 1914	1G
5	Harry Hooper	AL	BOS	Jun 24, 1915	
5	Ty Cobb	AL	DET	Jul 30, 1917	
5	Tris Speaker	AL	CLE	Aug 11, 1919	
5	George Sisler	AL	STL	May 30, 1921	1G
5	Earl Sheely	AL	CHI	Sep 9, 1921	
5	Bill Wambsganss	AL	CLE	Sep 10, 1921	2G
5	Charlie Jamieson	AL	CLE	Sep 15, 1921	1G
5	George Sisler	AL	STL	Apr 19, 1922	
5	Ross Youngs	NL	NY	Apr 29, 1922	
5	Reb Russell	NL	PIT	Aug 8, 1922	1G
5	Cotton Tierney	NL	PIT	Aug 8, 1922	1G
5	Lu Blue	AL	DET	Aug 22 1922, 2G	
5	Cliff Heathcote	AL	CHI	Aug 25, 1922	
5	Reb Russell	NL	PIT	Jul 7, 1923	
5	Sam Rice	AL	WAS	Aug 24, 1923	
5	Ty Cobb	AL	DET	Sep 21, 1923	2G
5	Eddie Moore	NL	PIT	Sep 25, 1923	Major League debut

(172) *(continued)*

5	Johnny Mostil	AL	CHI	Jun 30, 1924	
5	Rogers Hornsby	NL	STL	Apr 18, 1925	
5	Ira Flagstead	AL	BOS	May 8, 1925	
5	Kiki Cuyler	NL	PIT	May 12, 1925	2G
5	Kiki Cuyler	NL	PIT	Jun 20, 1925	
5	Babe Ruth	AL	NY	Apr 20, 1926	
5	Taylor Douthit	NL	STL	Sep 16, 1926	1G
5	Ben Paschal	AL	NY	Jun 13, 1927	
5	Hack Wilson	NL	CHI	Aug 24, 1927	2G
5	Ira Flagstead	AL	BOS	Aug 29, 1927	
5	Lou Gehrig	AL	NY	Jun 12, 1928	
5	Chuck Dressen	NL	CIN	Jul 4, 1928	2G
5	Johnny Frederick	NL	BRO	May 18, 1929	1G; 8 runs in DH
5	Al Simmons	AL	PHI	Jun 21, 1929	1G
5	Freddie Lindstrom	NL	NY	Aug 24, 1929	1G
5	George Watkins	NL	STL	May 7, 1930	
5	Bibb Falk	AL	CLE	May 11, 1930	
5	Tony Lazzeri	AL	NY	May 22, 1930	2G
5	Denny Sothern	NL	PHI	Jun 6, 1930	
5	Al Simmons	AL	PHI	Jun 23, 1930	2G
5	Curt Walker	NL	CIN	Jul 15, 1930	
5	Bob Meusel	NL	CIN	Jul 18, 1930	
5	George Grantham	NL	PIT	Jul 23, 1930	2G; 13 inn.
5	Woody English	NL	CHI	Aug 18, 1930	
5	Earle Combs	AL	NY	Sep 19, 1930	
5	Rabbit Maranville	NL	BOS	Jun 10, 1931	
5	Oscar Melillo	AL	STL	Jun 22, 1931	
5	Eddie Morgan	AL	CLE	Aug 28, 1931	
5	Jimmie Foxx	AL	PHI	May 5, 1932	
5	Bob L. Johnson	AL	PHI	Aug 25, 1933	
5	Ripper Collins	NL	STL	Jul 6, 1934	
5	Billy Werber	AL	BOS	Jul 6, 1934	
5	Lou Chiozza	NL	PHI	Apr 19, 1935	2G
5	Jimmie Foxx	AL	PHI	May 4, 1935	
5	Lloyd Waner	NL	PIT	May 15, 1935	1G
5	John Stone	AL	WAS	Jun 16, 1935	
5	Chuck Klein	NL	CHI	Aug 21, 1935	1G
5	Lou Gehrig	AL	NY	May 3, 1936	
5	Roy Hughes	AL	CLE	Jul 2, 1936	
5	Earl Averill	AL	CLE	Jul 24, 1936	
5	Lou Gehrig	AL	NY	Jul 28, 1936	
5	Fabian Gaffke	AL	BOS	Jul 14, 1937	
5	Mel Almada	AL	WAS	Jul 25, 1937	2G; 9 runs in DH
5	Jeff Heath	AL	CLE	Aug 20, 1938	
5	Dixie Walker	AL	DET	Apr 30, 1939	2G
5	Jimmie Foxx	AL	BOS	Jun 9, 1939	
5	Jim Tabor	AL	BOS	Jul 4, 1939	1G
5	Hank Greenberg	AL	DET	Jul 30, 1939	2G
5	Ben Chapman	AL	CLE	Sep 19, 1939	
5	Frank McCormick	NL	CIN	Jun 8, 1940	
5	Dom DiMaggio	AL	BOS	Sep 27, 1940	1G
5	Roy Cullenbine	AL	STL	Jul 31, 1941	2G

(172) *(continued)*

5	Rudy York	AL	DET	May 24, 1942	1G
5	Joe Medwick	NL	NY	Apr 30, 1944	1G
5	Phil Weintraub	NL	NY	Apr 30, 1944	
5	Mel Ott	NL	NY	Jun 12, 1944	
5	Phil Weintraub	NL	NY	Jun 12, 1944	
5	George Metkovich	AL	BOS	Sep 30, 1944	
5	Phil Cavarretta	NL	CHI	Jul 3	1945
5	Stan Hack	NL	CHI	Jul 3	1945
5	Don Johnson	NL	CHI	Jul 3, 1945	2G
5	Pete Coscarart	NL	PIT	Jul 15, 1945	1G
5	Snuffy Stirnweiss	AL	NY	May 25, 1947	
5	Vic Wertz	AL	DET	Sep 14, 1947	6 hits
5	Stan Musial	NL	STL	May 19, 1948	
5	Gene Woodling	AL	NY	May 8, 1949	1G
5	Pee Wee Reese	NL	BRO	May 21, 1949	
5	Hank Edwards	NL	CHI	Jun 30, 1949	
5	Walker Cooper	NL	CHI	Jul 6, 1949	
5	Dom DiMaggio	AL	BOS	Apr 30, 1950	
5	Gil Hodges	NL	BRO	Aug 31, 1950	
5	Walt Dropo	AL	BOS	Jun 8, 1950	
5	Wes Westrum	NL	NY	Jun 24, 1950	
5	Hoot Evers	AL	DET	Jul 7, 1951	
5	Bob Elliott	NL	BOS	Jul 21, 1951	1G
5	Solly Hemus	NL	STL	May 20, 1953	
5	Hank Bauer	AL	NY	Aug 12, 1953	
5	Jim Pendleton	NL	MIL	Aug 30, 1953	
5	Eddie Yost	AL	WAS	Sep 7, 1953	
5	Wally Moon	NL	STL	May 12, 1954	
5	Willie Mays	NL	NY	May 25, 1954	
5	Alvin Dark	NL	NY	Jun 3, 1954	
5	Joe Adcock	NL	MIL	Jul 31, 1954	
5	Chico Carrasquel	AL	CHI	Apr 23, 1955	
5	Minnie Minoso	AL	CHI	Apr 23, 1955	
5	Wally Post	NL	CIN	Jul 14, 1955	
5	Frank Bolling	AL	DET	May 18, 1959	
5	Rocky Colavito	AL	CLE	Jun 10, 1959	
5	Vada Pinson	NL	CIN	Jul 9, 1961	2G; 13 inn.
5	Don Demeter	NL	PHI	Sep 12, 1961	1G
5	Norm Siebern	AL	KC	May 5, 1962	
5	Frank Robinson	NL	CIN	Jul 8, 1962	2G
5	Carl Yastrzemski	AL	BOS	Jun 16, 1963	
5	Willie Mays	NL	SF	Apr 24, 1964	
5	Willie Mays	NL	SF	Sep 19, 1964	
5	Tommie Agee	AL	CHI	Apr 21, 1966	
5	Billy Grabarkewitz	NL	LA	May 26, 1970	
5	Walt Williams	AL	CHI	May 31, 1970	
5	Willie Stargell	NL	PIT	Aug 1, 1970	13 inn.
5	Lou Brock	NL	STL	Aug 22, 1971	
5	Bobby Murcer	AL	NY	Jun 3, 1972	
5	Ron Hunt	NL	MON	Jun 8, 1973	
5	Bill Madlock	NL	CHI	Apr 17, 1974	2 hits in 3 AB
5	Tony Solaita	AL	KC	Jun 18, 1975	

(172) *(continued)*

5	Rennie Stennett	NL	PIT	Sep 16, 1975	
5	Tom Poquette	AL	KC	Jun 15, 1976	
5	George Foster	NL	CIN	Apr 25, 1977	
5	Garry Templeton	NL	STL	Apr 27, 1977	
5	Larry Parrish	NL	MON	May 29, 1977	
5	Rod Carew	AL	MIN	Jun 26, 1977	
5	Joe Morgan	NL	CIN	Jun 30, 1977	10 inn.
5	Steve Garvey	NL	LA	Aug 28, 1977	
5	Lenny Randle	NL	NY	May 18, 1978	
5	Dave Cash	NL	MON	May 27, 1978	
5	Mike Edwards	AL	OAK	Sep 8, 1978	
5	Lee Mazzilli	NL	NY	Aug 14, 1979	
5	Mike Hargrove	AL	CLE	Jul 31, 1983	1G
5	Tim Teufel	AL	MIN	Sep 16, 1983	
5	Lou Whitaker	AL	DET	Jun 10, 1984	
5	Joe Carter	AL	CLE	Sep 6, 1986	
5	Eric Davis	NL	CIN	Sep 10, 1986	
5	Pete O'Brien	AL	TEX	May 29, 1987	
5	Jody Davis	NL	CHI	Jun 3, 1987	
5	Mark McGwire	AL	OAK	Jun 27, 1987	
5	Tim Raines	NL	MON	Aug 13, 1987	
5	Darryl Strawberry	NL	NY	Aug 16, 1987	
5	Dave Collins	NL	CIN	Oct 2, 1987	
5	Don Mattingly	AL	NY	Apr 30, 1988	
5	Kal Daniels	NL	CIN	Sep 6, 1988	
5	Luis Polonia	AL	OAK	Sep 9, 1988	
5	Lonnie Smith	NL	ATL	May 6, 1989	
5	John Kruk	NL	PHI	Aug 9, 1989	
5	Bobby Bonilla	NL	PIT	May 20, 1990	
5	Mariano Duncan	NL	PHI	May 3, 1992	11 inn.
5	Travis Fryman	AL	DET	Apr 17, 1993	
5	Kevin Mitchell	NL	CIN	Jun 22, 1993	
5	Barry Bonds	NL	SF	Aug 4, 1993	
5	Tim Raines	AL	CHI	Apr 18, 1994	
5	Bret Boone	NL	CIN	Aug 3, 1994	13 inn.; 6 hits
5	Rondell White	NL	MON	Jun 11, 1995	11 inn.
5	Craig Biggio	NL	HOU	Jul 4, 1995	
5	Walt Weiss	NL	COL	Sep 20, 1995	
5	Craig Biggio	NL	HOU	Sep 28, 1995	
5	Paul Molitor	AL	MIN	Apr 24, 1996	
5	Ken Griffey Jr.	AL	SEA	May 24, 1996	
5	Craig Biggio	NL	HOU	Jun 4, 1996	
5	Tim Naehring	AL	BOS	Jul 13, 1996	
5	Jeff Frye	AL	BOS	Jul 19, 1996	
5	Tino Martinez	AL	NY	Apr 2, 1997	
5	Kenny Lofton	NL	ATL	Apr 14, 1997	
5	Chipper Jones	NL	ATL	Aug 30, 1997	
5	Tim Salmon	AL	ANA	Apr 12, 1998	12 inn.
5	Bernard Gilkey	NL	NY	Apr 19, 1998	
5	Juan Encarnacion	AL	DET	Sep 14, 1998	6 hits
5	J.D. Drew	NL	STL	May 1, 1999	

(172) *(continued)*

5	Carlos Delgado	AL	TOR	May 3, 1999	
5	Edgar Martinez	AL	SEA	May 17, 1999	
5	Sean Casey	NL	CIN	May 19, 1999	
5	Jeffrey Hammonds	NL	CIN	May 19, 1999	
5	Cal Ripken	AL	BAL	Jun 13, 1999	
5	Darren Lewis	AL	BOS	Aug 13, 1999	
5	Al Martin	NL	SD	Apr 16, 2000	
5	Alex Rodriguez	AL	SEA	Apr 16, 2000	
5	Barry Bonds	NL	SF	Apr 18, 2000	
5	Jeff Cirillo	NL	COL	Jun 28, 2000	
5	Larry Walker	NL	COL	Jul 27, 2000	
5	Luis Alicea	AL	TEX	Aug 31, 2000	
5	Chipper Jones	NL	ATL	Jul 3, 2001	
5	Larry Walker	NL	COL	Sep 24, 2001	
5	Luis Rivas	AL	MIN	Jun 4, 2002	
5	Shannon Stewart	AL	TOR	Jun 25, 2002	
5	Brian Giles	NL	PIT	Sep 27, 2002	
5	Jason Giambi	AL	NY	Jul 24, 2002	
5	Kevin Mench	AL	TEX	Apr 25, 2004	
5	Orlando Hudson	AL	TOR	May 13, 2004	
5	J.T. Snow	AL	SF	Aug 13, 2004	
5	Angel Berroa	AL	KC	Sep 13, 2004	
5	Hideki Matsui	AL	NY	Oct 16, 2004	ALCS
5	Alex Rodriguez	AL	NY	Oct 16, 2004	ALCS
5	Alex Rodriguez	AL	NY	Apr 18, 2005	
5	Derek Jeter	AL	NY	Jun 21, 2005	
5	Mike Jacobs	NL	NY	Aug 24, 2005	

(173) Batters Hitting Two Triples in an Inning

				INN	OPP.	
Joe Hornung	NL	BOS	May 6, 1882	8	TRO	
Harry Wheeler	AA	CIN	Jun 28, 1882	11	BAL	
Harry Stovey	AA	PHI	Aug 18, 1884	8	BAL	5 hits; 3 triples
Heinie Peitz	NL	STL	Jul 2, 1895	1	CHI	STL has 4 triples in 11-run 1st inn.
Frank Shugart	NL	LOU	Jul 30, 1895	5	STL	3 triples
Buck Freeman	NL	BOS	Jul 25, 1900	1	STL	6-inning game
Bill Dahlen	NL	BRO	Aug 30, 1900	8	PHI	
Gavy Cravath	NL	PHI	Jun 22, 1912	4	BRO	
Curt Walker	NL	CIN	Jul 22, 1926	2	BOS	CIN has 4 triples in 11-run 2nd inn.
Al Zarilla	AL	STL	Jul 13, 1946	4	PHI	1st time in AL
Gil Coan	AL	WAS	Apr 21, 1951	6	NY	WAS scores 7 in 6th, but lose
Cory Sullivan	NL	COL	Apr 9, 2006	5	SD	

(174) Extra-inning Pinch-hit Grand Slams

				INN.	
Rogers Hornsby	NL	STL	Sep 13, 1931	11	1G
Harvey Hendrick	NL	CHI	Jul 23, 1933	10	1G
Frank Secory	NL	CHI	Jun 6, 1946	12	
Steve Souchock	AL	DET	Jul 26, 1952	11	
Rick Joseph	NL	PHI	Sep 16, 1967	11	
Roger Freed	NL	STL	May 1, 1979	11	
Mike Vail	NL	CHI	Jun 30, 1979	11	
Tim Teufel	NL	NY	Jun 10, 1986	11	
Mike Fitzgerald	NL	MON	Jul 26, 1988	11	
Greg Litton	NL	SF	Oct 4, 1992	13	
Todd Hundley	NL	NY	May 4, 1995	10	
Benny Agbayani	NL	NY	Mar 30, 2000	11	At Tokyo
Adam Dunn	NL	CIN	May 26, 2003	11	

TRANSCENDENTAL GRAPHICS

Joe Jackson

(175) Batters Hitting Two Home Runs in an Inning

				INN	OPP.	
Charley Jones	NL	BOS	Jun 10, 1880	8	BUF	
Lou Bierbauer	PL	BRO	Jul 12, 1890	3	BUF	
Ed Cartwright	AA	STL	Sep 23, 1890	3	PHI	
Bobby Lowe	NL	BOS	May 30, 1894	3	CIN	2G; Lowe hit 4 HR in this game
Jake Stenzel	NL	PIT	Jun 6, 1894	3	BOS	
Ken Williams	AL	STL	Aug 7, 1922	6	WAS	
Hack Wilson	NL	NY	Jul 1, 1925	3	PHI	2G
Bill Regan	AL	BOS	Jun 16, 1928	4	CHI	
Hank Leiber	NL	NY	Aug 24, 1935	2	CHI	
Joe DiMaggio	AL	NY	Jun 24, 1936	5	CHI	
Andy Seminick	NL	PHI	Jun 2, 1949	8	CIN	
Sid Gordon	NL	NY	Jul 31, 1949	2	CIN	2G
Al Kaline	AL	DET	Apr 17, 1955	6	KC	
Jim Lemon	AL	WAS	Sep 5, 1959	2	BOS	
Joe Pepitone	AL	NY	May 23, 1962	8	KC	
Rick Reichardt	AL	CAL	Apr 30, 1966	8	BOS	
Willie McCovey	NL	SF	Apr 12, 1973	4	HOU	
John Boccabella	NL	MON	Jul 6, 1973	6	HOU	1G
Lee May	NL	HOU	Apr 29, 1974	6	CHI	
Willie McCovey	NL	SF	Jun 27, 1977	6	CIN	
Cliff Johnson	AL	NY	Jun 30, 1977	8	TOR	
Andre Dawson	NL	MON	Jul 30, 1978	3	ATL	
Ray Knight	NL	CIN	May 13, 1980	5	NY	
Von Hayes	NL	PHI	Jun 11, 1985	1	NY	
Andre Dawson	NL	MON	Sep 24, 1985	5	CHI	
Dale Murphy	NL	ATL	Jul 27, 1989	6	SF	
Ellis Burks	AL	BOS	Aug 27, 1990	4	CLE	
Carlos Baerga	AL	CLE	Apr 8, 1993	7	NY	
Joe Carter	AL	TOR	Oct 3, 1993	2	BAL	Last game of season
Jeff Bagwell	NL	HOU	Jun 24, 1994	6	LA	
Jeff King	NL	PIT	Aug 8, 1995	2	SF	
Jeff King	NL	PIT	Apr 30, 1996	4	CIN	
Sammy Sosa	NL	CHI	May 16, 1996	7	HOU	
Dave Nilsson	AL	MIL	May 17, 1996	6	MIN	
Mark McGwire	AL	OAK	Sep 22, 1996	5	SEA	
Mike Lansing	NL	MON	May 7, 1997	6	SF	
Gary Sheffield	NL	FLA	Jul 13, 1997	4	PHI	
Fernando Tatis	NL	STL	Apr 23, 1999	3	LA	Both grand slams
Eric Karros	NL	LA	Aug 22, 2000	6	MON	
Bret Boone	AL	SEA	May 2, 2002	1	CHI	Same game and inn. as Mike Cameron
Mike Cameron	AL	SEA	May 2, 2002	1	CHI	Same game and inn. as Bret Boone
Jared Sandberg	AL	TB	Jun 11, 2002	5	LA (NL)	
Nomar Garciaparra	AL	BOS	Jul 23, 2002	3	TB	1G
Carl Everett	AL	TEX	Jul 26, 2002	7	OAK	
Aaron Boone	NL	CIN	Aug 9, 2002	1	SD	
Mark Bellhorn	NL	CHI	Aug 29, 2002	4	MIL	
Reggie Sanders	NL	PIT	Aug 20, 2003	5	STL	
Juan Rivera	NL	MON	Jun 19, 2004	2	CHI (AL)	
Julio Lugo	AL	TB	Jul 22, 2006	5	BAL	

(176) Most Plate Appearances by a Player in an Inning

				INN.		
3	Ned Williamson	NL	CHI	7	Sep 6, 1883	3 hits
3	Tom Burns	NL	CHI	7	Sep 6, 1883	3 hits
3	Fred Pfeffer	NL	CHI	7	Sep 6, 1883	3 hits
3	Fred Goldsmith	NL	CHI	7	Sep 6, 1883	
3	Billy Sunday	NL	CHI	7	Sep 6, 1883	
3	Larry Murphy	AA	WAS	1	Jun 17, 1891	
3	Bobby Lowe	NL	BOS	1	Jun 18, 1894	1G
3	Herman Long	NL	BOS	1	Jun 18, 1894	1G
3	Hugh Duffy	NL	BOS	1	Jun 18, 1894	
3	Tommy McCarthy	NL	BOS	1	Jun 18, 1894	
3	Marty Gallaghan	NL	CHI	4	Aug 25, 1922	
3	Ted Williams	AL	BOS	7	Jul 4, 1948	3 different pitchers
3	Billy Cox	NL	BRO	1	May 21, 1952	
3	Pee Wee Reese	NL	BRO	1	May 21, 1952	
3	Duke Snider	NL	BRO	1	May 21, 1952	
3	Sammy White	AL	BOS	7	Jun 18, 1953	
3	Gene Stephens	AL	BOS	7	Jun 18, 1953	3 hits
3	Tom Umphlett	AL	BOS	7	Jun 18, 1953	
3	Johnny Lipon	AL	BOS	7	Jun 18, 1953	
3	George Kell	AL	BOS	7	Jun 18, 1953	
3	Gil Hodges	NL	BRO	8	Aug 8, 1954	
3	Dusty Baker	NL	ATL	2	Sep 20, 1972	2G
3	Mariano Duncan	NL	CIN	1	Aug 3, 1989	
3	Luis Quinones	NL	CIN	1	Aug 3, 1989	
3	Darryl Hamilton	AL	TEX	8	Apr 19, 1996	
3	Stan Javier	NL	SF	7	Jul 15, 1997	
3	Johnny Damon	AL	BOS	1	Jun 27, 2003	3 hits

(177) Hit by Pitch Twice in One Inning

					NN.
Willard Schmidt	NL	CIN	Apr 26, 1959		3
Frank J. Thomas	NL	NY	Apr 29, 1962		4
Brady Anderson	AL	BAL	May 23, 1999		1

(178) Most At-bats in a Season, before 1893

660	Tom Brown	NL	LOU	1892	
649	Lou Bierbauer	NL	PIT	1892	
646	Herman Long	NL	BOS	1892	
627	Arlie Latham	AA	STL	1887	
623	Doggie Miller	NL	PIT	1892	
622	Arlie Latham	NL	CIN	1892	
619	Billy Shindle	NL	BAL	1892	
614	Jake Beckley	NL	PIT	1892	
614	John Ward	NL	BRO	1892	
613	Tommy Corcoran	NL	BRO	1892	
612	Hugh Duffy	NL	BOS	1892	
611	George Van Haltren	NL	BAL-PIT	1892	
			BAL (556); PIT (55)		

609	Sam Thompson	NL	PHI	1892
608	Jesse Burkett	NL	CLE	1892
605	Duke Farrell	NL	PIT	1892
604	Tommy McCarthy	AA	STL	1889
603	Ed McKean	NL	CLE	1891
603	Tommy McCarthy	NL	BOS	1892
602	Steve Brodie	NL	STL	1892
602	Bug Holliday	NL	CIN	1892
598	Bill Gleason	AA	STL	1887
598	Perry Werden	NL	STL	1892
597	George Pinkney	AA	BRO	1886
597	George Davis	NL	CLE	1892
596	Hugh Duffy	PL	CHI	1890
595	Bill McClellan	AA	BRO	1886

(179) Most At-bats in a Season, since 1893

705	Willie Wilson	AL	KC	1980
704	Ichiro Suzuki	AL	SEA	2004
701	Juan Samuel	NL	PHI	1984
699	Dave Cash	NL	PHI	1975
699	Juan Pierre	NL	CHI	2006
698	Matty Alou	NL	PIT	1969
696	Woody Jensen	NL	PIT	1936
696	Alfonso Soriano	AL	NY	2002
696	Jose Reyes	NL	NY	2005
695	Maury Wills	NL	LA	1962
695	Omar Moreno	NL	PIT	1979
695	Ichiro Suzuki	AL	SEA	2006
692	Bobby Richardson	AL	NY	1962
692	Ichiro Suzuki	AL	SEA	2001
691	Kirby Puckett	AL	MIN	1985
691	Michael Young	AL	TEX	2006
690	Neifi Perez	NL	COL	1999
690	Michael Young	AL	TEX	2004
689	Lou Brock	NL	STL	1967
689	Sandy Alomar Sr.	AL	CAL	1971
689	Jimmy Rollins	NL	PHI	2006
687	Dave Cash	NL	PHI	1974
687	Tony Fernandez	AL	TOR	1986
686	Horace Clarke	AL	NY	1970
686	Alex Rodriguez	AL	SEA	1998

684	Nomar Garciaparra	AL	BOS	1997
682	Lance Johnson	NL	NY	1996
682	Alfonso Soriano	AL	NY	2003
681	Lloyd Waner	NL	PIT	1931
681	Jo-Jo Moore	NL	NY	1935
680	Pete Rose	NL	CIN	1973
680	Frank Taveras	NL	PIT-NY	1979
			PIT (45); NY (635)	
680	Kirby Puckett	AL	MIN	1986
679	Harvey Kuenn	AL	DET	1953
679	Curt Flood	NL	STL	1964
679	Bobby Richardson	AL	NY	1964
679	Ichiro Suzuki	AL	SEA	2003
679	Ichiro Suzuki	AL	SEA	2005
678	Dick Groat	NL	PIT	1962
678	Doug Glanville	NL	PHI	1998
678	Vernon Wells	AL	TOR	2003
678	Juan Pierre	NL	FLA	2004
677	Matty Alou	NL	PIT	1970
677	Jim Rice	AL	BOS	1978
677	Don Mattingly	AL	NY	1986
677	Jimmy Rollins	NL	PHI	2005
676	Felix Millan	NL	NY	1975
676	Omar Moreno	NL	PIT	1980
676	Darin Erstad	AL	ANA	2000

(180) Most At-bats in a Season by a Left-handed Batter

704	Ichiro Suzuki	AL	SEA	2004		664	Lou Brock	NL	STL	1970
699	Juan Pierre	NL	CHI	2006		663	Bill Virdon	NL	PIT	1962
698	Matty Alou	NL	PIT	1969		662	Lloyd Waner	NL	PIT	1929
696	Woody Jensen	NL	PIT	1936		662	Richie Ashburn	NL	PHI	1949
695	Omar Moreno	NL	PIT	1979		662	Kenny Lofton	AL	CLE	1996
695	Ichiro Suzuki	AL	SEA	2006		661	Doc Cramer	AL	PHI	1933
692	Ichiro Suzuki	AL	SEA	2001		661	Doc Cramer	AL	BOS	1940
689	Lou Brock	NL	STL	1967		661	Cecil Cooper	AL	MIL	1983
682	Lance Johnson	NL	NY	1996		660	Tom Brown	NL	LOU	1892
681	Lloyd Waner	NL	PIT	1931		660	Doc Cramer	AL	WAS	1941
681	Jo-Jo Moore	NL	NY	1935		660	Lou Brock	NL	STL	1968
679	Ichiro Suzuki	AL	SEA	2003		659	Lloyd Waner	NL	PIT	1928
679	Ichiro Suzuki	AL	SEA	2005		659	Warren Cromartie	NL	MON	1979
678	Juan Pierre	NL	FLA	2004		658	Heinie Manush	AL	WAS	1933
677	Matty Alou	NL	PIT	1970		658	Doc Cramer	AL	BOS	1938
677	Don Mattingly	AL	NY	1986		658	Bill White	NL	STL	1963
676	Omar Moreno	NL	PIT	1980		658	Chase Utley	NL	PHI	2006
676	Darin Erstad	AL	ANA	2000		657	Bill Buckner	NL	CHI	1982
673	Bill Buckner	AL	BOS	1985		656	Buddy Lewis	AL	WAS	1938
673	B.J. Surhoff	AL	BAL	1999		656	Al Oliver	AL	TEX	1980
672	Tony Oliva	AL	MIN	1964		656	Juan Pierre	NL	FLA	2005
672	Garret Anderson	AL	ANA	2001		655	Lou Brock	NL	STL	1969
671	Jack Tobin	AL	STL	1921		655	Steve Finley	NL	SD	1996
669	Vada Pinson	NL	CIN	1965		655	Tony Womack	NL	PIT	1998
668	Buddy Lewis	AL	WAS	1937		655	Johnny Damon	AL	KC	2000
668	Ralph Garr	NL	ATL	1973		655	Grady Sizemore	AL	CLE	2006
668	Juan Pierre	NL	FLA	2003						

NATIONAL BASEBALL HALL OF FAME LIBRARY

Joe DiMaggio

(181) Most At-bats in a Season by a Right-handed Batter

701	Juan Samuel	NL	PHI	1984		671	Marquis Grissom	NL	ATL	1996
699	Dave Cash	NL	PHI	1975		670	Al Simmons	AL	PHI	1932
696	Alfonso Soriano	AL	NY	2002		670	Buddy Bell	AL	TEX	1979
692	Bobby Richardson	AL	NY	1962		668	Brooks Robinson	AL	BAL	1961
691	Kirby Puckett	AL	MIN	1985		668	Michael Young	AL	TEX	2005
691	Michael Young	AL	TEX	2006		667	Carl Furillo	NL	BRO	1951
690	Michael Young	AL	TEX	2004		666	Billy Herman	NL	CHI	1935
687	Dave Cash	NL	PHI	1974		666	Zoilo Versalles	AL	MIN	1965
686	Alex Rodriguez	AL	SEA	1998		666	Felipe Alou	NL	ATL	1966
684	Nomar Garciaparra	AL	BOS	1997		666	Dave Cash	NL	PHI	1976
682	Alfonso Soriano	AL	NY	2003		666	Ron LeFlore	AL	DET	1978
680	Frank Taveras	NL	PIT-NY	1979		666	Paul Molitor	AL	MIL	1982
	PIT (45); NY (635)					666	Michael Young	AL	TEX	2003
680	Kirby Puckett	AL	MIN	1986		665	Tommy Davis	NL	LA	1962
679	Harvey Kuenn	AL	DET	1953		665	Paul Molitor	AL	MIL	1991
679	Curt Flood	NL	STL	1964		664	Taylor Douthit	NL	STL	1930
679	Bobby Richardson	AL	NY	1964		664	Bobby Richardson	AL	NY	1965
678	Dick Groat	NL	PIT	1962		663	Jake Wood	AL	DET	1961
678	Doug Glanville	NL	PHI	1998		663	Bobby Bonds	NL	SF	1970
678	Vernon Wells	AL	TOR	2003		663	Rick Burleson	AL	BOS	1977
677	Jim Rice	AL	BOS	1978		663	Cal Ripken	AL	BAL	1983
676	Felix Millan	NL	NY	1975		663	Juan Samuel	NL	PHI	1985
673	Rennie Stennett	NL	PIT	1974		663	Joe Carter	AL	CLE	1986
672	Rabbit Maranville	NL	PIT	1922						

(182) Most At-bats in a Season by a Switch-hitter

705	Willie Wilson	AL	KC	1980		661	Ruben Sierra	AL	TEX	1991
696	Jose Reyes	NL	NY	2005		659	Red Schoendienst	NL	STL	1947
695	Maury Wills	NL	LA	1962		657	Carlos Baerga	AL	CLE	1992
690	Neifi Perez	NL	COL	1999		657	Jimmy Rollins	NL	PHI	2004
689	Sandy Alomar Sr.	AL	CAL	1971		656	Tito Fuentes	NL	SF	1973
689	Jimmy Rollins	NL	PHI	2006		656	Jimmy Rollins	NL	PHI	2001
687	Tony Fernandez	AL	TOR	1986		655	Don Kessinger	NL	CHI	1968
686	Horace Clarke	AL	NY	1970		655	Pete Rose	NL	CIN	1977
680	Pete Rose	NL	CIN	1973		655	Pete Rose	NL	CIN	1978
677	Jimmy Rollins	NL	PHI	2005		655	Pete Rose	NL	PHI	1980
672	Sandy Alomar Sr.	AL	CAL	1970		654	Pete Rose	NL	CIN	1966
672	Garry Templeton	NL	STL	1979		654	Larry Bowa	NL	PHI	1978
670	Pete Rose	NL	CIN	1965		654	Rafael Furcal	NL	LA	2006
670	Cesar Izturis	NL	LA	2004		653	Alfredo Griffin	AL	TOR	1980
669	Larry Bowa	NL	PHI	1974		652	Pete Rose	NL	CIN	1974
665	Pete Rose	NL	CIN	1976		651	Dave Bancroft	NL	NY	1922
664	Don Kessinger	NL	CHI	1969		651	Neifi Perez	NL	COL	2000
664	Rafael Furcal	NL	ATL	2003		650	Maury Wills	NL	LA	1965
663	Carlos Beltran	AL	KC	1999		650	Larry Bowa	NL	PHI	1971
662	Pete Rose	NL	CIN	1975						

(183) Most Plate Appearances in a Season, before 1893

712	Tom Brown	NL	LOU	1892
700	Tommy McCarthy	NL	BOS	1892
699	Doggie Miller	NL	PIT	1892
699	John Ward	NL	BRO	1892
698	Herman Long	NL	BOS	1892
689	George Van Haltren	NL	BAL-PIT	1892
		BAL (628); PIT (61)		
688	Dummy Hoy	AA	STL	1891
688	Dan Brouthers	NL	BRO	1892
687	Arlie Latham	NL	CIN	1892
686	Roger Connor	NL	PHI	1892
684	Cupid Childs	NL	CLE	1892
683	Dummy Hoy	NL	WAS	1892
679	Sam Thompson	NL	PHI	1892
677	Arlie Latham	AA	STL	1887
676	Jesse Burkett	NL	CLE	1892
674	Lou Bierbauer	NL	PIT	1892
673	Hugh Duffy	NL	BOS	1892
668	Ed McKean	NL	CLE	1891
667	George Pinkney	AA	BRO	1886
665	Herman Long	NL	BOS	1891
664	Bid McPhee	NL	CIN	1892
663	Tom Brown	AA	BOS	1891
662	Billy Shindle	NL	BAL	1892
661	Perry Werden	NL	STL	1892
660	Bug Holliday	NL	CIN	1892

(184) Most Plate Appearances in a Season, since 1893

773	Lenny Dykstra	NL	PHI	1993
771	Pete Rose	NL	CIN	1974
766	Dave Cash	NL	PHI	1975
764	Pete Rose	NL	CIN	1975
762	Ichiro Suzuki	AL	SEA	2004
759	Maury Wills	NL	LA	1962
759	Pete Rose	NL	CIN	1976
758	Wade Boggs	AL	BOS	1985
758	Jimmy Rollins	NL	PHI	2006
757	Frankie Crosetti	AL	NY	1938
757	Pete Rose	NL	CIN	1965
757	Omar Moreno	NL	PIT	1979
756	Dom DiMaggio	AL	BOS	1948
755	Woody English	NL	CHI	1930
754	Bobby Richardson	AL	NY	1962
752	Taylor Douthit	NL	STL	1928
752	Pete Rose	NL	CIN	1973
752	Paul Molitor	AL	MIL	1991
752	Mo Vaughn	AL	BOS	1996
752	Derek Jeter	AL	NY	2005
752	Ichiro Suzuki	AL	SEA	2006
751	Paul Molitor	AL	MIL	1982
751	Grady Sizemore	AL	CLE	2006
750	Juan Pierre	NL	CHI	2006
749	Brady Anderson	AL	BAL	1992
749	Craig Biggio	NL	HOU	1999
748	Taylor Douthit	NL	STL	1930
748	Augie Galan	NL	CHI	1935
748	Derek Jeter	AL	NY	1997
748	Alex Rodriguez	AL	SEA	1998
748	Juan Pierre	NL	FLA	2004
748	Michael Young	AL	TEX	2006
747	Rabbit Maranville	NL	PIT	1922
747	Darin Erstad	AL	ANA	2000
747	Juan Pierre	NL	FLA	2003
746	Matty Alou	NL	PIT	1969
746	Jim Rice	AL	BOS	1978
745	Dave Bancroft	NL	NY	1922
745	Lyn Lary	AL	STL	1936
745	Tommy Harper	NL	CIN	1965
745	Bobby Bonds	NL	SF	1970
745	Dave Cash	NL	PHI	1974
745	Willie Wilson	AL	KC	1980
745	Omar Moreno	NL	PIT	1980
744	Jo-Jo Moore	NL	NY	1935
744	Dwight Evans	AL	BOS	1985
744	Kirby Puckett	AL	MIN	1985
744	Craig Biggio	NL	HOU	1997
743	Frankie Crosetti	AL	NY	1939
743	Pee Wee Reese	NL	BRO	1949
743	Felix Millan	NL	NY	1975

(185) Most Plate Appearances in a Season by a Left-handed Batter

773	Lenny Dykstra	NL	PHI	1993		738	Al Bumbry	AL	BAL	1980
762	Ichiro Suzuki	AL	SEA	2004		738	Ichiro Suzuki	AL	SEA	2001
758	Wade Boggs	AL	BOS	1985		736	Kenny Lofton	AL	CLE	1996
757	Omar Moreno	NL	PIT	1979		734	Rusty Staub	AL	DET	1978
752	Mo Vaughn	AL	BOS	1996		733	Buddy Lewis	AL	WAS	1937
752	Ichiro Suzuki	AL	SEA	2006		733	Darrell Evans	NL	ATL	1973
751	Grady Sizemore	AL	CLE	2006		732	Brett Butler	NL	SF	1990
750	Juan Pierre	NL	CHI	2006		732	Rafael Palmeiro	AL	BAL	1996
749	Brady Anderson	AL	BAL	1992		731	Jack Tobin	AL	STL	1921
748	Juan Pierre	NL	FLA	2004		731	Lefty O'Doul	NL	PHI	1929
747	Darin Erstad	AL	ANA	2000		731	Charlie Gehringer	AL	DET	1936
747	Juan Pierre	NL	FLA	2003		731	Woody Jensen	NL	PIT	1936
746	Matty Alou	NL	PIT	1969		731	Red Rolfe	AL	NY	1939
745	Omar Moreno	NL	PIT	1980		730	Ted Williams	AL	BOS	1949
744	Jo-Jo Moore	NL	NY	1935		730	Brett Butler	NL	LA	1991
742	Charlie Jamieson	AL	CLE	1923		729	Richie Ashburn	NL	PHI	1957
742	Don Mattingly	AL	NY	1986		729	Lou Brock	NL	STL	1970
742	Wade Boggs	AL	BOS	1989		728	Burt Shotton	AL	STL	1916
741	Johnny Damon	AL	KC	2000		728	Richie Ashburn	NL	PHI	1949
740	Red Rolfe	AL	NY	1937		728	Don Blasingame	NL	STL	1957
739	Ichiro Suzuki	AL	SEA	2005		728	Vada Pinson	NL	CIN	1965
739	Chase Utley	NL	PHI	2006		728	Luis Gonzalez	NL	ARI	2001
738	Lou Gehrig	AL	NY	1931		728	Ichiro Suzuki	AL	SEA	2002

(186) Most Plate Appearances in a Season by a Right-handed Batter

766	Dave Cash	NL	PHI	1975		743	Frankie Crosetti	AL	NY	1939
757	Frankie Crosetti	AL	NY	1938		743	Pee Wee Reese	NL	BRO	1949
756	Dom DiMaggio	AL	BOS	1948		743	Felix Millan	NL	NY	1975
755	Woody English	NL	CHI	1930		741	Kiki Cuyler	NL	CHI	1930
754	Bobby Richardson	AL	NY	1962		741	Lyn Lary	AL	CLE	1937
752	Taylor Douthit	NL	STL	1928		741	Ron LeFlore	AL	DET	1978
752	Paul Molitor	AL	MIL	1991		741	Alfonso Soriano	AL	NY	2002
752	Derek Jeter	AL	NY	2005		740	Frankie Crosetti	AL	NY	1936
751	Paul Molitor	AL	MIL	1982		739	Curt Flood	NL	STL	1964
749	Craig Biggio	NL	HOU	1999		739	Derek Jeter	AL	NY	1999
748	Taylor Douthit	NL	STL	1930		739	Michael Young	AL	TEX	2004
748	Derek Jeter	AL	NY	1997		738	Chuck Schilling	AL	BOS	1961
748	Alex Rodriguez	AL	SEA	1998		738	Bobby Bonds	NL	SF	1973
748	Michael Young	AL	TEX	2006		738	Dwight Evans	AL	BOS	1984
747	Rabbit Maranville	NL	PIT	1922		738	Brian L. Hunter	AL	DET	1997
746	Jim Rice	AL	BOS	1978		738	Craig Biggio	NL	HOU	1998
745	Lyn Lary	AL	STL	1936		737	Juan Samuel	NL	PHI	1984
745	Tommy Harper	NL	CIN	1965		736	Brooks Robinson	AL	BAL	1961
745	Bobby Bonds	NL	SF	1970		735	Billy Herman	NL	CHI	1935
745	Dave Cash	NL	PHI	1974		735	Phil Rizzuto	AL	NY	1950
744	Dwight Evans	AL	BOS	1985		735	Dick Howser	AL	CLE	1964
744	Kirby Puckett	AL	MIN	1985		735	Doug Glanville	NL	PHI	1998
744	Craig Biggio	NL	HOU	1997		735	Vernon Wells	AL	TOR	2003

(187) Most Plate Appearances in a Season by a Switch-hitter

771	Pete Rose	NL	CIN	1974		732	Horace Clarke	AL	NY	1970
764	Pete Rose	NL	CIN	1975		732	Pete Rose	NL	CIN	1977
759	Maury Wills	NL	LA	1962		732	Pete Rose	NL	PHI	1979
759	Pete Rose	NL	CIN	1976		732	Neifi Perez	NL	COL	1999
758	Jimmy Rollins	NL	PHI	2006		732	Jimmy Rollins	NL	PHI	2005
757	Pete Rose	NL	CIN	1965		731	Pete Rose	NL	CIN	1969
752	Pete Rose	NL	CIN	1973		731	Pete Rose	NL	CIN	1972
748	Augie Galan	NL	CHI	1935		731	Tito Fuentes	NL	SF	1973
745	Dave Bancroft	NL	NY	1922		731	Pete Rose	NL	CIN	1978
745	Willie Wilson	AL	KC	1980		731	Tim Raines	NL	MON	1982
739	Sandy Alomar Sr.	AL	CAL	1971		730	Pete Rose	NL	CIN	1970
739	Pete Rose	NL	PHI	1980		730	Mark Teixeira	AL	TEX	2005
737	Don Kessinger	NL	CHI	1969		729	Roy Smalley Jr.	AL	MIN	1979
737	Harold Reynolds	AL	SEA	1990		728	Roy White	AL	NY	1976
736	Brian Roberts	AL	BAL	2004		728	Harold Reynolds	AL	SEA	1991
736	Rafael Furcal	NL	LA	2006		728	Cesar Izturis	NL	LA	2004
735	Sandy Alomar Sr.	AL	CAL	1970		727	Tony Fernandez	AL	TOR	1986
734	Rafael Furcal	NL	ATL	2003		727	Mark Teixeira	AL	TEX	2006
733	Tony Phillips	AL	DET	1992		726	Ruben Sierra	AL	TEX	1991
733	Jose Reyes	NL	NY	2005		725	Lu Blue	AL	CHI	1931
732	Max Carey	NL	PIT	1922		725	Jimmy Rollins	NL	CHI	2004

(188) Most Hits in a Season, before 1893

225	Tip O'Neill	AA	STL	1887		186	Spud Johnson	AA	COL	1890
220	Pete Browning	AA	LOU	1887		186	Sam Thompson	NL	PHI	1892
209	Denny Lyons	AA	PHI	1887		185	Fred Dunlap	UA	STL	1884
205	Jack Glasscock	NL	IND	1889		184	John Ward	NL	NY	1887
203	Sam Thompson	NL	DET	1887		184	Pete Browning	PL	CLE	1890
198	Arlie Latham	AA	STL	1887		184	Hugh Duffy	NL	BOS	1892
197	Jimmy Wolf	AA	LOU	1890		183	Dave Orr	AA	COL	1889
197	Dan Brouthers	NL	BRO	1892		183	Billy Hamilton	NL	PHI	1892
196	Tommy Tucker	AA	BAL	1889		182	Jimmy Ryan	NL	CHI	1888
193	Dave Orr	AA	NY	1886		182	Hugh Duffy	NL	CHI	1889
192	Tommy McCarthy	AA	STL	1890		181	Dan Brouthers	NL	DET	1886
191	Hugh Duffy	PL	CHI	1890		181	Dan Brouthers	NL	BOS	1889
190	Tip O'Neill	AA	STL	1886		181	Bug Holliday	AA	CIN	1889
189	Hardy Richardson	NL	DET	1886		181	Hardy Richardson	PL	BOS	1890
189	Billy Shindle	PL	PHI	1890		181	Herman Long	NL	BOS	1892
189	Tom Brown	AA	BOS	1891		180	Henry Larkin	AA	PHI	1886
188	Oyster Burns	AA	BAL	1887		180	Charlie Comiskey	AA	STL	1887
188	John Ward	NL	BRO	1890		180	Lou Bierbauer	PL	BRO	1890
187	Cap Anson	NL	CHI	1886		180	Hugh Duffy	AA	BOS	1891
187	Jimmy Ryan	NL	CHI	1889		180	George Van Haltren	AA	BAL	1891

(189) **Most Hits in a Season, since 1893**

262	Ichiro Suzuki	AL	SEA	2004		233	Joe Jackson	AL	CLE	1911
257	George Sisler	AL	STL	1920		232	Nap Lajoie	AL	PHI	1901
254	Lefty O'Doul	NL	PHI	1929		232	Earl Averill	AL	CLE	1936
254	Bill Terry	NL	NY	1930		231	Earle Combs	AL	NY	1927
253	Al Simmons	AL	PHI	1925		231	Freddie Lindstrom	NL	NY	1928
250	Rogers Hornsby	NL	STL	1922		231	Freddie Lindstrom	NL	NY	1930
250	Chuck Klein	NL	PHI	1930		231	Matty Alou	NL	PIT	1969
248	Ty Cobb	AL	DET	1911		230	Stan Musial	NL	STL	1948
246	George Sisler	AL	STL	1922		230	Tommy Davis	NL	LA	1962
242	Ichiro Suzuki	AL	SEA	2001		230	Joe Torre	NL	STL	1971
241	Heinie Manush	AL	STL	1928		230	Pete Rose	NL	CIN	1973
241	Babe Herman	NL	BRO	1930		230	Willie Wilson	AL	KC	1980
240	Jesse Burkett	NL	CLE	1896		229	Rogers Hornsby	NL	CHI	1929
240	Wade Boggs	AL	BOS	1985		228	Kiki Cuyler	NL	CHI	1930
240	Darin Erstad	AL	ANA	2000		228	Stan Musial	NL	STL	1946
239	Willie Keeler	NL	BAL	1897		227	Nap Lajoie	AL	CLE	1910
239	Rod Carew	AL	MIN	1977		227	Rogers Hornsby	NL	STL	1924
238	Ed Delahanty	NL	PHI	1899		227	Sam Rice	AL	WAS	1925
238	Don Mattingly	AL	NY	1986		227	Jim Bottomley	NL	STL	1925
237	Hugh Duffy	NL	BOS	1894		227	Billy Herman	NL	CHI	1935
237	Harry Heilmann	AL	DET	1921		227	Charlie Gehringer	AL	DET	1936
237	Paul Waner	NL	PIT	1927		227	Lance Johnson	NL	NY	1996
237	Joe Medwick	NL	STL	1937		226	Jesse Burkett	NL	STL	1901
236	Jack Tobin	AL	STL	1921		226	Joe Jackson	AL	CLE	1912
235	Rogers Hornsby	NL	STL	1921		226	Ty Cobb	AL	DET	1912
234	Lloyd Waner	NL	PIT	1929		226	Bill Terry	NL	NY	1929
234	Kirby Puckett	AL	MIN	1988		226	Chuck Klein	NL	PHI	1932

Edd Roush

(190) Most Hits in a Season by a Left-handed Batter

262	Ichiro Suzuki	AL	SEA	2004	226	Jesse Burkett	NL	STL	1901
257	George Sisler	AL	STL	1920	226	Joe Jackson	AL	CLE	1912
254	Lefty O'Doul	NL	PHI	1929	226	Ty Cobb	AL	DET	1912
254	Bill Terry	NL	NY	1930	226	Bill Terry	NL	NY	1929
250	Chuck Klein	NL	PHI	1930	226	Chuck Klein	NL	PHI	1932
248	Ty Cobb	AL	DET	1911	225	Billy Hamilton	NL	PHI	1894
246	George Sisler	AL	STL	1922	225	Jesse Burkett	NL	CLE	1895
242	Ichiro Suzuki	AL	SEA	2001	225	Ty Cobb	AL	DET	1917
241	Heinie Manush	AL	STL	1928	225	Bill Terry	NL	NY	1932
241	Babe Herman	NL	BRO	1930	224	Eddie Collins	AL	CHI	1920
240	Jesse Burkett	NL	CLE	1896	224	George Sisler	AL	STL	1925
240	Wade Boggs	AL	BOS	1985	224	Tommy Holmes	NL	BOS	1945
240	Darin Erstad	AL	ANA	2000	224	Ichiro Suzuki	AL	SEA	2006
239	Willie Keeler	NL	BAL	1897	223	Lloyd Waner	NL	PIT	1927
239	Rod Carew	AL	MIN	1977	223	Paul Waner	NL	PIT	1928
238	Don Mattingly	AL	NY	1986	223	Chuck Klein	NL	PHI	1933
237	Paul Waner	NL	PIT	1927	222	Sam Thompson	NL	PHI	1893
236	Jack Tobin	AL	STL	1921	222	Tris Speaker	AL	BOS	1912
234	Lloyd Waner	NL	PIT	1929	222	Charlie Jamieson	AL	CLE	1923
233	Joe Jackson	AL	CLE	1911	221	Jesse Burkett	NL	STL	1899
232	Earl Averill	AL	CLE	1936	221	Zack Wheat	NL	BRO	1925
231	Earle Combs	AL	NY	1927	221	Lloyd Waner	NL	PIT	1928
231	Matty Alou	NL	PIT	1969	221	Heinie Manush	AL	WAS	1933
230	Stan Musial	NL	STL	1948	221	Richie Ashburn	NL	PHI	1951
228	Stan Musial	NL	STL	1946	221	Juan Pierre	NL	FLA	2004
227	Jim Bottomley	NL	STL	1925	220	Lou Gehrig	AL	NY	1930
227	Sam Rice	AL	WAS	1925	220	Stan Musial	NL	STL	1943
227	Charlie Gehringer	AL	DET	1936	220	Tony Gwynn	NL	SD	1997
227	Lance Johnson	NL	NY	1996					

TRANSCENDENTAL GRAPHICS

Ralph Kiner

(191) Most Hits in a Season by a Right-handed Batter

253	Al Simmons	AL	PHI	1925		220	Pete Browning	AA	LOU	1887
250	Rogers Hornsby	NL	STL	1922		220	Jimmy Williams	NL	PIT	1899
238	Ed Delahanty	NL	PHI	1899		220	Kiki Cuyler	NL	PIT	1925
237	Hugh Duffy	NL	BOS	1894		219	Ed Delahanty	NL	PHI	1893
237	Harry Heilmann	AL	DET	1921		219	Dante Bichette	NL	COL	1998
237	Joe Medwick	NL	STL	1937		219	Derek Jeter	AL	NY	1999
235	Rogers Hornsby	NL	STL	1921		218	Rogers Hornsby	NL	STL	1920
234	Kirby Puckett	AL	MIN	1988		218	Beau Bell	AL	STL	1937
232	Nap Lajoie	AL	PHI	1901		218	George Kell	AL	DET	1950
231	Freddie Lindstrom	NL	NY	1928		218	Felipe Alou	NL	ATL	1966
231	Freddie Lindstrom	NL	NY	1930		217	Michael Young	AL	TEX	2006
230	Tommy Davis	NL	LA	1962		216	Baby Doll Jacobson	AL	STL	1920
230	Joe Torre	NL	STL	1971		216	George H. Burns	AL	CLE	1926
229	Rogers Hornsby	NL	CHI	1929		216	Al Simmons	AL	PHI	1932
228	Kiki Cuyler	NL	CHI	1930		216	Joe Vosmik	AL	CLE	1935
227	Nap Lajoie	AL	CLE	1910		216	Paul Molitor	AL	MIL	1991
227	Rogers Hornsby	NL	STL	1924		216	Michael Young	AL	TEX	2004
227	Billy Herman	NL	CHI	1935		215	Dale Alexander	AL	DET	1929
225	Tip O'Neill	AA	STL	1887		215	Joe DiMaggio	AL	NY	1937
225	Harry Heilmann	AL	DET	1925		215	Kirby Puckett	AL	MIN	1989
225	Johnny Hodapp	AL	CLE	1930		215	Alex Rodriguez	AL	SEA	1996
225	Paul Molitor	AL	MIN	1996		215	Vernon Wells	AL	TOR	2003
224	Joe Medwick	NL	STL	1935		214	Nap Lajoie	AL	CLE	1906
223	Joe Medwick	NL	STL	1936		214	Woody English	NL	CHI	1930
223	Hank Aaron	NL	MIL	1959		214	Derek Jeter	AL	NY	2006
223	Kirby Puckett	AL	MIN	1986		214	Miguel Tejada	AL	BAL	2006
221	Michael Young	AL	TEX	2005						

(192) Most Hits in a Season by a Switch-hitter

230	Pete Rose	NL	CIN	1973		208	Pete Rose	NL	PHI	1979
230	Willie Wilson	AL	KC	1980		207	Max Carey	NL	PIT	1922
223	Frankie Frisch	NL	NY	1923		205	Pete Rose	NL	CIN	1966
218	Pete Rose	NL	CIN	1969		205	Pete Rose	NL	CIN	1970
216	Willie McGee	NL	STL	1985		205	Carlos Baerga	AL	CLE	1992
215	Pete Rose	NL	CIN	1976		204	Pete Rose	NL	CIN	1977
213	Tony Fernandez	AL	TOR	1986		204	Bernie Williams	AL	NY	2002
211	Frankie Frisch	NL	NY	1921		203	Augie Galan	NL	CHI	1935
211	Garry Templeton	NL	STL	1979		203	Ruben Sierra	AL	TEX	1991
210	Pete Rose	NL	CIN	1968		202	Bernie Williams	AL	NY	1999
210	Pete Rose	NL	CIN	1975		200	Ripper Collins	NL	STL	1934
209	Dave Bancroft	NL	NY	1922		200	Red Schoendienst	NL	NY-MIL	1957
209	Pete Rose	NL	CIN	1965				NY (78); MIL (122)		
208	Buck Weaver	AL	CHI	1920		200	Garry Templeton	NL	STL	1977
208	Frankie Frisch	NL	NY	1927		200	Carlos Baerga	AL	CLE	1993
208	Maury Wills	NL	LA	1962		200	Jose Vidro	NL	MON	2000

(193) Most Singles in a Season, before 1893

165	Pete Browning	AA	LOU	1887	146	John Ward	NL	BRO	1892
162	John Ward	NL	NY	1887	145	Tip O'Neill	AA	STL	1886
158	Tommy Tucker	AA	BAL	1889	144	Billy Shindle	AA	BAL	1889
157	John Ward	NL	BRO	1890	144	Spud Johnson	AA	COL	1890
155	Jack Glasscock	NL	IND	1889	143	Hugh Duffy	AA	BOS	1891
155	Harry L. Taylor	AA	LOU	1890	142	Arlie Latham	AA	STL	1886
153	Jimmy Wolf	AA	LOU	1890	142	Tommy McCarthy	AA	STL	1889
152	Bill Gleason	AA	STL	1887	142	Hugh Duffy	NL	CHI	1889
152	Billy Hamilton	NL	PHI	1892	142	Tommy McCarthy	AA	STL	1891
151	Arlie Latham	AA	STL	1887	142	George Van Haltren	AA	BAL	1891
149	Charlie Comiskey	AA	STL	1887	142	Dan Brouthers	NL	BRO	1892
149	Tommy McCarthy	AA	STL	1890	141	Sam Thompson	NL	DET	1887
149	Cupid Childs	NL	CLE	1892	140	Hardy Richardson	NL	DET	1886
147	Billy Hamilton	NL	PHI	1891	140	Tip O'Neill	AA	STL	1887
146	Denny Lyons	AA	PHI	1887	140	Dummy Hoy	AA	STL	1891

Although the NL counted walks as both hits and at bats in 1887, this table does not include them as such in the calculation of 1887 batting averages.

(194) Most Singles in a Season, since 1893

225	Ichiro Suzuki	AL	SEA	2004	178	Curt Flood	NL	STL	1964
206	Willie Keeler	NL	BAL	1898	177	Bill Terry	NL	NY	1930
198	Lloyd Waner	NL	PIT	1927	177	Tony Gwynn	NL	SD	1984
193	Willie Keeler	NL	BAL	1897	176	George Sisler	AL	STL	1925
192	Ichiro Suzuki	AL	SEA	2001	176	Richie Ashburn	NL	PHI	1958
191	Jesse Burkett	NL	CLE	1896	175	Willie Keeler	NL	BRO	1900
190	Willie Keeler	NL	BRO	1899	174	Al Simmons	AL	PHI	1925
187	Wade Boggs	AL	BOS	1985	173	Hughie Jennings	NL	BAL	1896
186	Jesse Burkett	NL	CLE	1898	172	Fred Tenney	NL	BOS	1899
186	Ichiro Suzuki	AL	SEA	2006	172	Charlie Jamieson	AL	CLE	1923
185	Jesse Burkett	NL	CLE	1895	172	Lloyd Waner	NL	PIT	1931
185	Jesse Burkett	NL	STL	1899	172	Mickey Witek	NL	NY	1943
184	Willie Wilson	AL	KC	1980	172	Johnny Pesky	AL	BOS	1947
184	Juan Pierre	NL	FLA	2004	171	Steve Brodie	NL	BAL	1894
183	Matty Alou	NL	PIT	1969	171	Willie Keeler	NL	BAL	1896
182	Sam Rice	AL	WAS	1925	171	George Sisler	AL	STL	1920
181	Billy Hamilton	NL	PHI	1894	171	Matty Alou	NL	PIT	1970
181	Jesse Burkett	NL	STL	1901	171	Cesar Tovar	AL	MIN	1971
181	Lefty O'Doul	NL	PHI	1929	171	Rod Carew	AL	MIN	1977
181	Lloyd Waner	NL	PIT	1929	171	Steve Sax	AL	NY	1989
181	Richie Ashburn	NL	PHI	1951	170	Willie Keeler	NL	BAL	1895
181	Pete Rose	NL	CIN	1973	170	Jesse Burkett	NL	STL	1900
180	Lloyd Waner	NL	PIT	1928	170	Willie Keeler	NL	BRO	1901
180	Ralph Garr	NL	ATL	1971	170	Sam Rice	AL	WAS	1920
180	Rod Carew	AL	MIN	1974	170	Eddie Collins	AL	CHI	1920
179	Jack Tobin	AL	STL	1921	170	Milt Stock	NL	STL	1920
179	Maury Wills	NL	LA	1962	170	Doc Cramer	AL	PHI	1935
178	George Sisler	AL	STL	1922	170	Darin Erstad	AL	ANA	2000
178	Paul Waner	NL	PIT	1937					

(195) Most Singles in a Season by a Left-handed Batter

225	Ichiro Suzuki	AL	SEA	2004		177	Bill Terry	NL	NY	1930
206	Willie Keeler	NL	BAL	1898		177	Tony Gwynn	NL	SD	1984
198	Lloyd Waner	NL	PIT	1927		176	George Sisler	AL	STL	1925
193	Willie Keeler	NL	BAL	1897		176	Richie Ashburn	NL	PHI	1958
192	Ichiro Suzuki	AL	SEA	2001		175	Willie Keeler	NL	BRO	1900
191	Jesse Burkett	NL	CLE	1896		172	Fred Tenney	NL	BOS	1899
190	Willie Keeler	NL	BRO	1899		172	Charlie Jamieson	AL	CLE	1923
187	Wade Boggs	AL	BOS	1985		172	Lloyd Waner	NL	PIT	1931
186	Jesse Burkett	NL	CLE	1898		172	Johnny Pesky	AL	BOS	1947
186	Ichiro Suzuki	AL	SEA	2006		171	Steve Brodie	NL	BAL	1894
185	Jesse Burkett	NL	CLE	1895		171	Willie Keeler	NL	BAL	1896
185	Jesse Burkett	NL	STL	1899		171	George Sisler	AL	STL	1920
184	Juan Pierre	NL	FLA	2004		171	Matty Alou	NL	PIT	1970
183	Matty Alou	NL	PIT	1969		171	Rod Carew	AL	MIN	1977
182	Sam Rice	AL	WAS	1925		170	Willie Keeler	NL	BAL	1895
181	Billy Hamilton	NL	PHI	1894		170	Jesse Burkett	NL	STL	1900
181	Jesse Burkett	NL	STL	1901		170	Willie Keeler	NL	BRO	1901
181	Lefty O'Doul	NL	PHI	1929		170	Sam Rice	AL	WAS	1920
181	Lloyd Waner	NL	PIT	1929		170	Eddie Collins	AL	CHI	1920
181	Richie Ashburn	NL	PHI	1951		170	Doc Cramer	AL	PHI	1935
180	Lloyd Waner	NL	PIT	1928		170	Darin Erstad	AL	ANA	2000
180	Ralph Garr	NL	ATL	1971		169	Bill Everitt	NL	CHI	1898
180	Rod Carew	AL	MIN	1974		169	Fred Clarke	NL	LOU	1899
179	Jack Tobin	AL	STL	1921		169	Ty Cobb	AL	DET	1911
178	George Sisler	AL	STL	1922		169	Bill Terry	NL	NY	1934
178	Paul Waner	NL	PIT	1937		169	Richie Ashburn	NL	PHI	1953

(196) Most Singles in a Season by a Right-handed Batter

178	Curt Flood	NL	STL	1964		162	Chick Fullis	NL	PHI	1933
174	Al Simmons	AL	PHI	1925		162	Harvey Kuenn	AL	DET	1954
173	Hughie Jennings	NL	BAL	1896		162	Dave Cash	NL	PHI	1976
172	Mickey Witek	NL	NY	1943		161	Harry Heilmann	AL	DET	1921
171	Cesar Tovar	AL	MIN	1971		161	Hy Myers	NL	BRO	1922
171	Steve Sax	AL	NY	1989		161	Harry Heilmann	AL	DET	1925
170	Milt Stock	NL	STL	1920		161	Bob Dillinger	AL	STL	1948
169	Freddie Lindstrom	NL	NY	1928		160	Hal Chase	AL	NY	1906
167	Hugh Duffy	NL	BOS	1893		160	Stuffy McInnis	AL	PHI	1914
167	Harvey Kuenn	AL	DET	1953		160	Eddie Brown	NL	BOS	1926
167	Tommy Davis	NL	LA	1962		160	Luke Appling	AL	CHI	1936
167	Dave Cash	NL	PHI	1974		160	Frank McCormick	NL	CIN	1938
167	Paul Molitor	AL	MIN	1996		160	Dick Groat	NL	PIT	1962
166	Dave Cash	NL	PHI	1975		160	Curt Flood	NL	STL	1968
165	Pete Browning	AA	LOU	1887		160	Rafael Ramirez	NL	ATL	1983
165	Gene DeMontreville	NL	BAL	1898		159	Bill John Sweeney	NL	BOS	1912
165	Ed Delahanty	NL	PHI	1899		159	Baby Doll Jacobson	AL	STL	1920
165	Nap Lajoie	AL	CLE	1910		159	Jimmy Johnston	NL	BRO	1923
165	Sparky Adams	NL	CHI	1927		159	Frank Demaree	NL	CHI	1936
164	Buck Weaver	AL	CHI	1920		158	Lave Cross	NL	PHI	1894
164	Milt Stock	NL	BRO	1925		158	Jigger Statz	NL	CHI	1923
164	Joe Torre	NL	STL	1971		158	Pie Traynor	NL	PIT	1923
163	Freddie Lindstrom	NL	NY	1930		158	Bobby Richardson	AL	NY	1962
163	Kirby Puckett	AL	MIN	1988		158	Julio Franco	AL	CLE	1984

(197) Most Singles in a Season by a Switch-hitter

184	Willie Wilson	AL	KC	1980	
181	Pete Rose	NL	CIN	1973	
179	Maury Wills	NL	LA	1962	
169	Frankie Frisch	NL	NY	1923	
165	Maury Wills	NL	LA	1965	
162	Maury Wills	NL	PIT	1967	
162	Willie McGee	NL	STL	1985	
161	Tony Fernandez	AL	TOR	1986	
160	Red Schoendienst	NL	STL	1949	
160	Luis Castillo	NL	FLA	2002	
159	Dave Bancroft	NL	NY	1922	
159	Pete Rose	NL	PHI	1979	
158	Tommy Tucker	AA	BAL	1889	
158	Pete Rose	NL	CIN	1969	
158	Luis Castillo	NL	FLA	2000	
157	Max Carey	NL	PIT	1922	
157	Pete Rose	NL	CIN	1976	
157	Willie Wilson	AL	KC	1982	
156	Frankie Frisch	NL	STL	1927	
156	Maury Wills	NL	PIT	1968	
156	Tito Fuentes	AL	DET	1977	

156	Luis Castillo	NL	FLA	2003	
155	Frankie Frisch	NL	NY	1921	
155	Garry Templeton	NL	STL	1977	
154	Larry Bowa	NL	PHI	1974	
154	Willie McGee	NL-AL	STL-OAK	1990	
			STL (128); OAK (26)		
153	Larry Bowa	NL	PHI	1978	
153	Vince Coleman	NL	STL	1987	
152	Pete Rose	NL	CIN	1965	
152	Pete Rose	NL	CIN	1968	
152	Pete Rose	NL	CIN	1975	
152	Carlos Baerga	AL	CLE	1992	
151	Kid Gleason	NL	NY	1897	
151	Maury Wills	NL	LA	1964	
151	Garry Templeton	NL	STL	1979	
151	Harold Reynolds	AL	SEA	1989	
151	Otis Nixon	AL	TEX	1995	
150	Jimmy Brown	NL	STL	1939	
150	Maury Wills	NL	LA	1961	
150	Pete Rose	NL	CIN	1972	
150	Pete Rose	NL	CIN	1977	

(198) Most Doubles in a Season, before 1893

52	Tip O'Neill	AA	STL	1887
49	Ned Williamson	NL	CHI	1883
43	Denny Lyons	AA	PHI	1887
41	Dan Brouthers	NL	BUF	1883
41	King Kelly	NL	BOS	1889
41	Sam Thompson	NL	PHI	1890
40	Orator Shafer	UA	STL	1884
40	Dan Brouthers	NL	DET	1886
40	Jack Glasscock	NL	IND	1889
40	Pete Browning	PL	CLE	1890
39	Sam Barkley	AA	TOL	1884
39	Fred Dunlap	UA	STL	1884
39	Curt Welch	AA	PHI	1889
38	Harry Stovey	AA	PHI	1889
38	Jake Beckley	PL	PIT	1890
37	King Kelly	NL	CHI	1882
37	Tom Burns	NL	CHI	1883
37	Henry Larkin	AA	PHI	1885
37	Jim O'Rourke	PL	NY	1890

37	Roger Connor	NL	PHI	1892
36	Cap Anson	NL	CHI	1883
36	Paul Hines	NL	PRO	1884
36	Henry Larkin	AA	PHI	1886
36	Dan Brouthers	NL	DET	1887
36	Jim O'Rourke	NL	NY	1889
36	Denny Lyons	AA	PHI	1889
36	Sam Thompson	NL	PHI	1889
36	Dan Brouthers	PL	BOS	1890
36	Hugh Duffy	PL	CHI	1890
36	Mike Griffin	NL	BRO	1891
35	Cap Anson	NL	CHI	1885
35	Cap Anson	NL	CHI	1886
35	Pete Browning	AA	LOU	1887
35	John Reilly	AA	CIN	1887
35	Arlie Latham	AA	STL	1887
35	George Davis	NL	CLE	1891
35	Jocko Milligan	AA	PHI	1891

(199) Most Doubles in a Season, since 1893

67	Earl Webb	AL	BOS	1931		53	Grady Sizemore	AL	CLE	2006
64	George H. Burns	AL	CLE	1926		53	Freddy Sanchez	NL	PIT	2006
64	Joe Medwick	NL	STL	1936		52	Tris Speaker	AL	CLE	1921
63	Hank Greenberg	AL	DET	1934		52	Tris Speaker	AL	CLE	1926
62	Paul Waner	NL	PIT	1932		52	Lou Gehrig	AL	NY	1927
60	Charlie Gehringer	AL	DET	1936		52	Johnny Frederick	NL	BRO	1929
59	Tris Speaker	AL	CLE	1923		52	Enos Slaughter	NL	STL	1939
59	Chuck Klein	NL	PHI	1930		52	Edgar Martinez	AL	SEA	1995
59	Todd Helton	NL	COL	2000		52	Albert Belle	AL	CLE	1995
57	Billy Herman	NL	CHI	1935		52	Edgar Martinez	AL	SEA	1996
57	Billy Herman	NL	CHI	1936		52	Luis Gonzalez	NL	ARI	2006
57	Carlos Delgado	AL	TOR	2000		52	Michael Young	AL	TEX	2006
56	Joe Medwick	NL	STL	1937		51	Hugh Duffy	NL	BOS	1894
56	George Kell	AL	DET	1950		51	Nap Lajoie	AL	CLE	1910
56	Craig Biggio	NL	HOU	1999		51	Baby Doll Jacobson	AL	STL	1926
56	Nomar Garciaparra	AL	BOS	2002		51	George H. Burns	AL	CLE	1927
56	Garret Anderson	AL	ANA	2002		51	Johnny Hodapp	AL	CLE	1930
55	Ed Delahanty	NL	PHI	1899		51	Beau Bell	AL	STL	1937
55	Gee Walker	AL	DET	1936		51	Joe Cronin	AL	BOS	1938
55	Lance Berkman	NL	HOU	2001		51	Stan Musial	NL	STL	1944
54	Hal McRae	AL	KC	1977		51	Mickey Vernon	AL	WAS	1946
54	John Olerud	AL	TOR	1993		51	Frank Robinson	NL	CIN	1962
54	Alex Rodriguez	AL	SEA	1996		51	Pete Rose	NL	CIN	1978
54	Mark Grudzielanek	NL	MON	1997		51	Wade Boggs	AL	BOS	1989
54	Todd Helton	NL	COL	2001		51	Mark Grace	NL	CHI	1995
53	Tris Speaker	AL	BOS	1912		51	Craig Biggio	NL	HOU	1998
53	Al Simmons	AL	PHI	1926		51	Nomar Garciaparra	AL	BOS	2000
53	Paul Waner	NL	PIT	1936		51	Jose Vidro	NL	MON	2000
53	Stan Musial	NL	STL	1953		51	Alfonso Soriano	AL	NY	2002
53	Don Mattingly	AL	NY	1986		51	Albert Pujols	NL	STL	2003
53	Jeff Cirillo	NL	COL	2000		51	Albert Pujols	NL	STL	2004
53	Lyle Overbay	NL	MIL	2004						

(200) Most Doubles in a Season by a Left-handed Batter

67	Earl Webb	AL	BOS	1931		50	Tris Speaker	AL	CLE	1920
62	Paul Waner	NL	PIT	1932		50	Paul Waner	NL	PIT	1928
60	Charlie Gehringer	AL	DET	1936		50	Chuck Klein	NL	PHI	1932
59	Tris Speaker	AL	CLE	1923		50	Charlie Gehringer	AL	DET	1934
59	Chuck Klein	NL	PHI	1930		50	Stan Musial	NL	STL	1946
59	Todd Helton	NL	COL	2000		50	Stan Spence	AL	WAS	1946
57	Carlos Delgado	AL	TOR	2000		50	Bobby Abreu	NL	PHI	2002
56	Garret Anderson	AL	ANA	2002		49	George Sisler	AL	STL	1920
54	John Olerud	AL	TOR	1993		49	Heinie Manush	AL	STL-WAS	1930
54	Todd Helton	NL	COL	2001				STL (16); WAS (33)		
53	Tris Speaker	AL	BOS	1912		49	Rafael Palmeiro	AL	TEX	1991
53	Paul Waner	NL	PIT	1936		49	Tony Gwynn	NL	SD	1997
53	Stan Musial	NL	STL	1953		49	Shawn Green	NL	LA	2003
53	Don Mattingly	AL	NY	1986		49	Todd Helton	NL	COL	2003
53	Lyle Overbay	NL	MIL	2004		49	Garret Anderson	AL	ANA	2003
53	Grady Sizemore	AL	CLE	2006		49	Todd Helton	NL	COL	2004
52	Tris Speaker	AL	CLE	1921		48	Tris Speaker	AL	CLE	1922
52	Tris Speaker	AL	CLE	1926		48	Joe Sewell	AL	CLE	1927
52	Lou Gehrig	AL	NY	1927		48	Babe Herman	NL	BRO	1930
52	Johnny Frederick	NL	BRO	1929		48	Earl Averill	AL	CLE	1934
52	Enos Slaughter	NL	STL	1939		48	Wally Moses	AL	PHI	1937
52	Luis Gonzalez	NL	ARI	2006		48	Stan Musial	NL	STL	1943
51	Stan Musial	NL	STL	1944		48	Keith Hernandez	NL	STL	1979
51	Mickey Vernon	AL	WAS	1946		48	Don Mattingly	AL	NY	1985
51	Wade Boggs	AL	BOS	1989		48	Bobby Abreu	NL	PHI	2001
51	Mark Grace	NL	CHI	1995						

TRANSCENDENTAL GRAPHICS

Jackie Robinson

(201) Most Doubles in a Season by a Right-handed Batter

64	George H. Burns	AL	CLE	1926		51	Albert Pujols	NL	STL	2003
64	Joe Medwick	NL	STL	1936		51	Albert Pujols	NL	STL	2004
63	Hank Greenberg	AL	DET	1934		50	Harry Heilmann	AL	DET	1927
57	Billy Herman	NL	CHI	1935		50	Kiki Cuyler	NL	CHI	1930
57	Billy Herman	NL	CHI	1936		50	Ben Chapman	AL	NY-WAS	1936
56	Joe Medwick	NL	STL	1937				NY (14); WAS (36)		
56	George Kell	AL	DET	1950		50	Odell Hale	AL	CLE	1936
56	Craig Biggio	NL	HOU	1999		50	Hank Greenberg	AL	DET	1940
56	Nomar Garciaparra	AL	BOS	2002		50	Juan Gonzalez	AL	TEX	1998
55	Ed Delahanty	NL	PHI	1899		50	Derrek Lee	NL	CHI	2005
55	Gee Walker	AL	DET	1936		50	Miguel Tejada	AL	BAL	2005
54	Hal McRae	AL	KC	1977		50	Miguel Cabrera	NL	FLA	2006
54	Alex Rodriguez	AL	SEA	1996		49	Ned Williamson	NL	CHI	1883
54	Mark Grudzielanek	NL	MON	1997		49	Ed Delahanty	NL	PHI	1895
53	Al Simmons	AL	PHI	1926		49	Nap Lajoie	AL	CLE	1904
53	Jeff Cirillo	NL	COL	2000		49	Riggs Stephenson	NL	CHI	1932
53	Freddy Sanchez	NL	PIT	2006		49	Hank Greenberg	AL	DET	1937
52	Tip O'Neill	AA	STL	1887		49	Robin Yount	AL	MIL	1980
52	Edgar Martinez	AL	SEA	1995		49	Jeff Kent	NL	SF	2001
52	Albert Belle	AL	CLE	1995		49	Scott Rolen	NL	STL	2003
52	Edgar Martinez	AL	SEA	1996		49	Vernon Wells	AL	TOR	2003
52	Michael Young	AL	TEX	2006		49	Marcus Giles	NL	ATL	2003
51	Hugh Duffy	NL	BOS	1894		48	Joe Kelley	NL	BAL	1894
51	Nap Lajoie	AL	CLE	1910		48	Nap Lajoie	AL	PHI	1901
51	Baby Doll Jacobson	AL	STL	1926		48	Nap Lajoie	AL	CLE	1906
51	George H. Burns	AL	CLE	1927		48	Dick Bartell	NL	PHI	1932
51	Johnny Hodapp	AL	CLE	1930		48	Joe Medwick	NL	STL	1939
51	Beau Bell	AL	STL	1937		48	Jeff Bagwell	NL	HOU	1996
51	Joe Cronin	AL	BOS	1938		48	Albert Belle	AL	CHI	1998
51	Frank Robinson	NL	CIN	1962		48	Dante Bichette	NL	COL	1998
51	Craig Biggio	NL	HOU	1998		48	Ron Belliard	AL	CLE	2004
51	Nomar Garciaparra	AL	BOS	2000		48	Scott Rolen	NL	STL	2006
51	Alfonso Soriano	AL	NY	2002		48	Garrett Atkins	NL	COL	2006

(202) Most Doubles in a Season by a Switch-hitter

55	Lance Berkman	NL	HOU	2001		42	David Segui	AL	TEX-CLE	2000
51	Pete Rose	NL	CIN	1978				TEX (29); CLE (13)		
51	Jose Vidro	NL	MON	2000		42	Ray Durham	AL	CHI	2001
50	Brian Roberts	AL	BAL	2004		42	Jimmy Rollins	NL	PHI	2003
48	Dmitri Young	NL	CIN	1998		42	Coco Crisp	AL	CLE	2005
47	Wes Parker	NL	LA	1970		41	Dave Bancroft	NL	NY	1922
47	Pete Rose	NL	CIN	1975		41	Augie Galan	NL	CHI	1935
46	John Anderson	AL	MIL	1901		41	Tony Fernandez	AL	TOR	1988
46	Frankie Frisch	NL	STL	1930		41	Howard Johnson	NL	NY	1989
45	Walt Wilmot	NL	CHI	1894		41	Roberto Alomar	AL	TOR	1991
45	Pete Rose	NL	CIN	1974		41	Chipper Jones	NL	ATL	1997
45	Jose Vidro	NL	MON	1999		41	Chipper Jones	NL	ATL	1999
45	Bill Mueller	AL	BOS	2003		41	Tony Fernandez	AL	TOR	1999
45	Brian Roberts	AL	BAL	2005		41	Carlos Guillen	AL	DET	2006
45	Jimmy Rollins	NL	PHI	2006		40	Bill Kenworthy	FL	KC	1914
45	Mark Teixeira	AL	TEX	2006		40	Frankie Frisch	NL	STL	1929
44	Bobby Bonilla	NL	PIT	1991		40	Lu Blue	AL	STL	1929
44	Ruben Sierra	AL	TEX	1991		40	Ripper Collins	NL	STL	1934
44	Carlos Beltran	AL	KC	2002		40	Red Schoendienst	NL	STL	1952
44	Gary Mathews Jr.	AL	TEX	2006		40	Ted Simmons	NL	STL	1978
43	Augie Galan	NL	BRO	1944		40	Pete Rose	NL	PHI	1979
43	Red Schoendienst	NL	STL	1950		40	Ozzie Smith	NL	STL	1987
43	Roberto Alomar	AL	BAL	1996		40	Gregg Jefferies	NL	NY	1990
43	Jose Vidro	NL	MON	2002		40	Devon White	AL	TOR	1991
43	Jimmy Rollins	NL	PHI	2004		40	Felix Jose	NL	STL	1991
42	Billy Rogell	AL	DET	1933		40	Mariano Duncan	NL	PHI	1992
42	Pete Rose	NL	CIN	1968		40	Joey Cora	AL	SEA	1997
42	Pete Rose	NL	CIN	1976		40	Roberto Alomar	AL	CLE	1999
42	Pete Rose	NL	PHI	1980		40	Roberto Alomar	AL	CLE	2000
42	Johnny Ray	AL	CAL	1988		40	Jorge Posada	AL	NY	2002
42	Devon White	AL	TOR	1993		40	Lance Berkman	NL	HOU	2004

(203) Most Triples in a Season, before 1893

31	Dave Orr	AA	NY	1886		21	Ed Delahanty	NL	PHI	1892
26	John Reilly	NL	CIN	1890		20	Buck Ewing	NL	NY	1884
23	Harry Stovey	AA	PHI	1884		20	Roger Connor	NL	NY	1886
23	Sam Thompson	NL	DET	1887		20	Dan Brouthers	NL	DET	1887
22	Roger Connor	NL	NY	1887		20	Dick Johnston	NL	BOS	1887
22	Joe Visner	PL	PIT	1890		20	Harry Stovey	AA	PHI	1888
22	Bid McPhee	NL	CIN	1890		20	Perry Werden	AA	TOL	1890
22	Jake Beckley	PL	PIT	1890		20	Jocko Fields	PL	PIT	1890
21	Dave Orr	AA	NY	1885		20	Harry Stovey	NL	BOS	1891
21	Mike Tiernan	NL	NY	1890		20	Jake Virtue	NL	CLE	1892
21	Billy Shindle	PL	PHI	1890		20	Dan Brouthers	NL	BRO	1892
21	Tom Brown	AA	BOS	1891						

(204) Most Triples in a Season, since 1893

36	Chief Wilson	NL	PIT	1912		23	Ty Cobb	AL	DET	1912
31	Heinie Reitz	NL	BAL	1894		23	Sam Crawford	AL	DET	1913
29	Perry Werden	NL	STL	1893		23	Earle Combs	AL	NY	1927
28	Sam Thompson	NL	PHI	1894		23	Adam Comorosky	NL	PIT	1930
28	Harry Davis	NL	PIT	1897		23	Dale Mitchell	AL	CLE	1949
28	Jimmy Williams	NL	PIT	1899		22	Willie Keeler	NL	BAL	1894
27	George Davis	NL	NY	1893		22	Kip Selbach	NL	WAS	1895
26	George Treadway	NL	BRO	1894		22	John Anderson	NL	BRO-WAS	1898
26	Joe Jackson	AL	CLE	1912					BRO (4); WAS (18)	
26	Sam Crawford	AL	DET	1914		22	Honus Wagner	NL	PIT	1900
26	Kiki Cuyler	NL	PIT	1925		22	Sam Crawford	NL	CIN	1902
25	Roger Connor	NL	NY-STL	1894		22	Tommy Leach	NL	PIT	1902
			All with STL			22	Bill Bradley	AL	CLE	1903
25	Buck Freeman	NL	WAS	1899		22	Elmer Flick	NL	CLE	1906
25	Sam Crawford	AL	DET	1903		22	Mike Mitchell	NL	CIN	1911
25	Larry Doyle	NL	NY	1911		22	Birdie Cree	AL	NY	1911
25	Tom Long	NL	STL	1915		22	Tris Speaker	AL	BOS	1913
24	Ed McKean	NL	CLE	1893		22	Hy Myers	NL	BRO	1920
24	Ty Cobb	AL	DET	1911		22	Jake Daubert	NL	CIN	1922
24	Ty Cobb	AL	DET	1917		22	Paul Waner	NL	PIT	1926
23	Elmer Smith	NL	PIT	1893		22	Earle Combs	AL	NY	1930
23	Dan Brouthers	NL	BAL	1894		22	Snuffy Stirnweiss	AL	NY	1945
23	Nap Lajoie	NL	PHI	1897						

(205) Most Triples in a Season by a Left-handed Batter

36	Chief Wilson	NL	PIT	1912		22	Willie Keeler	NL	BAL	1894
31	Heinie Reitz	NL	BAL	1894		22	Sam Crawford	NL	CIN	1902
28	Sam Thompson	NL	PHI	1894		22	Elmer Flick	NL	CLE	1906
26	George Treadway	NL	BRO	1894		22	Tris Speaker	AL	BOS	1913
26	Joe Jackson	AL	CLE	1912		22	Jake Daubert	NL	CIN	1922
26	Sam Crawford	AL	DET	1914		22	Paul Waner	NL	PIT	1926
25	Roger Connor	NL	NY-STL	1894		22	Earle Combs	AL	NY	1930
			All with STL			21	Mike Tiernan	NL	NY	1890
25	Buck Freeman	NL	WAS	1899		21	Tom Brown	AA	BOS	1891
25	Sam Crawford	AL	DET	1903		21	Mike Tiernan	NL	NY	1895
25	Larry Doyle	NL	NY	1911		21	Sam Thompson	NL	PHI	1895
24	Ty Cobb	AL	DET	1911		21	George Van Haltren	NL	NY	1896
24	Ty Cobb	AL	DET	1917		21	Bill Keister	AL	BAL	1901
23	Sam Thompson	NL	DET	1887		21	Cy Seymour	NL	CIN	1905
23	Elmer Smith	NL	PIT	1893		21	Frank Schulte	NL	CHI	1911
23	Dan Brouthers	NL	BAL	1894		21	Sam Crawford	AL	DET	1912
23	Ty Cobb	AL	DET	1912		21	Frank Baker	AL	PHI	1912
23	Sam Crawford	AL	DET	1913		21	Vic Saier	NL	CHI	1913
23	Earle Combs	AL	NY	1927		21	Joe Jackson	AL	CHI	1916
23	Dale Mitchell	AL	CLE	1949		21	Edd Roush	NL	CIN	1924
22	Roger Connor	NL	NY	1887		21	Earle Combs	AL	NY	1928
22	Jake Beckley	PL	PIT	1890		21	Lance Johnson	NL	NY	1996
22	Joe Visner	PL	PIT	1890						

(206) Most Triples in a Season by a Right-handed Batter

31	Dave Orr	AA	NY	1886		21	Billy Shindle	PL	PHI	1890
29	Perry Werden	NL	STL	1893		21	Ed Delahanty	NL	PHI	1892
28	Harry Davis	NL	PIT	1897		21	Bobby Wallace	NL	CLE	1897
28	Jimmy Williams	NL	PIT	1899		21	Jimmy Williams	AL	BAL	1901
26	John Reilly	NL	CIN	1890		21	Jimmy Williams	AL	BAL	1902
26	Kiki Cuyler	NL	PIT	1925		20	Buck Ewing	NL	NY	1884
25	Tom Long	NL	STL	1915		20	Dick Johnston	NL	BOS	1887
24	Ed McKean	NL	CLE	1893		20	Harry Stovey	AA	PHI	1888
23	Harry Stovey	AA	PHI	1884		20	Perry Werden	AA	TOL	1890
23	Nap Lajoie	NL	PHI	1897		20	Jocko Fields	PL	PIT	1890
23	Adam Comorosky	NL	PIT	1930		20	Harry Stovey	NL	BOS	1891
22	Bid McPhee	NL	CIN	1890		20	Jake Stenzel	NL	PIT	1894
22	Kip Selbach	NL	WAS	1895		20	Tommy Corcoran	NL	BRO	1894
22	Honus Wagner	NL	PIT	1900		20	Joe Kelley	NL	BAL	1894
22	Tommy Leach	NL	PIT	1902		20	Honus Wagner	NL	PIT	1912
22	Bill Bradley	AL	CLE	1903		20	Red Murray	NL	NY	1912
22	Birdie Cree	AL	NY	1911		20	Dots Miller	NL	PIT	1913
22	Mike Mitchell	NL	CIN	1911		20	Rogers Hornsby	NL	STL	1920
22	Hy Myers	NL	BRO	1920		20	Rabbit Maranville	NL	PIT	1924
22	Snuffy Stirnweiss	AL	NY	1945		20	Joe Vosmik	AL	CLE	1935
21	Dave Orr	AA	NY	1885		20	Willie Mays	NL	NY	1957

(207) Most Triples in a Season by a Switch-hitter

27	George Davis	NL	NY	1893		17	Tony Fernandez	AL	TOR	1990
22	John Anderson	NL	BRO-WAS	1898		17	Chone Figgins	AL	ANA	2004
			BRO (4); WAS (18)			17	Jose Reyes	NL	NY	2005
21	Tom McCreery	NL	LOU	1896		17	Jose Reyes	NL	NY	2006
21	Willie Wilson	AL	KC	1985		16	Candy LaChance	NL	BRO	1897
20	Jake Virtue	NL	CLE	1892		15	Dan McGann	AL-NL	BAL-NY	1902
20	Cristian Guzman	AL	MIN	2000					BAL (8); NY (7)	
19	Walt Wilmot	NL	CHI	1889		15	George Davis	AL	CHI	1904
19	George Davis	NL	NY	1894		15	Dave Bancroft	NL	NY	1921
19	Max Carey	NL	PIT	1923		15	Frankie Frisch	NL	NY	1924
19	Garry Templeton	NL	STL	1979		15	Lu Blue	AL	CHI	1931
18	Garry Templeton	NL	STL	1977		15	Willie Wilson	AL	KC	1980
18	Willie McGee	NL	STL	1985		15	Alfredo Griffin	AL	TOR	1980
17	John Anderson	NL	BRO	1896		15	Willie Wilson	AL	KC	1982
17	Max Carey	NL	PIT	1914		15	Dave Collins	AL	TOR	1984
17	Frankie Frisch	NL	STL	1921		15	Willie Wilson	AL	KC	1987
17	Jim Gilliam	NL	BRO	1953						

(208) Highest Batting Average in a Season, before 1893
(min. 3.1 PA per scheduled game)

.435	Tip O'Neill	AA	STL	1887	.368	Dan Brouthers	NL	BUF	1882
.429	Ross Barnes	NL	CHI	1876	.367	Denny Lyons	AA	PHI	1887
.412	Fred Dunlap	UA	STL	1884	.366	George Hall	NL	PHI	1876
.402	Pete Browning	AA	LOU	1887	.363	Jimmy Wolf	AA	LOU	1890
.399	Cap Anson	NL	CHI	1881	.362	Jim O'Rourke	NL	BOS	1877
.388	King Kelly	NL	CHI	1886	.362	Cap Anson	NL	CHI	1882
.387	Deacon White	NL	BOS	1877	.362	Pete Browning	AA	LOU	1885
.378	John Cassidy	NL	HAR	1877	.360	George Gore	NL	CHI	1880
.378	Pete Browning	AA	LOU	1882	.360	Orator Shaffer	UA	STL	1884
.374	Dan Brouthers	NL	BUF	1883	.360	Jim O'Rourke	PL	NY	1890
.373	Dan Brouthers	NL	BOS	1889	.359	Dan Brouthers	NL	BUF	1885
.373	Pete Browning	PL	CLE	1890	.358	Paul Hines	NL	PRO	1878
.372	Sam Thompson	NL	DET	1887	.357	Paul Hines	NL	PRO	1879
.372	Tommy Tucker	AA	BAL	1889	.357	Roger Connor	NL	NY	1883
.371	Roger Connor	NL	NY	1885	.357	Bob Caruthers	AA	STL	1887
.371	Cap Anson	NL	CHI	1886	.357	Dave Foutz	AA	STL	1887
.371	Dave Orr	PL	BRO	1890	.356	Cap Anson	NL	CHI	1876
.370	Dan Brouthers	NL	DET	1886	.356	Ed Swartwood	AA	PIT	1883
.368	Cal McVey	NL	CHI	1877	.355	Roger Connor	NL	NY	1886

Although the NL counted walks as both hits and at bats in 1887, this table does not include them as such in the calculation of 1887 batting averages.

Nap Lajoie

(209) Highest Batting Average in a Season, since 1893
(min. 3.1 PA per scheduled game)

.440	Hugh Duffy	NL	BOS	1894		.394	Tony Gwynn	NL	SD	1994
.426	Nap Lajoie	AL	PHI	1901		.393	Joe Kelley	NL	BAL	1894
.424	Willie Keeler	NL	BAL	1897		.393	Babe Ruth	AL	NY	1923
.424	Rogers Hornsby	NL	STL	1924		.393	Harry Heilmann	AL	DET	1925
.420	Ty Cobb	AL	DET	1911		.393	Babe Herman	NL	BRO	1930
.420	George Sisler	AL	STL	1922		.392	Sam Thompson	NL	PHI	1895
.415	Sam Thompson	NL	PHI	1894		.391	John McGraw	NL	BAL	1899
.410	Jesse Burkett	NL	CLE	1896		.390	Fred Clarke	NL	PIT	1897
.410	Ed Delahanty	NL	PHI	1899		.390	Ty Cobb	AL	DET	1913
.409	Ty Cobb	AL	DET	1912		.390	Al Simmons	AL	PHI	1931
.408	Joe Jackson	AL	CLE	1911		.390	George Brett	AL	KC	1980
.407	George Sisler	AL	STL	1920		.389	Bill Lange	NL	CHI	1895
.406	Ted Williams	AL	BOS	1941		.389	Billy Hamilton	NL	PHI	1895
.405	Jesse Burkett	NL	CLE	1895		.389	Ty Cobb	AL	DET	1921
.404	Ed Delahanty	NL	PHI	1894		.389	Tris Speaker	AL	CLE	1925
.404	Ed Delahanty	NL	PHI	1895		.388	Tris Speaker	AL	CLE	1920
.403	Billy Hamilton	NL	PHI	1894		.388	Luke Appling	AL	CHI	1936
.403	Harry Heilmann	AL	DET	1923		.388	Ted Williams	AL	BOS	1957
.403	Rogers Hornsby	NL	STL	1925		.388	Rod Carew	AL	MIN	1977
.401	Hughie Jennings	NL	BAL	1896		.388	Deacon White	NL	BOS	1877
.401	Rogers Hornsby	NL	STL	1922		.387	Lave Cross	NL	PHI	1894
.401	Ty Cobb	AL	DET	1922		.387	Al Simmons	AL	PHI	1925
.401	Bill Terry	NL	NY	1930		.387	Rogers Hornsby	NL	BOS	1928
.398	Harry Heilmann	AL	DET	1927		.386	Hughie Jennings	NL	BAL	1895
.398	Lefty O'Doul	NL	PHI	1929		.386	Willie Keeler	NL	BAL	1896
.397	Ed Delahanty	NL	PHI	1896		.386	Tris Speaker	AL	CLE	1916
.397	Rogers Hornsby	NL	STL	1921		.386	Chuck Klein	NL	PHI	1930
.396	Jesse Burkett	NL	STL	1899		.385	Willie Keeler	NL	BAL	1898
.395	Joe Jackson	AL	CLE	1912		.385	Arky Vaughan	NL	PIT	1935
.394	Harry Heilmann	AL	DET	1921						

(210) Highest Batting Average in a Season by a Left-handed Batter (min. 3.1 PA per scheduled game)

.424	Willie Keeler	NL	BAL	1897	.389	Tris Speaker	AL	CLE	1925
.420	George Sisler	AL	STL	1922	.389	Billy Hamilton	NL	PHI	1895
.420	Ty Cobb	AL	DET	1911	.389	Ty Cobb	AL	DET	1921
.415	Sam Thompson	NL	PHI	1894	.388	Ted Williams	AL	BOS	1957
.410	Jesse Burkett	NL	CLE	1896	.388	Rod Carew	AL	MIN	1977
.409	Ty Cobb	AL	DET	1912	.388	Tris Speaker	AL	CLE	1920
.408	Joe Jackson	AL	CLE	1911	.387	Deacon White	NL	BOS	1877
.407	George Sisler	AL	STL	1920	.386	Tris Speaker	AL	CLE	1916
.406	Ted Williams	AL	BOS	1941	.386	Willie Keeler	NL	BAL	1896
.405	Jesse Burkett	NL	CLE	1895	.386	Chuck Klein	NL	PHI	1930
.403	Billy Hamilton	NL	PHI	1894	.385	Willie Keeler	NL	BAL	1898
.401	Bill Terry	NL	NY	1930	.385	Arky Vaughan	NL	PIT	1935
.401	Ty Cobb	AL	DET	1922	.384	Ty Cobb	AL	DET	1919
.398	Lefty O'Doul	NL	PHI	1929	.383	Ty Cobb	AL	DET	1910
.396	Jesse Burkett	NL	STL	1899	.383	Jesse Burkett	NL	CLE	1897
.395	Joe Jackson	AL	CLE	1912	.383	Tris Speaker	AL	BOS	1912
.394	Tony Gwynn	NL	SD	1994	.383	Ty Cobb	AL	DET	1917
.393	Babe Ruth	AL	NY	1923	.383	Lefty O'Doul	NL	PHI	1930
.393	Babe Herman	NL	BRO	1930	.382	Joe Jackson	AL	CHI	1920
.392	Sam Thompson	NL	PHI	1895	.382	Ty Cobb	AL	DET	1918
.391	John McGraw	NL	BAL	1899	.381	Babe Herman	NL	BRO	1929
.390	Ty Cobb	AL	DET	1913	.380	Paul Waner	NL	PIT	1927
.390	Fred Clarke	NL	PIT	1897	.380	Billy Hamilton	NL	PHI	1893
.390	George Brett	AL	KC	1980	.380	Tris Speaker	AL	CLE	1923

George Wright

(211) Highest Batting Average in a Season by a Right-handed Batter
(min. 3.1 PA per scheduled game)

.440	Hugh Duffy	NL	BOS	1894	.387	Rogers Hornsby	NL	BOS	1928
.435	Tip O'Neill	AA	STL	1887	.386	Hughie Jennings	NL	BAL	1895
.429	Ross Barnes	NL	CHI	1876	.384	Nap Lajoie	AL	CLE	1910
.426	Nap Lajoie	AL	PHI	1901	.384	Rogers Hornsby	NL	STL	1923
.424	Rogers Hornsby	NL	STL	1924	.381	Honus Wagner	NL	PIT	1900
.412	Fred Dunlap	UA	STL	1884	.381	Al Simmons	AL	PHI	1930
.410	Ed Delahanty	NL	PHI	1899	.381	Joe DiMaggio	AL	NY	1939
.404	Ed Delahanty	NL	PHI	1894	.380	Rogers Hornsby	NL	CHI	1929
.404	Ed Delahanty	NL	PHI	1895	.379	Freddie Lindstrom	NL	NY	1930
.403	Harry Heilmann	AL	DET	1923	.378	John Cassidy	NL	HAR	1877
.403	Rogers Hornsby	NL	STL	1925	.378	Pete Browning	AA	LOU	1882
.402	Pete Browning	AA	LOU	1887	.377	Ed Delahanty	NL	PHI	1897
.401	Hughie Jennings	NL	BAL	1896	.376	Bug Holliday	NL	CIN	1894
.401	Rogers Hornsby	NL	STL	1922	.376	Ed Delahanty	AL	WAS	1902
.399	Cap Anson	NL	CHI	1881	.376	Nap Lajoie	AL	CLE	1904
.398	Harry Heilmann	AL	DET	1927	.374	Joe Medwick	NL	STL	1937
.397	Ed Delahanty	NL	PHI	1896	.373	Pete Browning	PL	CLE	1890
.397	Rogers Hornsby	NL	STL	1921	.373	Dave Orr	PL	BRO	1890
.394	Harry Heilmann	AL	DET	1921	.372	Bug Holliday	NL	CIN	1894
.393	Joe Kelley	NL	BAL	1894	.372	Heinie Zimmerman	NL	CHI	1912
.393	Harry Heilmann	AL	DET	1925	.372	Nomar Garciaparra	AL	BOS	2000
.390	Al Simmons	AL	PHI	1931	.371	Cap Anson	NL	CHI	1886
.389	Bill Lange	NL	CHI	1895	.371	Dave Orr	PL	BRO	1890
.388	King Kelly	NL	CHI	1886	.371	Jake Stenzel	NL	PIT	1895
.388	Luke Appling	AL	CHI	1936	.370	Rogers Hornsby	NL	STL	1920
.387	Lave Cross	NL	PHI	1894	.370	Andres Galarraga	NL	COL	1993
.387	Al Simmons	AL	PHI	1925					

Honus Wagner

(212) Highest Batting Average in a Season by a Switch-hitter
(min. 3.1 PA per scheduled game)

.372	Tommy Tucker	AA	BAL	1889		.335	Pete Rose	NL	CIN	1968
.365	Mickey Mantle	AL	NY	1957		.334	Frankie Frisch	NL	STL	1929
.355	George Davis	NL	NY	1893		.334	Tim Raines	NL	MON	1986
.353	George Davis	NL	NY	1897		.334	David Segui	AL	TEX-CLE	2000
.353	Mickey Mantle	AL	NY	1956			TEX (.336); CLE (.332)			
.353	Willie McGee	NL	STL	1985		.334	Luis Castillo	NL	FLA	2000
.352	George Davis	NL	NY	1894		.333	Tommy Tucker	NL	BOS-WAS	1897
.351	Bob Ferguson	NL	CHI	1878			BOS (.214); WAS (.338)			
.351	Tom McCreery	NL	LOU	1896		.333	Ripper Collins	NL	STL	1934
.348	Frankie Frisch	NL	NY	1923		.333	Omar Vizquel	AL	CLE	1999
.348	Pete Rose	NL	CIN	1969		.333	Bernie Williams	AL	NY	2002
.346	Frankie Frisch	NL	STL	1930		.332	Ted Simmons	NL	STL	1975
.343	Max Carey	NL	PIT	1925		.332	Willie Wilson	AL	KC	1980
.342	Red Schoendienst	NL	STL	1953		.331	Buck Weaver	AL	CHI	1920
.342	Gregg Jefferies	NL	STL	1993		.331	Frankie Frisch	NL	NY	1925
.342	Bernie Williams	AL	NY	1999		.331	Pete Rose	NL	PHI	1979
.339	Tom Daly	NL	BRO	1894		.331	Lance Berkman	NL	HOU	2001
.341	Frankie Frisch	NL	NY	1921		.330	Tommy Tucker	NL	BOS	1894
.341	Miguel Dilone	AL	CLE	1980		.330	John Anderson	AL	MIL	1901
.340	George Davis	NL	NY	1895		.330	Tim Raines	NL	MON	1987
.339	Bernie Williams	AL	NY	1998		.330	Eddie Murray	NL	LA	1990
.338	Pete Rose	NL	CIN	1973		.330	Jose Vidro	NL	MON	2000
.337	Frankie Frisch	NL	NY	1927		.330	Chipper Jones	NL	ATL	2001
.336	Roberto Alomar	AL	CLE	2001						

(213) Highest On Base Percentage in a Season, before 1893
(min. 3.1 PA per scheduled game)

.490	Tip O'Neill	AA	STL	1887		.450	Roger Connor	PL	NY	1890
.483	King Kelly	NL	CHI	1886		.448	Fred Dunlap	UA	STL	1884
.471	Dan Brouthers	AA	BOS	1891		.447	Mike Tiernan	NL	NY	1889
.466	Dan Brouthers	PL	BOS	1890		.445	Dan Brouthers	NL	DET	1886
.464	Pete Browning	AA	LOU	1887		.445	Yank Robinson	AA	STL	1887
.463	Bob Caruthers	AA	STL	1887		.445	Denny Lyons	AA	STL	1891
.462	Ross Barnes	NL	CHI	1876		.444	Ed Swartwood	AA	TOL	1890
.462	Dan Brouthers	NL	BOS	1889		.443	Cap Anson	NL	CHI	1890
.459	Pete Browning	PL	CLE	1890		.443	Cupid Childs	NL	CLE	1892
.453	Billy Hamilton	NL	PHI	1891		.442	Cap Anson	NL	CHI	1881
.450	Tommy Tucker	AA	BAL	1889		.440	Cap Anson	NL	CHI	1889

(214) Highest On Base Percentage in a Season, since 1893
(min. 3.1 PA per scheduled game)

.609	Barry Bonds	NL	SF	2004		.494	Babe Ruth	AL	NY	1931
.582	Barry Bonds	NL	SF	2002		.493	Babe Ruth	AL	NY	1930
.553	Ted Williams	AL	BOS	1941		.491	Arky Vaughan	NL	PIT	1935
.547	John McGraw	NL	BAL	1899		.490	Billy Hamilton	NL	PHI	1893
.545	Babe Ruth	AL	NY	1923		.490	Billy Hamilton	NL	PHI	1895
.532	Babe Ruth	AL	NY	1920		.490	Ted Williams	AL	BOS	1949
.529	Barry Bonds	NL	SF	2003		.489	Rogers Hornsby	NL	STL	1925
.526	Ted Williams	AL	BOS	1957		.489	Babe Ruth	AL	NY	1932
.522	Billy Hamilton	NL	PHI	1894		.487	Norm Cash	AL	DET	1961
.516	Babe Ruth	AL	NY	1926		.487	Frank E. Thomas	AL	CHI	1994
.515	Barry Bonds	NL	SF	2001		.486	Ty Cobb	AL	DET	1915
.513	Babe Ruth	AL	NY	1924		.486	Babe Ruth	AL	NY	1927
.513	Ted Williams	AL	BOS	1954		.486	Mickey Mantle	AL	NY	1962
.512	Babe Ruth	AL	NY	1921		.483	Tris Speaker	AL	CLE	1920
.512	Mickey Mantle	AL	NY	1957		.482	Jesse Burkett	NL	CLE	1895
.507	Rogers Hornsby	NL	STL	1924		.481	Harry Heilmann	AL	DET	1923
.505	John McGraw	NL	STL	1900		.480	Billy Hamilton	NL	BOS	1898
.502	Joe Kelley	NL	BAL	1894		.479	Tris Speaker	AL	CLE	1925
.502	Hugh Duffy	NL	BOS	1894		.479	Ted Williams	AL	BOS	1956
.500	Ed Delahanty	NL	PHI	1895		.479	Edgar Martinez	AL	SEA	1995
.499	Ted Williams	AL	BOS	1942		.478	Billy Hamilton	NL	BOS	1896
.499	Ted Williams	AL	BOS	1947		.478	Lou Gehrig	AL	NY	1936
.498	Rogers Hornsby	NL	BOS	1928		.477	Jason Giambi	AL	OAK	2001
.497	Ted Williams	AL	BOS	1946		.476	Wade Boggs	AL	BOS	1988
.497	Ted Williams	AL	BOS	1948		.476	Jason Giambi	AL	OAK	2000
.496	Bill Joyce	NL	WAS	1894						

(215) Highest On Base Percentage in a Season by a Left-handed Batter
(min. 3.1 PA per scheduled game)

.609	Barry Bonds	NL	SF	2004		.489	Babe Ruth	AL	NY	1932
.582	Barry Bonds	NL	SF	2002		.487	Norm Cash	AL	DET	1961
.553	Ted Williams	AL	BOS	1941		.486	Ty Cobb	AL	DET	1915
.547	John McGraw	NL	BAL	1899		.486	Babe Ruth	AL	NY	1927
.545	Babe Ruth	AL	NY	1923		.483	Tris Speaker	AL	CLE	1920
.532	Babe Ruth	AL	NY	1920		.482	Jesse Burkett	NL	CLE	1895
.529	Barry Bonds	NL	SF	2003		.480	Billy Hamilton	NL	BOS	1898
.526	Ted Williams	AL	BOS	1957		.478	Billy Hamilton	NL	BOS	1896
.522	Billy Hamilton	NL	PHI	1894		.479	Tris Speaker	AL	CLE	1925
.516	Babe Ruth	AL	NY	1926		.479	Ted Williams	AL	BOS	1956
.515	Barry Bonds	NL	SF	2001		.478	Lou Gehrig	AL	NY	1936
.513	Babe Ruth	AL	NY	1924		.477	Jason Giambi	AL	OAK	2001
.513	Ted Williams	AL	BOS	1954		.476	Wade Boggs	AL	BOS	1988
.512	Babe Ruth	AL	NY	1921		.476	Jason Giambi	AL	OAK	2000
.505	John McGraw	NL	STL	1900		.475	Cupid Childs	NL	CLE	1894
.499	Ted Williams	AL	BOS	1942		.475	John McGraw	NL	BAL	1898
.499	Ted Williams	AL	BOS	1947		.474	Tris Speaker	AL	CLE	1922
.497	Ted Williams	AL	BOS	1946		.474	Lou Gehrig	AL	NY	1927
.497	Ted Williams	AL	BOS	1948		.473	Lou Gehrig	AL	NY	1930
.496	Bill Joyce	NL	WAS	1894		.473	Lou Gehrig	AL	NY	1937
.494	Babe Ruth	AL	NY	1931		.473	John Olerud	AL	TOR	1993
.493	Babe Ruth	AL	NY	1930		.471	John McGraw	NL	BAL	1897
.491	Arky Vaughan	NL	PIT	1935		.470	Bill Joyce	NL	WAS-NY	1896
.490	Billy Hamilton	NL	PHI	1893				WAS (.452); NY (.502)		
.490	Billy Hamilton	NL	PHI	1895		.470	Tris Speaker	AL	CLE	1916
.490	Ted Williams	AL	BOS	1949		.470	Carlos Delgado	AL	TOR	2000

Frank Baker

(216) Highest On Base Percentage in a Season by a Right-handed Batter
(min. 3.1 PA per scheduled game)

.507	Rogers Hornsby	NL	STL	1924		.463	Hughie Jennings	NL	BAL	1897
.502	Joe Kelley	NL	BAL	1894		.463	Nap Lajoie	AL	PHI	1901
.502	Hugh Duffy	NL	BOS	1894		.463	Jimmie Foxx	AL	PHI	1929
.500	Ed Delahanty	NL	PHI	1895		.462	Ross Barnes	NL	CHI	1876
.498	Rogers Hornsby	NL	BOS	1928		.462	Jimmie Foxx	AL	BOS	1938
.490	Tip O'Neill	AA	STL	1887		.461	Jimmie Foxx	AL	PHI	1935
.489	Rogers Hornsby	NL	STL	1925		.460	Eddie Stanky	NL	NY	1950
.487	Frank E. Thomas	AL	CHI	1994		.459	Pete Browning	PL	CLE	1890
.483	King Kelly	NL	CHI	1886		.459	Rogers Hornsby	NL	STL	1922
.481	Harry Heilmann	AL	DET	1923		.459	Rogers Hornsby	NL	STL	1923
.479	Edgar Martinez	AL	SEA	1995		.459	Rogers Hornsby	NL	CHI	1929
.475	Ed Delahanty	NL	PHI	1894		.459	Jack Clark	NL	STL	1987
.475	Harry Heilmann	AL	DET	1927		.459	Frank E. Thomas	AL	CHI	1996
.474	Luke Appling	AL	CHI	1936		.458	Rogers Hornsby	NL	STL	1921
.472	Hughie Jennings	NL	BAL	1896		.457	Harry Heilmann	AL	DET	1925
.472	Ed Delahanty	NL	PHI	1896		.457	Manny Ramirez	AL	CLE	2000
.470	Mark McGwire	NL	STL	1998		.456	Bill Lange	NL	CHI	1895
.469	Joe Kelley	NL	BAL	1896		.456	Joe Kelley	NL	BAL	1895
.469	Jimmie Foxx	AL	PHI	1932		.456	Frank E. Thomas	AL	CHI	1997
.467	Mark McGwire	AL	OAK	1996		.456	Edgar Martinez	AL	SEA	1997
.465	Gary Sheffield	NL	FLA	1996		.454	Hughie Jennings	NL	BAL	1898
.464	Pete Browning	AA	LOU	1887		.454	Hack Wilson	NL	CHI	1930
.464	Ed Delahanty	NL	PHI	1899		.454	Frank E. Thomas	AL	CHI	1995
.464	Jimmie Foxx	AL	BOS	1939		.454	Rico Carty	NL	ATL	1970
.464	Edgar Martinez	AL	SEA	1996		.454	Jeff Bagwell	NL	HOU	1999

(217) Highest On Base Percentage in a Season by a Switch-hitter
(min. 3.1 PA per scheduled game)

.512	Mickey Mantle	AL	NY	1957		.438	Ken Singleton	AL	BAL	1977
.486	Mickey Mantle	AL	NY	1962		.435	Bernie Williams	AL	NY	1999
.464	Mickey Mantle	AL	NY	1956		.435	Chipper Jones	NL	ATL	2002
.452	Roy Cullenbine	AL	STL	1941		.434	George Davis	NL	NY	1894
.450	Tommy Tucker	AA	BAL	1889		.433	Tom Daly	NL	BRO	1894
.450	Lance Berkman	NL	HOU	2004		.432	Miller Huggins	NL	STL	1913
.448	Mickey Mantle	AL	NY	1961		.431	Mickey Mantle	AL	NY	1955
.447	Piggy Ward	NL	WAS	1894		.430	Lu Blue	AL	CHI	1931
.443	Mickey Mantle	AL	NY	1958		.430	Lance Berkman	NL	HOU	2001
.443	Tony Phillips	AL	DET	1993		.429	Tim Raines	NL	MON	1987
.441	Chipper Jones	NL	ATL	1999		.429	Chili Davis	AL	CAL	1995

(218) Highest Slugging Average in a Season, before 1893
(min. 3.1 PA per scheduled game)

.691	Tip O'Neill	AA	STL	1887		.545	Deacon White	NL	BOS	1877
.621	Fred Dunlap	UA	STL	1884		.545	Harry Stovey	AA	PHI	1884
.590	Ross Barnes	NL	CHI	1876		.544	Cap Anson	NL	CHI	1886
.581	Dan Brouthers	NL	DET	1886		.543	Cap Anson	NL	CHI	1884
.572	Dan Brouthers	NL	BUF	1883		.543	Dan Brouthers	NL	BUF	1885
.565	Sam Thompson	NL	DET	1887		.543	Dave Orr	AA	NY	1885
.563	Dan Brouthers	NL	BUF	1884		.541	Dan Brouthers	NL	BUF	1881
.562	Dan Brouthers	NL	DET	1887		.541	Roger Connor	NL	NY	1887
.554	Ned Williamson	NL	CHI	1884		.540	Roger Connor	NL	NY	1886
.551	John Reilly	AA	CIN	1884		.539	Dave Orr	AA	NY	1884
.548	Roger Connor	PL	NY	1890		.535	Jake Beckley	PL	PIT	1890
.547	Dan Brouthers	NL	BUF	1882		.534	King Kelly	NL	CHI	1886
.547	Bob Caruthers	AA	STL	1887		.534	Dave Orr	PL	BRO	1890
.547	Pete Browning	AA	LOU	1887		.530	Roger Connor	NL	TRO	1882
.545	George Hall	NL	PHI	1876		.530	Pete Browning	AA	LOU	1885

(219) Highest Slugging Average in a Season, since 1893
(min. 3.1 PA per scheduled game)

.863	Barry Bonds	NL	SF	2001		.721	Lou Gehrig	AL	NY	1930
.847	Babe Ruth	AL	NY	1920		.720	Larry Walker	NL	COL	1997
.846	Babe Ruth	AL	NY	1921		.714	Albert Belle	AL	CLE	1994
.812	Barry Bonds	NL	SF	2004		.710	Larry Walker	NL	COL	1999
.799	Barry Bonds	NL	SF	2002		.709	Babe Ruth	AL	NY	1928
.772	Babe Ruth	AL	NY	1927		.708	Al Simmons	AL	PHI	1930
.765	Lou Gehrig	AL	NY	1927		.706	Lou Gehrig	AL	NY	1934
.764	Babe Ruth	AL	NY	1923		.705	Mickey Mantle	AL	NY	1956
.756	Rogers Hornsby	NL	STL	1925		.704	Jimmie Foxx	AL	BOS	1938
.752	Mark McGwire	NL	STL	1998		.703	Jimmie Foxx	AL	PHI	1933
.750	Jeff Bagwell	NL	HOU	1994		.702	Stan Musial	NL	STL	1948
.749	Jimmie Foxx	AL	PHI	1932		.700	Babe Ruth	AL	NY	1931
.749	Barry Bonds	NL	SF	2003		.698	Todd Helton	NL	COL	2000
.739	Babe Ruth	AL	NY	1924		.697	Babe Ruth	AL	NY	1929
.737	Babe Ruth	AL	NY	1926		.697	Mark McGwire	NL	STL	1999
.737	Sammy Sosa	NL	CHI	2001		.697	Manny Ramirez	AL	CLE	2000
.735	Ted Williams	AL	BOS	1941		.696	Sam Thompson	NL	PHI	1894
.732	Babe Ruth	AL	NY	1930		.696	Rogers Hornsby	NL	STL	1924
.731	Ted Williams	AL	BOS	1957		.696	Lou Gehrig	AL	NY	1936
.730	Mark McGwire	AL	OAK	1996		.694	Hugh Duffy	NL	BOS	1894
.729	Frank E. Thomas	AL	CHI	1994		.694	Jimmie Foxx	AL	BOS	1939
.723	Hack Wilson	NL	CHI	1930		.690	Albert Belle	AL	CLE	1995
.722	Rogers Hornsby	NL	STL	1922						

(220) Highest Slugging Average in a Season by a Left-handed Batter
(min. 3.1 PA per scheduled game)

.863	Barry Bonds	NL	SF	2001	.688	Barry Bonds	NL	SF	2000
.847	Babe Ruth	AL	NY	1920	.688	Luis Gonzalez	NL	ARI	2001
.846	Babe Ruth	AL	NY	1921	.687	Chuck Klein	NL	PHI	1930
.812	Barry Bonds	NL	SF	2004	.685	Todd Helton	NL	COL	2001
.799	Barry Bonds	NL	SF	2002	.678	Babe Herman	NL	BRO	1930
.772	Babe Ruth	AL	NY	1927	.677	Barry Bonds	NL	SF	1993
.765	Lou Gehrig	AL	NY	1927	.677	Jim Thome	AL	CLE	2002
.764	Babe Ruth	AL	NY	1923	.674	Ken Griffey Jr.	AL	SEA	1994
.749	Barry Bonds	NL	SF	2003	.672	Babe Ruth	AL	NY	1922
.739	Babe Ruth	AL	NY	1924	.667	Ted Williams	AL	BOS	1946
.737	Babe Ruth	AL	NY	1926	.664	George Brett	AL	KC	1980
.735	Ted Williams	AL	BOS	1941	.664	Carlos Delgado	AL	TOR	2000
.732	Babe Ruth	AL	NY	1930	.662	Lou Gehrig	AL	NY	1931
.731	Ted Williams	AL	BOS	1957	.662	Norm Cash	AL	DET	1961
.721	Lou Gehrig	AL	NY	1930	.662	Larry Walker	NL	COL	2001
.720	Larry Walker	NL	COL	1997	.661	Babe Ruth	AL	NY	1932
.710	Larry Walker	NL	COL	1999	.660	Jason Giambi	AL	OAK	2001
.709	Babe Ruth	AL	NY	1928	.659	Ryan Howard	NL	PHI	2006
.706	Lou Gehrig	AL	NY	1934	.659	Travis Hafner	AL	CLE	2006
.702	Stan Musial	NL	STL	1948	.657	Babe Ruth	AL	BOS	1919
.700	Babe Ruth	AL	NY	1931	.657	Chuck Klein	NL	PHI	1929
.698	Todd Helton	NL	COL	2000	.656	Willie McCovey	NL	SF	1969
.697	Babe Ruth	AL	NY	1929	.654	Sam Thompson	NL	PHI	1895
.696	Sam Thompson	NL	PHI	1894	.650	Ted Williams	AL	BOS	1949
.696	Lou Gehrig	AL	NY	1936					

Babe Herman and Hack Wilson

(221) Highest Slugging Average in a Season by a Right-handed Batter
(min. 3.1 PA per scheduled game)

.756	Rogers Hornsby	NL	STL	1925		.670	Hank Greenberg	AL	DET	1940
.752	Mark McGwire	NL	STL	1998		.669	Hank Aaron	NL	ATL	1971
.750	Jeff Bagwell	NL	HOU	1994		.668	Hank Greenberg	AL	DET	1937
.749	Jimmie Foxx	AL	PHI	1932		.667	Willie Mays	NL	SF	1954
.737	Sammy Sosa	NL	CHI	2001		.667	Albert Pujols	NL	STL	2003
.730	Mark McGwire	AL	OAK	1996		.664	Vladimir Guerrero	NL	MON	2000
.729	Frank E. Thomas	AL	CHI	1994		.663	Manny Ramirez	AL	CLE	1999
.723	Hack Wilson	NL	CHI	1930		.662	Derrek Lee	NL	CHI	2005
.722	Rogers Hornsby	NL	STL	1922		.659	Willie Mays	NL	SF	1955
.714	Albert Belle	AL	CLE	1994		.658	Ralph Kiner	NL	PIT	1949
.708	Al Simmons	AL	PHI	1930		.657	Albert Pujols	NL	STL	2004
.704	Jimmie Foxx	AL	BOS	1938		.655	Albert Belle	AL	CHI	1998
.703	Jimmie Foxx	AL	PHI	1933		.653	Jimmie Foxx	AL	PHI	1934
.697	Mark McGwire	NL	STL	1999		.652	Chick Hafey	NL	STL	1930
.697	Manny Ramirez	AL	CLE	2000		.647	Sammy Sosa	NL	CHI	1998
.696	Rogers Hornsby	NL	STL	1924		.647	Manny Ramirez	AL	BOS	2002
.694	Hugh Duffy	NL	BOS	1894		.645	Willie Mays	NL	SF	1965
.694	Jimmie Foxx	AL	BOS	1939		.644	Mike Schmidt	NL	PHI	1981
.691	Tip O'Neill	AA	STL	1887		.643	Nap Lajoie	AL	PHI	1901
.690	Albert Belle	AL	CLE	1995		.643	Joe DiMaggio	AL	NY	1941
.683	Hank Greenberg	AL	DET	1938		.643	Juan Gonzalez	AL	TEX	1996
.683	Kevin Mitchell	NL	CIN	1994		.643	Gary Sheffield	NL	LA	2000
.679	Rogers Hornsby	NL	CHI	1929		.642	Al Simmons	AL	PHI	1929
.673	Joe DiMaggio	AL	NY	1937		.641	Al Simmons	AL	PHI	1931
.671	Joe DiMaggio	AL	NY	1939		.641	Joe Medwick	NL	STL	1937
.671	Albert Pujols	NL	STL	2006						

(222) Highest Slugging Average in a Season by a Switch-hitter
(min. 3.1 PA per scheduled game)

.705	Mickey Mantle	AL	NY	1956		.576	Reggie Smith	NL	LA	1977
.687	Mickey Mantle	AL	NY	1961		.576	Bobby Bonilla	NL-AL	NY-BAL	1995
.665	Mickey Mantle	AL	NY	1957				NY (.599); BAL (.544)		
.633	Chipper Jones	NL	ATL	1999		.575	Bernie Williams	AL	NY	1998
.621	Ken Caminiti	NL	SD	1996		.575	Mark Teixeira	AL	TEX	2005
.621	Lance Berkman	NL	HOU	2006		.571	Carl Everett	NL	HOU	1999
.620	Lance Berkman	NL	HOU	2001		.566	Chipper Jones	NL	ATL	2000
.615	Ripper Collins	NL	STL	1934		.566	Bernie Williams	AL	NY	2000
.611	Mickey Mantle	AL	NY	1955		.566	Lance Berkman	NL	HOU	2004
.605	Mickey Mantle	AL	NY	1962		.561	Chili Davis	AL	CAL	1994
.605	Chipper Jones	NL	ATL	2001		.560	Mark Teixeira	AL	TEX	2004
.594	Carlos Beltran	NL	NY	2006		.559	Reggie Smith	NL	LA	1978
.592	Mickey Mantle	AL	NY	1958		.559	Howard Johnson	NL	NY	1989
.591	Mickey Mantle	AL	NY	1964		.558	Mickey Mantle	AL	NY	1960
.587	Carl Everett	AL	BOS	2000		.554	George Davis	NL	NY	1893
.578	Lance Berkman	NL	HOU	2002		.550	Todd Hundley	NL	NY	1996

(223) Highest On Base Percentage Plus Slugging Average in a Season, before 1893
(min. 3.1 PA per scheduled game)

1.180	Tip O'Neill	AA	STL	1887		.969	Dan Brouthers	NL	BUF	1883
1.069	Fred Dunlap	UA	STL	1884		.969	Dan Brouthers	NL	BOS	1889
1.052	Ross Barnes	NL	CHI	1876		.955	Roger Connor	NL	NY	1889
1.026	Dan Brouthers	NL	DET	1886		.952	Cap Anson	NL	CHI	1881
1.018	King Kelly	NL	CHI	1886		.951	Dan Brouthers	NL	BUF	1885
1.011	Pete Browning	AA	LOU	1887		.950	Deacon White	NL	BOS	1877
1.010	Bob Caruthers	AA	STL	1887		.950	Dan Brouthers	NL	BUF	1882
.998	Roger Connor	PL	NY	1890		.948	Dave Orr	PL	BRO	1890
.988	Dan Brouthers	NL	DET	1887		.945	Roger Connor	NL	NY	1886
.983	Dan Brouthers	AA	BOS	1891		.944	Mike Tiernan	NL	NY	1889
.982	Sam Thompson	NL	DET	1887		.943	Denny Lyons	AA	PHI	1887
.977	Cap Anson	NL	CHI	1886		.941	Dan Brouthers	NL	BUF	1884
.976	Pete Browning	PL	CLE	1890		.940	Pete Browning	AA	LOU	1882

(224) Highest On Base Percentage Plus Slugging Average in a Season, since 1893
(min. 3.1 PA per scheduled game)

1.422	Barry Bonds	NL	SF	2004		1.177	Hack Wilson	NL	CHI	1930
1.381	Barry Bonds	NL	SF	2002		1.177	Mickey Mantle	AL	NY	1957
1.379	Babe Ruth	AL	NY	1920		1.174	Lou Gehrig	AL	NY	1936
1.379	Barry Bonds	NL	SF	2001		1.174	Sammy Sosa	NL	CHI	2001
1.359	Babe Ruth	AL	NY	1921		1.172	Babe Ruth	AL	NY	1928
1.309	Babe Ruth	AL	NY	1923		1.172	Lou Gehrig	AL	NY	1934
1.287	Ted Williams	AL	BOS	1941		1.172	Larry Walker	NL	COL	1997
1.278	Barry Bonds	NL	SF	2003		1.169	Mickey Mantle	AL	NY	1956
1.258	Babe Ruth	AL	NY	1927		1.168	Larry Walker	NL	COL	1999
1.257	Ted Williams	AL	BOS	1957		1.166	Jimmie Foxx	AL	BOS	1938
1.253	Babe Ruth	AL	NY	1926		1.164	Ted Williams	AL	BOS	1946
1.252	Babe Ruth	AL	NY	1924		1.162	Todd Helton	NL	COL	2000
1.245	Rogers Hornsby	NL	STL	1925		1.161	Sam Thompson	NL	PHI	1894
1.240	Lou Gehrig	AL	NY	1927		1.158	Jimmie Foxx	AL	BOS	1939
1.225	Babe Ruth	AL	NY	1930		1.154	Manny Ramirez	AL	BOS	2000
1.222	Mark McGwire	NL	STL	1998		1.153	Jimmie Foxx	AL	PHI	1933
1.218	Jimmie Foxx	AL	PHI	1932		1.152	Stan Musial	NL	STL	1948
1.217	Frank E. Thomas	AL	CHI	1994		1.152	Albert Belle	AL	CLE	1994
1.203	Rogers Hornsby	NL	STL	1924		1.150	Babe Ruth	AL	NY	1932
1.201	Jeff Bagwell	NL	HOU	1994		1.148	Ted Williams	AL	BOS	1954
1.198	Mark McGwire	AL	OAK	1996		1.148	Norm Cash	AL	DET	1961
1.196	Hugh Duffy	NL	BOS	1894		1.147	Ted Williams	AL	BOS	1942
1.194	Lou Gehrig	AL	NY	1930		1.143	Bill Joyce	NL	WAS	1894
1.195	Babe Ruth	AL	NY	1931		1.141	Ted Williams	AL	BOS	1949
1.181	Rogers Hornsby	NL	STL	1922		1.139	Rogers Hornsby	NL	CHI	1929

(225) Highest On Base Percentage plus Slugging Average in a Season by a Left-handed Batter (min. 3.1 PA per scheduled game)

1.422	Barry Bonds	NL	SF	2004	1.150	Babe Ruth	AL	NY	1932
1.381	Barry Bonds	NL	SF	2002	1.148	Ted Williams	AL	BOS	1954
1.379	Babe Ruth	AL	NY	1920	1.148	Norm Cash	AL	DET	1961
1.379	Barry Bonds	NL	SF	2001	1.147	Ted Williams	AL	BOS	1942
1.359	Babe Ruth	AL	NY	1921	1.143	Bill Joyce	NL	WAS	1894
1.309	Babe Ruth	AL	NY	1923	1.141	Ted Williams	AL	BOS	1949
1.287	Ted Williams	AL	BOS	1941	1.137	Jason Giambi	AL	OAK	2001
1.278	Barry Bonds	NL	SF	2003	1.136	Barry Bonds	NL	SF	1993
1.258	Babe Ruth	AL	NY	1927	1.134	Carlos Delgado	AL	TOR	2000
1.257	Ted Williams	AL	BOS	1957	1.133	Ted Williams	AL	BOS	1947
1.253	Babe Ruth	AL	NY	1926	1.132	Babe Herman	NL	BRO	1930
1.252	Babe Ruth	AL	NY	1924	1.128	Babe Ruth	AL	NY	1929
1.240	Lou Gehrig	AL	NY	1927	1.127	Barry Bonds	NL	SF	2000
1.225	Babe Ruth	AL	NY	1930	1.123	Chuck Klein	NL	PHI	1930
1.194	Lou Gehrig	AL	NY	1930	1.123	Jason Giambi	AL	OAK	2000
1.194	Babe Ruth	AL	NY	1931	1.122	Jim Thome	AL	CLE	2002
1.174	Lou Gehrig	AL	NY	1936	1.118	George Brett	AL	KC	1980
1.172	Babe Ruth	AL	NY	1928	1.117	Luis Gonzalez	NL	ARI	2001
1.172	Lou Gehrig	AL	NY	1934	1.116	Lou Gehrig	AL	NY	1937
1.172	Larry Walker	NL	COL	1997	1.116	Todd Helton	NL	COL	2001
1.168	Larry Walker	NL	COL	1999	1.115	Lou Gehrig	AL	NY	1928
1.164	Ted Williams	AL	BOS	1946	1.113	Babe Ruth	AL	BOS	1919
1.162	Todd Helton	NL	COL	2000	1.112	Ted Williams	AL	BOS	1948
1.161	Sam Thompson	NL	PHI	1894	1.111	Larry Walker	NL	COL	2001
1.152	Stan Musial	NL	STL	1948					

Bill White

(226) Highest On Base Percentage plus Slugging Average in a Season by a Right-handed Batter (min. 3.1 PA per scheduled game)

1.245	Rogers Hornsby	NL	STL	1925		1.107	Edgar Martinez	AL	SEA	1995
1.222	Mark McGwire	NL	STL	1998		1.106	Nap Lajoie	AL	PHI	1901
1.218	Jimmie Foxx	AL	PHI	1932		1.106	Albert Pujols	NL	STL	2003
1.217	Frank E. Thomas	AL	CHI	1994		1.105	Hank Greenberg	AL	DET	1937
1.203	Rogers Hornsby	NL	STL	1924		1.105	Manny Ramirez	AL	CLE	1999
1.201	Jeff Bagwell	NL	HOU	1994		1.104	Joe Kelley	NL	BAL	1894
1.198	Mark McGwire	AL	OAK	1996		1.103	Ed Delahanty	NL	PHI	1896
1.196	Hugh Duffy	NL	BOS	1894		1.103	Hank Greenberg	AL	DET	1940
1.181	Rogers Hornsby	NL	STL	1922		1.102	Jimmie Foxx	AL	PHI	1934
1.180	Tip O'Neill	AA	STL	1887		1.102	Albert Pujols	NL	STL	2006
1.177	Hack Wilson	NL	CHI	1930		1.097	Rogers Hornsby	NL	STL	1921
1.174	Sammy Sosa	NL	CHI	2001		1.097	Manny Ramirez	AL	BOS	2002
1.166	Jimmie Foxx	AL	BOS	1938		1.096	Jimmie Foxx	AL	PHI	1935
1.158	Jimmie Foxx	AL	BOS	1939		1.091	Harry Heilmann	AL	DET	1927
1.154	Manny Ramirez	AL	BOS	2000		1.091	Albert Belle	AL	CLE	1995
1.153	Jimmie Foxx	AL	PHI	1933		1.090	Gary Sheffield	NL	FLA	1996
1.152	Albert Belle	AL	CLE	1994		1.089	Ralph Kiner	NL	PIT	1949
1.139	Rogers Hornsby	NL	CHI	1929		1.088	Jimmie Foxx	AL	PHI	1929
1.130	Rogers Hornsby	NL	BOS	1928		1.086	Rogers Hornsby	NL	STL	1923
1.130	Al Simmons	AL	PHI	1930		1.085	Al Simmons	AL	PHI	1931
1.122	Hank Greenberg	AL	DET	1938		1.085	Joe DiMaggio	AL	NY	1937
1.120	Mark McGwire	NL	STL	1999		1.085	Frank E. Thomas	AL	CHI	1996
1.119	Joe DiMaggio	AL	NY	1939		1.083	Joe DiMaggio	AL	NY	1941
1.117	Ed Delahanty	NL	PHI	1895		1.081	Gary Sheffield	NL	LA	2000
1.113	Harry Heilmann	AL	DET	1923		1.080	Mike Schmidt	NL	PHI	1981
1.110	Kevin Mitchell	NL	CIN	1994		1.080	Derrek Lee	NL	CHI	2005

(227) Highest On Base Percentage plus Slugging Average in a Season by a Switch-hitter (min. 3.1 PA per scheduled game)

1.177	Mickey Mantle	AL	NY	1957		.972	Chipper Jones	NL	ATL	2002
1.169	Mickey Mantle	AL	NY	1956		.971	Chili Davis	AL	CAL	1994
1.135	Mickey Mantle	AL	NY	1961		.971	Bernie Williams	AL	NY	1999
1.091	Mickey Mantle	AL	NY	1962		.970	Chipper Jones	NL	ATL	2000
1.074	Chipper Jones	NL	ATL	1999		.969	Carl Everett	NL	HOU	1999
1.051	Lance Berkman	NL	HOU	2001		.964	George Davis	NL	NY	1893
1.042	Mickey Mantle	AL	NY	1955		.963	Bobby Bonilla	NL-AL	NY-BAL	1995
1.041	Lance Berkman	NL	HOU	2006				NY (.984); BAL (.936)		
1.035	Mickey Mantle	AL	NY	1958		.959	Carl Everett	AL	BOS	2000
1.032	Chipper Jones	NL	ATL	2001		.957	Mickey Mantle	AL	NY	1960
1.028	Ken Caminiti	NL	SD	1996		.957	Bernie Williams	AL	NY	2000
1.016	Lance Berkman	NL	HOU	2004		.956	Tom McCreery	NL	LOU	1896
1.015	Mickey Mantle	AL	NY	1964		.956	Roberto Alomar	AL	CLE	2001
1.008	Ripper Collins	NL	STL	1934		.955	Tim Raines	NL	MON	1987
1.003	Reggie Smith	NL	LA	1977		.955	Roberto Alomar	AL	CLE	1999
.997	Bernie Williams	AL	NY	1998		.954	Mark Teixeira	AL	TEX	2005
.982	Lance Berkman	NL	HOU	2002		.952	Bernie Williams	AL	NY	1997
.982	Carlos Beltran	NL	NY	2006		.951	Chipper Jones	NL	ATL	1998
.976	George Davis	NL	NY	1894						

(228) Most RBI in a Season, before 1893

166	Sam Thompson	NL	DET	1887		118	Dan Brouthers	NL	BOS	1889
147	Cap Anson	NL	CHI	1886		117	Cap Anson	NL	CHI	1889
146	Hardy Richardson	PL	BOS	1890		115	Jim O'Rourke	PL	NY	1890
130	Roger Connor	NL	NY	1889		113	Dave Foutz	AA	BRO	1889
128	Oyster Burns	NL	BRO	1890		113	Spud Johnson	AA	COL	1890
124	Dave Orr	PL	BRO	1890		112	Dave Orr	AA	NY	1884
124	Dan Brouthers	NL	BRO	1892		112	Jerry Denny	NL	IND	1889
123	Tip O'Neill	AA	STL	1887		112	Henry Larkin	PL	CLE	1890
120	Jake Beckley	PL	PIT	1890		111	Sam Thompson	NL	DET	1889
120	Cap Anson	NL	CHI	1891		110	Tip O'Neill	AA	STL	1889
119	Harry Stovey	AA	PHI	1889		110	Hugh Duffy	AA	BOS	1891
118	Pete Browning	AA	LOU	1887		110	Duke Farrell	AA	BOS	1891

RBI before 1920 was not an official league statistic and were calculated retroactively.

(229) Most RBI in a Season, since 1893

191	Hack Wilson	NL	CHI	1930		155	Ken Williams	AL	STL	1922
184	Lou Gehrig	AL	NY	1931		155	Joe DiMaggio	AL	NY	1948
183	Hank Greenberg	AL	DET	1937		154	Babe Ruth	AL	NY	1929
175	Lou Gehrig	AL	NY	1927		154	Joe Medwick	NL	STL	1937
175	Jimmie Foxx	AL	BOS	1938		153	Babe Ruth	AL	NY	1930
174	Lou Gehrig	AL	NY	1930		153	Tommy Davis	NL	LA	1962
171	Babe Ruth	AL	NY	1921		152	Rogers Hornsby	NL	STL	1922
170	Chuck Klein	NL	PHI	1930		152	Lou Gehrig	AL	NY	1936
170	Hank Greenberg	AL	DET	1935		152	Albert Belle	AL	CHI	1998
169	Jimmie Foxx	AL	PHI	1932		151	Mel Ott	NL	NY	1929
167	Joe DiMaggio	AL	NY	1937		151	Lou Gehrig	AL	NY	1932
165	Sam Thompson	NL	PHI	1895		151	Al Simmons	AL	PHI	1932
165	Al Simmons	AL	PHI	1930		150	Hank Greenberg	AL	DET	1940
165	Lou Gehrig	AL	NY	1934		150	Andres Galarraga	NL	COL	1996
165	Manny Ramirez	AL	CLE	1999		150	Miguel Tejada	AL	BAL	2004
164	Babe Ruth	AL	NY	1927		149	Rogers Hornsby	NL	CHI	1929
163	Babe Ruth	AL	NY	1931		149	George Foster	NL	CIN	1977
163	Jimmie Foxx	AL	PHI	1933		149	Ryan Howard	NL	PHI	2006
162	Hal Trosky	AL	CLE	1936		148	Johnny Bench	NL	CIN	1970
160	Sammy Sosa	NL	CHI	2001		148	Albert Belle	AL	CLE	1996
159	Hack Wilson	NL	CHI	1929		148	Rafael Palmeiro	AL	TEX	1999
159	Lou Gehrig	AL	NY	1937		148	David Ortiz	AL	BOS	2005
159	Vern Stephens	AL	BOS	1949		147	Sam Thompson	NL	PHI	1894
159	Ted Williams	AL	BOS	1949		147	Ken Griffey Jr.	AL	SEA	1997
158	Sammy Sosa	NL	CHI	1998		147	Mark McGwire	NL	STL	1998
157	Al Simmons	AL	PHI	1929		147	Mark McGwire	NL	STL	1999
157	Juan Gonzalez	AL	TEX	1998		147	Todd Helton	NL	COL	2000
156	Jimmie Foxx	AL	PHI	1930						

RBI before 1920 was not an official league statistic and were calculated retroactively.

(230) Most RBI in a Season by a Left-handed Batter

184	Lou Gehrig	AL	NY	1931	146	Babe Ruth	AL	NY	1926
175	Lou Gehrig	AL	NY	1927	146	Ken Griffey Jr.	AL	SEA	1998
174	Lou Gehrig	AL	NY	1930	146	Todd Helton	NL	COL	2001
171	Babe Ruth	AL	NY	1921	145	Chuck Klein	NL	PHI	1929
170	Chuck Klein	NL	PHI	1930	145	Ted Williams	AL	BOS	1939
166	Sam Thompson	NL	DET	1887	145	Don Mattingly	AL	NY	1985
165	Sam Thompson	NL	PHI	1895	145	Carlos Delgado	AL	TOR	2003
165	Lou Gehrig	AL	NY	1934	143	Earl Averill	AL	CLE	1931
164	Babe Ruth	AL	NY	1927	143	Don Hurst	NL	PHI	1932
163	Babe Ruth	AL	NY	1931	143	Mo Vaughn	AL	BOS	1996
162	Hal Trosky	AL	CLE	1936	142	Lou Gehrig	AL	NY	1928
159	Lou Gehrig	AL	NY	1937	142	Babe Ruth	AL	NY	1928
159	Ted Williams	AL	BOS	1949	142	Hal Trosky	AL	CLE	1934
155	Ken Williams	AL	STL	1922	142	Roger Maris	AL	NY	1961
154	Babe Ruth	AL	NY	1929	142	Rafael Palmeiro	AL	BAL	1996
153	Babe Ruth	AL	NY	1930	142	Luis Gonzalez	NL	ARI	2001
152	Lou Gehrig	AL	NY	1936	141	Ted Kluszewski	NL	CIN	1954
151	Mel Ott	NL	NY	1929	141	Jim Gentile	AL	BAL	1961
151	Lou Gehrig	AL	NY	1932	141	Tino Martinez	AL	NY	1997
149	Ryan Howard	NL	PHI	2006	140	Ken Griffey Jr.	AL	SEA	1996
148	Rafael Palmeiro	AL	TEX	1999	139	Lou Gehrig	AL	NY	1933
147	Ken Griffey Jr.	AL	SEA	1997	139	David Ortiz	AL	BOS	2004
147	Todd Helton	NL	COL	2000					

GEORGE BRACE

Ernie Banks

(231) Most RBI in a Season by a Right-handed Batter

191	Hack Wilson	NL	CHI	1930		148	Johnny Bench	NL	CIN	1970
183	Hank Greenberg	AL	DET	1937		148	Albert Belle	AL	CLE	1996
175	Jimmie Foxx	AL	BOS	1938		147	Cap Anson	NL	CHI	1886
170	Hank Greenberg	AL	DET	1935		147	Mark McGwire	NL	STL	1998
169	Jimmie Foxx	AL	PHI	1932		147	Mark McGwire	NL	STL	1999
167	Joe DiMaggio	AL	NY	1937		146	Hardy Richardson	PL	BOS	1890
165	Al Simmons	AL	PHI	1930		146	Ed Delahanty	NL	PHI	1893
165	Manny Ramirez	AL	CLE	1999		146	Hank Greenberg	AL	DET	1938
163	Jimmie Foxx	AL	PHI	1933		145	Hugh Duffy	NL	BOS	1894
160	Sammy Sosa	NL	CHI	2001		145	Al Rosen	AL	CLE	1953
159	Hack Wilson	NL	CHI	1929		145	Manny Ramirez	AL	CLE	1998
159	Vern Stephens	AL	BOS	1949		145	Edgar Martinez	AL	SEA	2000
158	Sammy Sosa	NL	CHI	1998		144	Vern Stephens	AL	BOS	1950
157	Al Simmons	AL	PHI	1929		144	Walt Dropo	AL	BOS	1950
157	Juan Gonzalez	AL	TEX	1998		144	Juan Gonzalez	AL	TEX	1996
156	Jimmie Foxx	AL	PHI	1930		144	Vinny Castilla	NL	COL	1998
155	Joe DiMaggio	AL	NY	1948		144	Mike Sweeney	AL	KC	2000
154	Joe Medwick	NL	STL	1937		144	Manny Ramirez	AL	BOS	2005
153	Tommy Davis	NL	LA	1962		143	Rogers Hornsby	NL	STL	1925
152	Rogers Hornsby	NL	STL	1922		143	Jimmie Foxx	AL	BOS	1936
152	Albert Belle	AL	CHI	1998		143	Ernie Banks	NL	CHI	1959
151	Al Simmons	AL	PHI	1932		143	Frank E. Thomas	AL	CHI	2000
150	Hank Greenberg	AL	DET	1940		142	Roy Campanella	NL	BRO	1953
150	Andres Galarraga	NL	COL	1996		142	Orlando Cepeda	NL	SF	1961
150	Miguel Tejada	AL	BAL	2004		142	Matt Williams	NL	ARI	1999
149	Rogers Hornsby	NL	CHI	1929		142	Alex Rodriguez	AL	TEX	2002
149	George Foster	NL	CIN	1977						

(232) Most RBI in a Season by a Switch-hitter

144	Mark Teixeira	AL	TEX	2005		115	Bernie Williams	AL	NY	1999
136	Lance Berkman	NL	HOU	2006		114	Frankie Frisch	NL	STL	1930
135	George Davis	NL	NY	1897		114	Carlos Baerga	AL	CLE	1993
130	Walt Wilmot	NL	CHI	1894		112	Chili Davis	AL	CAL	1993
130	Mickey Mantle	AL	NY	1956		112	Todd Hundley	NL	NY	1996
130	Ken Caminiti	NL	SD	1996		112	Mark Teixeira	AL	TEX	2004
128	Ripper Collins	NL	STL	1934		111	Candy LaChance	NL	BRO	1895
128	Mickey Mantle	AL	NY	1961		111	Frankie Frisch	NL	NY	1923
128	Lance Berkman	NL	HOU	2002		111	Mickey Mantle	AL	NY	1964
126	Lance Berkman	NL	HOU	2001		111	Wes Parker	NL	LA	1970
124	Eddie Murray	AL	BAL	1985		111	Ken Singleton	AL	BAL	1979
122	Ripper Collins	NL	STL	1935		111	Eddie Murray	AL	BAL	1983
121	Bernie Williams	AL	NY	2000		111	Chipper Jones	NL	ATL	1997
120	Bobby Bonilla	NL	PIT	1990		111	Chipper Jones	NL	ATL	2000
120	Roberto Alomar	AL	CLE	1999		110	Duke Farrell	AA	BOS	1891
119	George Davis	NL	NY	1893		110	Eddie Murray	AL	BAL	1982
119	Ruben Sierra	AL	TEX	1989		110	Eddie Murray	AL	BAL	1984
117	Howard Johnson	NL	NY	1991		110	Tom Herr	NL	STL	1985
117	Tony Clark	AL	DET	1997		110	Mickey Tettleton	AL	DET	1993
116	Eddie Murray	AL	BAL	1980		110	Chipper Jones	NL	ATL	1996
116	Ruben Sierra	AL	TEX	1991		110	Chipper Jones	NL	ATL	1999
116	Bobby Bonilla	AL	BAL	1996		110	Mark Teixeira	AL	TEX	2006
116	Carlos Beltran	NL	NY	2006						

(233) Most Runs in a Season, before 1893

177	Tom Brown	AA	BOS	1891		140	Jim McTamany	AA	COL	1890
167	Tip O'Neill	AA	STL	1887		139	Dan Brouthers	NL	DET	1886
163	Arlie Latham	AA	STL	1887		139	Bid McPhee	AA	CIN	1886
161	Hugh Duffy	PL	CHI	1890		139	Charlie Comiskey	AA	STL	1887
160	Fred Dunlap	UA	STL	1884		139	Hub Collins	AA	BRO	1889
155	King Kelly	NL	CHI	1886		137	Bid McPhee	AA	CIN	1887
153	Dan Brouthers	NL	DET	1887		137	Pete Browning	AA	LOU	1887
152	Arlie Latham	AA	STL	1886		137	Herman Long	AA	KC	1889
152	Harry Stovey	AA	PHI	1889		137	Tommy McCarthy	AA	STL	1890
152	Mike Griffin	AA	BAL	1889		136	Tommy McCarthy	AA	STL	1889
150	George Gore	NL	CHI	1886		136	George Van Haltren	AA	BAL	1891
148	Hub Collins	NL	BRO	1890		136	Cupid Childs	NL	CLE	1892
147	Mike Tiernan	NL	NY	1889		135	Bill Gleason	AA	STL	1887
146	William "Darby" O'Brien	AA	BRO	1889		135	Jack Rowe	NL	DET	1887
146	Tom Brown	PL	BOS	1890		135	Denny Lyons	AA	PHI	1889
144	Hugh Duffy	NL	CHI	1889		134	George Pinkney	AA	BRO	1888
144	Billy Hamilton	AA	KC	1889		134	Curt Welch	AA	PHI	1889
142	Mike Griffin	AA	BAL	1887		134	John Ward	PL	BRO	1890
142	Harry Stovey	PL	BOS	1890		134	Cliff Carroll	NL	CHI	1890
141	Billy Hamilton	NL	PHI	1891		134	Dummy Hoy	AA	STL	1891
140	Tom Poorman	AA	PHI	1887		134	Hugh Duffy	AA	BOS	1891
140	Jimmy Ryan	NL	CHI	1889						

(234) Most Runs in a Season, since 1893

198	Billy Hamilton	NL	PHI	1894	151	Babe Ruth	AL	NY	1923
177	Babe Ruth	AL	NY	1921	151	Jimmie Foxx	AL	PHI	1932
167	Lou Gehrig	AL	NY	1936	151	Joe DiMaggio	AL	NY	1937
166	Billy Hamilton	NL	PHI	1895	150	Bill Dahlen	NL	CHI	1894
165	Joe Kelley	NL	BAL	1894	150	Jake Stenzel	NL	PIT	1894
165	Willie Keeler	NL	BAL	1894	150	Babe Ruth	AL	NY	1930
163	Babe Ruth	AL	NY	1928	150	Ted Williams	AL	BOS	1949
163	Lou Gehrig	AL	NY	1931	149	Herman Long	NL	BOS	1893
162	Willie Keeler	NL	BAL	1895	149	Ed Delahanty	NL	PHI	1895
160	Hugh Duffy	NL	BOS	1894	149	Lou Gehrig	AL	NY	1927
160	Jesse Burkett	NL	CLE	1896	149	Babe Ruth	AL	NY	1931
159	Hughie Jennings	NL	BAL	1895	148	Ed Delahanty	NL	PHI	1894
158	Bobby Lowe	NL	BOS	1894	148	Joe Kelley	NL	BAL	1895
158	Babe Ruth	AL	NY	1920	148	Joe Kelley	NL	BAL	1896
158	Babe Ruth	AL	NY	1927	147	Hugh Duffy	NL	BOS	1893
158	Chuck Klein	NL	PHI	1930	147	Patsy Donovan	NL	PIT	1894
156	John McGraw	NL	BAL	1894	147	Ty Cobb	AL	DET	1911
156	Rogers Hornsby	NL	CHI	1929	146	Hack Wilson	NL	CHI	1930
155	Kiki Cuyler	NL	CHI	1930	146	Rickey Henderson	AL	NY	1985
153	Jesse Burkett	NL	CLE	1895	146	Craig Biggio	NL	HOU	1997
153	Willie Keeler	NL	BAL	1896	146	Sammy Sosa	NL	CHI	2001
153	Billy Hamilton	NL	BOS	1896	145	Ed Delahanty	NL	PHI	1893
152	Billy Hamilton	NL	BOS	1897	145	Cupid Childs	NL	CLE	1893
152	Lefty O'Doul	NL	PHI	1929	145	Jesse Burkett	NL	CLE	1893
152	Woody English	NL	CHI	1930	145	Willie Keeler	NL	BAL	1897
152	Al Simmons	AL	PHI	1930	145	Nap Lajoie	AL	PHI	1901
152	Chuck Klein	NL	PHI	1932	145	Harlond Clift	AL	STL	1936
152	Jeff Bagwell	NL	HOU	2000					

Sam Crawford

(235) Most Runs in a Season by a Left-handed Batter

198	Billy Hamilton	NL	PHI	1894		149	Babe Ruth	AL	NY	1931
177	Tom Brown	AA	BOS	1891		147	Mike Tiernan	NL	NY	1889
177	Babe Ruth	AL	NY	1921		147	Patsy Donovan	NL	PIT	1894
167	Lou Gehrig	AL	NY	1936		147	Ty Cobb	AL	DET	1911
166	Billy Hamilton	NL	PHI	1895		146	Tom Brown	PL	BOS	1890
165	Willie Keeler	NL	BAL	1894		145	Cupid Childs	NL	CLE	1893
163	Babe Ruth	AL	NY	1928		145	Jesse Burkett	NL	CLE	1893
163	Lou Gehrig	AL	NY	1931		145	Willie Keeler	NL	BAL	1897
162	Willie Keeler	NL	BAL	1895		144	Billy Hamilton	AA	KC	1889
160	Jesse Burkett	NL	CLE	1896		144	Ty Cobb	AL	DET	1915
158	Babe Ruth	AL	NY	1920		144	Charlie Gehringer	AL	DET	1930
158	Babe Ruth	AL	NY	1927		144	Charlie Gehringer	AL	DET	1936
158	Chuck Klein	NL	PHI	1930		143	Cupid Childs	NL	CLE	1894
156	John McGraw	NL	BAL	1894		143	John McGraw	NL	BAL	1898
153	Dan Brouthers	NL	DET	1887		143	Babe Ruth	AL	NY	1924
153	Jesse Burkett	NL	CLE	1895		143	Lou Gehrig	AL	NY	1930
153	Willie Keeler	NL	BAL	1896		143	Babe Herman	NL	BRO	1930
153	Billy Hamilton	NL	BOS	1896		143	Earle Combs	AL	NY	1932
152	Mike Griffin	AA	BAL	1889		143	Red Rolfe	AL	NY	1937
152	Billy Hamilton	NL	BOS	1897		143	Lenny Dykstra	NL	PHI	1993
152	Lefty O'Doul	NL	PHI	1929		143	Larry Walker	NL	COL	1997
152	Chuck Klein	NL	PHI	1932		142	Mike Griffin	AA	BAL	1887
151	Babe Ruth	AL	NY	1923		142	Jesse Burkett	NL	STL	1901
150	George Gore	NL	CHI	1886		142	Paul Waner	NL	PIT	1928
150	Babe Ruth	AL	NY	1930		142	Ted Williams	AL	BOS	1946
150	Ted Williams	AL	BOS	1949		141	Billy Hamilton	NL	PHI	1891
149	Herman Long	NL	BOS	1893		141	Ted Williams	AL	BOS	1942
149	Lou Gehrig	AL	NY	1927						

(236) Most Runs in a Season by a Right-handed Batter

167	Tip O'Neill	AA	STL	1887		147	Hugh Duffy	NL	BOS	1893
165	Joe Kelley	NL	BAL	1894		146	William "Darby" O'Brien	AA	BRO	1889
163	Arlie Latham	AA	STL	1887		146	Hack Wilson	NL	CHI	1930
161	Hugh Duffy	PL	CHI	1890		146	Rickey Henderson	AL	NY	1985
160	Fred Dunlap	UA	STL	1884		146	Craig Biggio	NL	HOU	1997
160	Hugh Duffy	NL	BOS	1894		146	Sammy Sosa	NL	CHI	2001
159	Hughie Jennings	NL	BAL	1895		145	Ed Delahanty	NL	PHI	1893
158	Bobby Lowe	NL	BOS	1894		145	Nap Lajoie	AL	PHI	1901
156	Rogers Hornsby	NL	CHI	1929		145	Harlond Clift	AL	STL	1936
155	King Kelly	NL	CHI	1886		144	Hugh Duffy	NL	CHI	1889
155	Kiki Cuyler	NL	CHI	1930		144	Kiki Cuyler	NL	PIT	1925
152	Arlie Latham	AA	STL	1886		144	Al Simmons	AL	PHI	1932
152	Harry Stovey	AA	PHI	1889		144	Hank Greenberg	AL	DET	1938
152	Al Simmons	AL	PHI	1930		143	Jeff Bagwell	NL	HOU	1999
152	Woody English	NL	CHI	1930		142	Harry Stovey	PL	BOS	1890
152	Jeff Bagwell	NL	HOU	2000		142	Ellis Burks	NL	COL	1996
151	Jimmie Foxx	AL	PHI	1932		141	Rogers Hornsby	NL	STL	1922
151	Joe DiMaggio	AL	NY	1937		141	Alex Rodriguez	AL	SEA	1996
150	Bill Dahlen	NL	CHI	1894		140	Jimmy Ryan	NL	CHI	1889
150	Jake Stenzel	NL	PIT	1894		140	Jim McTamany	AA	COL	1890
149	Ed Delahanty	NL	PHI	1895		140	Chuck Knoblauch	AL	MIN	1996
148	Hub Collins	NL	BRO	1890		139	Bid McPhee	AA	CIN	1886
148	Ed Delahanty	NL	PHI	1894		139	Charlie Comiskey	AA	STL	1887
148	Joe Kelley	NL	BAL	1895		139	Hub Collins	AA	BRO	1889
148	Joe Kelley	NL	BAL	1896		139	Jimmie Foxx	AL	BOS	1938

Chuck Klein

(237) Most Runs in a Season by a Switch-hitter

140	Max Carey	NL	PIT	1922	121	Mickey Mantle	AL	NY	1955
138	Roberto Alomar	AL	CLE	1999	121	Mickey Mantle	AL	NY	1957
136	Walt Wilmot	NL	CHI	1894	121	Vince Coleman	NL	STL	1987
135	Tom Daly	NL	BRO	1894	121	Ray Durham	AL	CHI	2000
134	Cliff Carroll	NL	CHI	1890	121	Carlos Beltran	AL-NLKC-HOU		2004
133	Augie Galan	NL	CHI	1935			KC (51); HOU (70)		
133	Willie Wilson	AL	KC	1980	120	Bob Bescher	NL	CIN	1912
133	Tim Raines	NL	MON	1983	120	Max Carey	NL	PIT	1923
132	Mickey Mantle	AL	NY	1956	120	Pete Rose	NL	CIN	1969
132	Mickey Mantle	AL	NY	1961	120	Pete Rose	NL	CIN	1970
132	Roberto Alomar	AL	BAL	1996	119	Lu Blue	AL	CHI	1931
131	Lu Blue	AL	DET	1922	119	Mickey Mantle	AL	NY	1960
130	Maury Wills	NL	LA	1962	119	Tony Phillips	AL	CAL	1995
130	Pete Rose	NL	CIN	1976	119	Tony Phillips	AL	CHI	1996
130	Rafael Furcal	NL	ATL	2003	119	Jimmy Rollins	NL	PHI	2004
129	Mickey Mantle	AL	NY	1954	118	Chipper Jones	NL	ATL	2000
127	Mickey Mantle	AL	NY	1958	117	Miller Huggins	NL	CIN	1905
127	Carlos Beltran	NL	NY	2006	117	Dave Bancroft	NL	NY	1922
127	Jimmy Rollins	NL	PHI	2006	117	Pete Rose	NL	CIN	1965
126	Donie Bush	AL	DET	1911	116	Frankie Frisch	NL	NY	1923
126	Ray Durham	AL	CHI	1998	116	Lu Blue	AL	STL	1928
125	George Davis	NL	NY	1894	116	Ripper Collins	NL	STL	1934
125	Jim Gilliam	NL	BRO	1953	116	Devon White	AL	TOR	1993
123	Tim Raines	NL	MON	1987	116	Chipper Jones	NL	ATL	1999
123	Chipper Jones	NL	ATL	1998	116	Bernie Williams	AL	NY	1999
122	Jose Reyes	NL	NY	2006	115	George Davis	NL	CLE	1891
121	Frankie Frisch	NL	NY	1921	115	Pete Rose	NL	CIN	1973
121	Dave Bancroft	NL	NY	1921	115	Eddie Murray	AL	BAL	1983
121	Frankie Frisch	NL	NY	1924	115	Tim Raines	NL	MON	1985
121	Frankie Frisch	NL	STL	1930					

(238) Most Extra-base Hits in a Season, before 1893

85	Tip O'Neill	AA	STL	1887		59	Jimmy Ryan	NL	CHI	1888
70	Harry Stovey	AA	PHI	1889		59	Hugh Duffy	PL	CHI	1890
69	Jake Beckley	PL	PIT	1890		59	Mike Tiernan	NL	NY	1890
68	Dan Brouthers	NL	DET	1887		58	Jocko Milligan	AA	PHI	1891
67	Harry Stovey	NL	BOS	1891		58	Mike Tiernan	NL	NY	1891
66	Dan Brouthers	NL	DET	1886		57	Jerry Denny	NL	IND	1887
65	Roger Connor	NL	NY	1887		57	John Reilly	NL	CIN	1890
63	Dave Orr	AA	NY	1886		57	Ed Delahanty	NL	PHI	1892
63	Denny Lyons	AA	PHI	1887		56	Ned Williamson	NL	CHI	1883
62	Sam Thompson	NL	DET	1887		56	Dave Orr	AA	NY	1885
62	Jimmy Ryan	NL	CHI	1889		56	Roger Connor	NL	NY	1886
62	Roger Connor	NL	NY	1889		56	Cap Anson	NL	CHI	1886
61	Dan Brouthers	NL	BUF	1883		56	Tom Brown	AA	BOS	1891
61	Oyster Burns	AA	BAL	1887		55	John Morrill	NL	BOS	1883
61	Dick Johnston	NL	BOS	1888		55	Harry Stovey	AA	PHI	1884
60	Fred Dunlap	UA	STL	1884		55	George Wood	NL	PHI	1887
60	Sam Thompson	NL	PHI	1889		55	Pete Browning	AA	LOU	1887
60	Roger Connor	NL	PHI	1892		55	John Reilly	AA	CIN	1888
59	Henry Larkin	AA	PHI	1885		55	King Kelly	NL	BOS	1889
59	John Reilly	AA	CIN	1887		55	Dan Brouthers	NL	BRO	1892

(239) Most Extra-base Hits in a Season, since 1893

119	Babe Ruth	AL	NY	1921		97	Juan Gonzalez	AL	TEX	1998
117	Lou Gehrig	AL	NY	1927		96	Hank Greenberg	AL	DET	1934
107	Chuck Klein	NL	PHI	1930		96	Hal Trosky	AL	CLE	1936
107	Barry Bonds	NL	SF	2001		96	Joe DiMaggio	AL	NY	1937
105	Todd Helton	NL	COL	2001		95	Lou Gehrig	AL	NY	1934
103	Chuck Klein	NL	PHI	1932		95	Joe Medwick	NL	STL	1936
103	Hank Greenberg	AL	DET	1937		95	Albert Pujols	NL	STL	2003
103	Stan Musial	NL	STL	1948		94	Rogers Hornsby	NL	CHI	1929
103	Albert Belle	AL	CLE	1995		94	Chuck Klein	NL	PHI	1929
103	Todd Helton	NL	COL	2000		94	Babe Herman	NL	BRO	1930
103	Sammy Sosa	NL	CHI	2001		94	Jimmie Foxx	AL	PHI	1933
102	Rogers Hornsby	NL	STL	1922		94	Lance Berkman	NL	HOU	2001
100	Lou Gehrig	AL	NY	1930		93	Jim Bottomley	NL	STL	1928
100	Jimmie Foxx	AL	PHI	1932		93	Al Simmons	AL	PHI	1930
100	Luis Gonzalez	NL	ARI	2001		93	Lou Gehrig	AL	NY	1936
99	Babe Ruth	AL	NY	1920		93	Ellis Burks	NL	COL	1996
99	Babe Ruth	AL	NY	1923		93	Ken Griffey Jr.	AL	SEA	1997
99	Hank Greenberg	AL	DET	1940		92	Babe Ruth	AL	NY	1924
99	Larry Walker	NL	COL	1997		92	Lou Gehrig	AL	NY	1931
99	Albert Belle	AL	CHI	1998		92	Jimmie Foxx	AL	BOS	1938
99	Carlos Delgado	AL	TOR	2000		92	Stan Musial	NL	STL	1953
99	Albert Pujols	NL	STL	2004		92	Hank Aaron	NL	MIL	1959
99	Derrek Lee	NL	CHI	2005		92	Frank Robinson	NL	CIN	1962
98	Hank Greenberg	AL	DET	1935		92	Brady Anderson	AL	BAL	1996
97	Babe Ruth	AL	NY	1927		92	Ken Griffey Jr.	AL	SEA	1998
97	Hack Wilson	NL	CHI	1930		92	Alfonso Soriano	AL	NY	2002
97	Joe Medwick	NL	STL	1937		92	Grady Sizemore	AL	CLE	2006

(240) Most Extra-base Hits in a Season by a Left-handed Batter

119	Babe Ruth	AL	NY	1921	91	Babe Ruth	AL	NY	1928
117	Lou Gehrig	AL	NY	1927	91	David Ortiz	AL	BOS	2004
107	Chuck Klein	NL	PHI	1930	90	Stan Musial	NL	STL	1949
107	Barry Bonds	NL	SF	2001	90	Willie Stargell	NL	PIT	1973
105	Todd Helton	NL	COL	2001	89	Hal Trosky	AL	CLE	1934
103	Chuck Klein	NL	PHI	1932	89	Duke Snider	NL	BRO	1954
103	Stan Musial	NL	STL	1948	88	Barry Bonds	NL	SF	1993
103	Todd Helton	NL	COL	2000	88	Barry Bonds	NL	SF	1998
100	Lou Gehrig	AL	NY	1930	88	Garret Anderson	AL	ANA	2002
100	Luis Gonzalez	NL	ARI	2001	88	David Ortiz	AL	BOS	2005
99	Babe Ruth	AL	NY	1920	87	Tris Speaker	AL	CLE	1923
99	Babe Ruth	AL	NY	1923	87	Lou Gehrig	AL	NY	1928
99	Larry Walker	NL	COL	1997	87	Charlie Gehringer	AL	DET	1936
99	Carlos Delgado	AL	TOR	2000	87	Johnny Mize	NL	STL	1940
97	Babe Ruth	AL	NY	1927	87	Shawn Green	AL	TOR	1999
96	Hal Trosky	AL	CLE	1936	87	Jason Giambi	AL	OAK	2001
95	Lou Gehrig	AL	NY	1934	87	Todd Helton	NL	COL	2003
94	Chuck Klein	NL	PHI	1929	86	George Sisler	AL	STL	1920
94	Babe Herman	NL	BRO	1930	86	Babe Ruth	AL	NY	1930
93	Jim Bottomley	NL	STL	1928	86	Wally Moses	AL	PHI	1937
93	Lou Gehrig	AL	NY	1936	86	Johnny Mize	NL	STL	1939
93	Ken Griffey Jr.	AL	SEA	1997	86	Ted Williams	AL	BOS	1939
92	Babe Ruth	AL	NY	1924	86	Stan Musial	NL	STL	1946
92	Lou Gehrig	AL	NY	1931	86	Eddie Mathews	NL	MIL	1953
92	Stan Musial	NL	STL	1953	86	Reggie Jackson	AL	OAK	1969
92	Brady Anderson	AL	BAL	1996	86	Don Mattingly	AL	NY	1985
92	Ken Griffey Jr.	AL	SEA	1998	86	Don Mattingly	AL	NY	1986
92	Grady Sizemore	AL	CLE	2006	86	Ken Griffey Jr.	AL	SEA	1993

(241) Most Extra-base Hits in a Season by a Right-handed Batter

103	Hank Greenberg	AL	DET	1937	91	Mark McGwire	NL	STL	1998
103	Albert Belle	AL	CLE	1995	90	Rogers Hornsby	NL	STL	1925
103	Sammy Sosa	NL	CHI	2001	90	Willie Mays	NL	SF	1962
102	Rogers Hornsby	NL	STL	1922	89	Albert Belle	AL	CLE	1996
100	Jimmie Foxx	AL	PHI	1932	89	Andres Galarraga	NL	COL	1996
99	Hank Greenberg	AL	DET	1940	89	Sammy Sosa	NL	CHI	1999
99	Albert Belle	AL	CHI	1998	89	Sammy Sosa	NL	CHI	2000
99	Albert Pujols	NL	STL	2004	89	Richard Hidalgo	NL	HOU	2000
99	Derrek Lee	NL	CHI	2005	89	Alfonso Soriano	NL	WAS	2006
98	Hank Greenberg	AL	DET	1935	88	Joe DiMaggio	AL	NY	1936
97	Hack Wilson	NL	CHI	1930	88	Albert Pujols	NL	STL	2001
97	Joe Medwick	NL	STL	1937	87	Kiki Cuyler	NL	PIT	1925
97	Juan Gonzalez	AL	TEX	1998	87	Willie Mays	NL	NY	1954
96	Hank Greenberg	AL	DET	1934	87	Robin Yount	AL	MIL	1982
96	Joe DiMaggio	AL	NY	1937	87	Kevin Mitchell	NL	SF	1989
95	Joe Medwick	NL	STL	1936	87	Mark McGwire	NL	STL	1999
95	Albert Pujols	NL	STL	2003	87	Frank E. Thomas	AL	CHI	2000
94	Rogers Hornsby	NL	CHI	1929	87	Alex Rodriguez	AL	TEX	2001
94	Jimmie Foxx	AL	PHI	1933	87	Vernon Wells	AL	TOR	2003
93	Al Simmons	AL	PHI	1930	87	Manny Ramirez	AL	BOS	2004
93	Ellis Burks	NL	COL	1996	86	Hal McRae	AL	KC	1977
92	Jimmie Foxx	AL	BOS	1938	86	Jim Rice	AL	BOS	1978
92	Hank Aaron	NL	MIL	1959	86	Sammy Sosa	NL	CHI	1998
92	Frank Robinson	NL	CIN	1962	86	Jeff Bagwell	NL	HOU	2001
92	Alfonso Soriano	AL	NY	2002	86	Magglio Ordonez	AL	CHI	2002
91	Alex Rodriguez	AL	SEA	1996	86	Alex Rodriguez	AL	TEX	2002

Larry Walker

(242) Most Extra-base Hits in a Season by a Switch-hitter

94	Lance Berkman	NL	HOU	2001		74	Lance Berkman	NL	HOU	2006
87	Ripper Collins	NL	STL	1934		73	Mickey Mantle	AL	NY	1955
87	Chipper Jones	NL	ATL	1999		73	Bobby Bonilla	NL-AL	NY-BAL	1995
87	Mark Teixeira	AL	TEX	2005					NY (47); BAL (26)	
83	Carlos Beltran	AL-NL	KC-HOU	2004		73	Bernie Williams	AL	NY	2000
		KC (36); HOU (47)				73	Lance Berkman	NL	HOU	2004
80	Howard Johnson	NL	NY	1989		72	Ray Durham	AL	CHI	2001
80	Carlos Beltran	AL	KC	2002		71	Bobby Bonilla	NL	PIT	1989
80	Carlos Beltran	NL	NY	2006		71	Tony Clark	AL	DET	1998
79	Mickey Mantle	AL	NY	1956		70	Eddie Murray	AL	BAL	1980
79	Ken Caminiti	NL	SD	1996		70	Carl Everett	AL	BOS	2000
79	Lance Berkman	NL	HOU	2002		70	Dmitri Young	AL	DET	2003
79	Jimmy Rollins	NL	PHI	2006		69	Bill Kenworthy	FL	KC	1914
79	Mark Teixeira	AL	TEX	2006		69	Ripper Collins	NL	STL	1935
78	Ruben Sierra	AL	TEX	1989		69	Eddie Murray	AL	BAL	1985
78	Bobby Bonilla	NL	PIT	1990		69	Ruben Sierra	AL	TEX	1987
77	Jose Vidro	NL	MON	2000		69	Roberto Alomar	AL	BAL	1996
76	Mickey Mantle	AL	NY	1961		69	Bill Mueller	AL	BOS	2003
76	Howard Johnson	NL	NY	1991		69	Jimmy Rollins	NL	PHI	2004
76	Chipper Jones	NL	ATL	2001		68	Mickey Mantle	AL	NY	1957
76	Jose Cruz Jr.	AL	TOR	2001		68	Bobby Bonilla	NL	PIT	1991
75	Chipper Jones	NL	ATL	2000		68	Chipper Jones	NL	ATL	1998
74	Ruben Sierra	AL	TEX	1991		68	Jose Cruz Jr.	AL	TOR	2000
74	Todd Hundley	NL	NY	1996		68	Jose Valentin	AL	CHI	2000
74	Mark Teixeira	AL	TEX	2004		68	Carlos Beltran	AL	KC	2001

(243) Most Total Bases in a Season, before 1893

357	Tip O'Neill	AA	STL	1887		280	Hugh Duffy	PL	CHI	1890
308	Sam Thompson	NL	DET	1887		279	Fred Dunlap	UA	STL	1884
301	Dave Orr	AA	NY	1886		276	Dick Johnston	NL	BOS	1888
299	Pete Browning	AA	LOU	1887		276	Jake Beckley	PL	PIT	1890
298	Denny Lyons	AA	PHI	1887		276	Tom Brown	AA	BOS	1891
297	Jimmy Ryan	NL	CHI	1889		274	Cap Anson	NL	CHI	1886
292	Harry Stovey	AA	PHI	1889		274	Mike Tiernan	NL	NY	1890
286	Oyster Burns	AA	BAL	1887		274	Hardy Richardson	PL	BOS	1890
284	Dan Brouthers	NL	DET	1886		272	Jack Glasscock	NL	IND	1889
283	Jimmy Ryan	NL	CHI	1888		271	Hardy Richardson	NL	DET	1886
282	Billy Shindle	PL	PHI	1890		271	Harry Stovey	NL	BOS	1891
282	Dan Brouthers	NL	BRO	1892		271	Bug Holliday	NL	CIN	1892
281	Dan Brouthers	NL	DET	1887		268	Mike Tiernan	NL	NY	1891
280	Bug Holliday	AA	CIN	1889		265	Roger Connor	PL	NY	1890

(244) Most Total Bases in a Season, since 1893

457	Babe Ruth	AL	NY	1921		405	Hal Trosky	AL	CLE	1936
450	Rogers Hornsby	NL	STL	1922		405	Todd Helton	NL	COL	2000
447	Lou Gehrig	AL	NY	1927		403	Jimmie Foxx	AL	PHI	1933
445	Chuck Klein	NL	PHI	1930		403	Lou Gehrig	AL	NY	1936
438	Jimmie Foxx	AL	PHI	1932		402	Todd Helton	NL	COL	2001
429	Stan Musial	NL	STL	1948		400	Hank Aaron	NL	MIL	1959
425	Sammy Sosa	NL	CHI	2001		399	George Sisler	AL	STL	1920
423	Hack Wilson	NL	CHI	1930		399	Babe Ruth	AL	NY	1923
420	Chuck Klein	NL	PHI	1932		399	Albert Belle	AL	CHI	1998
419	Lou Gehrig	AL	NY	1930		398	Jimmie Foxx	AL	BOS	1938
419	Luis Gonzalez	NL	ARI	2001		397	Lefty O'Doul	NL	PHI	1929
418	Joe DiMaggio	AL	NY	1937		397	Hank Greenberg	AL	DET	1937
417	Babe Ruth	AL	NY	1927		397	Sammy Sosa	NL	CHI	1999
416	Babe Herman	NL	BRO	1930		394	Albert Pujols	NL	STL	2003
416	Sammy Sosa	NL	CHI	1998		393	Ken Griffey Jr.	AL	SEA	1997
411	Barry Bonds	NL	SF	2001		393	Alex Rodriguez	AL	TEX	2001
410	Lou Gehrig	AL	NY	1931		393	Derrek Lee	NL	CHI	2005
409	Rogers Hornsby	NL	CHI	1929		392	Al Simmons	AL	PHI	1925
409	Lou Gehrig	AL	NY	1934		392	Bill Terry	NL	NY	1930
409	Larry Walker	NL	COL	1997		392	Al Simmons	AL	PHI	1930
406	Joe Medwick	NL	STL	1937		392	Ellis Burks	NL	COL	1996
406	Jim Rice	AL	BOS	1978		391	Babe Ruth	AL	NY	1924
405	Chuck Klein	NL	PHI	1929						

(245) Most Total Bases in a Season by a Left-handed Batter

457	Babe Ruth	AL	NY	1921		392	Bill Terry	NL	NY	1930
447	Lou Gehrig	AL	NY	1927		391	Babe Ruth	AL	NY	1924
445	Chuck Klein	NL	PHI	1930		388	Babe Ruth	AL	NY	1920
429	Stan Musial	NL	STL	1948		388	Don Mattingly	AL	NY	1986
420	Chuck Klein	NL	PHI	1932		387	Ken Griffey Jr.	AL	SEA	1998
419	Lou Gehrig	AL	NY	1930		385	Earl Averill	AL	CLE	1936
419	Luis Gonzalez	NL	ARI	2001		383	Ryan Howard	NL	PHI	2006
417	Babe Ruth	AL	NY	1927		382	Stan Musial	NL	STL	1949
416	Babe Herman	NL	BRO	1930		380	Babe Ruth	AL	NY	1928
411	Barry Bonds	NL	SF	2001		379	Babe Ruth	AL	NY	1930
410	Lou Gehrig	AL	NY	1931		378	Duke Snider	NL	BRO	1954
409	Lou Gehrig	AL	NY	1934		378	Carlos Delgado	AL	TOR	2000
409	Larry Walker	NL	COL	1997		374	Babe Ruth	AL	NY	1931
405	Chuck Klein	NL	PHI	1929		374	Hal Trosky	AL	CLE	1934
405	Hal Trosky	AL	CLE	1936		374	Tony Oliva	AL	MIN	1964
405	Todd Helton	NL	COL	2000		373	Bill Terry	NL	NY	1932
403	Lou Gehrig	AL	NY	1936		373	Billy Williams	NL	CHI	1970
402	Todd Helton	NL	COL	2001		370	Lou Gehrig	AL	NY	1932
399	George Sisler	AL	STL	1920		370	Duke Snider	NL	BRO	1953
399	Babe Ruth	AL	NY	1923		370	Don Mattingly	AL	NY	1985
397	Lefty O'Doul	NL	PHI	1929		370	Mo Vaughn	AL	BOS	1996
393	Ken Griffey Jr.	AL	SEA	1997		370	Shawn Green	NL	LA	2001

(246) Most Total Bases in a Season by a Right-handed Batter

450	Rogers Hornsby	NL	STL	1922		388	George Foster	NL	CIN	1977
438	Jimmie Foxx	AL	PHI	1932		384	Hank Greenberg	AL	DET	1940
425	Sammy Sosa	NL	CHI	2001		384	Alex Rodriguez	AL	SEA	1998
423	Hack Wilson	NL	CHI	1930		383	Mark McGwire	NL	STL	1998
418	Joe DiMaggio	AL	NY	1937		383	Sammy Sosa	NL	CHI	2000
416	Sammy Sosa	NL	CHI	1998		382	Willie Mays	NL	NY	1955
409	Rogers Hornsby	NL	CHI	1929		382	Willie Mays	NL	SF	1962
406	Joe Medwick	NL	STL	1937		382	Jim Rice	AL	BOS	1977
406	Jim Rice	AL	BOS	1978		382	Juan Gonzalez	AL	TEX	1998
403	Jimmie Foxx	AL	PHI	1933		381	Rogers Hornsby	NL	STL	1925
400	Hank Aaron	NL	MIL	1959		381	Alfonso Soriano	AL	NY	2002
399	Albert Belle	AL	CHI	1998		380	Hank Greenberg	AL	DET	1938
398	Jimmie Foxx	AL	BOS	1938		380	Frank Robinson	NL	CIN	1962
397	Hank Greenberg	AL	DET	1937		380	Vinny Castilla	NL	COL	1998
397	Sammy Sosa	NL	CHI	1999		379	Ernie Banks	NL	CHI	1958
394	Albert Pujols	NL	STL	2003		379	Alex Rodriguez	AL	SEA	1996
393	Alex Rodriguez	AL	TEX	2001		379	Vladimir Guerrero	NL	MON	2000
393	Derrek Lee	NL	CHI	2005		378	Rogers Hornsby	NL	STL	1921
392	Al Simmons	AL	PHI	1925		377	Willie Mays	NL	NY	1954
392	Al Simmons	AL	PHI	1930		377	Albert Belle	AL	CLE	1995
392	Ellis Burks	NL	COL	1996		376	Andres Galarraga	NL	COL	1996
389	Hank Greenberg	AL	DET	1935		376	Adrian Beltre	NL	LA	2004
389	Alex Rodriguez	AL	TEX	2002		375	Albert Belle	AL	CLE	1996
389	Albert Pujols	NL	STL	2004						

(247) Most Total Bases in a Season by a Switch-hitter

376	Mickey Mantle	AL	NY	1956		323	Mark Teixeira	AL	TEX	2006
370	Mark Teixeira	AL	TEX	2005		322	Eddie Murray	AL	BAL	1980
369	Ripper Collins	NL	STL	1934		321	Pete Rose	NL	CIN	1969
359	Chipper Jones	NL	ATL	1999		319	Howard Johnson	NL	NY	1989
358	Lance Berkman	NL	HOU	2001		319	Bobby Bonilla	NL-ALNY-BAL	1995
353	Mickey Mantle	AL	NY	1961				NY (190); BAL (129)	
346	Chipper Jones	NL	ATL	2001		319	Carlos Beltran	AL	KC	2002
344	Ruben Sierra	AL	TEX	1989		317	Chipper Jones	NL	ATL	1996
339	Ken Caminiti	NL	SD	1996		317	Bernie Williams	AL	NY	1999
334	Lance Berkman	NL	HOU	2002		317	Carlos Beltran	AL	KC	2001
333	Lance Berkman	NL	HOU	2006		316	Mickey Mantle	AL	NY	1955
332	Ruben Sierra	AL	TEX	1991		315	Mickey Mantle	AL	NY	1957
329	Chipper Jones	NL	ATL	1998		315	Jose Reyes	NL	NY	2006
329	Jimmy Rollins	NL	PHI	2006		314	Tony Clark	AL	DET	1998
328	Chipper Jones	NL	ATL	2000		313	Eddie Murray	AL	BAL	1983
328	Carlos Beltran	AL-NLKC-HOU	2004		311	Frankie Frisch	NL	NY	1923
		KC (142); HOU (186)			311	Roberto Alomar	AL	CLE	2001
327	Jose Vidro	NL	MON	2000		310	Roberto Alomar	AL	BAL	1996
324	Bobby Bonilla	NL	PIT	1990						

(248) Most Batter Strikeouts in a Season, before 1893

96	Tom Brown	AA	BOS	1891		80	Bill B. Phillips	NL	CLE	1884
94	Tom Brown	NL	LOU	1892		80	Jim Lillie	NL	KC	1886
92	Jim McTamany	AA	COL-PHI	1891		79	Jim Galvin	NL	BUF	1883
			COL (48); PHI (44)			79	John Cahill	NL	STL	1886
89	Frank Meinke	NL	DET	1884		79	Jerry Denny	NL	IND	1888
87	John Morrill	NL	BOS	1884		78	John Morrill	NL	BOS	1885
86	John Morrill	NL	BOS	1884		78	Pop Smith	NL	PIT	1888
84	Tom Brown	NL	BOS	1890		78	Frank Fennelly	AA	PHI	1889
82	Charlie Bastian	NL	PHI	1885		77	Bill Joyce	PL	BRO	1890
82	Emmett Seery	NL	STL	1886		77	Pete Gilbert	AA	BAL	1891
81	John Morrill	NL	BOS	1886		77	Mike Lehane	AA	COL	1891
81	Charlie Duffee	AA	STL	1889		76	William "Darby" O'Brien	AA	BRO	1889
81	Pop Smith	NL	BOS	1890		75	George Wood	NL	DET	1884
80	Jim Galvin	NL	BUF	1884		75	George Wood	NL	PHI	1886
80	Joe Hornung	NL	BOS	1884						

Batter strikeouts in a season before 1893 were very much a function of the rules. By the mid-1880s it was possible to get a lot of strikeouts, before then, hardly any.

(249) Most Batter Strikeouts in a Season, since 1893

195	Adam Dunn	NL	CIN	2004		177	Mark Bellhorn	AL	BOS	2004
194	Adam Dunn	NL	CIN	2006		176	Mike Cameron	AL	SEA	2002
189	Bobby Bonds	NL	SF	1970		175	Dave Nicholson	AL	CHI	1963
188	Jose Hernandez	NL	MIL	2002		175	Gorman Thomas	AL	MIL	1979
187	Bobby Bonds	NL	SF	1969		175	Jose Canseco	AL	OAK	1986
187	Preston Wilson	NL	FLA	2000		175	Rob Deer	AL	DET	1991
186	Rob Deer	AL	MIL	1987		175	Jay Buhner	AL	SEA	1997
185	Pete Incaviglia	AL	TEX	1986		174	Sammy Sosa	NL	CHI	1997
185	Jose Hernandez	NL	MIL	2001		174	Curtis Granderson	AL	DET	2006
185	Jim Thome	AL	CLE	2001		172	Jim Presley	AL	SEA	1986
182	Cecil Fielder	AL	DET	1990		171	Bo Jackson	AL	KC	1989
182	Jim Thome	NL	PHI	2003		171	Reggie Jackson	AL	OAK	1968
181	Mo Vaughn	AL	ANA	2000		171	Sammy Sosa	NL	CHI	1998
181	Ryan Howard	NL	PHI	2006		171	Sammy Sosa	NL	CHI	1999
180	Mike Schmidt	NL	PHI	1975		171	Jim Thome	AL	CLE	1999
179	Rob Deer	AL	MIL	1986		171	Jim Thome	AL	CLE	2000
178	Richie Sexson	NL	MIL	2001		170	Gorman Thomas	AL	MIL	1980
177	Jose Hernandez	NL	COL-CHI-PIT	2003		170	Adam Dunn	NL	CIN	2002
			COL (95); CHI (26); PIT (56)							

(250) Most Batter Strikeouts in a Season by a Left-handed Batter

195	Adam Dunn	NL	CIN	2004		159	Ben Grieve	AL	TB	2001
194	Adam Dunn	NL	CIN	2006		158	Jeromy Burnitz	NL	MIL	1998
185	Jim Thome	AL	CLE	2001		157	Lee Stevens	NL	MON	2001
182	Jim Thome	NL	PHI	2003		156	Reggie Jackson	AL	CAL	1982
181	Mo Vaughn	AL	ANA	2000		155	Brad Wilkerson	NL	MON	2003
181	Ryan Howard	NL	PHI	2006		154	Willie Stargell	NL	PIT	1971
174	Curtis Granderson	AL	DET	2006		154	Mo Vaughn	AL	BOS	1996
171	Reggie Jackson	AL	OAK	1968		154	Mo Vaughn	AL	BOS	1997
171	Jim Thome	AL	CLE	1999		153	Grady Sizemore	AL	CLE	2006
171	Jim Thome	AL	CLE	2000		152	Geoff Jenkins	NL	MIL	2004
170	Adam Dunn	NL	CIN	2002		152	Brad Wilkerson	NL	MON	2004
168	Corey Patterson	NL	CHI	2004		151	Delino DeShields	NL	MON	1991
168	Adam Dunn	NL	CIN	2005		151	Ray Lankford	NL	STL	1998
167	Jim Edmonds	NL	STL	2000		150	Mo Vaughn	AL	BOS	1995
161	Reggie Jackson	AL	OAK	1971		150	Jeromy Burnitz	NL	MIL	2001
161	Brad Wilkerson	NL	MON	2002		150	Jim Edmonds	NL	STL	2004
160	Henry Rodriguez	NL	MON	1996						

(251) Most Batter Strikeouts in a Season by a Right-handed Batter

189	Bobby Bonds	NL	SF	1970		174	Sammy Sosa	NL	CHI	1997
188	Jose Hernandez	NL	MIL	2002		172	Jim Presley	AL	SEA	1986
187	Bobby Bonds	NL	SF	1969		171	Bo Jackson	AL	KC	1989
187	Preston Wilson	NL	FLA	2000		171	Sammy Sosa	NL	CHI	1998
186	Rob Deer	AL	MIL	1987		171	Sammy Sosa	NL	CHI	1999
185	Pete Incaviglia	AL	TEX	1986		170	Gorman Thomas	AL	MIL	1980
185	Jose Hernandez	NL	MIL	2001		169	Andres Galarraga	NL	MON	1990
182	Cecil Fielder	AL	DET	1990		169	Rob Deer	AL	DET-BOS	1993
180	Mike Schmidt	NL	PHI	1975					DET (120); BOS (49)	
179	Rob Deer	AL	MIL	1986		169	Craig Wilson	NL	PIT	2004
178	Richie Sexson	NL	MIL	2001		168	Juan Samuel	NL	PHI	1984
177	Jose Hernandez	NL	COL-CHI-PIT	2003		168	Pete Incaviglia	AL	TEX	1987
		COL (95); CHI 9(26); PIT (56)				168	Sammy Sosa	NL	CHI	2000
176	Mike Cameron	AL	SEA	2002		167	Richie Sexson	AL	SEA	2005
175	Dave Nicholson	AL	CHI	1963		166	Gary Alexander	AL	OAK-CLE	1978
175	Gorman Thomas	AL	MIL	1979					OAK (66); CLE (100)	
175	Jose Canseco	AL	OAK	1986		166	Steve Balboni	AL	KC	1985
175	Rob Deer	AL	DET	1991		166	Cory Snyder	AL	CLE	1987
175	Jay Buhner	AL	SEA	1997						

(252) Most Batter Strikeouts in a Season by a Switch-hitter

177	Mark Bellhorn	AL	BOS	2004
160	Mickey Tettleton	AL	BAL	1990
158	Melvin Nieves	AL	DET	1996
157	Melvin Nieves	AL	DET	1997
152	Nick Swisher	AL	OAK	2006
151	Jorge Posada	AL	NY	2000
146	Todd Hundley	NL	NY	1996
145	Jose Valentin	AL	MIL	1996
144	Tony Clark	AL	DET	1997
144	Mark Bellhorn	NL	CHI	2002
143	Jorge Posada	AL	NY	2002
139	Mickey Tettleton	AL	DET	1993
139	Jose Valentin	NL	CHI	2004
138	Jose Cruz Jr.	AL	TOR	2001
137	Mickey Tettleton	AL	DET	1992
137	Mickey Tettleton	AL	TEX	1996
135	Devon White	AL	CAL	1987
135	Devon White	AL	TOR	1991
135	Tony Phillips	AL	CAL	1995
135	Carlos Beltran	AL	KC	2002
133	Dale Sveum	AL	MIL	1987
133	Devon White	AL	TOR	1992
133	Tony Clark	AL	DET	1999
132	Gary Pettis	AL	CAL	1986
132	Tony Phillips	AL	CAL	1996
132	Jorge Posada	AL	NY	2001
131	Mickey Tettleton	AL	DET	1991

(253) Most Hit by Pitch in a Season

51	Hughie Jennings	NL	BAL	1896
50	Ron Hunt	NL	MON	1971
46	Hughie Jennings	NL	BAL	1897
46	Hughie Jennings	NL	BAL	1898
39	Dan McGann	NL	BAL	1898
37	Dan McGann	NL	BRO-WAS	1899
			BRO (19); WAS (18)	
36	Curt Welch	AA	BAL	1891
35	Don Baylor	AL	BOS	1986
34	Curt Welch	AA	PHI-BAL	1890
			PHI (32); BAL (2)	
34	Craig Biggio	NL	HOU	1997
33	Tommy Tucker	AA	BAL	1889
32	Hughie Jennings	NL	BAL	1895
31	Steve Evans	NL	STL	1910
31	Jason Kendall	NL	PIT	1997
31	Jason Kendall	NL	PIT	1998
30	Craig Wilson	NL	PIT	2004
29	Tommy Tucker	AA	BAL	1887
29	Curt Welch	AA	PHI	1888
29	Chief Roseman	NL	HOU	1890
29	Tommy Tucker	NL	BOS	1891
28	Pete Gilbert	AA	BAL	1891
28	Don Baylor	AL	BOS-MIN	1987
			BOS (24); MIN (4)	
28	Fernando Vina	NL	STL	2000
28	Craig Biggio	NL	HOU	2001
27	Hughie Jennings	NL	BAL	1894
27	Craig Biggio	NL	HOU	1996
27	David Eckstein	AL	ANA	2002
27	Craig Biggio	NL	HOU	2003
26	Tommy Tucker	NL	BOS	1892
26	Ron Hunt	NL	SF	1970
26	Ron Hunt	NL	MON	1972
25	Tommy Tucker	NL	BOS	1890
25	Eddie Burke	NL	NY	1893
25	Fred Clarke	NL	LOU	1897
25	Kid Elberfeld	AL	WAS	1911
25	Ron Hunt	NL	SF	1968
25	Ron Hunt	NL	SF	1969
25	F.P. Santangelo	NL	MON	1997
25	Fernando Vina	NL	MIL	1998
25	Andres Galarraga	NL	HOU	1998
25	Jason Kendall	NL	PIT	2003

(254) Most Batter Walks in a Season, before 1893

136	Jack Crooks	NL	STL	1892	101	Yank Robinson	NL	PIT	1890
123	Bill Joyce	NL	BRO	1890	101	Jim McTamany	AA	COL-PHI	1891
118	Yank Robinson	AA	STL	1889				COL (58); PHI (43)	
117	Dummy Hoy	AA	STL	1891	99	Dan Brouthers	PL	BOS	1890
117	Cupid Childs	NL	CLE	1892	97	Cupid Childs	NL	CLE	1891
116	Yank Robinson	AA	STL	1888	96	Mike Tiernan	NL	NY	1889
116	Jim McTamany	AA	COL	1890	96	Jack Crooks	AA	COL	1890
116	Roger Connor	NL	PHI	1892	96	Paul Radford	AA	BOS	1891
113	Cap Anson	NL	CHI	1890	94	Dummy Hoy	PL	BUF	1890
112	Jim McTamany	AA	COL	1890	93	Roger Connor	NL	NY	1889
106	Paul Radford	AA	NY	1887	93	Tommy McCarthy	NL	BOS	1892
103	Jack Crooks	AA	COL	1891	92	Yank Robinson	AA	STL	1887
102	George Gore	NL	CHI	1886	91	Mike Griffin	AA	BAL	1889
102	Billy Hamilton	NL	PHI	1891	91	Paul Radford	NL	CLE	1889

A walk consisted of four balls from 1889 forward. Before that there were various higher numbers of balls needed for a walk.

(255) Most Batter Walks in a Season, since 1893

232	Barry Bonds	NL	SF	2004	142	Babe Ruth	AL	NY	1924
198	Barry Bonds	NL	SF	2002	142	Gary Sheffield	NL	FLA	1996
177	Barry Bonds	NL	SF	2001	141	Eddie Yost	AL	WAS	1950
170	Babe Ruth	AL	NY	1923	138	Frank E. Thomas	AL	CHI	1991
162	Ted Williams	AL	BOS	1947	137	Babe Ruth	AL	NY	1927
162	Ted Williams	AL	BOS	1949	137	Babe Ruth	AL	NY	1928
162	Mark McGwire	NL	STL	1998	137	Eddie Stanky	NL	BRO	1946
156	Ted Williams	AL	BOS	1946	137	Roy Cullenbine	AL	DET	1947
151	Eddie Yost	AL	WAS	1956	137	Ralph Kiner	NL	PIT	1951
151	Barry Bonds	NL	SF	1996	137	Willie McCovey	NL	SF	1970
150	Babe Ruth	AL	NY	1920	137	Jason Giambi	AL	OAK	2000
149	Eddie Joost	AL	PHI	1949	136	Babe Ruth	AL	NY	1930
149	Jeff Bagwell	NL	HOU	1999	136	Ferris Fain	AL	PHI	1949
148	Eddie Stanky	NL	BRO	1945	136	Ted Williams	AL	BOS	1954
148	Jim Wynn	NL	HOU	1969	136	Jack Clark	NL	STL	1987
148	Barry Bonds	NL	SF	2003	136	Frank E. Thomas	AL	CHI	1995
147	Jimmy Sheckard	NL	CHI	1911	135	Eddie Yost	AL	DET	1959
147	Ted Williams	AL	BOS	1941	135	Jeff Bagwell	NL	HOU	1996
146	Mickey Mantle	AL	NY	1957	135	Brian Giles	NL	ATL	2002
145	Babe Ruth	AL	NY	1921	133	Ferris Fain	AL	PHI	1950
145	Ted Williams	AL	BOS	1942	133	Mark McGwire	NL	STL	1999
145	Harmon Killebrew	AL	MIN	1969	132	Lou Gehrig	AL	NY	1935
145	Barry Bonds	NL	SF	1997	132	Frank Howard	AL	WAS	1970
144	Babe Ruth	AL	NY	1926	132	Joe Morgan	NL	CIN	1975
144	Eddie Stanky	NL	NY	1950	132	Jack Clark	NL	STL	1989
144	Ted Williams	AL	BOS	1951	132	Tony Phillips	AL	DET	1993

(256) Most Batter Walks in a Season by a Left-handed Batter

232	Barry Bonds	NL	SF	2004		133	Ferris Fain	AL	PHI	1950
198	Barry Bonds	NL	SF	2002		132	Lou Gehrig	AL	NY	1935
177	Barry Bonds	NL	SF	2001		132	Joe Morgan	NL	CIN	1975
170	Babe Ruth	AL	NY	1923		130	Babe Ruth	AL	NY	1932
162	Ted Williams	AL	BOS	1947		130	Lou Gehrig	AL	NY	1936
162	Ted Williams	AL	BOS	1949		130	Barry Bonds	NL	SF	1998
156	Ted Williams	AL	BOS	1946		129	Lenny Dykstra	NL	PHI	1993
151	Barry Bonds	NL	SF	1996		129	Jason Giambi	AL	OAK	2001
150	Babe Ruth	AL	NY	1920		129	Jason Giambi	AL	NY	2003
148	Barry Bonds	NL	SF	2003		128	Billy Hamilton	NL	PHI	1894
147	Jimmy Sheckard	NL	CHI	1911		128	Max Bishop	AL	PHI	1929
147	Ted Williams	AL	BOS	1941		128	Max Bishop	AL	PHI	1930
145	Babe Ruth	AL	NY	1921		128	Babe Ruth	AL	NY	1931
145	Ted Williams	AL	BOS	1942		128	Carl Yastrzemski	AL	BOS	1970
145	Barry Bonds	NL	SF	1997		128	Adam Dunn	NL	CIN	2002
144	Babe Ruth	AL	NY	1926		127	Lou Gehrig	AL	NY	1937
144	Ted Williams	AL	BOS	1951		127	Barry Bonds	NL	PIT	1992
142	Babe Ruth	AL	NY	1924		127	Jim Thome	AL	CLE	1999
137	Babe Ruth	AL	NY	1927		127	Bobby Abreu	NL	PHI	2004
137	Babe Ruth	AL	NY	1928		127	Todd Helton	NL	COL	2004
137	Willie McCovey	NL	SF	1970		126	Ted Williams	AL	BOS	1948
137	Jason Giambi	AL	OAK	2000		126	Darrell Evans	NL	ATL	1974
136	Babe Ruth	AL	NY	1930		126	Barry Bonds	NL	SF	1993
136	Ferris Fain	AL	PHI	1949		125	Richie Ashburn	NL	PHI	1954
136	Ted Williams	AL	BOS	1954		125	Wade Boggs	AL	BOS	1988
135	Brian Giles	NL	ATL	2002		125	John Olerud	NL	NY	1999

COURTESY OF L. ROBERT DAVIDS

Willie Wilson

(257) Most Batter Walks in a Season by a Right-handed Batter

162	Mark McGwire	NL	STL	1998		128	Harmon Killebrew	AL	MIN	1970
151	Eddie Yost	AL	WAS	1956		128	Mike Schmidt	NL	PHI	1983
149	Eddie Joost	AL	PHI	1949		127	Eddie Stanky	NL	NY	1951
149	Jeff Bagwell	NL	HOU	1999		127	Jim Wynn	NL	ATL	1976
148	Eddie Stanky	NL	BRO	1945		127	Jeff Bagwell	NL	HOU	1997
148	Jim Wynn	NL	HOU	1969		126	Eddie Yost	AL	WAS	1951
145	Harmon Killebrew	AL	MIN	1969		126	Rickey Henderson	AL	NY-OAK	1989
144	Eddie Stanky	NL	NY	1950				NY (56); OAK(70)		
142	Gary Sheffield	NL	FLA	1996		125	Eddie Yost	AL	DET	1960
141	Eddie Yost	AL	WAS	1950		125	Gene Tenace	NL	SD	1977
138	Frank E. Thomas	AL	CHI	1991		125	Rickey Henderson	NL	SD	1996
137	Eddie Stanky	NL	BRO	1946		123	Eddie Yost	AL	WAS	1953
137	Ralph Kiner	NL	PIT	1951		123	Edgar Martinez	AL	SEA	1996
136	Jack Crooks	NL	STL	1892		122	Luke Appling	AL	CHI	1935
136	Jack Clark	NL	STL	1987		122	Ralph Kiner	NL	PIT	1950
136	Frank E. Thomas	AL	CHI	1995		122	Eddie Joost	AL	PHI	1952
135	Eddie Yost	AL	DET	1959		122	Frank E. Thomas	AL	CHI	1992
135	Jeff Bagwell	NL	HOU	1996		121	Jack Crooks	NL	STL	1893
133	Mark McGwire	NL	STL	1999		121	Luke Appling	AL	CHI	1949
132	Frank Howard	AL	WAS	1970		121	Gary Sheffield	NL	FLA	1997
132	Jack Clark	NL	STL	1989		120	Eddie Lake	AL	DET	1947
131	Bob Elliott	NL	BOS	1948		120	Mike Schmidt	NL	PHI	1979
131	Eddie Yost	AL	WAS	1954		120	Rickey Henderson	AL	OAK-TOR	1993
131	Harmon Killebrew	AL	MIN	1967				OAK (85); TOR (35)		
129	Eddie Yost	AL	WAS	1952						

(258) Most Batter Walks in a Season by a Switch-hitter

146	Mickey Mantle	AL	NY	1957		113	Mickey Mantle	AL	NY	1955
137	Roy Cullenbine	AL	DET	1947		113	Tony Phillips	AL	CAL	1995
132	Tony Phillips	AL	DET	1993		112	Donie Bush	AL	DET	1914
129	Mickey Mantle	AL	NY	1958		112	Mickey Mantle	AL	NY	1956
127	Lu Blue	AL	CHI	1931		111	Mickey Mantle	AL	NY	1960
127	Lance Berkman	NL	HOU	2004		109	Don Buford	AL	BAL	1970
126	Lu Blue	AL	STL	1929		109	Ken Singleton	AL	BAL	1979
126	Mickey Mantle	AL	NY	1961		109	Mickey Tettleton	AL	DET	1993
126	Chipper Jones	NL	ATL	1999		107	Mickey Mantle	AL	NY	1967
125	Tony Phillips	AL	CHI	1996		107	Ken Singleton	AL	BAL	1977
123	Ken Singleton	NL	MON	1973		107	Eddie Murray	AL	BAL	1984
122	Mickey Mantle	AL	NY	1962		107	Mickey Tettleton	AL	TEX	1995
122	Mickey Tettleton	AL	DET	1992		107	Jorge Posada	AL	NY	2000
121	Roy Cullenbine	AL	STL	1941		107	Lance Berkman	NL	HOU	2002
118	Donie Bush	AL	DET	1915		107	Chipper Jones	NL	ATL	2002
118	Ken Singleton	AL	BAL	1975		107	Lance Berkman	NL	HOU	2003
117	Donie Bush	AL	DET	1912		106	Mickey Mantle	AL	NY	1968
116	Miller Huggins	NL	STL	1910		106	Pete Rose	NL	CIN	1974
114	Tony Phillips	AL	DET	1992		106	Mickey Tettleton	AL	BAL	1990
113	Roy Cullenbine	AL	CLE-DET	1945		105	Miller Huggins	NL	STL	1914
		CLE (11); DET(102)				105	Lu Blue	AL	STL	1928

(259) Most Intentional Walks in a Season, since 1955

120	Barry Bonds	NL	SF	2004	27	Will Clark	NL	SF	1988
68	Barry Bonds	NL	SF	2002	27	Jeff Bagwell	NL	HOU	1997
61	Barry Bonds	NL	SF	2003	27	Ichiro Suzuki	AL	SEA	2002
45	Willie McCovey	NL	SF	1969	27	Albert Pujols	NL	STL	2005
43	Barry Bonds	NL	SF	1993	27	Miguel Cabrera	NL	FLA	2006
40	Willie McCovey	NL	SF	1970	26	Duke Snider	NL	BRO	1956
38	Barry Bonds	NL	SF	2006	26	Stan Musial	NL	STL	1958
37	Sammy Sosa	NL	CHI	2001	26	Tony Gwynn	NL	SD	1987
37	Ryan Howard	NL	PHI	2006	26	Tim Raines	NL	MON	1987
35	Barry Bonds	NL	SF	2001	26	Fred McGriff	NL	SD	1991
34	Barry Bonds	NL	SF	1997	26	Frank E. Thomas	AL	CHI	1996
33	Ted Williams	AL	BOS	1957	26	Jim Thome	NL	PHI	2004
33	John Olerud	AL	TOR	1993	26	Vladimir Guerrero	AL	LA	2005
32	Kevin Mitchell	NL	SF	1989	25	Ted Kluszewski	NL	CIN	1955
32	Barry Bonds	NL	PIT	1992	25	Leo Cardenas	NL	CIN	1965
32	Vladimir Guerrero	NL	MON	2002	25	Willie Stargell	NL	PIT	1967
31	George Brett	KC	AL	1985	25	Willie McCovey	NL	SF	1973
30	Barry Bonds	NL	SF	1996	25	Bill Russell	NL	LA	1974
29	Adolfo Phillips	NL	CHI	1967	25	Ted Simmons	NL	STL	1977
29	Frank Howard	AL	WAS	1970	25	Eddie Murray	AL	BAL	1984
29	Dale Murphy	NL	ATL	1987	25	Mike Schmidt	NL	PHI	1986
29	Frank E. Thomas	AL	CHI	1995	25	Howard Johnson	NL	NY	1988
29	Barry Bonds	NL	SF	1998	25	Spike Owen	NL	MON	1989
28	Ernie Banks	NL	CHI	1960	25	Barry Bonds	NL	PIT	1991
28	Mark McGwire	NL	STL	1998	25	Wade Boggs	AL	BOS	1991
28	Manny Ramirez	AL	BOS	2003	25	Ken Griffey Jr.	AL	SEA	1993
28	Albert Pujols	NL	STL	2006	25	Manny Ramirez	AL	BOS	2001
27	Roberto Clemente	NL	PIT	1968	25	Vladimir Guerrero	AL	LA	2006

(260) Batters with 20 Doubles, 20 Triples, and 20 Home Runs in a Season

				2B	3B	HR
George Brett	AL	KC	1979	42	20	23
Jim Bottomley	NL	STL	1928	42	20	31
Jeff Heath	AL	CLE	1941	32	20	24
Frank Schulte	NL	CHI	1911	30	21	21
Willie Mays	NL	NY	1957	26	20	35

(261) Lowest Batting Average for an RBI Leader

				BAV	RBI
Harmon Killebrew	AL	MIN	1962	.243	126
Cecil Fielder	AL	DET	1992	.244	124
Harmon Killebrew	AL	MIN	1971	.254	119
Jim Nealon	NL	PIT	1906	.255	83
Lee May	AL	BAL	1976	.258	109
Howard Johnson	NL	NY	1991	.259	117
Cecil Fielder	AL	DET	1991	.261	133
Dick Stuart	AL	BOS	1963	.261	118
Andruw Jones	NL	ATL	2005	.263	128
George Kelly	NL	NY	1920	.266	94
Del Pratt	AL	STL	1916	.267	103
Tony Armas Sr.	AL	BOS	1984	.268	123
Bill Dahlen	NL	NY	1904	.268	80
Gus Zernial	AL	CHI-PHI	1951	.268	129
			CHI (.105-4); PHI (.274-125)		
Roger Maris	AL	NY	1961	.269	142
Johnny Bench	NL	CIN	1972	.270	125
Hank Sauer	NL	CHI	1952	.270	121
Darren Daulton	NL	PHI	1992	.270	109

SPALDING

Frankie Frisch

(262) More Walks Received than Games Played in a Season (min. 100 walks)

				GAMES	WALKS
Babe Ruth	AL	NY	1920	142	148
Babe Ruth	AL	NY	1923	152	170
Ted Williams	AL	BOS	1941	143	145
Ted Williams	AL	BOS	1946	150	156
Ted Williams	AL	BOS	1947	156	162
Ted Williams	AL	BOS	1949	155	162
Eddie Joost	AL	PHI	1949	144	149
Ted Williams	AL	BOS	1954	117	136
Mickey Mantle	AL	NY	1957	144	146
Jack Clark	NL	STL	1987	131	136
Mark McGwire	NL	STL	1998	155	162
Barry Bonds	NL	SF	2001	153	177
Barry Bonds	NL	SF	2002	143	198
Barry Bonds	NL	SF	2003	130	148
Barry Bonds	NL	SF	2004	147	232

(263) Most RBI in a Season while Playing for Multiple Teams

138	Goose Goslin	AL	WAS-STL	1930	WAS (38); STL (100)
129	Gus Zernial	AL	CHI-PHI	1951	CHI (4); PHI (125)
123	Mark McGwire	AL-NL	OAK-STL	1997	OAK (81); STL (42)
118	David Justice	AL	CLE-NY	2000	CLE (58); NY (60)
117	Greg Vaughn	AL-NL	MIL-SD	1996	MIL (95); SD (22)
117	Cecil Fielder	AL	DET-NY	1996	DET (80); NY (37)
116	Ralph Kiner	NL	PIT-CHI	1953	PIT (29); CHI (87)
116	Carlos Lee	NL-AL	MIL-TEX	2006	MIL (81); TEX (35)
114	Ray Boone	AL	CLE-DET	1953	CLE (21); DET (93)
112	Moose Solters	AL	BOS-STL	1935	BOS (8); STL (104)
111	Mike Piazza	NL	LA-FLA-NY	1998	LA (30); FLA (5); NY (76)
110	Charlie Hickman	AL	BOS-CLE	1902	BOS (16); CLE (94)
110	Scott Rolen	NL	PHI-STL	2002	PHI (66); STL (44)
109	Buster Adams	NL	PHI-STL	1945	PHI (8); STL (101)
107	Bobby Abreu	NL-AL	PHI-NY	2006	PHI (65); NY (42)
106	Smead Jolley	AL	CHI-BOS	1932	CHI (7); BOS (99)
106	Jermaine Dye	AL	KC-OAK	2001	KC (47); OAK (59)
106	Aramis Ramirez	NL	PIT-CHI	2003	PIT (67); CHI (39)
104	Chuck Klein	NL	CHI-PHI	1936	CHI (18); PHI (86)
104	Carlos Beltran	AL-NL	KC-HOU	2004	KC (51); HOU (53)
103	Harold Baines	AL	BAL-CLE	1999	BAL (81); CLE (22)
103	David Segui	AL	TEX-CLE	2000	TEX (57); CLE (46)
102	Fred McGriff	AL-NL	TB-CHI	2001	TB (61); CHI (41)
101	Willie Montanez	NL	PHI-SF	1975	PHI (16); SF (85)
101	Fred McGriff	NL	SD-ATL	1993	SD (46); ATL (55)
100	Jack Glasscock	NL	STL-PIT	1893	STL (26); PIT (74)
100	Tony Batista	NL-AL	ARI-TOR	1999	ARI (21); TOR (79)

(264) Highest RBI Ratio per Games Played (min. 100 RBI)

					RBI	GAMES
1.387	Sam Thompson	NL	PHI	1895	165	119
1.382	Sam Thompson	NL	PHI	1894	141	102
1.307	Sam Thompson	NL	DET	1887	166	127
1.232	Hack Wilson	NL	CHI	1930	191	155
1.196	Al Simmons	AL	PHI	1930	165	138
1.188	Hank Greenberg	AL	DET	1937	183	154
1.187	Lou Gehrig	AL	NY	1931	184	155
1.176	Cap Anson	NL	CHI	1886	147	125
1.174	Jimmie Foxx	AL	BOS	1938	175	149
1.160	Hugh Duffy	NL	BOS	1894	145	125
1.159	Dave Orr	PL	BRO	1890	124	107
1.149	Ed Delahanty	NL	PHI	1894	131	114
1.141	Babe Ruth	AL	NY	1929	154	135
1.130	Lou Gehrig	AL	NY	1930	174	154
1.129	Lou Gehrig	AL	NY	1927	175	155
1.125	Babe Ruth	AL	NY	1921	171	152
1.124	Babe Ruth	AL	NY	1931	163	145
1.123	Hardy Richardson	PL	BOS	1890	146	130
1.122	Manny Ramirez	AL	CLE	1999	165	147
1.118	Hank Greenberg	AL	DET	1935	170	152
1.106	Ed Delahanty	NL	PHI	1893	146	132
1.106	Joe DiMaggio	AL	NY	1937	167	151
1.098	Al Simmons	AL	PHI	1929	157	143
1.097	Jimmie Foxx	AL	PHI	1932	169	154
1.094	Jimmie Foxx	AL	PHI	1933	163	149
1.090	Chuck Klein	NL	PHI	1930	170	156
1.086	Babe Ruth	AL	NY	1927	164	151
1.076	Oyster Burns	NL	BRO	1890	128	119
1.075	Juan Gonzalez	AL	TEX	1996	144	134
1.073	Hal Trosky	AL	CLE	1936	162	151
1.071	Lou Gehrig	AL	NY	1934	165	154
1.064	Ed McKean	NL	CLE	1893	133	125
1.060	Hack Wilson	NL	CHI	1929	159	150
1.059	Dave Foutz	AA	STL	1887	108	102
1.059	Walt Dropo	AL	BOS	1950	144	136
1.055	Babe Ruth	AL	NY	1930	153	145
1.055	Jeff Bagwell	NL	HOU	1994	116	110
1.052	Buck Ewing	NL	CLE	1893	122	116
1.050	Lave Cross	NL	PHI	1894	125	119
1.050	Joe DiMaggio	AL	NY	1939	126	120
1.046	George Davis	NL	NY	1897	136	130
1.041	Dan Brouthers	NL	BAL	1894	128	123
1.037	Kirby Puckett	AL	MIN	1994	112	108
1.036	Rogers Hornsby	NL	STL	1925	143	138
1.036	Jim O'Rourke	PL	NY	1890	115	111
1.034	Manny Ramirez	AL	CLE	2000	122	118
1.030	Babe Ruth	AL	NY	1932	137	133
1.029	Ken Williams	AL	STL	1925	105	102
1.026	Vern Stephens	AL	BOS	1949	159	155
1.026	Ted Williams	AL	BOS	1949	159	155

(264) *(continued)*

1.024	Ed Delahanty	NL	PHI	1896	126	123
1.023	Joe Kelley	NL	BAL	1895	134	131
1.023	Steve Brodie	NL	BAL	1895	134	131
1.020	Jimmie Foxx	AL	PHI	1930	156	153
1.019	Juan Gonzalez	AL	TEX	1998	157	154
1.019	Al Simmons	AL	PHI	1927	108	106
1.018	Dave Orr	AA	NY	1884	112	110
1.014	Hank Greenberg	AL	DET	1940	150	148
1.013	Ken Williams	AL	STL	1922	155	153
1.013	Joe DiMaggio	AL	NY	1948	155	153
1.013	Lou Gehrig	AL	NY	1937	159	157
1.009	George Brett	AL	KC	1980	118	117
1.008	Joe DiMaggio	AL	NY	1940	133	132
1.007	Mel Ott	NL	NY	1929	151	150
1.000	Nap Lajoie	NL	PHI	1897	127	127
1.000	Al Simmons	AL	PHI	1931	128	128
1.000	Ken Griffey Jr.	AL	SEA	1996	140	140
1.000	Sammy Sosa	NL	CHI	2001	160	160
1.000	Juan Gonzalez	AL	CLE	2001	140	140

(265) Players who Batted .300 in a Season after Age 40
(min. 3.1 PA per scheduled game)

BAV			AGE			PA
.362	2004	Barry Bonds	41	NL	SF	617
.357	1927	Ty Cobb	40	AL	PHI	574
.349	1930	Sam Rice	40	AL	WAS	668
.341	1996	Paul Molitor	40	AL	MIN	729
.341	2003	Barry Bonds	40	NL	SF	550
.335	1895	Cap Anson	43	NL	CHI	545
.331	1896	Cap Anson	44	NL	CHI	459
.330	1962	Stan Musial	41	NL	STL	505
.328	1958	Ted Williams	40	AL	BOS	517
.325	1981	Pete Rose	40	NL	PHI	486
.319	1941	Johnny Cooney	40	NL	BOS	478
.315	1999	Rickey Henderson	40	NL	NY	526
.314	1948	Luke Appling	41	AL	CHI	594
.306	1947	Luke Appling	40	AL	CHI	572
.305	1997	Paul Molitor	41	AL	MIN	597
.304	1892	Jim O'Rourke	42	NL	NY	483
.301	1949	Luke Appling	42	AL	CHI	619

Player turned 40 sometime during season.

(266) Batting Triple Crown Winners, since 1893

				BAV	HR	RBI
Nap Lajoie	AL	PHI	1901	.426	14	125
Ty Cobb	AL	DET	1909	.377	9	107
Rogers Hornsby	NL	STL	1922	.401	42	152
Rogers Hornsby	NL	STL	1925	.403	39	143
Jimmie Foxx	AL	PHI	1933	.356	48	163
Chuck Klein	NL	PHI	1933	.368	28	120
Lou Gehrig	AL	NY	1934	.363	49	165
Joe Medwick	NL	STL	1937	.374	31	154
Ted Williams	AL	BOS	1942	.356	36	137
Ted Williams	AL	BOS	1947	.343	32	114
Mickey Mantle	AL	NY	1956	.353	52	130
Frank Robinson	AL	BAL	1966	.316	49	122
Carl Yastrzemski	AL	BOS	1967	.326	44	121

Jimmie Foxx

(267) Batting Triple Crown Near Misses, since 1893
(Winning two categories and finishing second in other)

				BAV	HR	RBI	
Cy Seymour	NL	CIN	1905	.377	8	121	Fred Odwell led in HR with 9
Ty Cobb	AL	DET	1907	.350	5	119	Harry Davis led in HR with 8
Honus Wagner	NL	PIT	1908	.354	10	109	Tim Jordan led in HR with 12
Ty Cobb	AL	DET	1911	.420	8	127	Frank Baker led in HR with 11
Gavy Cravath	NL	PHI	1913	.341	19	128	Jake Daubert led in BAV with .350
Rogers Hornsby	NL	STL	1921	.397	21	126	George Kelly led in HR with 23
Babe Ruth	AL	NY	1923	.393	41	131	Harry Heilmann led in BAV with .403
Babe Ruth	AL	NY	1924	.378	46	121	Goose Goslin led in RBI with 129
Babe Ruth	AL	NY	1926	.372	47	146	Heinie Manush led in BAV with .378
Jimmie Foxx	AL	PHI	1932	.364	58	169	Dale Alexander led in BAV with .357
Jimmie Foxx	AL	BOS	1938	.349	50	175	Hank Greenberg led in HR with 58
Stan Musial	NL	STL	1948	.376	39	131	Ralph Kiner and Johnny Mize led in HR with 40
Ted Williams	AL	BOS	1949	.3428	43	159	George Kell led in BAV with .3429
Al Rosen	AL	CLE	1953	.336	43	145	Mickey Vernon led in BAV with .337

(268) Batting Triple Crown Losers (Qualified batters who finished last in all three categories)

				BAV	HR	RBI
George McBride	AL	WAS	1914	.203	0	24
Herbie Moran	NL	BOS	1915	.200	0	21
Jack Smith	NL	STL	1919	.223	0	15
Ivy Griffin	AL	PHI	1920	.238	0	20
Freddie Maguire	NL	BOS	1929	.252	0	41
Freddie Maguire	NL	BOS	1931	.223	0	26
Woody W. Williams	NL	CIN	1945	.237	0	27
Willy Miranda	AL	BAL	1956	.217	2	34
Mark Belanger	AL	CLE	1970	.218	1	36
Enzo Hernandez	NL	SD	1971	.222	0	12
Ozzie Smith	NL	SD	1979	.211	0	27
Ivan DeJesus	NL	CHI	1981	.194	0	13
Ramon Santiago	AL	DET	2003	.225	2	29

(269) Batters who Hit .400 in a Season (min. 3.1 PA per scheduled game)

Hugh Duffy	NL	BOS	1894	.440
Tip O'Neill	AA	STL	1887	.435
Ross Barnes	NL	CHI	1876	.429
Nap Lajoie	AL	PHI	1901	.426
Rogers Hornsby	NL	STL	1924	.424
Willie Keeler	NL	BAL	1897	.424
George Sisler	AL	STL	1922	.420
Ty Cobb	AL	DET	1911	.420
Sam Thompson	NL	PHI	1894	.415
Fred Dunlap	UA	STL	1884	.412
Ed Delahanty	NL	PHI	1899	.410
Jesse Burkett	NL	CLE	1896	.410
Ty Cobb	AL	DET	1912	.409
Joe Jackson	AL	CLE	1911	.408
George Sisler	AL	STL	1920	.407
Ted Williams	AL	BOS	1941	.406
Jesse Burkett	NL	CLE	1895	.405
Ed Delahanty	NL	PHI	1895	.404
Ed Delahanty	NL	PHI	1894	.404
Billy Hamilton	NL	PHI	1894	.403
Harry Heilmann	AL	DET	1923	.403
Rogers Hornsby	NL	STL	1925	.403
Pete Browning	AA	LOU	1887	.402
Bill Terry	NL	NY	1930	.401
Hughie Jennings	NL	BAL	1896	.401
Rogers Hornsby	NL	STL	1922	.401
Ty Cobb	AL	DET	1922	.401

(270) Batters who Led the League in Hits and Walks in the Same Season

				HITS	WALKS
Ross Barnes	NL	CHI	1876	138	20
Billy Hamilton	NL	PHI	1891	179	102
Rogers Hornsby	NL	STL	1924	227	89
Richie Ashburn	NL	PHI	1958	215	97
Carl Yastrzemski	AL	BOS	1963	183	95
Lenny Dykstra	NL	PHI	1993	194	129

(271) Batting Champions by Widest Margin

DIFF.	WINNER			BAV	RUNNER UP		BAV	
.086	Nap Lajoie	AL	PHI	.426	Mike Donlin	BAL	.340	1901
.071	Cap Anson	NL	CHI	.399	Joe Start	PRO	.328	1881
.063	Ross Barnes	NL	CHI	.429	George Hall	PHI	.366	1876
.052	Fred Dunlap	UA	STL	.412	Orator Shaffer	STL	.360	1884
.052	Rod Carew	AL	MIN	.388	Lyman Bostock	MIN	.336	1977
.049	Rogers Hornsby	NL	STL	.424	Zack Wheat	BRO	.375	1924
.048	Rod Carew	AL	MIN	.364	Jorge Orta	CHI	.316	1974
.047	Rogers Hornsby	NL	STL	.401	Ray Grimes	CHI	.354	1922
.047	Ted Williams	AL	BOS	.406	Cecil Travis	WAS	.359	1941
.046	Harry Walker	NL	STL-PHI	.363	Bob Elliott	BOS	.317	1947
.045	Rogers Hornsby	NL	STL	.397	Edd Roush	CIN	.352	1921
.044	Rod Carew	AL	MIN	.350	George Scott	MIL	.306	1973
.043	Stan Musial	NL	STL	.376	Richie Ashburn	PHI	.333	1948
.043	Larry Walker	NL	COL	.379	Luis Gonzalez	ARI	.336	1999
.041	Rico Carty	NL	ATL	.366	Joe Torre	STL	.325	1970

(272) Highest Batting Average in Two Consecutive Seasons (min. 800 AB)

.414	Ty Cobb	1911-12		.400	Hugh Duffy	1893-94
.413	Rogers Hornsby	1924-25		.400	Ed Delahanty	1895-96
.408	Jesse Burkett	1895-96		.399	Rogers Hornsby	1921-22
.407	Nap Lajoie	1901-02		.397	Jesse Burkett	1896-97
.406	Rogers Hornsby	1923-24		.396	Billy Hamilton	1894-95
.405	Willie Keeler	1896-97		.396	Hugh Duffy	1894-95
.404	Ed Delahanty	1894-95		.396	George Sisler	1921-22
.404	Willie Keeler	1897-98		.395	Ty Cobb	1921-22
.403	Ty Cobb	1910-11		.394	Billy Hamilton	1893-94
.402	Sam Thompson	1894-95		.394	Rogers Hornsby	1922-23
.402	Joe Jackson	1911-12		.393	Hughie Jennings	1895-96
.401	Ty Cobb	1912-13		.391	Lefty O'Doul	1929-30

(273) Highest Batting Average in Three Consecutive Seasons (min. 1,200 AB)

.408	Ty Cobb	1911-13		.393	Joe Jackson	1911-13
.405	Ty Cobb	1910-12		.392	Billy Hamilton	1893-95
.405	Rogers Hornsby	1923-25		.392	Jesse Burkett	1894-96
.404	Rogers Hornsby	1922-24		.392	Ed Delahanty	1895-97
.402	Ed Delahanty	1894-96		.392	Ty Cobb	1912-14
.401	Joe Jackson	1910-12		.390	Ed Delahanty	1893-95
.400	Jesse Burkett	1895-97		.390	Sam Thompson	1893-95
.400	George Sisler	1920-22		.390	Rogers Hornsby	1920-22
.398	Willie Keeler	1896-98		.386	Billy Hamilton	1894-96
.396	Willie Keeler	1895-97		.386	Harry Heilmann	1921-23
.396	Willie Keeler	1897-99		.386	Harry Heilmann	1925-27
.395	Rogers Hornsby	1921-23		.385	Nap Lajoie	1901-03
.394	Ty Cobb	1909-11				

(274) Highest Batting Average in Four Consecutive Seasons (min. 1,600 AB)

.404	Rogers Hornsby	1922-25		.389	George Sisler	1919-22
.402	Ty Cobb	1910-13		.389	Rogers Hornsby	1920-23
.402	Rogers Hornsby	1921-24		.388	Willie Keeler	1897-1900
.401	Ty Cobb	1911-14		.385	Billy Hamilton	1893-96
.398	Ty Cobb	1909-12		.385	Ty Cobb	1912-15
.395	Ed Delahanty	1894-97		.384	Jesse Burkett	1895-98
.393	Willie Keeler	1895-98		.383	Nap Lajoie	1899-1902
.393	Willie Keeler	1896-99		.383	Nap Lajoie	1901-04
.392	Ed Delahanty	1893-96		.382	Jesse Burkett	1893-96
.392	Joe Jackson	1910-13		.382	Jesse Burkett	1896-99
.390	Jesse Burkett	1894-97		.382	Rogers Hornsby	1923-26
.389	Willie Keeler	1894-97		.381	Joe Jackson	1911-14

(275) Highest Batting Average in Five Consecutive Seasons (min. 2,000 AB)

.402	Rogers Hornsby	1921-25		.381	George Sisler	1918-22
.397	Ty Cobb	1910-14		.381	Harry Heilmann	1923-27
.396	Ty Cobb	1909-13		.379	Jesse Burkett	1894-98
.395	Rogers Hornsby	1920-24		.379	Ty Cobb	1918-22
.394	Ty Cobb	1911-15		.379	Harry Heilmann	1921-25
.390	Willie Keeler	1895-99		.378	Jesse Burkett	1896-1900
.389	Ed Delahanty	1893-97		.378	Ty Cobb	1915-19
.388	Willie Keeler	1894-98		.378	Rogers Hornsby	1924-28
.387	Willie Keeler	1896-1900		.377	Billy Hamilton	1893-97
.386	Willie Keeler	1893-97		.377	Willie Keeler	1897-1901
.386	Jesse Burkett	1895-99		.377	Nap Lajoie	1901-05
.386	Rogers Hornsby	1922-26		.377	Rogers Hornsby	1923-27
.383	Ed Delahanty	1894-98		.376	Ed Delahanty	1892-96
.382	Jesse Burkett	1893-97		.376	Ty Cobb	1913-17
.382	Ed Delahanty	1895-99		.376	Ty Cobb	1917-21
.382	Ty Cobb	1908-12		.376	Rogers Hornsby	1919-23
.382	Ty Cobb	1912-16		.375	Al Simmons	1927-31
.381	Joe Jackson	1910-14				

(276) Most Consecutive Games Scoring a Run, since 1893

24	Billy Hamilton	NL	PHI	1894	Jul 6 to Aug 2
23	Jesse Burkett	NL	CLE	1896	Jun 13 to Jul 10 (1G)
22	Jimmy Bannon	NL	BOS	1894	Aug 2 to Aug 28
21	Joe Sullivan	NL	PHI	1895	Sep 2 to Sep 23
20	Herman Long	NL	BOS	1893	May 29 to Jun 26
20	Billy Hamilton	NL	PHI	1894	Aug 15 to Sep 3 (1G)
18	Billy Hamilton	NL	PHI	1893	May 12 to Jun 1
18	Jesse Burkett	NL	CLE	1894	Jun 30 to Jul 18
18	Ed Delahanty	NL	PHI	1895	Aug 23 (2G) to Sep 10
18	Red Rolfe	AL	NY	1939	Aug 9 to Aug 25 (2G)
18	Kenny Lofton	AL	CLE	2000	Aug 15 to Sep 3
17	Joe Kelley	NL	BAL	1894	Aug 27 to Sep 16 (1G)
17	Mike Griffin	NL	BRO	1895	Aug 16 (2G) to Sep 4
17	Rogers Hornsby	NL	STL	1921	Jul 3 to Jul 20
17	Ted Kluszewski	NL	CIN	1954	Aug 27 to Sep 13
17	Jim Thome	AL	CHI	2006	Apr 2 to Apr 22; from start of season

(277) Most Consecutive Games with an RBI, since 1893

17	Ray Grimes	NL	CHI	1922
15	Mike Piazza	NL	NY	2000
14	George Van Haltren	NL	NY	1895
13	Nap Lajoie	NL	PHI	1899
13	Taft Wright	AL	CHI	1941
13	Mike Sweeney	AL	KC	1999
12	Tuck Turner	NL	PHI	1894
12	Sam Thompson	NL	PHI	1895
12	Charlie Hickman	NL	NY	1900
12	Paul Waner	NL	PIT	1927
12	Mickey Cochrane	AL	DET	1934
12	Ripper Collins	NL	STL	1935
12	Joe Cronin	AL	BOS	1939
12	Rudy York	AL	DET	1940
12	Ted Williams	AL	BOS	1942

(278) Most Consecutive Games with a Base on Balls

22	Roy Cullenbine	AL	DET	1947	Jul 2 to Jul 22; Cullenbine had 33 more walks than hits in 1947
20	Barry Bonds	NL	SF	2002-03	Sep 9, 2002 to Apr 1, 2003; streak includes 16 IBB
19	Ted Williams	AL	BOS	1941	Aug 24 (2G) to Sep 14 (1G)
17	Babe Ruth	AL	NY	1921	Jun 1 to Jun 18

SPALDING

Paul Waner

(279) Most Consecutive Hits

12	Pinky Higgins	AL	BOS	1938		9	Max Carey	NL	PIT	1922
12	Walt Dropo	AL	DET	1952		9	Rogers Hornsby	NL	STL	1924
11	Tris Speaker	AL	CLE	1920		9	Ty Cobb	AL	DET	1925
11	Johnny Pesky	AL	BOS	1946		9	Sam Rice	AL	WAS	1925
11	Bernie Williams	AL	NY	2002		9	Taylor Douthit	NL	STL	1926
10	Jake Stenzel	NL	PIT	1893		9	Babe Herman	NL	BRO	1926
10	Tom Parrott	NL	CIN	1895		9	Hal Trosky	AL	CLE	1936
10	Ed Delahanty	NL	PHI	1897		9	Ted Williams	AL	BOS	1939
10	Jake Gettman	NL	WAS	1897		9	Billy Jurges	NL	NY	1941
10	Nap Lajoie	AL	PHI	1901		9	Terry Moore	NL	STL	1947
10	Ed Konetchy	NL	BRO	1919		9	Dick Sisler	NL	PHI	1950
10	George Sisler	AL	STL	1921		9	Eddie Waitkus	NL	PHI	1950
10	Harry Heilmann	AL	DET	1922		9	Dave Philley	NL	PHI	1958-59
10	Kiki Cuyler	NL	PIT	1925			All pinch hits; 8 in 1958 and 1 in 1959			
10	Harry McCurdy	AL	CHI	1926		9	Clay Dalrymple	NL	PHI	1961
10	Chick Hafey	NL	STL	1929		9	Felipe Alou	NL	SF	1962
10	Joe Medwick	NL	STL	1936		9	Willie Stargell	NL	PIT	1966
10	Rip Radcliff	AL	CHI	1938		9	Tony Oliva	AL	MIN	1967
10	Buddy Hassett	NL	BOS	1940		9	Rennie Stennett	NL	PIT	1975
10	Woody W. Williams	NL	CIN	1943		9	Ron Cey	NL	LA	1977
	Had only 26 hits for the season					9	Jorge Orta	AL	CLE	1980
10	Ken Singleton	AL	BAL	1981		9	Mickey Hatcher	AL	MIN	1985
10	Bip Roberts	NL	CIN	1992		9	Andres Galarraga	NL	COL	1993
10	Chris Stynes	AL-NL	KC-CIN	1996-97		9	Sammy Sosa	NL	CHI	1993
	KC (3); CIN (7)					9	Lance Johnson	AL	CHI	1995
10	Frank E. Thomas	AL	CHI	1997		9	Jose Vizcaino	NL	NY	1996
10	Joe Randa	AL	KC	1999		9	Barry Bonds	NL	SF	1998
10	Frank Catalanotto	AL	TEX	2000		9	John Olerud	NL	NY	1998
10	Matt Diaz	NL	ATL	2006		9	Todd Walker	AL	MIN	1998
9	George Van Haltren	BAL	NL	1892		9	Charles Johnson	AL	BAL	1999
9	Joe Kelley	NL	BAL	1894		9	Jim Edmonds	NL	STL	2000
9	Roger Connor	NL	STL	1895		9	Bengie Molina	AL	ANA	2001
9	Joe Kelley	NL	BAL	1898		9	Dmitri Young	NL	CIN	2001
9	George Stone	AL	STL	1907		9	Manny Ramirez	AL	BOS	2002
9	Johnny Bates	NL	CIN	1911		9	Marcus Giles	NL	ATL	2003
9	Doc Johnston	AL	CLE	1919		9	Raul Ibanez	AL	SEA	2004
9	Bobby Veach	AL	DET	1921						

(280) Most Consecutive Games with a Hit in a Single Season

56	Joe DiMaggio	AL	NY	1941	May 15 to Jul 16
44	Willie Keeler	NL	BAL	1897	Apr 22 to Jun 18
44	Pete Rose	NL	CIN	1978	Jun 14 to Jul 31
42	Bill Dahlen	NL	CHI	1894	Jun 20 to Aug 6
41	George Sisler	AL	STL	1922	Jul 27 to Sep 17
40	Ty Cobb	AL	DET	1911	May 15 to Jul 2
39	Paul Molitor	AL	MIL	1987	Jul 16 to Aug 25
37	Tommy Holmes	NL	BOS	1945	Jun 6 (1G) to Jul 8 (2G)
36	Jimmy Rollins	NL	PHI	2005	Aug 23 to Oct 2
35	Fred Clarke	NL	LOU	1895	Aug 5 to Sep 9
35	Ty Cobb	AL	DET	1917	May 31 to Jul 5
35	Luis Castillo	NL	FLA	2002	May 8 to Jun 21
35	Chase Utley	NL	PHI	2006	Jun 23 to Aug 3
34	George Sisler	AL	STL	1925	Apr 14 to May 19
34	George McQuinn	AL	STL	1938	Jul 24 (1G) to Aug 25 (1G)
34	Dom DiMaggio	AL	BOS	1949	Jun 29 to Aug 7
34	Benito Santiago	NL	SD	1987	Aug 25 to Oct 2
33	George Davis	NL	NY	1893	Aug 3 to Sep 9 (2G)
33	Hal Chase	AL	NY	1907	Jun 24 (1G) to Jul 26 (1G)
33	Rogers Hornsby	NL	STL	1922	Aug 13 to Sep 19
33	Heinie Manush	AL	WAS	1933	Jul 22 to Aug 25
31	Ed Delahanty	NL	PHI	1899	Jul 15 to Aug 18 (2G)
31	Nap Lajoie	AL	CLE	1906	Jun 4 to Jul 4 (2G)
31	Sam Rice	AL	WAS	1924	Aug 23 to Sep 24
31	Willie Davis	NL	LA	1969	Aug 1 to Sep 3
31	Rico Carty	NL	ATL	1970	Apr 8 to May 15
31	Ken Landreaux	AL	MIN	1980	Apr 23 to May 30
31	Vladimir Guerrero	NL	MON	1999	Jul 27 to Aug 26
30	Cal McVey	NL	CHI	1876	Jun 1 to Aug 8
30	Elmer Smith	NL	CIN	1898	Apr 15 to May 30
30	Tris Speaker	AL	BOS	1912	Jun 17 to Jul 16
30	Goose Goslin	AL	DET	1934	May 6 to Jun 5 (2G)
30	Stan Musial	NL	STL	1950	Jun 27 (1G) to Jul 26
30	Ron LeFlore	AL	DET	1976	Apr 17 to May 27
30	George Brett	AL	KC	1980	Jul 18 to Aug 18
30	Jerome Walton	NL	CHI	1989	Jul 21 to Aug 20
30	Sandy Alomar Jr.	AL	CLE	1997	May 25 to Jul 6
30	Nomar Garciaparra	AL	BOS	1997	Jul 26 to Aug 29
30	Eric Davis	AL	BAL	1998	Jul 12 to Aug 15
30	Luis Gonzalez	NL	ARI	1999	Apr 11 to May 18
30	Albert Pujols	NL	STL	2003	Jul 12 to Aug 16
30	Willy Taveras	NL	HOU	2006	Jul 27 to Aug 28

(281) Most Consecutive Games with a Hit over Two Seasons

56	Joe DiMaggio	AL	NY	1941	May 15 to Jul 16	
45	Willie Keeler	NL	BAL	1896-97	Sep 26, 1896 to Jun 18 1897;	1 game to end 1896 and 44 to begin 1897
44	Pete Rose	NL	CIN	1978	Jun 14 to Jul 31	
42	Bill Dahlen	NL	CHI	1894	Jun 20 to Aug 6	
41	George Sisler	AL	STL	1922	Jul 27 to Sep 17	
40	Ty Cobb	AL	DET	1911	May 15 to Jul 2	
39	Paul Molitor	AL	MIL	1987	Jul 16 to Aug 25	
38	Jimmy Rollins	NL	PHI	2005-06	Aug 23, 2005 to April 5, 2006;	36 games to end 2005 and 2 to begin 2006
37	Tommy Holmes	NL	BOS	1945	Jun 6 (1G) to Jul 8 (2G)	
36	Gene DeMontreville	NL	WAS	1896-97	Sep 7, 1896 (2G) to May 17, 1897;	17 games to end 1896 and 19 to begin 1897
35	Fred Clarke	NL	LOU	1895	Aug 5 to Sep 9	
35	Ty Cobb	AL	DET	1917	May 31 to Jul 5	
35	George Sisler	AL	STL	1924-25	Sep 27, 1924 to May 19, 1925;	1 game to end 1924 and 34 to begin 1925
35	Luis Castillo	NL	FLA	2002	May 8 to Jun 21	
35	Chase Utley	NL	PHI	2006	Jun 23 to Aug 3	
34	George McQuinn	AL	STL	1938	Jul 24 (1G) to Aug 25 (1G)	
34	Dom DiMaggio	AL	BOS	1949	Jun 29 to Aug 7	
34	Benito Santiago	NL	SD	1987	Aug 25 to Oct 2	
33	George Davis	NL	NY	1893	Aug 3 to Sep 9 (2G)	
33	Hal Chase	AL	NY	1907	Jun 24 (1G) to Jul 26 (1G)	
33	Rogers Hornsby	NL	STL	1922	Aug 13 to Sep 19	
33	Heinie Manush	AL	WAS	1933	Jul 22 to Aug 25	
32	Harry Heilmann	AL	DET	1922-23	Aug 17, 1922 to May 15 1923;	11 games to end 1922 and 21 to begin 1923
32	Hal Morris	NL	CIN	1996-97	Aug 27, 1996 to Apr 3, 1997;	29 games to end 1996 and 3 to begin 1997
31	Ed Delahanty	NL	PHI	1899	Jul 15 to Aug 18 (2G)	
31	Nap Lajoie	AL	CLE	1906	Jun 4 to Jul 4 (2G)	
31	Sam Rice	AL	WAS	1924	Aug 23 to Sep 24	
31	Vada Pinson	NL	CIN	1965-66	Sep 3, 1965 to April 18, 1966;	27 games to end 1965 and 4 to begin 1966
31	Willie Davis	NL	LA	1969	Aug 1 to Sep 3	
31	Rico Carty	NL	ATL	1970	Apr 8 to May 15	
31	Ron LeFlore	AL	DET	1975-76	Sep 27, 1975 to May 27 1976;	1 game to end 1975 and 30 to begin 1976
31	Ken Landreaux	AL	MIN	1980	Apr 23 to May 30	
31	Vladimir Guerrero	NL	MON	1999	Jul 27 to Aug 26	
30	Cal McVey	NL	CHI	1876	Jun 1 to Aug 8	
30	Elmer Smith	NL	CIN	1898	Apr 15 to May 30	
30	Tris Speaker	AL	BOS	1912	Jun 17 to Jul 16	
30	Charlie Grimm	NL	CHI	1922-23	Sep 24, 1922 to May 16, 1923;	5 games to end 1922 and 25 to begin 1923
30	Sam Rice	AL	WAS	1929-30	Oct 5, 1929 to May 17, 1930 (2G);	2 games to end 1929 and 28 to begin 1930
30	Goose Goslin	AL	DET	1934	May 6 to Jun 5 (2G)	
30	Stan Musial	NL	STL	1950	Jun 27 (1G) to Jul 26	
30	George Brett	AL	KC	1980	Jul 18 to Aug 18	
30	Jerome Walton	NL	CHI	1989	Jul 21 to Aug 20	
30	Sandy Alomar Jr.	AL	CLE	1997	May 25 to Jul 6	
30	Nomar Garciaparra	AL	BOS	1997	Jul 26 to Aug 29	
30	Eric Davis	AL	BAL	1998	Jul 12 to Aug 15	
30	Luis Gonzalez	NL	ARI	1999	Apr 11 to May 18	
30	Albert Pujols	NL	STL	2003	Jul 12 to Aug 16	
30	Willy Taveras	NL	HOU	2006	Jul 27 to Aug 28	

(282) Most Consecutive Games with an Extra-base Hit

14	Paul Waner	NL	PIT	1927	Jun 3 to Jun 19
14	Chipper Jones	NL	ATL	2006	Jun 26 to Jul 16
12	Tip O'Neill	AA	STL	1887	Aug 24 to Sep 5
12	Rogers Hornsby	NL	BOS	1928	May 27 (1G) to Jun 9 (1G)
11	Rogers Hornsby	NL	STL	1924	Aug 20 (1G) to Aug 27
11	Hank Greenberg	AL	DET	1935	Jun 21 to Jun 30 (1G)
11	Bob Bailey	NL	MON	1970	Jun 22 (2G) to Jul 12
11	Jesse Barfield	AL	TOR	1985	Aug 17 to Aug 27
11	Bobb Abreu	NL	PHI	2005	May 7 to May 18

(283) Longest Consecutive Game On-base Streaks

84	Ted Williams	AL	BOS	1949
74	Joe DiMaggio	AL	NY	1941
69	Ted Williams	AL	BOS	1941
64	Bill Joyce	AA	BOS	1891
63	Orlando Cabrera	AL	LA	2006
60	George Van Haltren	NL	PIT	1893
58	Duke Snider	NL	BRO	1954
58	Barry Bonds	NL	SF	2003
57	Cupid Childs	NL	CLE	1892
57	Jake Stenzel	NL	PIT	1895
57	George Kell	AL	DET	1950
57	Wade Boggs	AL	BOS	1985
56	Ed Delahanty	NL	PHI	1896
56	Bill Joyce	NL	WAS-NY	1896
			WAS (25), NY(31)	
56	Arky Vaughan	NL	PIT	1936
56	Ryan Klesko	NL	SD	2002
55	Billy Hamilton	NL	BOS	1896
55	Ty Cobb	AL	DET	1915
55	Stan Musial	NL	STL	1943
55	Jim Thome	AL	CLE	2002
54	Bill Joyce	NL	WAS	1894
54	Ray Blades	NL	STL	1925
53	Luke Appling	AL	CHI	1936

53	Derek Jeter	AL	NY	1999
53	Shawn Green	NL	LA	2000
53	Alex Rodriguez	AL	NY	2004
52	Denny Lyons	AA	PHI	1887
52	Ty Cobb	AL	DET	1914
52	Tris Speaker	AL	CLE	1920
52	Jack Tobin	AL	STL	1922
52	Lou Gehrig	AL	NY	1934
52	Mel Almada	AL	STL	1938
52	Jim Wynn	NL	HOU	1969
52	Greg Gross	NL	HOU	1975
52	Tony Phillips	AL	DET	1993
52	Frank E. Thomas	AL	CHI	1996
52	Gary Sheffield	NL	ATL	2002
51	Joe Kelley	NL	BAL	1896
51	Babe Ruth	AL	NY	1923
51	Ken Williams	AL	STL	1923
51	Joe DiMaggio	AL	NY	1937
51	George Brett	AL	KC	1980
50	Tommy McCarthy	NL	BOS	1895
50	Mike Griffin	NL	BRO	1895
50	Tris Speaker	AL	CLE	1926
50	Vince Coleman	NL	STL	1987
50	Lou Whitaker	AL	DET	1991

(284) Most Consecutive Games with a Home Run

GAMES					TOTAL HR	
8	Dale Long	NL	PIT	1956	8	
8	Don Mattingly	AL	NY	1987	10	Includes 2 grand slams
8	Ken Griffey Jr.	AL	SEA	1993	8	
7	Jim Thome	AL	CLE	2002	7	
7	Kevin Mench	AL	TEX	2006	7	Includes 2 grand slams
6	Ken Williams	AL	STL	1922	6	
6	George Kelly	NL	NY	1924	7	
6	Lou Gehrig	AL	NY	1931	6	Includes 3 grand slams
6	Walker Cooper	NL	NY	1947	7	
6	Willie Mays	NL	NY	1955	7	
6	Roy Sievers	AL	WAS	1957	6	HR in 6th game hit in 17th inn.
6	Roger Maris	AL	NY	1961	7	
6	Willie Mays	NL	SF	1965	6	
6	Frank Howard	AL	WAS	1968	10	10 in 6 games for record; 10 HRs in 20 AB.
6	Reggie Jackson	AL	BAL	1976	6	
6	Graig Nettles	NL	SD	1984	7	
6	Barry Bonds	NL	SF	2001	9	Bonds had two six-game streaks during 2001 season
6	Barry Bonds	NL	SF	2001	6	Bonds had two six-game streaks during 2001 season
6	Jose Cruz Jr.	AL	TOR	2001	6	
6	Travis Hafner	AL	CLE	2005	7	
6	Morgan Ensberg	NL	HOU	2006	6	
6	Jason Bay	NL	PIT	2006	7	
6	Frank E. Thomas	AL	OAK	2006	6	

(285) 40 Home Runs and 40 Stolen Bases in a Season

				HR	SB
Jose Canseco	AL	OAK	1988	42	40
Barry Bonds	NL	SF	1996	42	40
Alex Rodriguez	AL	SEA	1998	42	46
Alfonso Soriano	NL	WAS	2006	46	41

(286) 30 Home Runs and 30 Stolen Bases in a Season

				HR	SB
Ken Williams	AL	STL	1922	39	37
Willie Mays	NL	NY	1956	36	40
Willie Mays	NL	NY	1957	35	38
Hank Aaron	NL	MIL	1963	44	31
Bobby Bonds	NL	SF	1969	32	45
Tommy Harper	AL	MIL	1970	31	38
Bobby Bonds	NL	SF	1973	39	43
Bobby Bonds	AL	NY	1975	32	30
Bobby Bonds	AL	CAL	1977	37	41
Bobby Bonds	AL	CHI-TEX	1978	31	43
		CHI (2 HR, 6 SB); TEX (29 HR, 37 SB)			
Dale Murphy	NL	ATL	1983	36	30
Joe Carter	AL	CLE	1987	32	31
Darryl Strawberry	NL	NY	1987	39	36
Eric Davis	NL	CIN	1987	37	50
Howard Johnson	NL	NY	1987	36	32
Jose Canseco	AL	OAK	1988	42	40
Howard Johnson	NL	NY	1989	36	41
Barry Bonds	NL	PIT	1990	33	52
Ron Gant	NL	ATL	1990	32	33
Howard Johnson	NL	NY	1991	38	30
Ron Gant	NL	ATL	1991	32	34
Barry Bonds	NL	PIT	1992	34	39
Sammy Sosa	NL	CHI	1993	33	36
Barry Bonds	NL	SF	1995	33	31
Sammy Sosa	NL	CHI	1995	36	34
Barry Larkin	NL	CIN	1996	33	36
Barry Bonds	NL	SF	1996	42	40
Dante Bichette	NL	COL	1996	31	31
Ellis Burks	NL	COL	1996	40	32
Barry Bonds	NL	SF	1997	40	37
Larry Walker	NL	COL	1997	49	33
Raul Mondesi	NL	LA	1997	30	32
Jeff Bagwell	NL	HOU	1997	43	31
Alex Rodriguez	AL	SEA	1998	42	46
Shawn Green	AL	TOR	1998	35	35
Jeff Bagwell	NL	HOU	1999	42	30
Raul Mondesi	NL	LA	1999	33	36
Preston Wilson	NL	FLA	2000	31	36
Jose Cruz Jr.	AL	TOR	2001	34	32
Bobby Abreu	NL	PHI	2001	31	36
Vladimir Guerrero	NL	MON	2001	34	37
Alfonso Soriano	AL	NY	2002	39	41
Vladimir Guerrero	NL	MON	2002	39	40
Alfonso Soriano	AL	NY	2003	38	35
Bobby Abreu	NL	PHI	2004	30	40
Carlos Beltran	AL-NL	KC-HOU	2004	38	42
		KC (15 HR, 14 SB); HOU (23 HR, 28 SB)			
Alfonso Soriano	NL	WAS	2006	46	41

(287) 20 Home Runs and 50 Stolen Bases in a Season

				HR	SB
Lou Brock	NL	STL	1967	21	52
Cesar Cedeno	NL	HOU	1972	22	55
Cesar Cedeno	NL	HOU	1973	25	56
Joe Morgan	NL	CIN	1973	26	67
Cesar Cedeno	NL	HOU	1974	26	57
Joe Morgan	NL	CIN	1974	22	58
Joe Morgan	NL	CIN	1976	27	60
Ryne Sandberg	NL	CHI	1985	26	54
Rickey Henderson	AL	NY	1985	24	80
Eric Davis	NL	CIN	1986	27	80
Rickey Henderson	AL	NY	1986	28	87
Eric Davis	NL	CIN	1987	37	50
Rickey Henderson	AL	OAK	1990	28	65
Barry Bonds	NL	PIT	1990	33	52
Brady Anderson	AL	BAL	1992	21	53
Rickey Henderson	AL	OAK-TOR	1993	21	53
		OAK (17 HR, 31 SB); TOR (4 HR, 22 SB)			
Craig Biggio	NL	HOU	1998	20	50

Jeff Bagwell

(288) 40 Home Runs and 200 Hits in a Season

				HR	HITS
Babe Ruth	AL	NY	1921	59	204
Rogers Hornsby	NL	STL	1922	42	250
Babe Ruth	AL	NY	1923	41	205
Babe Ruth	AL	NY	1924	46	200
Lou Gehrig	AL	NY	1927	47	218
Chuck Klein	NL	PHI	1929	43	219
Hack Wilson	NL	CHI	1930	56	208
Lou Gehrig	AL	NY	1930	41	220
Chuck Klein	NL	PHI	1930	40	250
Lou Gehrig	AL	NY	1931	46	211
Jimmie Foxx	AL	PHI	1932	58	213
Jimmie Foxx	AL	PHI	1933	48	204
Lou Gehrig	AL	NY	1934	49	210
Hal Trosky	AL	CLE	1936	42	216
Lou Gehrig	AL	NY	1936	49	205
Joe DiMaggio	AL	NY	1937	46	215
Hank Greenberg	AL	DET	1937	40	200
Al Rosen	AL	CLE	1953	43	201
Hank Aaron	NL	Mil	1963	44	201
Billy Williams	NL	CHI	1970	42	205
Jim Rice	AL	BOS	1978	46	213
Mo Vaughn	AL	BOS	1996	44	207
Ellis Burks	NL	COL	1996	40	211
Larry Walker	NL	COL	1997	49	208
Mike Piazza	NL	LA	1997	40	201
Mo Vaughn	AL	BOS	1998	40	205
Albert Belle	AL	CHI	1998	49	200
Vinny Castilla	NL	COL	1998	46	206
Todd Helton	NL	STL	2000	42	216
Alex Rodriguez	AL	TEX	2001	52	201
Albert Pujols	NL	STL	2003	43	212
Adrian Beltre	NL	LA	2004	48	200

(289) 50 Home Runs and 150 RBI in a Season

				HR	RBI
Babe Ruth	AL	NY	1921	59	171
Babe Ruth	AL	NY	1927	60	164
Hack Wilson	NL	CHI	1930	56	191
Jimmie Foxx	AL	PHI	1932	58	169
Jimmie Foxx	AL	BOS	1938	50	175
Sammy Sosa	NL	CHI	1998	66	158
Sammy Sosa	NL	CHI	2001	64	160

(290) 40 Home Runs with Fewer than 100 RBI in a Season

				HR	RBI	
Duke Snider	NL	BRO	1957	40	92	
Mickey Mantle	AL	NY	1958	42	97	
Mickey Mantle	AL	NY	1960	40	94	
Harmon Killebrew	AL	MIN	1963	45	96	
Hank Aaron	NL	ATL	1969	44	97	
Rico Petrocelli	AL	BOS	1969	40	97	
Hank Aaron	NL	ATL	1973	40	96	
Davey Johnson	NL	ATL	1973	40	99	
Darrell Evans	AL	DET	1985	40	94	
Ken Griffey Jr.	AL	SEA	1994	40	90	Strike-shortened season
Matt Williams	NL	SF	1994	43	96	Strike-shortened season
Barry Bonds	NL	SF	2003	45	90	
Alfonso Soriano	NL	WAS	2006	46	95	
Adam Dunn	NL	CIN	2006	40	92	

(291) 50 Doubles and 30 Home Runs in a Season

				2B	HR
Lou Gehrig	AL	NY	1927	52	47
Chuck Klein	NL	PHI	1930	59	40
Chuck Klein	NL	PHI	1932	50	38
Joe Medwick	NL	STL	1937	56	31
Hank Greenberg	AL	DET	1940	50	41
Stan Musial	NL	STL	1953	53	30
Frank Robinson	NL	CIN	1962	51	39
Don Mattingly	AL	NY	1986	53	31
Albert Belle	AL	CLE	1995	52	50
Alex Rodriguez	AL	SEA	1996	54	36
Juan Gonzalez	AL	TEX	1998	50	45
Todd Helton	NL	COL	2000	59	42
Carlos Delgado	AL	TOR	2000	57	41
Lance Berkman	NL	HOU	2001	55	34
Todd Helton	NL	COL	2001	54	49
Alfonso Soriano	AL	NY	2002	51	39
Albert Pujols	NL	STL	2003	51	43
Albert Pujols	NL	STL	2004	51	46
Derrek Lee	NL	CHI	2005	50	46

(292) Most RBI in a Season with No Home Runs

121	Hughie Jennings	NL	BAL	1896	80	Lou Bierbauer	AA	PHI	1888
108	Lave Cross	AL	PHI	1902	80	George Davis	AL	CHI	1906
93	Ed McKean	NL	CLE	1892	79	George Stovall	AL	CLE	1911
91	Kitty Bransfield	NL	PIT	1901	79	Luke Appling	AL	CHI	1940
91	Cap Anson	NL	CHI	1893	78	Tommy Thevenow	NL	PHI	1930
91	Jack Doyle	NL	BRO	1903	77	John Ward	NL	NY	1894
91	Nap Lajoie	AL	CLE	1906	77	Lave Cross	AL	PHI	1905
90	Harry Swacina	FL	BAL	1914	76	Milt Stock	NL	STL	1920
90	Nap Lajoie	AL	CLE	1912	76	Hal Chase	AL	NY	1906
90	Duffy Lewis	AL	BOS	1913	76	Charlie Grimm	NL	PIT	1922
86	Gene DeMontreville	NL	BAL	1898	75	Ozzie Smith	NL	STL	1987
85	Blondie Purcell	AA	PHI	1899	75	Joe Tinker	NL	CHI	1912
82	Rebel Oakes	FL	PIT	1915	75	Willie Kamm	AL	CHI-CLE	1931
81	Tommy Corcoran	NL	CIN	1899				CHI (9); CLE (66)	

(293) Most At-bats in a Season with No Home Runs

672	Rabbit Maranville	NL	BOS	1922	619	Billy Herman	NL	CHI	1933
658	Doc Cramer	AL	BOS	1938	618	Eddie Foster	AL	WAS	1915
654	Frank Taveras	NL	PIT	1978	617	Harry Swacina	FL	BAL	1914
653	Marvell Wynne	NL	PIT	1984	616	Irv Hall	AL	PHI	1945
650	Maury Wills	NL	LA	1965	615	Joe Quinn	NL	CLE	1899
650	Larry Bowa	NL	PHI	1971	614	Freddy Spurgeon	AL	CLE	1926
650	Dave Cash	NL	MON	1977	613	Dave Bancroft	NL	PHI-NY	1920
648	Nellie Fox	AL	CHI	1952				PHI (171); NY (442)	
647	Sparky Adams	NL	CHI	1927	613	Harold Reynolds	AL	SEA	1989
646	Tom Oliver	AL	BOS	1930	612	Jack Perconte	AL	SEA	1984
643	Doc Cramer	AL	BOS	1936	610	Patsy Donovan	NL	PIT	1898
639	Milt Stock	NL	STL	1920	609	Jiggs Donahue	AL	CHI	1907
638	Roy Hughes	AL	CLE	1936	609	Ozzie Smith	NL	STL	1980
638	Johnny Pesky	AL	BOS	1947	606	Joe Gedeon	AL	STL	1920
636	Bill Wambsganss	AL	BOS	1924	606	Red Schoendienst	NL	STL	1946
636	Jerry Remy	AL	BOS	1982	604	Dick Bartell	NL	PHI	1934
630	Doc Cramer	AL	DET	1942	603	Charlie Hemphill	AL	STL	1907
627	Maury Wills	NL	PIT	1968	603	Ernie R. Johnson	AL	CHI	1922
626	Richie Ashburn	NL	PHI	1957	602	Freddy Parent	AL	BOS	1905
624	Jesse Burkett	NL	CLE	1898	602	Nap Lajoie	AL	CLE	1906
624	Jimmy Barrett	AL	DET	1904	601	Don Kessinger	NL	CHI	1975
624	Sparky Adams	NL	CHI	1926	601	Jason Kendall	AL	OAK	2005
624	Larry Bowa	NL	PHI	1976	600	Vince Coleman	NL	STL	1986
623	Nellie Fox	AL	CHI	1958	600	Ozzie Smith	NL	STL	1987
622	Arlie Latham	NL	CIN	1892					

(294) More Home Runs than Walks in a Season (min. 30 HR)

				HR	WALKS	
Dante Bichette	NL	COL	1995	40	22	
Alfonso Soriano	AL	NY	2002	39	23	
Matt Williams	NL	SF	1993	38	27	
Dave Kingman	NL	NY	1976	37	28	
Tony Armas Sr.	AL	BOS	1983	36	29	
Ivan Rodriguez	AL	TEX	1999	35	24	
Garret Anderson	AL	ANA	2000	35	24	
Walker Cooper	NL	NY	1947	35	24	
Bob Horner	NL	ATL	1980	35	27	
Tony Armas Sr.	AL	OAK	1980	35	29	
Bob Horner	NL	ATL	1979	33	22	
Tony Batista	NL	MON	2004	32	26	
Ernie Banks	NL	CHI	1968	32	27	
Joe Carter	AL	CLE	1987	32	27	
Andres Galarraga	NL	COL	1994	31	19	
Andre Dawson	NL	CHI	1991	31	22	
Felipe Alou	NL	ATL	1966	31	24	
Jose Guillen	NL-AL	CIN-OAK	2003	31	24	CIN (23 HR, 17 BB); OAK (8 HR, 7 BB)
Mack Jones	NL	MIL	1965	31	29	
Joe Pepitone	AL	NY	1966	31	29	
Butch Hobson	AL	BOS	1977	30	27	

(295) Hitting 49 Home Runs in a Season but never 50

Lou Gehrig	1934, 1936
Ted Kluszewski	1954
Harmon Killebrew	1964, 1969
Frank Robinson	1966
Andre Dawson	1987
Larry Walker	1997
Todd Helton	2001
Shawn Green	2001
Albert Pujols	2006

(296) Led Two Major Leagues in Home Runs in Different Seasons

Harry Stovey	NL	1880-1881	AA	1883, 1885, 1891	
Bug Holliday	AA	1889	NL	1892	
Buck Freeman	NL	1889	AL	1903	
Sam Crawford	NL	1901	AL	1908	
Mark McGwire	AL	1987, 1996	NL	1998-1999	
Fred McGriff	AL	1989	NL	1992	

(297) Most Home Runs by a Batter over Two Consecutive Seasons

135	Mark McGwire	NL	STL	1998-1999	
129	Sammy Sosa	NL	CHI	1998-1999	
128	Mark McGwire	AL-NL	OAK-STL	1997-1998	OAK (34); STL (94)
122	Barry Bonds	NL	SF	2000-2001	
119	Barry Bonds	NL	SF	2001-2002	
114	Babe Ruth	AL	NY	1927-1928	
114	Sammy Sosa	NL	CHI	2000-2001	
113	Babe Ruth	NL	NY	1920-1921	
113	Sammy Sosa	NL	CHI	1999-2000	
113	Sammy Sosa	NL	CHI	2001-2002	
112	Ken Griffey Jr.	AL	SEA	1997-1998	
110	Mark McGwire	AL-NL	OAK-STL	1996-1997	OAK (86); STL (24)
109	Alex Rodriguez	AL	TEX	2001-2002	
107	Babe Ruth	AL	NY	1926-1927	
106	Jimmie Foxx	AL	PHI	1932-1933	
105	Ken Griffey Jr.	AL	SEA	1996-1997	
104	Ken Griffey Jr.	AL	SEA	1998-1999	
104	Alex Rodriguez	AL	TEX	2002-2003	
102	Sammy Sosa	NL	CHI	1997-1998	
101	Ralph Kiner	NL	PIT	1949-1950	
101	Jim Thome	AL	CLE	2001-2002	
101	David Ortiz	AL	BOS	2005-2006	
100	Babe Ruth	AL	NY	1928-1929	
100	Roger Maris	AL	NY	1960-1961	

(298) Most Home Runs in each Month of the Season

March	Vinny Castilla	NL	COL	2	1998
March	Corey Patterson	NL	CHI	2	2003
March	Jorge Posada	AL	NY	2	2004
April	Albert Pujols	NL	STL	14	2006
May	Barry Bonds	NL	SF	17	2001
June	Sammy Sosa	NL	CHI	20	1998
July	Albert Belle	AL	CHI	16	1999
July	Mark McGwire	NL	STL	16	1999
August	Rudy York	AL	DET	18	1937
September	Babe Ruth	AL	NY	17	1927
September	Albert Belle	AL	CLE	17	1995
October	Sammy Sosa	NL	CHI	5	2001
October	Richie Sexson	NL	MIL	5	2001

(299) Pinch-hit Home Run and One Other Home Run in the Same Game

Les Mann	NL	STL	May 11, 1923		John Mayberry	AL	TOR	Jun 26, 1978
Goose Goslin	AL	WAS	Aug 24, 1933		Joe Lefebvre	NL	SD	Apr 30, 1981
Jeff Heath	NL	BOS	Aug 27, 1949		Thad Bosley	NL	CHI	Aug 12, 1985
Wally Post	NL	CIN	Jul 2, 1960		Marvell Wynne	NL	SD	Apr 13, 1986
Del Rice	AL	LA	Jun 18, 1961		Mark Ryal	AL	CAL	May 13, 1987
Roy Sievers	AL	CHI	Jun 21, 1961		Jack Howell	AL	CAL	May 27, 1987
			1G		Geno Petralli	AL	TEX	Sep 29, 1987
Don Mincher	AL	MIN	Apr 28, 1962		Steve Balboni	AL	NY	May 23, 1990
Joe Foy	AL	BOS	Jun 9, 1967		Jeff Bagwell	NL	HOU	May 10, 1992
Jim Gentile	AL	BAL	Jun 30, 1970		Darrin Jackson	AL	CHI	Apr 6, 1994
Tony Horton	AL	CLE	Jul 24, 1970		Kirk Gibson	AL	DET	May 28, 1994
			2G		Robin Ventura	AL	CHI	May 28, 1996
Frank Howard	AL	DET	Jul 26, 1973		Ryan Howard	NL	PHI	May 14, 2006
Steve Brye	AL	MIN	Sep 7, 1975		Jeff Salazar	AL	CHI	Sep 18, 2006

(300) Most Grand Slams in a Season

6	Don Mattingly	AL	NY	1987		4	Sid Gordon	NL	BOS	1950
6	Travis Hafner	AL	CLE	2006		4	Al Rosen	AL	CLE	1951
5	Ernie Banks	NL	CHI	1955		4	Ray Boone	AL	CLE-DET	1953
5	Jim Gentile	AL	BAL	1961					CLE (2); DET (2)	
5	Richie Sexson	AL	SEA	2006		4	Jim Northrup	AL	DET	1968
4	Frank Schulte	NL	CHI	1911		4	Albert Belle	AL	CHI	1997
4	Babe Ruth	AL	BOS	1919		4	Mike Piazza	NL	LA-FLA-NY	1998
4	Lou Gehrig	AL	NY	1934					LA (3): FLA (0); NY (1)	
4	Rudy York	AL	DET	1938		4	Edgar Martinez	AL	SEA	2000
4	Vince DiMaggio	NL	PHI	1945		4	Jason Giambi	AL	OAK	2000
4	Tommy Henrich	AL	NY	1948		4	Phil Nevin	NL	SD	2001
4	Ralph Kiner	NL	PIT	1949						

(301) Most Leadoff Home Runs in a Season

13	Alfonso Soriano	AL	NY	2003		8	Rick Monday	NL	CHI	1976
12	Brady Anderson	AL	BAL	1996		8	Kal Daniels	NL	CIN	1987
11	Bobby Bonds	NL	SF	1993		8	Barry Bonds	NL	PIT	1988
11	Jacque Jones	AL	MIN	2002		8	Rickey Henderson	AL	OAK-TOR	1993
9	Rickey Henderson	AL	NY	1986					OAK (7); TOR (1)	
9	Brad Wilkerson	NL	MON	2004		8	Chuck Knoblauch	AL	NY	1999
9	Ray Durham	NL	SF	2004		8	Craig Biggio	NL	HOU	2001
9	Alfonso Soriano	NL	WAS	2006		8	Alfonso Soriano	AL	NY	2002

(302) Most Extra-inning Home Runs in a Season

5	Charlie Maxwell	AL	DET	1960	3	Reggie Jackson	AL	OAK	1971
4	Willie Mays	NL	NY	1955	3	Ron Fairly	NL	MON	1973
4	Ron Gant	NL	CIN	1995	3	Dave May	AL	MIL	1973
4	Mark McGwire	NL	STL	1998	3	Tony Perez	NL	CIN	1973
4	Chipper Jones	NL	ATL	1999	3	Gene Tenace	AL	OAK	1973
4	Jim Thome	AL	CLE	2001	3	Joe Ferguson	NL	HOU	1977
3	Lou Gehrig	AL	NY	1935	3	Eddie Murray	AL	BAL	1978
3	Dolph Camilli	NL	BRO	1940	3	Joe Ferguson	NL	LA	1980
3	Babe Young	NL	NY	1941	3	Jack Clark	NL	SF	1981
3	Jeff Heath	AL	CLE	1943	3	Terry Harper	NL	ATL	1985
3	Rudy York	AL	DET	1943	3	Tony Pena	NL	PIT	1985
3	Ted Williams	AL	BOS	1946	3	Kevin Bass	NL	HOU	1987
3	Willie Mays	NL	NY	1951	3	Jack Clark	NL	STL	1987
3	Jackie Robinson	NL	BRO	1951	3	Mark McGwire	AL	OAK	1987
3	Andy Pafko	NL	BRO	1952	3	Bobby Bonilla	NL	PIT	1989
3	Ernie Banks	NL	CHI	1955	3	Jay Buhner	AL	SEA	1991
3	Roy Sievers	AL	WAS	1957	3	Felix Jose	NL	STL	1992
3	Ken Boyer	NL	STL	1958	3	Jeff Bagwell	NL	HOU	1992
3	Mickey Mantle	AL	NY	1959	3	Dante Bichette	NL	COL	1996
3	Frank Robinson	NL	CIN	1962	3	Barry Larkin	NL	CIN	1996
3	Bob Aspromonte	NL	HOU	1963	3	Rafael Palmeiro	AL	BAL	1998
3	Willie Kirkland	AL	CLE	1963	3	Troy Glaus	AL	ANA	2000
3	Willie Mays	NL	SF	1963	3	Lance Berkman	NL	HOU	2001
3	Bob Bailey	NL	PIT	1966	3	Raul Ibanez	AL	KC	2002
3	Ron Santo	NL	CHI	1966	3	Aaron Boone	NL	CIN	2002
3	Art Shamsky	NL	CIN	1966	3	Jose Vidro	NL	MON	2002
3	Willie Stargell	NL	PIT	1966	3	Alex S. Gonzalez	NL	CHI	2003
3	Frank Robinson	AL	BAL	1969	3	David Ortiz	AL	BOS	2003
3	Del Unser	AL	WAS	1969	3	Corey Patterson	NL	CHI	2004
3	Lee May	NL	CIN	1970	3	Craig Wilson	NL	PIT	2004

(303) Most Home Runs in a Season without Leading the League

66	Sammy Sosa	NL	CHI	1998	
64	Sammy Sosa	NL	CHI	2001	
63	Sammy Sosa	NL	CHI	1999	
58	Mark McGwire	AL-NL	OAK-STL	1997	OAK (34); STL (24); combined total highest for all players in 1997
57	Luis Gonzalez	NL	ARI	2001	

(304) Most Times Hitting Two or More Home Runs in One Game in a Season

11	Hank Greenberg	AL	DET	1938		8	Willie Mays	NL	SF	1964
11	Sammy Sosa	NL	CHI	1998		8	Reggie Jackson	AL	OAK	1969
10	Jimmie Foxx	AL	BOS	1938		8	George Foster	NL	CIN	1977
10	Ralph Kiner	NL	PIT	1947		8	Andre Dawson	NL	CHI	1987
10	Mark McGwire	NL	STL	1998		8	Albert Belle	AL	CLE	1995
10	Barry Bonds	NL	SF	2001		8	Andres Galarraga	NL	COL	1996
10	Sammy Sosa	NL	CHI	2001		8	Ken Griffey Jr.	AL	SEA	1997
10	Alex Rodriguez	AL	TEX	2002		8	Larry Walker	NL	COL	1997
9	Willie Mays	NL	NY	1955		8	Andres Galarraga	NL	ATL	1998
9	George A. Bell	AL	TOR	1987		8	Manny Ramirez	AL	CLE	1998
9	Mark McGwire	NL	STL	1999		8	Vladimir Guerrero	NL	MON	2000
9	Andruw Jones	NL	ATL	2005		8	Todd Helton	NL	COL	2000
9	David Ortiz	AL	BOS	2005		8	Luis Gonzalez	NL	ARI	2001
8	Babe Ruth	AL	NY	1927		8	Javy Lopez	NL	ARI	2003
8	Hack Wilson	NL	CHI	1930		8	Derrek Lee	NL	CHI	2005
8	Mickey Mantle	AL	NY	1961						

(305) Batters with 200 Hits and Less than a .300 Batting Average

				HITS	BAV
Juan Pierre	NL	CHI	2006	204	.292
Jo-Jo Moore	NL	NY	1935	201	.295
Matty Alou	NL	PIT	1970	201	.297
Maury Wills	NL	LA	1962	208	.299
Lou Brock	NL	STL	1967	206	.299
Bill Buckner	AL	BOS	1985	201	.299
Buddy Bell	AL	TEX	1979	200	.299
Ralph Garr	NL	ATL	1973	200	.299

COURTESY OF SOCIETY FOR AMERICAN BASEBALL RESEARCH

Gavy Cravath

(306) Greatest Home-Road Disparity in Home Runs in a Season

DIFF.					HOME	ROAD
25	Fred Pfeffer	NL	CHI	1884	25	0
25	Ken Williams	AL	STL	1922	32	7
23	Ned Williamson	NL	CHI	1884	25	2
22	Ralph Kiner	NL	PIT	1948	31	9
22	Dante Bichette	NL	COL	1995	31	9
20	Chuck Klein	NL	PHI	1932	29	9
20	Dolph Camilli	NL	PHI	1936	24	4
20	Hank Greenberg	AL	DET	1938	39	19
20	Jimmie Foxx	AL	BOS	1938	35	15
20	Frank E. Thomas	AL	CHI	2002	24	4
19	Cap Anson	NL	CHI	1884	20	1
19	Gavy Cravath	NL	PHI	1914	19	0
19	Bill Dickey	AL	NY	1938	23	4
19	Ted Kluszewski	NL	CIN	1954	34	15
19	Carlos Delgado	AL	TOR	2000	30	11
19	Moises Alou	NL	CHI	2004	29	10
18	Hal Trosky	AL	CLE	1936	30	12
18	Tommy Henrich	AL	NY	1938	20	2
18	Mel Ott	NL	NY	1943	18	0
18	Bob Horner	NL	ATL	1982	25	7
17	Cliff W. Lee	NL	PHI	1922	17	0
17	Mel Ott	NL	NY	1930	21	4
17	Johnny Mize	NL	STL	1938	22	5
17	Al Kaline	AL	DET	1963	22	5
17	Dick Allen	AL	CHI	1972	27	10
17	Fred Lynn	AL	BOS	1979	28	11
17	Jesse Barfield	AL	TOR	1983	22	5
17	Andres Galarraga	NL	COL	1996	32	15
17	Frank E. Thomas	AL	CHI	2000	30	13
17	Paul Konerko	AL	CHI	2004	29	12
17	Mark Teixeira	AL	TEX	2005	30	13

(307) Greatest Road–Home Disparity in Home Runs in a Season

DIFF.					ROAD	HOME
22	Leon Wagner	AL	LA	1963	24	2
22	Donn Clendenon	NL	PIT	1966	25	3
18	Matt Williams	AL	CLE	1997	25	7
18	Steve Finley	NL	SD	1997	23	5
18	Jeff Bagwell	NL	HOU	1999	30	12
18	Jose Guillen	NL	WAS	2005	21	3
17	Goose Goslin	AL	WAS	1926	17	0
17	Sid Gordon	NL	BOS	1950	22	5
17	Frank J. Thomas	NL	PIT	1958	26	9
17	Jason Giambi	AL	NY	2003	29	12
16	Willie McCovey	NL	SF	1977	22	6
16	Gene Tenace	NL	SD	1979	18	2
15	Alex Kampouris	NL	CIN	1937	16	1
15	Max West	NL	BOS	1939	17	2
15	Elston Howard	AL	NY	1962	18	3
15	Alex Rodriguez	AL	SEA	2000	28	13
15	Jacque Jones	AL	MIN	2002	21	6
15	Jeff Kent	NL	SF	2002	26	11

(308) Most Pinch-hit Home Runs in a Season

7	Dave Hansen	NL	LA	2000		4	Don Mincher	AL	MIN	1964
7	Craig Wilson	NL	PIT	2001		4	Hal Breeden	NL	MON	1973
6	Johnny Frederick	NL	BRO	1932		4	Mike Ivie	NL	SF	1978
5	Joe Cronin	AL	BOS	1943		4	Del Unser	NL	PHI	1979
5	Butch Nieman	NL	BOS	1945		4	Jeff Burroughs	AL	OAK	1982
5	Gene Freese	NL	PHI	1959		4	Danny Heep	NL	NY	1983
5	Jerry Lynch	NL	CIN	1961		4	Candy Maldonado	NL	SF	1986
5	Cliff Johnson	NL	HOU	1974		4	Mark Carreon	NL	NY	1989
5	Lee Lacy	NL	LA	1978		4	Tommy Gregg	NL	ATL	1990
5	Jerry Turner	NL	SD	1978		4	Ernie Riles	NL	SF	1990
5	Billy Ashley	NL	LA	1996		4	Howard Johnson	NL	COL	1994
5	David Dellucci	NL	ARI	2001		4	John Vander Wal	NL	COL	1995
5	Erubiel Durazo	NL	ARI	2001		4	Jack Howell	AL	CAL	1996
5	Mark Sweeney	NL	COL	2004		4	Mark Johnson	NL	PIT	1996
4	Ernie Lombardi	NL	NY	1946		4	Bob Hamelin	NL	MIL	1998
4	Del Wilber	AL	BOS	1953		4	Glenallen Hill	NL	CHI	1999
4	Bill Taylor	NL	NY	1955		4	Angel Echevarria	NL	COL	1999
4	Bob Thurman	NL	CIN	1957		4	Bubba Trammell	AL-NL	TB-NY	2000
4	Rip Repulski	NL	PHI	1958					TB (3); NY (1)	
4	George Crowe	NL	STL	1959		4	Orlando Merced	NL	HOU	2001
4	George Crowe	NL	STL	1960		4	Greg Norton	NL	COL	2003
4	Johnny Blanchard	AL	NY	1961		4	Matt LeCroy	NL	MIN	2004
4	Carl Sawatski	NL	STL	1961		4	Javier Valentin	NL	CIN	2006
4	Jerry Lynch	NL	CIN-PIT	1963		4	Daryle Ward	NL	WAS-ATL	2006
			CIN (2); PIT (2)						WAS (3); ATL (1)	

(309) Most Inside the Park Home Runs in a Season

12	Sam Crawford	NL	CIN	1901		8	Jake Beckley	NL	PIT	1892
9	John Reilly	AA	CIN	1888		8	Duke Farrell	NL	PIT	1892
9	Hobe Ferris	AL	BOS	1903		8	Jesse Burkett	NL	STL	1901
9	Ty Cobb	AL	DET	1909		8	Buck Freeman	AL	BOS	1901
9	Jake Stahl	AL	BOS	1910		8	Chief Wilson	NL	PIT	1911
9	Kiki Cuyler	NL	PIT	1925		8	Tony Boeckel	NL	BOS	1921

(310) Most Home Runs in a Season, before 1893

27	Ned Williamson	NL	CHI	1884		19	Bug Holliday	AA	CIN	1889
25	Fred Pfeffer	NL	CHI	1884		19	Harry Stovey	AA	PHI	1889
22	Abner Dalrymple	NL	CHI	1884		18	Jerry Denny	NL	IND	1889
21	Cap Anson	NL	CHI	1884		17	Roger Connor	NL	NY	1887
20	Sam Thompson	NL	PHI	1889		17	Jimmy Ryan	NL	CHI	1889
19	Billy O'Brien	NL	WAS	1887						

Distance to left field was just 180 feet at Chicago's White Stocking Park. Balls hit over the fence were doubles in 1883, but home runs in 1884.

(311) Most Home Runs in a Season, since 1893

73	Barry Bonds	NL	SF	2001		54	Babe Ruth	AL	NY	1928
70	Mark McGwire	NL	STL	1998		54	Ralph Kiner	NL	PIT	1949
66	Sammy Sosa	NL	CHI	1998		54	Mickey Mantle	AL	NY	1961
65	Mark McGwire	NL	STL	1999		54	David Ortiz	AL	BOS	2006
64	Sammy Sosa	NL	CHI	2001		52	Mickey Mantle	AL	NY	1956
63	Sammy Sosa	NL	CHI	1999		52	Willie Mays	NL	SF	1965
61	Roger Maris	AL	NY	1961		52	George Foster	NL	CIN	1977
60	Babe Ruth	AL	NY	1927		52	Mark McGwire	AL	OAK	1996
59	Babe Ruth	AL	NY	1921		52	Alex Rodriguez	AL	TEX	2001
58	Jimmie Foxx	AL	PHI	1932		52	Jim Thome	AL	CLE	2002
58	Hank Greenberg	AL	DET	1938		51	Johnny Mize	NL	NY	1947
58	Mark McGwire	AL-NL	OAK-STL	1997		51	Ralph Kiner	NL	PIT	1947
			OAK (34); STL (24)			51	Willie Mays	NL	NY	1955
58	Ryan Howard	NL	PHI	2006		51	Cecil Fielder	AL	DET	1990
57	Luis Gonzalez	NL	ARI	2001		51	Andruw Jones	NL	ATL	2005
57	Alex Rodriguez	AL	TEX	2002		50	Jimmie Foxx	AL	BOS	1938
56	Hack Wilson	NL	CHI	1930		50	Albert Belle	AL	CLE	1995
56	Ken Griffey Jr.	AL	SEA	1997		50	Brady Anderson	AL	BAL	1996
56	Ken Griffey Jr.	AL	SEA	1998		50	Greg Vaughn	NL	SD	1998
54	Babe Ruth	AL	NY	1920		50	Sammy Sosa	NL	CHI	2000

(312) Most Home Runs in a Season by a Left-handed Batter

73	Barry Bonds	NL	SF	2001		49	Ted Kluszewski	NL	CIN	1954
61	Roger Maris	AL	NY	1961		49	Ken Griffey Jr.	AL	SEA	1996
60	Babe Ruth	AL	NY	1927		49	Larry Walker	NL	COL	1997
59	Babe Ruth	AL	NY	1921		49	Barry Bonds	NL	SF	2000
58	Ryan Howard	NL	PHI	2006		49	Todd Helton	NL	COL	2001
57	Luis Gonzalez	NL	ARI	2001		49	Shawn Green	NL	LA	2001
56	Ken Griffey Jr.	AL	SEA	1997		49	Jim Thome	AL	CLE	2001
56	Ken Griffey Jr.	AL	SEA	1998		48	Willie Stargell	NL	PIT	1971
54	Babe Ruth	AL	NY	1920		48	Ken Griffey Jr.	AL	SEA	1999
54	Babe Ruth	AL	NY	1928		47	Babe Ruth	AL	NY	1926
54	David Ortiz	AL	BOS	2006		47	Lou Gehrig	AL	NY	1927
52	Jim Thome	AL	CLE	2002		47	Eddie Mathews	NL	MIL	1953
51	Johnny Mize	NL	NY	1947		47	Ted Kluszewski	NL	CIN	1955
50	Brady Anderson	AL	BAL	1996		47	Reggie Jackson	AL	OAK	1969
49	Babe Ruth	AL	NY	1930		47	Rafael Palmeiro	AL	TEX	1999
49	Lou Gehrig	AL	NY	1934		47	Rafael Palmeiro	AL	TEX	2001
49	Lou Gehrig	AL	NY	1936		47	Jim Thome	NL	PHI	2003

(313) Most Home Runs in a Season by a Right-handed Batter

70	Mark McGwire	NL	STL	1998		51	Willie Mays	NL	NY	1955
66	Sammy Sosa	NL	CHI	1998		51	Cecil Fielder	AL	DET	1990
65	Mark McGwire	NL	STL	1999		51	Andruw Jones	NL	ATL	2005
64	Sammy Sosa	NL	CHI	2001		50	Jimmie Foxx	AL	BOS	1938
63	Sammy Sosa	NL	CHI	1999		50	Albert Belle	AL	CLE	1995
58	Jimmie Foxx	AL	PHI	1932		50	Greg Vaughn	NL	SD	1998
58	Hank Greenberg	AL	DET	1938		50	Sammy Sosa	NL	CHI	2000
58	Mark McGwire	AL-NL	OAK-STL	1997		49	Willie Mays	NL	SF	1962
			OAK (34); STL (24)			49	Harmon Killebrew	AL	MIN	1964
57	Alex Rodriguez	AL	TEX	2002		49	Frank Robinson	AL	BAL	1966
56	Hack Wilson	NL	CHI	1930		49	Harmon Killebrew	AL	MIN	1969
54	Ralph Kiner	NL	PIT	1949		49	Mark McGwire	AL	OAK	1987
52	Willie Mays	NL	SF	1965		49	Andre Dawson	NL	CHI	1987
52	George Foster	NL	CIN	1977		49	Albert Belle	AL	CHI	1998
52	Mark McGwire	AL	OAK	1996		49	Sammy Sosa	NL	CHI	2002
52	Alex Rodriguez	AL	TEX	2001		49	Albert Pujols	NL	STL	2006
51	Ralph Kiner	NL	PIT	1947						

(314) Most Home Runs in a Season by a Switch-hitter

54	Mickey Mantle	AL	NY	1961		35	Mickey Mantle	AL	NY	1964
52	Mickey Mantle	AL	NY	1956		35	Ken Singleton	AL	BAL	1979
45	Chipper Jones	NL	ATL	1999		34	Bobby Bonilla	NL	NY	1993
45	Lance Berkman	NL	HOU	2006		34	Tony Clark	AL	DET	1998
42	Mickey Mantle	AL	NY	1958		34	Chipper Jones	NL	ATL	1998
42	Lance Berkman	NL	HOU	2002		34	Carl Everett	AL	BOS	2000
41	Todd Hundley	NL	NY	1996		34	Lance Berkman	NL	HOU	2001
41	Carlos Beltran	NL	NY	2006		34	Jose Cruz Jr.	AL	TOR	2001
40	Mickey Mantle	AL	NY	1960		33	Eddie Murray	AL	BAL	1983
40	Ken Caminiti	NL	SD	1996		33	Mark Teixeira	AL	TEX	2006
38	Howard Johnson	NL	NY	1991		32	Reggie Smith	NL	LA	1977
38	Chipper Jones	NL	ATL	2001		32	Eddie Murray	AL	BAL	1980
38	Mark Teixeira	AL	TEX	2004		32	Eddie Murray	AL	BAL	1982
38	Carlos Beltran	AL-NL	KC-HOU	2004		32	Bobby Bonilla	NL	PIT	1990
			KC (15); HOU (23)			32	Mickey Tettleton	AL	DET	1992
37	Mickey Mantle	AL	NY	1955		32	Mickey Tettleton	AL	DET	1993
36	Howard Johnson	NL	NY	1987		32	Mickey Tettleton	AL	TEX	1995
36	Chipper Jones	NL	ATL	2000		32	Tony Clark	AL	DET	1997
35	Ripper Collins	NL	STL	1934						

(315) Most Home Runs by a Pitcher in a Season

9	Wes Ferrell	AL	CLE	1931		6	Hal Schumacher	NL	NY	1934
7	Jack Stivetts	AA	STL	1890		6	Wes Ferrell	AL	BOS	1935
7	Wes Ferrell	AL	CLE	1933		6	Jack Harshman	AL	CHI	1956
7	Bob Lemon	AL	CLE	1949		6	Jack Harshman	AL	BAL	1958
7	Don Newcombe	NL	BRO	1955		6	Earl Wilson	AL	BOS	1965
7	Don Drysdale	NL	LA	1958		6	Earl Wilson	AL	BOS-DET	1966
7	Don Drysdale	NL	LA	1965					BOS (2); DET (4)	
7	Earl Wilson	AL	DET	1968		6	Ferguson Jenkins	NL	CHI	1971
7	Mike Hampton	NL	COL	2001		6	Rick Wise	NL	PHI	1971
6	John Clarkson	NL	CHI	1887		6	Sonny Siebert	AL	BOS	1971
6	Bill Hutchison	NL	CHI	1894		6	Carlos Zambrano	NL	CHI	2006

(316) Most Home Runs by a Catcher in a Season

42	Javy Lopez	NL	ATL	2003		32	Roy Campanella	NL	BRO	1955
41	Todd Hundley	NL	NY	1996		32	Lance Parrish	AL	DET	1982
40	Roy Campanella	NL	BRO	1953		31	Roy Campanella	NL	BRO	1950
40	Mike Piazza	NL	LA	1997		31	Gary Carter	NL	MON	1977
40	Mike Piazza	NL	NY	1999		31	Mike Piazza	NL	LA	1995
38	Johnny Bench	NL	CIN	1970		31	Mike Lieberthal	NL	PHI	1999
36	Gabby Hartnett	NL	CHI	1930		31	Charles Johnson	AL	BAL-CHI	2000
36	Mike Piazza	NL	LA	1996					BAL (21); CHI (10)	
35	Walker Cooper	NL	NY	1947		30	Yogi Berra	AL	NY	1952
35	Mike Piazza	NL	LA	1993		30	Yogi Berra	AL	NY	1956
35	Ivan Rodriguez	AL	TEX	1999		30	Gus Triandos	AL	BAL	1958
35	Mike Piazza	NL	NY	2000		30	Johnny Bench	NL	CIN	1977
34	Johnny Bench	NL	CIN	1972		30	Todd Hundley	NL	NY	1997
34	Terry Steinbach	AL	OAK	1996		30	Mike Piazza	NL	LA-FLA-NY	1998
34	Javy Lopez	NL	ATL	1998					LA (8); FLA (0); NY (22)	
34	Mike Piazza	NL	NY	2001		30	Mike Piazza	NL	NY	2002
33	Carlton Fisk	AL	CHI	1985		30	Jorge Posada	AL	NY	2003
32	Roy Campanella	NL	BRO	1951						

(317) Most Home Runs by a First Baseman in a Season

69	Mark McGwire	NL	STL	1998		47	Jeff Bagwell	NL	HOU	2000
65	Mark McGwire	NL	STL	1999		46	Lou Gehrig	AL	NY	1931
58	Hank Greenberg	AL	DET	1938		46	Jim Thome	NL	PHI	2003
57	Mark McGwire	AL-NL	OAK-STL	1997		46	Albert Pujols	NL	STL	2004
			OAK (34); STL (23)			46	Derrek Lee	NL	CHI	2005
57	Ryan Howard	NL	PHI	2006		45	Jim Gentile	AL	BAL	1961
51	Jimmie Foxx	AL	PHI	1932		45	Willie McCovey	NL	SF	1969
51	Johnny Mize	NL	NY	1947		45	Richie Sexson	NL	MIL	2001
50	Jimmie Foxx	AL	BOS	1938		45	Richie Sexson	NL	MIL	2003
49	Lou Gehrig	AL	NY	1934		44	Hank Greenberg	AL	DET	1946
49	Lou Gehrig	AL	NY	1936		44	Harmon Killebrew	AL	MIN	1967
49	Ted Kluszewski	NL	CIN	1954		44	Andres Galarraga	NL	ATL	1998
49	Todd Helton	NL	COL	2001		43	Johnny Mize	NL	STL	1940
49	Albert Pujols	NL	STL	2006		43	Tino Martinez	AL	NY	1997
48	Jimmie Foxx	AL	PHI	1933		43	Jeff Bagwell	NL	HOU	1997
48	Mark McGwire	AL	OAK	1987		43	Rafael Palmeiro	AL	BAL	1998
48	Cecil Fielder	AL	DET	1990		42	Gil Hodges	NL	BRO	1954
48	Jim Thome	AL	CLE	2001		42	Dick Stuart	AL	BOS	1963
48	Jim Thome	AL	CLE	2002		42	Mark McGwire	AL	OAK	1992
47	Lou Gehrig	AL	NY	1927		42	Mo Vaughn	AL	BOS	1996
47	Ted Kluszewski	CIN	NL	1955		42	Jeff Bagwell	NL	HOU	1999
47	Andres Galarraga	NL	COL	1996		42	Todd Helton	NL	COL	2000
47	Mark McGwire	AL	OAK	1996						

(318) Most Home Runs by a Second Baseman in a Season

42	Rogers Hornsby	NL	STL	1922	32	Jeff Kent	NL	SF	2000
42	Davey Johnson	NL	ATL	1973	31	Jeff Kent	NL	SF	1998
40	Ryne Sandberg	NL	CHI	1990	31	Chase Utley	NL	PHI	2006
39	Rogers Hornsby	NL	STL	1925	30	Joe Gordon	AL	NY	1940
39	Rogers Hornsby	NL	CHI	1929	30	Bobby Grich	AL	CAL	1979
39	Alfonso Soriano	AL	NY	2002	30	Ryne Sandberg	NL	CHI	1989
38	Alfonso Soriano	AL	NY	2003	29	Joe Gordon	AL	CLE	1947
36	Jay Bell	NL	ARI	1999	28	Joe Gordon	AL	NY	1939
36	Bret Boone	AL	SEA	2001	28	Davey Lopes	NL	LA	1979
36	Jeff Kent	NL	SF	2002	28	Juan Samuel	NL	PHI	1987
35	Bret Boone	AL	SEA	2003	28	Lou Whitaker	AL	DET	1989
35	Alfonso Soriano	AL	TEX	2005	28	Jeff Kent	NL	SF	1997
32	Joe Gordon	AL	CLE	1948	28	Jeff Kent	NL	LA	2005

(319) Most Home Runs by a Third Baseman in a Season

48	Mike Schmidt	NL	PHI	1980	39	Tony Perez	NL	CIN	1970
48	Adrian Beltre	NL	LA	2004	39	Darrell Evans	NL	ATL	1973
47	Eddie Mathews	NL	MIL	1953	38	Mike Schmidt	NL	PHI	1976
47	Alex Rodriguez	AL	NY	2005	38	Mike Schmidt	NL	PHI	1977
46	Eddie Mathews	NL	MIL	1959	38	Matt Williams	NL	SF	1993
46	Vinny Castilla	NL	COL	1998	38	Dean Palmer	AL	TEX	1996
46	Troy Glaus	AL	ANA	2000	38	Jim Thome	AL	CLE	1996
45	Mike Schmidt	NL	PHI	1979	38	Dean Palmer	AL	DET	1999
45	Chipper Jones	NL	ATL	1999	38	Aramis Ramirez	NL	CHI	2006
43	Al Rosen	AL	CLE	1953	37	Al Rosen	AL	CLE	1950
43	Matt Williams	NL	SF	1994	37	Eddie Mathews	NL	MIL	1956
42	Harmon Killebrew	AL	WAS	1959	37	Tony Perez	NL	CIN	1969
41	Tony Batista	AL	TOR	2000	37	Harmon Killebrew	AL	MIN	1970
41	Phil Nevin	NL	SD	2001	37	Mike Schmidt	NL	PHI	1975
41	Troy Glaus	AL	ANA	2001	37	Graig Nettles	AL	NY	1977
40	Eddie Mathews	NL	MIL	1955	37	Chipper Jones	NL	ATL	2001
40	Mike Schmidt	NL	PHI	1983	36	Mike Schmidt	NL	PHI	1974
40	Ken Caminiti	NL	SD	1996	36	Alex Rodriguez	AL	NY	2004
40	Vinny Castilla	NL	COL	1996	36	Aramis Ramirez	NL	CHI	2004
40	Vinny Castilla	NL	COL	1997	36	Troy Glaus	NL	ARI	2005
39	Eddie Mathews	NL	MIL	1954	36	Morgan Ensberg	NL	HOU	2005
39	Eddie Mathews	NL	MIL	1960					

(320) Most Home Runs by a Shortstop in a Season

57	Alex Rodriguez	AL	TEX	2002	36	Rich Aurilia	NL	SF	2001
52	Alex Rodriguez	AL	TEX	2001	35	Nomar Garciaparra	AL	BOS	1998
47	Ernie Banks	NL	CHI	1958	34	Cal Ripken	AL	BAL	1991
46	Alex Rodriguez	AL	TEX	2003	34	Miguel Tejada	AL	OAK	2002
45	Ernie Banks	NL	CHI	1959	34	Miguel Tejada	AL	BAL	2004
44	Ernie Banks	NL	CHI	1955	32	Barry Larkin	NL	CIN	1996
42	Alex Rodriguez	AL	SEA	1998	31	Tony Batista	NL-AL	ARI-TOR	1999
42	Alex Rodriguez	AL	SEA	1999				ARI (5); TOR (26)	
41	Ernie Banks	NL	CHI	1960	31	Miguel Tejada	AL	OAK	2001
41	Alex Rodriguez	AL	SEA	2000	30	Vern Stephens	AL	BOS	1950
40	Rico Petrocelli	AL	BOS	1969	30	Nomar Garciaparra	AL	BOS	1997
39	Vern Stephens	AL	BOS	1949	30	Miguel Tejada	AL	OAK	2000
36	Alex Rodriguez	AL	SEA	1998	30	Jose Valentin	AL	CHI	2004

(321) Most Home Runs by a Left Fielder in a Season

71	Barry Bonds	NL	SF	2001	45	Manny Ramirez	AL	BOS	2005
57	Luis Gonzalez	NL	ARI	2001	44	Carl Yastrzemski	AL	BOS	1967
54	Ralph Kiner	NL	PIT	1949	44	Juan Gonzalez	AL	TEX	1993
51	Babe Ruth	AL	NY	1921	44	Adam Dunn	NL	CIN	2004
51	Ralph Kiner	NL	PIT	1947	43	Ted Williams	AL	BOS	1949
50	Albert Belle	AL	CLE	1995	43	Willie Stargell	NL	PIT	1973
49	Harmon Killebrew	AL	MIN	1964	43	Greg Vaughn	NL	CIN	1999
49	Albert Belle	AL	CHI	1998	43	Gary Sheffield	NL	LA	2000
49	Barry Bonds	NL	SF	2000	43	Barry Bonds	NL	SF	2004
48	Willie Stargell	NL	PIT	1971	42	Billy Williams	NL	CHI	1970
48	Dave Kingman	NL	CHI	1979	42	Barry Bonds	NL	SF	1996
48	Greg Vaughn	NL	SD	1998	42	Barry Bonds	NL	SF	2003
47	Ralph Kiner	NL	PIT	1950	41	Hank Greenberg	AL	DET	1940
47	Albert Belle	AL	CLE	1996	41	Gus Zernial	AL	PHI	1953
46	Harmon Killebrew	AL	MIN	1962	41	Rocky Colavito	AL	DET	1961
46	Barry Bonds	NL	SF	1993	41	Greg Vaughn	AL-NL MIL-SD		1996
46	Alfonso Soriano	NL	WAS	2006			MIL (31); SD (10)		
45	Harmon Killebrew	AL	MIN	1963	40	Willie McCovey	NL	SF	1963
45	George A. Bell	AL	TOR	1987	40	Ben Oglivie	AL	MIL	1980
45	Kevin Mitchell	NL	SF	1989	40	Barry Bonds	NL	SF	1997
45	Barry Bonds	NL	SF	2002	40	Manny Ramirez	AL	BOS	2004

(322) Most Home Runs by a Center Fielder in a Season

56	Hack Wilson	NL	CHI	1930		40	Ken Griffey Jr.	AL	SEA	1993
56	Ken Griffey Jr.	AL	SEA	1998		40	Jim Edmonds	NL	STL	2004
54	Mickey Mantle	AL	NY	1961		39	Hack Wilson	NL	CHI	1929
54	Ken Griffey Jr.	AL	SEA	1997		39	Joe DiMaggio	AL	NY	1948
52	Mickey Mantle	AL	NY	1956		39	Willie Mays	NL	SF	1961
51	Willie Mays	NL	NY	1955		39	Gorman Thomas	AL	MIL	1982
51	Willie Mays	NL	SF	1965		39	Ken Griffey Jr.	NL	CIN	2000
51	Andruw Jones	NL	ATL	2005		38	Willie Mays	NL	SF	1963
50	Brady Anderson	AL	BAL	1996		38	Fred Lynn	AL	BOS	1979
49	Willie Mays	NL	SF	1962		38	Gorman Thomas	AL	MIL	1980
47	Ken Griffey Jr.	AL	SEA	1999		38	Tony Armas Sr.	AL	BOS	1984
46	Joe DiMaggio	AL	NY	1937		38	Carlos Beltran	AL-NL	KC-HOU	2004
46	Ken Griffey Jr.	AL	SEA	1996					KC (15); HOU (23)	
45	Willie Mays	NL	SF	1964		37	Mickey Mantle	AL	NY	1955
43	Gorman Thomas	AL	MIL	1979		37	Jim Wynn	NL	HOU	1967
42	Duke Snider	NL	BRO	1955		37	Dale Murphy	NL	ATL	1985
42	Duke Snider	NL	BRO	1956		37	Ken Griffey Jr.	AL	SEA	1994
41	Cy Williams	NL	PHI	1923		37	Richard Hidalgo	NL	HOU	2000
41	Duke Snider	NL	BRO	1953		37	Jim Edmonds	NL	STL	2003
41	Willie Mays	NL	NY	1954		36	Willie Mays	NL	NY	1956
41	Mickey Mantle	AL	NY	1958		36	Willie Mays	NL	SF	1966
41	Jim Edmonds	NL	STL	2000		36	Dale Murphy	NL	ATL	1984
41	Andruw Jones	NL	ATL	2006		36	Eric Davis	NL	CIN	1987
41	Carlos Beltran	NL	NY	2006		36	Andruw Jones	NL	ATL	2000
40	Duke Snider	NL	BRO	1954		36	Preston Wilson	NL	COL	2003
40	Duke Snider	NL	BRO	1957		36	Steve Finley	NL	ARI-LA	2004
40	Mickey Mantle	AL	NY	1960					ARI (23); LA (13)	

(323) Most Home Runs by a Right Fielder in a Season

65	Sammy Sosa	NL	CHI	1998		42	Mel Ott	NL	NY	1929
64	Sammy Sosa	NL	CHI	2001		42	Rocky Colavito	AL	CLE	1959
56	Roger Maris	AL	NY	1961		42	Gary Sheffield	NL	FLA	1996
51	Sammy Sosa	NL	CHI	1999		42	Shawn Green	AL	TOR	1999
49	Andre Dawson	NL	CHI	1987		42	Vladimir Guerrero	NL	MON	1999
49	Sammy Sosa	NL	CHI	2000		42	Shawn Green	NL	LA	2002
49	Shawn Green	NL	LA	2001		41	Hank Sauer	NL	CHI	1954
49	Sammy Sosa	NL	CHI	2002		41	Frank Robinson	AL	BAL	1966
47	Larry Walker	NL	COL	1997		41	Jeff Burroughs	NL	ATL	1977
45	Reggie Jackson	AL	OAK	1969		40	Chuck Klein	NL	PHI	1929
45	Manny Ramirez	AL	CLE	1998		40	Chuck Klein	NL	PHI	1930
44	Hank Aaron	NL	MIL	1963		40	Wally Post	NL	CIN	1955
44	Hank Aaron	NL	MIL	1969		40	Hank Aaron	NL	MIL	1960
44	Dale Murphy	NL	ATL	1987		40	David Justice	NL	ATL	1993
44	Manny Ramirez	AL	CLE	1999		40	Jay Buhner	AL	SEA	1995
44	Vladimir Guerrero	NL	MON	2000		40	Sammy Sosa	NL	CHI	1996
44	Jermaine Dye	AL	CHI	2006		40	Jay Buhner	AL	SEA	1997
43	Hank Aaron	NL	MIL	1966		40	Sammy Sosa	NL	CHI	2003

(324) Most Home Runs by a Designated Hitter in a Season

47	David Ortiz	AL	BOS	2006		32	Gorman Thomas	AL	SEA	1985
43	David Ortiz	AL	BOS	2005		32	Jose Canseco	AL	TB	1999
39	Frank E. Thomas	AL	OAK	2006		32	Brad Fullmer	AL	TOR	2000
39	Jim Thome	AL	CHI	2006		32	Ellis Burks	AL	CLE	2002
39	Travis Hafner	AL	CLE	2006		32	Travis Hafner	AL	CLE	2005
37	Rafael Palmeiro	AL	TEX	1999		31	Jose Canseco	AL	TEX	1994
37	Edgar Martinez	AL	SEA	2000		31	Rico Carty	AL	TOR-OAK	1978
35	Dave Kingman	AL	OAK	1984				TOR (20); OAK (11)		
35	Dave Kingman	AL	OAK	1986		31	Jim Rice	AL	BOS	1977
35	John Jaha	AL	OAK	1999		31	Andre Thornton	AL	CLE	1982
34	Frank E. Thomas	AL	CHI	2003		30	Don Baylor	AL	BOS	1986
33	David Ortiz	AL	BOS	2004		30	Chili Davis	AL	KC	1997
32	Greg Luzinski	AL	CHI	1983		30	Frank E. Thomas	AL	CHI	2000

(325) Progression of Season Home Run Record

5	George Hall	NL	PHI	1876		59	Babe Ruth	AL	NY	1921
9	Charley Jones	NL	BOS	1879		60	Babe Ruth	AL	NY	1927
14	Harry Stovey	AA	PHI	1883		61	Roger Maris	AL	NY	1961
27	Ned Williamsom	NL	CHI	1884		70	Mark McGwire	NL	STL	1998
29	Babe Ruth	AL	BOS	1919		73	Barry Bonds	NL	SF	2001
54	Babe Ruth	AL	NY	1920						

COURTESY OF SOCIETY FOR AMERICAN BASEBALL RESEARCH

Rogers Hornsby

(326) Most Seasons with 60+ Home Runs

3	Sammy Sosa	1	Roger Maris
2	Mark McGwire	1	Barry Bonds
1	Babe Ruth		

(327) Most Seasons with 50+ Home Runs

4	Sammy Sosa	2	Alex Rodriguez	1	George Foster
4	Babe Ruth	1	Johnny Mize	1	Cecil Fielder
4	Mark McGwire	1	Hack Wilson	1	Barry Bonds
2	Mickey Mantle	1	Brady Anderson	1	Albert Belle
2	Jimmie Foxx	1	Jim Thome	1	Roger Maris
2	Ken Griffey Jr.	1	Hank Greenberg	1	Andruw Jones
2	Ralph Kiner	1	Luis Gonzalez	1	Ryan Howard
2	Willie Mays	1	Greg Vaughn		

(328) Most Seasons with 40+ Home Runs

11	Babe Ruth	5	Duke Snider	3	Jason Giambi
8	Harmon Killebrew	5	Frank E. Thomas	3	Frank Howard
8	Barry Bonds	5	Jim Thome	3	Jeff Bagwell
8	Hank Aaron	5	Manny Ramirez	3	Carlos Delgado
7	Ken Griffey Jr.	4	Mickey Mantle	3	Rocky Colavito
7	Sammy Sosa	4	Eddie Mathews	3	Vinny Castilla
7	Alex Rodriguez	4	Hank Greenberg	3	Jose Canseco
6	Willie Mays	4	Rafael Palmeiro	3	Jay Buhner
6	Mark McGwire	4	Albert Pujols	3	Mike Schmidt
5	Ernie Banks	3	Andres Galarraga	3	Carl Yastrzemski
5	Jimmie Foxx	3	Greg Vaughn	3	Albert Belle
5	Lou Gehrig	3	Johnny Mize	3	David Ortiz
5	Juan Gonzalez	3	Shawn Green	3	Adam Dunn
5	Ralph Kiner	3	Ted Kluszewski		

(329) Most Seasons with 30+ Home Runs

15	Hank Aaron	10	Fred McGriff	8	Gary Sheffield
14	Barry Bonds	10	Rafael Palmeiro	8	Ken Griffey Jr.
13	Babe Ruth	10	Jim Thome	8	Vladimir Guerrero
13	Mike Schmidt	10	Carlos Delgado	7	Reggie Jackson
12	Jimmie Foxx	10	Alex Rodriguez	7	Rocky Colavito
11	Willie Mays	9	Jeff Bagwell	7	Willie McCovey
11	Sammy Sosa	9	Mickey Mantle	7	Joe DiMaggio
11	Mark McGwire	9	Mike Piazza	7	Ralph Kiner
11	Frank Robinson	9	Frank E. Thomas	7	Ernie Banks
11	Manny Ramirez	8	Albert Belle	7	Dave Kingman
10	Harmon Killebrew	8	Jose Canseco	7	Juan Gonzalez
10	Lou Gehrig	8	Ted Williams	7	Jason Giambi
10	Eddie Mathews	8	Mel Ott	7	Andruw Jones

(330) Most Seasons with 20+ Home Runs

20	Hank Aaron	13	Lou Gehrig	12	Manny Ramirez
18	Barry Bonds	13	Mark McGwire	11	Gil Hodges
17	Willie Mays	13	Andre Dawson	11	Juan Gonzalez
17	Frank Robinson	13	Ernie Banks	11	Harold Baines
16	Reggie Jackson	13	Gary Sheffield	11	Ron Santo
16	Ted Williams	12	Willie McCovey	11	Johnny Bench
16	Babe Ruth	12	Dave Kingman	11	Yogi Berra
16	Eddie Murray	12	Orlando Cepeda	11	Norm Cash
15	Mel Ott	12	Dale Murphy	11	Dwight Evans
15	Fred McGriff	12	Sammy Sosa	11	Graig Nettles
15	Dave Winfield	12	Jimmie Foxx	11	Jack Clark
15	Willie Stargell	12	Cal Ripken	11	Rocky Colavito
14	Mike Schmidt	12	Joe Carter	11	Lee May
14	Billy Williams	12	Jeff Bagwell	11	Joe DiMaggio
14	Rafael Palmeiro	12	Jose Canseco	11	Jim Rice
14	Mickey Mantle	12	Frank E. Thomas	11	Carlos Delgado
14	Eddie Mathews	12	Jim Thome	11	Alex Rodriguez
14	Ken Griffey Jr.	12	Mike Piazza	11	Jeff Kent
13	Harmon Killebrew	12	Chipper Jones		

(331) Most Seasons with 10+ Home Runs

23	Hank Aaron	18	Mickey Mantle	15	Will Clark
22	Carl Yastrzemski	18	Andre Dawson	15	Ellis Burks
21	Stan Musial	17	Graig Nettles	15	Johnny Bench
20	Dave Winfield	17	Ernie Banks	15	Joe Carter
20	Al Kaline	17	Fred McGriff	15	Tony Perez
20	Eddie Murray	17	Babe Ruth	15	Andres Galarraga
20	Harold Baines	17	Chili Davis	15	Dave Parker
20	Cal Ripken	17	Rafael Palmeiro	15	George Brett
20	Willie McCovey	17	Ken Griffey Jr.	15	Willie Horton
20	Reggie Jackson	16	Gary Gaetti	15	Dave Kingman
20	Barry Bonds	16	Mike Schmidt	15	Lance Parrish
19	Willie Mays	16	Billy Williams	15	Frank E. Thomas
19	Carlton Fisk	16	Yogi Berra	15	Luis Gonzalez
19	Frank Robinson	16	Jose Canseco	15	Reggie Sanders
19	Darrell Evans	16	Eddie Mathews	15	Jeff Kent
18	Mel Ott	16	Harmon Killebrew	15	Gary Sheffield
18	Willie Stargell	16	Joe Adcock	15	Sammy Sosa
18	Dwight Evans	15	Reggie Smith	15	Larry Walker
18	Ted Williams	15	Don Baylor		

(332) Most Seasons with a Home Run

25	Rickey Henderson	21	Babe Ruth	19	Gary Gaetti
24	Ty Cobb	21	Barry Bonds	19	Barry Larkin
23	Carlton Fisk	20	Andre Dawson	19	Gary Carter
23	Rusty Staub	20	Pete Rose	19	Gabby Hartnett
23	Hank Aaron	20	George Brett	19	Phil Cavarretta
23	Carl Yastrzemski	20	Bill Buckner	19	Darrell Evans
22	Dave Winfield	20	Robin Yount	19	Ken Griffey Sr.
22	Tony Perez	20	Mel Ott	19	Andres Galarraga
22	Stan Musial	20	Cal Ripken	19	Jimmy Dykes
22	Willie Mays	20	Honus Wagner	19	Joe Morgan
22	Brooks Robinson	20	Dwight Evans	19	Alan Trammell
22	Al Kaline	20	Harmon Killebrew	19	Ted Williams
22	Willie McCovey	20	Brian Downing	19	Lance Parrish
21	Graig Nettles	20	Rogers Hornsby	19	Ted Simmons
21	Eddie Murray	20	Paul Molitor	19	Willie Stargell
21	Tim Raines	20	Tony Gwynn	19	Ernie Banks
21	Harold Baines	20	Rafael Palmeiro	19	Dave Parker
21	Reggie Jackson	20	Julio Franco	19	Enos Slaughter
21	Ron Fairly	19	Gary Sheffield	19	Ruben Sierra
21	Frank Robinson	19	Craig Biggio		

(333) Most Home Runs by Two Teammates in a Season

115	AL	NY	1961	Roger Maris (61)	Mickey Mantle (54)
110	NL	SF	2001	Barry Bonds (73)	Rich Aurilia (37)
107	AL	NY	1927	Babe Ruth (60)	Lou Gehrig (47)
101	NL	STL	1998	Mark McGwire (70)	Ray Lankford (31)
100	AL	TEX	2002	Alex Rodriguez (57)	Rafael Palmeiro (43)

(334) Most Home Runs by Three Teammates in a Season

143	AL	NY	1961	Roger Maris (61)	Mickey Mantle (54)	Bill Skowron (28)
137	AL	NY	1961	Roger Maris (61)	Mickey Mantle (54)	Yogi Berra (22)
136	AL	NY	1961	Roger Maris (61)	Mickey Mantle (54)	Johnny Blanchard (21)
136	AL	NY	1961	Roger Maris (61)	Mickey Mantle (54)	Elston Howard (21)
132	NL	SF	2001	Barry Bonds (73)	Rich Aurilia (37)	Jeff Kent (22)

(335) Players Hitting Home Runs for the Most Different Teams

11	Todd Zeile	9	Rickey Henderson
10	Dan Brouthers	9	Dave Martinez
10	Tom Brown	9	Kenny Lofton
9	Tommy Davis		

(336) Best Career Home Runs to At-bats Ratio (min. 100 HR)

AB/HR		AB/HR	
10.61	Mark McGwire	13.96	Manny Ramirez
11.76	Babe Ruth	14.11	Ralph Kiner
12.95	Barry Bonds	14.22	Harmon Killebrew
13.57	Jim Thome	14.28	Adam Dunn
13.94	Albert Pujols	14.29	Sammy Sosa

(337) Most Career Home Runs by a Father and a Son (Each having at least one)

TOTAL	FATHER		SON	
1066	Bobby Bonds	332	Barry Bonds	734
715	Ken Griffey Sr.	152	Ken Griffey Jr.	563
525	Felipe Alou	206	Moises Alou	319
458	Tony Perez	379	Eduardo Perez	79
407	Gus Bell	206	Buddy Bell	201
407	Yogi Berra	358	Dale Berra	49
363	Jose Cruz Sr.	165	Jose Cruz Jr.	198
357	Bob Boone	105	Bret Boone	252
349	Cecil Fielder	319	Prince Fielder	30
324	Buddy Bell	201	David Bell	123
312	Gary Mathews Sr.	234	Gary Mathews Jr.	78
294	Hal McRae	191	Brian McRae	103
284	Randy Hundley	82	Todd Hundley	202
282	Earl Averill	238	Earl Averill Jr.	44
264	Jose Tartabull	2	Danny Tartabull	262
257	Dolph Camilli	239	Doug Camilli	18
256	Ray Boone	151	Bob Boone	105
251	Jeff Burroughs	240	Sean Burroughs	11

(338) Most Career Home Runs by a Grandfather and a Grandson (Each having at least one)

TOTAL	GRANDFATHER		GRANDSON	
403	Ray Boone	151	Bret Boone	252
382	Bert Griffith	4	Matt Williams	378
329	Gus Bell	206	David Bell	123
266	Ray Boone	151	Aaron Boone	115
208	Gus Bell	206	Mike Bell	2

(339) Most Career Home Runs by Two Brothers (Each having at least one)
TOTAL

Total	Player 1	HR 1	Player 2	HR 2
768	Hank Aaron	755	Tommie Aaron	13
508	Eddie Murray	504	Rich Murray	4
486	Joe DiMaggio	361	Vince DiMaggio	125
451	Cal Ripken	431	Billy Ripken	20
448	Joe DiMaggio	361	Dom DiMaggio	87
444	Lee May	354	Carlos May	90
444	Ken Boyer	282	Clete Boyer	162
406	Graig Nettles	390	Jim Nettles	16
402	Jason Giambi	350	Jeremy Giambi	52
367	Bret Boone	252	Aaron Boone	115
357	Dick Allen	351	Hank Allen	6
352	Dick Allen	351	Ron Allen	1
349	Vladimir Guerrero	338	Wilton Guerrero	11
332	Brian Giles	260	Marcus Giles	72
327	George Brett	317	Ken Brett	10
322	Roberto Alomar	210	Sandy Alomar Jr.	112
293	Hank Sauer	288	Ed Sauer	5
285	Jose Valentin	246	Javier Valentin	39
275	George A. Bell	265	Juan Bell	10
269	Sal Bando	242	Chris Bando	27
265	Joe Torre	252	Frank Torre	13
262	Bob Meusel	156	Irish Meusel	106
252	Tony Armas Sr.	251	Marcos Armas	1
238	Felipe Alou	206	Jesus Alou	32
237	Felipe Alou	206	Matty Alou	31

(340) Most Career Home Runs as a Teenager

24	Tony Conigliaro	11	Robin Yount
19	Mel Ott	8	Harmon Killebrew
16	Ken Griffey Jr.	8	Adrian Beltre
14	Phil Cavarretta	7	Jimmy Sheckard
13	Mickey Mantle	7	Cesar Cedeno
12	Ed Kranepool		

(341) Most Career Home Runs after Age 40

72	Carlton Fisk	46	Stan Musial
60	Darrell Evans	44	Ted Williams
59	Dave Winfield	42	Hank Aaron
51	Barry Bonds	40	Graig Nettles
49	Carl Yastrzemski	39	Hank Sauer

(342) Back to Back Pinch-hit Home Runs by a Team

					INN.	
AL	NY	Bob Cerv	Elston Howard	Jul 23, 1955	9	
NL	SF	Hank Sauer	Bob Schmidt	Jun 4, 1958	10	
NL	LA	Frank Howard	Bill Skowron	Aug 8, 1963	5	
AL	BAL	Vic Roznovsky	Boog Powell	Aug 26, 1966	9	
NL	LA	Willie Crawford	Lee Lacy	Jul 23, 1975	9	
AL	BAL	Wayne Gross	Larry Sheets	Aug 12, 1985	9	
AL	TEX	Oddibe McDowell	Darrell Porter	Sep 1, 1986	9	2G
NL	NY	Mackey Sasser	Mark Carreon	May 4, 1991	9	
NL	NY	Carl Everett	Butch Huskey	May 11, 1997	9	
NL	ATL	Keith Lockhart	Javy Lopez	May 25, 1999	9	
NL	SD	Phil Nevin	Carlos Baerga	Jul 2, 1999	9	
NL	SF	Barry Bonds	Shawon Dunston	Aug 23, 2001	9	
NL	FLA	Joe Borchard	Wes Helms	Jun 22, 2006	9	

(343) Two Pinch-hit Home Runs in One Inning by a Team

				OPP. PITCHER			OPP. PITCHER		INN.
NL	NY	Bobby Hofman	Vic Raschi		Dusty Rhodes	Cot Deal		Jun 20, 1954	6
AL	NY	Bob Cerv	Tom Gorman		Elston Howard	Alex Kellner		Jul 23, 1955	9
NL	SF	Hank Sauer	Ernie T. Johnson		Bob Schmidt	Ernie T. Johnson		Jun 4, 1958	10
NL	LA	Frank Howard	Bob Buhl		Bill Skowron	Don Elston		Aug 8, 1963	5
AL	BAL	Vic Roznovsky	Lee Stange		Boog Powell	Lee Stange		Aug 26, 1966	9
NL	LA	Willie Crawford	Bob Forsch		Lee Lacy	Bob Forsch		Jul 23, 1975	9
AL	SEA	Bob Stinson	Dick Tidrow		Dan Meyer	Dick Tidrow		Apr 27, 1979	8
AL	MIN	Mickey Hatcher	Tom Burgmeier		Dave Engle	Dave Beard		May 16, 1983	9
AL	BAL	Wayne Gross	Jerry Reed		Larry Sheets	Jerry Reed		Aug 12, 1985	9
AL	TEX	Oddibe McDowell	Steve Crawford		Darrell Porter	Steve Crawford		Sep 1, 1986	9
2G									
NL	NY	Mackey Sasser	Jeff Brantley		Mark Carreon	Jeff Brantley		May 4, 1991	9
NL	CIN	Eric Anthony	Mark Wohlers		Ed Taubensee	Pedro Borbon Jr.		Jun 22, 1995	8
NL	NY	Carl Everett	Dennis Eckersley		Butch Huskey	Dennis Eckersley		May 11, 1997	9
AL	BOS	Curtis Pride	Keith Foulke		Scott Hatteberg	Keith Foulke		Sep 19, 1997	9
NL	ATL	Keith Lockhart	Bob Wickman		Javy Lopez	Bob Wickman		May 25, 1999	9
NL	SD	Carlos Baerga	Dave Wainhouse		Phil Nevin	Dave Wainhouse		Jul 2, 1999	9
NL	SF	Shawon Dunston	Graeme Lloyd		Barry Bonds	Graeme Lloyd		Aug 23, 2001	9
AL	TOR	Eric Hinske	Carlos Almanzar		Chris Gomez	Ron Mahay		Sep 11, 2004	8
NL	FLA	Joe Borchard	Chris Ray		Wes Helms	Chris Ray		Jun 22, 2006	9

(344) Two Grand Slams in One Inning by a Team

					INN.
NL	CHI	Tom Burns	Malachi Kittridge	Aug 16, 1890	5
AL	MIN	Harmon Killebrew	Bob Allison	Jul 18, 1962	1
NL	HOU	Jim Wynn	Denis Menke	Jul 30, 1969	9
AL	MIL	Cecil Cooper	Don Money	Apr 12, 1980	2
AL	BAL	Jim Dwyer	Larry Sheets	Aug 6, 1986	4
NL	STL	Fernando Tatis	Fernando Tatis	Apr 23, 1999	3
NL	NY	Cliff Floyd	Carlos Beltran	Jul 16, 2006	6

(345) Most Home Runs by One Team in an Inning

				INN.
5	NY	NL	Jun 6, 1939	4
5	PHI	NL	Jun 2, 1949	8
5	SF	NL	Aug 23, 1961	9
5	MIN	AL	Jun 9, 1966	7
5	MIL	NL	Apr 22, 2006	4

(346) Most Home Runs by Two Teams in an Inning

				INN.	
5	PHI at STL	AL	Jun 8, 1928	9	
5	CIN at NY	NL	Jun 6, 1939	4	All by NY
5	CIN at PHI	NL	Jun 2, 1949	8	All by PHI
5	NY at DET	AL	Jun 23, 1950	4	
5	BOS at NY	NL	Jul 6, 1951	3	
5	BRO at CIN	NL	Jun 11, 1954	7	
5	SF at CIN	NL	Aug 23, 1961	9	All by SF
5	PHI at CHI	NL	Apr 17, 1964	5	
5	KC at MIN	AL	Jun 9, 1966	7	All by MIN
5	BAL at BOS	AL	May 17, 1967	7	
5	CHI at ATL	NL	Jul 3, 1967	1	
5	PIT at ATL	NL	Aug 1, 1970	7	
5	CIN at CHI	NL	Jul 28, 1977	1	
5	ATL at SF	NL	May 25, 1979	4	
5	OAK at MIN	AL	May 16, 1983	9	
5	TEX at CLE	AL	Jun 29, 1984	5	
5	BAL at BOS	AL	Sep 10, 1985	8	1G
5	CIN at ATL	NL	Jun 19, 1994	1	
5	CLE at MIL	AL	Apr 25, 1997	4	
5	PIT at SF	NL	Jul 27, 1997	9	2G
5	COL at STL	NL	Jul 31, 1999	3	
5	DET at BAL	AL	Apr 7, 2000	5	
5	SF at ATL	NL	May 20, 2001	7	
5	KC at SEA	AL	Aug 27, 2004	5	
5	CIN at MIL	NL	Apr 22, 2006	4	All by MIL

(347) Most Home Runs by One Team in a Game

10	AL	TOR	Sep 14, 1987		8	AL	TEX	May 21, 2005	
9	NL	CIN	Sep 4, 1999		8	AL	TEX	Jun 30, 2005	
8	AL	NY	Jun 28, 1939	1G	8	NL	ATL	May 28, 2006	
8	NL	MIL	Aug 30, 1953	1G	8	AL	DET	Jun 18, 2006	
8	NL	CIN	Aug 18, 1956		8	NL	MON	Jul 30, 1978	
8	NL	SF	Apr 30, 1961		8	AL	OAK	Jun 27, 1996	
8	AL	MIN	Aug 29, 1963	1G	8	AL	CLE	Apr 25, 1997	
8	AL	BOS	Jul 4, 1977		8	AL	DET	Jun 20, 2000	
8	NL	MON	Jul 30, 1978		8	NL	LA	May 23, 2002	
8	AL	OAK	Jun 27, 1996		8	AL	CLE	Jul 16, 2004	
8	AL	CLE	Apr 25, 1997		8	AL	TEX	May 21, 2005	
8	AL	DET	Jun 20, 2000		8	AL	TEX	Jun 30, 2005	
8	NL	LA	May 23, 2002		8	NL	ATL	May 28, 2006	
8	AL	CLE	Jul 16, 2004		8	AL	DET	Jun 18, 2006	

(348) Most Home Runs by Both Teams in a Game

12	AL	CHI at DET	May 28, 1995		11	AL	MIL at BOS	May 22, 1977	1G
12	AL	DET at CHI	Jul 2, 2002		11	NL	CIN at CHI	Jul 28, 1977	
11	AL	NY at DET	Jun 23, 1950		11	NL	PHI at CHI	May 17, 1979	
11	NL	PIT at CIN	Aug 12, 1966		11	AL	BAL at TOR	Sep 14, 1987	
11	NL	NY at CHI	Jun 11, 1967	2G	11	AL	CAL at BAL	Jul 1, 1994	
					11	AL	CLE at MIL	Apr 25, 1997	

Joe Cronin

(349) Most Grand Slams by One Team in a Game

2	NL	CHI	Aug 16, 1890	
2	NL	BOS	May 28, 1894	
2	AL	CHI	May 1, 1901	
2	NL	BRO	Sep 23, 1901	
2	NL	BOS	Aug 12, 1903	2G
2	NL	PHI	Apr 28, 1921	
2	NL	NY	Sep 5, 1924	2G
2	NL	PIT	Jun 22, 1925	
2	NL	STL	Jul 6, 1929	
2	NL	PIT	May 1, 1933	
2	AL	BOS	May 13, 1934	
2	AL	NY	May 24, 1936	Both by Tony Lazzeri
2	NL	BOS	Apr 30, 1938	
2	NL	NY	Jul 4, 1938	2G
2	AL	BOS	Jul 4, 1939	Both by Jim Tabor
2	AL	BOS	Jul 27, 1946	Both by Rudy York
2	NL	NY	Jul 13, 1951	
2	AL	DET	Jun 11, 1954	
2	NL	CIN	Jul 29, 1955	
2	AL	BAL	Apr 24, 1960	
2	AL	BOS	May 10, 1960	
2	AL	BAL	May 9, 1961	Both by Jim Gentile
2	AL	MIN	Jul 18, 1962	
2	NL	ATL	Jul 3, 1966	Both by Tony Cloninger
2	AL	DET	Jun 24, 1968	Both by Jim Northrup
2	NL	HOU	Jul 30, 1969	1G
2	NL	SF	Apr 26, 1970	1G
2	AL	BAL	Jun 26, 1970	Both by Frank Robinson
2	AL	MIL	Jun 17, 1973	
2	AL	MIL	Apr 12, 1980	
2	NL	PIT	Sep 14, 1982	
2	AL	CAL	Apr 27, 1983	
2	AL	BOS	Aug 7, 1984	1G
2	NL	LA	Aug 23, 1985	
2	AL	CAL	Jul 31, 1986	
2	AL	BAL	Aug 6, 1986	
2	NL	ATL	May 2, 1987	
2	NL	CHI	Jun 3, 1987	
2	AL	BOS	Jun 10, 1987	
2	AL	NY	Jun 29, 1987	
2	AL	CLE	Apr 22, 1988	
2	NL	CIN	Apr 24, 1993	
2	AL	BOS	May 2, 1995	
2	AL	CHI	Sep 4, 1995	Both by Robin Ventura
2	NL	PIT	Apr 16, 1996	
2	NL	MON	Apr 28, 1996	
2	AL	CHI	May 19, 1996	
2	NL	FLA	Apr 28, 1997	
2	NL	ATL	Jul 14, 1997	
2	NL	PHI	Aug 18, 1997	
2	AL	BAL	Aug 14, 1998	Both by Chris Hoiles
2	NL	SF	Sep 19, 1998	
2	NL	STL	Apr 23, 1999	Both by Fernando Tatis in same inn.
2	AL	BOS	May 10, 1999	
2	NL	CIN	Aug 21, 1999	
2	AL	NY	Sep 14, 1999	
2	AL	CLE	Sep 24, 1999	Both by Manny Ramirez
2	NL	LA	May 21, 2000	
2	AL	SEA	Aug 8, 2000	
2	NL	MIL	May 12, 2002	
2	AL	BOS	Jul 29, 2003	Both by Bill Mueller
2	AL	OAK	Aug 24, 2003	
2	NL	PHI	Sep 9, 2003	
2	AL	TEX	Jul 4, 2004	
2	AL	KC	Aug 13, 2004	
2	AL	BAL	Jun 4, 2005	
2	NL	NY	Jul 16, 2006	

(350) Most Grand Slams by Both Teams in a Game

3	AL	TEX at BAL	Aug 6, 1986
3	NL	HOU at CHI	Jun 3, 1987

(351) Most Pinch-hit Home Runs by One Team in a Game

2	NL	PHI	May 30, 1925	2G
2	NL	PHI	Jun 2, 1928	
2	NL	STL	Jul 21, 1930	1G
2	AL	CLE	May 26, 1937	
2	NL	STL	May 12, 1951	2G
2	NL	NY	Aug 5, 1952	
2	NL	CHI	Jun 9, 1954	2G
2	NL	NY	Jun 20, 1955	
2	AL	NY	Jul 23, 1955	
2	NL	SF	Jun 4, 1958	
2	NL	PHI	Aug 13, 1958	
2	NL	NY	Aug 15, 1962	2G
2	NL	LA	Aug 8, 1963	
2	NL	NY	Sep 17, 1963	
2	AL	CLE	Aug 15, 1965	
2	NL	NY	Aug 4, 1966	
2	AL	BAL	Aug 26, 1966	
2	AL	DET	Aug 11, 1968	
2	AL	SEA	Aug 2, 1969	
2	AL	MIN	Jul 31, 1970	
2	NL	MON	Jul 13, 1973	1G
2	AL	MIN	Jul 28, 1974	2G
2	NL	CHI	Sep 10, 1974	
2	NL	LA	Jul 23, 1975	
2	NL	CHI	Aug 23, 1975	
2	AL	SEA	Apr 27, 1979	
2	AL	CHI	Jul 6, 1980	
2	NL	LA	Aug 27, 1982	
2	AL	MIN	May 16, 1983	
2	AL	BAL	May 5, 1984	
2	AL	BAL	Aug 12, 1985	
2	AL	TOR	Jun 14, 1986	
2	AL	TEX	Sep 1, 1986	
2	AL	CAL	Jun 28, 1987	
2	NL	SF	Sep 28, 1987	
2	NL	NY	May 4, 1991	
2	NL	COL	May 6, 1995	
2	NL	CIN	Jun 22, 1995	
2	NL	HOU	Sep 28, 1995	
2	NL	ATL	Jul 22, 1996	
2	NL	NY	May 11, 1997	
2	NL	CHI	Jul 13, 1997	
2	AL	BOS	Sep 19, 1997	
2	NL	CHI	Sep 12, 1998	
2	NL	ATL	May 25, 1999	
2	NL'	SD	Jul 2, 1999	
2	NL	ARI	Apr 12, 2001	
2	NL	SF	Aug 23, 2001	
2	AL	BOS	Jun 7, 2003	
2	NL	MIL	Jun 25, 2003	
2	AL	TOR	Sep 11, 2004	
2	NL	FLA	Jun 22, 2006	
2	NL	CIN	Sep 18, 2006	

(352) Most Pinch-hit Home Runs by Both Teams in a Game

3	NL	STL at PHI	Jun 2, 1928
3	NL	STL at BRO	Jul 21, 1930
3	NL	LA at COL	May 6, 1995
3	NL	SD at COL	Jul 2, 1999

(353) Most Home Runs by a Team in a Season

264	AL	SEA	1997	240	AL	NY	1961	235	NL	CHI	2004
260	AL	TEX	2005	239	NL	COL	1997	234	AL	SEA	1998
257	AL	BAL	1996	239	AL	OAK	2000	230	AL	TEX	1999
249	NL	HOU	2000	239	AL	TEX	2003	230	AL	TEX	2002
246	AL	TEX	2001	238	AL	BOS	2003	230	AL	NY	2003
245	AL	SEA	1996	236	AL	ANA	2000	229	AL	NY	2005
244	AL	SEA	1999	236	AL	CHI	2006	227	AL	TEX	2004
244	AL	TOR	2000	235	AL	OAK	1999	226	NL	SF	2000
243	AL	OAK	1996	235	NL	STL	2000	225	AL	MIN	1963
242	AL	CHI	2004	235	NL	SF	2001	225	AL	DET	1987
242	AL	NY	2004	235	NL	ATL	2003				

(354) Most Pinch-hit Home Runs by a Team in a Season

14	NL	ARI	2001	12	NL	LA	2000	11	NL	COL	1995
14	NL	SF	2001	11	NL	PHI	1958	11	NL	CIN	1996
13	NL	CIN	2006	11	NL	SF	1977	11	NL	NY	1997
12	NL	CIN	1957	11	AL	BAL	1982	11	NL	COL	2004
12	NL	NY	1983	11	NL	SF	1987				

(355) Teams with the Most Double-digit Home Runs Hitters In a Season

11	AL	DET	2004	10	AL	BAL	2000
10	AL	BAL	1998	10	NL	CIN	2000
10	AL	NY	1998	10	AL	TEX	2004
10	NL	CIN	1999	10	AL	TB	2006
10	AL	DET	1999				

(356) Teams with Most Batters with 100 RBI in a Season

5	AL	NY	1936	Lou Gehrig (152)	Joe DiMaggio (125)	Tony Lazzeri (109)	Bill Dickey (107)	George Selkirk (107)
4	AL	STL	1922	Ken Williams (155)	Marty McManus (109)	George Sisler (105)	Baby Doll Jacobson (102)	
4	NL	PIT	1925	Glenn Wright (121)	Clyde Barnhart (114)	Pie Traynor (106)	Kiki Cuyler (102)	
4	AL	NY	1927	Lou Gehrig (175)	Babe Ruth (164)	Bob Meusel (103)	Tony Lazzeri (102)	
4	NL	CHI	1929	Hack Wilson (159)	Rogers Hornsby (149)	Riggs Stephenson (110)	Kiki Cuyler (102)	
4	NL	PHI	1929	Chuck Klein (145)	Don Hurst (125)	Lefty O'Doul (122)	Pinky Whitney (115)	
4	AL	NY	1931	Lou Gehrig (184)	Babe Ruth (163)	Ben Chapman (122)	Lyn Lary (107)	
4	AL	NY	1932	Lou Gehrig (151)	Babe Ruth (137)	Tony Lazzeri (113)	Ben Chapman (107)	
4	AL	DET	1934	Hank Greenberg (139)	Charlie Gehringer (127)	Billy Rogell (100)	Goose Goslin (100)	
4	AL	DET	1936	Goose Goslin (125)	Charlie Gehringer (116)	Al Simmons (112)	Marv Owen (105)	
4	AL	NY	1939	Joe DiMaggio (126)	Joe Gordon (111)	Bill Dickey (105)	George Selkirk (101)	
4	AL	BOS	1940	Jimmie Foxx (119)	Ted Williams (113)	Joe Cronin (111)	Bobby Doerr (105)	
4	AL	BOS	1977	Jim Rice (114)	Butch Hobson (112)	Carlton Fisk (102)	Carl Yastrzemski (102)	
4	AL	MIL	1982	Cecil Cooper (121)	Robin Yount (114)	Gorman Thomas (112)	Ben Oglivie (102)	
4	AL	BAL	1996	Rafael Palmeiro (142)	Bobby Bonilla (116)	Brady Anderson (110)	Cal Ripken (102)	
4	NL	COL	1996	Andres Galarraga (150)	Dante Bichette (141)	Ellis Burks (128)	Vinny Castilla (113)	
4	AL	SEA	1996	Ken Griffey Jr. (140)	Jay Buhner (138)	Alex Rodriguez (123)	Edgar Martinez (103)	
4	NL	COL	1997	Andres Galarraga (140)	Larry Walker (130)	Dante Bichette (118)	Vinny Castilla (113)	
4	AL	CLE	1999	Manny Ramirez (165)	Roberto Alomar (120)	Richie Sexson (116)	Jim Thome (108)	
4	AL	NY	1999	Bernie Williams (115)	Paul O'Neill (110)	Tino Martinez (105)	Derek Jeter (102)	
4	AL	TEX	1999	Rafael Palmeiro (148)	Juan Gonzalez (128)	Ivan Rodriguez (113)	Rusty Greer (101)	
4	NL	ARI	1999	Matt Williams (142)	Jay Bell (112)	Luis Gonzalez (111)	Steve Finley (103)	
4	NL	COL	1999	Dante Bichette (133)	Larry Walker (115)	Todd Helton (113)	Vinny Castilla (102)	
4	AL	ANA	2000	Mo Vaughn (117)	Garret Anderson (117	Troy Glaus (102)	Darin Erstad (100)	
4	NL	ATL	2003	Gary Sheffield (131)	Andruw Jones (116)	Javy Lopez (109)	Chipper Jones (106)	

(357) Teams with Most Batters with 200 Hits in a Season

4	NL	PHI	1929	Lefty O'Doul (254)	Chuck Klein (219)	Fresco Thompson (202)	Pinky Whitney (200)
4	AL	DET	1937	Gee Walker (213)	Charlie Gehringer (209)	Pete Fox (208)	Hank Greenberg (200)
3	AL	CHI	1920	Eddie Collins (224)	Joe Jackson (218)	Buck Weaver (208)	
3	AL	STL	1920	George Sisler (257)	Baby Doll Jacobson (216)	Jack Tobin (202)	
3	AL	STL	1921	Jack Tobin (236)	George Sisler (216)	Baby Doll Jacobson (211)	
3	AL	DET	1929	Dale Alexander (215)	Charlie Gehringer (215)	Roy Johnson (201)	
3	NL	CHI	1930	Kiki Cuyler (228)	Woody English (214)	Hack Wilson (208)	
3	NL	PHI	1930	Chuck Klein (250)	Pinky Whitney (207)	Lefty O'Doul (202)	
3	NL	NY	1935	Hank Leiber (203)	Bill Terry (203)	Jo-Jo Moore (201	
3	NL	STL	1963	Dick Groat (201)	Curt Flood (200)	Bill White (200)	
3	AL	MIL	1982	Robin Yount (210)	Cecil Cooper (205)	Paul Molitor (201)	
3	AL	TEX	1991	Rafael Palmeiro (203)	Ruben Sierra (203)	Julio Franco (201)	

(358) Highest Batting Average in a Season by a Runner-Up without Winning the Batting Title, since 1893 (min. 3.1 PA per scheduled game)

Year	Player	Lg	Team	AVG	TRAILED BY		Year	Player	Lg	Team	AVG	TRAILED BY
1894	Tuck Turner	NL	PHI	.418	.022		1898	Billy Hamilton	NL	BOS	.369	.016
1911	Joe Jackson	AL	CLE	.408	.012		1994	Jeff Bagwell	NL	HOU	.368	.026
1895	Ed Delahanty	NL	PHI	.404	.001		1900	Elmer Flick	NL	PHI	.367	.014
1896	Hughie Jennings	NL	BAL	.401	.009		1925	Jim Bottomley	NL	STL	.367	.036
1922	Ty Cobb	AL	DET	.401	.019		1997	Larry Walker	NL	COL	.366	.006
1899	Jesse Burkett	NL	STL	.396	.014		1929	Al Simmons	AL	PHI	.365	.004
1912	Joe Jackson	AL	CLE	.395	.014		1957	Mickey Mantle	AL	NY	.365	.023
1923	Babe Ruth	AL	NY	.393	.010		1932	Jimmie Foxx	AL	PHI	.364	.003
1930	Babe Herman	NL	BRO	.393	.008		1937	Johnny Mize	NL	STL	.364	.013
1927	Al Simmons	AL	PHI	.392	.006		1905	Honus Wagner	NL	PIT	.363	.014
1897	Fred Clarke	NL	LOU	.390	.034		1927	Rogers Hornsby	NL	NY	.361	.019
1921	Ty Cobb	AL	DET	.389	.005		1939	Jimmie Foxx	AL	BOS	.360	.021
1925	Tris Speaker	AL	CLE	.389	.004		1924	Charlie Jamieson	AL	CLE	.359	.019
1920	Tris Speaker	AL	CLE	.388	.019		1941	Cecil Travis	AL	WAS	.359	.047
1910	Nap Lajoie	AL	CLE	.384	.001		1993	Tony Gwynn	NL	SD	.358	.012
1929	Babe Herman	NL	BRO	.381	.017		2003	Todd Helton	NL	COL	.358	.001
1930	Lou Gehrig	AL	NY	.379	.002		1994	Albert Belle	AL	CLE	.357	.002
1928	Heinie Manush	AL	STL	.378	.001		1934	Charlie Gehringer	AL	DET	.356	.007
1936	Earl Averill	AL	CLE	.378	.010		1988	Kirby Puckett	AL	MIN	.356	.010
1924	Zack Wheat	NL	BRO	.375	.049		1906	Nap Lajoie	AL	CLE	.355	.003
1913	Joe Jackson	AL	CLE	.373	.017		1919	Bobby Veach	AL	DET	.355	.029
1931	Babe Ruth	AL	NY	.373	.017		1948	Lou Boudreau	AL	CLE	.355	.014
1926	Babe Ruth	AL	NY	.372	.006		2000	Darin Erstad	AL	ANA	.355	.017
1916	Ty Cobb	AL	DET	.371	.015		2000	Moises Alou	NL	HOU	.355	.017
1928	Paul Waner	NL	PIT	.370	.017							

Although Lajoie batted .384 to Cobb's .383, Cobb is still recognized by MLB as the 1910 batting champion due to suspicious circumstances regarding Lajoie's eight hits in eight at bats against St. Louis on October 9.

(359) Most At-bats in a Season without a Hit by a Non-Pitcher

35	Hal Finney	NL	PIT	1936
23	Larry Littleton	AL	CLE	1981
22	Sandy Alomar Sr.	NL	NY	1967
22	Barry Foote	NL	CHI	1981
21	Ed Whiting	NL	WAS	1886
21	Dave Campbell	NL	STL	1973

(360) Most At-bats in a Season without a Hit by a Pitcher

69	Bob Buhl	NL	CHI	1962
61	Bill Wight	AL	CHI	1950
47	Ron Herbel	NL	SF	1964
46	Karl Drews	AL	STL	1949
41	Ernie Koob	AL	STL	1916
41	Randy Tate	NL	NY	1975
40	Joey Hamilton	NL	SD	1994

(361) Lowest Batting Average in a Season (min. 400 AB)

.166	Jim Canavan	NL	CHI	1892
.171	Ben Conroy	AA	PHI	1890
.175	Jim Lillie	NL	KC	1886
.179	Rob Deer	AL	DET	1991
.183	Jack Boyle	NL	NY	1892
.184	Bill Hallman	NL	PHI	1901
.185	John Gochnaur	AL	CLE	1902
.185	John Gochnaur	AL	CLE	1903
.185	Eddie Zimmerman	NL	BRO	1911
.185	Eddie Joost	NL	BOS	1943
.185	Ed Brinkman	AL	WAS	1965
.189	Monte Cross	AL	PHI	1904

(362) Pitchers who Won 20 Games and Batted .300 in the same Season (min. 25 hits)

				WINS	BAV	AB	HITS
Walter Johnson	AL	WAS	1925	20	.433	97	42
Curt Davis	NL	STL	1939	22	.381	105	40
Billy Taylor	UA	STL	1884	25	.366	186	68
George Uhle	AL	CLE	1923	26	.361	144	52
Don Newcombe	NL	BRO	1955	20	.359	117	42
Bob Caruthers	AA	STL	1887	29	.357	364	130
Dave Foutz	AA	STL	1887	25	.357	423	151
Catfish Hunter	AL	OAK	1971	21	.350	103	36
Wes Ferrell	AL	BOS	1935	25	.347	150	52
Wilbur Cooper	NL	PIT	1924	20	.346	104	36
Johnny Sain	NL	BOS	1947	21	.346	107	37
Jack Stivetts	NL	BOS	1896	22	.344	221	76
Carl Mays	AL	NY	1921	27	.343	143	49
Guy Hecker	AA	LOU	1886	26	.341	343	117

(362) *(continued)*

				WINS	BAV	AB	HITS
Charlie Ferguson	NL	PHI	1887	22	.337	264	89
Jesse Tannehill	NL	PIT	1900	20	.336	110	37
Bob Caruthers	AA	STL	1886	30	.334	317	106
Jack B. Taylor	NL	PHI	1894	23	.333	144	48
Warren Spahn	NL	Mil	1958	22	.333	108	36
Jack Stivetts	NL	BOS	1894	26	.328	244	80
Joe Bush	AL	NY	1922	26	.326	95	31
Babe Ruth	AL	BOS	1917	24	.325	123	40
Bucky Walters	NL	CIN	1939	27	.325	120	39
Fred Klobedanz	NL	BOS	1897	26	.324	148	48
Scott Stratton	AA	LOU	1890	34	.323	189	61
Jim Whitney	NL	BOS	1882	24	.323	251	81
Claude Hendrix	NL	PIT	1912	24	.322	121	39
Cy Young	AL	BOS	1903	28	.321	137	44
Burleigh Grimes	NL	PIT	1928	25	.321	131	42
Ed Killian	AL	DET	1907	25	.320	122	39
Clark Griffith	NL	CHI	1895	26	.319	144	46
Jack Coombs	AL	PHI	1911	28	.319	141	45
Wes Ferrell	AL	CLE	1931	22	.319	116	37
Joe Shaute	AL	CLE	1924	20	.318	107	34
Win Mercer	NL	WAS	1897	20	.317	139	44
Charlie Sweeney	UA	STL	1884	24	.316	171	54
Jim Devlin	NL	LOU	1876	30	.315	298	94
Al Spalding	NL	CHI	1876	47	.312	292	91
Ted Lyons	AL	CHI	1930	22	.311	122	38
Pete Donohue	NL	CIN	1926	20	.311	106	33
Mike Hampton	NL	HOU	1999	22	.311	74	23
Pink Hawley	NL	PIT	1895	31	.308	185	57
Red Ruffing	AL	NY	1939	21	.307	114	35
Charlie Ferguson	NL	PHI	1885	26	.306	235	72
Burleigh Grimes	NL	BRO	1920	23	.306	111	34
Dick Burns	UA	CIN	1884	23	.306	350	107
Ned Garver	AL	STL	1951	20	.305	95	29
Jack Stivetts	AA	STL	1891	33	.305	302	92
Brickyard Kennedy	NL	BRO	1894	24	.304	161	49
Bill Hoffer	NL	BAL	1896	25	.304	125	38
Clark Griffith	AL	CHI	1901	24	.303	89	27
Schoolboy Rowe	AL	DET	1934	24	.303	109	33
Bob Gibson	NL	STL	1970	23	.303	109	33
Brickyard Kennedy	NL	BRO	1900	20	.301	123	37
Adonis Terry	AA	BRO	1889	22	.300	160	48
Don Drysdale	NL	LA	1965	23	.300	130	39

(363) Most Career Pinch Hits

212	Lenny Harris	114	Red Lucas	96	Dave Clark
150	Manny Mota	113	Steve Braun	95	Larry Biittner
145	Smoky Burgess	108	Terry Crowley	95	Vic Davalillo
143	Greg Gross	108	Denny Walling	95	Gerald Perry
139	Dave Hansen	107	Gates Brown	94	Jerry Hairston Sr.
139	Mark Sweeney	105	Orlando Palmeiro	93	Dave Philley
126	John Vander Wal	103	Mike Lum	93	Joel Youngblood
123	Jose Morales	102	Jim Dwyer	92	Jay Johnstone
116	Jerry Lynch	100	Rusty Staub	92	Dave Magadan

(364) Most Pinch Hits in a Season

28	John Vander Wal	NL	COL	1995	21	Doc Miller	NL	PHI	1913
26	Lenny Harris	NL	COL-ARI	1999	21	Smoky Burgess	AL	CHI	1966
			COL (20); ARI (6)		21	Merv Rettenmund	NL	SD	1977
25	Jose Morales	NL	MON	1976	21	Lenny Harris	NL	NY	2001
24	Dave Philley	AL	BAL	1961	20	Ed Coleman	AL	STL	1936
24	Vic Davalillo	NL	STL	1970	20	Frenchy Bordagaray	NL	STL	1938
24	Rusty Staub	NL	NY	1983	20	Joe Frazier	NL	STL	1954
24	Gerald Perry	NL	STL	1993	20	Smoky Burgess	AL	CHI	1965
23	Greg Norton	NL	COL	2003	20	Ken Boswell	NL	HOU	1976
22	Sam Leslie	NL	NY	1932	20	Jerry Turner	NL	SD	1978
22	Peanuts Lowrey	NL	STL	1953	20	Thad Bosley	NL	CHI	1985
22	Red Schoendienst	NL	STL	1962	20	Chris Chambliss	NL	ATL	1986
22	Wallace Johnson	NL	MON	1988	20	Dave Clark	NL	CHI	1997
22	Mark Sweeney	NL	STL-SD	1997	20	Jacob Cruz	NL	CIN	2005
			STL (5); SD (17)		20	Orlando Palmeiro	NI	HOU	2006
22	Lenny Harris	NL	MIL	2002					
22	Daryle Ward	NL	WAS-ATL	2006					
			WAS (14); ATL (8)						

(365) Highest Career Batting Average as a Pinch Hitter (min. 150 AB)

.320	Alex Arias	.300	Bob Fothergill	.289	Chip Hale
.320	Tommy Davis	.299	Dave Philley	.288	Manny Sanguillen
.312	Frenchy Bordagaray	.297	Manny Mota	.287	Midre Cummings
.311	Harold Baines	.296	Ted Easterly	.287	Glenallen Hill
.310	Greg Colbrunn	.295	Harvey Hendrick	.286	Rick Miller
.307	Frank Baumholtz	.294	Larry Herndon	.286	Carlos Baerga
.306	Sid Bream	.292	Rance Mulliniks	.286	Smoky Burgess
.306	Mark Carreon	.291	Marlon Anderson		
.303	Red Schoendienst	.289	Terry Puhl		

(366) Highest Batting Average as a Pinch Hitter in a Season (min. 30 AB)

.486	Ed Kranepool	NL	NY	1974		.429	Joe Cronin	AL	BOS	1943
.467	Smead Jolley	AL	CHI	1931		.429	Don Dillard	AL	CLE	1961
.465	Frenchy Bordagaray	NL	STL	1938		.425	Candy Maldonado	NL	SF	1986
.457	Rick Miller	AL	BOS	1983		.419	Richie Ashburn	NL	NY	1962
.455	Bill Spiers	NL	HOU	1997		.419	Dick Williams	AL	BAL	1962
.455	Jorge Piedra	NL	COL	2005		.415	Merritt Ranew	NL	CHI	1963
.452	Elmer Valo	AL	KC	1955		.415	Carl Taylor	NL	PIT	1969
.452	Jose Pagan	NL	PIT	1969		.412	Kurt Bevacqua	NL	SD	1983
.452	Mark Johnson	NL	PIT	1996		.408	Jerry Turner	NL	SD	1978
.450	Gates Brown	AL	DET	1968		.406	Bob Bowman	NL	PHI	1958
.433	Ted Easterly	AL	CLE-CHI	1912		.406	Chico Walker	NL	CHI	1991
			CLE (.417); CHI (.444)			.406	Sid Bream	NL	HOU	1994
.433	Milt Thompson	NL	ATL	1985		.405	Frank Baumholtz	NL	CHI	1955
.433	Randy Bush	AL	MIN	1986						

(367) Most RBI in First 10 Seasons

1277	Joe DiMaggio	1936-42, 1946-48		1040	Frank E. Thomas	1990-1999
1275	Al Simmons	1924-1933		1036	Manny Ramirez	1993-2002
1258	Ted Williams	1939-42, 1946-51		1029	Del Ennis	1946-1955
1141	Lou Gehrig	1923-1932		1019	Albert Belle	1989-1998
1121	Hank Aaron	1954-1963		1018	Ken Griffey Jr.	1989-1998
1096	Johnny Mize	1936-42, 1946-48		1015	Hank Greenberg	1930, 1933-41
1093	Jeff Bagwell	1991-2000		1015	Ralph Kiner	1946-1955
1078	Earl Averill	1929-1938		1015	Eddie Murray	1977-1986
1057	Jim Bottomley	1922-1931		1013	Sam Thompson	1885-1894
1047	Joe Medwick	1932-1941		1009	Frank Robinson	1956-1965
1041	Chuck Klein	1928-1937		1008	Hugh Duffy	1888-1897
1040	Bob L. Johnson	1933-1942		1005	Bob Meusel	1920-1929

(368) Grounded into the Most Double Plays in a Season

36	Jim Rice	AL	BOS	1984		29	Brooks Robinson	AL	BAL	1960
35	Jim Rice	AL	BOS	1985		29	Frank Howard	AL	WAS	1969
32	Jackie Jensen	AL	BOS	1954		29	Frank Howard	AL	WAS	1971
32	Cal Ripken	AL	BAL	1985		29	Ted Simmons	NL	STL	1973
32	Ivan Rodriguez	AL	TEX	1999		29	Jim Rice	AL	BOS	1982
31	Bobby Doerr	AL	BOS	1949		29	Jim Presley	AL	SEA	1985
31	Jim Rice	AL	BOS	1983		29	George A. Bell	AL	CHI	1992
31	Tony Armas Sr.	AL	BOS	1983		28	George Kell	AL	PHI	1944
31	Ben Grieve	AL	OAK	2000		28	Sid Gordon	NL	BOS	1951
30	Ernie Lombardi	NL	CIN	1938		28	Harmon Killebrew	AL	MIN	1970
30	Billy Hitchcock	AL	PHI	1950		28	Julio Franco	AL	CLE	1986
30	Carl Yastrzemski	AL	BOS	1964		28	Cal Ripken	AL	BAL	1996
30	Dave Winfield	AL	NY	1983		28	Magglio Ordonez	AL	CHI	2000
30	Brad Ausmus	NL	HOU	2002		28	Paul Konerko	AL	CHI	2003
29	Jimmy Bloodworth	AL	DET	1943		28	Miguel Tejada	AL	BAL	2006
29	Dave Philley	AL	PHI	1952						

(369) Highest Percentage of Games Played over a 10-year Period

			GAMES	TEAM'S GAMES
1.0000	Cal Ripken	1983 - 1992	1617	1617
1.0000	Lou Gehrig	1926 - 1935	1538	1538
.9974	Pete Rose	1972 - 1981	1554	1558
.9938	Billy Williams	1962 - 1971	1614	1624
.9913	Cap Anson	1883 - 1892	1258	1269
.9904	Nellie Fox	1952 - 1961	1544	1559
.9890	Stan Musial	1946 - 1955	1533	1550
.9874	George J. Burns	1914 - 1923	1487	1506
.9866	John Morrill	1878 - 1887	957	970
.9865	George Van Haltren	1891 - 1900	1393	1412
.9859	Dale Murphy	1980 - 1989	1537	1559
.9858	Richie Ashburn	1949 - 1958	1524	1546
.9858	Rafael Palmeiro	1992 - 2001	1531	1553
.9858	Ron Santo	1961 - 1970	1595	1618
.9845	Roger Connor	1880 - 1889	1083	1100
.9836	Jim O'Rourke	1876 - 1885	839	853
.9834	Willie Mays	1954 - 1963	1536	1562
.9803	Jimmie Foxx	1929 - 1938	1495	1525
.9795	Brooks Robinson	1960 - 1969	1578	1611
.9790	Hugh Duffy	1889 - 1898	1352	1381
.9786	Sam Crawford	1905 - 1914	1510	1543
.9775	Joe Carter	1988 - 1997	1520	1555
.9768	Paul Hines	1877 - 1886	886	907
.9764	Hank Aaron	1955 - 1964	1534	1571
.9753	Mel Ott	1929 - 1938	1498	1536
.9748	Jesse Burkett	1893 - 1902	1354	1389
.9743	Craig Biggio	1990 - 1999	1515	1555
.9743	Fred Pfeffer	1882 - 1891	1176	1207
.9742	Gil Hodges	1949 - 1958	1509	1549
.9739	Jimmy Wolf	1882 - 1891	1193	1225
.9735	Bobby Veach	1913 - 1922	1467	1507
.9733	Sal Bando	1968 - 1977	1569	1612
.9723	Ned Williamson	1878 - 1887	949	976
.9719	Sam Rice	1919 - 1928	1487	1530
.9714	Paul Waner	1928 - 1937	1493	1537
.9707	Ken Boyer	1955 - 1964	1523	1569
.9703	Lou Brock	1964 - 1973	1566	1614

(370) Most Runs by One Team in an Inning

		OPP.			INN.					OPP.			INN.	
18	NL	CHI	DET	Sep 6, 1883	7			13	NL	NY	STL	May 13, 1911	1	
17	AL	BOS	DET	Jun 18, 1953	7			13	AL	CLE	BOS	Jul 7, 1923	6	1G
16	NL	BOS	BAL	Jun 18, 1894	1			13	AL	PHI	CLE	Jun 15, 1925	8	
16	AL	TEX	BAL	Apr 19, 1996	8			13	AL	DET	NY	Jun 17, 1925	6	
15	NL	HAR	NY	May, 13, 1876	4			13	AL	CHI	WAS	Sep 26, 1943	4	1G
15	NL	BRO	CIN	May 21, 1952	1			13	AL	NY	BOS	Jun 21, 1945	5	
14	NL	CLE	WAS	Aug 7, 1889	3			13	NL	BRO	CIN	Aug 8, 1954	8	
14	PL	PHI	BUF	Jun 26, 1890	6			13	AL	KC	CHI	Apr 21, 1956	2	
14	AA	WAS	BAL	Jun 17, 1891	1			13	NL	SF	STL	May 7, 1966	3	
14	NL	CIN	LOU	Jun 18, 1893	1			13	NL	ATL	HOU	Sep 20, 1972	2	
14	NL	BAL	BOS	Apr 24, 1894	9			13	AL	CLE	BOS	Apr 10, 1977	8	
14	AL	NY	WAS	Jul 6, 1920	5			13	AL	CAL	TEX	Sep 14, 1978	9	
14	NL	CHI	PHI	Aug 25, 1922	4			13	AL	MIL	CAL	Jul 8, 1990	5	
14	AL	BOS	PHI	Jul 4, 1948	7			13	NL	SD	STL	Aug 24, 1993	1	
14	AL	CLE	PHI	Jun 18, 1950	1	2G		13	NL	SD	PIT	May 31, 1994	2	
14	NL	CIN	HOU	Aug 3, 1989	1			13	AL	OAK	CAL	Jul 5, 1996	1	
14	AL	BOS	FLA	Jun 27, 2003	1			13	NL	MON	SF	May 7, 1997	6	
13	NL	CHI	CIN	Aug 7, 1877	2			13	AL	ANA	CHI	May 12, 1997	7	
13	NL	PRO	DET	Jun 22, 1882	3			13	NL	SF	SD	Jul 15, 1997	7	
13	NL	NY	PHI	Sep 8, 1883	3			13	AL	DET	TEX	Aug 8, 2001	9	
13	PL	CHI	BRO	Jun 24, 1890	4			13	NL	PHI	CIN	Apr 13, 2003	4	
13	NL	NY	CLE	Jul 19, 1890	2			13	AL	NY	TB	Apr 18, 2005	2	
13	NL	CHI	PIT	Aug 16, 1890	5			13	AL	NY	TB	Jun 21, 2005	8	
13	NL	BOS	STL	Jul 25, 1900	1									

Johnny Mize

PITCHING RECORDS

Pitching Records

(371) Most Career Games by a Pitcher

1252	Jesse Orosco	880	Jeff Reardon	777	Gaylord Perry
1119	John Franco	874	Don McMahon	774	Don Sutton
1109	Mike Stanton	874	Todd Jones	765	Darold Knowles
1071	Dennis Eckersley	864	Phil Niekro	765	Mark Guthrie
1070	Hoyt Wilhelm	858	Charlie Hough	760	Tommy John
1064	Dan Plesac	848	Roy Face	756	Jack Quinn
1050	Kent Tekulve	846	Doug Jones	754	David Weathers
1022	Lee Smith	841	Paul Quantrill	751	Ron Reed
1005	Mike Jackson	833	Steve Reed	750	Warren Spahn
1002	Goose Gossage	824	Tug McGraw	745	Gary Lavelle
987	Lindy McDaniel	821	Trevor Hoffman	745	Tom Burgmeier
966	Jose Mesa	811	Mike Myers	744	Willie Hernandez
961	Mike Timlin	809	Tom Gordon	741	Steve Carlton
960	Roberto Hernandez	807	Nolan Ryan	737	Ron Perranoski
944	Rollie Fingers	802	Walter Johnson	736	Ron Kline
931	Gene Garber	798	Jeff Nelson	732	Rick Aguilera
906	Cy Young	797	Rick Honeycutt	732	Steve Bedrosian
899	Sparky Lyle	786	Buddy Groom	731	Clay Carroll
898	Jim Kaat	781	Eddie Guardado		
884	Paul Assenmacher	778	Bob Wickman		

(372) Most Career Games by a Right-handed Pitcher

1071	Dennis Eckersley	848	Roy Face	732	Steve Bedrosian
1070	Hoyt Wilhelm	846	Doug Jones	731	Clay Carroll
1050	Kent Tekulve	841	Paul Quantrill	723	Roger McDowell
1022	Lee Smith	833	Steve Reed	723	Mike G. Marshall
1005	Mike Jackson	821	Trevor Hoffman	720	Mariano Rivera
1002	Goose Gossage	809	Tom Gordon	716	Danny Darwin
987	Lindy McDaniel	807	Nolan Ryan	714	Eric Plunk
966	Jose Mesa	802	Walter Johnson	711	Johnny Klippstein
961	Mike Timlin	798	Jeff Nelson	710	Greg Minton
960	Roberto Hernandez	778	Bob Wickman	704	Stu Miller
944	Rollie Fingers	777	Gaylord Perry	704	Rod Beck
931	Gene Garber	774	Don Sutton	703	Greg A. Harris
906	Cy Young	765	Mark Guthrie	702	Joe Niekro
880	Jeff Reardon	756	Jack Quinn	700	Bill Campbell
874	Don McMahon	754	David Weathers	700	Julian Tavarez
874	Todd Jones	751	Ron Reed	700	Jeff Montgomery
864	Phil Niekro	736	Ron Kline		
858	Charlie Hough	732	Rick Aguilera		

(373) Most Career Games by a Left-handed Pitcher

1252	Jesse Orosco	745	Gary Lavelle	685	Terry Mulholland
1119	John Franco	745	Tom Burgmeier	677	Rheal Cormier
1109	Mike Stanton	744	Willie Hernandez	677	Kent Mercker
1064	Dan Plesac	741	Steve Carlton	665	Dennis Cook
899	Sparky Lyle	737	Ron Perranoski	664	Greg Swindell
898	Jim Kaat	728	Randy Myers	655	Paul Lindblad
884	Paul Assenmacher	728	Steve James Kline	654	Billy Wagner
824	Tug McGraw	721	Kenny Rogers	654	Chuck McElroy
811	Mike Myers	720	Jeff Fassero	651	Wilbur Wood
797	Rick Honeycutt	718	Dave Righetti	647	Dave LaRoche
786	Buddy Groom	708	Alan Embree	639	Mike Remlinger
781	Eddie Guardado	698	Bob McClure	638	Frank Tanana
765	Darold Knowles	696	Craig Lefferts	635	Tom Glavine
760	Tommy John	692	Eppa Rixey	628	Jerry Reuss
750	Warren Spahn	692	Grant Jackson	625	Woodie Fryman

(374) Most Career Games Started by a Pitcher

815	Cy Young	625	Jim Kaat	529	Eddie Plank
773	Nolan Ryan	616	Frank Tanana	529	Rick Reuschel
756	Don Sutton	612	Early Wynn	527	Jack Morris
716	Phil Niekro	609	Robin Roberts	527	Jerry Koosman
709	Steve Carlton	600	Grover Alexander	521	Jim Palmer
700	Tommy John	594	Ferguson Jenkins	519	Jim Bunning
690	Gaylord Perry	594	Tim Keefe	518	Jamie Moyer
690	Roger Clemens	562	Dennis Martinez	518	John Clarkson
685	Bert Blyleven	562	Kid Nichols	516	Jack Powell
681	Jim Galvin	554	Eppa Rixey	505	Gus Weyhing
673	Greg Maddux	552	Christy Mathewson	504	Tony Mullane
666	Walter Johnson	549	Mickey Welch	502	Charley Radbourn
665	Warren Spahn	547	Jerry Reuss	500	Joe Niekro
647	Tom Seaver	546	Randy Johnson		
635	Tom Glavine	538	Red Ruffing		

(375) Most Career Games Started by a Right-handed Pitcher

815	Cy Young	562	Kid Nichols	485	Jim McCormick
773	Nolan Ryan	552	Christy Mathewson	484	Bob Feller
756	Don Sutton	549	Mickey Welch	484	Luis Tiant
716	Phil Niekro	538	Red Ruffing	484	Ted Lyons
690	Gaylord Perry	529	Rick Reuschel	483	Red Faber
690	Roger Clemens	527	Jack Morris	483	Bobo Newsom
685	Bert Blyleven	521	Jim Palmer	482	Bob Gibson
681	Jim Galvin	519	Jim Bunning	476	Kevin Brown
673	Greg Maddux	518	John Clarkson	476	Catfish Hunter
666	Walter Johnson	516	Jack Powell	475	Mike Mussina
647	Tom Seaver	505	Gus Weyhing	471	Vic Willis
612	Early Wynn	504	Tony Mullane	466	Orel Hershiser
609	Robin Roberts	502	Charley Radbourn	465	Don Drysdale
600	Grover Alexander	500	Joe Niekro	465	Milt Pappas
594	Ferguson Jenkins	497	Bob Friend	464	Doyle Alexander
594	Tim Keefe	497	Burleigh Grimes	462	Bob Welch
562	Dennis Martinez	487	Sam P. Jones		

(376) Most Career Games Started by a Left-handed Pitcher

709	Steve Carlton	467	Chuck Finley	406	Wilbur Cooper
700	Tommy John	462	Curt Simmons	404	Mike Flanagan
665	Warren Spahn	460	David Wells	396	Dave McNally
635	Tom Glavine	457	Lefty Grove	392	Paul Splittorff
625	Jim Kaat	438	Whitey Ford	389	Jimmy Key
616	Frank Tanana	433	Carl Hubbell	383	Larry French
554	Eppa Rixey	433	Kenny Rogers	382	Al Leiter
547	Jerry Reuss	432	Billy Pierce	379	Mike Cuellar
546	Randy Johnson	428	Mark Langston	374	Hal Newhouser
529	Eddie Plank	424	Fernando Valenzuela	363	Floyd Bannister
527	Jerry Koosman	420	Frank Viola	363	Doc White
518	Jamie Moyer	419	Herb Pennock	360	Rudy May
496	Mickey Lolich	413	Bob Knepper	359	Andy Pettitte
488	Claude Osteen	410	Ken Holtzman	359	Bruce Hurst
473	Earl Whitehill	408	Tom Zachary	356	John Candelaria
473	Vida Blue	407	Rube Marquard		

(377) Most Career Complete Games

749	Cy Young	388	Vic Willis	306	Bill Dinneen
639	Jim Galvin	382	Warren Spahn	305	Robin Roberts
554	Tim Keefe	377	Jim Whitney	303	Gaylord Perry
532	Kid Nichols	367	Adonis Terry	301	Ted Breitenstein
531	Walter Johnson	356	Ted Lyons	298	Lefty Grove
525	Mickey Welch	353	George Mullin	298	Bob Caruthers
488	Charley Radbourn	351	Charlie Buffinton	297	Ed Morris
485	John Clarkson	342	Chick Fraser	297	Pink Hawley
468	Tony Mullane	337	Clark Griffith	295	Mark Baldwin
466	Jim McCormick	335	Red Ruffing	294	Tommy Bond
449	Gus Weyhing	328	Silver King	294	Brickyard Kennedy
437	Grover Alexander	324	Al Orth	290	Eppa Rixey
435	Christy Mathewson	321	Bill Hutchison	290	Early Wynn
422	Jack Powell	314	Joe McGinnity	289	Bobby Mathews
410	Eddie Plank	314	Burleigh Grimes	289	Bill Donovan
394	Will White	312	Red Donahue	287	Bert Cunningham
393	Amos Rusie	312	Guy Hecker		

(378) Most Career Complete Games by a Right-handed Pitcher

749	Cy Young	388	Vic Willis	306	Bill Dinneen
639	Jim Galvin	377	Jim Whitney	305	Robin Roberts
554	Tim Keefe	367	Adonis Terry	303	Gaylord Perry
532	Kid Nichols	356	Ted Lyons	298	Bob Caruthers
531	Walter Johnson	353	George Mullin	297	Pink Hawley
525	Mickey Welch	351	Charlie Buffinton	295	Mark Baldwin
488	Charley Radbourn	342	Chick Fraser	294	Tommy Bond
485	John Clarkson	337	Clark Griffith	294	Brickyard Kennedy
468	Tony Mullane	335	Red Ruffing	290	Early Wynn
466	Jim McCormick	328	Silver King	289	Bobby Mathews
449	Gus Weyhing	324	Al Orth	289	Bill Donovan
437	Grover Alexander	321	Bill Hutchison	287	Bert Cunningham
435	Christy Mathewson	314	Joe McGinnity	279	Bob Feller
422	Jack Powell	314	Burleigh Grimes	279	Sadie McMahon
394	Will White	312	Red Donahue	279	Jack W. Taylor
393	Amos Rusie	312	Guy Hecker	278	Jack Stivetts

(379) Most Career Complete Games by a Left-handed Pitcher

410	Eddie Plank	225	Toad Ramsey	179	Lefty Tyler
382	Warren Spahn	214	Hippo Vaughn	173	Lefty Gomez
301	Ted Breitenstein	212	Noodles Hahn	172	Mike Cuellar
298	Lefty Grove	212	Hal Newhouser	169	Frank Foreman
297	Ed Morris	206	Case Patten	164	Ed Lopat
290	Eppa Rixey	198	Larry French	163	Curt Simmons
279	Wilbur Cooper	197	Rube Marquard	162	Tommy John
264	Matt Kilroy	196	Dupee Shaw	161	Lee Richmond
264	Jesse Tannehill	195	Mickey Lolich	159	Bill Sherdel
262	Doc White	193	Billy Pierce	156	Whitey Ford
261	Rube Waddell	189	Slim Sallee	155	Thornton Lee
260	Carl Hubbell	186	Nap Rucker	155	Dutch Ruether
254	Steve Carlton	186	Tom Zachary	154	Hooks Wiltse
253	Frank Killen	182	Dan Casey	152	Duke Esper
247	Herb Pennock	181	Art Nehf	152	Hubert "Dutch" Leonard
226	Earl Whitehill	180	Jim Kaat		

(380) Most Career Innings Pitched

7356.0	Cy Young	4783.0	Tom Seaver	4188.1	Frank Tanana
5941.1	Jim Galvin	4710.1	Tommy John	4180.0	Burleigh Grimes
5914.1	Walter Johnson	4688.2	Robin Roberts	4161.0	Ted Lyons
5404.0	Phil Niekro	4616.1	Greg Maddux	4149.2	Tom Glavine
5386.0	Nolan Ryan	4564.0	Early Wynn	4086.2	Red Faber
5350.0	Gaylord Perry	4536.1	John Clarkson	3999.2	Dennis Martinez
5282.1	Don Sutton	4531.1	Tony Mullane	3996.0	Vic Willis
5243.2	Warren Spahn	4530.1	Jim Kaat	3948.0	Jim Palmer
5217.2	Steve Carlton	4527.1	Charley Radbourn	3940.2	Lefty Grove
5190.0	Grover Alexander	4500.2	Ferguson Jenkins	3920.1	Jack Quinn
5067.1	Kid Nichols	4495.2	Eddie Plank	3884.1	Bob Gibson
5049.2	Tim Keefe	4494.2	Eppa Rixey	3883.0	Sam P. Jones
4970.0	Bert Blyleven	4389.0	Jack Powell	3839.1	Jerry Koosman
4817.2	Roger Clemens	4344.0	Red Ruffing	3827.0	Bob Feller
4802.0	Mickey Welch	4337.0	Gus Weyhing	3824.0	Jack Morris
4788.2	Christy Mathewson	4275.2	Jim McCormick	3801.1	Charlie Hough

(381) Most Career Innings Pitched by a Right-handed Pitcher

7356.0	Cy Young	4564.0	Early Wynn	3883.0	Sam P. Jones
5941.1	Jim Galvin	4536.1	John Clarkson	3827.0	Bob Feller
5914.1	Walter Johnson	4531.1	Tony Mullane	3824.0	Jack Morris
5404.0	Phil Niekro	4527.1	Charley Radbourn	3801.1	Charlie Hough
5386.0	Nolan Ryan	4500.2	Ferguson Jenkins	3778.2	Amos Rusie
5350.0	Gaylord Perry	4389.0	Jack Powell	3762.1	Waite Hoyt
5282.1	Don Sutton	4344.0	Red Ruffing	3760.1	Jim Bunning
5190.0	Grover Alexander	4337.0	Gus Weyhing	3759.1	Bobo Newsom
5067.1	Kid Nichols	4275.2	Jim McCormick	3686.2	George Mullin
5049.2	Tim Keefe	4180.0	Burleigh Grimes	3645.0	Paul Derringer
4970.0	Bert Blyleven	4161.0	Ted Lyons	3611.0	Bob Friend
4817.2	Roger Clemens	4086.2	Red Faber	3584.1	Joe Niekro
4802.0	Mickey Welch	3999.2	Dennis Martinez	3548.1	Rick Reuschel
4788.2	Christy Mathewson	3996.0	Vic Willis	3542.2	Will White
4783.0	Tom Seaver	3948.0	Jim Palmer	3514.1	Adonis Terry
4688.2	Robin Roberts	3920.1	Jack Quinn	3507.0	Juan Marichal
4616.1	Greg Maddux	3884.1	Bob Gibson		

(382) Most Career Innings Pitched by a Left-handed Pitcher

5243.2	Warren Spahn	3590.1	Carl Hubbell	3152.0	Larry French
5217.2	Steve Carlton	3571.2	Herb Pennock	3126.1	Tom Zachary
4710.1	Tommy John	3564.2	Earl Whitehill	3066.0	Kenny Rogers
4530.1	Jim Kaat	3480.0	Wilbur Cooper	3041.0	Doc White
4495.2	Eddie Plank	3460.2	Claude Osteen	2993.0	Hal Newhouser
4494.2	Eppa Rixey	3351.0	Jamie Moyer	2973.1	Ted Breitenstein
4188.1	Frank Tanana	3348.1	Curt Simmons	2962.2	Mark Langston
4149.2	Tom Glavine	3343.1	Vida Blue	2961.1	Rube Waddell
3940.2	Lefty Grove	3306.2	Rube Marquard	2930.0	Fernando Valenzuela
3839.1	Jerry Koosman	3306.2	Billy Pierce	2867.1	Ken Holtzman
3798.2	Randy Johnson	3281.2	David Wells	2836.1	Frank Viola
3669.2	Jerry Reuss	3197.1	Chuck Finley	2821.2	Slim Sallee
3638.1	Mickey Lolich	3170.1	Whitey Ford	2808.0	Mike Cuellar

(383) Most Career Games Won by a Pitcher

511	Cy Young	311	Tom Seaver	266	Eppa Rixey
417	Walter Johnson	309	Charley Radbourn	265	Jim McCormick
373	Christy Mathewson	307	Mickey Welch	264	Gus Weyhing
373	Grover Alexander	300	Lefty Grove	260	Ted Lyons
363	Warren Spahn	300	Early Wynn	254	Jack Morris
361	Kid Nichols	290	Tom Glavine	254	Red Faber
361	Jim Galvin	288	Tommy John	253	Carl Hubbell
348	Roger Clemens	287	Bert Blyleven	251	Bob Gibson
342	Tim Keefe	286	Robin Roberts	249	Vic Willis
333	Greg Maddux	284	Tony Mullane	247	Jack Quinn
329	Steve Carlton	284	Ferguson Jenkins	246	Joe McGinnity
328	John Clarkson	283	Jim Kaat	246	Amos Rusie
326	Eddie Plank	280	Randy Johnson	245	Jack Powell
324	Nolan Ryan	273	Red Ruffing	245	Dennis Martinez
324	Don Sutton	270	Burleigh Grimes	243	Juan Marichal
318	Phil Niekro	268	Jim Palmer	241	Herb Pennock
314	Gaylord Perry	266	Bob Feller	240	Frank Tanana

Walter Johnson

(384) Most Career Games Won by a Right-handed Pitcher

511	Cy Young	287	Bert Blyleven	245	Jack Powell
417	Walter Johnson	286	Robin Roberts	245	Dennis Martinez
373	Christy Mathewson	284	Tony Mullane	243	Juan Marichal
373	Grover Alexander	284	Ferguson Jenkins	239	Mordecai Brown
361	Kid Nichols	273	Red Ruffing	239	Mike Mussina
361	Jim Galvin	270	Burleigh Grimes	237	Waite Hoyt
348	Roger Clemens	268	Jim Palmer	237	Clark Griffith
342	Tim Keefe	266	Bob Feller	233	Charlie Buffinton
333	Greg Maddux	265	Jim McCormick	229	Sam P. Jones
328	John Clarkson	264	Gus Weyhing	229	Will White
324	Nolan Ryan	260	Ted Lyons	229	Luis Tiant
324	Don Sutton	254	Jack Morris	228	George Mullin
318	Phil Niekro	254	Red Faber	224	Jim Bunning
314	Gaylord Perry	251	Bob Gibson	224	Catfish Hunter
311	Tom Seaver	249	Vic Willis	223	Paul Derringer
309	Charley Radbourn	247	Jack Quinn	223	Mel Harder
307	Mickey Welch	246	Joe McGinnity	223	Hooks Dauss
300	Early Wynn	246	Amos Rusie	221	Joe Niekro

(385) Most Career Games Won by a Left-handed Pitcher

363	Warren Spahn	216	Wilbur Cooper	185	Mike Cuellar
329	Steve Carlton	216	Jamie Moyer	184	Art Nehf
326	Eddie Plank	211	Billy Pierce	184	Dave McNally
300	Lefty Grove	209	Vida Blue	179	Mark Langston
290	Tom Glavine	207	Hal Newhouser	178	Hippo Vaughn
288	Tommy John	207	Kenny Rogers	177	John Candelaria
283	Jim Kaat	201	Rube Marquard	176	Frank Viola
280	Randy Johnson	200	Chuck Finley	174	Ken Holtzman
266	Eppa Rixey	197	Larry French	174	Slim Sallee
253	Carl Hubbell	197	Jesse Tannehill	173	Fernando Valenzuela
241	Herb Pennock	196	Claude Osteen	171	Ed Morris
240	Frank Tanana	193	Curt Simmons	170	Ron Guidry
236	Whitey Ford	193	Rube Waddell	167	Mike Flanagan
230	David Wells	189	Lefty Gomez	166	Paul Splittorff
222	Jerry Koosman	189	Doc White	166	Ed Lopat
220	Jerry Reuss	186	Tom Zachary	165	Bill Sherdel
218	Earl Whitehill	186	Jimmy Key	165	Sandy Koufax
217	Mickey Lolich	186	Andy Pettitte		

(386) Most Career Games Lost by a Pitcher

316	Cy Young	237	Jim Kaat	214	Jim McCormick
308	Jim Galvin	236	Frank Tanana	213	Red Faber
292	Nolan Ryan	232	Gus Weyhing	212	Chick Fraser
279	Walter Johnson	231	Tommy John	212	Paul Derringer
274	Phil Niekro	230	Ted Lyons	212	Burleigh Grimes
265	Gaylord Perry	230	Bob Friend	210	Mickey Welch
256	Don Sutton	226	Ferguson Jenkins	209	Jerry Koosman
254	Jack Powell	225	Tim Keefe	208	Grover Alexander
251	Eppa Rixey	225	Red Ruffing	208	Kid Nichols
250	Bert Blyleven	222	Bobo Newsom	205	Vic Willis
245	Robin Roberts	220	Tony Mullane	205	Tom Seaver
245	Warren Spahn	218	Jack Quinn	204	Jim Whitney
244	Early Wynn	217	Sam P. Jones	204	Joe Niekro
244	Steve Carlton	216	Charlie Hough	203	Greg Maddux

(387) Most Career Games Lost by a Right-handed Pitcher

316	Cy Young	218	Jack Quinn	193	Dennis Martinez
308	Jim Galvin	217	Sam P. Jones	191	Rick Reuschel
292	Nolan Ryan	216	Charlie Hough	189	Al Orth
279	Walter Johnson	214	Jim McCormick	188	Christy Mathewson
274	Phil Niekro	213	Red Faber	186	Jack Morris
265	Gaylord Perry	212	Chick Fraser	186	Mel Harder
256	Don Sutton	212	Paul Derringer	186	Mike Morgan
254	Jack Powell	212	Burleigh Grimes	184	Jim Bunning
250	Bert Blyleven	210	Mickey Welch	184	Joe Bush
245	Robin Roberts	208	Grover Alexander	183	Larry Jackson
244	Early Wynn	208	Kid Nichols	182	Waite Hoyt
232	Gus Weyhing	205	Vic Willis	182	Hooks Dauss
230	Ted Lyons	205	Tom Seaver	182	Danny Darwin
230	Bob Friend	204	Jim Whitney	181	Emil "Dutch" Leonard
226	Ferguson Jenkins	204	Joe Niekro	181	Murry Dickson
225	Tim Keefe	203	Greg Maddux	181	Rick Wise
225	Red Ruffing	196	George Mullin	180	Lee Meadows
222	Bobo Newsom	196	Adonis Terry		
220	Tony Mullane	194	Charley Radbourn		

(388) Most Career Games Lost by a Left-handed Pitcher

251	Eppa Rixey	173	Chuck Finley	150	Ken Holtzman
245	Warren Spahn	171	Larry French	150	Frank Viola
244	Steve Carlton	170	Ted Breitenstein	148	David Wells
237	Jim Kaat	169	Billy Pierce	147	Earl Hamilton
236	Frank Tanana	166	Jamie Moyer	147	Randy Johnson
231	Tommy John	162	Herb Pennock	146	Bill Sherdel
209	Jerry Koosman	161	Vida Blue	146	Ed Brandt
195	Claude Osteen	158	Mark Langston	144	Rube Benton
194	Eddie Plank	156	Rudy May	143	Paul Splittorff
191	Jerry Reuss	156	Wilbur Wood	143	Rube Waddell
191	Tom Zachary	156	Doc White	143	Floyd Bannister
191	Mickey Lolich	155	Woodie Fryman	143	Rick Honeycutt
191	Tom Glavine	155	Bob Knepper	143	Slim Sallee
185	Earl Whitehill	154	Ken Raffensberger	143	Mike Flanagan
183	Curt Simmons	154	Carl Hubbell	142	Terry Mulholland
178	Wilbur Cooper	153	Fernando Valenzuela	141	Rube Walberg
177	Rube Marquard	150	Hal Newhouser	141	Lefty Grove

(389) Best Career Winning Percentage by a Pitcher (min. 100 wins)

.717	Spud Chandler	.651	Ron Guidry	.627	Jesse Tannehill
.691	Pedro Martinez	.649	Lefty Gomez	.627	Ray Kremer
.690	Dave Foutz	.648	John Clarkson	.627	Firpo Marberry
.690	Whitey Ford	.648	Mordecai Brown	.627	Eddie Plank
.688	Bob Caruthers	.644	Dizzy Dean	.627	Tommy Bond
.686	Don Gullett	.644	Mark Mulder	.625	Chief Bender
.680	Lefty Grove	.642	Grover Alexander	.623	Don Newcombe
.672	Joe Wood	.641	Andy Pettitte	.623	Nig Cuppy
.667	Vic Raschi	.641	Mike Mussina	.623	Carl Mays
.665	Tim Hudson	.638	Jim Palmer	.623	Addie Joss
.665	Larry Corcoran	.634	Kid Nichols	.622	Fred Goldsmith
.665	Christy Mathewson	.634	Deacon Phillippe	.622	Doc Crandall
.662	Roger Clemens	.634	Joe McGinnity	.622	Carl Hubbell
.660	Sam Leever	.634	Dwight Gooden	.621	Greg Maddux
.657	Sal Maglie	.632	Ed Reulbach	.621	Monte Pearson
.656	Randy Johnson	.631	Juan Marichal	.621	Bob Feller
.655	Sandy Koufax	.631	Mort Cooper	.621	Mel Parnell
.654	Johnny Allen	.630	Allie Reynolds	.620	Freddy Garcia

(390) Best Career Winning Percentage by a Right-handed Pitcher (min. 100 wins)

.717	Spud Chandler	.638	Jim Palmer	.622	Doc Crandall
.691	Pedro Martinez	.634	Kid Nichols	.621	Greg Maddux
.690	Dave Foutz	.634	Deacon Phillippe	.621	Bob Feller
.688	Bob Caruthers	.634	Joe McGinnity	.621	Monte Pearson
.672	Joe Wood	.634	Dwight Gooden	.620	Freddy Garcia
.667	Vic Raschi	.632	Ed Reulbach	.619	Clark Griffith
.665	Tim Hudson	.631	Juan Marichal	.618	Bob Lemon
.665	Larry Corcoran	.631	Mort Cooper	.618	Cy Young
.665	Christy Mathewson	.630	Allie Reynolds	.617	Bartolo Colon
.662	Roger Clemens	.627	Ray Kremer	.615	Urban Shocker
.660	Sam Leever	.627	Firpo Marberry	.615	Jeff Tesreau
.657	Sal Maglie	.627	Tommy Bond	.615	Jim Maloney
.654	Johnny Allen	.625	Chief Bender	.614	Charley Radbourn
.648	John Clarkson	.623	Don Newcombe	.614	John Ward
.648	Mordecai Brown	.623	Nig Cuppy	.613	Lon Warneke
.644	Dizzy Dean	.623	Carl Mays	.611	Gary Nolan
.642	Grover Alexander	.623	Addie Joss	.610	Schoolboy Rowe
.641	Mike Mussina	.622	Fred Goldsmith	.610	Carl Erskine

(391) Best Career Winning Percentage by a Left-handed Pitcher (min. 100 wins)

.690	Whitey Ford	.619	John Tudor	.592	John Candelaria
.686	Don Gullett	.618	Barry Zito	.591	Harry Brecheen
.680	Lefty Grove	.614	Jimmy Key	.591	Dutch Ruether
.656	Randy Johnson	.608	David Wells	.587	Mike Cuellar
.655	Sandy Koufax	.607	Dave McNally	.586	Kirk Rueter
.651	Ron Guidry	.607	Hooks Wiltse	.584	Ed Morris
.649	Lefty Gomez	.605	Art Nehf	.580	Noodles Hahn
.644	Mark Mulder	.602	Preacher Roe	.580	Hal Newhouser
.641	Andy Pettitte	.602	Tom Glavine	.577	Tom Browning
.627	Jesse Tannehill	.598	Herb Pennock	.577	Mike Hampton
.627	Eddie Plank	.598	Kenny Rogers	.574	Rube Waddell
.622	Carl Hubbell	.597	Ed Lopat	.574	Steve Carlton
.621	Mel Parnell	.597	Warren Spahn	.574	Denny Neagle

(392) Lowest Career Earned Run Average by a Pitcher (min. 1,500 IP)

1.82	Ed Walsh	2.43	Jeff Tesreau	2.63	Tim Keefe
1.89	Addie Joss	2.43	Jim McCormick	2.63	Cy Young
2.06	Mordecai Brown	2.43	Terry Larkin	2.63	Vic Willis
2.10	John Ward	2.46	Chief Bender	2.63	Red Ames
2.13	Christy Mathewson	2.47	Sam Leever	2.65	Claude Hendrix
2.16	Rube Waddell	2.47	Hooks Wiltse	2.65	Jack W. Taylor
2.17	Walter Johnson	2.47	Lefty Leifield	2.66	Joe McGinnity
2.23	Orval Overall	2.49	Hippo Vaughn	2.66	Dick Rudolph
2.25	Tommy Bond	2.49	Bob Ewing	2.67	Nick Altrock
2.28	Will White	2.50	George Bradley	2.67	Carl Weilman
2.28	Ed Reulbach	2.52	Hoyt Wilhelm	2.67	Charlie Ferguson
2.30	Jim Scott	2.55	Noodles Hahn	2.68	Charley Radbourn
2.35	Eddie Plank	2.56	Grover Alexander	2.68	Cy Falkenberg
2.36	Larry Corcoran	2.56	Slim Sallee	2.68	Jack Chesbro
2.38	Eddie Cicotte	2.59	Deacon Phillippe	2.69	Fred Toney
2.38	George McQuillan	2.59	Frank E. Smith	2.69	Bill Donovan
2.38	Ed Killian	2.60	Ed Siever	2.70	Larry Cheney
2.39	Doc White	2.61	Bob Rhoads		
2.42	Nap Rucker	2.63	Barney Pelty		

Earned run average did not become an official statistic until 1912 in the National League and 1913 in the American League.

(393) Lowest Career Earned Run Average by a Right-handed Pitcher (min. 1,500 IP)

1.82	Ed Walsh	2.43	Terry Larkin	2.65	Jack W. Taylor
1.89	Addie Joss	2.46	Chief Bender	2.66	Joe McGinnity
2.06	Mordecai Brown	2.47	Sam Leever	2.66	Dick Rudolph
2.10	John Ward	2.49	Bob Ewing	2.67	Charlie Ferguson
2.13	Christy Mathewson	2.50	George Bradley	2.68	Charley Radbourn
2.17	Walter Johnson	2.52	Hoyt Wilhelm	2.68	Cy Falkenberg
2.23	Orval Overall	2.56	Grover Alexander	2.68	Jack Chesbro
2.25	Tommy Bond	2.59	Deacon Phillippe	2.69	Fred Toney
2.28	Will White	2.59	Frank E. Smith	2.69	Bill Donovan
2.28	Ed Reulbach	2.61	Bob Rhoads	2.70	Larry Cheney
2.30	Jim Scott	2.63	Barney Pelty	2.71	Mickey Welch
2.36	Larry Corcoran	2.63	Tim Keefe	2.73	Fred Goldsmith
2.38	Eddie Cicotte	2.63	Cy Young	2.74	Harry Howell
2.38	George McQuillan	2.63	Vic Willis	2.75	Dummy Taylor
2.43	Jeff Tesreau	2.63	Red Ames	2.75	Howie Camnitz
2.43	Jim McCormick	2.65	Claude Hendrix	2.76	Babe Adams

(394) Lowest Career Earned Run Average by a Left-handed Pitcher (min. 1,500 IP)

2.16	Rube Waddell		2.82	Ed Morris		3.14	Mike Cuellar	
2.35	Eddie Plank		2.88	Willie Mitchell		3.15	Eppa Rixey	
2.38	Ed Killian		2.89	Wilbur Cooper		3.16	Earl Hamilton	
2.39	Doc White		2.92	Harry Brecheen		3.17	Sam McDowell	
2.42	Nap Rucker		2.95	Lefty Tyler		3.18	Dan Casey	
2.47	Hooks Wiltse		2.98	Carl Hubbell		3.18	Jon Matlack	
2.47	Lefty Leifield		3.01	Max Lanier		3.20	Art Nehf	
2.49	Hippo Vaughn		3.06	Hal Newhouser		3.21	Ed Lopat	
2.55	Noodles Hahn		3.06	Lefty Grove		3.22	Randy Johnson	
2.56	Slim Sallee		3.06	Lee Richmond		3.22	Steve Carlton	
2.60	Ed Siever		3.07	Bob Veale		3.22	Al Downing	
2.67	Nick Altrock		3.08	Rube Marquard		3.23	George Mogridge	
2.67	Carl Weilman		3.09	Warren Spahn		3.24	Dave McNally	
2.75	Whitey Ford		3.09	Rube Benton		3.24	Wilbur Wood	
2.76	Sandy Koufax		3.10	Dupee Shaw		3.25	Gary Peters	
2.76	Hubert "Dutch" Leonard		3.12	John Tudor				
2.80	Jesse Tannehill		3.14	Tug McGraw				

(395) Most Career Shutouts

110	Walter Johnson		52	Juan Marichal		44	Babe Adams	
90	Grover Alexander		50	Rube Waddell		44	Bob Feller	
79	Christy Mathewson		50	Vic Willis		43	Milt Pappas	
76	Cy Young		49	Ferguson Jenkins		42	Catfish Hunter	
69	Eddie Plank		49	Early Wynn		42	Bucky Walters	
63	Warren Spahn		49	Don Drysdale		41	Mickey Welch	
61	Nolan Ryan		49	Luis Tiant		41	Mickey Lolich	
61	Tom Seaver		48	Kid Nichols		41	Hippo Vaughn	
60	Bert Blyleven		46	Jack Powell		40	Chief Bender	
58	Don Sutton		46	Tommy John		40	Sandy Koufax	
57	Ed Walsh		46	Roger Clemens		40	Larry French	
57	Jim Galvin		45	Doc White		40	Jim Bunning	
56	Bob Gibson		45	Whitey Ford		40	Mel Stottlemyre	
55	Mordecai Brown		45	Robin Roberts		40	Claude Osteen	
55	Steve Carlton		45	Red Ruffing		40	Ed Reulbach	
53	Jim Palmer		45	Phil Niekro				
53	Gaylord Perry		45	Addie Joss				

(396) Most Career Shutouts by a Right-handed Pitcher

110	Walter Johnson	49	Ferguson Jenkins	41	Mickey Welch
90	Grover Alexander	49	Early Wynn	40	Chief Bender
79	Christy Mathewson	49	Don Drysdale	40	Jim Bunning
76	Cy Young	49	Luis Tiant	40	Mel Stottlemyre
61	Nolan Ryan	48	Kid Nichols	40	Ed Reulbach
61	Tom Seaver	46	Jack Powell	39	Sam Leever
60	Bert Blyleven	46	Roger Clemens	39	Tim Keefe
58	Don Sutton	45	Robin Roberts	38	Stan Coveleski
57	Ed Walsh	45	Red Ruffing	37	Larry Jackson
57	Jim Galvin	45	Phil Niekro	37	Steve Rogers
56	Bob Gibson	45	Addie Joss	37	John Clarkson
55	Mordecai Brown	44	Babe Adams	36	Will White
53	Jim Palmer	44	Bob Feller	36	Sam P. Jones
53	Gaylord Perry	43	Milt Pappas	36	Bob Friend
52	Juan Marichal	42	Bucky Walters	36	Allie Reynolds
50	Vic Willis	42	Catfish Hunter	36	Camilo Pascual

(397) Most Career Shutouts by a Left-handed Pitcher

69	Eddie Plank	38	Billy Pierce	33	Dave McNally
63	Warren Spahn	38	Nap Rucker	33	Jerry Koosman
55	Steve Carlton	37	Eppa Rixey	33	Hal Newhouser
50	Rube Waddell	37	Randy Johnson	33	Hubert "Dutch" Leonard
46	Tommy John	37	Vida Blue	32	Lefty Leifield
45	Doc White	36	Carl Hubbell	31	Fernando Valenzuela
45	Whitey Ford	36	Curt Simmons	31	Ken Raffensberger
41	Mickey Lolich	36	Mike Cuellar	31	Jim Kaat
41	Hippo Vaughn	35	Wilbur Cooper	31	Ken Holtzman
40	Sandy Koufax	35	Herb Pennock	30	Rube Marquard
40	Larry French	35	Lefty Grove	30	Jon Matlack
40	Claude Osteen	34	Frank Tanana	30	Bob Knepper
39	Jerry Reuss	34	Jesse Tannehill	30	Lefty Tyler

(398) Most Career Saves

482	Trevor Hoffman	310	Goose Gossage	217	Gregg Olson
478	Lee Smith	304	Jeff Montgomery	216	Dave Smith
424	John Franco	303	Doug Jones	203	Jeff Shaw
413	Mariano Rivera	300	Bruce Sutter	201	Bobby Thigpen
390	Dennis Eckersley	286	Rod Beck	193	Mike Henneman
367	Jeff Reardon	280	Armando Benitez	193	Roy Face
347	Randy Myers	263	Todd Jones	192	Mitch Williams
341	Rollie Fingers	256	Todd Worrell	190	Keith Foulke
330	John Wetteland	252	Dave Righetti	188	Mike G. Marshall
326	Roberto Hernandez	249	Jason Isringhausen	186	Jeff Russell
324	Troy Percival	247	Bob Wickman	184	Steve Bedrosian
324	Billy Wagner	244	Dan Quisenberry	184	Kent Tekulve
320	Jose Mesa	238	Sparky Lyle	183	Eddie Guardado
318	Rick Aguilera	237	Ugueth Urbina	182	Danny Graves
314	Robb Nen	227	Hoyt Wilhelm	180	Tug McGraw
311	Tom Henke	218	Gene Garber		

(399) Most Career Saves by a Right-handed Pitcher

482	Trevor Hoffman	286	Rod Beck	188	Mike G. Marshall
478	Lee Smith	280	Armando Benitez	186	Jeff Russell
413	Mariano Rivera	263	Todd Jones	184	Steve Bedrosian
390	Dennis Eckersley	256	Todd Worrell	184	Kent Tekulve
367	Jeff Reardon	249	Jason Isringhausen	182	Danny Graves
341	Rollie Fingers	247	Bob Wickman	177	Bryan Harvey
330	John Wetteland	244	Dan Quisenberry	172	Lindy McDaniel
326	Roberto Hernandez	237	Ugueth Urbina	172	Jeff Brantley
324	Troy Percival	227	Hoyt Wilhelm	163	Billy Koch
320	Jose Mesa	218	Gene Garber	161	Eric Gagne
318	Rick Aguilera	217	Gregg Olson	159	Roger McDowell
314	Robb Nen	216	Dave Smith	155	Jay Howell
311	Tom Henke	203	Jeff Shaw	154	John Smoltz
310	Goose Gossage	201	Bobby Thigpen	154	Stu Miller
304	Jeff Montgomery	193	Mike Henneman	153	Don McMahon
303	Doug Jones	193	Roy Face	150	Tom Gordon
300	Bruce Sutter	190	Keith Foulke	150	Greg Minton

(400) Most Career Saves by a Left-handed Pitcher

424	John Franco	180	Tug McGraw	132	Jim Brewer
347	Randy Myers	179	Ron Perranoski	127	Terry Forster
324	Billy Wagner	158	Dan Plesac	126	Dave LaRoche
252	Dave Righetti	147	Willie Hernandez	125	John Hiller
238	Sparky Lyle	144	Jesse Orosco	115	Tippy Martinez
192	Mitch Williams	143	Darold Knowles	102	Tom Burgmeier
183	Eddie Guardado	136	Gary Lavelle	101	Craig Lefferts

(401) Most Career Walks by a Pitcher, before 1893

1297	Mickey Welch	671	Toad Ramsey	496	Larry Corcoran
1165	Mark Baldwin	650	Bert Cunningham	496	Will White
1153	Tim Keefe	650	Jack Stivetts	492	Guy Hecker
1119	Tony Mullane	633	Kid Gleason	486	John "Darby" O'Brien
1050	John Clarkson	602	Charlie Getzien	479	Phenomenal Smith
998	Gus Weyhing	599	John Healy	479	Henry Gruber
937	Amos Rusie	597	Bob Caruthers	466	Henry Porter
875	Charley Radbourn	578	Hank O'Day	459	Stump Wiedman
857	Elton Chamberlain	574	George Haddock	451	Ed Seward
856	Charlie Buffinton	564	Jersey Bakely	429	Frank Foreman
847	Adonis Terry	562	Sadie McMahon	420	Harry Staley
837	Ed Crane	543	Dan Casey	418	Elmer Smith
797	Silver King	526	Lee Viau	415	Al Mays
749	Jim McCormick	522	Hardie Henderson	413	Hank Gastright
744	Jim Galvin	521	Phil Knell	411	Jim Whitney
685	Bill Hutchison	501	Dave Foutz		
681	Matt Kilroy	498	Ed Morris		

A walk consisted of four balls from 1889 forward. Before that there were various higher numbers of balls needed for a walk.

(402) Most Career Walks by a Pitcher, since 1893

2795	Nolan Ryan	1379	Gaylord Perry	1255	Frank Tanana
1833	Steve Carlton	1375	Bobby Witt	1251	Bob Lemon
1809	Phil Niekro	1371	Mike Torrez	1249	Hal Newhouser
1775	Early Wynn	1363	Walter Johnson	1238	George Mullin
1764	Bob Feller	1343	Don Sutton	1213	Red Faber
1732	Bobo Newsom	1338	Chick Fraser	1212	Vic Willis
1665	Charlie Hough	1336	Bob Gibson	1198	Jerry Koosman
1549	Roger Clemens	1332	Chuck Finley	1192	Tommy Bridges
1541	Red Ruffing	1322	Bert Blyleven	1187	Lefty Grove
1442	Bump Hadley	1312	Sam McDowell	1185	Vida Blue
1434	Warren Spahn	1311	Jim Palmer	1178	Billy Pierce
1431	Earl Whitehill	1295	Burleigh Grimes	1165	Dennis Martinez
1409	Randy Johnson	1289	Mark Langston	1163	Al Leiter
1399	Tom Glavine	1263	Joe Bush	1156	Mike Moore
1396	Sam P. Jones	1262	Joe Niekro	1151	Fernando Valenzuela
1390	Jack Morris	1261	Allie Reynolds		
1390	Tom Seaver	1259	Tommy John		

(403) Most Career Walks by a Right-handed Pitcher, since 1893

2795	Nolan Ryan	1343	Don Sutton	1137	David Cone
1809	Phil Niekro	1338	Chick Fraser	1121	Ted Lyons
1775	Early Wynn	1336	Bob Gibson	1121	Bucky Walters
1764	Bob Feller	1322	Bert Blyleven	1118	Mel Harder
1732	Bobo Newsom	1311	Jim Palmer	1108	Earl Moore
1665	Charlie Hough	1295	Burleigh Grimes	1106	Brickyard Kennedy
1549	Roger Clemens	1263	Joe Bush	1105	Bob Buhl
1541	Red Ruffing	1262	Joe Niekro	1104	Luis Tiant
1442	Bump Hadley	1261	Allie Reynolds	1088	Virgil Trucks
1396	Sam P. Jones	1251	Bob Lemon	1081	Rick Sutcliffe
1390	Jack Morris	1238	George Mullin	1069	Camilo Pascual
1390	Tom Seaver	1213	Red Faber	1068	Bob Turley
1379	Gaylord Perry	1212	Vic Willis	1067	Hooks Dauss
1375	Bobby Witt	1192	Tommy Bridges	1059	Bill Donovan
1371	Mike Torrez	1165	Dennis Martinez	1058	Murry Dickson
1363	Walter Johnson	1156	Mike Moore		

(404) Most Career Walks by a Left-handed Pitcher, since 1893

1833	Steve Carlton	1151	Fernando Valenzuela	946	Jamie Moyer
1434	Warren Spahn	1132	Johnny Vander Meer	940	Claude Osteen
1431	Earl Whitehill	1127	Jerry Reuss	933	Al Downing
1409	Randy Johnson	1099	Mickey Lolich	922	Ray Sadecki
1399	Tom Glavine	1095	Lefty Gomez	916	Herb Pennock
1332	Chuck Finley	1086	Whitey Ford	914	Tom Zachary
1312	Sam McDowell	1083	Jim Kaat	910	Ken Holtzman
1289	Mark Langston	1082	Eppa Rixey	890	Mike Flanagan
1259	Tommy John	1079	Kenny Rogers	890	Woodie Fryman
1255	Frank Tanana	1072	Eddie Plank	888	Juan Pizarro
1249	Hal Newhouser	1063	Curt Simmons	864	Frank Viola
1198	Jerry Koosman	1045	Ted Breitenstein	858	Rube Marquard
1187	Lefty Grove	1037	Tommy Byrne	858	Bob Veale
1185	Vida Blue	1031	Rube Walberg	857	Bob Knepper
1178	Billy Pierce	958	Rudy May	853	Wilbur Cooper
1163	Al Leiter	950	Steve Barber		

(405) Most Career Strikeouts by a Pitcher, before 1893

2508	Tim Keefe	1112	Silver King	846	Hugh Daily
1888	John Clarkson	1110	Guy Hecker	822	John Healy
1850	Mickey Welch	1103	Larry Corcoran	787	Dave Foutz
1830	Charley Radbourn	1091	Amos Rusie	745	Sadie McMahon
1799	Jim Galvin	1070	Charlie Getzien	743	Dan Casey
1704	Jim McCormick	1041	Will White	728	Charlie Ferguson
1700	Charlie Buffinton	1015	Elton Chamberlain	703	Ed Crane
1662	Tony Mullane	1005	Bill Hutchison	669	Jersey Bakely
1571	Jim Whitney	950	Dupee Shaw	663	Hank O'Day
1515	Toad Ramsey	930	Hardie Henderson	659	Henry Porter
1298	Adonis Terry	920	John Ward	654	Kid Nichols
1249	Mark Baldwin	910	Stump Wiedman	625	Harry Staley
1217	Ed Morris	900	Bob Caruthers	611	George Bradley
1208	Gus Weyhing	871	Jack Stivetts	608	Kid Gleason
1199	Bobby Mathews	860	Tommy Bond	607	Ed Cushman
1137	Matt Kilroy	859	Jack Lynch	602	Henry Boyle

Strikeouts between 1876-1892 were a function of the rules governing the number of strikes needed for a strikeout. The rule was solidified at three strikes in 1888.

(406) Most Career Strikeouts by a Pitcher, since 1893

5714	Nolan Ryan	2778	John Smoltz	2401	Dennis Eckersley
4604	Roger Clemens	2773	Frank Tanana	2397	Kevin Brown
4544	Randy Johnson	2668	David Cone	2396	Sandy Koufax
4136	Steve Carlton	2610	Chuck Finley	2362	Charlie Hough
3701	Bert Blyleven	2583	Warren Spahn	2357	Robin Roberts
3640	Tom Seaver	2581	Bob Feller	2334	Early Wynn
3574	Don Sutton	2572	Mike Mussina	2316	Rube Waddell
3534	Gaylord Perry	2556	Jerry Koosman	2303	Juan Marichal
3509	Walter Johnson	2507	Christy Mathewson	2293	Dwight Gooden
3342	Phil Niekro	2486	Don Drysdale	2266	Lefty Grove
3192	Ferguson Jenkins	2481	Tom Glavine	2246	Eddie Plank
3169	Greg Maddux	2478	Jack Morris	2245	Tommy John
3117	Bob Gibson	2464	Mark Langston	2212	Jim Palmer
3015	Curt Schilling	2461	Jim Kaat	2198	Grover Alexander
2998	Pedro Martinez	2453	Sam McDowell	2175	Vida Blue
2855	Jim Bunning	2449	Cy Young	2167	Camilo Pascual
2832	Mickey Lolich	2416	Luis Tiant	2149	Dennis Martinez

(407) Most Career Strikeouts by a Right-handed Pitcher, since 1893

5714	Nolan Ryan	2581	Bob Feller	2167	Camilo Pascual
4604	Roger Clemens	2572	Mike Mussina	2149	Dennis Martinez
3701	Bert Blyleven	2507	Christy Mathewson	2082	Bobo Newsom
3640	Tom Seaver	2486	Don Drysdale	2045	Dazzy Vance
3574	Don Sutton	2478	Jack Morris	2015	Rick Reuschel
3534	Gaylord Perry	2449	Cy Young	2014	Orel Hershiser
3509	Walter Johnson	2416	Luis Tiant	2012	Catfish Hunter
3342	Phil Niekro	2401	Dennis Eckersley	2000	Andy Benes
3192	Ferguson Jenkins	2397	Kevin Brown	1994	Kevin Appier
3169	Greg Maddux	2362	Charlie Hough	1987	Red Ruffing
3117	Bob Gibson	2357	Robin Roberts	1969	Bob Welch
3015	Curt Schilling	2334	Early Wynn	1955	Bobby Witt
2998	Pedro Martinez	2303	Juan Marichal	1942	Danny Darwin
2855	Jim Bunning	2293	Dwight Gooden	1915	Hideo Nomo
2778	John Smoltz	2212	Jim Palmer		
2668	David Cone	2198	Grover Alexander		

(408) Most Career Strikeouts by a Left-handed Pitcher, since 1893

4544	Randy Johnson	2074	Fernando Valenzuela	1673	John Candelaria
4136	Steve Carlton	1999	Billy Pierce	1643	Jeff Fassero
2832	Mickey Lolich	1992	Jamie Moyer	1639	Al Downing
2773	Frank Tanana	1974	Al Leiter	1632	Mike Cuellar
2610	Chuck Finley	1956	Whitey Ford	1629	Chris Short
2583	Warren Spahn	1907	Jerry Reuss	1614	Ray Sadecki
2556	Jerry Koosman	1850	Kenny Rogers	1612	Claude Osteen
2481	Tom Glavine	1844	Frank Viola	1601	Ken Holtzman
2464	Mark Langston	1796	Hal Newhouser	1593	Rube Marquard
2461	Jim Kaat	1778	Ron Guidry	1587	Woodie Fryman
2453	Sam McDowell	1760	Rudy May	1575	Harvey Haddix
2396	Sandy Koufax	1743	Sid Fernandez	1542	Greg Swindell
2316	Rube Waddell	1723	Floyd Bannister	1538	Jimmy Key
2266	Lefty Grove	1703	Andy Pettitte	1522	Juan Pizarro
2246	Eddie Plank	1703	Bob Veale	1516	Jon Matlack
2245	Tommy John	1697	Curt Simmons	1512	Dave McNally
2175	Vida Blue	1689	Bruce Hurst		
2119	David Wells	1677	Carl Hubbell		

Kid Nichols

(409) Most Career Strikeouts by a Pitcher per Nine Innings (min. 1,500 IP)

10.77	Randy Johnson	7.96	Bob Veale	7.35	Chuck Finley
10.20	Pedro Martinez	7.91	John Smoltz	7.29	Kevin Millwood
9.55	Nolan Ryan	7.81	Jim Maloney	7.27	Jeff Fassero
9.28	Sandy Koufax	7.81	Javier Vazquez	7.22	Bob Gibson
8.86	Sam McDowell	7.77	Chan Ho Park	7.21	Mike Mussina
8.74	Hideo Nomo	7.69	Jose Rijo	7.18	Andy Benes
8.73	Curt Schilling	7.56	Jose DeLeon	7.14	Bobby Witt
8.60	Roger Clemens	7.54	Mario Soto	7.13	Steve Carlton
8.40	Sid Fernandez	7.54	Sam Jones	7.08	Dave Burba
8.37	J.R. Richard	7.49	Mark Langston	7.05	Shane Reynolds
8.28	David Cone	7.47	Goose Gossage	7.04	Rube Waddell
8.26	Tom Gordon	7.43	Al Leiter	7.03	Bartolo Colon
7.96	Jason Schmidt	7.37	Dwight Gooden	7.01	Mickey Lolich

(410) Most Career Strikeouts per Nine Innings by a Right-handed Pitcher (min. 1,500 IP)

10.20	Pedro Martinez	7.47	Goose Gossage	6.80	Erik Hanson
9.55	Nolan Ryan	7.37	Dwight Gooden	6.77	Ramon J. Martinez
8.74	Hideo Nomo	7.29	Kevin Millwood	6.71	Bobby Bolin
8.73	Curt Schilling	7.22	Bob Gibson	6.70	Bert Blyleven
8.60	Roger Clemens	7.21	Mike Mussina	6.69	Ray Culp
8.37	J.R. Richard	7.18	Andy Benes	6.66	Stan Williams
8.28	David Cone	7.14	Bobby Witt	6.65	Camilo Pascual
8.26	Tom Gordon	7.08	Dave Burba	6.65	Bob Turley
7.96	Jason Schmidt	7.05	Shane Reynolds	6.62	Kevin Brown
7.91	John Smoltz	7.03	Bartolo Colon	6.60	Don Wilson
7.81	Jim Maloney	6.93	Darryl Kile	6.58	Freddy Garcia
7.81	Javier Vazquez	6.91	Kevin Appier	6.58	Dennis Eckersley
7.77	Chan Ho Park	6.89	Chris Carpenter	6.56	Andy Messersmith
7.69	Jose Rijo	6.87	Rollie Fingers	6.52	Don Drysdale
7.56	Jose DeLeon	6.85	Tom Seaver	6.52	Todd Stottlemyre
7.54	Mario Soto	6.83	Jim Bunning	6.48	Russ Ortiz
7.54	Sam Jones	6.82	Pedro Astacio		

(411) Most Career Strikeouts per Nine Innings by a Left-handed Pitcher (min. 1,500 IP)

10.77	Randy Johnson	6.73	Juan Pizarro	6.21	Greg Swindell
9.28	Sandy Koufax	6.69	Ron Guidry	6.14	Gary Peters
8.86	Sam McDowell	6.63	Andy Pettitte	6.06	John Smiley
8.40	Sid Fernandez	6.59	Tug McGraw	6.05	Fred Norman
7.96	Bob Veale	6.57	Denny Lemaster	6.04	Rudy May
7.49	Mark Langston	6.56	Shawn Estes	5.99	Jerry Koosman
7.43	Al Leiter	6.50	Al Downing	5.96	John Candelaria
7.35	Chuck Finley	6.49	Floyd Bannister	5.96	Frank Tanana
7.27	Jeff Fassero	6.49	Toad Ramsey	5.92	Woodie Fryman
7.13	Steve Carlton	6.42	Eric Milton	5.89	Steve Barber
7.04	Rube Waddell	6.37	Fernando Valenzuela	5.85	Vida Blue
7.01	Mickey Lolich	6.34	Harvey Haddix	5.85	Frank Viola
6.85	Wilson Alvarez	6.31	Chris Short		
6.74	Denny Neagle	6.29	Bruce Hurst		

(412) Most Seasons with 30 or More Wins

7	Kid Nichols	4	Silver King	2	Frank Killen
6	Tim Keefe	4	Tommy Bond	2	Guy Hecker
6	John Clarkson	4	Larry Corcoran	2	Jack Stivetts
5	Cy Young	3	Grover Alexander	2	Jim Devlin
5	Tony Mullane	3	Jim Galvin	2	Joe McGinnity
5	Will White	3	Charley Radbourn	2	John Ward
4	Amos Rusie	3	Bobby Mathews	2	Sadie McMahon
4	Christy Mathewson	3	Bob Caruthers	2	Toad Ramsey
4	Gus Weyhing	3	Bill Hutchison	2	Walter Johnson
4	Mickey Welch	3	Ed Morris	2	Jim Whitney
4	Jim McCormick	2	Dave Foutz		

(413) Most Seasons with 20 or More Wins

15	Cy Young	7	Clark Griffith	5	Carl Mays
13	Warren Spahn	7	Charlie Buffinton	5	Catfish Hunter
13	Christy Mathewson	7	Gus Weyhing	5	Bob Gibson
12	Walter Johnson	7	Tim Keefe	5	Carl Hubbell
11	Kid Nichols	7	Bob Lemon	5	Early Wynn
10	Jim Galvin	7	Ferguson Jenkins	5	Tommy Bond
9	Charley Radbourn	6	Jesse Tannehill	5	Jim Whitney
9	Grover Alexander	6	Deacon Phillippe	5	George Mullin
9	Mickey Welch	6	Wes Ferrell	5	Hippo Vaughn
8	Amos Rusie	6	Robin Roberts	5	Jack Chesbro
8	Lefty Grove	6	Jack Stivetts	5	Tom Seaver
8	John Clarkson	6	Steve Carlton	5	Tom Glavine
8	Jim McCormick	6	Juan Marichal	5	Will White
8	Jim Palmer	6	Bob Feller	5	Stan Coveleski
8	Eddie Plank	6	Bob Caruthers	5	Larry Corcoran
8	Joe McGinnity	6	Roger Clemens	5	Silver King
8	Vic Willis	6	Mordecai Brown	5	Gaylord Perry
8	Tony Mullane	5	Burleigh Grimes		

(414) Most Seasons with 15 or More Wins

18	Cy Young	11	Red Ruffing	9	David Wells
18	Greg Maddux	11	Jim Galvin	9	Charley Radbourn
16	Warren Spahn	11	Burleigh Grimes	9	Chief Bender
16	Walter Johnson	11	Tim Keefe	9	Frank Dwyer
15	Grover Alexander	11	Randy Johnson	9	George Mullin
15	Eddie Plank	10	Whitey Ford	9	Jack Powell
13	Gaylord Perry	10	Bob Feller	9	Joe Bush
13	Christy Mathewson	10	Bob Gibson	9	John Clarkson
13	Phil Niekro	10	Gus Weyhing	9	Wilbur Cooper
13	Tom Seaver	10	Early Wynn	9	Larry French
12	Jack Morris	10	Bert Blyleven	9	Mordecai Brown
12	Roger Clemens	10	Mickey Welch	9	Stan Coveleski
12	Jim Palmer	10	Ferguson Jenkins	9	Tony Mullane
12	Don Sutton	10	Robin Roberts	9	Vic Willis
12	Steve Carlton	10	Mike Mussina	9	Joe McGinnity
12	Kid Nichols	10	Tom Glavine		
11	Lefty Grove	9	Bob Lemon		

(415) Most Seasons with 10 or More Wins

21	Don Sutton	15	Early Wynn	13	David Wells
20	Nolan Ryan	15	Carl Hubbell	13	Earl Whitehill
19	Phil Niekro	15	Dennis Martinez	13	Kevin Brown
19	Cy Young	15	Ferguson Jenkins	13	Eddie Cicotte
19	Roger Clemens	15	Mike Mussina	13	Bobo Newsom
19	Greg Maddux	15	Randy Johnson	13	Herb Pennock
18	Steve Carlton	14	Jack Morris	13	Jack Powell
18	Walter Johnson	14	Milt Pappas	13	Jerry Koosman
17	Grover Alexander	14	Frank Tanana	13	Jim Bunning
17	Bert Blyleven	14	Eppa Rixey	13	Whitey Ford
17	Warren Spahn	14	Hooks Dauss	13	Luis Tiant
17	Tom Seaver	14	Kid Nichols	13	Mel Harder
17	Ted Lyons	14	Lefty Grove	13	Orel Hershiser
17	Gaylord Perry	14	Burleigh Grimes	13	Paul Derringer
17	Tommy John	14	Jim Galvin	13	Red Ruffing
17	Tom Glavine	14	Red Faber	13	Rick Reuschel
16	Robin Roberts	14	Bob Gibson	13	Jim Palmer
16	Eddie Plank	14	Christy Mathewson		
15	Jim Kaat	14	Kenny Rogers		

(416) Most Seasons with a Win

26	Nolan Ryan	21	Red Ruffing	19	Mel Harder
25	Tommy John	21	Ted Lyons	19	Randy Johnson
23	Dennis Eckersley	21	Walter Johnson	19	Rick Honeycutt
23	Dennis Martinez	20	David Wells	19	Robin Roberts
23	Don Sutton	20	Jesse Orosco	19	Sam P. Jones
23	Jim Kaat	20	Lindy McDaniel	19	Waite Hoyt
23	Phil Niekro	20	Mike Morgan	18	Dan Plesac
23	Roger Clemens	20	Red Faber	18	Dolf Luque
22	Bert Blyleven	20	Goose Gossage	18	Freddie Fitzsimmons
22	Charlie Hough	20	Tom Glavine	18	Jack Morris
22	Cy Young	20	Tom Seaver	18	Jerry Koosman
22	Early Wynn	20	Warren Spahn	18	Jesse Haines
22	Gaylord Perry	19	Burleigh Grimes	18	Jim Palmer
22	Jack Quinn	19	Curt Simmons	18	John Candelaria
22	Joe Niekro	19	Doyle Alexander	18	Jose Mesa
22	Steve Carlton	19	Emil "Dutch" Leonard	18	Kenny Rogers
21	Danny Darwin	19	Ferguson Jenkins	18	Rick Reuschel
21	Eppa Rixey	19	Grover Alexander	18	Ron Reed
21	Frank Tanana	19	Hoyt Wilhelm	18	Scott Sanderson
21	Greg Maddux	19	Jamie Moyer	18	Terry Mulholland
21	Herb Pennock	19	Kevin Brown	18	Tom Zachary
21	Jerry Reuss	19	Luis Tiant	18	Tug McGraw

(417) Most Career Games in Relief

1248	Jesse Orosco		873	Todd Jones		736	Ron Perranoski
1119	John Franco		872	Don McMahon		733	Willie Hernandez
1108	Mike Stanton		871	Jose Mesa		727	Steve James Kline
1050	Dan Plesac		842	Doug Jones		722	Mark Guthrie
1050	Kent Tekulve		833	Steve Reed		721	Roger McDowell
1018	Hoyt Wilhelm		821	Roy Face		716	Randy Myers
1016	Lee Smith		821	Trevor Hoffman		710	Mariano Rivera
998	Mike Jackson		811	Mike Myers		710	Dennis Eckersley
965	Goose Gossage		798	Jeff Nelson		704	Rod Beck
957	Roberto Hernandez		785	Tug McGraw		704	Alan Embree
957	Mike Timlin		777	Paul Quantrill		703	Clay Carroll
922	Gene Garber		771	Buddy Groom		703	Greg Minton
913	Lindy McDaniel		757	Darold Knowles		699	Mike G. Marshall
907	Rollie Fingers		756	Eddie Guardado		699	Armando Benitez
899	Sparky Lyle		750	Bob Wickman		699	Jeff Montgomery
883	Paul Assenmacher		742	Tom Burgmeier			
880	Jeff Reardon		742	Gary Lavelle			

(418) Most Career Wins in Relief

124	Hoyt Wilhelm		79	Tom Burgmeier		64	Al Hrabosky
119	Lindy McDaniel		79	Stu Miller		63	Roberto Hernandez
115	Goose Gossage		79	Ron Perranoski		63	Darold Knowles
107	Rollie Fingers		73	Johnny Murphy		63	Clem Labine
99	Sparky Lyle		73	Jeff Reardon		63	Dave LaRoche
96	Roy Face		72	John Hiller		63	Eric Plunk
94	Gene Garber		71	Mark Clear		62	Jim Brewer
94	Kent Tekulve		71	Dick Hall		62	Turk Farrell
92	Mike G. Marshall		71	Lee Smith		62	Eddie Fisher
90	John Franco		70	Willie Hernandez		62	Grant Jackson
90	Don McMahon		70	Roger McDowell		62	Paul Lindblad
89	Tug McGraw		69	Pedro Borbon Sr.		62	Frank Linzy
88	Clay Carroll		68	Bruce Sutter		62	Dan Plesac
87	Jesse Orosco		68	Mike Timlin		61	Paul Assenmacher
85	Bob Stanley		67	Mike Stanton		61	Mike Jackson
80	Bill Campbell		66	Doug Jones		60	Joe Heving
80	Gary Lavelle		65	Steve Bedrosian			

(419) Most Career Losses in Relief

108	Gene Garber	71	Bruce Sutter	57	Todd Jones
103	Hoyt Wilhelm	69	Roger McDowell	57	Frank Linzy
101	Rollie Fingers	69	Tug McGraw	57	Randy Myers
98	Mike G. Marshall	68	Roberto Hernandez	56	Mitch Williams
90	Kent Tekulve	67	Stu Miller	55	Willie Hernandez
88	Lindy McDaniel	67	Dan Plesac	55	Trevor Hoffman
87	Lee Smith	66	Clay Carroll	54	Craig Lefferts
87	John Franco	66	Don McMahon	53	Tom Burgmeier
85	Goose Gossage	66	Jose Mesa	53	Ron Davis
82	Roy Face	66	Mike Timlin	53	Greg A. Harris
78	Doug Jones	65	Bill Campbell	53	Dave Smith
78	Jesse Orosco	63	Mike Jackson	52	Rick Aguilera
77	Jeff Reardon	62	Greg Minton	52	Jim Kern
76	Sparky Lyle	61	Steve Bedrosian	52	Randy Moffitt
75	Gary Lavelle	61	Bob Stanley	52	Dave Righetti
74	Ron Perranoski	60	Mike Stanton	52	Todd Worrell
71	Darold Knowles	58	John Hiller		

(420) Most Career Innings Pitched in Relief

1871.0	Hoyt Wilhelm	1177.1	Bill Campbell	1016.1	Pedro Borbon Sr.
1694.0	Lindy McDaniel	1170.2	Ron Perranoski	1013.2	Roberto Hernandez
1556.2	Goose Gossage	1159.0	Bob Stanley	1003.0	Dan Plesac
1500.1	Rollie Fingers	1154.2	Mike Jackson	994.1	Willie Hernandez
1452.2	Gene Garber	1132.1	Jeff Reardon	992.2	Bob L. Miller
1436.2	Kent Tekulve	1097.1	Doug Jones	990.2	Larry Andersen
1390.1	Sparky Lyle	1094.2	Stu Miller	976.0	Dave LaRoche
1301.1	Tug McGraw	1087.1	Greg Minton	970.0	Ted Abernathy
1297.0	Don McMahon	1080.2	Mike Timlin	964.2	Todd Jones
1277.0	Jesse Orosco	1077.2	Gary Lavelle	962.2	John Hiller
1259.1	Mike G. Marshall	1052.1	Darold Knowles	933.1	Jose Mesa
1252.1	Lee Smith	1052.1	Mike Stanton	931.0	Steve Bedrosian
1248.2	Tom Burgmeier	1043.1	Paul Lindblad	922.1	Greg A. Harris
1245.2	John Franco	1043.1	Dan Quisenberry	920.0	Eric Plunk
1212.1	Roy Face	1042.0	Bruce Sutter	905.0	Elias Sosa
1204.2	Clay Carroll	1040.2	Johnny Klippstein	901.1	Dale Murray
1186.0	Eddie Fisher	1039.2	Roger McDowell		

(421) Most 20-Loss Seasons

10	Jim Galvin	5	Mark Baldwin	5	Charley Radbourn
7	Gus Weyhing	5	Chick Fraser	5	Amos Rusie
7	Jim Whitney	5	Brickyard Kennedy	5	Stump Wiedman
6	Jim McCormick	5	Tony Mullane		

(422) Pitchers whose Careers Lasted 10 or More Seasons and never Had a Losing Record

13	Deacon Phillippe	1899-1911	11	Spud Chandler	1937-1947
13	Urban Shocker	1916-1928	11	Jay Powell	1995-2005
12	Dizzy Dean	1930, 1932-41, 1947	10	Joe McGinnity	1899-1908
12	Andy Pettitte	1995-2006	10	Babe Ruth	1914-21, 1930, 1933
11	Dave Foutz	1884-1894			

(423) Most Career Wins with No 20-win Seasons but at least One 20-loss Season

161	Bump Hadley	Two 20-loss seasons	107	Chuck Stobbs	
158	Steve Rogers		106	Turk Farrell	
150	Rube Benton		105	Jim Tobin	
131	Harry Howell	Three 20-loss seasons	105	Case Patten	Three 20-loss seasons
127	Bob Rush		103	Jack Scott	Two 20-loss seasons
127	Lefty Tyler		101	Si Johnson	
121	Ed Brandt		97	Milt Gaston	
119	Ken Raffensberger		95	Slim Harriss	Two 20-loss seasons
117	Pedro Ramos				

(424) Most Wins after Age 40

121	Phil Niekro	52	Jamie Moyer	33	Connie Marrero
96	Jack Quinn	51	Tommy John	33	Dazzy Vance
75	Cy Young	50	Randy Johnson	32	Babe Adams
75	Warren Spahn	47	Gaylord Perry	31	Jerry Koosman
71	Nolan Ryan	46	Grover Alexander	29	Early Wynn
67	Charlie Hough	45	David Wells	28	Joe Niekro
55	Roger Clemens	44	Don Sutton	28	Satchel Paige
54	Hoyt Wilhelm	36	Red Faber		

(425) Most Career Games with 18 or More Strikeouts

5	Nolan Ryan	2	Sandy Koufax
4	Randy Johnson	2	Jack Coombs
3	Roger Clemens		

(426) Most Career Games with 15 or More Strikeouts

29	Randy Johnson	5	Steve Carlton	3	Mickey Lolich
26	Nolan Ryan	5	Sam McDowell	3	J.R. Richard
10	Roger Clemens	5	Tom Seaver	3	Frank Tanana
10	Pedro Martinez	4	Bob Feller	3	Luis Tiant
8	Sandy Koufax	4	Dwight Gooden	3	Dazzy Vance
8	Rube Waddell	4	Curt Schilling	3	Bob Veale
7	Toad Ramsey	3	Bob Gibson	3	Don Wilson

(427) Most Career Games with 10 or More Walks

4	Steve Barber	3	Wiley Piatt	2	Bill Hallahan
4	Bob Feller	3	J.R. Richard	2	Randy Johnson
4	Bill George	2	Sandy Burk	2	Nolan Ryan
4	Cy Seymour	2	Ken Chase	2	Chuck Stobbs
4	Dick Weik	2	Harry Coveleski	2	Johnny Vander Meer
3	Tommy Byrne	2	Ed Crane	2	Bobby Witt
3	Sam McDowell	2	Lefty Gomez		

COURTESY OF CHICAGO CUBS

Greg Maddux

(428) Most Batters Hit in a Career

278	Gus Weyhing	148	Adonis Terry	126	Jack W. Taylor
219	Chick Fraser	146	Silver King	126	Chan Ho Park
210	Pink Hawley	146	Tim Wakefield	125	Willie Sudhoff
205	Walter Johnson	144	Win Mercer	125	Greg Maddux
190	Eddie Plank	142	Frank Foreman	123	Mark Baldwin
185	Tony Mullane	141	Ed Doheny	123	Phil Niekro
179	Joe McGinnity	139	Red Ehret	122	Jim Kaat
178	Randy Johnson	139	Kevin Brown	122	Dennis Martinez
174	Charlie Hough	137	Howard Ehmke	121	Hooks Dauss
171	Clark Griffith	136	Phil Knell	120	Jack Powell
161	Cy Young	131	Matt Kilroy	120	Doc White
160	Jim Bunning	130	George Mullin	117	Orel Hershiser
158	Nolan Ryan	130	Jesse Tannehill	117	Darryl Kile
156	Vic Willis	129	Kid Nichols	117	Al Leiter
155	Bert Blyleven	129	Dave Stieb	117	Kenny Rogers
154	Don Drysdale	129	Frank Tanana	115	Rube Waddell
154	Roger Clemens	129	Pedro Martinez		
148	Bert Cunningham	126	Kid Carsey		

(429) Most Career Consecutive Wins by a Pitcher

24	Carl Hubbell	NL	NY	1936-37		16	Bill Donovan	AL	DET	1907-08
22	Roy Face	NL	PIT	1958-59		16	Walter Johnson	AL	WAS	1912
20	Rube Marquard	NL	NY	1911-12		16	Joe Wood	AL	BOS	1912
20	Roger Clemens	AL	TOR	1998-99		16	Lefty Grove	AL	PHI	1931
19	Tim Keefe	NL	NY	1888		16	Alvin Crowder	AL	WAS	1932-33
18	Charley Radbourn	NL	PRO	1884		16	Schoolboy Rowe	AL	DET	1934
18	Pat Luby	NL	CHI	1890-91		16	Ewell Blackwell	NL	CIN	1947
17	Mickey Welch	NL	NY	1885		16	Jack Sanford	NL	SF	1962
17	Johnny Allen	AL	CLE	1936-37		16	Tom Seaver	NL	NY	1969-70
17	Dave McNally	AL	BAL	1968-69		16	Rick Sutcliffe	NL	CHI	1984-85
17	Jose Contreras	AL	CHI	2005-06		16	Randy Johnson	AL	SEA	1995-97
16	Tim Keefe	NL	TRO	1880-81		16	Roger Clemens	AL	NY	2001
16	Jim McCormick	NL	CHI	1886						

(430) Most Career 1-0 Games Won

38	Walter Johnson	12	Stan Coveleski	10	Paul Derringer
17	Grover Alexander	12	Gaylord Perry	10	Bill Doak
15	Bert Blyleven	12	Eddie Plank	10	Addie Joss
14	Christy Mathewson	11	Ferguson Jenkins	10	Sandy Koufax
13	Dean Chance	11	Greg Maddux	10	Dick Rudolph
13	Ed Walsh	11	Kid Nichols	10	Warren Spahn
13	Doc White	11	Nap Rucker	10	Lefty Tyler
13	Cy Young	11	Nolan Ryan	10	Virgil Trucks
12	Steve Carlton	10	Joe Bush	10	Hippo Vaughn

(431) Most Career Games Allowing One or No Hits

		NO-HITTERS	ONE-HITTERS				NO-HITTERS	ONE-HITTERS
12	Nolan Ryan	7	5		5	Jim Maloney	2	3
12	Bob Feller	3	9		5	Jim Palmer	1	4
7	Walter Johnson	1	6		5	Tom Seaver	1	4
7	Addie Joss	1	6		5	Dave Stieb	1	4
7	Charley Radbourn	1	6		5	Ed Walsh	1	4
6	Mordecai Brown	0	6		5	Grover Alexander	0	5
6	Steve Carlton	0	6		5	Tim Keefe	0	5
6	Randy Johnson	2	4		5	Don Sutton	0	5
5	Bert Blyleven	1	4		5	Doc White	0	5

(432) Most Opening Day Starts

16	Tom Seaver	12	Grover Alexander	9	Phil Niekro
14	Steve Carlton	12	Bert Blyleven	9	Gaylord Perry
14	Walter Johnson	11	Ferguson Jenkins	9	Steve Rogers
14	Jack Morris	11	Dennis Martinez	9	Nolan Ryan
14	Cy Young	10	Bob Gibson	9	Rick Sutcliffe
14	Randy Johnson	10	Juan Marichal	9	Don Sutton
13	Roger Clemens	10	George Mullin	9	Brad Radke
13	Robin Roberts	10	Warren Spahn		

(433) Most Opening Day Wins

9	Walter Johnson	6	John Clarkson	5	Jim Palmer
8	Grover Alexander	6	Dwight Gooden	5	Don Drysdale
8	Jack Morris	6	Kid Nichols	5	Nolan Ryan
7	Tom Seaver	6	Roger Clemens	5	Rick Sutcliffe
7	Jimmy Key	6	Mickey Lolich	5	George Mullin
7	Randy Johnson	6	Juan Marichal	5	Robin Roberts
6	Greg Maddux	6	Cy Young		
6	Wes Ferrell	5	Lon Warneke		

(434) Most Career Innings as a Starting Pitcher

7034.2	Cy Young	4957.1	Bert Blyleven
5872.2	Jim Galvin	4891.1	Kid Nichols
5550.1	Walter Johnson	4815.2	Roger Clemens
5326.0	Nolan Ryan	4776.0	Tom Seaver
5248.1	Don Sutton	4753.1	Christy Mathewson
5165.0	Steve Carlton	4749.0	Mickey Welch
5161.2	Gaylord Perry	4622.0	Tommy John
5149.1	Phil Niekro	4614.0	Greg Maddux
5106.2	Warren Spahn	4567.1	Robin Roberts
5021.1	Tim Keefe	4491.1	John Clarkson
4983.1	Grover Alexander	4419.0	Charley Radbourn

(435) Most Career Grand Slams Allowed

10	Mike Jackson	8	Willie Blair	8	Jim Kaat
10	Nolan Ryan	8	Bert Blyleven	8	Johnny Klippstein
9	Ned Garver	8	Brian Boehringer	8	Lindy McDaniel
9	Jim Kaat	8	Jim Brewer	8	Tug McGraw
9	Milt Pappas	8	Roy Face	8	Jesse Orosco
9	Jerry Reuss	8	Bob Feller	8	Kenny Rogers
9	Lee Smith	8	Alex Fernandez	8	Frank Tanana
9	Frank Viola	8	Jimmy Haynes	8	Early Wynn

(436) Most Career Home Runs Allowed

505	Robin Roberts	374	Catfish Hunter	321	Danny Darwin
484	Ferguson Jenkins	372	Jim Bunning	320	Juan Marichal
482	Phil Niekro	372	Dennis Martinez	319	Steve Trachsel
472	Don Sutton	361	Randy Johnson	318	Greg Maddux
448	Frank Tanana	354	Roger Clemens	316	Pedro Ramos
434	Warren Spahn	347	Dennis Eckersley	315	Tim Wakefield
430	Bert Blyleven	347	Mickey Lolich	311	Mark Langston
414	Steve Carlton	346	Luis Tiant	309	Kenny Rogers
414	Jamie Moyer	345	Mike Mussina	308	Jim Perry
399	Gaylord Perry	338	Early Wynn	304	Chuck Finley
395	Jim Kaat	326	Curt Schilling	303	Jim Palmer
389	Jack Morris	326	Brad Radke	302	Tommy John
385	David Wells	324	Doyle Alexander	302	Murry Dickson
383	Charlie Hough	322	Tom Glavine		
380	Tom Seaver	321	Nolan Ryan		

(437) Most Career Wild Pitches

277	Nolan Ryan	169	Kid Nichols	144	John Ward
274	Mickey Welch	168	Will White	140	Sam McDowell
233	Tim Keefe	165	Tony Mullane	139	George Bradley
226	Phil Niekro	161	John Healy	136	Roger Clemens
223	Jim Galvin	160	Gaylord Perry	135	Mike Moore
217	Charley Radbourn	157	Jim McCormick	135	Chick Fraser
214	Jim Whitney	156	Red Ames	135	John Smoltz
206	Jack Morris	156	Cy Young	130	Chuck Finley
187	Tommy John	155	Walter Johnson	130	Gus Weyhing
183	Steve Carlton	154	Charlie Buffinton	128	Jim Kaat
183	Mark Baldwin	153	Amos Rusie	128	Bobby Witt
182	John Clarkson	149	David Cone	126	Tom Seaver
179	Charlie Hough	148	Adonis Terry		
172	Joe Niekro	145	Ed Crane		

(438) Best Career Strikeout to Walk Ratio (min. 2,000 strikeouts)

4.38	Curt Schilling	2.97	Roger Clemens	2.66	Kevin Brown
4.28	Pedro Martinez	2.96	Christy Mathewson	2.64	Cy Young
3.58	Mike Mussina	2.96	John Smoltz	2.62	Tom Seaver
3.36	Greg Maddux	2.93	Sandy Koufax	2.61	Robin Roberts
3.25	Dennis Eckersley	2.91	Don Drysdale	2.58	Mickey Lolich
3.25	Juan Marichal	2.88	Rube Waddell	2.57	Walter Johnson
3.22	Randy Johnson	2.86	Jim Bunning	2.56	Gaylord Perry
3.20	Ferguson Jenkins	2.80	Bert Blyleven		
3.13	David Wells	2.66	Don Sutton		

(439) Lowest Career Batting Average by Opponents (min. 1,500 IP)

.204	Nolan Ryan	.226	Larry Corcoran	.233	Mordecai Brown
.205	Sandy Koufax	.226	Tim Keefe	.233	Charlie Ferguson
.209	Pedro Martinez	.226	Tom Seaver	.233	Charlie Hough
.209	Sid Fernandez	.227	Walter Johnson	.234	John Smoltz
.212	Andy Messersmith	.228	Bob Gibson	.234	Dean Chance
.212	J.R. Richard	.228	Goose Gossage	.234	Larry Cheney
.215	Sam McDowell	.228	Rube Waddell	.234	Denny McLain
.216	Hoyt Wilhelm	.228	Don Wilson	.234	Toad Ramsey
.217	Randy Johnson	.228	Roger Clemens	.234	Amos Rusie
.218	Ed Walsh	.230	Sam P. Jones	.234	John Ward
.220	Mario Soto	.230	Jim Palmer	.235	Ray Culp
.220	Bob Turley	.231	Bobby Bolin	.235	Rollie Fingers
.223	Addie Joss	.231	Bob Feller	.235	Whitey Ford
.223	Orval Overall	.231	Catfish Hunter	.235	Dave Foutz
.223	Jeff Tesreau	.232	David Cone	.235	Ed Morris
.224	Jose DeLeon	.232	Al Downing	.235	Tony Mullane
.224	Jim Maloney	.232	Johnny Vander Meer		
.224	Ed Reulbach	.232	Stan Williams		

(440) Lowest Career On-base Percentage by Opponents (min. 1,500 IP)

.254	John Ward	.277	Juan Marichal	.286	Dave Foutz
.260	Addie Joss	.278	Mordecai Brown	.286	Don Sutton
.262	George Bradley	.278	Charley Radbourn	.287	Ferguson Jenkins
.263	Terry Larkin	.279	Walter Johnson	.287	Andy Messersmith
.264	Larry Corcoran	.279	Dupee Shaw	.287	Cy Young
.264	Ed Walsh	.281	Guy Hecker	.288	Grover Alexander
.267	Tommy Bond	.281	Jumbo McGinnis	.288	Rube Waddell
.268	Will White	.283	Deacon Phillippe	.288	Hoyt Wilhelm
.270	Pedro Martinez	.283	Tom Seaver	.289	Tiny Bonham
.270	Charlie Ferguson	.284	Babe Adams	.289	Henry Boyle
.273	Christy Mathewson	.284	Jim Galvin	.289	Noodles Hahn
.273	Ed Morris	.285	Curt Schilling	.289	Jack Lynch
.274	Jim McCormick	.285	Bob Caruthers	.289	Bret Saberhagen
.275	Fred Goldsmith	.285	Catfish Hunter	.290	Greg Maddux
.275	Tim Keefe	.285	Bobby Mathews	.290	Dennis Eckersley
.275	Sandy Koufax	.285	Gary Nolan	.290	Denny McLain
.275	Jim Whitney	.286	Sid Fernandez	.290	Hooks Wiltse

(441) Fewest Career Hits Allowed per Nine Innings (min. 1,500 IP)

6.56	Nolan Ryan	7.30	Addie Joss	7.69	Johnny Vander Meer
6.79	Sandy Koufax	7.38	Jose DeLeon	7.72	Catfish Hunter
6.85	Pedro Martinez	7.39	Jim Maloney	7.72	Al Downing
6.85	Sid Fernandez	7.45	Goose Gossage	7.73	Jim Scott
6.88	J.R. Richard	7.47	Tom Seaver	7.77	Charlie Hough
6.94	Andy Messersmith	7.48	Walter Johnson	7.77	David Cone
7.01	Hoyt Wilhelm	7.48	Rube Waddell	7.79	Bobby Bolin
7.03	Sam McDowell	7.60	Bob Gibson	7.79	Stan Williams
7.12	Ed Walsh	7.61	Don Wilson	7.80	Rollie Fingers
7.14	Randy Johnson	7.63	Jim Palmer	7.81	Dean Chance
7.18	Bob Turley	7.63	Roger Clemens	7.82	Frank E. Smith
7.22	Orval Overall	7.68	Larry Cheney	7.83	Tug McGraw
7.24	Jeff Tesreau	7.68	Mordecai Brown	7.84	Barney Pelty
7.24	Ed Reulbach	7.68	Sam P. Jones	7.85	Denny McLain
7.26	Mario Soto	7.69	Bob Feller	7.85	Whitey Ford

(442) Fewest Career Hits Allowed per Nine Innings by a Right-handed Pitcher
(min. 1,500 IP)

6.56 Nolan Ryan	7.45 Goose Gossage	7.77 David Cone
6.85 Pedro Martinez	7.47 Tom Seaver	7.79 Bobby Bolin
6.88 J.R. Richard	7.48 Walter Johnson	7.79 Stan Williams
6.94 Andy Messersmith	7.60 Bob Gibson	7.80 Rollie Fingers
7.01 Hoyt Wilhelm	7.61 Don Wilson	7.81 Dean Chance
7.12 Ed Walsh	7.63 Jim Palmer	7.82 Frank E. Smith
7.18 Bob Turley	7.63 Roger Clemens	7.84 Barney Pelty
7.22 Orval Overall	7.68 Larry Cheney	7.85 John Smoltz
7.24 Jeff Tesreau	7.68 Mordecai Brown	7.85 Denny McLain
7.24 Ed Reulbach	7.68 Sam P. Jones	7.89 Chief Bender
7.26 Mario Soto	7.69 Bob Feller	7.89 George McQuillan
7.30 Addie Joss	7.72 Catfish Hunter	7.89 Jack Coombs
7.38 Jose DeLeon	7.73 Jim Scott	7.90 Moe Drabowsky
7.39 Jim Maloney	7.77 Charlie Hough	

(443) Fewest Career Hits Allowed per Nine Innings by a Left-handed Pitcher
(min. 1,500 IP)

6.79 Sandy Koufax	8.04 Hal Newhouser	8.25 Carl Weilman
6.85 Sid Fernandez	8.06 Steve Carlton	8.27 Ron Guidry
7.03 Sam McDowell	8.06 Hooks Wiltse	8.27 Mark Langston
7.14 Randy Johnson	8.07 Willie Mitchell	8.28 Max Lanier
7.48 Rube Waddell	8.10 Al Leiter	8.29 Warren Spahn
7.69 Johnny Vander Meer	8.10 Doc White	8.29 Ed Morris
7.72 Al Downing	8.11 Hippo Vaughn	8.30 Hubert "Dutch" Leonard
7.83 Tug McGraw	8.13 Mike Cuellar	8.31 Fred Norman
7.85 Whitey Ford	8.14 Billy Pierce	8.32 Toad Ramsey
7.87 Bob Veale	8.17 Harry Brecheen	8.33 Mickey Lolich
7.91 Vida Blue	8.19 Steve Barber	8.35 Bobby Shantz
7.92 Nap Rucker	8.19 Gary Peters	8.35 Fernando Valenzuela
7.92 Eddie Plank	8.19 Lefty Leifield	8.36 Wilson Alvarez
7.94 Rudy May	8.20 Dave McNally	8.40 John Tudor
7.99 Juan Pizarro	8.23 Lefty Gomez	
8.03 Lefty Tyler	8.24 Ed Killian	

(444) Highest Career Percentage of Starts that Were Shutouts (min. 20 shutouts)

18.10 Ed Walsh	14.13 Spud Chandler	12.40 Doc White
17.72 Joe Wood	13.87 Nap Rucker	12.35 Hippo Vaughn
17.31 Addie Joss	13.81 Mort Cooper	12.22 Ed Killian
16.57 Mordecai Brown	13.33 Ed Reulbach	12.13 Hubert "Dutch" Leonard
16.52 Walter Johnson	13.06 Jack Coombs	11.98 Chief Bender
16.48 Orval Overall	13.04 Eddie Plank	11.95 Hooks Wiltse
16.22 Reb Russell	13.04 Sam Leever	11.92 Bob Porterfield
15.00 Grover Alexander	13.04 Jeff Tesreau	11.67 Jake Weimer
14.82 Lefty Leifield	13.04 Irv Young	11.65 Allie Reynolds
14.71 Rube Waddell	12.99 Pol Perritt	11.62 Bob Gibson
14.60 Lew Richie	12.74 Sandy Koufax	11.50 Jim Scott
14.31 Christy Mathewson	12.42 Babe Adams	

(445) **Most Games Pitched in a Season, before 1893**

76	Will White	NL	CIN	1879	67	Dupee Shaw	NL-UA	DET-BOS	1884
76	Jim Galvin	NL	BUF	1883				DET (28); BOS (39)	
76	Charley Radbourn	NL	PRO	1883	67	Toad Ramsey	AA	LOU	1886
75	Guy Hecker	AA	LOU	1884	67	Amos Rusie	NL	NY	1890
75	Charley Radbourn	NL	PRO	1884	66	Jim Galvin	NL	BUF	1879
75	Bill Hutchison	NL	CHI	1892	66	Jim Whitney	NL	BOS	1881
74	Jim McCormick	NL	CLE	1880	66	Jim McCormick	NL-UA	CLE-CIN	1884
74	Lee Richmond	NL	WOR	1880				CLE (42); CIN (24)	
73	John Clarkson	NL	BOS	1889	66	Silver King	AA	STL	1888
72	Jim Galvin	NL	BUF	1884	66	Bill Hutchison	NL	CHI	1891
71	Bill Hutchison	NL	CHI	1890	65	Mickey Welch	NL	TRO	1880
70	John Ward	NL	PRO	1879	65	Will White	AA	CIN	1883
70	John Ward	NL	PRO	1880	65	John Coleman	NL	PHI	1883
70	John Clarkson	NL	CHI	1885	65	Mickey Welch	NL	NY	1884
69	Matt Kilroy	AA	BAL	1887	65	Toad Ramsey	AA	LOU	1887
68	Jim Devlin	NL	LOU	1876	65	Amos Rusie	NL	NY	1892
68	Jim McCormick	NL	CLE	1882	64	George Bradley	NL	STL	1876
68	Tim Keefe	AA	NY	1883	64	Tommy Bond	NL	BOS	1879
68	Matt Kilroy	AA	BAL	1886	64	Ed Morris	AA	PIT	1886
67	Tony Mullane	AA	TOL	1884	64	Tim Keefe	NL	NY	1886
67	Charlie Buffinton	NL	BOS	1884	64	Jack Stivetts	AA	STL	1891

Juan Marichal

(446) Most Games Pitched in a Season, since 1893

106	Mike G. Marshall	NL	LA	1974		84	Dick Tidrow	NL	CHI	1980
94	Kent Tekulve	NL	PIT	1979		84	Dan Quisenberry	AL	KC	1985
94	Salomon Torres	NL	PIT	2006		84	Stan Belinda	NL	CIN	1997
92	Mike G. Marshall	NL	MON	1973		84	Graeme Lloyd	NL	MON	2001
91	Kent Tekulve	NL	PIT	1978		84	Billy Koch	AL	OAK	2002
90	Wayne Granger	NL	CIN	1969		84	Salomon Torres	NL	PIT	2004
90	Mike G. Marshall	AL	MIN	1979		84	Rheal Cormier	NL	PHI	2004
90	Kent Tekulve	NL	PHI	1987		84	Chris Reitsma	NL	ATL	2004
89	Mark Eichhorn	AL	TOR	1987		84	Bob Howry	NL	CHI	2006
89	Julian Tavarez	NL	SF	1997		83	Ken Sanders	AL	MIL	1971
89	Steve James Kline	NL	STL	2001		83	Craig Lefferts	NL	SD	1986
89	Paul Quantrill	NL	LA	2003		83	Mike Myers	AL	DET	1996
89	Jim Brower	NL	SF	2004		83	Eddie Guardado	AL	MIN	1996
88	Wilbur Wood	AL	CHI	1968		83	Steve James Kline	NL	MON	2000
88	Mike Myers	AL	DET	1997		83	Kelly Wunsch	AL	CHI	2000
88	Sean Runyan	AL	DET	1998		83	Octavio Dotel	NL	HOU	2002
87	Rob Murphy	NL	CIN	1987		83	Scott Eyre	NL	SF	2004
86	Paul Quantrill	NL	LA	2002		83	Mike Stanton	NL	NY	2004
86	Oscar Villarreal	NL	ARI	2003		83	Scott Proctor	AL	NY	2006
86	Ray King	NL	STL	2004		82	Eddie Fisher	AL	CHI	1965
86	Paul Quantrill	AL	NY	2004		82	Bill Campbell	NL	CHI	1983
86	Scott Eyre	NL	SF	2005		82	Juan Agosto	NL	HOU	1990
85	Kent Tekulve	NL	PIT	1982		82	Paul Quantrill	AL	TOR	1998
85	Mitch Williams	AL	TEX	1987		82	Steve James Kline	NL	MON	1999
85	Frank Williams	NL	CIN	1987		82	Ray King	NL	MIL	2001
85	Matt Capps	NL	PIT	2006		82	Jeff Fassero	NL	CHI	2001
85	Jon Rauch	NL	WAS	2006		82	Mike Stanton	NL	WAS-SF	2006
84	Ted Abernathy	NL	CHI	1965					WAS (56); SF (26)	
84	Enrique Romo	NL	PIT	1979						

TRANSCENDENTAL GRAPHICS

Bob Gibson

(447) Most Games Pitched in a Season by a Right-handed Pitcher, since 1893

106	Mike G. Marshall	NL	LA	1974		82	Bill Campbell	NL	CHI	1983
94	Kent Tekulve	NL	PIT	1979		82	Paul Quantrill	AL	TOR	1998
94	Salomon Torres	NL	PIT	2006		81	John Wyatt	AL	KC	1964
92	Mike G. Marshall	NL	MON	1973		81	Dale Murray	NL	MON	1976
91	Kent Tekulve	NL	PIT	1978		81	Jeff D. Robinson	NL	SF-PIT	1987
90	Wayne Granger	NL	CIN	1969					SF (63); PIT (18)	
90	Mike G. Marshall	AL	MIN	1979		81	Duane Ward	AL	TOR	1991
90	Kent Tekulve	NL	PHI	1987		81	Joe Boever	NL	HOU	1992
89	Mark Eichhorn	AL	TOR	1987		81	Mike Jackson	NL	SF	1993
89	Julian Tavarez	NL	SF	1997		81	Brad Clontz	NL	ATL	1996
89	Paul Quantrill	NL	LA	2003		81	Rod Beck	NL	CHI	1998
89	Jim Brower	NL	SF	2004		81	Luis Ayala	NL	MON	2004
86	Paul Quantrill	NL	LA	2002		81	Ugueth Urbina	AL-NL	DET-PHI	2005
86	Oscar Villarreal	NL	ARI	2003					DET (25); PHI (56)	
86	Paul Quantrill	AL	NY	2004		81	Mike Timlin	AL	BOS	2005
85	Kent Tekulve	NL	PIT	1982		81	Todd Coffey	NL	CIN	2006
85	Frank Williams	NL	CIN	1987		81	Geoff Geary	NL	PHI	2006
85	Matt Capps	NL	PIT	2006		81	Chad Qualls	NL	HOU	2006
85	Jon Rauch	NL	WAS	2006		80	Mudcat Grant	AL-NL	OAK-PIT	1970
84	Ted Abernathy	NL	CHI	1965					OAK (72); PIT (8)	
84	Enrique Romo	NL	PIT	1979		80	Pedro Borbon Sr.	NL	CIN	1973
84	Dick Tidrow	NL	CHI	1980		80	Doug Jones	NL	HOU	1992
84	Dan Quisenberry	AL	KC	1985		80	Greg A. Harris	AL	BOS	1993
84	Stan Belinda	NL	CIN	1997		80	Turk Wendell	NL	NY	1999
84	Billy Koch	AL	OAK	2002		80	David Weathers	NL	MIL-CHI	2001
84	Salomon Torres	NL	PIT	2004					MIL (52); CHI (28)	
84	Chris Reitsma	NL	ATL	2004		80	Paul Quantrill	AL	TOR	2001
84	Bob Howry	NL	CHI	2006		80	Felix Rodriguez	NL	SF	2001
83	Ken Sanders	AL	MIL	1971		80	Tim Worrell	NL	SF	2002
83	Octavio Dotel	NL	HOU	2002		80	Tom Gordon	AL	NY	2004
83	Scott Proctor	AL	NY	2006		80	Brad Lidge	NL	HOU	2004
82	Eddie Fisher	AL	CHI	1965						

(448) Most Games Pitched in a Season by a Left-handed Pitcher, since 1893

89	Steve James Kline	NL	STL	2001
88	Wilbur Wood	AL	CHI	1968
88	Mike Myers	AL	DET	1997
88	Sean Runyan	AL	DET	1998
87	Rob Murphy	NL	CIN	1987
86	Ray King	NL	STL	2004
86	Scott Eyre	NL	SF	2005
85	Mitch Williams	AL	TEX	1987
84	Graeme Lloyd	NL	MON	2001
84	Rheal Cormier	NL	PHI	2004
83	Craig Lefferts	NL	SD	1986
83	Mike Myers	AL	DET	1996
83	Eddie Guardado	AL	MIN	1996
83	Steve James Kline	NL	MON	2000
83	Kelly Wunsch	AL	CHI	2000
83	Scott Eyre	NL	SF	2004
83	Mike Stanton	NL	NY	2004
82	Juan Agosto	NL	HOU	1990
82	Steve James Kline	NL	MON	1999
82	Ray King	NL	MIL	2001
82	Jeff Fassero	NL	CHI	2001
82	Mike Stanton	NL	WAS-SF	2006
			WAS (56); SF (26)	
81	Kenny Rogers	AL	TEX	1992
81	Mike Stanton	AL	BOS-TEX	1996
			BOS (59); TEX (22)	
81	Greg Swindell	AL	MIN-BOS	1998
			MIN (52); BOS (29)	
81	J.C. Romero	AL	MIN	2002
80	Willie Hernandez	AL	DET	1984
80	Mitch Williams	AL	TEX	1986
80	Tom Martin	NL	LA	2003
80	Ray King	NL	ATL	2003
80	Scott Schoeneweis	AL	TOR	2005
79	Bob Patterson	NL	CHI	1996
79	Eddie Guardado	AL	MIN	1998
79	Mike Stanton	AL	NY	2002
79	Trever Miller	AL	TOR	2003
79	Scott Sauerbeck	NL-AL	PIT-BOS	2003
			PIT (53); BOS (26)	
78	Hal Woodeshick	NL	HOU-STL	1965
			HOU (27); STL (51)	
78	Ed Vande Berg	AL	SEA	1982
78	Buddy Groom	AL	OAK	1997
78	Dan Plesac	AL	TOR	1998
78	Chuck McElroy	NL	COL	1998
78	Steve James Kline	NL	MON	1998
78	Mike Myers	NL	COL	2000
78	Scott Sauerbeck	NL	PIT	2002
78	Steve James Kline	NL	STL	2003
78	Jamie Walker	AL	DET	2003
78	Billy Wagner	NL	HOU	2003
78	Brian Fuentes	NL	COL	2005
78	Kent Mercker	NL	CIN	2005
78	Will Ohman	NL	CHI	2006
77	Wilbur Wood	AL	CHI	1970
77	Gary Lavelle	NL	SF	1984
77	Mark Davis	NL	SF	1985
77	Craig Lefferts	NL	SD-SF	1987
			SD (33): SF (44)	
77	Mike Venafro	AL	TEX	2000
77	Mike Matthews	NL	SD	2003

(449) Most Games Started in a Season, before 1893

75	Will White	NL	CIN	1879
75	Jim Galvin	NL	BUF	1883
74	Jim McCormick	NL	CLE	1880
73	Charley Radbourn	NL	PRO	1884
73	Guy Hecker	AA	LOU	1884
72	Jim Galvin	NL	BUF	1884
72	John Clarkson	NL	BOS	1889
70	John Clarkson	NL	CHI	1885
70	Bill Hutchison	NL	CHI	1892
69	Matt Kilroy	AA	BAL	1887
68	Jim Devlin	NL	LOU	1876
68	Charley Radbourn	NL	PRO	1883
68	Tim Keefe	AA	NY	1883
68	Matt Kilroy	AA	BAL	1886
67	John Ward	NL	PRO	1880
67	Jim McCormick	NL	CLE	1882
67	Charlie Buffinton	NL	BOS	1884
67	Toad Ramsey	AA	LOU	1886
66	Jim Galvin	NL	BUF	1879
66	Lee Richmond	NL	WOR	1880
66	Dupee Shaw	NL-AA	DET-BOS	1884
			DET (28); BOS (38)	
66	Bill Hutchison	NL	CHI	1890
65	Tony Mullane	AA	TOL	1884
65	Mickey Welch	NL	NY	1884
65	Jim McCormick	NL-UA	CLE-CIN	1884
			CLE (41); CIN (24)	
64	George Bradley	NL	STL	1876
64	Tommy Bond	NL	BOS	1879
64	Mickey Welch	NL	TRO	1880
64	Will White	AA	CIN	1883
64	Tim Keefe	NL	NY	1886
64	Toad Ramsey	AA	LOU	1887
64	Silver King	AA	STL	1888

(450) Most Games Started in a Season, since 1893

52	Amos Rusie	NL	NY	1893		46	Vic Willis	NL	BOS	1902
51	Ted Breitenstein	NL	STL	1895		46	Rube Waddell	AL	PHI	1904
51	Jack Chesbro	AL	NY	1904		46	Christy Mathewson	NL	NY	1904
50	Amos Rusie	NL	NY	1894		46	Ed Walsh	AL	CHI	1907
50	Ted Breitenstein	NL	STL	1894		46	Dave Davenport	FL	STL	1915
50	Pink Hawley	NL	PIT	1895		45	Kid Gleason	NL	STL	1893
50	Frank Killen	NL	PIT	1896		45	Win Mercer	NL	WAS	1896
49	Jouett Meekin	NL	NY	1894		45	Jack Powell	AL	NY	1904
49	Ed Walsh	AL	CHI	1908		45	Grover Alexander	NL	PHI	1916
49	Wilbur Wood	AL	CHI	1972		45	Mickey Lolich	AL	DET	1971
48	Frank Killen	NL	PIT	1893		44	Kid Nichols	NL	BOS	1893
48	Joe McGinnity	NL	NY	1903		44	Brickyard Kennedy	NL	BRO	1893
48	Wilbur Wood	AL	CHI	1973		44	Joe McGinnity	NL	NY	1904
47	Cy Young	NL	CLE	1894		44	George Mullin	AL	DET	1904
47	Amos Rusie	NL	NY	1895		44	Christy Mathewson	NL	NY	1908
47	Jack B. Taylor	NL	STL	1898		44	Grover Alexander	NL	PHI	1917
46	Cy Young	NL	CLE	1893		44	George Uhle	AL	CLE	1923
46	Kid Nichols	NL	BOS	1894		44	Phil Niekro	NL	ATL	1979
46	Cy Young	NL	CLE	1896						

(451) Most Games Started in a Season by a Right-handed Pitcher, since 1893

52	Amos Rusie	NL	NY	1893		44	Kid Nichols	NL	BOS	1893
51	Jack Chesbro	AL	NY	1904		44	Brickyard Kennedy	NL	BRO	1893
50	Pink Hawley	NL	NY	1895		44	Joe McGinnity	NL	NY	1904
50	Amos Rusie	NL	NY	1894		44	George Mullin	AL	DET	1904
49	Jouett Meekin	NL	NY	1894		44	Christy Mathewson	NL	NY	1908
49	Ed Walsh	AL	CHI	1908		44	Grover Alexander	NL	PHI	1917
48	Joe McGinnity	NL	NY	1903		44	George Uhle	AL	CLE	1923
47	Cy Young	NL	CLE	1894		44	Phil Niekro	NL	ATL	1979
47	Amos Rusie	NL	NY	1895		43	Kid Nichols	NL	BOS	1895
47	Jack B. Taylor	NL	STL	1898		43	Pink Hawley	NL	PIT	1896
46	Cy Young	NL	CLE	1893		43	Kid Nichols	NL	BOS	1896
46	Kid Nichols	NL	BOS	1894		43	Win Mercer	NL	WAS	1897
46	Cy Young	NL	CLE	1896		43	Bill Carrick	NL	NY	1899
46	Vic Willis	NL	BOS	1902		43	Jack Powell	NL	STL	1899
46	Christy Mathewson	NL	NY	1904		43	Joe McGinnity	AL	BAL	1901
46	Ed Walsh	AL	CHI	1907		43	Dummy Taylor	NL	NY	1901
46	Dave Davenport	FL	STL	1915		43	Cy Young	AL	BOS	1902
45	Kid Gleason	NL	STL	1893		43	Vic Willis	NL	BOS	1904
45	Win Mercer	NL	WAS	1896		43	Cy Falkenberg	FL	IND	1914
45	Jack Powell	AL	NY	1904		43	Dick Rudolph	NL	BOS	1915
45	Grover Alexander	NL	PHI	1916		43	Phil Niekro	NL	ATL	1977

(452) Most Games Started in a Season by a Left-handed Pitcher, since 1893

51	Ted Breitenstein	NL	STL	1895		41	Jim Kaat	AL	MIN	1966
50	Ted Breitenstein	NL	STL	1894		41	Sandy Koufax	NL	LA	1966
50	Frank Killen	NL	PIT	1896		41	Claude Osteen	NL	LA	1969
49	Wilbur Wood	AL	CHI	1972		41	Steve Carlton	NL	PHI	1972
48	Frank Killen	NL	PIT	1893		41	Mickey Lolich	AL	DET	1972
48	Wilbur Wood	AL	CHI	1973		41	Mickey Lolich	AL	DET	1974
46	Rube Waddell	AL	PHI	1904		41	Jim Kaat	AL	CHI	1975
45	Mickey Lolich	AL	DET	1971		40	Eddie Plank	AL	PHI	1903
43	Ted Breitenstein	NL	STL	1896		40	Eddie Plank	AL	PHI	1907
43	Cy Seymour	NL	NY	1898		40	Lefty Williams	AL	CHI	1919
43	Eddie Plank	AL	PHI	1904		40	Johnny Podres	NL	LA	1962
43	Wilbur Wood	AL	CHI	1975		40	Sandy Koufax	NL	LA	1963
42	Ted Breitenstein	NL	STL	1893		40	Chris Short	NL	PHI	1965
42	Noodles Hahn	NL	CIN	1901		40	Claude Osteen	NL	LA	1965
42	Irv Young	NL	BOS	1905		40	Dave McNally	AL	BAL	1969
42	Jim Kaat	AL	MIN	1965		40	Dave McNally	AL	BAL	1970
42	Wilbur Wood	AL	CHI	1971		40	Mike Cuellar	AL	BAL	1970
42	Mickey Lolich	AL	DET	1973		40	Ken Holtzman	AL	OAK	1973
42	Wilbur Wood	AL	CHI	1974		40	Steve Carlton	NL	PHI	1973
41	Frank Killen	NL	PIT	1897		40	Jerry Reuss	NL	HOU	1973
41	Eddie Plank	AL	PHI	1905		40	Vida Blue	AL	OAK	1974
41	Irv Young	NL	BOS	1906		40	Randy Jones	NL	SD	1976
41	Babe Ruth	AL	BOS	1916		40	Mike Flanagan	AL	BAL	1978
41	Sandy Koufax	NL	LA	1965						

Whitey Ford

(453) Most Complete Games in a Season, before 1893

75	Will White	NL	CIN	1879		67	Bill Hutchison	NL	CHI	1892
73	Charley Radbourn	NL	PRO	1884		66	Jim Devlin	NL	LOU	1876
72	Jim McCormick	NL	CLE	1880		66	Charley Radbourn	NL	PRO	1883
72	Jim Galvin	NL	BUF	1883		66	Matt Kilroy	AA	BAL	1886
72	Guy Hecker	AA	LOU	1884		66	Toad Ramsey	AA	LOU	1886
71	Jim Galvin	NL	BUF	1884		66	Matt Kilroy	AA	BAL	1887
68	Tim Keefe	AA	NY	1883		65	Jim Galvin	NL	BUF	1879
68	John Clarkson	NL	CHI	1885		65	Jim McCormick	NL	CLE	1882
68	John Clarkson	NL	BOS	1889		65	Bill Hutchison	NL	CHI	1890

(454) Most Complete Games in a Season, 1893-1920

50	Amos Rusie	NL	NY	1893		42	George Mullin	AL	DET	1904
48	Jack Chesbro	AL	NY	1904		42	Ed Walsh	AL	CHI	1908
47	Ted Breitenstein	NL	STL	1895		41	Jouett Meekin	NL	NY	1894
46	Ted Breitenstein	NL	STL	1894		41	Bert Cunningham	NL	LOU	1898
45	Amos Rusie	NL	NY	1894		41	Noodles Hahn	NL	CIN	1901
45	Vic Willis	NL	BOS	1902		41	Cy Young	AL	BOS	1902
44	Cy Young	NL	CLE	1894		41	Irv Young	NL	BOS	1905
44	Pink Hawley	NL	PIT	1895		40	Brickyard Kennedy	NL	BRO	1893
44	Frank Killen	NL	PIT	1896		40	Kid Nichols	NL	BOS	1894
44	Joe McGinnity	NL	NY	1903		40	Cy Young	NL	CLE	1898
43	Kid Nichols	NL	BOS	1893		40	Doc McJames	NL	BAL	1898
43	Kid Nichols	NL	BOS	1895		40	Kid Nichols	NL	BOS	1898
42	Cy Young	NL	CLE	1893		40	Cy Young	NL	STL	1899
42	Amos Rusie	NL	NY	1895		40	Bill Carrick	NL	NY	1899
42	Cy Young	NL	CLE	1896		40	Jack Powell	NL	STL	1899
42	Jack B. Taylor	NL	STL	1898		40	Cy Young	AL	BOS	1904

(455) Most Complete Games in a Season, since 1921

36	Bob Feller	AL	CLE	1946		30	Robin Roberts	NL	PHI	1952
33	Burleigh Grimes	NL	BRO	1923		30	Juan Marichal	NL	SF	1968
33	Dizzy Trout	AL	DET	1944		30	Ferguson Jenkins	NL	CHI	1971
33	Robin Roberts	NL	PHI	1953		30	Steve Carlton	NL	PHI	1972
32	Red Faber	AL	CHI	1921		30	Catfish Hunter	AL	NY	1975
32	George Uhle	AL	CLE	1926		29	Wilbur Cooper	NL	PIT	1921
31	Red Faber	AL	CHI	1922		29	Urban Shocker	AL	STL	1922
31	Wes Ferrell	AL	BOS	1935		29	George Uhle	AL	CLE	1923
31	Bobo Newsom	AL	STL	1938		29	Ted Lyons	AL	CHI	1930
31	Bucky Walters	NL	CIN	1939		29	Dizzy Dean	NL	STL	1935
31	Bob Feller	AL	CLE	1940		29	Bucky Walters	NL	CIN	1940
30	Burleigh Grimes	NL	BRO	1921		29	Hal Newhouser	AL	DET	1945
30	Carl Mays	AL	NY	1921		29	Hal Newhouser	AL	DET	1946
30	Urban Shocker	AL	STL	1921		29	Robin Roberts	NL	PHI	1954
30	Dazzy Vance	NL	BRO	1924		29	Mickey Lolich	AL	DET	1971
30	Burleigh Grimes	NL	BRO	1924		29	Gaylord Perry	AL	CLE	1972
30	Ted Lyons	AL	CHI	1927		29	Gaylord Perry	AL	CLE	1973
30	Thornton Lee	AL	CHI	1941		29	Ferguson Jenkins	AL	TEX	1974

(456) Most Innings Pitched in a Season, before 1893

680.0	Will White	NL	CIN	1879	587.0	John Ward	NL	PRO	1879
678.2	Charley Radbourn	NL	PRO	1884	587.0	Charlie Buffinton	NL	BOS	1884
670.2	Guy Hecker	AA	LOU	1884	584.2	Silver King	AA	STL	1888
657.2	Jim McCormick	NL	CLE	1880	583.0	Matt Kilroy	AA	BAL	1886
656.1	Jim Galvin	NL	BUF	1883	581.0	Ed Morris	AA	PIT	1885
636.1	Jim Galvin	NL	BUF	1884	577.0	Will White	AA	CIN	1883
632.1	Charley Radbourn	NL	PRO	1883	574.0	Mickey Welch	NL	TRO	1880
623.0	John Clarkson	NL	CHI	1885	573.0	George Bradley	NL	STL	1876
622.0	Jim Devlin	NL	LOU	1876	569.0	Jim McCormick	NL-UA	CLE-CIN	1884
622.0	Bill Hutchison	NL	CHI	1892			CLE (359.0); CIN (210.0)		
620.0	John Clarkson	NL	BOS	1889	567.0	Tony Mullane	AA	TOL	1884
619.0	Tim Keefe	AA	NY	1883	561.0	Toad Ramsey	AA	LOU	1887
603.0	Bill Hutchison	NL	CHI	1890	561.0	Bill Hutchison	NL	CHI	1891
595.2	Jim McCormick	NL	CLE	1882	559.0	Jim Devlin	NL	LOU	1877
595.0	John Ward	NL	PRO	1880	557.1	Mickey Welch	NL	NY	1884
593.0	Jim Galvin	NL	BUF	1879	555.1	Tommy Bond	NL	BOS	1879
590.2	Lee Richmond	NL	WOR	1880	555.1	Ed Morris	AA	PIT	1886
589.1	Matt Kilroy	AA	BAL	1887	552.1	Jim Whitney	NL	BOS	1881
588.2	Toad Ramsey	AA	LOU	1886					

(457) Most Innings Pitched in a Season, since 1893

482.0	Amos Rusie	NL	NY	1893	390.2	Christy Mathewson	NL	NY	1908
464.0	Ed Walsh	AL	CHI	1908	390.1	Jack Powell	AL	NY	1904
454.2	Jack Chesbro	AL	NY	1904	389.1	Togie Pittinger	NL	BOS	1902
447.1	Ted Breitenstein	NL	STL	1894	389.0	Grover Alexander	NL	PHI	1916
444.1	Pink Hawley	NL	PIT	1895	388.0	Kid Nichols	NL	BOS	1898
444.0	Amos Rusie	NL	NY	1894	388.0	Grover Alexander	NL	PHI	1917
438.2	Ted Breitenstein	NL	STL	1895	384.2	Cy Young	AL	BOS	1902
434.0	Joe McGinnity	NL	NY	1903	383.0	Rube Waddell	AL	PHI	1904
432.1	Frank Killen	NL	PIT	1896	382.2	Ted Breitenstein	NL	STL	1893
425.0	Kid Nichols	NL	BOS	1893	382.2	Brickyard Kennedy	NL	BRO	1893
422.2	Cy Young	NL	CLE	1893	382.1	George Mullin	AL	DET	1904
422.1	Ed Walsh	AL	CHI	1907	382.0	Joe McGinnity	AL	BAL	1901
418.0	Jouett Meekin	NL	NY	1894	380.1	Kid Gleason	NL	STL	1893
415.0	Frank Killen	NL	PIT	1893	380.0	Cy Young	AL	BOS	1904
414.1	Cy Young	NL	CLE	1896	379.0	Sam Leever	NL	PIT	1899
410.0	Vic Willis	NL	BOS	1902	378.0	Pink Hawley	NL	PIT	1896
408.2	Cy Young	NL	CLE	1894	378.0	Irv Young	NL	BOS	1905
408.0	Joe McGinnity	NL	NY	1904	377.2	Cy Young	NL	CLE	1898
407.0	Kid Nichols	NL	BOS	1894	377.1	Cy Falkenberg	FL	IND	1914
397.1	Jack B. Taylor	NL	STL	1898	377.0	Oscar Jones	NL	BRO	1904
393.1	Amos Rusie	NL	NY	1895	376.2	Wilbur Wood	AL	CHI	1972
393.0	Ed Walsh	AL	CHI	1912	376.1	Grover Alexander	NL	PHI	1915
392.2	Pink Hawley	NL	STL	1894	376.0	Mickey Lolich	AL	DET	1971
392.2	Dave Davenport	FL	STL	1915	375.1	Noodles Hahn	NL	CIN	1901
390.2	Kid Nichols	NL	BOS	1895					

(458) Most Innings Pitched in a Season by a Right-handed Pitcher, since 1893

482.0	Amos Rusie	NL	NY	1893		389.0	Grover Alexander	NL	PHI	1916
464.0	Ed Walsh	AL	CHI	1908		388.0	Kid Nichols	NL	BOS	1898
454.2	Jack Chesbro	AL	NY	1904		388.0	Grover Alexander	NL	PHI	1917
444.1	Pink Hawley	NL	PIT	1895		384.2	Cy Young	AL	BOS	1902
444.0	Amos Rusie	NL	NY	1894		382.2	Brickyard Kennedy	NL	BRO	1893
434.0	Joe McGinnity	NL	NY	1903		382.1	George Mullin	AL	DET	1904
425.0	Kid Nichols	NL	BOS	1893		382.0	Joe McGinnity	AL	BAL	1901
422.2	Cy Young	NL	CLE	1893		380.1	Kid Gleason	NL	STL	1893
422.1	Ed Walsh	AL	CHI	1907		380.0	Cy Young	AL	BOS	1904
418.0	Jouett Meekin	NL	NY	1894		379.0	Sam Leever	NL	PIT	1899
414.1	Cy Young	NL	CLE	1896		378.0	Pink Hawley	NL	PIT	1896
410.0	Vic Willis	NL	BOS	1902		377.2	Cy Young	NL	CLE	1898
408.2	Cy Young	NL	CLE	1894		377.1	Cy Falkenberg	FL	IND	1914
408.0	Joe McGinnity	NL	NY	1904		377.0	Oscar Jones	NL	BRO	1904
407.0	Kid Nichols	NL	BOS	1894		376.1	Grover Alexander	NL	PHI	1915
397.1	Jack B. Taylor	NL	STL	1898		374.0	Doc McJames	NL	BAL	1898
393.1	Amos Rusie	NL	NY	1895		373.0	Jack Powell	NL	STL	1899
393.0	Ed Walsh	CHI	AL	1912		372.1	Kid Nichols	NL	BOS	1896
392.2	Pink Hawley	NL	STL	1894		371.2	Walter Johnson	AL	WAS	1914
392.2	Dave Davenport	FL	STL	1915		371.1	Cy Young	AL	BOS	1901
390.2	Kid Nichols	NL	BOS	1895		371.1	Bill Dinneen	AL	BOS	1902
390.2	Christy Mathewson	NL	NY	1908		371.1	Bob Feller	AL	CLE	1946
390.1	Jack Powell	AL	NY	1904		370.0	Walter Johnson	AL	WAS	1910
389.1	Togie Pittinger	NL	BOS	1902						

(459) Most Innings Pitched in a Season by a Left-handed Pitcher, since 1893

447.1	Ted Breitenstein	NL	STL	1894		334.1	Duke Esper	NL	WAS	1893
438.2	Ted Breitenstein	NL	STL	1895		334.0	Wilbur Wood	AL	CHI	1971
432.1	Frank Killen	NL	PIT	1896		333.2	Otto Hess	AL	CLE	1906
415.0	Frank Killen	NL	PIT	1893		333.1	Nap Rucker	NL	BRO	1908
383.0	Rube Waddell	AL	PHI	1904		331.2	Ed Killian	AL	DET	1904
382.2	Ted Breitenstein	NL	STL	1893		330.0	Hooks Wiltse	NL	NY	1908
378.0	Irv Young	NL	BOS	1905		328.2	Rube Waddell	AL	PHI	1905
376.2	Wilbur Wood	AL	CHI	1972		327.1	Mickey Lolich	AL	DET	1972
376.0	Mickey Lolich	AL	DET	1971		327.0	Wilbur Cooper	NL	PIT	1920
375.1	Noodles Hahn	NL	CIN	1901		327.0	Wilbur Cooper	NL	PIT	1921
359.1	Wilbur Wood	AL	CHI	1973		326.2	Jesse Tannehill	NL	PIT	1898
358.1	Irv Young	NL	BOS	1906		326.1	Babe Ruth	AL	BOS	1917
357.2	Case Patten	AL	WAS	1904		324.1	Harry Coveleski	AL	DET	1916
357.1	Eddie Plank	AL	PHI	1904		324.0	Rube Waddell	AL	PHI	1903
356.2	Cy Seymour	NL	NY	1898		323.2	Babe Ruth	AL	BOS	1916
346.2	Eddie Plank	AL	PHI	1905		323.0	Sandy Koufax	NL	LA	1966
346.1	Steve Carlton	NL	PHI	1972		321.0	Noodles Hahn	NL	CIN	1902
343.2	Eddie Plank	AL	PHI	1907		321.0	Claude Osteen	NL	LA	1969
339.2	Ted Breitenstein	NL	STL	1896		320.1	Ted Breitenstein	NL	CIN	1897
337.1	Frank Killen	NL	PIT	1897		320.1	Nap Rucker	NL	BRO	1910
336.0	Eddie Plank	AL	PHI	1903		320.1	Wilbur Wood	AL	CHI	1974
335.2	Sandy Koufax	NL	LA	1965						

(460) Most Wins in a Season, before 1893

59	Charley Radbourn	NL		PRO	1884	43	Will White	AA	CIN	1883
53	John Clarkson	NL		CHI	1885	43	Billy Taylor	UA-AA	STL-PHI	1884
52	Guy Hecker	AA		LOU	1884				STL (25); PHI (18)	
49	John Clarkson	NL		BOS	1889	42	Tim Keefe	NL	NY	1886
48	Charley Radbourn	NL		PRO	1883	42	Lady Baldwin	NL	DET	1886
48	Charlie Buffinton	NL		BOS	1884	42	Bill Hutchison	NL	CHI	1890
47	Al Spalding	NL		CHI	1876	41	Tim Keefe	AA	NY	1883
47	John Ward	NL		PRO	1879	41	Charlie Sweeney	NL-UA	PRO-STL	1884
46	Jim Galvin	NL		BUF	1883				PRO(17); STL (24)	
46	Jim Galvin	NL		BUF	1884	41	Ed Morris	AA	PIT	1886
46	Matt Kilroy	AA		BAL	1887	41	Dave Foutz	AA	STL	1886
45	George Bradley	NL		STL	1876	40	Tommy Bond	NL	BOS	1877
45	Jim McCormick	NL		CLE	1880	40	Tommy Bond	NL	BOS	1878
45	Silver King	AA		STL	1888	40	Will White	AA	CIN	1882
44	Mickey Welch	NL		NY	1885	40	Jim McCormick	NL-UA	CLE-CIN	1884
44	Bill Hutchison	NL		CHI	1891				CLE (19); CIN (21)	
43	Will White	NL		CIN	1879	40	Bill J. Sweeney	UA	BAL	1884
43	Tommy Bond	NL		BOS	1879	40	Bob Caruthers	AA	STL	1885
43	Larry Corcoran	NL		CHI	1880	40	Bob Caruthers	AA	BRO	1889

(461) Most Wins in a Season, since 1893

41	Jack Chesbro	AL	NY	1904	31	Denny McLain	AL	DET	1968
40	Ed Walsh	AL	CHI	1908	30	Kid Nichols	NL	BOS	1896
37	Christy Mathewson	NL	NY	1908	30	Frank Killen	NL	PIT	1896
36	Frank Killen	NL	PIT	1893	30	Christy Mathewson	NL	NY	1903
36	Amos Rusie	NL	NY	1894	30	Grover Alexander	NL	PHI	1917
36	Walter Johnson	AL	WAS	1913	30	Dizzy Dean	NL	STL	1934
35	Cy Young	NL	CLE	1895	29	Mordecai Brown	NL	CHI	1908
35	Joe McGinnity	NL	NY	1904	29	George Mullin	AL	DET	1909
34	Cy Young	NL	CLE	1893	29	Claude Hendrix	FL	CHI	1914
34	Kid Nichols	NL	BOS	1893	29	Eddie Cicotte	AL	CHI	1919
34	Joe Wood	AL	BOS	1912	29	Hal Newhouser	AL	DET	1944
33	Amos Rusie	NL	NY	1893	28	Cy Young	NL	CLE	1896
33	Jouett Meekin	NL	NY	1894	28	Amos Rusie	NL	NY	1897
33	Cy Young	AL	BOS	1901	28	Bert Cunningham	NL	LOU	1898
33	Christy Mathewson	NL	NY	1904	28	Jay Hughes	NL	BRO	1899
33	Walter Johnson	AL	WAS	1912	28	Joe McGinnity	NL	BAL	1899
33	Grover Alexander	NL	PHI	1916	28	Joe McGinnity	NL	BRO	1900
32	Kid Nichols	NL	BOS	1894	28	Jack Chesbro	NL	PIT	1902
32	Cy Young	AL	BOS	1902	28	Cy Young	AL	BOS	1903
31	Bill Hoffer	NL	BAL	1895	28	Grover Alexander	NL	PHI	1911
31	Pink Hawley	NL	PIT	1895	28	Jack Coombs	AL	PHI	1911
31	Kid Nichols	NL	BOS	1897	28	Walter Johnson	AL	WAS	1914
31	Kid Nichols	NL	BOS	1898	28	Eddie Cicotte	AL	CHI	1917
31	Joe McGinnity	NL	NY	1903	28	Dazzy Vance	NL	BRO	1924
31	Christy Mathewson	NL	NY	1905	28	Lefty Grove	AL	PHI	1930
31	Jack Coombs	AL	PHI	1910	28	Dizzy Dean	NL	STL	1935
31	Grover Alexander	NL	PHI	1915	28	Robin Roberts	NL	PHI	1952
31	Jim Bagby Sr.	AL	CLE	1920					
31	Lefty Grove	AL	PHI	1931					

(462) Most Wins in a Season by a Right-handed Pitcher, since 1893

41	Jack Chesbro	AL	NY	1904
40	Ed Walsh	CHI	AL	1908
37	Christy Mathewson	NL	NY	1908
36	Amos Rusie	NL	NY	1894
36	Walter Johnson	AL	WAS	1913
35	Cy Young	NL	CLE	1895
35	Joe McGinnity	NL	NY	1904
34	Cy Young	NL	CLE	1893
34	Kid Nichols	NL	BOS	1893
34	Joe Wood	AL	BOS	1912
33	Amos Rusie	NL	NY	1893
33	Jouett Meekin	NL	NY	1894
33	Cy Young	AL	BOS	1901
33	Christy Mathewson	NL	NY	1904
33	Walter Johnson	AL	WAS	1912
33	Grover Alexander	NL	PHI	1916
32	Kid Nichols	NL	BOS	1894
32	Cy Young	AL	BOS	1902
31	Bill Hoffer	NL	BAL	1895
31	Pink Hawley	NL	PIT	1895
31	Kid Nichols	NL	BOS	1897
31	Kid Nichols	NL	BOS	1898
31	Joe McGinnity	NL	NY	1903
31	Christy Mathewson	NL	NY	1905
31	Jack Coombs	AL	PHI	1910
31	Grover Alexander	NL	PHI	1915
31	Jim Bagby Sr.	AL	CLE	1920
31	Denny McLain	AL	DET	1968
30	Kid Nichols	NL	BOS	1896
30	Christy Mathewson	NL	NY	1903
30	Grover Alexander	NL	PHI	1917
30	Dizzy Dean	NL	STL	1934
29	Mordecai Brown	NL	CHI	1908
29	George Mullin	AL	DET	1909
29	Claude Hendrix	FL	CHI	1914
29	Eddie Cicotte	AL	CHI	1919
28	Cy Young	NL	CLE	1896
28	Amos Rusie	NL	NY	1897
28	Bert Cunningham	NL	LOU	1898
28	Jay Hughes	NL	BRO	1899
28	Joe McGinnity	NL	BAL	1899
28	Joe McGinnity	NL	BRO	1900
28	Jack Chesbro	NL	PIT	1902
28	Cy Young	AL	BOS	1903
28	Grover Alexander	NL	PHI	1911
28	Jack Coombs	AL	PHI	1911
28	Walter Johnson	AL	WAS	1914
28	Eddie Cicotte	AL	CHI	1917
28	Dazzy Vance	NL	BRO	1924
28	Dizzy Dean	NL	STL	1935
28	Robin Roberts	NL	PHI	1952

Grover Alexander

(463) Most Wins in a Season by a Left-handed Pitcher, since 1893

36	Frank Killen	NL	PIT	1893		25	Sandy Koufax	NL	LA	1963
31	Lefty Grove	AL	PHI	1931		25	Jim Kaat	AL	MIN	1966
30	Frank Killen	NL	PIT	1896		25	Mickey Lolich	AL	DET	1971
29	Hal Newhouser	AL	DET	1944		25	Ron Guidry	AL	NY	1978
28	Lefty Grove	AL	PHI	1930		24	Wiley Piatt	NL	PHI	1898
27	Ted Breitenstein	NL	STL	1894		24	Jesse Tannehill	NL	PIT	1899
27	Rube Waddell	AL	PHI	1905		24	Rube Waddell	AL	PHI	1902
27	Doc White	AL	CHI	1907		24	Eddie Plank	AL	PHI	1905
27	Sandy Koufax	NL	LA	1966		24	Eddie Plank	AL	PHI	1907
27	Steve Carlton	NL	PHI	1972		24	Rube Marquard	NL	NY	1911
26	Fred Klobedanz	NL	BOS	1897		24	Babe Ruth	AL	BOS	1917
26	Eddie Plank	AL	PHI	1904		24	Wilbur Cooper	NL	PIT	1920
26	Eddie Plank	AL	PHI	1912		24	Lefty Grove	AL	PHI	1928
26	Rube Marquard	NL	NY	1912		24	Lefty Gomez	AL	NY	1932
26	Lefty Gomez	AL	NY	1934		24	Lefty Grove	AL	PHI	1933
26	Carl Hubbell	NL	NY	1936		24	Bobby Shantz	AL	PHI	1952
26	Hal Newhouser	AL	DET	1946		24	Whitey Ford	AL	NY	1963
26	Sandy Koufax	NL	LA	1965		24	Dave McNally	AL	BAL	1970
25	Cy Seymour	NL	NY	1898		24	Mike Cuellar	AL	BAL	1970
25	Jesse Tannehill	NL	PIT	1898		24	Vida Blue	AL	OAK	1971
25	Rube Waddell	AL	PHI	1904		24	Wilbur Wood	AL	CHI	1972
25	Ed Killian	AL	DET	1907		24	Ron Bryant	NL	SF	1973
25	Eppa Rixey	NL	CIN	1922		24	Wilbur Wood	AL	CHI	1973
25	Lefty Grove	AL	PHI	1932		24	Steve Carlton	NL	PHI	1980
25	Hal Newhouser	AL	DET	1945		24	Frank Viola	AL	MIN	1988
25	Mel Parnell	AL	BOS	1949		24	Randy Johnson	NL	ARI	2002
25	Whitey Ford	AL	NY	1961						

(464) Most Losses in a Season, before 1893

48	John Coleman	NL	PHI	1883		34	Matt Kilroy	AA	BAL	1886
42	Will White	NL	CIN	1880		34	Al Mays	AA	NY	1887
41	Larry McKeon	AA	IND	1884		34	Mark Baldwin	AA	COL	1889
40	Jim McCormick	NL	CLE	1879		34	Amos Rusie	NL	NY	1890
40	George Bradley	NL	TRO	1879		33	Harry McCormick	NL	SYR	1879
37	Henry Porter	AA	KC	1888		33	Jim Whitney	NL	BOS	1881
37	Kid Carsey	AA	WAS	1891		33	Lee Richmond	NL	WOR	1882
37	George Cobb	NL	BAL	1892		33	Frank Mountain	AA	COL	1883
36	Stump Wiedman	NL	KC	1886		33	Hardie Henderson	NL-AA	PHI-BAL	1883
36	Bill Hutchison	NL	CHI	1892					PHI (1); BAL (32)	
35	Jim Devlin	NL	LOU	1876		33	Dupee Shaw	NL-UA	DET-BOS	1884
35	Jim Galvin	NL	BUF	1880					DET (18); BOS (15)	
35	Fleury Sullivan	AA	PIT	1884		33	Jersey Bakely	AA	CLE	1888
35	Adonis Terry	AA	BRO	1884		32	Lee Richmond	NL	WOR	1880
35	Hardie Henderson	AA	BAL	1885		32	John Harkins	NL	CLE	1884
34	Bobby Mathews	NL	NY	1876		32	Jim Whitney	NL	BOS	1885
34	Bob Barr	AA	WAS-IND	1884		32	Jim Whitney	NL	KC	1886
			WAS (23); IND (11)							

(465) Most Losses in a Season, since 1893

35	Red Donahue	NL	STL	1897
30	Ted Breitenstein	NL	STL	1895
30	Jim Hughey	NL	CLE	1899
29	Bill Hart	NL	STL	1896
29	Jack B. Taylor	NL	STL	1898
29	Vic Willis	NL	BOS	1905
28	Duke Esper	NL	WAS	1893
28	Bill Hill	NL	LOU	1896
27	Pink Hawley	NL	STL	1894
27	Chick Fraser	NL	LOU	1896
27	Bill Hart	NL	STL	1897
27	Willie Sudhoff	NL	STL	1898
27	Bill Carrick	NL	NY	1899
27	Dummy Taylor	NL	NY	1901
27	George G. Bell	NL	BRO	1910
27	Paul Derringer	NL	STL-CIN	1933
			STL (2); CIN (25)	
26	Ted Breitenstein	NL	STL	1896
26	Gus Weyhing	NL	WAS	1898
26	Happy Townsend	NL	WAS	1904
26	Gus Dorner	NL	CIN-BOS	1906
			CIN (1); BOS (25)	
26	Bob Groom	AL	WAS	1909
25	Jock Menefee	NL	LOU-PIT	1894
			LOU (17); PIT (8)	
25	Pete Dowling	AL	MIL-CLE	1901
			MIL (3); CLE (22)	
25	Patsy Flaherty	AL	CHI	1903
25	Vic Willis	NL	BOS	1904
25	Oscar Jones	NL	BRO	1904
25	Harry McIntire	NL	BRO	1905
25	Fred Glade	AL	STL	1905
25	Irv Young	NL	BOS	1906
25	Stoney McGlynn	NL	STL	1907
25	Bugs Raymond	NL	STL	1908
25	Walter Johnson	AL	WAS	1909
25	Scott Perry	AL	PHI	1920
25	Red Ruffing	AL	BOS	1928
25	Ben Cantwell	NL	BOS	1935
24	Ted Breitenstein	NL	STL	1893
24	Bill Hutchison	NL	CHI	1893
24	Dad Clarke	NL	NY	1896
24	Red Donahue	NL	STL	1896
24	Jim Hughey	NL	STL	1898
24	Chick Fraser	NL	PHI	1904
24	Cliff Curtis	NL	BOS	1910
24	Joe Bush	AL	PHI	1916
24	Pat Caraway	AL	CHI	1931
24	Sam Gray	AL	STL	1931
24	Roger Craig	NL	NY	1962
24	Jack Fisher	NL	NY	1965

Hal Newhouser

(466) Most Losses in a Season by a Right-handed Pitcher, since 1893

35	Red Donahue	NL	STL	1897		24	Dad Clarke	NL	NY	1896
30	Jim Hughey	NL	CLE	1899		24	Red Donahue	NL	STL	1896
29	Bill Hart	NL	STL	1896		24	Jim Hughey	NL	STL	1898
29	Jack B. Taylor	NL	STL	1898		24	Chick Fraser	NL	PHI	1904
29	Vic Willis	NL	BOS	1905		24	Cliff Curtis	NL	BOS	1910
27	Pink Hawley	NL	STL	1894		24	Joe Bush	AL	PHI	1916
27	Chick Fraser	NL	LOU	1896		24	Sam Gray	AL	STL	1931
27	Bill Hart	NL	STL	1897		24	Roger Craig	NL	NY	1962
27	Willie Sudhoff	NL	STL	1898		24	Jack Fisher	NL	NY	1965
27	Bill Carrick	NL	NY	1899		23	Scott Stratton	NL	LOU	1893
27	Dummy Taylor	NL	NY	1901		23	Win Mercer	NL	WAS	1894
27	George G. Bell	NL	BRO	1910		23	Win Mercer	NL	WAS	1895
27	Paul Derringer	NL	STL-CIN	1933		23	Amos Rusie	NL	NY	1895
			STL (2); CIN (25)			23	Doc McJames	NL	WAS	1897
26	Gus Weyhing	NL	WAS	1898		23	Sam Leever	NL	PIT	1899
26	Happy Townsend	NL	WAS	1904		23	Tom J. Hughes	NL	CHI	1901
26	Gus Dorner	NL	CIN-BOS	1906		23	Tom J. Hughes	AL	NY-WAS	1904
			CIN (1); BOS (25)						NY (11); WAS (12)
26	Bob Groom	AL	WAS	1909		23	Jack Cronin	NL	BRO	1904
25	Jock Menefee	NL	LOU-PIT	1894		23	George Mullin	AL	DET	1904
			LOU (17); PIT (8)			23	Kaiser Wilhelm	NL	BOS	1905
25	Vic Willis	NL	BOS	1904		23	Orval Overall	NL	CIN	1905
25	Oscar Jones	NL	BRO	1904		23	Vive Lindaman	NL	BOS	1906
25	Fred Glade	AL	STL	1905		23	George Ferguson	NL	BOS	1909
25	Harry McIntire	NL	BRO	1905		23	Buster Brown	NL	BOS	1910
25	Stoney McGlynn	NL	STL	1907		23	Red Ames	NL	CIN	1914
25	Bugs Raymond	NL	STL	1908		23	Elmer Myers	AL	PHI	1916
25	Walter Johnson	AL	WAS	1909		23	Lee Meadows	NL	STL	1916
25	Scott Perry	AL	PHI	1920		23	Rollie Naylor	AL	PHI	1920
25	Red Ruffing	AL	BOS	1928		23	Eddie Rommel	AL	PHI	1921
25	Ben Cantwell	NL	BOS	1935		23	Dolf Luque	NL	CIN	1922
24	Bill Hutchison	NL	CHI	1893						

(467) Most Losses in a Season by a Left-handed Pitcher, since 1893

30	Ted Breitenstein	NL	STL	1895		21	Ed Brandt	NL	BOS	1928
28	Duke Esper	NL	WAS	1893		21	Mickey Lolich	AL	DET	1974
28	Bill Hill	NL	LOU	1896		21	Mike Maroth	AL	DET	2003
26	Ted Breitenstein	NL	STL	1896		20	Bert Inks	NL	LOU	1895
25	Pete Dowling	AL	MIL-CLE	1901		20	Pete Dowling	NL	LOU	1898
			MIL (3); CLE (22)			20	Frank Killen	NL	PIT-WAS	1898
25	Patsy Flaherty	AL	CHI	1903					PIT (11); WAS (9)	
25	Irv Young	NL	BOS	1906		20	Noodles Hahn	NL	CIN	1900
24	Ted Breitenstein	NL	STL	1893		20	Doc White	NL	PHI	1902
24	Pat Caraway	AL	CHI	1931		20	Jim Pastorius	NL	BRO	1908
23	Ted Breitenstein	NL	STL	1894		20	Rube Benton	NL	CIN	1912
23	Frank Killen	NL	PIT	1897		20	Henry Keupper	FL	STL	1914
23	Beany Jacobson	AL	WAS	1904		20	Bill Bailey	FL	BAL-CHI	1915
23	Case Patten	AL	WAS	1904					BAL (19); CHI (1)	
23	Irv Young	NL	BOS	1907		20	Eddie Smith	AL	CHI	1942
22	Case Patten	AL	WAS	1903		20	Ken Raffensberger	NL	PHI	1944
22	Lefty Tyler	NL	BOS	1912		20	Bill Wight	AL	CHI	1948
22	Rube Marquard	NL	NY	1914		20	Alex Kellner	AL	PHI	1950
22	Eppa Rixey	NL	PHI	1920		20	Chuck Stobbs	AL	WAS	1957
22	Dick Ellsworth	NL	CHI	1966		20	Dick Ellsworth	NL	CHI	1962
22	Randy Jones	NL	SD	1974		20	Al Jackson	NL	NY	1962
21	Phil Knell	NL	PIT-LOU	1894		20	Al Jackson	NL	NY	1965
			PIT (0); LOU (21)			20	Steve Carlton	NL	PHI	1973
21	Case Patten	AL	WAS	1905		20	Wilbur Wood	AL	CHI	1973
21	Irv Young	NL	BOS	1905		20	Clyde Wright	AL	MIL	1974
21	Nap Rucker	NL	BRO	1912		20	Wilbur Wood	AL	CHI	1975
21	Eppa Rixey	NL	PHI	1917		20	Jerry Koosman	NL	NY	1977
21	Harry Harper	AL	WAS	1919						

(468) Highest Winning Percentage in a Season, since 1893 (min. 20 wins)

.893	Ron Guidry	AL	NY	1978		.833	King Cole	NL	CHI	1910
.886	Lefty Grove	AL	PHI	1931		.833	Spud Chandler	AL	NY	1943
.880	Preacher Roe	NL	BRO	1951		.833	Randy Johnson	AL	SEA	1997
.872	Joe Wood	AL	BOS	1912		.833	Pedro Martinez	AL	BOS	2002
.870	David Cone	NL	NY	1988		.828	Randy Johnson	NL	ARI	2002
.870	Roger Clemens	AL	NY	2001		.824	Jay Hughes	NL	BRO	1899
.862	Bill Donovan	AL	DET	1907		.824	Jack Chesbro	NL	PIT	1902
.862	Whitey Ford	AL	NY	1961		.824	Dazzy Vance	NL	BRO	1924
.857	Dwight Gooden	NL	NY	1985		.821	Chief Bender	AL	PHI	1910
.857	Roger Clemens	AL	BOS	1986		.821	Bob Purkey	NL	CIN	1962
.852	Pedro Martinez	AL	BOS	1999		.821	Barry Zito	AL	OAK	2002
.848	Lefty Grove	AL	PHI	1930		.818	Bob Welch	AL	OAK	1990
.846	Mike Hampton	NL	HOU	1999		.814	Joe McGinnity	NL	NY	1904
.839	Lefty Gomez	AL	NY	1934		.813	Mordecai Brown	NL	CHI	1906
.838	Bill Hoffer	NL	BAL	1895		.813	Russ Ford	AL	NY	1910
.838	Denny McLain	AL	DET	1968		.813	Eddie Plank	AL	PHI	1912
.837	Walter Johnson	AL	WAS	1913		.813	Carl Hubbell	NL	NY	1936
.833	Sandy Koufax	NL	LA	1963		.811	Dizzy Dean	NL	STL	1934

(469) Highest Winning Percentage in a Season, since 1893 (min. 15 wins)

.947	Roy Face	NL	PIT	1959		.850	John Smoltz	NL	ATL	1998
.938	Johnny Allen	AL	CLE	1937		.848	Lefty Grove	AL	PHI	1930
.905	Greg Maddux	NL	ATL	1995		.846	Mike Hampton	NL	HOU	1999
.900	Randy Johnson	AL	SEA	1995		.842	Tom L. Hughes	NL	BOS	1916
.893	Ron Guidry	AL	NY	1978		.842	Emil Yde	NL	PIT	1924
.889	Freddie Fitzsimmons	NL	BRO	1940		.842	Schoolboy Rowe	AL	DET	1940
.886	Lefty Grove	AL	PHI	1931		.842	Sandy Consuegra	AL	CHI	1954
.882	Bob Stanley	AL	BOS	1978		.842	Ralph Terry	AL	NY	1961
.880	Preacher Roe	NL	BRO	1951		.842	Ron Perranoski	NL	LA	1963
.872	Joe Wood	AL	BOS	1912		.839	Lefty Gomez	AL	NY	1934
.870	David Cone	NL	NY	1988		.838	Bill Hoffer	NL	BAL	1895
.870	Roger Clemens	AL	NY	2001		.838	Denny McLain	AL	DET	1968
.864	Orel Hershiser	NL	LA	1985		.837	Walter Johnson	AL	WAS	1913
.862	Bill Donovan	AL	DET	1907		.833	King Cole	NL	CHI	1910
.862	Whitey Ford	AL	NY	1961		.833	Spud Chandler	AL	NY	1943
.857	Dwight Gooden	NL	NY	1985		.833	Hoyt Wilhelm	NL	NY	1952
.857	Roger Clemens	AL	BOS	1986		.833	Sandy Koufax	NL	LA	1963
.852	Pedro Martinez	AL	BOS	1999		.833	Randy Johnson	AL	SEA	1997
.850	Chief Bender	AL	PHI	1914		.833	Pedro Martinez	AL	BOS	2002

Don Drysdale

(470) Lowest Earned Run Average in a Season, before 1893
(min. 1.0 IP per scheduled game)

0.86	Tim Keefe	NL	TRO	1880		1.70	Charlie Sweeney	NL-UA PRO-STL	1884	
1.21	Denny Driscoll	AA	PIT	1882				PRO (1.55); STL (1.83)		
1.23	George Bradley	NL	STL	1876		1.74	John Ward	NL	PRO	1880
1.30	Guy Hecker	AA	LOU	1882		1.74	Henry Boyle	UA	STL	1884
1.38	George Bradley	NL	PRO	1880		1.74	Tim Keefe	NL	NY	1888
1.38	Charley Radbourn	NL	PRO	1884		1.75	Al Spalding	NL	CHI	1876
1.51	John Ward	NL	PRO	1878		1.75	Fred Goldsmith	NL	CHI	1880
1.52	Harry McCormick	AA	CIN	1882		1.76	Henry Boyle	NL	STL	1886
1.54	Will White	AA	CIN	1882		1.79	Will White	NL	CIN	1878
1.56	Jim Devlin	NL	LOU	1876		1.80	Guy Hecker	AA	LOU	1884
1.58	Tim Keefe	NL	NY	1885		1.84	Jim McCormick	NL	CLE	1883
1.63	Silver King	AA	STL	1888		1.85	Jim McCormick	NL	CLE	1880
1.66	Mickey Welch	NL	NY	1885		1.85	John Clarkson	NL	CHI	1885
1.67	Candy Cummings	NL	HAR	1876		1.86	Lady Baldwin	NL	DET	1885
1.68	Tommy Bond	NL	HAR	1876		1.88	Tony Mullane	AA	LOU	1882
1.69	Jim McCormick	NL	IND	1878		1.90	Ben Sanders	NL	PHI	1888

Earned run average did not become an official statistic until 1912 in the National League and 1913 in the American League.

(471) Lowest Earned Run Average in a Season, since 1893
(min. 1.0 IP per scheduled game)

0.96	Hubert "Dutch" Leonard	AL	BOS	1914		1.43	Christy Mathewson	NL	NY	1908
1.04	Mordecai Brown	NL	CHI	1906		1.44	Fred Anderson	NL	NY	1917
1.12	Bob Gibson	NL	STL	1968		1.47	Mordecai Brown	NL	CHI	1908
1.14	Christy Mathewson	NL	NY	1909		1.48	Rube Waddell	AL	PHI	1905
1.14	Walter Johnson	AL	WAS	1913		1.49	Joe Wood	AL	BOS	1915
1.15	Jack Pfiester	NL	CHI	1907		1.49	Walter Johnson	AL	WAS	1919
1.16	Addie Joss	AL	CLE	1908		1.51	Jack Pfiester	NL	CHI	1906
1.17	Carl Lundgren	NL	CHI	1907		1.52	Doc White	AL	CHI	1906
1.22	Grover Alexander	NL	PHI	1915		1.53	George McQuillan	NL	PHI	1908
1.26	Cy Young	AL	BOS	1908		1.53	Eddie Cicotte	AL	CHI	1917
1.27	Ed Walsh	AL	CHI	1910		1.53	Dwight Gooden	NL	NY	1985
1.27	Walter Johnson	AL	WAS	1918		1.55	Cy Morgan	AL	PHI	1910
1.28	Christy Mathewson	NL	NY	1905		1.55	Walter Johnson	AL	WAS	1915
1.29	Jack W. Taylor	NL	CHI	1902		1.55	Grover Alexander	NL	PHI	1916
1.30	Jack Coombs	AL	PHI	1910		1.56	Howie Camnitz	NL	PIT	1908
1.31	Mordecai Brown	NL	CHI	1909		1.56	Greg Maddux	NL	ATL	1994
1.36	Walter Johnson	AL	WAS	1910		1.58	Chief Bender	AL	PHI	1910
1.39	Mordecai Brown	NL	CHI	1907		1.58	Eddie Cicotte	AL	CHI	1913
1.39	Harry Krause	AL	PHI	1909		1.58	Fred Toney	NL	CIN	1915
1.39	Walter Johnson	AL	WAS	1912		1.58	Rube Marquard	NL	BRO	1916
1.41	Ed Walsh	AL	CHI	1909		1.59	Addie Joss	AL	CLE	1904
1.42	Ed Reulbach	NL	CHI	1905		1.59	Barney Pelty	AL	STL	1906
1.42	Ed Walsh	AL	CHI	1908		1.60	Ed Walsh	AL	CHI	1907
1.42	Orval Overall	NL	CHI	1909		1.60	Luis Tiant	AL	CLE	1968

Earned run average did not become an official statistic until 1912 in the National League and 1913 in the American League.

(472) Lowest Earned Run Average in a Season by a Right-handed Pitcher, since 1893 (min. 1.0 IP per scheduled game)

1.04	Mordecai Brown	NL	CHI	1906		1.44	Fred Anderson	NL	NY	1917
1.12	Bob Gibson	NL	STL	1968		1.47	Mordecai Brown	NL	CHI	1908
1.14	Christy Mathewson	NL	NY	1909		1.49	Joe Wood	AL	BOS	1915
1.14	Walter Johnson	AL	WAS	1913		1.49	Walter Johnson	AL	WAS	1919
1.16	Addie Joss	AL	CLE	1908		1.53	George McQuillan	NL	PHI	1908
1.17	Carl Lundgren	NL	CHI	1907		1.53	Eddie Cicotte	AL	CHI	1917
1.22	Grover Alexander	NL	PHI	1915		1.53	Dwight Gooden	NL	NY	1985
1.26	Cy Young	AL	BOS	1908		1.55	Cy Morgan	AL	PHI	1910
1.27	Ed Walsh	AL	CHI	1910		1.55	Walter Johnson	AL	WAS	1915
1.27	Walter Johnson	AL	WAS	1918		1.55	Grover Alexander	NL	PHI	1916
1.28	Christy Mathewson	NL	NY	1905		1.56	Howie Camnitz	NL	PIT	1908
1.30	Jack Coombs	AL	PHI	1910		1.56	Greg Maddux	NL	ATL	1994
1.31	Mordecai Brown	NL	CHI	1909		1.58	Chief Bender	AL	PHI	1910
1.33	Jack W. Taylor	NL	CHI	1902		1.58	Eddie Cicotte	AL	CHI	1913
1.36	Walter Johnson	AL	WAS	1910		1.58	Fred Toney	NL	CIN	1915
1.39	Mordecai Brown	NL	CHI	1907		1.59	Addie Joss	AL	CLE	1904
1.39	Walter Johnson	AL	WAS	1912		1.59	Barney Pelty	AL	STL	1906
1.41	Ed Walsh	AL	CHI	1909		1.60	Ed Walsh	AL	CHI	1907
1.42	Ed Reulbach	NL	CHI	1905		1.60	Luis Tiant	AL	CLE	1968
1.42	Ed Walsh	AL	CHI	1908		1.61	Joe McGinnity	NL	NY	1904
1.42	Orval Overall	NL	CHI	1909		1.62	Cy Young	AL	BOS	1901
1.43	Christy Mathewson	NL	NY	1908		1.62	Howie Camnitz	NL	PIT	1909

(473) Lowest Earned Run Average in a Season by a Left-handed Pitcher, since 1893 (min. 1.0 IP per scheduled game)

0.96	Hubert "Dutch" Leonard	AL	BOS	1914		1.77	Noodles Hahn	NL	CIN	1902
1.15	Jack Pfiester	NL	CHI	1907		1.78	Doc White	AL	CHI	1904
1.39	Harry Krause	AL	PHI	1909		1.78	Ed Killian	AL	DET	1907
1.48	Rube Waddell	AL	PHI	1905		1.79	Hippo Vaughn	NL	CHI	1919
1.51	Jack Pfiester	NL	CHI	1906		1.80	Vean Gregg	AL	CLE	1911
1.52	Doc White	AL	CHI	1906		1.81	Hal Newhouser	AL	DET	1945
1.58	Rube Marquard	NL	BRO	1916		1.81	Sam McDowell	AL	CLE	1968
1.62	Rube Waddell	AL	PHI	1904		1.82	Dutch Ruether	NL	CIN	1919
1.62	Ray Collins	AL	BOS	1910		1.82	Vida Blue	AL	OAK	1971
1.66	Carl Hubbell	NL	NY	1933		1.83	Otto Hess	AL	CLE	1906
1.70	Bill Burns	AL	WAS	1908		1.83	Hippo Vaughn	AL	NY	1910
1.71	Ed Killian	AL	DET	1909		1.85	Eppa Rixey	NL	PHI	1916
1.72	Doc White	AL	CHI	1909		1.87	Lefty Leifield	NL	PIT	1906
1.73	Sandy Koufax	NL	LA	1966		1.87	Wilbur Cooper	NL	PIT	1916
1.74	Hippo Vaughn	NL	CHI	1918		1.88	Nick Altrock	AL	CHI	1905
1.74	Sandy Koufax	NL	LA	1964		1.88	Sandy Koufax	NL	LA	1963
1.74	Ron Guidry	AL	NY	1978		1.89	Rube Waddell	AL	PHI	1908
1.75	Babe Ruth	AL	BOS	1916		1.90	Reb Russell	AL	CHI	1913
1.76	Doc White	AL	CHI	1905		1.90	Max Lanier	NL	STL	1943
1.76	Eddie Plank	AL	PHI	1909						

(474) Most Shutouts in a Season, before 1893

16	George Bradley	NL	STL	1876		8	Charlie Buffinton	NL	BOS	1884
12	Jim Galvin	NL	BUF	1884		8	Tim Keefe	NL	NY	1888
12	Ed Morris	AA	PIT	1886		8	Ben Sanders	NL	PHI	1888
11	Tommy Bond	NL	BOS	1879		8	John Clarkson	NL	BOS	1889
11	Charley Radbourn	NL	PRO	1884		7	Jim McCormick	NL	CLE	1880
11	Dave Foutz	AA	STL	1886		7	Tony Mullane	AA	TOL	1884
10	Jim McCormick	NL-UA	CLE-CIN	1884		7	Will White	AA	CIN	1884
			CLE (3); CIN (7)			7	Larry Corcoran	NL	CHI	1884
10	John Clarkson	NL	CHI	1885		7	Mickey Welch	NL	NY	1885
9	Tommy Bond	NL	BOS	1878		7	Ed Morris	AA	PIT	1885
9	George Derby	NL	DET	1881		7	Tim Keefe	NL	NY	1885
9	Cy Young	NL	CLE	1892		7	Lady Baldwin	NL	DET	1886
8	Al Spalding	NL	CHI	1876		7	Bob Caruthers	AA	BRO	1889
8	John Ward	NL	PRO	1880		7	Kid Nichols	NL	BOS	1890
8	Will White	AA	CIN	1882						

(475) Most Shutouts in a Season, since 1893

16	Grover Alexander	NL	PHI	1916		9	Joe McGinnity	NL	NY	1904
13	Jack Coombs	AL	PHI	1910		9	Addie Joss	AL	CLE	1906
13	Bob Gibson	NL	STL	1968		9	Mordecai Brown	NL	CHI	1906
12	Grover Alexander	NL	PHI	1915		9	Addie Joss	AL	CLE	1908
11	Christy Mathewson	NL	NY	1908		9	Mordecai Brown	NL	CHI	1908
11	Ed Walsh	AL	CHI	1908		9	Orval Overall	NL	CHI	1909
11	Walter Johnson	AL	WAS	1913		9	Grover Alexander	NL	PHI	1913
11	Sandy Koufax	NL	LA	1963		9	Walter Johnson	AL	WAS	1914
11	Dean Chance	AL	LA	1964		9	Cy Falkenberg	FL	IND	1914
10	Cy Young	AL	BOS	1904		9	Babe Ruth	AL	BOS	1916
10	Ed Walsh	AL	CHI	1906		9	Stan Coveleski	AL	CLE	1917
10	Joe Wood	AL	BOS	1912		9	Grover Alexander	NL	CHI	1919
10	Dave Davenport	FL	STL	1915		9	Bill C. Lee	NL	CHI	1938
10	Carl Hubbell	NL	NY	1933		9	Bob Porterfield	AL	WAS	1953
10	Mort Cooper	NL	STL	1942		9	Luis Tiant	AL	CLE	1968
10	Bob Feller	AL	CLE	1946		9	Denny McLain	AL	DET	1969
10	Bob Lemon	AL	CLE	1948		9	Don Sutton	NL	LA	1972
10	Juan Marichal	NL	SF	1965		9	Nolan Ryan	LA	CAL	1972
10	Jim Palmer	AL	BAL	1975		9	Bert Blyleven	AL	MIN	1973
10	John Tudor	NL	STL	1985		9	Ron Guidry	AL	NY	1978

(476) Most Shutouts In a Season by a Right-handed Pitcher, since 1893

16	Grover Alexander	NL	PHI	1916		9	Addie Joss	AL	CLE	1906
13	Jack Coombs	AL	PHI	1910		9	Mordecai Brown	NL	CHI	1906
13	Bob Gibson	NL	STL	1968		9	Addie Joss	AL	CLE	1908
12	Grover Alexander	NL	PHI	1915		9	Mordecai Brown	NL	CHI	1908
11	Christy Mathewson	NL	NY	1908		9	Orval Overall	NL	CHI	1909
11	Ed Walsh	CHI	AL	1908		9	Grover Alexander	NL	PHI	1913
11	Walter Johnson	AL	WAS	1913		9	Walter Johnson	AL	WAS	1914
11	Dean Chance	AL	LA	1964		9	Cy Falkenberg	FL	IND	1914
10	Cy Young	AL	BOS	1904		9	Stan Coveleski	AL	CLE	1917
10	Ed Walsh	CHI	AL	1906		9	Grover Alexander	NL	CHI	1919
10	Joe Wood	AL	BOS	1912		9	Bill C. Lee	NL	CHI	1938
10	Dave Davenport	FL	STL	1915		9	Bob Porterfield	AL	WAS	1953
10	Mort Cooper	NL	STL	1942		9	Luis Tiant	AL	CLE	1968
10	Bob Feller	AL	CLE	1946		9	Denny McLain	AL	DET	1969
10	Bob Lemon	AL	CLE	1948		9	Don Sutton	NL	LA	1972
10	Juan Marichal	NL	SF	1965		9	Nolan Ryan	LA	CAL	1972
10	Jim Palmer	AL	BAL	1975		9	Bert Blyleven	AL	MIN	1973
9	Joe McGinnity	NL	NY	1904						

(477) Most Shutouts in a Season by a Left-handed Pitcher, since 1893

11	Sandy Koufax	NL	LA	1963		7	Rube Waddell	AL	PHI	1905
10	Carl Hubbell	NL	NY	1933		7	Otto Hess	AL	CLE	1906
10	John Tudor	NL	STL	1985		7	Doc White	AL	CHI	1906
9	Babe Ruth	AL	BOS	1916		7	Rube Waddell	AL	PHI	1907
9	Ron Guidry	AL	NY	1978		7	Hooks Wiltse	NL	NY	1908
8	Rube Waddell	AL	PHI	1904		7	Harry Krause	AL	PHI	1909
8	Ed Killian	AL	DET	1905		7	Eddie Plank	AL	PHI	1913
8	Rube Waddell	AL	PHI	1906		7	Hubert "Dutch" Leonard	AL	BOS	1914
8	Lefty Leifield	NL	PIT	1906		7	Wilbur Cooper	NL	PIT	1917
8	Eddie Plank	AL	PHI	1907		7	Warren Spahn	NL	BOS	1947
8	Reb Russell	AL	CHI	1913		7	Harry Brecheen	NL	STL	1948
8	Hippo Vaughn	NL	CHI	1918		7	Warren Spahn	NL	BOS	1951
8	Hal Newhouser	AL	DET	1945		7	Billy Pierce	AL	CHI	1953
8	Steve Barber	AL	BAL	1961		7	Billy Hoeft	AL	DET	1955
8	Whitey Ford	AL	NY	1964		7	Whitey Ford	AL	NY	1958
8	Sandy Koufax	NL	LA	1965		7	Warren Spahn	NL	MIL	1963
8	Vida Blue	AL	OAK	1971		7	Sandy Koufax	NL	LA	1964
8	Wilbur Wood	AL	CHI	1972		7	Bob Veale	NL	PIT	1965
8	Steve Carlton	NL	PHI	1972		7	Jerry Koosman	NL	NY	1968
8	Fernando Valenzuela	NL	LA	1981		7	Claude Osteen	NL	LA	1969
7	Eddie Plank	AL	PHI	1904		7	Wilbur Wood	AL	CHI	1971
7	Doc White	AL	CHI	1904		7	Jon Matlack	NL	NY	1974
7	Irv Young	NL	BOS	1905		7	Frank Tanana	AL	CAL	1977

(478) Most Saves in a Season

57	Bobby Thigpen	AL	CHI	1990
55	John Smoltz	NL	ATL	2002
55	Eric Gagne	NL	LA	2003
53	Randy Myers	NL	CHI	1993
53	Trevor Hoffman	NL	SD	1998
53	Mariano Rivera	AL	NY	2004
52	Eric Gagne	NL	LA	2002
51	Dennis Eckersley	AL	OAK	1992
51	Rod Beck	NL	CHI	1998
50	Mariano Rivera	AL	NY	2001
49	Francisco Cordero	AL	TEX	2004
48	Dennis Eckersley	AL	OAK	1990
48	Rod Beck	NL	SF	1993
48	Jeff Shaw	NL	CIN-LA	1998
			CIN (23); LA (25)	
47	Lee Smith	NL	STL	1991
47	Armando Benitez	NL	FLA	2004
47	Jason Isringhausen	NL	STL	2004
47	Chad Cordero	NL	WAS	2005
47	Francisco Rodriguez	AL	LA	2006
46	Dave Righetti	AL	NY	1986
46	Bryan Harvey	AL	CAL	1991
46	Lee Smith	NL-AL	STL-NY	1993
			STL (43); NY (3)	
46	Jose Mesa	AL	CLE	1995
46	Tom Gordon	AL	BOS	1998
46	Mike Williams	NL	PIT	2002

46	Trevor Hoffman	NL	SD	2006
45	Dan Quisenberry	AL	KC	1983
45	Bruce Sutter	NL	STL	1984
45	Dennis Eckersley	AL	OAK	1988
45	Bryan Harvey	NL	FLA	1993
45	Jeff Montgomery	AL	KC	1993
45	Duane Ward	AL	TOR	1993
45	Randy Myers	AL	BAL	1997
45	Mariano Rivera	AL	NY	1999
45	Antonio Alfonseca	NL	FLA	2000
45	Robb Nen	NL	SF	2001
45	Kazuhiro Sasaki	AL	SEA	2001
45	Jose Mesa	NL	PHI	2002
45	Eddie Guardado	AL	MIN	2002
45	John Smoltz	NL	ATL	2003
45	Eric Gagne	NL	LA	2004
45	Francisco Rodriguez	AL	LA	2005
45	Bob Wickman	AL	CLE	2005
44	Dan Quisenberry	AL	KC	1984
44	Mark Davis	NL	SD	1989
44	Jeff Brantley	NL	CIN	1996
44	Todd Worrell	NL	LA	1996
44	Billy Koch	AL	OAK	2002
44	Billy Wagner	NL	HOU	2003
44	John Smoltz	NL	ATL	2004
44	Joe Nathan	AL	MIN	2004

Joe McGinnity

(479) Most Saves in a Season by a Right-handed Pitcher

57	Bobby Thigpen	AL	CHI	1990		46	Mike Williams	NL	PIT	2002
55	John Smoltz	NL	ATL	2002		46	Trevor Hoffman	NL	SD	2006
55	Eric Gagne	NL	LA	2003		45	Dan Quisenberry	AL	KC	1983
53	Trevor Hoffman	NL	SD	1998		45	Bruce Sutter	NL	STL	1984
53	Mariano Rivera	AL	NY	2004		45	Dennis Eckersley	AL	OAK	1988
52	Eric Gagne	NL	LA	2002		45	Bryan Harvey	NL	FLA	1993
51	Dennis Eckersley	AL	OAK	1992		45	Jeff Montgomery	AL	KC	1993
51	Rod Beck	NL	CHI	1998		45	Duane Ward	AL	TOR	1993
50	Mariano Rivera	AL	NY	2001		45	Mariano Rivera	AL	NY	1999
49	Francisco Cordero	AL	TEX	2004		45	Antonio Alfonseca	NL	FLA	2000
48	Dennis Eckersley	AL	OAK	1990		45	Robb Nen	NL	SF	2001
48	Rod Beck	NL	SF	1993		45	Kazuhiro Sasaki	AL	SEA	2001
48	Jeff Shaw	NL	CIN-LA	1998		45	Jose Mesa	NL	PHI	2002
			CIN (23); LA (25)			45	John Smoltz	NL	ATL	2003
47	Lee Smith	NL	STL	1991		45	Eric Gagne	NL	LA	2004
47	Armando Benitez	NL	FLA	2004		45	Francisco Rodriguez	AL	LA	2005
47	Jason Isringhausen	NL	STL	2004		45	Bob Wickman	AL	CLE	2005
47	Chad Cordero	NL	WAS	2005		44	Dan Quisenberry	AL	KC	1984
47	Francisco Rodriguez	AL	LA	2006		44	Jeff Brantley	NL	CIN	1996
46	Bryan Harvey	AL	CAL	1991		44	Todd Worrell	NL	LA	1996
46	Lee Smith	NL-AL	STL-NY	1993		44	Billy Koch	AL	OAK	2002
			STL (43); NY (3)			44	John Smoltz	NL	ATL	2004
46	Jose Mesa	AL	CLE	1995		44	Joe Nathan	AL	MIN	2004
46	Tom Gordon	AL	BOS	1998						

(480) Most Saves in a Season by a Left-handed Pitcher

53	Randy Myers	NL	CHI	1993		38	Randy Myers	NL	SD	1992
46	Dave Righetti	AL	NY	1986		38	John Hiller	AL	DET	1973
45	Randy Myers	AL	BAL	1997		38	John Franco	NL	NY	1998
45	Eddie Guardado	AL	MIN	2002		38	Billy Wagner	NL	PHI	2005
44	Mark Davis	NL	SD	1989		38	Randy Myers	NL	CHI	1995
44	Billy Wagner	NL	HOU	2003		38	B.J. Ryan	AL	TOR	2006
43	Mitch Williams	NL	PHI	1993		36	Dave Righetti	AL	NY	1990
41	Eddie Guardado	AL	MIN	2003		36	Eddie Guardado	AL	SEA	2005
40	Billy Wagner	NL	NY	2006		36	Mitch Williams	NL	CHI	1989
39	John Franco	NL	CIN	1988		36	John Franco	NL	NY	1997
39	Billy Wagner	NL	HOU	1999		36	B.J. Ryan	AL	BAL	2005
39	Billy Wagner	NL	HOU	2001		35	Billy Wagner	NL	HOU	2002
38	John Rocker	NL	ATL	1999		35	Sparky Lyle	AL	NY	1972

(481) Fewest Hits per 9 Innings in a Season, before 1893
(min. 1.0 IP per scheduled game)

5.83	Tim Keefe	NL	TRO	1880		6.69	Adonis Terry	Aa	BRO	1888
6.49	Guy Hecker	AA	LOU	1882		6.70	Silver King	AA	STL	1888
6.57	Tim Keefe	NL	NY	1888		6.73	Frank Knauss	AA	COL	1890
6.59	Charlie Sweeney	NL-UA	PRO-STL	1884		6.73	Ed Seward	AA	PHI	1888
		PRO (6.23); STL (6.87)				6.75	Tim Keefe	NL	NY	1885
						6.77	Tony Mullane	NL	CIN	1892

(482) Fewest Hits per 9 Innings in a Season, since 1893
(min. 1.0 IP per scheduled game)

5.26	Nolan Ryan	AL	CAL	1972		5.84	Al Downing	AL	NY	1963
5.30	Luis Tiant	AL	CLE	1968		5.85	Herb Score	AL	CLE	1956
5.31	Nolan Ryan	AL	TEX	1991		5.85	Bob Gibson	NL	STL	1968
5.31	Pedro Martinez	AL	BOS	2000		5.87	Sam McDowell	AL	CLE	1965
5.33	Ed Reulbach	NL	CHI	1906		5.89	Ed Walsh	AL	CHI	1910
5.57	Hubert "Dutch" Leonard	AL	BOS	1914		5.89	Pedro Martinez	NL	MON	1997
5.65	Carl Lundgren	NL	CHI	1907		5.95	Mike Scott	NL	HOU	1986
5.71	Sid Fernandez	NL	NY	1985		5.96	Nolan Ryan	AL	CAL	1977
5.74	Tommy Byrne	AL	NY	1949		5.96	Mario Soto	NL	CIN	1980
5.77	Dave McNally	AL	BAL	1968		5.96	Floyd Youmans	NL	MON	1986
5.79	Sandy Koufax	NL	LA	1965		5.98	Nolan Ryan	AL	CAL	1974
5.83	Russ Ford	AL	NY	1910		5.98	Nolan Ryan	NL	HOU	1981
5.83	Hideo Nomo	NL	LA	1995						

(483) Fewest Hits per 9 Innings in a Season by a Right-handed Pitcher, since 1893
(min. 1.0 IP per scheduled game)

5.26	Nolan Ryan	AL	CAL	1972		5.98	Nolan Ryan	NL	HOU	1981
5.30	Luis Tiant	AL	CLE	1968		6.02	Nolan Ryan	NL	HOU	1986
5.31	Nolan Ryan	AL	TEX	1991		6.03	Walter Johnson	AL	WAS	1913
5.31	Pedro Martinez	AL	BOS	2000		6.04	Nolan Ryan	AL	TEX	1990
5.33	Ed Reulbach	NL	CHI	1906		6.05	Grover Alexander	NL	PHI	1915
5.65	Carl Lundgren	NL	CHI	1907		6.07	Joe Horlen	AL	CHI	1964
5.83	Russ Ford	AL	NY	1910		6.08	Andy Messersmith	AL	CAL	1969
5.83	Hideo Nomo	NL	LA	1995		6.09	Stan Coveleski	AL	CLE	1917
5.85	Bob Gibson	NL	STL	1968		6.09	Catfish Hunter	AL	OAK	1972
5.89	Ed Walsh	AL	CHI	1910		6.09	Nolan Ryan	AL	TEX	1989
5.89	Pedro Martinez	NL	MON	1997		6.11	Nolan Ryan	AL	CAL	1976
5.95	Mike Scott	NL	HOU	1986		6.12	Bob Turley	AL	NY	1957
5.96	Nolan Ryan	AL	CAL	1977		6.13	Bob Turley	AL	NY	1955
5.96	Mario Soto	NL	CIN	1980		6.14	Don Sutton	NL	LA	1972
5.96	Floyd Youmans	NL	MON	1986		6.14	Nolan Ryan	NL	HOU	1983
5.98	Nolan Ryan	AL	CAL	1974		6.17	Mordecai Brown	NL	CHI	1908

(484) Fewest Hits per 9 Innings in a Season by a Left-handed Pitcher, since 1893 (min. 1.0 IP per scheduled game)

5.57	Hubert "Dutch" Leonard	AL	BOS	1914	6.06	Sam McDowell	AL	CLE	1968
5.71	Sid Fernandez	NL	NY	1985	6.11	Sid Fernandez	NL	NY	1988
5.74	Tommy Byrne	AL	NY	1949	6.15	Ron Guidry	AL	NY	1978
5.77	Dave McNally	AL	BAL	1968	6.16	Johan Santana	AL	MIN	2004
5.79	Sandy Koufax	NL	LA	1965	6.19	Sandy Koufax	NL	LA	1963
5.84	Al Downing	AL	NY	1963	6.21	Jack Pfiester	NL	CHI	1906
5.85	Herb Score	AL	CLE	1956	6.21	Randy Johnson	AL	SEA	1997
5.87	Sam McDowell	AL	CLE	1965	6.22	Sandy Koufax	NL	LA	1964
6.02	Sam McDowell	AL	CLE	1966	6.26	Herb Score	AL	CLE	1955
6.03	Vida Blue	AL	OAK	1971					

(485) Most Relief Wins in a Season

18	Roy Face	NL	PIT	1959	14	Jim Slaton	AL	MIL	1983
17	John Hiller	AL	DET	1974	14	Mark Eichhorn	AL	TOR	1986
17	Bill Campbell	AL	MIN	1976	14	Roger McDowell	NL	NY	1986
16	Jim Konstanty	NL	PHI	1950	13	Wilcy Moore	AL	NY	1927
16	Ron Perranoski	NL	LA	1963	13	Clyde Shoun	NL	CIN	1943
16	Dick Radatz	AL	BOS	1964	13	Earl Caldwell	AL	CHI	1946
16	Tom Johnson	AL	MIN	1977	13	Joe Page	AL	NY	1949
15	Mace Brown	NL	PIT	1938	13	Clyde King	NL	BRO	1951
15	Hoyt Wilhelm	NL	NY	1952	13	Lindy McDaniel	NL	STL	1959
15	Luis Arroyo	AL	NY	1961	13	Gerry Staley	AL	CHI	1960
15	Dick Radatz	AL	BOS	1963	13	Larry Sherry	NL	LA	1960
15	Eddie Fisher	AL	CHI	1965	13	Lindy McDaniel	NL	CHI	1963
15	Mike G. Marshall	NL	LA	1974	13	Al Hrabosky	NL	STL	1975
15	Dale Murray	NL	MON	1975	13	Rollie Fingers	AL	OAK	1976
14	Joe Page	AL	NY	1947	13	Bill Campbell	AL	BOS	1977
14	Joe Black	NL	BRO	1952	13	Sparky Lyle	AL	NY	1977
14	Hershell Freeman	NL	CIN	1956	13	Bob Stanley	AL	BOS	1978
14	Stu Miller	NL	SF	1961	13	Gary Lavelle	NL	SF	1978
14	Stu Miller	AL	BAL	1965	13	Dick Tidrow	AL-NL	NY-CHI	1979
14	Phil Regan	NL	LA	1966				NY (2); CHI (11)	
14	Frank Linzy	NL	SF	1969	13	Jim Kern	AL	TEX	1979
14	Mike G. Marshall	NL	MON	1972	13	Ron Reed	NL	PHI	1979
14	Mike G. Marshall	NL	MON	1973	13	Aurelio Lopez	AL	DET	1980
14	Ron Davis	AL	NY	1979	13	Jesse Orosco	NL	NY	1983
14	Mark Clear	AL	BOS	1982	13	Goose Gossage	AL	NY	1983

(486) Most Relief Losses in a Season

16	Gene Garber	NL	ATL	1979
14	Darold Knowles	AL	WAS	1970
14	John Hiller	AL	DET	1974
14	Mike G. Marshall	NL	LA	1975
14	Mike G. Marshall	AL	MIN	1979
13	Wilbur Wood	AL	CHI	1970
13	Rollie Fingers	NL	SD	1978
13	Skip Lockwood	NL	NY	1978
12	Roy Face	NL	PIT	1956
12	Roy Face	NL	PIT	1961
12	Ken Sanders	AL	MIL	1971
12	Mike G. Marshall	NL	LA	1974
12	Gene Garber	NL	PHI	1975
12	Jim Willoughby	AL	BOS	1976
12	Charlie Hough	NL	LA	1977
12	Mike G. Marshall	AL	MIN	1978
12	Kent Tekulve	NL	PIT	1980
12	Ken Howell	NL	LA	1986
12	Roger Mason	NL	SD	1993

12	Luis Ayala	NL	MON	2004
11	Nelson Potter	NL	BOS	1949
11	Frank Funk	AL	CLE	1961
11	Dick Radatz	AL	BOS	1965
11	Frank Linzy	NL	SF	1966
11	Wilbur Wood	AL	CHI	1968
11	Wilbur Wood	AL	CHI	1969
11	Mike G. Marshall	NL	MON	1973
11	Rollie Fingers	AL	OAK	1976
11	Goose Gossage	AL	NY	1978
11	Dave Heaverlo	AL	OAK	1979
11	Mark Clear	AL	CAL	1980
11	Greg Minton	NL	SF	1983
11	Ron Davis	AL	MIN	1984
11	Mark Davis	NL	SD	1985
11	Joe Boever	NL	ATL	1989
11	Jose Paniagua	AL	SEA	1999
11	Scot Shields	AL	LA	2005

Warren Spahn

(487) Most Games Pitched in Relief in a Season

106	Mike G. Marshall	NL	LA	1974		86	Paul Quantrill	AL	NY	2004
94	Kent Tekulve	NL	PIT	1979		86	Scott Eyre	NL	SF	2005
94	Salomon Torres	NL	PIT	2006		85	Kent Tekulve	NL	PIT	1982
92	Mike G. Marshall	NL	MON	1973		85	Frank Williams	NL	CIN	1987
91	Kent Tekulve	NL	PIT	1978		85	Oscar Villarreal	NL	ARI	2003
90	Wayne Granger	NL	CIN	1969		85	Matt Capps	NL	PIT	2006
90	Kent Tekulve	NL	PHI	1987		85	Jon Rauch	NL	WAS	2006
89	Mike G. Marshall	AL	MIN	1979		84	Ted Abernathy	NL	CHI	1965
89	Mark Eichhorn	AL	TOR	1987		84	Enrique Romo	NL	PIT	1979
89	Julian Tavarez	NL	SF	1997		84	Dick Tidrow	NL	CHI	1980
89	Steve James Kline	NL	STL	2001		84	Dan Quisenberry	AL	KC	1985
89	Paul Quantrill	NL	LA	2003		84	Mitch Williams	AL	TEX	1987
89	Jim Brower	NL	SF	2004		84	Stan Belinda	NL	CIN	1997
88	Mike Myers	AL	DET	1997		84	Graeme Lloyd	NL	MON	2001
88	Sean Runyan	AL	DET	1998		84	Billy Koch	AL	OAK	2002
87	Rob Murphy	NL	CIN	1987		84	Rheal Cormier	NL	PHI	2004
86	Wilbur Wood	AL	CHI	1968		84	Chris Reitsma	NL	ATL	2004
86	Paul Quantrill	NL	LA	2002		84	Salomon Torres	NL	PIT	2004
86	Ray King	NL	STL	2004		84	Bob Howry	NL	CHI	2006

(488) Most Innings Pitched in Relief in a Season

208.1	Mike G. Marshall	NL	LA	1974		144.1	Steve Foucault	AL	TEX	1974
179.0	Mike G. Marshall	NL	MON	1973		144.0	Hoyt Wilhelm	AL	CHI	1965
168.1	Bob Stanley	AL	BOS	1982		143.0	Jim Kern	AL	TEX	1979
167.2	Bill Campbell	AL	MIN	1976		142.2	Charlie Hough	NL	LA	1976
166.2	Andy Karl	NL	PHI	1945		141.2	Goose Gossage	AL	CHI	1975
165.1	Eddie Fisher	AL	CHI	1965		140.2	Mike G. Marshall	AL	MIN	1979
159.1	Hoyt Wilhelm	NL	NY	1952		140.1	Sammy Stewart	AL	BAL	1983
157.0	Dick Radatz	AL	BOS	1964		140.1	Willie Hernandez	AL	DET	1984
157.0	Mark Eichhorn	AL	TOR	1986		140.0	Bill Campbell	AL	BOS	1977
152.0	Jim Konstanty	NL	PHI	1950		139.2	Jack Lamabe	AL	BOS	1963
150.0	John Hiller	AL	DET	1974		139.0	Pedro Borbon Sr.	NL	CIN	1974
146.2	Tom Johnson	AL	MIN	1977		139.0	Dan Quisenberry	AL	KC	1983
146.0	Garland Braxton	AL	WAS	1927		138.1	Lindy McDaniel	AL	NY	1973
145.1	Bob Stanley	AL	BOS	1983		137.2	Aurelio Lopez	AL	DET	1984
145.0	Hoyt Wilhelm	NL	NY	1953		137.1	Clay Carroll	NL	ATL	1966
145.0	Wilbur Wood	AL	CHI	1968		137.0	Sparky Lyle	AL	NY	1977
144.2	Allan Russell	AL	WAS	1923		137.0	Tom Hume	NL	CIN	1980
144.2	Wayne Granger	NL	CIN	1969						

(489) Most Innings Pitched in a Season, all in Relief

208.1	Mike G. Marshall	NL	LA	1974		141.2	Goose Gossage	AL	CHI	1975
179.0	Mike G. Marshall	NL	MON	1973		140.1	Willie Hernandez	AL	DET	1984
168.1	Bob Stanley	AL	BOS	1982		140.0	Bill Campbell	AL	BOS	1977
167.2	Bill Campbell	AL	MIN	1976		139.0	Pedro Borbon Sr.	NL	CIN	1974
165.1	Eddie Fisher	AL	CHI	1965		139.0	Dan Quisenberry	AL	KC	1983
159.1	Hoyt Wilhelm	NL	NY	1952		137.2	Aurelio Lopez	AL	DET	1984
157.0	Dick Radatz	AL	BOS	1964		137.0	Sparky Lyle	AL	NY	1977
157.0	Mark Eichhorn	AL	TOR	1986		137.0	Tom Hume	NL	CIN	1980
152.0	Jim Konstanty	NL	PHI	1950		136.2	Dan Quisenberry	AL	KC	1982
150.0	John Hiller	AL	DET	1974		136.1	Ted Abernathy	NL	CHI	1965
146.2	Tom Johnson	AL	MIN	1977		136.1	Ken Sanders	AL	MIL	1971
145.1	Bob Stanley	AL	BOS	1983		136.1	Doug Corbett	AL	MIN	1980
145.0	Hoyt Wilhelm	NL	NY	1953		135.1	Joe Page	AL	NY	1949
144.2	Wayne Granger	NL	CIN	1969		135.1	Ted Abernathy	NL	CIN	1968
144.1	Steve Foucault	AL	TEX	1974		135.1	Mudcat Grant	AL-NL	OAK-PIT	1970
144.0	Hoyt Wilhelm	AL	CHI	1965			OAK (123.1); PIT (12.0)			
143.0	Jim Kern	AL	TEX	1979		135.1	Kent Tekulve	NL	PIT	1978
142.2	Charlie Hough	NL	LA	1976						

(490) Most Pitcher Walks in a Season, before 1893

289	Amos Rusie	NL	NY	1890		207	Toad Ramsey	AA	LOU	1886
274	Mark Baldwin	AA	COL	1889		206	Elton Chamberlain	AA	PHI	1891
270	Amos Rusie	NL	NY	1892		205	Mike Morrison	AA	CLE	1887
262	Amos Rusie	NL	NY	1891		204	Henry Gruber	PL	CLE	1890
249	Mark Baldwin	PL	CHI	1890		203	John Clarkson	NL	BOS	1889
232	Jack Stivetts	AA	STL	1891		203	Ed Crane	AA-NL	CIN-CIN	1891
227	Mark Baldwin	NL	PIT	1891			CIN-AA (139); CIN-NL (64)			
226	Phil Knell	AA	COL	1891		201	Bert Cunningham	PL	PHI-BUF	1890
219	Bob Barr	AA	ROC	1890			PHI (67); BUF (134)			
212	Gus Weyhing	AA	PHI	1889		199	Bill Hutchison	NL	CHI	1890
208	Ed Crane	PL	NY	1890		194	Mark Baldwin	NL	PIT	1892

A walk consisted of four balls from 1889 forward. Before that there were various higher numbers of balls needed for a walk.

(491) Most Pitcher Walks in a Season, since 1893

218	Amos Rusie	NL	NY	1893		177	Bob Turley	AL	NY	1955
213	Cy Seymour	NL	NY	1898		176	Jouett Meekin	NL	NY	1894
208	Bob Feller	AL	CLE	1938		175	George Hemming	NL	LOU	1893
204	Nolan Ryan	AL	CAL	1977		171	Bump Hadley	AL	CHI-STL	1932
202	Nolan Ryan	AL	CAL	1974				CHI (8); STL (163)		
200	Amos Rusie	NL	NY	1894		170	Ed Stein	NL	BRO	1894
194	Bob Feller	AL	CLE	1941		170	Cy Seymour	NL	NY	1899
192	Bobo Newsom	AL	STL	1938		168	Brickyard Kennedy	NL	BRO	1893
191	Ted Breitenstein	NL	STL	1894		168	Cy Seymour	NL	NY	1897
189	Tony Mullane	NL	CIN-BAL	1893		168	Elmer Myers	AL	PHI	1916
		CIN (65); BAL (124)				167	Bobo Newsom	AL	WAS-BOS	1937
187	Kid Gleason	NL	STL	1893				WAS (48); BOS (119)		
185	Sam Jones	NL	CHI	1955		166	Chick Fraser	NL	LOU	1896
183	Nolan Ryan	AL	CAL	1976		165	Weldon Wyckoff	AL	PHI	1915
182	Ted Breitenstein	NL	STL	1895		164	Earl Moore	NL	PHI	1911
181	Willie McGill	NL	CHI	1893		164	Phil Niekro	NL	ATL	1977
181	Bob Harmon	NL	STL	1911		162	Johnny Vander Meer	NL	CIN	1943
181	Bob Turley	AL	STL	1954		162	Nolan Ryan	AL	CAL	1973
179	Tommy Byrne	AL	NY	1949		160	Tommy Byrne	AL	NY	1950

(492) Most Walks in a Season by a Right-handed Pitcher, since 1893

218	Amos Rusie	NL	NY	1893		167	Bobo Newsom	AL	WAS-BOS	1937
208	Bob Feller	AL	CLE	1938				WAS (48); BOS (119)		
204	Nolan Ryan	AL	CAL	1977		166	Chick Fraser	NL	LOU	1896
202	Nolan Ryan	AL	CAL	1974		165	Weldon Wyckoff	AL	PHI	1915
200	Amos Rusie	NL	NY	1894		164	Earl Moore	NL	PHI	1911
194	Bob Feller	AL	CLE	1941		164	Phil Niekro	NL	ATL	1977
192	Bobo Newsom	AL	STL	1938		162	Nolan Ryan	AL	CAL	1973
189	Tony Mullane	NL	CIN-BAL	1893		159	George Hemming	NL	LOU-BAL	1894
		CIN (65); BAL (124)						LOU (133); BAL (26)		
187	Kid Gleason	NL	STL	1893		159	Amos Rusie	NL	NY	1895
185	Sam Jones	NL	CHI	1955		159	Marty O'Toole	NL	PIT	1912
183	Nolan Ryan	AL	CAL	1976		158	Joe Coleman Jr.	AL	DET	1974
181	Bob Harmon	NL	STL	1911		157	Pink Hawley	NL	PIT	1896
181	Bob Turley	AL	STL	1954		157	Grover Lowdermilk	AL	STL-DET	1915
177	Bob Turley	AL	NY	1955				STL (133); DET (24)		
176	Jouett Meekin	NL	NY	1894		157	Nolan Ryan	AL	CAL	1972
175	George Hemming	NL	LOU	1893		156	Sadie McMahon	NL	BAL	1893
171	Bump Hadley	AL	CHI-STL	1932		156	Bill Hutchison	NL	CHI	1893
		CHI (8); STL (163)				153	Bob Feller	AL	CLE	1946
170	Ed Stein	NL	BRO	1894		152	Bill Donovan	NL	BRO	1901
168	Brickyard Kennedy	NL	BRO	1893		151	J.R. Richard	NL	HOU	1976
168	Elmer Myers	AL	PHI	1916						

There are so many high walk totals from the 1893 season and the following few seasons because 1893 was the year the pitching distance was increased to 60 feet 6 inches.

(493) Most Walks in a Season by a Left-handed Pitcher, since 1893

213	Cy Seymour	NL	NY	1898		150	Tommy Byrne	AL	NY-STL	1951
191	Ted Breitenstein	NL	STL	1894				NY (36); STL (114)		
182	Ted Breitenstein	NL	STL	1895		149	Al Schulz	FL	BUF	1915
181	Willie McGill	NL	CHI	1893		144	Randy Johnson	AL	SEA	1992
179	Tommy Byrne	AL	NY	1949		143	Ken Chase	AL	WAS	1940
170	Cy Seymour	NL	NY	1899		140	Frank Killen	NL	PIT	1893
168	Cy Seymour	NL	NY	1897		139	Danny Friend	NL	CHI	1896
162	Johnny Vander Meer	NL	CIN	1943		138	Ted Breitenstein	NL	STL	1896
160	Tommy Byrne	AL	NY	1950		137	Hal Newhouser	AL	DET	1941
158	Ed Doheny	NL	NY	1899		137	Billy Pierce	AL	CHI	1950
156	Ted Breitenstein	NL	STL	1893		136	Steve Carlton	NL	PHI	1974
156	Duke Esper	NL	WAS	1893		135	Bill Wight	AL	CHI	1948
155	Bill Hill	NL	LOU	1896		134	Mel Parnell	AL	BOS	1949
154	Herb Score	AL	CLE	1955		132	Sam McDowell	AL	CLE	1965
153	Sam McDowell	AL	CLE	1971		131	Lefty Grove	AL	PHI	1925
152	Randy Johnson	AL	SEA	1991		131	Sam McDowell	AL	CLE	1970
						130	Steve Barber	AL	BAL	1961

There are so many high walk totals from the 1893 season and the following few seasons because 1893 was the year the pitching distance was increased to 60 feet 6 inches.

(494) Most Pitcher Strikeouts in a Season, before 1893

513	Matt Kilroy	AA	BAL	1886		343	Jim McCormick	NL-UA	CLE-CIN	1884
499	Toad Ramsey	AA	LOU	1886				CLE (182); CIN (161)		
483	Hugh Daily	UA	CP-WAS	1884		341	Amos Rusie	NL	NY	1890
		CP (469); WAS (14)				337	Charlie Sweeney	NL-UA	PRO-STL	1884
451	Dupee Shaw	NL-UA	DET-BOS	1884				PRO (145); STL (192)		
		DET (142); BOS (309)				337	Amos Rusie	NL	NY	1891
441	Charley Radbourn	NL	PRO	1884		335	Tim Keefe	NL	NY	1888
417	Charlie Buffinton	NL	BOS	1884		334	Tim Keefe	AA	NY	1884
385	Guy Hecker	AA	LOU	1884		326	Ed Morris	AA	PIT	1886
374	Bill J. Sweeney	UA	BAL	1884		325	Tony Mullane	AA	TOL	1884
369	Jim Galvin	NL	BUF	1884		323	Lady Baldwin	NL	DET	1886
368	Mark Baldwin	AA	COL	1889		315	Charley Radbourn	NL	PRO	1883
359	Tim Keefe	AA	NY	1883		314	Bill Hutchison	NL	CHI	1892
355	Toad Ramsey	AA	LOU	1887		313	John Clarkson	NL	CHI	1886
346	Hardie Henderson	AA	BAL	1884		308	Larry McKeon	AA	IND	1884
345	Jim Whitney	NL	BOS	1883		308	John Clarkson	NL	CHI	1885
345	Mickey Welch	NL	NY	1884		304	Amos Rusie	NL	NY	1892
						302	Ed Morris	AA	COL	1884

Strikeouts between 1876-1892 were a function of the rules governing the number of strikes needed for a strikeout. By the mid 1880s it was possible to get a lot of strikeouts, before then, hardly any.

(495) Most Pitcher Strikeouts in a Season, since 1893

383	Nolan Ryan	AL	CAL	1973		304	Sam McDowell	AL	CLE	1970
382	Sandy Koufax	NL	LA	1965		303	Walter Johnson	AL	WAS	1912
372	Randy Johnson	NL	ARI	2001		303	J.R. Richard	NL	HOU	1978
367	Nolan Ryan	AL	CAL	1974		302	Rube Waddell	AL	PHI	1903
364	Randy Johnson	NL	ARI	1999		301	Vida Blue	AL	OAK	1971
349	Rube Waddell	AL	PHI	1904		301	Nolan Ryan	AL	TEX	1989
348	Bob Feller	AL	CLE	1946		300	Curt Schilling	NL	PHI	1998
347	Randy Johnson	NL	ARI	2000		294	Randy Johnson	AL	SEA	1995
341	Nolan Ryan	AL	CAL	1977		293	Curt Schilling	NL	ARI	2001
334	Randy Johnson	NL	ARI	2002		292	Roger Clemens	AL	BOS	1997
329	Nolan Ryan	AL	CAL	1972		291	Roger Clemens	AL	BOS	1988
329	Randy Johnson	AL-NL	SEA-HOU	1998		291	Randy Johnson	AL	SEA	1997
		SEA (213); HOU (116)				290	Randy Johnson	NL	ARI	2004
327	Nolan Ryan	AL	CAL	1976		289	Tom Seaver	NL	NY	1971
325	Sam McDowell	AL	CLE	1965		287	Rube Waddell	AL	PHI	1905
319	Curt Schilling	NL	PHI	1997		286	Steve Carlton	NL	PHI	1980
317	Sandy Koufax	NL	LA	1966		286	Steve Carlton	NL	PHI	1982
316	Curt Schilling	NL	ARI	2002		284	Pedro Martinez	AL	BOS	2000
313	Walter Johnson	AL	WAS	1910		283	Sam McDowell	AL	CLE	1968
313	J.R. Richard	NL	HOU	1979		283	Tom Seaver	NL	NY	1970
313	Pedro Martinez	AL	BOS	1999		280	Denny McLain	AL	DET	1968
310	Steve Carlton	NL	PHI	1972		279	Sam McDowell	AL	CLE	1969
308	Mickey Lolich	AL	DET	1971		276	Bob Veale	NL	PIT	1965
308	Randy Johnson	AL	SEA	1993		276	Dwight Gooden	NL	NY	1984
306	Sandy Koufax	NL	LA	1963		276	John Smoltz	NL	ATL	1996
306	Mike Scott	NL	HOU	1986		275	Hal Newhouser	AL	DET	1946
305	Pedro Martinez	NL	MON	1997		275	Steve Carlton	NL	PHI	1983

Eddie Plank

(496) Most Strikeouts in a Season by a Right-handed Pitcher, since 1893

383	Nolan Ryan	AL	CAL	1973		274	Ferguson Jenkins	NL	CHI	1970
367	Nolan Ryan	AL	CAL	1974		274	Bob Gibson	NL	STL	1970
348	Bob Feller	AL	CLE	1946		274	Mario Soto	NL	CIN	1982
341	Nolan Ryan	AL	CAL	1977		273	Ferguson Jenkins	NL	CHI	1969
329	Nolan Ryan	AL	CAL	1972		271	Roger Clemens	AL	TOR	1998
327	Nolan Ryan	AL	CAL	1976		270	Bob Gibson	NL	STL	1965
319	Curt Schilling	NL	PHI	1997		270	Nolan Ryan	NL	HOU	1987
316	Curt Schilling	NL	ARI	2002		269	Ed Walsh	AL	CHI	1908
313	Walter Johnson	AL	WAS	1910		269	Bob Gibson	NL	STL	1969
313	J.R. Richard	NL	HOU	1979		268	Jim Bunning	NL	PHI	1965
313	Pedro Martinez	AL	BOS	1999		268	Bob Gibson	NL	STL	1968
306	Mike Scott	NL	HOU	1986		268	Dwight Gooden	NL	NY	1985
305	Pedro Martinez	NL	MON	1997		267	Christy Mathewson	NL	NY	1903
303	Walter Johnson	AL	WAS	1912		266	Kerry Wood	NL	CHI	2003
303	J.R. Richard	NL	HOU	1978		265	Jim Maloney	NL	CIN	1963
301	Nolan Ryan	AL	TEX	1989		264	Luis Tiant	AL	CLE	1968
300	Curt Schilling	NL	PHI	1998		264	Ben Sheets	NL	MIL	2004
293	Curt Schilling	NL	ARI	2001		263	Ferguson Jenkins	NL	CHI	1971
292	Roger Clemens	AL	BOS	1997		262	Dazzy Vance	NL	BRO	1924
291	Roger Clemens	AL	BOS	1988		262	Phil Niekro	NL	ATL	1977
289	Tom Seaver	NL	NY	1971		261	Bob Feller	AL	CLE	1940
284	Pedro Martinez	AL	BOS	2000		261	David Cone	NL-AL	NY-TOR	1992
283	Tom Seaver	NL	NY	1970					NY (214); TOR (47)	
280	Denny McLain	AL	DET	1968		260	Bob Feller	AL	CLE	1941
276	Dwight Gooden	NL	NY	1984		260	Ferguson Jenkins	NL	CHI	1968
276	John Smoltz	NL	ATL	1996		260	Nolan Ryan	AL	CAL	1978

(497) Most Strikeouts in a Season by a Left-handed Pitcher, since 1893

382	Sandy Koufax	NL	LA	1965		290	Randy Johnson	NL	ARI	2004
372	Randy Johnson	NL	ARI	2001		287	Rube Waddell	AL	PHI	1905
364	Randy Johnson	NL	ARI	1999		286	Steve Carlton	NL	PHI	1980
349	Rube Waddell	AL	PHI	1904		286	Steve Carlton	NL	PHI	1982
347	Randy Johnson	NL	ARI	2000		283	Sam McDowell	AL	CLE	1968
334	Randy Johnson	NL	ARI	2002		279	Sam McDowell	AL	CLE	1969
329	Randy Johnson	AL-NL	SEA-HOU	1998		276	Bob Veale	NL	PIT	1965
		SEA (213); HOU (116)				275	Hal Newhouser	AL	DET	1946
325	Sam McDowell	AL	CLE	1965		275	Steve Carlton	NL	PHI	1983
317	Sandy Koufax	NL	LA	1966		271	Mickey Lolich	AL	DET	1969
310	Steve Carlton	NL	PHI	1972		269	Sandy Koufax	NL	LA	1961
308	Mickey Lolich	AL	DET	1971		269	Frank Tanana	AL	CAL	1975
308	Randy Johnson	AL	SEA	1993		265	Johan Santana	AL	MIN	2004
306	Sandy Koufax	NL	LA	1963		263	Herb Score	AL	CLE	1956
304	Sam McDowell	AL	CLE	1970		262	Mark Langston	AL	SEA	1987
302	Rube Waddell	AL	PHI	1903		261	Frank Tanana	AL	CAL	1976
301	Vida Blue	AL	OAK	1971		250	Bob Veale	NL	PIT	1964
294	Randy Johnson	AL	SEA	1995		250	Mickey Lolich	AL	DET	1972
291	Randy Johnson	AL	SEA	1997						

(498) Most Walks per 9 Innings in a Season, since 1893
(min. 1.0 IP per scheduled game)

8.22	Tommy Byrne	AL	NY	1949		6.29	Johnny Lindell	NL	PIT-PHI	1953
7.13	Hal Newhouser	AL	DET	1941			PIT (5.94); PHI (8.87)			
7.08	Tommy Byrne	AL	NY	1950		6.24	Byron Houck	AL	PHI	1913
6.97	Adonis Terry	NL	PIT-CHI	1894		6.24	Hal Gregg	NL	BRO	1944
	No walks in .2 IP for PIT					6.20	Bump Hadley	AL	CHI-STL	1932
6.89	Sam Jones	NL	CHI	1955			CHI (3.95); STL (6.39)			
6.87	Todd Van Poppel	AL	OAK	1994		6.16	Randy Johnson	AL	SEA	1992
6.79	Randy Johnson	AL	SEA	1991		6.14	Nolan Ryan	AL	CAL	1977
6.74	Bob Feller	AL	CLE	1938		6.12	Frank Bates	NL	CLE-STL	1899
6.59	Bob Turley	AL	BAL	1954			CLE (6.18); STL (5.19)			
6.46	Bob Turley	AL	NY	1955		6.12	J.R. Richard	NL	HOU	1975
6.44	Herb Score	AL	CLE	1959		6.10	Herb Score	AL	CLE	1955
6.41	Sam McDowell	AL	CLE	1971		6.05	Dave Morehead	AL	BOS	1964
6.34	Jose DeJesus	NL	PHI	1991		6.00	Nolan Ryan	AL	CAL	1975

(499) Fewest Walks per 9 Innings in a Season, since 1893
(min. 1.0 IP per scheduled game)

0.43	Carlos Silva	AL	MIN	2005		0.86	Deacon Phillippe	NL	PIT	1902
0.62	Christy Mathewson	NL	NY	1913		0.86	La Marr Hoyt	NL	SD	1985
0.62	Babe Adams	NL	PIT	1920		0.89	Grover Alexander	NL	CHI	1923
0.66	Christy Mathewson	NL	NY	1914		0.90	Cy Young	AL	BOS	1901
0.66	Bret Saberhagen	NL	NY	1994		0.90	Deacon Phillippe	NL	PIT	1903
0.69	Cy Young	AL	BOS	1904		0.92	Jon Lieber	AL	NY	2004
0.74	Red Lucas	NL	CIN	1933		0.92	David Wells	NL	SD	2004
0.77	Bob Tewksbury	NL	STL	1992		0.96	Tiny Bonham	AL	NY	1942
0.77	Greg Maddux	NL	ATL	1997		0.97	Jesse Tannehill	NL	PIT	1902
0.78	Cy Young	AL	BOS	1906		0.97	Cy Young	AL	BOS	1903
0.79	Babe Adams	NL	PIT	1919		0.97	Christy Mathewson	NL	NY	1908
0.79	Slim Sallee	NL	CIN	1919		0.97	Christy Mathewson	NL	NY	1915
0.79	Babe Adams	NL	PIT	1922		0.98	Cy Young	NL	CLE	1898
0.82	Slim Sallee	NL	NY	1918		0.99	Bill Burns	AL	WAS	1908
0.83	Addie Joss	AL	CLE	1908		0.99	Christy Mathewson	NL	NY	1912
0.84	Cy Young	AL	BOS	1905		0.99	Walter Johnson	AL	WAS	1913
0.84	Bob Tewksbury	NL	STL	1993		0.99	Greg Maddux	NL	ATL	1995
0.85	David Wells	AL	NY	2003						

(500) Most Strikeouts per 9 Innings in a Season, since 1893
(min. 1.0 IP per scheduled game)

13.41	Randy Johnson	NL	ARI	2001	10.97	Oliver Perez	NL	PIT	2004
13.20	Pedro Martinez	AL	BOS	1999	10.86	Randy Johnson	AL	SEA	1993
12.58	Kerry Wood	NL	CHI	1998	10.79	Pedro Martinez	AL	BOS	2002
12.56	Randy Johnson	NL	ARI	2000	10.71	Sam McDowell	AL	CLE	1965
12.35	Randy Johnson	AL	SEA	1995	10.67	Randy Johnson	AL	SEA	1994
12.30	Randy Johnson	AL	SEA	1997	10.62	Randy Johnson	NL	ARI	2004
12.12	Randy Johnson	AL-NL	SEA-HOU	1998	10.57	Nolan Ryan	AL	CAL	1973
	SEA (11.98); HOU (12.38)				10.56	Nolan Ryan	AL	TEX	1991
12.06	Randy Johnson	NL	ARI	1999	10.55	Sandy Koufax	NL	LA	1962
11.78	Pedro Martinez	AL	BOS	2000	10.46	Johan Santana	AL	MIN	2004
11.56	Randy Johnson	NL	ARI	2002	10.43	Nolan Ryan	AL	CAL	1972
11.48	Nolan Ryan	NL	HOU	1987	10.43	Mark Prior	NL	CHI	2003
11.39	Dwight Gooden	NL	NY	1984	10.42	Sam McDowell	AL	CLE	1966
11.37	Pedro Martinez	NL	MON	1997	10.39	Roger Clemens	AL	TOR	1998
11.35	Kerry Wood	NL	CHI	2003	10.39	Curt Schilling	NL	ARI	2003
11.32	Nolan Ryan	AL	TEX	1989	10.35	Nolan Ryan	AL	CAL	1976
11.29	Curt Schilling	NL	PHI	1997	10.31	Randy Johnson	AL	SEA	1992
11.20	Kerry Wood	NL	CHI	2001	10.27	Curt Schilling	NL	ARI	2001
11.10	Hideo Nomo	NL	LA	1995	10.26	Nolan Ryan	AL	CAL	1977
10.97	Curt Schilling	NL	ARI	2002	10.25	David Cone	AL	NY	1997

(501) Fewest Strikeouts per 9 Innings in a Season, since 1893
(min. 1.0 IP per scheduled game)

0.72	Frank Bates	NL	CLE-STL	1899	1.14	Edgar McNabb	NL	BAL	1893
	All strikeouts with CLE				1.14	Sloppy Thurston	AL	CHI	1924
0.85	Bert Cunningham	NL	LOU	1898	1.14	Sherry Smith	AL	CLE	1925
0.95	Slim Sallee	NL	CIN	1919	1.16	Al Maul	NL	BAL	1898
0.95	Ernie Wingard	AL	STL	1924	1.16	Bill Beckmann	AL	PHI	1939
1.00	Bert Cunningham	NL	LOU	1899	1.19	Sherry Smith	AL	CLE	1926
1.01	Walt Woods	NL	LOU	1899	1.19	George Blaeholder	AL	STL-PHI	1935
1.06	Al Orth	NL	PHI	1896		All strikeouts with PHI			
1.06	Les German	NL	NY-WAS	1896	1.21	Jack Russell	AL	BOS	1928
	All strikeouts with WAS				1.21	Benny Frey	NL	CIN	1934
1.06	Ted Wingfield	AL	BOS	1925	1.23	Scott Stratton	NL	LOU	1893
1.08	Jack Dunn	NL	BRO	1897	1.23	Bill C. Lee	NL	CHI	1945
1.09	Frank Dwyer	NL	CIN	1898	1.24	Dan Daub	NL	BRO	1897
1.09	Walt Woods	NL	CHI	1898	1.24	Sherry Smith	AL	CLE	1924
1.10	Duke Esper	NL	BAL	1896					
1.13	Jack Dunn	NL	BRO-PHI	1900					
	BRO (0.86); PHI (1.35)								

(502) Best Strikeout to Walk Ratio in a Season, before 1893
(min. 1.0 IP per scheduled game)

10.00	Jim Whitney	NL	BOS	1884		6.71	Hugh Daily	UA	CP-WAS	1884
9.86	Jim Whitney	NL	BOS	1883				CP (6.60); WAS (14.00)		
9.00	George Bradley	NL	STL	1880		6.64	John Ward	NL	PRO	1879
8.80	Henry Boyle	UA	STL	1884		6.64	John Murphy	UA	WIL-ALT	1884
8.23	James Burke	UA	BOS	1884				WIL (13.50); ALT (5.11)		
8.02	Charlie Sweeney	NL-UA	PRO-STL	1884		6.60	Guy Hecker	AA	LOU	1882
		PRO (5.0); STL (14.77)				6.55	Bobby Mathews	AA	PHI	1883
7.94	Tommy Bond	UA-AA	BOS-IND	1884		6.46	Tommy Bond	NL	BOS	1879
		BOS (9.14); IND (3.75)				5.92	Ed Morris	AA	COL	1884
7.30	George Bradley	UA	CIN	1884		5.86	Jim Galvin	NL	BUF	1884
6.95	Bobby Mathews	NL	BOS	1882		5.84	Bobby Mathews	AA	PHI	1884
6.95	Jack Lynch	AA	NY	1884		5.63	Charley Radbourn	NL	PRO	1883
6.88	Guy Hecker	AA	LOU	1884		5.58	Jim Galvin	NL	BUF	1883
6.77	Tommy Bond	NL	HAR	1876		5.52	Tommy Bond	NL	BOS	1878

(503) Best Strikeout to Walk Ratio in a Season, since 1893
(min. 1.0 IP per scheduled game)

11.00	Bret Saberhagen	NL	NY	1994		6.14	Greg Maddux	NL	ATL	1996
9.58	Curt Schilling	NL	ARI	2002		6.06	Curt Schilling	NL	ARI	2003
8.88	Pedro Martinez	AL	BOS	2000		5.98	Pedro Martinez	AL	BOS	2002
8.85	Greg Maddux	NL	ATL	1997		5.80	Curt Schilling	AL	BOS	2004
8.46	Pedro Martinez	AL	BOS	1999		5.67	Jon Lieber	AL	NY	2004
8.25	Ben Sheets	NL	MIL	2004		5.62	David Wells	AL	NY	1998
7.89	Carlos Silva	AL	MIN	2005		5.60	Cy Young	AL	BOS	1906
7.87	Greg Maddux	NL	ATL	1995		5.50	Curt Schilling	NL	PHI	1997
7.51	Curt Schilling	NL	ARI	2001		5.50	Brad Radke	AL	MIN	2004
7.11	Ferguson Jenkins	NL	CHI	1971		5.45	Greg Swindell	AL	CLE	1991
7.00	Cy Young	AL	BOS	1905		5.38	Sandy Koufax	NL	LA	1965
6.90	Cy Young	AL	BOS	1904		5.37	Jim Merritt	AL	MIN	1967
6.59	Randy Johnson	NL	ARI	2004		5.35	David Wells	AL	TOR	2000
6.54	Curt Schilling	AL	BOS	2006		5.32	Shane Reynolds	NL	HOU	1999
6.41	Greg Maddux	NL	ATL	2001		5.29	Johan Santana	AL	MIN	2005
6.39	Walter Johnson	AL	WAS	1913		5.28	Sandy Koufax	NL	LA	1963
6.38	Roy Halladay	AL	TOR	2003		5.28	Jose Lima	NL	HOU	1998
6.17	Christy Mathewson	NL	NY	1908		5.28	Rick Reed	NL	NY	1998
6.17	Juan Marichal	NL	SF	1966		5.27	Brad Radke	AL	MIN	2001
6.16	Dennis Eckersley	NL	CHI	1985						

(504) Fewest Base Runners Allowed per 9 Innings in a Season, since 1893
(min. 1.0 IP per scheduled game)

7.22	Pedro Martinez	AL	BOS	2000		8.17	Babe Adams	NL	PIT	1919
7.26	Walter Johnson	AL	WAS	1913		8.28	Eddie Cicotte	AL	CHI	1917
7.31	Addie Joss	AL	CLE	1908		8.29	Hubert "Dutch" Leonard	AL	BOS	1914
7.45	Christy Mathewson	NL	NY	1909		8.30	Denny McLain	AL	DET	1968
7.47	Ed Walsh	AL	CHI	1910		8.32	Catfish Hunter	AL	OAK	1972
7.47	Greg Maddux	NL	ATL	1995		8.33	Doc White	AL	CHI	1906
7.51	Christy Mathewson	NL	NY	1908		8.33	Greg Maddux	NL	ATL	1994
7.72	Mordecai Brown	NL	CHI	1908		8.35	Grover Alexander	NL	CHI	1919
7.82	Grover Alexander	NL	PHI	1915		8.35	Sandy Koufax	NL	LA	1964
7.83	Sandy Koufax	NL	LA	1965		8.35	Juan Marichal	NL	SF	1965
7.88	Juan Marichal	NL	SF	1966		8.35	Don Sutton	NL	LA	1972
7.89	Bob Gibson	NL	STL	1968		8.37	Mike Scott	NL	HOU	1986
7.89	Roger Nelson	AL	KC	1972		8.42	Christy Mathewson	NL	NY	1905
7.91	Ed Walsh	AL	CHI	1908		8.46	Randy Johnson	NL	ARI	2004
7.91	Dave McNally	AL	BAL	1968		8.49	Addie Joss	AL	CLE	1906
7.96	Sandy Koufax	NL	LA	1963		8.51	Reb Russell	AL	CHI	1916
7.98	Luis Tiant	AL	CLE	1968		8.53	Cy Young	AL	BOS	1904
8.03	Cy Young	AL	BOS	1905		8.53	Mordecai Brown	NL	CHI	1906
8.04	Mordecai Brown	NL	CHI	1909		8.54	Walter Johnson	AL	WAS	1910
8.07	Cy Young	AL	BOS	1908		8.55	Claude Hendrix	FL	CHI	1914
8.17	Russ Ford	AL	NY	1910		8.55	Ron Guidry	AL	NY	1978

(505) Fewest Base Runners Allowed per 9 Innings in a Season
by a Right-handed Pitcher, since 1893 (min. 1.0 IP per scheduled game)

7.22	Pedro Martinez	AL	BOS	2000		8.35	Grover Alexander	NL	CHI	1919
7.26	Walter Johnson	AL	WAS	1913		8.35	Juan Marichal	NL	SF	1965
7.31	Addie Joss	AL	CLE	1908		8.35	Don Sutton	NL	LA	1972
7.45	Christy Mathewson	NL	NY	1909		8.37	Mike Scott	NL	HOU	1986
7.47	Ed Walsh	AL	CHI	1910		8.42	Christy Mathewson	NL	NY	1905
7.47	Greg Maddux	NL	ATL	1995		8.49	Addie Joss	AL	CLE	1906
7.51	Christy Mathewson	NL	NY	1908		8.53	Cy Young	AL	BOS	1904
7.72	Mordecai Brown	NL	CHI	1908		8.53	Mordecai Brown	NL	CHI	1906
7.82	Grover Alexander	NL	PHI	1915		8.54	Walter Johnson	AL	WAS	1910
7.88	Juan Marichal	NL	SF	1966		8.55	Claude Hendrix	FL	CHI	1914
7.89	Bob Gibson	NL	STL	1968		8.56	Walter Johnson	AL	WAS	1912
7.89	Roger Nelson	AL	KC	1972		8.56	Warren Hacker	NL	CHI	1952
7.91	Ed Walsh	AL	CHI	1908		8.57	Jack Chesbro	AL	NY	1904
7.98	Luis Tiant	AL	CLE	1968		8.59	Joe Horlen	AL	CHI	1964
8.03	Cy Young	AL	BOS	1905		8.60	Ed Walsh	AL	CHI	1909
8.04	Mordecai Brown	NL	CHI	1909		8.60	Chief Bender	AL	PHI	1910
8.07	Cy Young	AL	BOS	1908		8.64	Addie Joss	AL	CLE	1909
8.17	Russ Ford	AL	NY	1910		8.64	Tom Seaver	NL	NY	1971
8.17	Babe Adams	NL	PIT	1919		8.66	Russ Ford	FL	BUF	1914
8.28	Eddie Cicotte	AL	CHI	1917		8.68	Bill Bernhard	AL	PHI-CLE	1902
8.30	Denny McLain	AL	DET	1968			PHI (12.86); CLE (8.63)			
8.32	Catfish Hunter	AL	OAK	1972		8.69	Pedro Martinez	AL	BOS	1999
8.33	Greg Maddux	NL	ATL	1994						

(506) Fewest Base Runners Allowed per 9 Innings in a Season by a Left-handed Pitcher, since 1893 (min. 1.0 IP per scheduled game)

7.83	Sandy Koufax	NL	LA	1965	8.62	Bill Burns	AL	WAS	1908
7.91	Dave McNally	AL	BAL	1968	8.64	Johan Santana	AL	MIN	2004
7.96	Sandy Koufax	NL	LA	1963	8.68	Vida Blue	AL	OAK	1971
8.29	Hubert "Dutch" Leonard	AL	BOS	1914	8.78	Johan Santana	AL	MIN	2005
8.33	Doc White	AL	CHI	1906	8.86	Sandy Koufax	NL	LA	1966
8.35	Sandy Koufax	NL	LA	1964	8.92	Carl Hubbell	NL	NY	1933
8.46	Randy Johnson	NL	ARI	2004	8.94	Jack Pfiester	NL	CHI	1906
8.51	Reb Russell	AL	CHI	1916	8.97	Gary Peters	AL	CHI	1966
8.55	Ron Guidry	AL	NY	1978	8.97	Steve Carlton	NL	PHI	1972
8.61	John Tudor	NL	STL	1985					

Orel Hershiser

(507) Most Wild Pitches in a Season, since 1893

30	Red Ames	NL	NY	1905		21	Brickyard Kennedy	NL	BRO	1894
29	Tony Mullane	NL	CIN-BAL	1893		21	Pink Hawley	NL	STL	1894
			CIN (8); BAL (21)			21	Doc McJames	NL	WAS	1897
27	Chick Fraser	NL	LOU	1896		21	Ed Doheny	NL	NY	1899
27	Tony Cloninger	NL	ATL	1966		21	Walter Johnson	AL	WAS	1910
26	Amos Rusie	NL	NY	1893		21	Earl Wilson	AL	BOS	1963
26	Larry Cheney	NL	CHI	1914		21	Nolan Ryan	AL	CAL	1977
26	Juan Guzman	AL	TOR	1993		21	Joe Niekro	NL-AL	HOU-NY	1985
24	Doc McJames	NL	WAS	1896					All with HOU	
24	Jack Morris	AL	DET	1987		21	Ken Howell	NL	PHI	1989
23	Christy Mathewson	NL	NY	1901		21	Scott Williamson	NL	CIN	2000
23	Tim Leary	AL	NY	1990		20	Red Ames	NL	NY	1907
23	Matt Clement	NL	SD	2000		20	Denny Lemaster	NL	MIL	1964
22	Jouett Meekin	NL	NY	1894		20	Larry Dierker	NL	HOU	1968
22	Chick Fraser	NL	LOU	1897		20	J.R. Richard	NL	HOU	1975
22	Jack Hamilton	NL	PHI	1962		20	Dave Lemanczyk	AL	TOR	1977
22	Tony Cloninger	NL	MIL	1965		20	John Smoltz	NL	ATL	1991
22	Bobby Witt	AL	TEX	1986		20	Jose Contreras	AL	CHI	2005
22	Mike Moore	AL	OAK	1992		20	Freddy Garcia	AL	CHI	2005

(508) Most Hit Batters in a Season, before 1893

54	Phil Knell	AA	COL	1891		24	Ed Seward	AA	PHI	1887
43	Frank Foreman	AA	WAS	1891		24	Tom Sullivan	AA	KC	1888
42	Gus Weyhing	AA	PHI	1888		24	Phenomenal Smith	AA	BAL-PHI	1888
40	Frank Foreman	AA	BAL	1889					BAL (24); PHI (0)	
37	Gus Weyhing	AA	PHI	1887		24	John "Darby" O'Brien	NL	CLE	1889
35	Will White	AA	CIN	1884		24	John Healy	AA	TOL	1890
34	Gus Weyhing	AA	PHI	1889		23	Matt Kilroy	AA	BAL	1888
32	Tony Mullane	AA	TOL	1884		23	Henry Porter	AA	KC	1888
32	Tony Mullane	AA	CIN	1887		23	Park Swartzel	AA	KC	1889
31	Gus Weyhing	AA	PHI	1891		23	Mark Baldwin	NL	PIT	1891
30	Bert Cunningham	AA	BAL	1888		22	Al Atkinson	AA	PHI	1886
30	Silver King	AA	STL	1888		22	Mike Morrison	AA	CLE	1887
29	Tony Mullane	AA	CIN	1888		22	Ed Seward	AA	PHI	1888
29	Tom Vickery	NL	PHI	1890		22	Billy Rhines	NL	CIN	1891
28	Phil Knell	AA	PHI	1890		22	Mark Baldwin	NL	PIT	1892
28	Kid Carsey	AA	WAS	1891		22	Red Ehret	NL	PIT	1892
27	Will White	AA	CIN	1885		22	Phil Knell	NL	WAS-PHI	1892
27	Matt Kilroy	AA	BAL	1889					WAS (11); PHI (11)	
27	Kid Madden	AA	BOS-BAL	1891		21	Jumbo McGinnis	AA	STL-BAL	1886
			BOS (3); BAL (24)						STL (7); BAL (14)	
26	Gus Shallix	AA	CIN	1884		21	Silver King	NL	NY	1889
26	Amos Rusie	NL	NY	1890		21	Frank Knauss	AA	COL	1890
26	Sadie McMahon	AA	PHI-BAL	1890		21	George Van Haltren	PL	BRO	1890
			PHI (20); BAL (6)			21	Jack Easton	AA	COL-STL	1891
26	Ed Daily	AA-NL-AA	BRO-NY-LOU	1890					COL (17); STL (4)	
			BRO (18); NY (4); LOU (4)			21	Silver King	NL	NY	1892
25	John Keefe	AA	SYR	1890						

(509) Most Hit Batters in a Season, since 1893

40	Joe McGinnity	NL	BRO	1900		23	Jake Weimer	NL	CIN	1907
39	Danny Friend	NL	CHI	1896		23	Howard Ehmke	AL	DET	1922
37	Ed Doheny	NL	NY	1899		22	Clark Griffith	NL	CHI	1895
33	Pink Hawley	NL	PIT	1895		22	Red Donahue	NL	STL	1897
32	Cy Seymour	NL	NY	1898		22	Chick Fraser	AL	PHI	1897
32	Chick Fraser	AL	PHI	1901		22	Cy Seymour	NL	NY	1897
30	Vic Willis	NL	BOS	1899		22	Pete Dowling	NL	LOU	1898
29	Chick Fraser	NL	LOU	1896		22	Pink Hawley	NL	CIN	1898
29	Vic Willis	NL	BOS	1898		22	Chick Fraser	AL	PHI	1899
29	Chick Fraser	NL	LOU-CLE	1898		22	Jim Hughey	NL	CLE	1899
	LOU (23); CLE (6)					22	Jack W. Taylor	NL	CHI	1899
28	Pink Hawley	NL	PIT	1896		22	Willie Sudhoff	NL	CLE-STL	1899
28	Win Mercer	NL	WAS	1897			CLE (7); STL (15)			
28	Jack B. Taylor	NL	PHI	1897		22	Nixey Callahan	NL	CHI	1900
28	Gus Weyhing	NL	WAS	1899		22	Ed Doheny	NL	NY	1900
27	Willie Sudhoff	NL	STL	1898		22	Cy Morgan	AL	BOS-PHI	1909
26	Pink Hawley	NL	PIT	1897			BOS (6); PHI (16)			
26	Joe McGinnity	NL	BAL	1899		21	Pink Hawley	NL	STL	1894
26	Jack Warhop	AL	NY	1909		21	Kid Carsey	NL	PHI	1895
25	Jack B. Taylor	NL	STL	1898		21	Billy Rhines	NL	CIN	1895
25	Chief Bender	AL	PHI	1903		21	Joe Corbett	NL	BAL	1897
24	Nixey Callahan	NL	CHI	1899		21	Doc McJames	NL	WAS	1897
24	Eddie Plank	AL	PHI	1905		21	Doc Newton	NL	CIN-BRO	1901
24	Otto Hess	AL	CLE	1906			CIN (14); BRO (7)			
23	Red Ehret	NL	PIT	1893		21	Joe McGinnity	AL	BAL	1901
23	Fred Klobedanz	NL	BOS	1897		21	Jack Chesbro	NL	PIT	1902
23	Wiley Piatt	NL	PHI	1899		21	Henry Schmidt	NL	BRO	1903
23	Frank Bates	NL	CLE-STL	1899		21	Harry McIntire	NL	BRO	1909
	CLE (23); STL (0)					21	Cy Morgan	AL	PHI	1911
23	Bill Magee	NL	LOU-PHI-WAS	1899		21	Tom Murphy	AL	CAL	1969
	LOU (9); PHI (7); WAS (7)					21	Kerry Wood	NL	CHI	2003
23	Eddie Plank	AL	PHI	1903						

(510) Pitching Triple Crown Winners (Leading league in wins, ERA, and strikeouts)

				WINS	ERA	K
Tommy Bond	NL	BOS	1877	40	2.11	170
Charley Radbourn	NL	PRO	1884	59	1.38	441
Guy Hecker	AA	LOU	1884	52	1.80	385
Tim Keefe	NL	NY	1888	35	1.74	335
John Clarkson	NL	BOS	1889	49	2.73	284
Amos Rusie	NL	NY	1894	36	2.78	195
Cy Young	AL	BOS	1901	33	1.62	158
Rube Waddell	AL	PHI	1905	27	1.48	287
Christy Mathewson	NL	NY	1905	31	1.28	206
Christy Mathewson	NL	NY	1908	37	1.43	259
Walter Johnson	AL	WAS	1913	36	1.14	243
Grover Alexander	NL	PHI	1915	31	1.22	241
Grover Alexander	NL	PHI	1916	33	1.55	167
Grover Alexander	NL	PHI	1917	30	1.83	200
Walter Johnson	AL	WAS	1918	23	1.27	162
Hippo Vaughn	NL	CHI	1918	22	1.74	148
Grover Alexander	NL	CHI	1920	27	1.91	173
Walter Johnson	AL	WAS	1924	23	2.72	158
Dazzy Vance	NL	BRO	1924	28	2.16	262
Lefty Grove	AL	PHI	1930	28	2.54	209
Lefty Grove	AL	PHI	1931	31	2.06	175
Lefty Gomez	AL	NY	1934	26	2.33	158
Lefty Gomez	AL	NY	1937	21	2.33	194
Bucky Walters	NL	CIN	1939	27	2.29	137
Bob Feller	AL	CLE	1940	27	2.61	261
Hal Newhouser	AL	DET	1945	25	1.81	212
Sandy Koufax	NL	LA	1963	25	1.88	306
Sandy Koufax	NL	LA	1965	26	2.04	382
Sandy Koufax	NL	LA	1966	27	1.73	317
Steve Carlton	NL	PHI	1972	27	1.97	310
Dwight Gooden	NL	NY	1985	24	1.53	268
Roger Clemens	AL	TOR	1997	21	2.05	292
Roger Clemens	AL	TOR	1998	20	2.65	271
Pedro Martinez	AL	BOS	1999	23	2.07	313
Randy Johnson	NL	ARI	2002	24	2.32	334
Johan Santana	AL	MIN	2006	19	2.77	245

(511) Pitching Triple Crown Near Misses (Winning two categories and finishing second in other)

				WINS	ERA	K	
Silver King	AA	STL	1888	45	1.63	258	Ed Seward led in K with 272
Walter Johnson	AL	WAS	1912	33	1.39	303	Joe Wood led in Wins with 34
Walter Johnson	AL	WAS	1915	27	1.55	203	Joe Wood led in ERA with 1.49
Eddie Cicotte	AL	CHI	1917	28	1.53	150	Walter Johnson led in K with 188
Dolf Luque	NL	CIN	1923	27	1.93	151	Dazzy Vance led in K with 197
Carl Hubbell	NL	NY	1933	23	1.66	156	Dizzy Dean led in K with 199
Dizzy Dean	NL	STL	1934	30	2.66	195	Carl Hubbell led in ERA with 2.30
Mort Cooper	NL	STL	1942	22	1.78	152	Johnny Vander Meer led in K with 186
Hal Newhouser	AL	DET	1944	29	2.22	187	Dizzy Trout led in ERA with 2.12
Hal Newhouser	AL	DET	1946	26	1.94	275	Bob Feller led in K with 348
Ewell Blackwell	NL	CIN	1947	22	2.47	193	Warren Spahn led in ERA with 2.33
Harry Brecheen	NL	STL	1948	20	2.24	149	Johnny Sain led in Wins with 24
Robin Roberts	NL	PHI	1953	23	2.75	198	Warren Spahn led in ERA with 2.10
Sam Jones	NL	SF	1959	21	2.83	209	Don Drysdale led in K with 242
Bob Gibson	NL	STL	1968	22	1.12	268	Juan Marichal led in Wins with 26
Tom Seaver	NL	NY	1971	20	1.76	289	Ferguson Jenkins led in Wins with 24
Tom Seaver	NL	NY	1973	19	2.08	251	Ron Bryant led in Wins with 24
Ron Guidry	AL	NY	1978	25	1.74	248	Nolan Ryan led in K with 260
J.R. Richard	NL	HOU	1979	18	2.71	313	Phil Niekro and Joe Niekro tied for lead in Wins with 21
Steve Carlton	NL	PHI	1980	24	2.34	286	Don Sutton led in ERA with 2.20
Roger Clemens	AL	BOS	1986	24	2.48	238	Mark Langston led in K with 245
Randy Johnson	AL	SEA	1995	18	2.48	294	Mike Mussina led in Wins with 19
Randy Johnson	NL	ARI	2001	21	2.49	372	Matt Morris and Curt Schilling led in Wins with 22
Johan Santana	AL	MIN	2004	20	2.61	265	Curt Schilling led in Wins with 21

(512) Highest ERA in a Season (min. 1.0 IP per scheduled game)

7.71	Les Sweetland	NL	PHI	1930
7.60	Bill Rhodes	NL	LOU	1893
7.60	Jack Wadsworth	NL	LOU	1894
7.39	Jim DeShaies	AL	MIN	1994
7.29	Jack Knott	AL	STL	1936
7.23	Tom Colcolough	NL	PIT	1894
6.99	Jose Lima	AL	KC	2005
6.90	Frank Bates	NL	CLE-STL	1899
	CLE (7.24); STL (1.04)			
6.81	Harry Staley	NL	BOS	1894
6.66	La Troy Hawkins	AL	MIN	1999
6.65	Greg W Harris	NL	COL	1994

6.65	Jose Lima	NL	HOU	2000
6.61	Chubby Dean	AL	PHI	1940
6.61	Darryl Kile	NL	COL	1999
6.60	Nelson Potter	AL	PHI	1939
6.59	Tony Mullane	NL	BAL-CLE	1894
	BAL (6.31); CLE (7.64)			
6.56	Ernie Wingard	AL	STL	1927
6.56	George Caster	AL	PHI	1940
6.51	Scott Stratton	NL	LOU-CHI	1894
	LOU (8.47); CHI (5.89)			
6.51	Bill Kissinger	NL	BAL-STL	1895

(513) Pitchers with Highest ERA in a 20-win Season

ERA	Pitcher	Lg	Team	Year	WINS
5.08	Bobo Newsom	AL	STL	1938	20
5.02	Ray Kremer	NL	PIT	1930	20
4.92	Brickyard Kennedy	NL	BRO	1894	24
4.92	Clark Griffith	NL	CHI	1894	21
4.92	Kid Carsey	NL	PHI	1895	24
4.90	Jack Stivetts	NL	BOS	1894	26
4.81	Kid Carsey	NL	PHI	1893	20
4.80	Adonis Terry	NL	CHI	1895	21
4.79	Ted Breitenstein	NL	STL	1894	27
4.79	Jack B. Taylor	NL	PHI	1896	20
4.75	Kid Nichols	NL	BOS	1894	32
4.74	Gus Weyhing	NL	PHI	1893	23
4.63	Ed Stein	NL	BRO	1894	26
4.63	Vern Kennedy	AL	CHI	1936	21
4.61	Kid Gleason	NL	STL	1893	21
4.60	Fred Klobedanz	NL	BOS	1897	26
4.56	Nig Cuppy	NL	CLE	1894	24
4.55	Charley Radbourn	NL	BOS	1887	24
4.49	Jack B. Taylor	NL	PHI	1895	26
4.44	George Earnshaw	AL	PHI	1930	22
4.41	Jack Stivetts	NL	BOS	1893	20
4.41	Rick Helling	AL	TEX	1998	20

(514) Most Home Runs Allowed in a Season

HR	Pitcher	Lg	Team	Year
50	Bert Blyleven	AL	MIN	1986
48	Jose Lima	NL	HOU	2000
46	Robin Roberts	NL	PHI	1956
46	Bert Blyleven	AL	MIN	1987
44	Jamie Moyer	AL	SEA	2004
43	Pedro Ramos	AL	WAS	1957
43	Eric Milton	NL	PHI	2004
42	Denny McLain	AL	DET	1966
41	Robin Roberts	NL	PHI	1955
41	Phil Niekro	NL	ATL	1979
41	Rick Helling	AL	TEX	1999
40	Robin Roberts	NL	PHI	1957
40	Ralph Terry	AL	NY	1962
40	Orlando Pena	AL	KC	1964
40	Phil Niekro	NL	ATL	1970
40	Ferguson Jenkins	AL	TEX	1979
40	Jack Morris	AL	DET	1986
40	Bill Gullickson	NL-AL	CIN-NY	1987
			CIN (33); NY (7)	
40	Brad Radke	AL	MIN	1996
40	Shawn Boskie	AL	CAL	1996
40	Ramon Ortiz	AL	ANA	2002
40	Eric Milton	NL	CIN	2005
39	Murry Dickson	NL	STL	1948
39	Pedro Ramos	AL	MIN	1961
39	Jim Perry	AL	MIN	1971
39	Catfish Hunter	AL	OAK	1973
39	Jack Morris	AL	DET	1987
39	Brian Anderson	NL	ARI	1998
39	Pedro Astacio	NL	COL	1998
38	Warren Hacker	NL	CHI	1955
38	Pedro Ramos	AL	WAS	1958
38	Lew Burdette	NL	MIL	1959
38	Jim Bunning	AL	DET	1963
38	Don Sutton	NL	LA	1970
38	Mickey Lolich	AL	DET	1974
38	Matt Keough	AL	OAK	1982
38	Curt Young	AL	OAK	1987
38	Don Sutton	AL	CAL	1987
38	Floyd Bannister	AL	CHI	1987
38	Tim Wakefield	AL	BOS	1996
38	Pedro Astacio	NL	COL	1999
38	Brian Anderson	NL	ARI	2000
38	Rick Helling	AL	TEX	2001
38	Bartolo Colon	AL	ANA	2004
38	Darrell May	AL	KC	2004
38	Carlos Silva	AL	MIN	2006

(515) Most Innings Pitched in a Season without Allowing a Home Run, since 1893

369.2	Walter Johnson	AL	WAS	1916	279.0	Deacon Phillippe	NL	PIT	1905
353.0	Jack Coombs	AL	PHI	1910	275.0	Bob Rhoads	AL	CLE	1907
331.2	Ed Killian	AL	DET	1904	274.0	Frank Corridon	NL	PHI	1907
323.2	Babe Ruth	AL	BOS	1916	271.1	Jim Bagby Sr.	AL	CLE	1918
322.0	Vic Willis	NL	PIT	1906	269.1	Eddie Cicotte	AL	CHI	1914
317.0	Rube Vickers	AL	PHI	1908	260.0	Harry Gaspar	NL	CIN	1909
313.1	Ed Killian	AL	DET	1905	259.1	Hubert "Dutch" Leonard	AL	BOS	1913
304.2	Jake Weimer	NL	CIN	1906	259.0	Hugh Bedient	AL	BOS	1913
291.2	Frank E. Smith	AL	CHI	1905	258.2	Charlie Smith	AL	WAS	1907
290.2	Cy Morgan	AL	PHI	1910	258.0	Billy Rhines	NL	PIT	1898
290.1	Walter Johnson	AL	WAS	1919	256.1	Walter Johnson	AL	WAS	1908
287.2	Nick Altrock	AL	CHI	1906	250.1	Jim Scott	AL	CHI	1909
285.2	Rube Waddell	AL	STL	1908					

(516) 20 Wins with a Last-place Team

29	Matt Kilroy	1886	AA		BAL	21	Phil Niekro	1979	NL (W)	ATL
27	Steve Carlton	1972	NL (E)		PHI	21	Roger Clemens	1997	AL (E)	TOR
25	Lee Richmond	1881	NL		WOR	20	Scott Perry	1918	AL	PHI
25	Hardie Henderson	1885	AA		BAL	20	Howard Ehmke	1923	AL	BOS
22	Mark Baldwin	1891	NL		PIT	20	Sloppy Thurston	1924	AL	CHI
22	Noodles Hahn	1901	NL		CIN	20	Ned Garver	1951	AL	STL
22	Nolan Ryan	1974	AL (W)		CAL					

(517) Highest Percentage of Teams Wins, since 1893

					WINS	TEAM WINS
48.7	Ted Breitenstein	1895	NL	STL	19	39
48.5	Amos Rusie	1893	NL	NY	33	68
48.2	Ted Breitenstein	1894	NL	STL	27	56
46.6	Cy Young	1893	NL	CLE	34	73
45.8	Steve Carlton	1972	NL	PHI	27	59
45.5	Ed Walsh	1908	AL	CHI	40	88
45.5	Frank Killen	1896	NL	PIT	30	66
45.0	Ted Breitenstein	1896	NL	STL	18	40
44.6	Jack Chesbro	1904	AL	NY	41	92
44.4	Frank Killen	1893	NL	PIT	36	81
43.7	Pink Hawley	1895	NL	PIT	31	71
43.1	Win Mercer	1896	NL	WAS	25	58
42.3	Noodles Hahn	1901	NL	CIN	22	52
41.8	Cy Young	1901	AL	BOS	33	79
41.7	Joe Bush	1916	AL	PHI	15	36
41.7	Cy Young	1895	NL	CLE	35	84
41.6	Cy Young	1902	AL	BOS	32	77
41.5	Eddie Rommel	1922	AL	PHI	27	65
40.9	Amos Rusie	1894	NL	NY	36	88
40.6	Jouett Meekin	1896	NL	NY	26	64
40.5	Kid Nichols	1896	NL	BOS	30	74
40.3	Red Faber	1921	AL	CHI	25	62
40.0	Walter Johnson	1913	AL	WAS	36	90

(518) Pitchers Winning 20 Games in a Season They Were Traded

43	Billy Taylor	1884	UA	STL (25)	AA	PHI (18)			
41	Charlie Sweeney	1884	NL	PRO (17)	UA	STL (24)			
40	Jim McCormick	1884	NL	CLE (19)	UA	CIN (21)			
36	Sadie McMahon	1890	AA	PHI (29)	AA	BAL (7)			
30	Dupee Shaw	1884	NL	DET (9)	UA	BOS (21)			
28	Hugh Daily	1884	UA	CHI-PIT (27)	UA	WAS (1)			
25	Elton Chamberlain	1888	AA	LOU (14)	AA	STL (11)			
25	John Clarkson	1892	NL	BOS (8)	NL	CLE (17)			
23	Red Barrett	1945	NL	BOS (2)	NL	STL (21)			
22	Frank Dwyer	1892	NL	STL (2)	NL	CIN (20)			
21	Jim McCormick	1885	NL	PRO (1)	NL	CHI (20)			
21	Joe McGinnity	1902	AL	BAL (13)	NL	NY (8)			
21	Hank Borowy	1945	AL	NY (10)	NL	CHI (11)			
21	Tom Seaver	1977	NL	NY (7)	NL	CIN (14)			
20	Al Atkinson	1884	AA	PHI (11)	UA	CHI-PIT (6)	UA	BAL (3)	
20	Willie McGill	1891	AA	CIN (2)	AA	STL (18)			
20	Bob Wicker	1903	NL	STL (0)	NL	CIN (20)			
20	Patsy Flaherty	1904	AL	CHI (1)	NL	PIT (19)			
20	Jack W. Taylor	1906	NL	STL (8)	NL	CHI (12)			
20	Bobo Newsom	1939	AL	STL (3)	AL	DET (17)			
20	Virgil Trucks	1953	AL	STL (5)	AL	CHI (15)			
20	Rick Sutcliffe	1984	AL	CLE (4)	NL	CHI (16)			
20	Bartolo Colon	2002	AL	CLE (10)	NL	MON (10)			

Sandy Koufax

(519) Undefeated Seasons with Eight or More Wins

12	Tom Zachary	AL	NY	1929	
11	Dennis Lamp	AL	TOR	1985	
10	Howie Krist	NL	STL	1941	
10	Aaron Small	AL	NY	2005	
9	Joe Pate	AL	PHI	1926	
9	Frank DiPino	NL	STL	1989	
9	Ken Holtzman	NL	CHI	1967	

8	Kirk Rueter	NL	MON	1993
8	Grant Jackson	AL	BAL	1973
8	Rheal Cormier	NL	PHI	2003
8	Arthur Rhodes	AL	SEA	2001
8	Ted Wilks	NL	STL	1946
8	Pat Mahomes	NL	NY	1999

(520) Most Wins by Age in a Season, Since 1893 (Age as of July 1)

AGE					WINS
17	Bob Feller	AL	CLE	1936	5
18	Bob Feller	AL	CLE	1937	9
19	Wally Bunker	AL	BAL	1964	19
20	Bob Feller	AL	CLE	1939	24
21	Bob Feller	AL	CLE	1940	27
22	Frank Killen	NL	PIT	1893	36
23	Amos Rusie	NL	NY	1894	36
24	Walter Johnson	AL	WAS	1912	33
25	Walter Johnson	AL	WAS	1913	36
26	Cy Young	NL	CLE	1893	34
27	Ed Walsh	AL	CHI	1908	40
28	Cy Young	NL	CLE	1895	35
29	Grover Alexander	NL	PHI	1916	33
30	Jack Chesbro	AL	NY	1904	41
31	Lefty Grove	AL	PHI	1931	31
32	Joe McGinnity	NL	NY	1903	31
33	Joe McGinnity	NL	NY	1904	35
34	Cy Young	AL	BOS	1901	33

AGE					WINS
35	Cy Young	AL	BOS	1902	32
36	Cy Young	AL	BOS	1903	28
37	Cy Young	AL	BOS	1904	26
38	Randy Johnson	NL	ARI	2002	22
39	Early Wynn	AL	CHI	1959	22
40	Cy Young	AL	BOS	1907	21
40	Grover Alexander	NL	STL	1927	21
40	Warren Spahn	NL	MIL	1961	21
40	Phil Niekro	NL	ATL	1979	21
40	Jamie Moyer	AL	SEA	2003	21
41	Cy Young	AL	BOS	1908	21
42	Warren Spahn	NL	MIL	1963	23
43	Phil Niekro	NL	ATL	1982	17
44	Jack Quinn	AL	PHI	1928	18
45	Phil Niekro	AL	NY	1984	16
46	Phil Niekro	AL	NY	1985	16
47	Phil Niekro	AL	CLE	1986	11
48	Phil Niekro	AL	CLE	1987	7

TRANSCENDENTAL GRAPHICS

Eddie Rommel

(521) Lowest Winning Percentage in a Season (min. 12 losses)

					RECORD	
.000	Terry Felton	AL	MIN	1982	0-13	
.000	Russ Miller	NL	PHI	1928	0-12	
.000	Steve Gerkin	AL	PHI	1945	0-12	
.048	Jack Nabors	AL	PHI	1916	1-20	
.053	Frank Bates	NL	CLE-STL	1899	1-18	CLE (1-18); STL (0-0)
.059	Art Hagan	NL	PHI-BUF	1883	1-16	PHI (1-14); BUF (0-2)
.059	Tom Sheehan	AL	PHI	1916	1-16	
.059	Mike Parrott	AL	SEA	1980	1-16	
.059	Anthony Young	NL	NY	1993	1-16	
.067	Howie Judson	AL	CHI	1949	1-14	
.067	Kyle Abbott	NL	PHI	1992	1-14	
.067	Adam Bernero	AL-NL	DET-COL	2003	1-14	DET (1-12); COL (0-2)
.071	Fred Corey	NL	WOR	1882	1-13	
.071	Jim McElroy	NL-UA	PHI-WIL	1884	1-13	PHI (1-12); WIL (0-1)
.071	Tony Madigan	NL	WAS	1886	1-13	
.071	Guy Morton	AL	CLE	1914	1-13	
.071	Roy Moore	AL	PHI	1920	1-13	
.071	George Gill	AL	DET-STL	1939	1-13	DET (0-1); STL (1-12)
.071	Troy Herriage	AL	KC	1956	1-13	
.071	Steve Hargan	AL	CLE	1971	1-13	
.071	Pascual Perez	NL	ATL	1985	1-13	
.071	Zane Smith	NL	ATL-MON	1989	1-13	ATL (1-12); MON (0-1)
.077	Tricky Nichols	AA	BAL	1882	1-12	
.077	John McPherson	NL	PHI	1904	1-12	
.077	Walt Leverenz	AL	STL	1914	1-12	
.077	Wally Hebert	AL	STL	1932	1-12	
.077	Jim Walkup	AL	STL	1938	1-12	
.077	Carl Scheib	AL	PHI	1951	1-12	
.077	Bob L. Miller	NL	NY	1962	1-12	
.077	Glendon Rusch	NL	MIL	2003	1-12	

(522) Most Consecutive Scoreless Innings

59.0	Orel Hershiser	NL	LA	Aug 30 to Sep 28, 1988
58.0	Don Drysdale	NL	LA	May 14 to Jun 8, 1968
55.2	Walter Johnson	AL	WAS	Apr 10 to May 14, 1913
53.0	Jack Coombs	AL	PHI	Sep 5 to Sep 25, 1910
47.0	Bob Gibson	NL	STL	Jun 2 to Jun 26, 1968
45.1	Carl Hubbell	NL	NY	Jul 13 to Aug 1, 1933
45.0	Cy Young	AL	BOS	Apr 25 to May 17, 1904
45.0	Doc White	AL	CHI	Sep 12 to Sep 30, 1904
45.0	Sal Maglie	NL	NY	Aug 16 to Sep 3, 1950
44.0	Ed Reulbach	NL	CHI	Sep 17 to Oct 3, 1908
43.2	Rube Waddell	AL	PHI	Aug 22 to Sep 5, 1905
42.0	Rube Foster	AL	BOS	May 1 to May 26, 1914
41.0	Jack Chesbro	NL	PIT	Jun 26 to Jul 16, 1902
41.0	Grover Alexander	NL	PHI	Sep 7 to Sep 24, 1911
41.0	Art Nehf	NL	BOS	Sep 13 to Oct 4, 1917
41.0	Ted Lyons	AL	CHI	Aug 9 to Aug 26, 1926
41.0	Luis Tiant	AL	CLE	Apr 28 to May 17, 1968
40.0	Walter Johnson	AL	WAS	May 7 to May 26, 1918
40.0	Gaylord Perry	NL	SF	Aug 28 to Sep 10, 1967
40.0	Luis Tiant	AL	BOS	Aug 19 to Sep 8, 1972
39.2	Mordecai Brown	NL	CHI	Jun 8 to Jul 8, 1908
39.2	Billy Pierce	AL	CHI	Aug 3 to Aug 19, 1953
39.1	Greg Maddux	NL	ATL	Sep 2 to Sep 28, 2000
39.0	Christy Mathewson	NL	NY	May 3 to May 21, 1901
39.0	Al Orth	AL	NY	Jun 29 to Jul 21, 1905
39.0	Ed Walsh	AL	CHI	Aug 10 to Aug 22, 1906
39.0	Barney Pelty	AL	STL	Jun 6 to Jun 22, 1907
39.0	Don Newcombe	NL	BRO	Jul 25 to Aug 11, 1956
39.0	Ray Culp	AL	BOS	Sep 7 to Sep 25, 1968
39.0	Gaylord Perry	NL	SF	Sep 1 to Sep 23, 1970
39.0	Kenny Rogers	AL	TEX	May 6 to Jun 1, 1995

Partial innings are not included, except when they are relief appearances.

(523) Most Consecutive Wins in a Season

19	Tim Keefe	NL	NY	1888		15	Steve Carlton	NL	PHI	1972
19	Rube Marquard	NL	NY	1912		15	Gaylord Perry	AL	CLE	1974
18	Charley Radbourn	NL	PRO	1884		15	Roger Clemens	AL	TOR	1998
17	Mickey Welch	NL	NY	1885		15	Roy Halladay	AL	TOR	2003
17	Pat Luby	NL	CHI	1890		14	Jim McCormick	UA	CIN	1884
17	Roy Face	NL	PIT	1959		14	John Lynch	AA	NY	1884
16	Jim McCormick	NL	CHI	1886		14	Jim McCormick	NL	CHI	1885
16	Walter Johnson	AL	WAS	1912		14	John Flynn	NL	CHI	1886
16	Joe Wood	AL	BOS	1912		14	Jack Chesbro	AL	NY	1904
16	Lefty Grove	AL	PHI	1931		14	Joe McGinnity	NL	NY	1904
16	Schoolboy Rowe	AL	DET	1934		14	Ed Reulbach	NL	CHI	1909
16	Carl Hubbell	NL	NY	1936		14	Walter Johnson	AL	WAS	1913
16	Ewell Blackwell	NL	CIN	1947		14	Chief Bender	AL	PHI	1914
16	Jack Sanford	NL	SF	1962		14	Lefty Grove	AL	PHI	1928
16	Roger Clemens	AL	NY	2001		14	Whitey Ford	AL	NY	1961
15	Scott Stratton	AA	LOU	1890		14	Steve Stone	AL	BAL	1980
15	Dazzy Vance	NL	BRO	1924		14	Rick Sutcliffe	NL	CHI	1984
15	Alvin Crowder	AL	WAS	1932		14	Dwight Gooden	NL	NY	1985
15	Johnny Allen	AL	CLE	1937		14	Roger Clemens	AL	BOS	1986
15	Bob Gibson	NL	STL	1968		14	John Smoltz	NL	ATL	1996
15	Dave McNally	AL	BAL	1969						

(524) Pitchers who Completed all Their Starts in a Season, before 1893 (min. 40 starts)

75	Will White	NL	CIN	1879		50	Jim Whitney	NL	BOS	1885
73	Charley Radbourn	NL	PRO	1884		50	Jack Lynch	AA	NY	1886
68	Tim Keefe	AA	NY	1883		49	Tony Mullane	AA	STL	1883
64	Mickey Welch	NL	TRO	1880		49	Charley Radbourn	NL	PRO	1885
64	Will White	AA	CIN	1883		48	Henry Porter	AA	BRO	1886
63	Ed Morris	AA	PIT	1885		47	Mickey Welch	NL	NY	1888
63	Ed Morris	AA	PIT	1886		47	Kid Nichols	NL	BOS	1890
61	Jim Devlin	NL	LOU	1877		46	Dave Foutz	AA	STL	1885
59	Billy Taylor	AA-UA	STL-PHI	1884		46	Hank O'Day	NL	WAS	1888
			STL (29); PHI (30)			45	Tommy Bond	NL	HAR	1876
58	Tommy Bond	NL	BOS	1877		45	Tim Keefe	NL	TRO	1881
57	Ed Seward	AA	PHI	1888		45	Fred Goldsmith	NL	CHI	1882
56	Terry Larkin	NL	CHI	1878		45	Charlie Ferguson	NL	PHI	1885
55	George Derby	NL	DET	1881		45	Billy Crowell	AA	CLE	1887
55	Mickey Welch	NL	NY	1885		45	Billy Rhines	NL	CIN	1890
53	Jack Lynch	AA	NY	1884		43	Jack Lynch	AA	NY	1885
53	Bob Caruthers	AA	STL	1885		42	Lee Viau	AA	CIN	1888
52	Will White	NL	CIN	1878		41	Sam Weaver	AA	PHI	1882
52	Will White	AA	CIN	1884		41	Sam Kimber	AA	BRO	1884
52	Ed Seward	AA	PHI	1887		41	Bill Stemmeyer	NL	BOS	1886
51	Fleury Sullivan	AA	PIT	1884		40	Mickey Welch	NL	TRO	1881
51	Gus Weyhing	AA	PHI	1891		40	Mickey Hughes	AA	BRO	1888
50	Bob Emslie	AA	BAL	1884						

(525) Pitchers who Completed all Their Starts in a Season, since 1893 (min. 20 starts)

39	Jack W. Taylor	NL	STL	1904		31	Addie Joss	AL	CLE	1903
37	Bill Dinneen	AL	BOS	1904		28	Roy Evans	NL	NY-BRO	1902
35	Kid Nichols	NL	STL	1904					NY (17); BRO (11)	
34	Bill Donovan	AL	DET	1903		28	Frank Kitson	AL	DET	1903
34	Noodles Hahn	NL	CIN	1903		28	Patsy Flaherty	NL	PIT	1904
34	Jack W. Taylor	NL	STL	1905		27	Earl Moore	AL	CLE	1903
33	George Hemming	NL	LOU	1893		24	Mike Lynch	NL	PIT	1904
33	George Hemming	NL	LOU	1894		21	Jack Dunn	NL	BRO	1897
33	Red Donahue	NL	PHI	1901		21	Win Mercer	NL	WAS	1899
33	Jack W. Taylor	NL	CHI	1902		20	Ted Lyons	AL	CHI	1942
33	Jack W. Taylor	NL	CHI	1903						

(526) Teams with Four 20-Game Winners

1920	AL	CHI	Red Faber	23-13	Lefty Williams	22-14	Dickie Kerr	21-9	Eddie Cicotte	21-10
1971	AL	BAL	Dave McNally	21-5	Pat Dobson	20-8	Jim Palmer	20-9	Mike Cuellar	20-9

Hippo Vaughn

(527) Teams with Three 20-Game Winners, before 1893

1884	UA	CIN	George Bradley	25-15	Dick Burns	23-15	Jim McCormick	21-3
1886	NL	CHI	John Clarkson	36-17	Jim McCormick	31-11	John Flynn	23-6
1887	NL	PHI	Dan Casey	28-13	Charlie Ferguson	22-10	Charlie Buffinton	21-17
1887	AA	STL	Silver King	32-12	Bob Caruthers	29-9	Dave Foutz	25-12
1888	AA	CIN	Lee Viau	27-14	Tony Mullane	26-16	Elmer Smith	22-17
1890	NL	BRO	Tom Lovett	30-11	Adonis Terry	26-16	Bob Caruthers	23-11
1890	NL	BOS	Kid Nichols	27-19	John Clarkson	26-18	Charlie Getzein	23-17
1891	NL	BOS	John Clarkson	33-19	Kid Nichols	30-17	Harry Staley	20-8
1892	NL	BOS	Jack Stivetts	35-16	Kid Nichols	35-16	Harry Staley	22-10

(528) Teams with Three 20-Game Winners, since 1893

1897	NL	BOS	Kid Nichols	31-11	Fred Klobedanz	26-7	Ed Lewis	21-12
1897	NL	BAL	Joe Corbett	24-8	Bill Hoffer	22-11	Jerry Nops	20-6
1897	NL	NY	Amos Rusie	28-10	Jouett Meekin	20-11	Cy Seymour	20-14
1898	NL	BOS	Kid Nichols	31-12	Ed Lewis	26-8	Vic Willis	25-13
1898	NL	BAL	Doc McJames	27-15	Jay Hughes	23-12	Al Maul	20-7
1899	NL	BRO	Jay Hughes	28-6	Jack Dunn	23-13	Brickyard Kennedy	22-9
1899	NL	PHI	Wiley Platt	23-15	Frank Donahue	21-8	Chick Fraser	21-12
1902	NL	PIT	Jack Chesbro	28-6	Jesse Tannehill	20-6	Deacon Phillippe	20-9
1903	AL	BOS	Cy Young	28-9	Bill Dinneen	21-13	Tom J. Hughes	20-7
1903	NL	CHI	Jack W. Taylor	21-14	Jake Weimer	20-8	Bob Wicker	20-9
1904	AL	BOS	Cy Young	26-16	Bill Dinneen	23-14	Jesse Tannehill	21-11
1904	NL	NY	Joe McGinnity	35-8	Christy Mathewson	33-12	Dummy Taylor	21-15
1905	NL	NY	Christy Mathewson	31-9	Red Ames	22-8	Joe McGinnity	21-15
1906	AL	CLE	Bob Rhoads	22-10	Addie Joss	21-9	Otto Hess	20-17
1907	AL	DET	Bill Donovan	25-4	Ed Killian	25-13	George Mullin	20-20
1907	AL	CHI	Doc White	27-13	Ed Walsh	24-18	Frank E. Smith	22-11
1912	AL	BOS	Joe Wood	34-5	Hugh Bedient	20-9	Tom O'Brien	20-13
1913	NL	NY	Christy Mathewson	25-11	Rube Marquard	23-10	Jeff Tesreau	22-13
1914	FL	STL	Dave Davenport	22-18	Eddie Plank	21-11	Doc Crandall	21-15
1920	AL	CLE	Jim Bagby Sr.	31-12	Stan Coveleski	24-14	Ray Caldwell	20-10
1920	NL	NY	Fred Toney	21-11	Art Nehf	21-12	Jesse Barnes	20-15
1923	NL	CIN	Dolf Luque	27-8	Pete Donohue	21-15	Eppa Rixey	20-15
1931	AL	PHI	Lefty Grove	31-4	George Earnshaw	21-7	Rube Walberg	20-12
1951	AL	CLE	Bob Feller	22-8	Mike Garcia	20-13	Early Wynn	20-13
1952	AL	CLE	Early Wynn	23-12	Mike Garcia	22-11	Bob Lemon	22-11
1956	AL	CLE	Herb Score	20-9	Early Wynn	20-9	Bob Lemon	20-9
1970	AL	BAL	Mike Cuellar	24-8	Dave McNally	24-9	Jim Palmer	20-10
1973	AL	OAK	Catfish Hunter	21-5	Ken Holtzman	21-13	Vida Blue	20-9

(529) Most Wins in a Season by a Right-handed and Left-handed Pitcher Duo (min. 15 wins each)

TOTAL WINS				RIGHT-HANDED PITCHER	WINS	LEFT-HANDED PITCHER	WINS
72	1886	NL	DET	Charlie Getzein	30	Lady Baldwin	42
70	1886	AA	PIT	Jim Galvin	29	Ed Morris	41
65	1887	AA	CIN	Tony Mullane	31	Elmer Smith	34
64	1886	AA	LOU	Guy Hecker	26	Toad Ramsey	38
60	1908	NL	NY	Christy Mathewson	37	Hooks Wiltse	23
58	1908	AL	CHI	Ed Walsh	40	Doc White	18
57	1884	AA	COL	Frank Mountain	23	Ed Morris	34
57	1897	NL	BOS	Kid Nichols	31	Fred Klobedanz	26
56	1944	AL	DET	Dizzy Trout	27	Hal Newhouser	29
55	1887	AA	LOU	Elton Chamberlain	18	Toad Ramsey	37
55	1887	AA	LOU	Guy Hecker	18	Toad Ramsey	37
55	1916	NL	PHI	Grover Alexander	33	Eppa Rixey	22
54	1886	NL	PHI	Charlie Ferguson	30	Dan Casey	24
54	1893	NL	PIT	Red Ehret	18	Frank Killen	36
53	1913	AL	WAS	Walter Johnson	36	Joe Boehling	17
52	1888	NL	PIT	Jim Galvin	23	Ed Morris	29
52	1891	AA	STL	Jack Stivetts	33	Willie McGill	19
52	1896	NL	PIT	Pink Hawley	22	Frank Killen	30
52	1919	AL	CHI	Eddie Cicotte	29	Lefty Williams	23
52	1931	AL	PHI	George Earnshaw	21	Lefty Grove	31
51	1885	NL	PRO	Charley Radbourn	28	Dupee Shaw	23
51	1890	AA	STL	Jack Stivetts	27	Toad Ramsey	24
51	1907	AL	CHI	Ed Walsh	24	Doc White	27
51	1911	AL	PHI	Jack Coombs	28	Eddie Plank	23
50	1887	NL	PHI	Charlie Ferguson	22	Dan Casey	28
50	1888	AA	PHI	Ed Seward	35	Mike Mattimore	15
50	1898	NL	BOS	Kid Nichols	31	Fred Klobedanz	19
50	1907	AL	DET	Bill Donovan	25	Ed Killian	25
50	1907	AL	CHI	Frank E. Smith	23	Doc White	27
50	1911	NL	NY	Christy Mathewson	26	Rube Marquard	24
50	1930	AL	PHI	George Earnshaw	22	Lefty Grove	28

(530) Most Seasons with 20 Wins, 200 Strikeouts, and an ERA below 3.00

7	Walter Johnson	1910-16	3	Jim McCormick	1880, 1882, 1884
6	Juan Marichal	1963-66, 68-69	3	Charley Radbourn	1882-84
5	Tim Keefe	1883-86, 1888	3	Ed Morris	1884-86
5	Christy Mathewson	1901, 03-05, 08	3	Mickey Welch	1884-86
5	Roger Clemens	1986-87, 90, 97-98	3	Gus Weyhing	1888-89, 1892
4	John Clarkson	1885-86, 1888-89	3	Bill Hutchison	1890-92
4	Rube Waddell	1902-05	3	Amos Rusie	1890-92
4	Ed Walsh	1907-08, 11-12	3	Bob Feller	1939-40, 46
4	Grover Alexander	1911, 14-15, 17	3	Sandy Koufax	1963, 65-66
4	Ferguson Jenkins	1967-68, 71, 74	3	Bob Gibson	1966, 68-69
4	Tom Seaver	1969, 71-72, 75	3	Gaylord Perry	1966, 72, 74
3	Larry Corcoran	1880, 1883-84	3	Randy Johnson	1997, 2001-2

(531) Pitchers with Shutouts in Their First Two or More Starts

				OPP.	DATE	OPP.	DATE	OPP.	DATE	
George McQuillan	NL	PHI	1907	STL	Sep 22 (2G)	CHI	Sep 25 (2G)	CIN	Sep 29 (1G)	Pitched 1 scoreless inning in relief on May 8
Jay Hughes	NL	BAL	1898	WAS	Apr 18	BOS	Apr 22			Apr 18 was ML debut; Apr 22 a no-hitter
Joe Doyle	AL	NY	1906	CLE	Aug 25 (1G)	WAS	Aug 30 (1G)			Aug 25 was ML debut
Buck O'Brien	AL	BOS	1911	PHI	Sep 9	CLE	Sep 16 (2G)			Pitched 1.2 scoreless inning in relief on Sep 12; Sep 9 was ML debut
George Dumont	AL	WAS	1915	CLE	Sep 14	STL	Sep 20			Allowed runs in relief on Sep 17; Sep 14 was ML debut
Johnny Marcum	AL	PHI	1933	CLE	Sep 7	CHI	Sep 11 (2G)			Sep 7 was ML debut
Bill C. Lee	NL	CHI	1934	PHI	May 7	BRO	May 12			Allowed 2 runs in 2 previous relief appearances
Hal White	AL	DET	1942	STL	Apr 18	CHI	Apr 23			Allowed 6 runs in 4 relief appearances in 1941
Dave Ferriss	AL	BOS	1945	PHI	Apr 29 (1G)	NY	May 6 (1G)			Apr 29 was ML debut
Fred Sanford	AL	STL	1946	NY	Sep 15 (1G)	CHI	Sep 22 (1G)			Allowed 2 runs in 3 relief appearances in 1943
Al Worthington	NL	NY	1953	PHI	Jul 6	BRO	Jul 11			Jul 6 was ML debut
Karl Spooner	NL	BRO	1954	NY	Sep 22	PIT	Sep 26			Sep 22 was ML debut
Tom Phoebus	AL	BAL	1966	CAL	Sep 15 (1G)	KC	Sep 20			Sep 15 was ML debut
John Hiller	AL	DET	1967	CLE	Aug 20 (2G)	KC	Aug 25			Allowed 8 runs in 17 relief appearances in 1965-67

(532) Two Relief Wins in One Day

		OPP.	
Rube Waddell	AL	PHI	BAL	Sep 10, 1902
Hub Perdue	NL	STL	NY	Aug 23, 1915
Dickie Kerr	AL	CHI	NY	Jul 21, 1919
Ted Lyons	AL	CHI	CLE	Oct 6, 1923
Guy Bush	NL	CHI	CIN	Jul 4, 1927
Bill Harris	NL	PIT	NY	Jul 27, 1932
Johnny Murphy	AL	NY	WAS	Sep 24, 1940
Howie Krist	NL	STL	CHI	Jun 27, 1943
Harry Brecheen	NL	STL	BOS	Sep 21, 1944
Joe Berry	AL	PHI	CLE	Oct 1, 1944
Tom Ferrick	AL	STL	PHI	Aug 4, 1946
Al Brazle	NL	STL	CIN	Sep 2, 1946
Bill Voiselle	NL	BOS	CHI	Jun 17, 1948
Gerry Staley	NL	STL	CHI	Jul 5, 1948
Jim Hearn	NL	STL	NY	Aug 28, 1948
Gerry Staley	NL	STL	PIT	May 30, 1950
Emil "Dutch" Leonard	NL	CHI	BOS	May 20, 1951
Clyde King	NL	BRO	STL	Aug 22, 1951
Hershell Freeman	NL	CIN	NY	Jul 15, 1956
Tom Acker	NL	CIN	PIT	May 19, 1957
Ed Roebuck	NL	BRO	CHI	Jul 31, 1957
Ernie Broglio	NL	STL	MIL	Jul 1, 1960
Gerry Staley	AL	CHI	WAS	Aug 7, 1960
Jim Coates	AL	NY	DET	May 14, 1961
Craig Anderson	NL	NY	MIL	May 12, 1962
Wes Stock	AL	BAL	CLE	May 26, 1963
Jack Baldschun	NL	PHI	STL	Apr 14, 1963
John Wyatt	AL	KC	MIN	May 3, 1964
Chi Chi Olivo	NL	MIL	NY	Jul 26, 1964
Willard Hunter	NL	NY	CHI	Aug 23, 1964
Don McMahon	AL	BOS	NY	Jul 6, 1966
Phil Regan	NL	LA	NY	Apr 21, 1968
Phil Regan	NL	CHI	PIT	Jul 7, 1968
Jim Brewer	NL	LA	CIN	Sep 16, 1969
Bob L. Miller	NL	SD	HOU	Jun 23, 1971
John Hiller	AL	DET	MIL	Jun 1, 1976
Joe Kerrigan	NL	MON	STL	Sep 8, 1976
Ken Forsch	NL	HOU	MON	Jul 14, 1978
Kent Tekulve	NL	PIT	PHI	Sep 29, 1978
Jeff Reardon	NL	MON	HOU	Aug 26, 1982
Jesse Orosco	NL	NY	PIT	Jul 31, 1983
Frank Williams	NL	SF	NY	Aug 24, 1984
David Wells	AL	TOR	CAL	Jul 17, 1989
Cory Bailey	AL	KC	TEX	May 26, 2002
Terry Adams	NL	PHI	CIN	Sep 21, 2002

(533) Extra-inning One-hitters

				INN.	BATTER	OPP.	
Toad Ramsey	AA	LOU	Jul 31, 1886	12	Chris Fulmer	BAL	Double in 6th
Doc White	AL	CHI	Sep 9, 1903	10	Bill Bradley	CLE	Double in 9th
Orval Overall	NL	CIN	Jul 17, 1905	10	Red Dooin	PHI	Single in 6th
Jack Pfiester	NL	CHI	Sep 25, 1906	10	Bill Bergen	BRO	Single in 8th
Frank Corridon	NL	STL	May 7, 1907	10	Frank Burke	BOS	Single in 4th
Red Ames	NL	STL	Sep 19, 1915	10	Possum Whitted	PHI	Single in 8th
Bobo Newsom	AL	STL	Sep 18, 1934	10	Roy Johnson	BOS	Single in 10th
Harvey Haddix	NL	PIT	May 26, 1959	12.1	Joe Adcock	MIL	Single in 13th
Bob Veale	NL	PIT	Sep 19, 1965	10	Tony Taylor	PHI	Single in 6th
Randy Jones	NL	SD	May 19, 1975	10	Luis Melendez	STL	Single in 7th
Bert Blyleven	AL	TEX	Jun 21, 1976	10	Ken McMullen	OAK	Single in 5th
Terry Leach	NL	NY	Oct 1, 1982	10	Luis Aguayo	PHI	Triple in 5th

(534) Most Walks Allowed by a Pitcher in a Game, before 1893

16	Bill George	NL	NY	May 30, 1887	1G
16	George Van Haltren	NL	CHI	Jun 27, 1887	
16	Henry Gruber	PL	CLE	Apr 19, 1890	
14	Ed Crane	NL	WAS	Sep 1, 1886	
13	Bill George	NL	NY	May 17, 1887	
13	John Kirby	NL	IND	Jun 9, 1887	
13	Jesse Burkett	NL	NY	Sep 23, 1890	2G

(535) Most Walks Allowed by a Pitcher in a Game, since 1893

16	Bruno Haas	AL	PHI	Jun 23, 1915	
16	Tommy Byrne	AL	STL	Aug 22, 1951	13 inn.
15	Carroll Brown	AL	PHI	Jul 12, 1913	7.2 inn.
14	Charlie Hickman	NL	BOS	Aug 16, 1899	2G
14	Henry Mathewson	NL	NY	Oct 5, 1906	
14	Skipper Friday	AL	WAS	Jun 17, 1923	11 inn.
13	Cy Seymour	NL	NY	May 24, 1899	10 inn.
13	Mal Eason	NL	BOS	Sep 3, 1902	
13	Pete Schneider	NL	CIN	Jul 6, 1918	
13	George Turbeville	AL	PHI	Aug 24, 1935	15 inn.
13	Tommy Byrne	AL	NY	Jun 8, 1949	11 inn.
13	Dick Weik	AL	WAS	Sep 1, 1949	
13	Bud Podbielan	NL	CIN	May 18, 1953	10 inn.

(536) Most Strikeouts in a Nine-inning Game

20	Roger Clemens	AL	BOS	Apr 29, 1986	
20	Roger Clemens	AL	BOS	Sep 18, 1996	
20	Kerry Wood	NL	CHI	May 6, 1998	
19	Charlie Sweeney	NL	PRO	Jun 7, 1884	
19	Hugh Daily	UA	CHI	Jul 7, 1884	
19	Steve Carlton	NL	STL	Sep 15, 1969	
19	Tom Seaver	NL	NY	Apr 22, 1970	
19	Nolan Ryan	AL	CAL	Aug 12, 1974	
19	David Cone	NL	NY	Oct 6, 1991	
19	Randy Johnson	AL	SEA	Jun 24, 1997	
19	Randy Johnson	AL	SEA	Aug 8, 1997	
18	Dupee Shaw	UA	BOS	Jul 19, 1884	
18	Henry Porter	UA	Mil	Oct 3, 1884	
18	Bob Feller	AL	CLE	Oct 2, 1938	1G
18	Sandy Koufax	NL	LA	Aug 31, 1959	
18	Sandy Koufax	NL	LA	Apr 24, 1962	
18	Don Wilson	NL	HOU	Jul 14, 1968	
18	Nolan Ryan	AL	CAL	Sep 10, 1976	
18	Ron Guidry	AL	NY	Jun 17, 1978	
18	Bill Gullickson	NL	MON	Sep 10, 1980	
18	Ramon J. Martinez	NL	LA	Jun 4, 1990	
18	Randy Johnson	AL	SEA	Sep 27, 1992	
18	Roger Clemens	AL	TOR	Aug 25, 1998	
18	Ben Sheets	NL	MIL	May 16, 2004	

(537) Most Strikeouts in an Extra-inning Game

21	Tom Cheney	AL	WAS	Sep 12, 1962	16 inn.	
20	Randy Johnson	NL	ARI	May 8, 2001	11 inn.	Johnson pitched first 9 inn.
19	Luis Tiant	AL	CLE	Jul 3, 1968	10 inn.	
19	Nolan Ryan	AL	CAL	Jun 14, 1974	15 inn.	Ryan pitched first 13 inn.
19	Nolan Ryan	AL	CAL	Aug 20, 1974	11 inn.	
19	Nolan Ryan	AL	CAL	Jun 8, 1977	13 inn.	Ryan pitched first 10 inn.
18	Jim Whitney	NL	BOS	Jun 14, 1884	15 inn.	
18	Jack Coombs	AL	PHI	Sep 1, 1906	24 inn.	
18	Jack Coombs	AL	PHI	Aug 4, 1910	16 inn.	
18	Warren Spahn	NL	BOS	Jun 14, 1952	15 inn.	
18	Jim Maloney	NL	CIN	Jun 14, 1965	11 inn.	
18	Chris Short	NL	PHI	Oct 2, 1965	18 inn.	Short pitched first 15 inn.

(538) Most Consecutive Strikeouts

					OPP.	
10	Tom Seaver	NL	NY	Apr 22, 1970	SD	Last 10 batters, 19 overall
9	Mickey Welch	NL	NY	Aug 28, 1884	PIT	First 9 batters
8	Charlie Buffinton	NL	BOS	Sep 2, 1884	CLE	17 overall
8	Ed Cushman	AA	NY	Sep 16, 1885	PIT	
8	Max Surkont	NL	MIL	May 25, 1953	CIN	2G
8	Johnny Podres	NL	LA	Jul 2, 1962	PHI	1G
8	Jim Maloney	NL	CIN	May 21, 1963	MIL	16 overall
8	Don Wilson	NL	HOU	Jul 14, 1968	CIN	2G; First 9 batters (one walk); 18 overall
8	Nolan Ryan	AL	CAL	Jul 9, 1972	BOS	One hitter
8	Nolan Ryan	AL	CAL	Jul 15, 1973	DET	No hitter; 17 overall
8	Ron Davis	AL	NY	May 4, 1981	CAL	Last 8 batters; relief pitcher record
8	Roger Clemens	AL	BOS	Apr 29, 1986	SEA	20 overall
8	Jim Deshaies	NL	HOU	Sep 23, 1986	LA	First 8 batters; a post-1893 record
8	Blake Stein	AL	KC	Jun 17, 2001	MIL	11 K in 5.2 IP
7	John Clarkson	NL	CHI	Sep 30, 1884	NY	
7	Jack Stivetts	AA	STL	May 3, 1890	LOU	
7	Hooks Wiltse	NL	NY	May 15, 1906	CIN	
7	Dazzy Vance	NL	BRO	Aug 1, 1924	CHI	14 overall
7	Van Mungo	NL	BRO	Jun 25, 1936	CIN	1G
7	Ryne Duren	AL	LA	Jun 9, 1961	BOS	11 overall
7	Juan Marichal	NL	SF	Sep 6, 1964	PHI	13 overall
7	Denny McLain	AL	DET	Jun 15, 1965	BOS	First inn. reliever; first 7 batters; 14 overall in 6 2/3
7	Pete Richert	AL	WAS	Apr 24, 1966	DET	1G
7	Phil Ortega	AL	WAS	May 29, 1966	BOS	
7	Jim Merritt	AL	MIN	Jul 21, 1966	WAS	
7	John Hiller	AL	DET	Oct 1, 1970	CLE	
7	Steve Renko	NL	MON	Oct 3, 1972	NY	
7	Al Downing	NL	LA	Jul 14, 1973	CHI	
7	Sammy Stewart	AL	BAL	Sep 1, 1978	CLE	Major League debut
7	Mark Langston	AL	SEA	Jun 15, 1984	BOS	
7	Joe Cowley	AL	CHI	May 28, 1986	TEX	First 7 batters in 2nd Major League start
7	Jamie Moyer	NL	CHI	Jul 3, 1987	SF	
7	Sid Fernandez	NL	NY	July 20, 1990	ATL	
7	Nolan Ryan	AL	TEX	Jul 7, 1991	CAL	
7	Roger Clemens	AL	BOS	Sep 7, 1992	TEX	
7	Curt Schilling	NL	PHI	Aug 26, 1996	SF	
7	Pedro Martinez	NL	MON	Aug 20, 1997	STL	
7	Kerry Wood	NL	CHI	May 6, 1998	HOU	20 overall; Shane Reynolds (HOU) had 10 K for combined record
7	Jesus Sanchez	NL	FLA	Sep 13, 1998	ATL	
7	Randy Johnson	NL	ARI	May 8, 2001	CIN	11 Inn.; 20 K in first 9 inn.
7	Randy Johnson	NL	ARI	Jul 4, 2001	HOU	13 overall in 6 IP
7	Randy Johnson	NL	ARI	Jul 18, 2001	SD	16 K in 7 inn. to break Walter Johnson's relief record
7	Mark Prior	NL	CHI	Aug 15, 2002	HOU	12 overall in 6 IP

(539) Most At-bats Allowed by One Pitcher in a Nine-inning Game

					OPP.	
64	Jack Wadsworth	NL	LOU	Aug 17, 1894	PHI	Wadsworth pitched 9 inn.; allowed 30 H, 3 BB, 29 R
53	Roy Patterson	AL	CHI	May 5, 1901	MIL	Patterson pitched 9 inn. in losing 21-7
49	Bill C. Phillips	NL	CIN	Jun 24, 1901	PHI	Phillips pitched only 8 inn.
48	Doc Parker	NL	CIN	Jun 21, 1901	BRO	Parker's last ML game; pitched only 8 inn.
47	Hod Lisenbee	AL	PHI	Sep 11, 1936	CHI	Lisenbee pitched only 8 inn.

(540) Most At-bats Allowed by One Pitcher in an Extra-inning Game

					OPP.	
86	Leon Cadore	NL	BRO	May 1, 1920	BOS	26 inn.; game ended in 1-1 tie; longest game in history
85	Joe Oeschger	NL	BOS	May 1, 1920	BRO	26 inn.; game ended in 1-1 tie; longest game in history
82	Joe Harris	AL	BOS	Sep 1, 1906	PHI	24 inn.; Harris tossed a complete game, losing 4-1
79	Jack Coombs	AL	PHI	Sep 1, 1906	BOS	24 inn.; Coombs tossed a complete-game victory, 4-1
78	Ted Lyons	AL	CHI	May 24, 1929	DET	21 inn.; Lyons pitched 21 inn. and lost 1-0 in Chicago
76	Eddie Rommel	AL	PHI	Jul 10, 1932	CLE	18 inn.; Rommel pitched 17 inn. in relief and won, 18-17
76	Lefty Tyler	NL	CHI	Jul 17, 1918	PHI	21 inn.; Tyler went distance and won, 2-1
75	Milt Watson	NL	PHI	Jul 17, 1918	CHI	21 inn.; Watson went distance and lost, 2-1
75	Burleigh Grimes	NL	BRO	Apr 30, 1919	PHI	20 inn.; tied 6-6, each team scored 3 in 19th; darkness ended 9-9 tie
75	Joe Oeschger	NL	PHI	Apr 30, 1919	BRO	20 inn.; tied 6-6, each team scored 3 in 19th; darkness ended 9-9 tie

Carl Hubbell

(541) Most Batters Faced by One Pitcher in a Nine-inning Game

					OPP.	
67	Jack Wadsworth	NL	LOU	Aug 17, 1894	LOU	Wadsworth pitched 9 inn., lost 29-4
57	Roy Patterson	AL	CHI	May 5, 1901	MIL	Patterson pitched 9 inn., lost 21-7
55	Bill C. Phillips	NL	CIN	Jun 24, 1901	PHI	Phillips pitched only 8 inn.; lost 19-1
53	Bruno Haas	AL	PHI	Jun 23, 1915	NY	Haas pitched a 9-inn. complete game; lost 15-7
52	Doc Parker	NL	CIN	Jun 21, 1901	BRO	Parker's last ML game; pitched only 8 inn.; lost 21-3
52	Al Travers	AL	DET	May 18, 1912	PHI	Travers pitched only 8 inn.; lost 24-2
51	Elton Chamberlain	NL	CIN	May 30, 1894	BOS	(2G); Chamberlain pitched only 8 inn.; lost 20-11
51	Hod Lisenbee	AL	PHI	Sep 11, 1936	CHI	Lisenbee pitched only 8 inn.; lost 17-2

(542) Most Batters Faced by One Pitcher in an Extra-inning Game

					OPP.	
96	Leon Cadore	NL	BRO	May 1, 1920	BOS	26 inn.; game ended in 1-1 tie; longest game in history
90	Joe Oeschger	NL	BOS	May 1, 1920	BRO	26 inn.; game ended in 1-1 tie; longest game in history
89	Jack Coombs	AL	PHI	Sep 1, 1906	BOS	24 inn.; Coombs tossed a complete-game victory, 4-1
89	Bob Smith	NL	BOS	May 17, 1927	CHI	22 inn.; Smith pitched 22 inn. and lost 4-3 in Boston
87	Joe Harris	AL	BOS	Sep 1, 1906	PHI	24 inn.; Harris tossed a complete game, losing 4-1
87	Eddie Rommel	AL	PHI	Jul 10, 1932	CLE	18 inn.; Rommel pitched 17 inn. in relief and won, 18-17
86	Joe Oeschger	NL	PHI	Apr 30, 1919	BRO	20 inn.; tied 6-6, each team scored 3 in 19th; darkness ended 9-9 tie
85	Ted Lyons	AL	CHI	May 24, 1929	DET	21 inn.; Lyons pitched 21 inn. and lost 1-0 in Chicago
83	Burleigh Grimes	NL	BRO	Apr 30, 1919	PHI	20 inn.; tied 6-6, each team scored 3 in 19th; darkness ended 9-9 tie

(543) Perfect Games Broken up with Two Outs in the Ninth Inning

				BATTER	OPP.	
Hooks Wiltse	NL	NY	Jul 4, 1908	George McQuillan	PHI	1G; HBP
Tommy Bridges	AL	DET	Aug 5, 1932	Dave Harris	WAS	Single
Billy Pierce	AL	CHI	Jun 27, 1958	Ed Fitzgerald	WAS	Double
Milt Pappas	NL	CHI	Sep 2, 1972	Larry Stahl	SD	Walk
Milt Wilcox	AL	DET	Apr 15, 1983	Jerry Hairston Sr.	CHI	Single
Ron Robinson	NL	CIN	May 2, 1988	Wallace Johnson	MON	Single
Dave Stieb	AL	TOR	Aug 4, 1989	Roberto Kelly	NY	Double
Brian Holman	AL	SEA	Apr 20, 1990	Ken Phelps	OAK	Home run
Mike Mussina	AL	NY	Sep 2, 2001	Carl Everett	BOS	Single

(544) Opposing One-Hitters

	WINNER		LOSER				
AA	Matt Kilroy	BAL	Joe Miller	PHI	Aug 20, 1886	1-0	
NL	Mordecai Brown	CHI	Lefty Leifield	PIT	Jul 4, 1906	1-0	1G
AL	Bob Cain	STL	Bob Feller	CLE	Apr 23, 1952	1-0	
AL	Jack Harshman	CHI	Connie Johnson	BAL	Jun 21, 1956	1-0	Johnson 7 IP; George Zuverink 1 IP
AL	Frank Bertaina	BAL	Bob Meyer	KC	Sep 12, 1964	1-0	

FIELDING RECORDS

Fielding Records

(545) Most Career Games by a First Baseman

2413	Eddie Murray	2045	Willie McCovey	1778	Tony Perez
2380	Jake Beckley	2014	Keith Hernandez	1773	George Scott
2239	Fred McGriff	2002	Jake Daubert	1763	Mark McGwire
2237	Mickey Vernon	1995	Stuffy McInnis	1759	Roger Connor
2162	Mark Grace	1971	George Sisler	1698	Eric Karros
2139	Rafael Palmeiro	1962	Chris Chambliss	1683	Orlando Cepeda
2137	Lou Gehrig	1943	Norm Cash	1671	George H. Burns
2131	Charlie Grimm	1919	Jimmie Foxx	1670	Tommy Tucker
2111	Jeff Bagwell	1913	Wally Joyner	1667	Johnny Mize
2106	Andres Galarraga	1908	Gil Hodges	1656	J.T. Snow
2084	Joe Judge	1889	Will Clark	1634	Don Mattingly
2073	Ed Konetchy	1885	Jim Bottomley	1633	Dan Brouthers
2059	Steve Garvey	1869	Tino Martinez	1628	Harry Davis
2059	Cap Anson	1819	Wally Pipp	1609	Kent Hrbek
2057	Joe Kuhel	1815	Hal Chase		
2053	John Olerud	1810	Fred Tenney		

(546) Most Career Assists by a First Baseman

1865	Eddie Murray	1301	Joe Judge	1087	Lou Gehrig
1704	Jeff Bagwell	1294	Will Clark	1078	Vic Power
1682	Keith Hernandez	1292	Ed Konetchy	1074	George McQuinn
1665	Mark Grace	1281	Gil Hodges	1064	Pete O'Brien
1587	Rafael Palmeiro	1238	Stuffy McInnis	1049	Kent Hrbek
1529	George Sisler	1222	Jimmie Foxx	1049	Hal Chase
1470	Wally Joyner	1222	Willie McCovey	1042	Mark McGwire
1448	Mickey Vernon	1214	Charlie Grimm	1032	Johnny Mize
1447	Fred McGriff	1163	Joe Kuhel	1026	Steve Garvey
1418	John Olerud	1159	Tino Martinez	1022	Mike Hargrove
1376	Andres Galarraga	1152	Wally Pipp	1016	Lu Blue
1363	Fred Tenney	1148	Todd Helton	1016	J.T. Snow
1359	Eric Karros	1132	George Scott	1012	Orlando Cepeda
1351	Bill Buckner	1128	Jake Daubert	1001	Frank McCormick
1351	Chris Chambliss	1108	Bill Terry	1000	Cecil Cooper
1317	Norm Cash	1104	Don Mattingly		
1316	Jake Beckley	1094	George H. Burns		

(547) Most Career Putouts by a First Baseman

23731	Jake Beckley	18337	Jim Bottomley	16081	Wally Joyner
21361	Ed Konetchy	18244	Andres Galarraga	15972	Bill Terry
21255	Eddie Murray	18185	Hal Chase	15666	Harry Davis
20798	Cap Anson	17909	Keith Hernandez	15644	Lu Blue
20711	Charlie Grimm	17903	Fred Tenney	15419	Fred Merkle
19962	Stuffy McInnis	17771	Chris Chambliss	15405	George Scott
19808	Mickey Vernon	17738	Rafael Palmeiro	15344	Gil Hodges
19634	Jake Daubert	17612	Roger Connor	15157	Norm Cash
19510	Lou Gehrig	17545	Jeff Bagwell	15001	Tino Martinez
19386	Joe Kuhel	17207	Jimmie Foxx	14850	Johnny Mize
19264	Joe Judge	17170	Willie McCovey	14481	Tony Perez
18985	Fred McGriff	16892	George H. Burns	14459	Orlando Cepeda
18844	Steve Garvey	16695	Will Clark	14451	Mark McGwire
18837	George Sisler	16401	Tommy Tucker	14232	George Kelly
18779	Wally Pipp	16365	Dan Brouthers	14148	Don Mattingly
18503	Mark Grace	16165	John Olerud	14056	Eric Karros

Nellie Fox

(548) Most Career Errors by a First Baseman

583	Cap Anson	252	Fred Merkle	181	Jake Daubert
512	Dan Brouthers	245	George H. Burns	180	Dick Hoblitzel
481	Jake Beckley	236	Kitty Bransfield	176	Andres Galarraga
419	Roger Connor	233	Willie McCovey	173	Joe Kuhel
403	Charlie Comiskey	227	Dave Orr	169	Dick Stuart
402	Hal Chase	224	Ed Konetchy	168	Dan McGann
393	Tommy Tucker	223	Jim Bottomley	168	Wally Pipp
343	Harry Davis	211	Mickey Vernon	167	Fred McGriff
327	Fred Tenney	209	Henry Larkin	167	Eddie Murray
324	Bill B. Phillips	208	Jack Fournier	165	George Scott
316	John Reilly	207	Candy LaChance	162	Orlando Cepeda
294	Joe Start	201	Fred Luderus	162	Charlie Grimm
285	John Morrill	194	George Stovall	160	Stuffy McInnis
277	Jack Doyle	193	Lou Gehrig	159	Perry Werden
269	George Sisler	191	Lu Blue	155	Jimmie Foxx
262	Sid Farrar	183	Tom Jones	150	Jake Stahl

(549) Best Career Fielding Average by a First Baseman (min. 1,000 G)

.997	Travis Lee	.994	Wally Joyner	.993	Chris Chambliss
.996	Steve Garvey	.994	Rafael Palmeiro	.993	Joe Judge
.996	Don Mattingly	.994	Keith Hernandez	.993	Eric Karros
.996	Wes Parker	.994	Vic Power	.993	Ted Kluszewski
.996	J.T. Snow	.994	Kent Hrbek	.993	Eddie Murray
.996	Todd Helton	.994	Joe Adcock	.993	Eddie Waitkus
.995	David Segui	.994	Mike Jorgensen	.993	Tony Clark
.995	John Olerud	.994	Pete O'Brien	.993	Charlie Grimm
.995	Tino Martinez	.994	Ernie Banks	.993	Walter Holke
.995	Dan Driessen	.994	John Mayberry	.993	Elbie Fletcher
.995	Sean Casey	.994	Ed Kranepool	.993	Stuffy McInnis
.995	Jim Spencer	.994	Lee May	.993	Will Clark
.995	Frank McCormick	.994	Jim Thome	.993	Gil Hodges
.995	Mark Grace	.993	Mark McGwire	.993	Tony Perez
.994	Derrek Lee	.993	Jeff Bagwell		

(550) Most Career Double Plays by a First Baseman

2044	Mickey Vernon	1533	Mark Grace	1320	Johnny Mize
2033	Eddie Murray	1528	Jimmie Foxx	1309	Stuffy McInnis
1782	Rafael Palmeiro	1500	Don Mattingly	1307	John Mayberry
1775	Fred McGriff	1500	Joe Judge	1306	Todd Helton
1769	Joe Kuhel	1498	Steve Garvey	1298	J.T. Snow
1733	Charlie Grimm	1480	George Scott	1290	Wally Pipp
1687	Chris Chambliss	1468	George Sisler	1273	Carlos Delgado
1654	Keith Hernandez	1408	Mark McGwire	1269	Ted Kluszewski
1648	Andres Galarraga	1405	Willie McCovey	1266	Bill Skowron
1618	Jeff Bagwell	1398	Tino Martinez	1265	George McQuinn
1614	Gil Hodges	1348	Cecil Cooper	1257	Eric Karros
1611	Wally Joyner	1347	Norm Cash	1235	Lee May
1581	John Olerud	1342	Tony Perez	1228	Joe Adcock
1575	Lou Gehrig	1334	Bill Terry	1221	Frank McCormick
1571	Will Clark	1331	Kent Hrbek	1200	Bill Buckner
1562	Jim Bottomley	1327	Jake Beckley		

(551) Most Career Games by a Second Baseman

2650	Eddie Collins	1813	Billy Herman	1519	Joe Gordon
2527	Joe Morgan	1785	Jeff Kent	1518	Manny Trillo
2320	Roberto Alomar	1765	Bobby Grich	1518	Frank Bolling
2308	Lou Whitaker	1763	Bret Boone	1498	Tony Taylor
2295	Nellie Fox	1762	Frankie Frisch	1486	George Cutshaw
2206	Charlie Gehringer	1735	Johnny Evers	1479	Claude Ritchey
2152	Willie Randolph	1728	Larry Doyle	1456	Tony Lazzeri
2151	Frank White	1688	Del Pratt	1455	Cupid Childs
2129	Bid McPhee	1679	Steve Sax	1453	Hughie Critz
2094	Bill Mazeroski	1624	Ray Durham	1450	Felix Millan
2035	Nap Lajoie	1585	Kid Gleason	1449	Jim Gantner
1995	Ryne Sandberg	1561	Rogers Hornsby	1447	Cookie Rojas
1875	Craig Biggio	1552	Julian Javier	1418	Davey Lopes
1852	Bobby Doerr	1538	Fred Pfeffer	1416	Tom Herr
1834	Red Schoendienst	1530	Miller Huggins		

(552) Most Career Assists by a Second Baseman

7630	Eddie Collins	5381	Bobby Grich	4655	Larry Doyle
7068	Charlie Gehringer	5243	Red Schoendienst	4589	Bret Boone
6967	Joe Morgan	5181	Craig Biggio	4563	Lou Bierbauer
6919	Bid McPhee	5166	Rogers Hornsby	4479	Claude Ritchey
6685	Bill Mazeroski	5138	Hughie Critz	4473	George Cutshaw
6653	Lou Whitaker	5124	Johnny Evers	4448	Oscar Melillo
6524	Roberto Alomar	5108	Fred Pfeffer	4445	Tony Lazzeri
6373	Nellie Fox	5075	Del Pratt	4444	Glenn Hubbard
6363	Ryne Sandberg	4805	Steve Sax	4436	Ray Durham
6336	Willie Randolph	4776	Kid Gleason	4347	Jim Gantner
6267	Nap Lajoie	4706	Joe Gordon	4171	Bobby Lowe
6253	Frank White	4699	Manny Trillo	4113	Julian Javier
6026	Frankie Frisch	4698	Jeff Kent	4068	Buddy Myer
5710	Bobby Doerr	4697	Miller Huggins	4019	Frank Bolling
5681	Billy Herman	4679	Cupid Childs		

(553) Most Career Putouts by a Second Baseman

6552	Bid McPhee	4217	Bobby Grich	3446	Hughie Critz
6526	Eddie Collins	4069	Del Pratt	3444	Claude Ritchey
6090	Nellie Fox	3887	Kid Gleason	3443	Bret Boone
5742	Joe Morgan	3865	Cupid Childs	3437	Oscar Melillo
5496	Nap Lajoie	3807	Ryne Sandberg	3425	Miller Huggins
5369	Charlie Gehringer	3801	Craig Biggio	3423	Frank Bolling
4974	Bill Mazeroski	3762	George Cutshaw	3412	Bucky Harris
4928	Bobby Doerr	3758	Johnny Evers	3403	Manny Trillo
4859	Willie Randolph	3726	Lou Bierbauer	3380	Julian Javier
4780	Billy Herman	3635	Larry Doyle	3351	Tony Lazzeri
4771	Lou Whitaker	3613	Jeff Kent	3336	Bobby Lowe
4742	Frank White	3600	Joe Gordon	3319	Joe Quinn
4719	Fred Pfeffer	3574	Steve Sax	3274	Tony Taylor
4616	Red Schoendienst	3495	Felix Millan	3226	Jerry Priddy
4458	Roberto Alomar	3487	Buddy Myer	3206	Rogers Hornsby
4348	Frankie Frisch	3447	Cub Stricker		

(554) Most Career Errors by a Second Baseman

857	Fred Pfeffer	430	Al Myers	287	Otto Knabe
792	Bid McPhee	423	Johnny Evers	280	Frankie Frisch
701	Cub Stricker	418	Tom Daly	271	Hobe Ferris
646	Cupid Childs	409	Joe Quinn	263	Bucky Harris
574	Lou Bierbauer	389	Bobby Lowe	263	Tony Lazzeri
571	Kid Gleason	385	Bill Hallman	260	Joe Gordon
543	Jack Burdock	381	Del Pratt	250	George Grantham
543	Joe Gerhardt	376	Miller Huggins	245	Danny Richardson
498	Fred Dunlap	355	Claude Ritchey	244	Joe Morgan
477	Jack Farrell	354	Billy Herman	237	Billy Gilbert
471	Yank Robinson	309	Charlie Gehringer	234	Willie Randolph
469	Pop Smith	307	Rogers Hornsby	231	Hughie Critz
451	Nap Lajoie	299	George Cutshaw	228	Ralph Young
443	Larry Doyle	292	Bill Wambsganss	224	Dick Padden
435	Eddie Collins	292	Jimmy Williams		

(555) Best Career Fielding Average by a Second Baseman (min. 1,000 G)

.989	Ryne Sandberg	.984	Craig Biggio	.982	Frank Bolling
.989	Tom Herr	.984	Cookie Rojas	.982	Chuck Knoblauch
.989	Mickey Morandini	.984	Dave Cash	.981	Joe Morgan
.988	Jose Lind	.984	Fernando Vina	.981	Manny Trillo
.988	Jody Reed	.984	Nellie Fox	.981	Mark McLemore
.986	Bret Boone	.983	Tommy Helms	.981	Jerry Remy
.985	Jose Vidro	.983	Dick Green	.981	Jeff Kent
.985	Jim Gantner	.983	Bill Doran	.980	Ron Oester
.984	Frank White	.983	Red Schoendienst	.980	Bobby Doerr
.984	Bobby Grich	.983	Robby Thompson	.980	Davey Johnson
.984	Luis Castillo	.983	Bill Mazeroski	.980	Bobby Knoop
.984	Damion Easley	.983	Glenn Hubbard	.980	Felix Millan
.984	Roberto Alomar	.983	Julio Cruz	.980	Willie Randolph
.984	Lou Whitaker	.983	Horace Clarke		
.984	Jerry Lumpe	.982	Johnny Ray		

(556) Most Career Double Plays by a Second Baseman

1706	Bill Mazeroski	1160	Joe Gordon	965	Oscar Melillo
1619	Nellie Fox	1158	Ryne Sandberg	963	Buddy Myer
1547	Willie Randolph	1132	Jeff Kent	963	Bobby Richardson
1527	Lou Whitaker	1099	Craig Biggio	960	Hughie Critz
1507	Bobby Doerr	1085	Bret Boone	953	Cookie Rojas
1505	Joe Morgan	1062	Frankie Frisch	950	Tony Taylor
1444	Charlie Gehringer	1050	Nap Lajoie	948	Harold Reynolds
1407	Roberto Alomar	1050	Ray Durham	907	Julian Javier
1382	Frank White	1036	Jim Gantner	906	Jerry Priddy
1368	Red Schoendienst	1003	Frank Bolling	901	Dave Cash
1302	Bobby Grich	998	Steve Sax	894	Fred Pfeffer
1215	Eddie Collins	991	Tom Herr	892	Rogers Hornsby
1188	Bid McPhee	975	Glenn Hubbard	873	Robby Thompson
1177	Billy Herman	973	Manny Trillo	855	Felix Millan

(557) Most Career Games by a Third Baseman

2870	Brooks Robinson	1863	Pie Traynor	1656	Vinny Castilla
2412	Graig Nettles	1836	Stan Hack	1614	Willie Jones
2282	Gary Gaetti	1785	Ken Boyer	1573	Arlie Latham
2215	Wade Boggs	1785	Terry Pendleton	1550	Harlond Clift
2212	Mike Schmidt	1768	Pinky Higgins	1548	Frank Baker
2183	Buddy Bell	1743	Matt Williams	1543	Doug DeCinces
2181	Eddie Mathews	1724	Lave Cross	1500	Ken Keltner
2130	Ron Santo	1720	Carney Lansford	1498	Todd Zeile
2054	Tim Wallach	1692	George Brett	1487	Ossie Bluege
2008	Eddie Yost	1692	George Kell	1465	Billy Nash
1989	Ron Cey	1683	Jimmy Collins	1442	Darrell Evans
1983	Aurelio Rodriguez	1676	Ken Caminiti	1440	Bill Madlock
1896	Sal Bando	1674	Willie Kamm	1439	Clete Boyer
1887	Robin Ventura	1656	Larry Gardner	1431	Jimmy Austin

(558) Most Career Assists by a Third Baseman

6205	Brooks Robinson	3674	George Brett	3215	Doug DeCinces
5279	Graig Nettles	3659	Eddie Yost	3155	Frank Baker
5045	Mike Schmidt	3652	Ken Boyer	3127	Ken Caminiti
4925	Buddy Bell	3552	Robin Ventura	3123	Darrell Evans
4581	Ron Santo	3546	Arlie Latham	3122	Billy Nash
4531	Gary Gaetti	3521	Pie Traynor	3070	Ken Keltner
4322	Eddie Mathews	3494	Stan Hack	3040	Ossie Bluege
4246	Wade Boggs	3408	Larry Gardner	2949	Jimmy Austin
4150	Aurelio Rodriguez	3376	Matt Williams	2943	Bill Bradley
4018	Ron Cey	3345	Willie Kamm	2934	Willie Jones
3992	Tim Wallach	3303	George Kell	2891	Billy Shindle
3891	Terry Pendleton	3262	Harlond Clift	2889	Scott Rolen
3720	Sal Bando	3261	Vinny Castilla	2887	Doug Rader
3715	Lave Cross	3258	Pinky Higgins	2884	Frank Malzone
3702	Jimmy Collins	3218	Clete Boyer	2805	Harry Steinfeldt

(559) Most Career Putouts by a Third Baseman

2697	Brooks Robinson	1898	Graig Nettles	1591	Mike Schmidt
2372	Jimmy Collins	1848	Pinky Higgins	1576	Ken Keltner
2356	Eddie Yost	1825	George Kell	1567	Ken Boyer
2310	Lave Cross	1815	Billy Shindle	1551	Ossie Bluege
2289	Pie Traynor	1798	Buddy Bell	1550	Wade Boggs
2222	Billy Nash	1789	Larry Gardner	1529	Aurelio Rodriguez
2154	Frank Baker	1777	Harlond Clift	1500	Ron Cey
2151	Willie Kamm	1777	Jerry Denny	1471	Robin Ventura
2049	Eddie Mathews	1776	Harry Steinfeldt	1470	Clete Boyer
2045	Willie Jones	1755	Bill Bradley	1456	Bobby Byrne
2042	Jimmy Austin	1699	Gary Gaetti	1456	Heinie Groh
1976	Arlie Latham	1675	Denny Lyons	1455	Pinky Whitney
1955	Ron Santo	1662	Tim Wallach	1450	Hick Carpenter
1944	Stan Hack	1647	Sal Bando		

(560) Most Career Errors by a Third Baseman

822	Arlie Latham	365	Harry Steinfeldt	293	Eddie Mathews
615	Billy Nash	358	Jimmy Austin	287	Larry Gardner
591	Hick Carpenter	356	Pinky Higgins	280	John McGraw
570	Billy Shindle	344	Tommy Leach	279	Harlond Clift
552	Jerry Denny	344	Art Whitney	278	Eddie Foster
509	Denny Lyons	336	Bill Bradley	270	Eddie Yost
475	Joe Mulvey	327	Tom Burns	264	Ken Boyer
465	Jimmy Collins	325	Doc Casey	263	Brooks Robinson
444	Deacon White	324	Pie Traynor	263	Harry Wolverton
439	Bill Joyce	322	Frank Baker	261	George Brett
401	Ned Williamson	318	Jim Donnelly	258	Bobby Byrne
397	Lave Cross	317	Ron Santo	257	Art Devlin
387	George Pinkney	313	Mike Schmidt	254	Buddy Bell
373	Frank Hankinson	309	Ezra Sutton	253	Darrell Evans
373	Bill Kuehne	295	Graig Nettles	251	Charlie Irwin

(561) Best Career Fielding Average by a Third Baseman (min. 1,000 G)

.977	Mike Lowell	.965	Ken Keltner	.958	Brook Jacoby
.971	Brooks Robinson	.964	Jim Davenport	.958	Robin Ventura
.970	Ken Reitz	.964	Buddy Bell	.958	Doug DeCinces
.969	George Kell	.964	Aurelio Rodriguez	.957	Ray Knight
.968	Steve Buechele	.964	Matt Williams	.957	Eddie Yost
.968	Don Money	.963	Willie Jones	.957	Terry Pendleton
.968	Eric Chavez	.963	Toby Harrah	.957	Joe Dugan
.968	Don Wert	.962	Joe Randa	.957	Stan Hack
.967	Willie Kamm	.962	Wade Boggs	.957	Ossie Bluege
.967	Heinie Groh	.961	Pinky Whitney	.956	Eddie Mathews
.967	Jeff Cirillo	.961	Ron Cey	.956	Red Rolfe
.966	Scott Rolen	.961	Ken McMullen	.956	Doug Rader
.966	Carney Lansford	.961	Graig Nettles	.955	Frank Malzone
.965	Clete Boyer	.960	Bob Aspromonte	.955	Mike Schmidt
.965	Gary Gaetti	.959	Tim Wallach	.955	Mike Pagliarulo
.965	Travis Fryman	.959	Sal Bando	.955	Adrian Beltre
.965	Ken Oberkfell	.959	Don Hoak		
.965	Vinny Castilla	.958	Bill Mueller		

(562) Most Career Double Plays by a Third Baseman

618	Brooks Robinson	315	Clete Boyer	266	Billy Nash
470	Graig Nettles	315	Matt Williams	259	Frank Baker
460	Gary Gaetti	312	Terry Pendleton	258	Ken McMullen
450	Mike Schmidt	309	Harlond Clift	256	Doug Rader
430	Buddy Bell	307	George Brett	256	Carney Lansford
423	Wade Boggs	306	George Kell	255	Stan Hack
408	Aurelio Rodriguez	306	Ken Keltner	255	Scott Rolen
395	Ron Santo	303	Pie Traynor	253	Arlie Latham
369	Eddie Mathews	299	Willie Kamm	252	Bob Elliott
359	Robin Ventura	289	Frank Malzone	246	Larry Gardner
355	Ken Boyer	288	Pinky Higgins	238	Todd Zeile
345	Eddie Yost	280	Ken Caminiti	233	Mike Lowell
345	Sal Bando	278	Heine Groh	231	Charlie Hayes
331	Doug DeCinces	273	Willie Jones	230	Travis Fryman
331	Vinny Castilla	271	Jeff Cirillo	229	Jimmy Austin
319	Tim Wallach	270	Darrell Evans	227	Don Hoak
315	Ron Cey	266	Ossie Bluege	227	Adrian Beltre

(563) Most Career Games by a Shortstop

2581	Luis Aparicio	1984	Royce Clayton	1795	Ed Brinkman
2511	Ozzie Smith	1982	Roger Peckinpaugh	1795	Herman Long
2427	Omar Vizquel	1964	Garry Templeton	1765	Greg Gagne
2302	Cal Ripken	1955	Don Kessinger	1746	Bill Russell
2222	Larry Bowa	1942	Mark Belanger	1743	Joe Tinker
2218	Luke Appling	1900	Chris Speier	1679	Dick Bartell
2178	Dave Concepcion	1896	Ozzie Guillen	1678	Monte Cross
2153	Rabbit Maranville	1887	Honus Wagner	1670	Derek Jeter
2139	Alan Trammell	1877	Dick Groat	1667	Germany Smith
2133	Bill Dahlen	1873	Dave Bancroft	1647	Phil Rizzuto
2097	Bert Campaneris	1866	Donie Bush	1643	Everett Scott
2085	Barry Larkin	1861	Alfredo Griffin	1629	Jack Glasscock
2075	Tommy Corcoran	1843	Leo Cardenas	1626	George McBride
2028	Roy McMillan	1843	Joe Cronin	1625	Mickey Doolan
2014	Pee Wee Reese	1826	Bobby Wallace		

(564) Most Career Assists by a Shortstop

8375	Ozzie Smith	6172	Alan Trammell	5632	Jack Glasscock
8016	Luis Aparicio	6166	Germany Smith	5590	Dick Bartell
7505	Bill Dahlen	6160	Bert Campaneris	5546	Bill Russell
7354	Rabbit Maranville	6137	Herman Long	5466	Ed Brinkman
7218	Luke Appling	6119	Donie Bush	5375	Monte Cross
7110	Tommy Corcoran	6041	Honus Wagner	5335	Ozzie Guillen
6977	Cal Ripken	6041	Garry Templeton	5303	Leo Cardenas
6924	Omar Vizquel	5891	Pee Wee Reese	5290	Mickey Doolan
6857	Larry Bowa	5858	Barry Larkin	5274	George McBride
6594	Dave Concepcion	5856	Joe Tinker	5186	Alfredo Griffin
6561	Dave Bancroft	5814	Joe Cronin	5134	Art Fletcher
6337	Roger Peckinpaugh	5811	Dick Groat	5053	Everett Scott
6303	Bobby Wallace	5786	Mark Belanger	4959	Billy Jurges
6212	Don Kessinger	5781	Chris Speier	4930	Greg Gagne
6191	Roy McMillan	5723	Royce Clayton		

NATIONAL BASEBALL HALL OF FAME LIBRARY

Ozzie Smith

(565) Most Career Putouts by a Shortstop

5139	Rabbit Maranville	3768	Joe Tinker	3219	Phil Rizzuto
4856	Bill Dahlen	3733	Omar Vizquel	3218	Leo Cardenas
4623	Dave Bancroft	3705	Roy McMillan	3207	Alfredo Griffin
4576	Honus Wagner	3696	Joe Cronin	3151	Don Kessinger
4553	Tommy Corcoran	3670	Dave Concepcion	3150	Barry Larkin
4548	Luis Aparicio	3651	Cal Ripken	3133	Billy Jurges
4398	Luke Appling	3608	Bert Campaneris	3132	Lou Boudreau
4249	Ozzie Smith	3585	George McBride	3097	Leo Durocher
4225	Herman Long	3578	Mickey Doolan	3061	Frankie Crosetti
4142	Bobby Wallace	3505	Dick Groat	3057	Chris Speier
4040	Pee Wee Reese	3393	Garry Templeton	3022	Royce Clayton
4038	Donie Bush	3391	Alan Trammell	3005	Mark Belanger
3980	Monte Cross	3351	Everett Scott	2995	Arky Vaughan
3919	Roger Peckinpaugh	3314	Larry Bowa	2986	Marty Marion
3872	Dick Bartell	3239	George Davis	2976	Eddie Miller

(566) Most Career Errors by a Shortstop

1070	Herman Long	594	Arthur Irwin	455	Doc Lavan
975	Bill Dahlen	590	Frank Fennelly	439	Wally Gerber
973	Germany Smith	578	Bones Ely	417	Ivy Olson
957	Tommy Corcoran	570	Mickey Doolan	402	Frankie Crosetti
857	Ed McKean	553	Roger Peckinpaugh	397	Arky Vaughan
832	Jack Glasscock	535	Bill Gleason	388	Pee Wee Reese
812	Monte Cross	530	John Ward	384	Garry Templeton
689	Donie Bush	521	Art Fletcher	381	Travis Jackson
685	Bobby Wallace	511	George Davis	374	Dick Groat
676	Honus Wagner	485	Joe Cronin	366	Luis Aparicio
660	Dave Bancroft	484	George McBride	366	Al Bridwell
643	Luke Appling	473	Freddy Parent	365	Bert Campaneris
635	Joe Tinker	471	Dick Bartell	364	Jack Rowe
631	Rabbit Maranville	470	Hughie Jennings	356	Heinie Wagner
595	Shorty Fuller	458	Kid Elberfeld	351	Glenn Wright

(567) Best Career Fielding Average by a Shortstop (min. 1,000 G)

.984	Omar Vizquel	.976	Dick Schofield Jr.	.972	Chris Gomez
.982	Mike Bordick	.976	Roger Metzger	.972	Eddie Miller
.980	Larry Bowa	.975	Jay Bell	.972	Luis Aparicio
.980	Tony Fernandez	.975	Derek Jeter	.972	Roy McMillan
.979	Cal Ripken	.975	Alex S. Gonzalez	.971	Rick Burleson
.978	Ozzie Smith	.975	Barry Larkin	.971	Bobby Wine
.978	Orlando Cabrera	.974	Royce Clayton	.971	Dave Concepcion
.978	Deivi Cruz	.974	Rich Aurilia	.971	Leo Cardenas
.978	Neifi Perez	.974	Ozzie Guillen	.971	Miguel Tejada
.977	Alex Rodriguez	.973	Gary DiSarcina	.970	Ed Brinkman
.977	Spike Owen	.973	Tim Foli	.970	Chris Speier
.977	Alan Trammell	.973	Dal Maxvill	.970	Walt Weiss
.977	Mark Belanger	.973	Lou Boudreau	.970	Ernie Banks
.976	Bucky Dent	.972	Greg Gagne		

(568) Most Career Double Plays by a Shortstop

1590	Ozzie Smith	1180	Lou Boudreau	1004	Freddie Patek
1567	Omar Vizquel	1170	Don Kessinger	978	Marty Marion
1565	Cal Ripken	1165	Joe Cronin	967	Greg Gagne
1553	Luis Aparicio	1164	Garry Templeton	952	Roger Peckinpaugh
1424	Luke Appling	1094	Ozzie Guillen	946	Eddie Miller
1307	Alan Trammell	1092	Barry Larkin	944	Frankie Crosetti
1304	Roy McMillan	1072	Dick Bartell	943	Tony Fernandez
1290	Dave Concepcion	1055	Mike Bordick	943	Miguel Tejada
1265	Larry Bowa	1054	Mark Belanger	941	Robin Yount
1246	Pee Wee Reese	1053	Alfredo Griffin	933	Alvin Dark
1237	Dick Groat	1043	Chris Speier	930	Edgar Renteria
1217	Phil Rizzuto	1036	Leo Cardenas	929	Billy Jurges
1194	Royce Clayton	1028	Tim Foli	928	Eddie Joost
1186	Bert Campaneris	1017	Dave Bancroft	909	Bill Russell
1183	Rabbit Maranville	1005	Ed Brinkman	900	Dick Schofield Jr.

(569) Most Career Games by an Outfielder

2934	Ty Cobb	2323	Andre Dawson	2142	Al Simmons
2842	Willie Mays	2313	Mel Ott	2132	Frank Robinson
2826	Rickey Henderson	2299	Sam Crawford	2123	Tim Raines
2764	Barry Bonds	2288	Paul Waner	2115	Ken Griffey Jr.
2760	Hank Aaron	2284	Harry Hooper	2104	Richie Ashburn
2698	Tris Speaker	2270	Sam Rice	2102	Reggie Jackson
2507	Lou Brock	2241	Babe Ruth	2088	Billy Williams
2488	Al Kaline	2229	Luis Gonzalez	2088	Marquis Grissom
2469	Dave Winfield	2193	Fred Clarke	2076	Carl Yastrzemski
2459	Steve Finley	2187	Goose Goslin	2071	Jimmy Sheckard
2421	Max Carey	2187	Sammy Sosa	2064	Enos Slaughter
2403	Vada Pinson	2159	Brett Butler	2054	Jesse Burkett
2370	Roberto Clemente	2156	Jose Cruz Sr.	2039	Willie Keeler
2337	Zack Wheat	2151	Ted Williams	2031	Willie Wilson
2326	Tony Gwynn	2146	Dwight Evans	2019	Mickey Mantle
2323	Willie Davis	2142	Doc Cramer		

(570) Most Career Assists by an Outfielder

449	Tris Speaker	270	Jesse Burkett	228	Jimmy Wolf
392	Ty Cobb	268	Sam Crawford	226	Hugh Nicol
375	Jimmy Ryan	266	Tommy McCarthy	226	Cy Williams
349	George Van Haltren	266	Roberto Clemente	225	Fielder Jones
348	Tom Brown	265	Patsy Donovan	224	Pop Corkhill
344	Harry Hooper	258	Willie Keeler	223	Dode Paskert
339	Max Carey	256	Mel Ott	222	Edd Roush
307	Jimmy Sheckard	254	Fred Clarke	221	Tilly Walker
294	Clyde Milan	243	George Gore	221	Goose Goslin
289	Orator Shafer	243	Mike Griffin	221	Paul Hines
285	King Kelly	241	Paul Waner	217	Paul Radford
283	Sam Thompson	241	Hugh Duffy	216	Jim O'Rourke
278	Sam Rice	238	Ed Delahanty	212	Joe Kelley
273	Dummy Hoy	232	Zack Wheat	210	Duffy Lewis

5552251252522252222555522

(571) Most Career Putouts by an Outfielder

7095	Willie Mays
6788	Tris Speaker
6468	Rickey Henderson
6363	Max Carey
6361	Ty Cobb
6089	Richie Ashburn
5618	Steve Finley
5539	Hank Aaron
5475	Barry Bonds
5449	Willie Davis
5412	Doc Cramer
5296	Brett Butler
5158	Andre Dawson
5097	Vada Pinson
5083	Ken Griffey Jr.
5060	Willie Wilson
5035	Al Kaline
4996	Zack Wheat
4993	Chet Lemon
4988	Al Simmons
4975	Dave Winfield
4936	Amos Otis
4880	Marquis Grissom
4872	Paul Waner
4860	Lloyd Waner
4795	Fred Clarke
4792	Goose Goslin
4774	Sam Rice
4739	Devon White
4710	Bernie Williams
4696	Roberto Clemente
4586	Kenny Lofton
4556	Fred Lynn
4537	Edd Roush
4516	Joe DiMaggio
4512	Tony Gwynn
4511	Mel Ott
4490	Sammy Sosa
4449	Garry Maddox
4444	Babe Ruth
4438	Mickey Mantle
4394	Lou Brock
4392	Kirby Puckett
4391	Jose Cruz Sr.
4371	Dwight Evans
4343	Paul Blair
4300	Sam West

(572) Most Career Errors by an Outfielder

490	Tom Brown
394	Dummy Hoy
383	Jesse Burkett
368	George Gore
366	Jimmy Ryan
358	George Van Haltren
350	Ned Hanlon
332	Paul Hines
289	Billy Hamilton
285	Abner Dalrymple
276	George Wood
271	Ty Cobb
269	Pete Browning
268	Jim O'Rourke
262	Tommy McCarthy
259	King Kelly
256	Fred Clarke
248	Charley Jones
246	Pete Hotaling
244	Orator Shafer
241	Blondie Purcell
235	Max Carey
229	Harry Stovey
228	Walt Wilmot
222	Tris Speaker
220	Hugh Duffy
216	Clyde Milan
214	Kip Selbach
209	Goose Goslin
203	Emmett Seery
201	Patsy Donovan
200	Elmer Smith
197	Jimmy Sheckard
196	Lou Brock
194	Cliff Carroll
193	Dick Johnston
187	Ed Swartwood
187	Mike Tiernan
185	Curt Welch
184	Burt Shotton
184	Sam Rice
183	Zack Wheat
181	Tom York
179	Paul Radford
178	Joe Hornung
177	Cy Seymour
174	Mike Griffin
173	Jack Manning
172	Sam Thompson

(573) Best Career Fielding Average by an Outfielder (min. 1,000 G)

.995	Darryl Hamilton	.989	Ken Berry	.988	Tim Raines
.994	Darren Lewis	.989	Johnny Damon	.988	Andy Van Slyke
.993	Terry Puhl	.989	Garret Anderson	.988	Roy White
.993	Brett Butler	.989	Brady Anderson	.988	Jim Busby
.991	Pete Rose	.989	Otis Nixon	.988	Jay Buhner
.991	Torii Hunter	.989	Tommy Holmes	.988	Steve Finley
.991	Randy Winn	.989	Kirby Puckett	.987	Magglio Ordonez
.991	Tom Goodwin	.989	Jim Edmonds	.987	Dwayne Murphy
.991	Amos Otis	.989	Gene Woodling	.987	Lenny Dykstra
.991	Doug Glanville	.988	Cesar Geronimo	.987	Dwight Evans
.991	Joe Rudi	.988	Fred Lynn	.987	Curt Flood
.991	Mickey Stanley	.988	Mike Devereaux	.987	Willie Wilson
.990	Robin Yount	.988	Stan Javier	.987	Tony Gwynn
.990	Jim Piersall	.988	Paul O'Neill	.987	Mark Kotsay
.990	Bernie Williams	.988	Brian Jordan	.987	Johnny Groth
.990	Andruw Jones	.988	Paul Blair	.987	Tony Gonzalez
.990	Brian McRae	.988	Jim Eisenreich	.987	Kevin McReynolds
.989	Jim Landis	.988	Marquis Grissom		

(574) Most Career Double Plays by an Outfielder

139	Tris Speaker	60	Tommy McCarthy	50	Elmer Flick
107	Ty Cobb	60	Mel Ott	49	Curt Welch
86	Max Carey	60	Willie Mays	49	Dode Paskert
85	Tom Brown	60	Willie Keeler	48	Jesse Barfield
81	Harry Hooper	59	Sam Crawford	48	Babe Ruth
80	Jimmy Sheckard	58	Clyde Milan	48	Kip Selbach
75	Mike Griffin	57	Jimmy Slagle	48	Roy Thomas
72	Dummy Hoy	55	Billy Hamilton	48	Curt Walker
71	Jimmy Ryan	54	Zack Wheat	48	Chief Wilson
70	Fielder Jones	53	Paul Waner	47	Pop Corkhill
69	Patsy Donovan	53	Steve Brodie	47	Hugh Duffy
67	Sam Rice	52	Cy Seymour	47	George Gore
64	George Van Haltren	52	Ginger Beaumont	47	Goose Goslin
62	Jesse Burkett	51	Burt Shotton	47	Ned Hanlon
61	Sam Thompson	51	Paul Hines	47	Ross Youngs

(575) Most Career Games by a Catcher

2226	Carlton Fisk	1696	Brad Ausmus	1435	Wally Schang
2225	Bob Boone	1633	Rick Dempsey	1410	Muddy Ruel
2056	Gary Carter	1629	Mike Piazza	1395	Mike Scioscia
1950	Tony Pena	1629	Jim Hegan	1392	Johnny Edwards
1934	Ivan Rodriguez	1612	Deacon McGuire	1387	Tim McCarver
1927	Jim Sundberg	1581	Bill Freehan	1381	Terry Steinbach
1918	Al Lopez	1571	Sherm Lollar	1378	Terry Kennedy
1917	Benito Santiago	1562	Luke Sewell	1360	Gus Mancuso
1818	Lance Parrish	1544	Ernie Lombardi	1351	Jimmie Wilson
1806	Rick Ferrell	1532	Steve O'Neill	1351	Javy Lopez
1793	Gabby Hartnett	1506	Darrell Porter	1348	Jerry Grote
1771	Ted Simmons	1493	Jason Kendall	1338	Bob O'Farrell
1742	Johnny Bench	1482	Rollie Hemsley	1318	Sandy Alomar Jr.
1727	Ray Schalk	1479	Del Crandall	1316	Wilbert Robinson
1708	Bill Dickey	1476	John Roseboro	1311	Frankie Hayes
1699	Yogi Berra	1451	Mickey Cochrane		

(576) Most Career Assists by a Catcher

1859	Deacon McGuire	1332	Frank Snyder	1079	Jack Clements
1811	Ray Schalk	1319	Bill Killefer	1072	Frank Bowerman
1698	Steve O'Neill	1314	Billy Sullivan Sr.	1071	Silver Flint
1590	Red Dooin	1309	John Warner	1053	Otto Miller
1580	Chief Zimmer	1254	Gabby Hartnett	1048	Charlie Bennett
1552	Johnny Kling	1231	Bill Rariden	1048	Carlton Fisk
1487	Ivey Wingo	1203	Gary Carter	1045	Tony Pena
1454	Wilbert Robinson	1195	Roger Bresnahan	1037	Cy Perkins
1444	Bill Bergen	1174	Bob Boone	1024	Ed McFarland
1444	Pop Snyder	1136	Muddy Ruel	1017	Buck Ewing
1420	Wally Schang	1127	Rick Ferrell	1013	Bill Holbert
1417	Duke Farrell	1115	Al Lopez	1007	Jim Sundberg
1386	George Gibson	1112	Hank Severeid	1001	Doc Bushong
1381	Oscar Stanage	1094	Heinie Peitz	1000	Hank Gowdy
1363	Malachi Kittridge	1088	Eddie Ainsmith		
1342	Lou Criger	1084	Luke Sewell		

(577) Most Career Putouts by a Catcher

11785	Gary Carter	8906	Ted Simmons	7248	Rick Ferrell
11676	Ivan Rodriguez	8738	Yogi Berra	7218	Charles Johnson
11369	Carlton Fisk	8335	Mike Scioscia	7168	Ray Schalk
11282	Brad Ausmus	8206	Tim McCarver	7118	Mike Matheny
11260	Bob Boone	8109	Dan Wilson	7086	Alan Ashby
11212	Tony Pena	8081	Jerry Grote	7059	Sherm Lollar
10846	Mike Piazza	7965	Bill Dickey	7012	Tom Haller
10817	Benito Santiago	7805	Jorge Posada	6852	Deacon McGuire
9941	Bill Freehan	7693	Mike Lieberthal	6756	Darrell Porter
9767	Jim Sundberg	7638	Sandy Alomar Jr.	6709	Jason Varitek
9647	Lance Parrish	7619	Joe Girardi	6678	Darrin Fletcher
9543	Jason Kendall	7506	Jim Hegan	6644	Al Lopez
9291	John Roseboro	7505	Terry Steinbach	6555	Terry Kennedy
9249	Johnny Bench	7367	Rick Dempsey	6548	Rick Cerone
8990	Javy Lopez	7352	Del Crandall	6534	Todd Hundley
8925	Johnny Edwards	7292	Gabby Hartnett	6520	Roy Campanella

(578) Most Career Errors by a Catcher

679	Pop Snyder	233	Pop Schriver	166	Ossee Schreckengost
577	Deacon McGuire	229	Oscar Stanage	165	Joe Sugden
456	Silver Flint	223	Wally Schang	161	Bill Bergen
412	Wilbert Robinson	217	Steve O'Neill	155	Carlton Fisk
412	Doc Bushong	210	Johnny Kling	154	Rollie Hemsley
392	Jack Clements	205	John Warner	153	George Gibson
379	Charlie Bennett	193	Eddie Ainsmith	151	Benito Santiago
365	Duke Farrell	190	Boileryard Clarke	150	Bill Rariden
328	Chief Zimmer	187	Heinie Peitz	150	Luke Sewell
322	Buck Ewing	182	Frank Bowerman	148	Bill Killefer
320	Red Dooin	178	Bob Boone	148	Gus Mancuso
285	Doggie Miller	177	Jack O'Connor	148	Billy Sullivan Sr.
281	Connie Mack	175	Ray Schalk	146	Chief Meyers
264	Malachi Kittridge	170	Lou Criger	144	Ed McFarland
234	Ivey Wingo	167	Roger Bresnahan	143	Ernie Lombardi

(579) Best Career Fielding Average by a Catcher (min. 1,000 G)

.995	Dan Wilson	.991	Lance Parrish	.989	John Roseboro
.994	Mike Matheny	.991	Jerry Grote	.989	Joe Oliver
.994	Brad Ausmus	.991	Ernie Whitt	.989	Butch Wynegar
.993	Charles Johnson	.991	Ivan Rodriguez	.989	Del Crandall
.993	Darrin Fletcher	.991	Gary Carter	.989	Terry Steinbach
.993	Bill Freehan	.991	Joe Girardi	.989	Yogi Berra
.993	Brent Mayne	.991	Tony Pena	.988	Roy Campanella
.993	Elston Howard	.990	Johnny Bench	.988	Bill Dickey
.993	Jason Varitek	.990	Randy Hundley	.988	Rick Dempsey
.993	Jim Sundberg	.990	Rick Cerone	.988	Jeff Reed
.993	Javy Lopez	.990	Earl Battey	.988	Carlton Fisk
.992	Sherm Lollar	.990	Tim McCarver	.988	Pat Borders
.992	Mike Macfarlane	.990	Jim Hegan	.988	Smoky Burgess
.992	Jorge Posada	.990	Jason Kendall	.988	Todd Hundley
.992	Mike Lieberthal	.989	Sandy Alomar Jr.	.988	Mike Scioscia
.992	Tom Haller	.989	Mike Piazza		
.992	Johnny Edwards	.989	John Flaherty		

(580) Most Career Double Plays by a Catcher

226	Ray Schalk	137	Al Lopez	112	Wilbert Robinson
193	Steve O'Neill	136	Jim Hegan	111	Billy Sullivan Sr.
175	Yogi Berra	135	Muddy Ruel	111	Rick Dempsey
163	Gabby Hartnett	135	Chief Zimmer	111	John Roseboro
156	Tony Pena	133	Lance Parrish	107	Ernie Lombardi
154	Bob Boone	130	Benito Santiago	107	Oscar Stanage
153	Jimmie Wilson	129	Bill Killefer	107	Charles Johnson
149	Gary Carter	128	Ivan Rodriguez	106	Frank Snyder
149	Wally Schang	127	Johnny Bench	106	Frankie Hayes
147	Carlton Fisk	126	Johnny Kling	106	Bill Bergen
145	Jim Sundberg	122	Red Dooin	105	Johnny Edwards
142	Deacon McGuire	120	Brad Ausmus	105	Larry McLean
141	Ivey Wingo	116	Del Crandall	104	Ted Simmons
141	Rollie Hemsley	116	Jason Kendall	104	Mickey Cochrane
139	Rick Ferrell	114	Charlie Bennett	104	Darrell Porter
138	Luke Sewell	112	George Gibson	103	Frank Bowerman
137	Bill Dickey	112	Heinie Peitz		

(581) Most Career Passed Balls by a Catcher, since 1893

199	Deacon McGuire	138	Gus Triandos	118	Malachi Kittridge
192	Lance Parrish	135	Jack O'Connor	117	Joe Azcue
192	Ted Simmons	132	Tim McCarver	113	Alan Ashby
176	Ed McFarland	132	Darrell Porter	111	John Roseboro
165	Frank Bowerman	131	Wally Schang	110	Mike Grady
163	Heinie Peitz	130	Jim Sundberg	110	Eddie Ainsmith
157	Benito Santiago	129	Carlton Fisk	106	Bill Freehan
155	Duke Farrell	129	Roger Bresnahan	105	Tony Pena
152	Ernie Lombardi	128	Boileryard Clarke	104	John Bateman
148	Wilbert Robinson	126	Gabby Hartnett	103	John Grim
147	John Warner	126	Johnny Kling	102	Johnny Edwards
145	Steve O'Neill	125	Ed Herrmann	101	Oscar Stanage
142	Rick Ferrell	121	Tom Haller	101	George Gibson
140	Billy Sullivan Sr.	121	J.C. Martin	100	Mike Macfarlane
139	Frankie Hayes	120	Chief Zimmer	100	Joe Sugden
139	Red Dooin	120	Lou Criger		

(582) Most Career Assists by a Pitcher

2014	Cy Young	1108	Red Faber	942	Freddie Fitzsimmons
1503	Christy Mathewson	1086	Greg Maddux	939	Chick Fraser
1419	Grover Alexander	1060	Tim Keefe	934	Bill Doak
1382	Jim Galvin	1041	Tony Mullane	929	Joe McGinnity
1351	Walter Johnson	1031	Kid Nichols	922	Jim McCormick
1252	Burleigh Grimes	1028	Tommy John	903	Red Donahue
1244	George Mullin	1000	Red Ames	878	Phil Niekro
1240	Jack Quinn	999	Warren Spahn	877	Gaylord Perry
1207	Ed Walsh	998	Eddie Cicotte	874	Sam P. Jones
1195	Eppa Rixey	967	Jack Powell	874	Amos Rusie
1143	John Clarkson	966	Doc White	863	Clark Griffith
1138	Carl Mays	965	Harry Howell	853	Howard Ehmke
1128	Hooks Dauss	957	Al Orth	851	Charlie Buffinton
1124	Vic Willis	943	Ted Lyons	851	Stan Coveleski
1108	Eddie Plank	942	Charley Radbourn	850	Lee Meadows

(583) Most Career Putouts by a Pitcher

510	Greg Maddux	316	Roger Clemens	263	Jim McCormick
388	Kevin Brown	313	Kid Nichols	262	Jim Kaat
387	Jack Morris	293	John Smoltz	260	Tim Keefe
386	Phil Niekro	292	Jim Palmer	257	Larry Jackson
363	Ferguson Jenkins	291	Bob Gibson	255	Dan Petry
349	Gaylord Perry	291	Juan Marichal	253	Joe Niekro
334	Don Sutton	287	Bert Blyleven	252	Tom Glavine
332	Orel Hershiser	281	Christy Mathewson	245	Mike Boddicker
328	Rick Reuschel	278	Mike Moore	245	Ted Breitenstein
328	Tom Seaver	276	Walter Johnson	245	Lew Burdette
326	Tony Mullane	272	Dave Stieb	245	Milt Pappas
324	Jim Galvin	271	Vic Willis	244	Adonis Terry
319	Dennis Martinez	266	Doug Drabek	243	Bob Welch
317	Chick Fraser	264	Doyle Alexander	242	Mel Stottlemyre
316	Robin Roberts	263	Bob Lemon		

(584) Most Career Errors by a Pitcher

166	Tim Keefe	99	Jim McCormick	76	Stump Wiedman
162	John Clarkson	99	Jim Whitney	74	Hippo Vaughn
161	Jim Galvin	94	Red Ehret	74	Red Ames
146	Cy Young	94	Chick Fraser	74	Bill Hutchison
133	Mickey Welch	94	Charlie Buffinton	72	Jack Powell
128	Gus Weyhing	91	Rube Waddell	71	Jack Lynch
122	Tony Mullane	91	Matt Kilroy	71	Ed Crane
122	Amos Rusie	90	Nolan Ryan	71	Jersey Bakely
111	Charley Radbourn	84	Win Mercer	71	Burleigh Grimes
111	Bert Cunningham	83	Al Orth	71	Red Faber
107	Toad Ramsey	82	Frank Killen	70	Ed Morris
106	Will White	82	George Mullin	70	Sadie McMahon
104	Adonis Terry	78	George Bradley	70	Eddie Cicotte
101	Bobby Mathews	77	Jack B. Taylor	70	Pink Hawley
100	Joe McGinnity	77	Mark Baldwin		

(585) Best Career Fielding Average by a Pitcher (min. 1,500 IP)

.990	Don Mossi	.983	Harry Brecheen	.979	Jamie Moyer
.990	Gary Nolan	.982	Kevin Tapani	.979	Mike Flanagan
.989	Rick Rhoden	.982	Rick Wise	.979	Harry Gumbert
.988	Lon Warneke	.982	John Burkett	.979	Frank Tanana
.988	Russ Ortiz	.981	Red Lucas	.979	Mike Mussina
.988	Jim Wilson	.981	Ron Guidry	.978	Chris Carpenter
.988	Kirk Rueter	.981	Bob Smith	.978	Livan Hernandez
.988	Woodie Fryman	.980	Urban Shocker	.978	Shane Reynolds
.987	Brad Radke	.980	Dan Petry	.978	Hoyt Wilhelm
.986	Larry Gura	.980	Scott McGregor	.978	Eppa Rixey
.985	Grover Alexander	.980	Tom Glavine	.978	Frank Sullivan
.984	Alvin Crowder	.980	Bob Tewksbury	.978	Mark Gardner
.984	Bill Monbouquette	.980	Walt Terrell	.978	Ken Heintzelman

(586) Most Career Double Plays by a Pitcher

89	Greg Maddux	56	Eppa Rixey	49	Livan Hernandez
83	Phil Niekro	55	Lew Burdette	48	Bert Blyleven
82	Warren Spahn	55	Don Drysdale	48	Art Nehf
79	Freddie Fitzsimmons	55	Carl Hubbell	48	Sam P. Jones
78	Bob Lemon	54	Willis Hudlin	48	Bobby Shantz
76	Bucky Walters	54	Murry Dickson	47	Early Wynn
74	Burleigh Grimes	54	Tom Seaver	47	Jamie Moyer
72	Walter Johnson	54	Kirk Rueter	46	Bob Gibson
69	Tommy John	54	Kenny Rogers	46	John Denny
65	Jim Kaat	53	Jim Palmer	46	Rick Wise
64	Tom Glavine	51	Eddie Rommel	46	Larry Jackson
63	Dizzy Trout	51	Red Ruffing	45	Dave Stieb
61	Dennis Martinez	50	Grover Alexander	45	Stan Coveleski
58	Gaylord Perry	50	Joe Bush	45	Herb Pennock
57	Ted Lyons	49	Paul Splittorff	45	Ferguson Jenkins
56	Carl Mays	49	Whitey Ford	45	Robin Roberts

(587) Most Career Triple Plays Participated in

9	Bid McPhee	All at 2B	7	Bill B. Phillips	All at 1B
	Also involved in three as a runner		7	George Davis	6 at SS; 1 at 3B
9	Donie Bush	All at SS	7	Tommy Tucker	All at 1B
8	John Morrill	7 at 1B; 1 at 3B	7	George Sisler	All at 1B
8	Roger Connor	7 at 1B; 1 at 3B	7	Jim Bottomley	All at 1B
8	Germany Smith	All at SS	7	Gary Gaetti	All at 3B
8	Jake Beckley	All at 1B		Two in one game on Jul 17, 1990	

Bill Bergen

(588) Unassisted Triple Plays

Neal Ball (SS)	AL	CLE	Jul 19, 1909	1G	
Bill Wambsganss (2B)	AL	CLE	Oct 10, 1920	World Series	
George H. Burns (1B)	AL	BOS	Sep 14, 1923		
Ernie Padgett (SS)	NL	BOS	Oct 6, 1923	2G	
Glenn Wright (SS)	NL	PIT	May 7, 1925		
Jimmy Cooney Jr. (SS)	NL	CHI	May 30, 1927	1G	
Johnny Neun (1B)	AL	DET	May 31, 1927	
Ron Hansen (SS)	AL	WAS	Jul 30, 1968	
Mickey Morandini (2B)	NL	PHI	Sep 20, 1992	
John Valentin (SS)	AL	BOS	Jul 8, 1994	
Randy Velarde (2B)	AL	OAK	May 29, 2000	
Rafael Furcal (SS)	NL	ATL	Aug 10, 2003	

(589) Best Fielding Average by a First Baseman in a Season (min. 125 G)

1.0000	Steve Garvey	NL	SD	1984		.9980	Mark Teixeira	AL	TEX	2005
.9994	Stuffy McInnis	AL	BOS	1921		.9978	Travis Lee	NL	ARI	1998
.9992	Frank McCormick	NL	PHI	1946		.9978	Don Mattingly	AL	NY	1993
.9991	J.T. Snow	NL	SF	1998		.9977	Mark Grace	NL	CHI	1992
.9991	David Segui	AL	SEA	1998		.9977	Dan Driessen	NL	CIN	1982
.9991	Jim Spencer	AL	CAL-TEX	1973		.9977	Travis Lee	AL	TB	2003
	CAL (26 games); TEX (99 games)					.9976	Wally Joyner	AL	KC	1995
.9986	Todd Helton	NL	COL	2001		.9975	John Olerud	AL	SEA	2003
.9985	Jim Spencer	AL	CHI	1976		.9975	Kevin Young	NL	PIT	1993
.9984	Sean Casey	NL	CIN	2005		.9975	Rico Brogna	NL	NY	1995
.9982	Steve Garvey	NL	LA	1976		.9975	Mark Teixeira	AL	TEX	2006

(590) Worst Fielding Average by a First Baseman in a Season, since 1946 (min. 125 G)

.9788	Dick Stuart	AL	BOS	1963		.9845	Ferris Fain	AL	PHI	1952
.9814	Dick Stuart	AL	BOS	1964		.9845	Jack Graham	AL	STL	1949
.9819	Dale Long	NL	PIT	1956		.9845	Mike Hargrove	AL	TEX	1976
.9835	Dick Stuart	NL	PIT	1961		.9845	Ferris Fain	AL	PHI	1949
.9837	Donn Clendenon	NL	PIT	1965		.9846	Orlando Cepeda	NL	SF	1963
.9840	Dale Murphy	NL	ATL	1978		.9847	Donn Clendenon	NL	PIT	1966
.9842	Willie McCovey	NL	SF	1966		.9849	George Scott	AL	BOS	1977
.9843	Lee Thomas	AL	BOS	1965		.9849	Ferris Fain	AL	PHI	1947
.9843	Mo Vaughn	NL	NY	2002		.9850	Kevin Young	NL	PIT	1999
.9844	Frank Robinson	NL	CIN	1959						

(591) Most Errors by a First Baseman in a Season, since 1946

29	Dick Stuart	AL	BOS	1963	22	Willie McCovey	NL	SF	1966
28	Donn Clendenon	NL	PIT	1965	22	Willie Montanez	NL	SF-ATL	1976
24	Dale Long	NL	PIT	1956				SF (7); ATL (15)	
24	Dick Stuart	AL	BOS	1964	21	Earl Torgeson	NL	BOS	1950
24	Donn Clendenon	NL	PIT	1966	21	Dick Stuart	NL	PIT	1961
24	George Scott	AL	BOS	1977	21	Orlando Cepeda	NL	SF	1963
23	Kevin Young	NL	PIT	1999	21	Willie McCovey	NL	SF	1968
22	Ferris Fain	AL	PHI	1949	21	Mike Hargrove	AL	TEX	1976
22	Ferris Fain	AL	PHI	1952	21	Willie Upshaw	AL	TOR	1983
22	Dick Stuart	NL	PIT	1959	20	Tom McCraw	AL	CHI	1968
22	Tito Francona	AL	CLE	1962	20	Dale Murphy	NL	ATL	1978

(592) Fewest Errors by a First Baseman in a Season (min. 125 G)

0	Steve Garvey	NL	SD	1984	3	Pete O'Brien	AL	SEA	1991
1	Stuffy McInnis	AL	BOS	1921	3	Kevin Young	NL	PIT	1993
1	Frank McCormick	NL	PHI	1946	3	Don Mattingly	AL	NY	1993
1	Jim Spencer	AL	CAL-TEX	1973	3	Rico Brogna	NL	NY	1995
			CAL (0); TEX (1)		3	Wally Joyner	AL	KC	1995
1	J.T. Snow	NL	SF	1998	3	Travis Lee	NL	ARI	1998
1	David Segui	AL	SEA	1998	3	Scott Spiezio	AL	ANA	2002
2	Jim Spencer	AL	CHI	1976	3	John Olerud	AL	SEA	2003
2	Todd Helton	NL	COL	2001	3	Travis Lee	AL	TB	2003
2	Sean Casey	NL	CIN	2005	3	Tino Martinez	NL	STL	2003
3	Steve Garvey	NL	LA	1976	3	Mark Teixeira	AL	TEX	2005
3	Dan Driessen	NL	CIN	1982					

(593) Most Assists by a First Baseman in a Season

184	Bill Buckner	AL	BOS	1985	146	Rudy York	AL	DET	1942
180	Mark Grace	NL	CHI	1990	146	Keith Hernandez	NL	STL	1979
167	Mark Grace	NL	CHI	1991	146	Pete O'Brien	AL	TEX	1987
166	Sid Bream	PIT	PIT	1986	146	Todd Helton	NL	COL	1998
161	Bill Buckner	NL	CHI	1983	145	Vic Power	AL	CLE	1960
159	Bill Buckner	NL	CHI	1982	145	Eddie Murray	AL	BAL	1987
157	Bill Buckner	AL	BOS	1986	145	Wally Joyner	AL	KC	1993
156	Todd Helton	NL	COL	2003	144	Todd Helton	NL	COL	2004
155	Mickey Vernon	AL	CLE	1949	143	Rafael Palmeiro	AL	TEX	1992
152	Fred Tenney	NL	BOS	1905	143	Chick Gandil	AL	WAS	1914
152	Eddie Murray	AL	BAL	1985	143	Wally Joyner	AL	CAL	1988
150	Ferris Fain	AL	PHI	1952	143	Eddie Murray	AL	BAL	1984
149	Rudy York	AL	DET	1943	143	Jeff Bagwell	NL	HOU	2001
149	Keith Hernandez	NL	NY	1986	142	Vic Power	AL	CLE	1961
149	Keith Hernandez	NL	NY	1987	142	Keith Hernandez	NL	NY	1984
149	Todd Helton	NL	COL	2000	141	Rico Brogna	NL	PHI	1998
147	Keith Hernandez	NL	STL-NY	1983	141	Mark Grace	NL	CHI	1992
			STL (51); NY (96)		140	Pete O'Brien	AL	TEX	1988
147	Rafael Palmeiro	AL	TEX	1993	140	Jiggs Donahue	AL	CHI	1907
147	Eric Karros	NL	LA	1993	140	George Sisler	AL	STL	1920
147	Jeff King	AL	KC	1997	140	Sid Bream	NL	PIT	1988

(594) Most Putouts by a First Baseman in a Season

1846	Jiggs Donahue	AL	CHI	1907		1642	George Kelly	NL	NY	1922
1759	George Kelly	NL	NY	1920		1637	Earl Sheely	AL	CHI	1921
1755	Phil Todt	AL	BOS	1926		1635	Walter Holke	NL	NY	1917
1710	Wally Pipp	NL	CIN	1926		1626	Ed Konetchy	NL	BOS	1916
1697	Jiggs Donahue	AL	CHI	1906		1626	Chris Chambliss	NL	ATL	1980
1691	Candy LaChance	AL	BOS	1904		1624	Fred Tenney	NL	NY	1908
1687	Tom Jones	AL	STL	1907		1624	Wally Pipp	AL	NY	1921
1682	Ernie Banks	NL	CHI	1965		1622	Vic Saier	NL	CHI	1916
1667	Wally Pipp	AL	NY	1922		1621	Bill Terry	NL	NY	1927
1662	Lou Gehrig	AL	NY	1927		1616	Tom Jones	AL	STL	1908
1658	Stuffy McInnis	PHI	AL	1917		1616	Harry Swacina	FL	BAL	1914
1656	Jim Bottomley	STL	NL	1927		1614	Fred Beck	FL	CHI	1914
1652	Ed Konetchy	NL	STL	1911		1610	Ed Konetchy	NL	STL	1908
1652	Jake Daubert	NL	CIN	1922		1609	Wally Pipp	AL	NY	1917
1649	Wally Pipp	AL	NY	1920		1607	Jim Bottomley	NL	STL	1926
1645	Jiggs Donahue	AL	CHI	1905		1606	Steve Garvey	NL	LA	1977

(595) Most Double Plays by a First Baseman in a Season

194	Ferris Fain	AL	PHI	1949		168	Mickey Vernon	AL	CLE	1949
192	Ferris Fain	AL	PHI	1950		167	Carlos Delgado	AL	TOR	2001
182	Donn Clendenon	NL	PIT	1966		166	Ted Kluszewski	NL	CIN	1954
176	Andres Galarraga	NL	COL	1997		163	Rudy York	AL	DET	1944
175	Ron Jackson	AL	MIN	1979		161	Donn Clendenon	NL	PIT	1965
175	Albert Pujols	NL	STL	2005		161	Rod Carew	AL	MIN	1977
171	Gil Hodges	NL	BRO	1951		160	Cecil Cooper	AL	MIL	1980

(596) Best Fielding Average by a Second Baseman in a Season (min. 125 G)

.9967	Bret Boone	NL	CIN	1997		.9937	Manny Trillo	NL	PHI	1982
.9956	Jose Oquendo	NL	STL	1990		.9937	Jose Lind	AL	KC	1993
.9949	Ryne Sandberg	NL	CHI	1991		.9937	Mark Loretta	AL	BOS	2006
.9947	Bobby Grich	AL	BAL	1973		.9937	Mark Grudzielanek	AL	KC	2006
.9945	Frank White	AL	KC	1988		.9935	Johnny Ray	NL	PIT	1986
.9941	Jose Oquendo	NL	STL	1989		.9935	Lou Whitaker	AL	DET	1991
.9941	Bret Boone	NL	CIN	1995		.9931	Tito Fuentes	NL	SF	1973
.9940	Jody Reed	NL	SD	1995		.9931	Ryne Sandberg	NL	CHI	1984
.9939	Jerry Adair	AL	BAL	1964		.9930	Joe Morgan	NL	CIN	1977
.9938	Ryne Sandberg	NL	CHI	1986		.9930	Snuffy Stirnweiss	AL	NY	1948
.9938	Roberto Alomar	AL	TOR	1995						

(597) Worst Fielding Average by a Second Baseman in a Season, since 1946 (min. 125 games)

.9566	Luis Alicea	NL	STL	1996		.9633	Emil Verban	NL	PHI	1946
.9600	Rod Carew	AL	MIN	1974		.9638	Don Blasingame	NL	STL	1958
.9605	Steve Sax	NL	LA	1983		.9641	Tito Fuentes	NL	SF	1972
.9616	Juan Samuel	NL	PHI	1984		.9641	Mike Edwards	AL	OAK	1978
.9616	Alan Wiggins	NL	SD	1984		.9643	Chuck Hiller	NL	SF	1962
.9618	Jerry Priddy	AL	WAS	1946		.9643	Cass Michaels	AL	WAS	1951
.9623	Delino DeShields	NL	MON	1991		.9649	Dick McAuliffe	AL	DET	1967
.9627	Granny Hamner	NL	PHI	1957		.9649	Jack Dittmer	NL	MIL	1953
.9631	Chuck Knoblauch	AL	NY	1999						

(598) Most Errors by a Second Baseman in a Season, since 1946

33	Juan Samuel	NL	PHI	1984		29	Jim Morrison	AL	CHI	1980
33	Rod Carew	AL	MIN	1974		28	Emil Verban	NL	STL-PHI	1946
32	Jerry Priddy	AL	WAS	1946					STL (0); PHI (28)	
32	Alan Wiggins	NL	SD	1984		28	Bobby Avila	AL	CLE	1952
30	Gene Baker	NL	CHI	1955		28	Roberto Alomar	NL	SD	1989
30	Davey Johnson	NL	ATL	1973		27	Al Kozar	AL	WAS	1948
30	Steve Sax	NL	LA	1983		27	Jerry Priddy	AL	STL	1949
29	Jerry Priddy	AL	STL	1948		27	Julian Javier	NL	STL	1964
29	Chuck Hiller	NL	SF	1962		27	Joe Morgan	NL	HOU	1965
29	Tito Fuentes	NL	SF	1972		27	Pedro Garcia	AL	MIL	1973
29	Manny Trillo	NL	CHI	1975		27	Delino DeShields	NL	MON	1991

(599) Fewest Errors by a Second Baseman in a Season (min. 125 G)

2	Bret Boone	NL	CIN	1997		5	Bobby Grich	AL	BAL	1973
3	Jose Oquendo	NL	STL	1990		5	Joe Morgan	NL	CIN	1977
4	Frank White	AL	KC	1988		5	Manny Trillo	NL	PHI	1982
4	Ryne Sandberg	NL	CHI	1991		5	Ryne Sandberg	NL	CHI	1986
4	Lou Whitaker	AL	DET	1991		5	Johnny Ray	NL	PIT	1986
4	Jose Lind	AL	KC	1993		5	Jose Oquendo	NL	STL	1989
4	Bret Boone	NL	CIN	1995		5	Roberto Alomar	AL	TOR	1992
4	Jody Reed	NL	SD	1995		5	Jody Reed	NL	LA	1993
4	Roberto Alomar	AL	TOR	1995		5	Mickey Morandini	NL	CHI	1998
4	Mark Loretta	AL	BOS	2006		5	Edgardo Alfonzo	NL	NY	1999
4	Mark Grudzielanek	AL	KC	2006		5	Mickey Morandini	NL	CHI	1999
5	Snuffy Stirnweiss	AL	NY	1948		5	Roberto Alomar	AL	CLE	2001
5	Jerry Adair	AL	BAL	1964		5	Adam Kennedy	AL	LA	2005

(600) Most Assists by a Second Baseman in a Season

641	Frankie Frisch	NL	NY	1927		542	Jerry Priddy	AL	DET	1950
588	Hughie Critz	NL	CIN	1926		541	Hughie Critz	NL	NY	1933
582	Rogers Hornsby	NL	NY	1927		539	Glenn Hubbard	NL	ATL	1985
572	Oscar Melillo	AL	STL	1930		539	Ryne Sandberg	NL	CHI	1992
571	Ryne Sandberg	NL	CHI	1983		538	Nap Lajoie	AL	CLE	1908
568	Rabbit Maranville	NL	PIT	1924		538	Bill Mazeroski	NL	PIT	1966
562	Frank Parkinson	NL	PHI	1922		537	Frankie Frisch	NL	NY	1924
559	Tony Cuccinello	NL	BOS	1936		527	Billy Herman	NL	CHI	1932
557	Johnny Hodapp	AL	CLE	1930		527	Manny Trillo	NL	CHI	1976
555	Lou Bierbauer	NL	PIT	1892		526	Oscar Melillo	AL	STL	1932
554	Pep Young	NL	PIT	1938		526	Bump Wills	AL	TEX	1978
552	Burgess Whitehead	NL	NY	1936		525	Miller Huggins	NL	CIN	1905
551	Sparky Adams	NL	CHI	1925		525	Tony Cuccinello	NL	BRO	1932
550	Ryne Sandberg	NL	CHI	1984		524	Rogers Hornsby	NL	STL	1920
547	Rogers Hornsby	NL	NY	1929		524	Freddie Maguire	NL	CHI	1928
543	Hod Ford	NL	PHI	1924		524	Charlie Gehringer	AL	DET	1936
543	Oscar Melillo	AL	STL	1931		524	Tony Cuccinello	NL	BOS	1937
543	Bill Mazeroski	NL	PIT	1964		522	Jimmy Dykes	AL	PHI	1921
542	Hughie Critz	NL	CIN	1925		522	Bobby Knoop	AL	LA	1964
542	Charlie Gehringer	AL	DET	1933		522	Ryne Sandberg	NL	CHI	1988
542	Woody W. Williams	NL	CIN	1944		520	Billy Herman	NL	CHI	1935

(601) Most Putouts by a Second Baseman in a Season

529	Bid McPhee	AA	CIN	1886		443	Bobby Doerr	AL	BOS	1950
484	Bobby Grich	AL	BAL	1974		442	Bid McPhee	AA	CIN	1887
483	Bucky Harris	AL	WAS	1922		442	Nap Lajoie	NL	PHI	1898
478	Nellie Fox	AL	CHI	1956		442	Burgess Whitehead	NL	NY	1936
472	Lou Bierbauer	AA	PHI	1889		441	Rennie Stennett	NL	PIT	1974
466	Billy Herman	NL	CHI	1933		441	Fred Pfeffer	PL	CHI	1890
463	Bill Wambsganss	AL	BOS	1924		440	Marty McManus	AL	STL	1925
461	Cub Stricker	AA	CLE	1887		440	Jerry Priddy	AL	DET	1950
460	Buddy Myer	AL	WAS	1935		438	Del Pratt	AL	STL	1916
459	Bill John Sweeney	NL	BOS	1912		437	Bill Kenworthy	FL	KC	1914
457	Billy Herman	NL	CHI	1936		437	Jerry Priddy	AL	DET	1951
455	George Cutshaw	NL	BRO	1914		434	Cub Stricker	NL	CLE	1889
453	Nellie Fox	AL	CHI	1957		434	Jimmy Dykes	AL	PHI	1921
452	Fred Pfeffer	NL	CHI	1889		433	Snuffy Stirnweiss	AL	NY	1944
451	Bid McPhee	NL	CIN	1892		432	Snuffy Stirnweiss	AL	NY	1945
451	Nellie Fox	AL	CHI	1953		432	Gene Baker	NL	CHI	1955
450	Nap Lajoie	AL	CLE	1908		431	Joe Quinn	PL	BOS	1890
450	Emil Verban	NL	PHI	1947		431	Bobby Grich	AL	BAL	1973
449	Eddie Collins	AL	CHI	1920		430	Rennie Stennett	NL	PIT	1976
444	Nellie Fox	AL	CHI	1958						

(602) Most Double Plays by a Second Baseman in a Season

161	Bill Mazeroski	NL	PIT	1966		135	Bobby Knoop	AL	CAL	1966
150	Jerry Priddy	AL	DET	1950		135	Fernando Vina	NL	MIL	1998
144	Bill Mazeroski	NL	PIT	1961		134	Bobby Doerr	AL	BOS	1949
141	Nellie Fox	AL	CHI	1957		133	Jackie Robinson	NL	BRO	1950
141	Dave Cash	NL	PHI	1974		133	Harold Reynolds	AL	SEA	1991
138	Buddy Myer	AL	WAS	1935		132	Bobby Doerr	AL	BOS	1943
138	Bill Mazeroski	NL	PIT	1962		132	Jerry Priddy	AL	STL	1948
138	Carlos Baerga	AL	CLE	1992		132	Bobby Grich	AL	BAL	1974
137	Jerry Coleman	AL	NY	1950		131	Bill Mazeroski	NL	PIT	1963
137	Jackie Robinson	NL	BRO	1951		131	Bill Mazeroski	NL	PIT	1967
137	Red Schoendienst	NL	STL	1954		130	Bobby Doerr	AL	BOS	1950
136	Bobby Richardson	AL	NY	1961		130	Tommy Helms	NL	CIN	1971
135	Cass Michaels	AL	CHI	1949		130	Bobby Grich	AL	BAL	1973

(603) Best Fielding Average by a Third Baseman in a Season (min. 125 G)

.9894	Don Money	AL	MIL	1974		.9831	George Kell	AL	PHI-DET	1946
.9883	Hank Majeski	AL	PHI	1947				PHI (26 games); DET (105 games)			
.9872	Eric Chavez	AL	OAK	2006		.9827	Carney Lansford	AL	CAL	1979
.9871	Aurelio Rodriguez	AL	DET	1978		.9824	George Kell	AL	DET	1950
.9870	Mike Lowell	AL	BOS	2006		.9823	Mike Lowell	NL	FLA	2004
.9865	Vinny Castilla	NL	COL	2004		.9822	Vinny Castilla	NL	ATL	2002
.9842	Willie Kamm	AL	CLE	1933		.9822	Jeff Cirillo	NL	COL	2001
.9833	Steve Buechele	AL-NL	TEX-PIT	1991		.9816	Pinky Whitney	NL	PHI	1937
		TEX (111 games); PIT (31 games)				.9805	Brooks Robinson	AL	BAL	1967
.9831	Heinie Groh	NL	NY	1924		.9802	Carney Lansford	AL	OAK	1987
.9831	Mike Lowell	NL	FLA	2005		.9801	Robin Ventura	NL	NY	1999
						.9800	Ken Reitz	NL	STL	1977
						.9800	Jimmy Dykes	AL	PHI	1932

(604) Worst Fielding Average by a Third Baseman in a Season, since 1946 (min. 125 G)

.8991	Butch Hobson	AL	BOS	1978		.9199	Ed Sprague Jr.	NL	PIT	1999
.8994	Gary Sheffield	NL	SD-FLA	1993		.9209	Dean Palmer	AL	KC	1998
		SD (67 games); FLA (66 games)				.9212	Dick Allen	NL	PHI	1964
.9062	Russ Davis	AL	SEA	1998		.9212	Ed Sprague Jr.	AL	TOR-OAK	1998
.9101	Howard Johnson	NL	NY	1989				TOR (105 games); OAK (23 games)			
.9134	Mike Lamb	AL	TEX	2000		.9218	Dave Hollins	AL	ANA	1997
.9143	Dave Hollins	NL	PHI	1993		.9220	Dean Palmer	AL	TEX	1993
.9152	Dan Driessen	NL	CIN	1974		.9225	Todd Zeile	NL	STL	1993
.9188	Larry Parrish	NL	MON	1975		.9226	Tony Perez	NL	CIN	1970
.9194	Jim Ray Hart	NL	SF	1965		.9234	Pete Ward	AL	CHI	1963

(605) Most Errors by a Third Baseman in a Season, since 1946

43	Butch Hobson	AL	BOS	1978		33	Aramis Ramirez	NL	PIT-CHI	2003
41	Dick Allen	NL	PHI	1964					PIT (23); CHI (10)	
38	Pete Ward	AL	CHI	1963		32	Bob Bailey	NL	PIT	1963
36	Darrell Evans	NL	ATL	1975		32	Jim Ray Hart	NL	SF	1965
36	Joel Youngblood	NL	SF	1984		32	Tony Perez	NL	CIN	1969
35	Dick Allen	NL	PHI	1967		32	Bobby Bonilla	NL	PIT	1988
35	Tony Perez	NL	CIN	1970		32	Russ Davis	AL	SEA	1998
35	Larry Parrish	NL	MON	1975		31	Frankie Gustine	NL	PIT	1947
35	Bobby Bonilla	NL	PIT	1989		31	Ron Santo	NL	CHI	1961
34	Ray Jablonski	NL	STL	1954		30	Eddie Yost	AL	WAS	1950
34	Ken Boyer	NL	STL	1963		30	Eddie Mathews	NL	MIL	1953
34	Gary Sheffield	NL	SD-FLA	1993		30	Harmon Killebrew	AL	WAS	1959
			SD (15); FLA (19)			30	Joe Foy	AL	BOS	1968
33	Todd Zeile	NL	STL	1993		30	Paul Schaal	AL	KC	1973
33	Mike Lamb	AL	TEX	2000		30	Darrell Evans	NL	SF	1979
33	Troy Glaus	AL	ANA	2000		30	George Brett	AL	KC	1979
						30	Pedro Guerrero	NL	LA	1983

JOHN THORN

Tris Speaker

(606) Fewest Errors by a Third Baseman in a Season (min. 125 G)

4	Aurelio Rodriguez	AL	DET	1978		7	George Kell	AL	PHI-DET	1946
5	Hank Majeski	AL	PHI	1947					PHI (2); DET (5)	
5	Don Money	AL	MIL	1974		7	Carney Lansford	AL	CAL	1979
5	Eric Chavez	AL	OAK	2006		7	Buddy Bell	NL	CIN	1987
6	Willie Kamm	AL	CLE	1933		7	Carney Lansford	AL	OAK	1987
6	Vinny Castilla	NL	ATL	2002		7	Ken Oberkfell	NL	ATL	1987
6	Vinny Castilla	NL	COL	2004		7	Carney Lansford	AL	OAK	1988
6	Mike Lowell	NL	FLA	2005		7	Steve Buechele	AL-NL	TEX-PIT	1991
6	Mike Lowell	AL	BOS	2006					TEX (3); PIT (4)	
7	Heinie Groh	NL	NY	1924		7	Gary Gaetti	NL	STL	1997
7	Pinky Whitney	NL	PHI	1937		7	Jeff Cirillo	NL	COL	2001
						7	Joe Randa	AL	KC	2003
						7	Mike Lowell	NL	FLA	2004

(607) Most Assists by a Third Baseman in a Season

412	Graig Nettles	AL	CLE	1971		381	Darrell Evans	NL	ATL	1975
410	Brooks Robinson	AL	BAL	1974		379	Graig Nettles	AL	NY	1975
410	Graig Nettles	AL	NY	1973		378	Frank Malzone	AL	BOS	1958
405	Harlond Clift	AL	STL	1937		378	Ron Santo	NL	CHI	1968
405	Brooks Robinson	AL	BAL	1967		377	Aurelio Rodriguez	AL	CAL-WAS	1970
404	Mike Schmidt	NL	PHI	1974					CAL (41); WAS (336)	
399	Doug DeCinces	AL	CAL	1982		377	Graig Nettles	AL	NY	1974
398	Brandon Inge	AL	DET	2006		377	Mike Schmidt	NL	PHI	1976
396	Mike Schmidt	NL	PHI	1977		376	Jimmy Collins	NL	BOS	1899
396	Clete Boyer	AL	NY	1962		375	Aurelio Rodriguez	AL	DET	1975
396	Buddy Bell	AL	TEX	1982		374	Ron Santo	NL	CHI	1963
393	Ron Santo	NL	CHI	1967		373	Ron Santo	NL	CHI	1965
392	Terry Pendleton	STL	NL	1989		373	George Brett	AL	KC	1979
391	Ron Santo	NL	CHI	1966		372	Mike Schmidt	NL	PHI	1980
389	Vinny Castilla	NL	COL	1996		372	Robin Ventura	AL	CHI	1992
389	Aurelio Rodriguez	AL	DET	1974		371	Tommy Leach	NL	PIT	1904
385	Ossie Vitt	AL	DET	1916		371	Bill Melton	AL	CHI	1971
383	Buddy Bell	AL	TEX	1983		371	Terry Pendleton	NL	STL	1986
383	Graig Nettles	AL	NY	1976		370	Arlie Latham	NL	CIN	1891
383	Tim Wallach	NL	MON	1985		370	Frank Malzone	AL	BOS	1957
382	Billy Shindle	NL	BAL	1892		370	Brooks Robinson	AL	BAL	1969

(608) Most Putouts by a Third Baseman in a Season

255	Denny Lyons	AA	PHI	1887	219	Jimmy Austin	AL	STL	1912
251	Jimmy Williams	NL	PIT	1899	219	Tony Boeckel	NL	BOS	1920
251	Jimmy Collins	NL	BOS	1900	218	Billy Shindle	AA	BAL	1888
243	Jimmy Collins	NL	BOS	1898	218	Howard Shanks	AL	WAS	1921
243	Willie Kamm	AL	CHI	1928	217	Jimmy Collins	NL	BOS	1899
236	Willie Kamm	AL	CHI	1927	217	Ed Gremminger	NL	BOS	1903
233	Frank Baker	AL	PHI	1913	217	Frank Baker	AL	PHI	1911
232	Bill Coughlin	AL	WAS	1901	217	Frank Baker	AL	PHI	1912
229	Ernie Courtney	NL	PHI	1905	216	Jimmy Austin	AL	STL	1913
228	Jimmy Austin	AL	STL	1911	216	Willie Jones	NL	PHI	1952
226	Pie Traynor	NL	PIT	1925	215	Lave Cross	NL	STL	1898
225	Tom Burns	NL	CHI	1889	214	Denny Lyons	NL	PIT	1893
225	Billy Shindle	AA	BAL	1889	214	Jimmy Collins	NL	BOS	1897
223	Charlie Irwin	NL	CIN	1898	214	Bobby Byrne	NL	STL-PIT	1909
223	Lave Cross	NL	CLE-STL	1899			STL (164); PIT (50)		
	CLE (66); STL (157)				213	Billy Nash	NL	BOS	1891
222	Ed Gremminger	NL	BOS	1902	212	Tommy Leach	NL	PIT	1904
222	Hobe Ferris	AL	STL	1908	212	Bobby Byrne	NL	STL	1907
221	Will Smalley	NL	CLE	1890	212	Pie Traynor	NL	PIT	1927
221	Frank Baker	AL	PHI	1914	212	Eddie Yost	AL	WAS	1952
221	Willie Kamm	AL	CHI	1929	210	Jack Crooks	NL	STL	1893
220	Red Smith	NL	BRO-BOS	1914	210	Billy Lauder	NL	PHI	1899
	BRO (136); BOS (84)								

(609) Most Double Plays by a Third Baseman in a Season

54	Graig Nettles	AL	CLE	1971	41	Pie Traynor	NL	PIT	1925
50	Harlond Clift	AL	STL	1937	41	Ken Boyer	NL	STL	1958
48	Johnny Pesky	AL	BOS	1949	41	Ron Santo	NL	CHI	1961
48	Paul Molitor	AL	MIL	1982	41	Clete Boyer	AL	NY	1962
46	Sammy Hale	AL	PHI	1927	41	Aurelio Rodriguez	AL	CAL-WAS	1970
46	Clete Boyer	AL	NY	1965			CAL (7); WAS (34)		
46	Gary Gaetti	AL	MIN	1983	41	Darrell Evans	NL	ATL	1975
45	Eddie Yost	AL	WAS	1950	41	Doug DeCinces	AL	BAL	1980
45	Frank Malzone	AL	BOS	1961	41	Doug DeCinces	AL	CAL	1982
45	Darrell Evans	NL	ATL	1974	41	Vinny Castilla	NL	COL	1997
45	Jeff Cirillo	NL	MIL	1998	41	Jeff Cirillo	NL	COL	2000
44	Buddy Bell	AL	CLE	1973	41	Scott Rolen	NL	PHI-STL	2002
44	Brooks Robinson	AL	BAL	1974			PHI (23); STL (18)		
43	Hank Thompson	NL	NY	1950	41	Brandon Inge	AL	DET	2005
43	Brooks Robinson	AL	BAL	1963	40	Ken Keltner	AL	CLE	1939
43	Vinny Castilla	NL	COL	1996	40	Frank Malzone	AL	BOS	1959
43	Eric Chavez	AL	OAK	2006	40	Brooks Robinson	AL	BAL	1964
42	Aurelio Rodriguez	AL	CAL	1969	40	Graig Nettles	AL	CLE	1970
42	Don Money	AL	MIL	1974	40	Mike Schmidt	NL	PHI	1974
42	Aaron Boone	NL	CIN	2002	40	Aurelio Rodriguez	AL	DET	1974
41	Gene Robertson	AL	STL	1925	40	Wade Boggs	AL	BOS	1983

(610) Best Fielding Average by a Shortstop in a Season (min. 125 G)

.9956	Cal Ripken	AL	BAL	1990		.9912	Larry Bowa	NL	PHI	1979
.9954	Omar Vizquel	AL	CLE	2000		.9905	Ed Brinkman	AL	DET	1972
.9941	Rey Sanchez	AL	KC	2000		.9902	Cal Ripken	AL	BAL	1989
.9938	Rey Ordonez	NL	NY	1999		.9898	Mike Bordick	AL	BAL	1998
.9933	Omar Vizquel	NL	SF	2006		.9898	Adam Everett	NL	HOU	2006
.9931	Omar Vizquel	AL	CLE	1998		.9897	Omar Vizquel	AL	CLE	2002
.9919	Tony Fernandez	AL	TOR	1989		.9893	Spike Owen	NL	MON	1990
.9915	Rey Sanchez	AL-NL	KC-ATL	2001		.9891	Omar Vizquel	AL	CLE	2001
	KC (100 games); ATL (48 games)									

(611) Worst Fielding Average by a Shortstop in a Season, since 1946 (min. 125 G)

.9352	Jose Offerman	NL	LA	1992		.9438	Mike Tyson	NL	STL	1973
.9359	Alan Bannister	AL	CHI	1977		.9438	Granny Hamner	NL	PHI	1950
.9388	Robin Yount	AL	MIL	1975		.9441	Alvin Dark	NL	NY	1951
.9415	Wil Cordero	NL	MON	1993		.9444	Mike Caruso	AL	CHI	1998
.9423	Zoilo Versalles	AL	MIN	1966		.9448	Roy Smalley	NL	CHI	1950
.9426	George Strickland	NL	PIT	1951		.9450	Rafael Ramirez	NL	HOU	1989
.9428	Desi Relaford	NL	PHI-SD	2000		.9453	Maury Wills	NL	LA	1960
	PHI (81 games); SD (45 games)					.9455	Daryl Spencer	NL	STL	1960
.9428	Eddie Lake	AL	DET	1947		.9459	Frank Taveras	NL	PIT	1978
.9434	Sonny Jackson	NL	HOU	1967						

(612) Most Errors by a Shortstop in a Season, since 1946

51	Roy Smalley	NL	CHI	1950		39	Luke Appling	AL	CHI	1946
48	Granny Hamner	NL	PHI	1950		39	Roy Smalley	NL	CHI	1949
45	Alvin Dark	NL	NY	1951		39	Zoilo Versalles	AL	MIN	1965
44	Robin Yount	AL	MIL	1975		39	Bill Russell	NL	LA	1974
43	Eddie Lake	AL	DET	1947		39	Rafael Ramirez	NL	ATL	1983
42	Jose Offerman	NL	LA	1992		38	Eddie Joost	AL	PHI	1947
41	Bill Almon	NL	SD	1977		38	Granny Hamner	NL	PHI	1952
40	Maury Wills	NL	LA	1960		38	Dick Howser	AL	KC	1961
40	Dick Groat	NL	STL	1964		38	Dick Groat	NL	PIT	1962
40	Alan Bannister	AL	CHI	1977		38	Frank Taveras	NL	PIT	1978
40	Garry Templeton	NL	STL	1978		38	Rafael Ramirez	NL	ATL	1982
39	Billy Cox	NL	PIT	1946						

(613) Fewest Errors by a Shortstop in a Season (min. 125 G)

3	Cal Ripken	AL	BAL	1990		7	Ed Brinkman	AL	DET	1972
3	Omar Vizquel	AL	CLE	2000		7	Dick Schofield Jr.	AL-NL	CAL-NY	1992
4	Rey Ordonez	NL	NY	1999					CAL (0); NY (7)	
4	Rey Sanchez	AL	KC	2000		7	Omar Vizquel	AL	SEA	1992
4	Omar Vizquel	NL	SF	2006		7	Manuel Lee	AL	TOR	1992
5	Omar Vizquel	AL	CLE	1998		7	Cal Ripken	AL	BAL	1995
6	Larry Bowa	NL	PHI	1979		7	Mike Bordick	AL	BAL	1998
6	Tony Fernandez	AL	TOR	1989		7	Omar Vizquel	AL	CLE	2001
6	Spike Owen	NL	MON	1990		7	Royce Clayton	AL	CHI	2001
6	Rey Sanchez	AL-NL	KC-ATL	2001		7	Omar Vizquel	AL	CLE	2002
			KC (3); ATL (3)			7	Orlando Cabrera	AL	LA	2005
6	David Eckstein	AL	ANA	2004		7	Adam Everett	NL	HOU	2006

(614) Most Assists by a Shortstop in a Season

621	Ozzie Smith	NL	SD	1980		556	Donie Bush	AL	DET	1911
601	Glenn Wright	NL	PIT	1924		556	Luke Appling	AL	CHI	1935
598	Dave Bancroft	NL	PHI-NY	1920		555	Ozzie Smith	NL	SD	1979
			PHI (153); NY (445)			554	Tommy Thevenow	NL	PHI	1930
597	Tommy Thevenow	NL	STL	1926		553	Bill Dahlen	NL	BOS	1908
595	Ivan DeJesus	NL	CHI	1977		552	Travis Jackson	NL	NY	1929
583	Cal Ripken	AL	BAL	1984		552	Mark Belanger	AL	BAL	1974
581	Whitey Wietelmann	NL	BOS	1943		551	Luis Aparicio	AL	CHI	1960
579	Dave Bancroft	NL	NY	1922		549	Ozzie Smith	NL	STL	1985
574	Rabbit Maranville	NL	BOS	1914		548	Ozzie Smith	NL	SD	1978
573	Don Kessinger	NL	CHI	1968		547	Donie Bush	AL	DET	1912
572	Roy Smalley Jr.	AL	MIN	1979		547	Travis Jackson	NL	NY	1928
570	Terry Turner	AL	CLE	1906		546	George McBride	AL	WAS	1911
570	Joe Tinker	NL	CHI	1908		546	Dave Bancroft	NL	NY	1921
570	Leo Cardenas	AL	MIN	1969		545	Mark Belanger	AL	BAL	1976
570	Ozzie Guillen	AL	CHI	1988		544	Donie Bush	AL	DET	1914
569	Heinie Wagner	AL	BOS	1908		544	Art Fletcher	NL	NY	1915
569	Ed Brinkman	AL	WAS	1970		544	Eddie Miller	NL	CIN	1944
568	George McBride	AL	WAS	1908		543	Eddie Miller	NL	CIN	1943
567	Donie Bush	AL	DET	1909		543	Bucky Dent	AL	CHI	1975
565	Art Fletcher	NL	NY	1917		542	Bobby Wallace	NL	STL	1901
563	Luis Aparicio	AL	CHI	1969		542	Arky Vaughan	NL	PIT	1940
561	Germany Smith	NL	CIN	1892		542	Don Kessinger	NL	CHI	1969
561	Tommy Corcoran	NL	CIN	1898		541	Luke Appling	AL	CHI	1937
560	Larry Bowa	NL	PHI	1971		541	Roy Smalley	NL	CHI	1950
560	Bill Russell	NL	LA	1973		540	Doc Lavan	NL	STL	1921
559	Dick Bartell	NL	NY	1936		540	Vern Stephens	AL	BOS	1948
558	Ivan DeJesus	NL	CHI	1978						

(615) Most Putouts by a Shortstop in a Season

425	Hughie Jennings	NL	BAL	1895		373	Monte Cross	AL	PHI	1902
425	Donie Bush	AL	DET	1914		373	Heinie Wagner	AL	BOS	1908
408	Joe Cassidy	AL	WAS	1905		372	George McBride	AL	WAS	1908
407	Rabbit Maranville	NL	BOS	1914		372	Donie Bush	AL	DET	1911
405	Dave Bancroft	NL	NY	1922		371	Dave Bancroft	NL	NY	1922
405	Eddie Miller	NL	BOS	1940		371	Tommy Thevenow	NL	STL	1926
404	Monte Cross	NL	PHI	1898		370	Monte Cross	NL	PHI	1899
396	Dave Bancroft	NL	NY	1921		370	Charlie Babb	NL	BRO	1904
395	Mickey Doolan	NL	PHI	1906		370	George McBride	AL	WAS	1910
392	Buck Weaver	AL	CHI	1913		370	Eddie Joost	AL	PHI	1947
391	Rabbit Maranville	NL	BOS	1915		369	Bill Dahlen	NL	CHI	1898
391	Buck Herzog	NL	CIN	1915		367	Ed Abbaticchio	NL	BOS	1904
386	Ed Abbaticchio	NL	BOS	1905		367	George McBride	AL	WAS	1914
386	Rabbit Maranville	NL	BOS	1916		367	Buck Weaver	AL	CHI	1920
385	Bobby Wallace	AL	STL	1905		362	Dave Bancroft	NL	PHI-NY	1920
382	Doc Lavan	NL	STL	1921			PHI (106); NY (256)			
381	Dick Bartell	NL	PHI	1933		361	Rabbit Maranville	NL	BOS	1919
380	Everett Scott	AL	BOS	1921		361	Joe Sewell	AL	CLE	1927
378	Ray Chapman	AL	CLE	1915		360	Ray Chapman	AL	CLE	1917
377	Hughie Jennings	NL	BAL	1896						

(616) Most Double Plays by a Shortstop in a Season

147	Rick Burleson	AL	BOS	1980		126	Alfredo Griffin	AL	TOR	1980
144	Roy Smalley Jr.	AL	MIN	1979		126	Jack Wilson	NL	PIT	2005
137	Bobby Wine	NL	MON	1970		125	Jim Fregosi	AL	CAL	1966
134	Lou Boudreau	AL	CLE	1944		125	Dick Schofield Jr.	AL	CAL	1988
133	Spike Owen	AL	SEA-BOS	1986		124	Alfredo Griffin	AL	TOR	1979
	SEA (99); BOS (34)					124	Neifi Perez	NL	COL	1999
132	Mike Bordick	AL	BAL	1999		123	Phil Rizzuto	AL	NY	1950
130	Rafael Ramirez	NL	ATL	1982		123	Cal Ripken	AL	BAL	1985
130	Rey Sanchez	AL-NL	KC-ATL	2001		122	Eddie Miller	NL	BOS	1940
	KC (99); ATL (31)					122	Lou Boudreau	AL	CLE	1943
129	Roy McMillan	NL	CIN	1954		122	Cal Ripken	AL	BAL	1984
129	Jack Wilson	NL	PIT	2004		122	Alex S. Gonzalez	AL	TOR	1996
128	Hod Ford	NL	CIN	1928		122	Alex Rodriguez	AL	SEA	2000
128	Vern Stephens	AL	BOS	1949		122	David Eckstein	NL	STL	2005
128	Gene Alley	NL	PIT	1966		121	Eddie Miller	NL	CIN	1943
127	Dick Groat	NL	PIT	1958		121	Roy Smalley Jr.	AL	MIN	1978
127	Zoilo Versalles	AL	MIN	1962		121	Mike Bordick	AL	OAK	1996
127	Neifi Perez	NL	COL	1998		120	Frankie Crosetti	AL	NY	1938
126	Eddie Joost	AL	PHI	1949		120	Lou Boudreau	AL	CLE	1947
126	Johnny Lipon	AL	DET	1950		120	Neifi Perez	NL	COL	2000
126	Dick Groat	NL	PIT	1962		120	Alex S. Gonzalez	AL	TOR	2001
126	Leo Cardenas	AL	MIN	1969						

(617) Best Fielding Average by an Outfielder in a Season (min. 125 G)

1.0000	Danny Litwhiler	NL	PHI	1942	1.0000	Darryl Hamilton	AL	TEX	1996
1.0000	Willard Marshall	NL	BOS	1951	1.0000	Paul O'Neill	AL	NY	1996
1.0000	Rocky Colavito	AL	CLE	1965	1.0000	B.J. Surhoff	AL	BAL	1999
1.0000	Curt Flood	NL	STL	1966	1.0000	Darryl Hamilton	NL	COL-NY	1999
1.0000	Ken Harrelson	AL	BOS	1968			COL (82 games); NY (52 games)		
1.0000	Mickey Stanley	AL	DET	1968	1.0000	Eric Owens	NL	SD	2000
1.0000	Mickey Stanley	AL	DET	1970	1.0000	Bernie Williams	AL	NY	2000
1.0000	Roy White	AL	NY	1971	1.0000	Luis Gonzalez	NL	ARI	2001
1.0000	Al Kaline	AL	DET	1971	1.0000	Kenny Lofton	AL-NL	CHI-SF	2002
1.0000	Carl Yastrzemski	AL	BOS	1977			CHI (92 games); SF (44 games)		
1.0000	Terry Puhl	NL	HOU	1979	1.0000	Juan Encarnacion	NL	FLA	2003
1.0000	Brian Downing	AL	CAL	1982	1.0000	Carlos Lee	AL	CHI	2004
1.0000	Brian Downing	AL	CAL	1984	1.0000	Shawn Green	NL	ARI	2005
1.0000	Brett Butler	NL	LA	1991	1.0000	Vernon Wells	AL	TOR	2005
1.0000	Brett Butler	NL	LA	1993	1.0000	Juan Pierre	NL	CHI	2006
1.0000	Darren Lewis	NL	SF	1993	1.0000	Dave Roberts	NL	SD	2006

(618) Worst Fielding Average by an Outfielder in a Season, since 1946 (min. 125 G)

.9265	Alex Johnson	NL	CIN	1969	.9458	Roman Mejias	NL	HOU	1962
.9360	Lou Brock	NL	STL	1966	.9464	Greg Luzinski	NL	PHI	1979
.9409	Lonnie Smith	NL	STL	1983	.9472	Alex Johnson	NL	CIN	1968
.9419	Willie McCovey	NL	SF	1963	.9481	Vladimir Guerrero	NL	MON	1999
.9421	Chili Davis	AL	CAL	1988	.9484	Lonnie Smith	NL	STL	1984
.9433	Del Ennis	NL	STL	1957	.9492	Reggie Jackson	AL	NY	1977
.9450	Willie Stargell	NL	PIT	1966	.9493	Lou Brock	NL	STL	1969
.9451	Rusty Staub	NL	MON	1971	.9500	Billy Williams	NL	CHI	1964
.9451	Pete Incaviglia	AL	TEX	1987	.9500	Reggie Smith	NL	LA	1978
.9457	George A. Bell	AL	TOR	1988					

(619) Most Errors by an Outfielder in a Season, since 1946

19	Lou Brock	NL	STL	1966	17	Vladimir Guerrero	NL	MON	1998
19	Chili Davis	AL	CAL	1988	15	Willie Davis	NL	LA	1962
19	Vladimir Guerrero	NL	MON	1999	15	Dave Parker	NL	PIT	1977
18	Alex Johnson	NL	CIN	1969	15	Dave Parker	NL	PIT	1979
18	Rusty Staub	NL	MON	1971	15	Lonnie Smith	NL	STL	1983
17	Willie McGee	NL-AL	STL-OAK	1990	15	Larry Herndon	AL	DET	1983
		STL (16); OAK (1)			15	George A. Bell	AL	TOR	1988

(620) Fewest Errors by an Outfielder in a Season (min. 125 G)

0	Danny Litwhiler	NL	PHI	1942	0	Darryl Hamilton	AL	TEX	1996
0	Willard Marshall	NL	BOS	1951	0	Paul O'Neill	AL	NY	1996
0	Rocky Colavito	AL	CLE	1965	0	B.J. Surhoff	AL	BAL	1999
0	Curt Flood	NL	STL	1966	0	Darryl Hamilton	NL	COL-NY	1999
0	Ken Harrelson	AL	BOS	1968				COL (0); NY (0)	
0	Mickey Stanley	AL	DET	1968	0	Eric Owens	NL	SD	2000
0	Mickey Stanley	AL	DET	1970	0	Bernie Williams	AL	NY	2000
0	Roy White	AL	NY	1971	0	Luis Gonzalez	NL	ARI	2001
0	Al Kaline	AL	DET	1971	0	Kenny Lofton	AL-NL	CHI-SF	2002
0	Carl Yastrzemski	AL	BOS	1977				CHI (0); SF (0)	
0	Terry Puhl	NL	HOU	1979	0	Juan Encarnacion	NL	FLA	2003
0	Brian Downing	AL	CAL	1982	0	Carlos Lee	AL	CHI	2004
0	Brian Downing	AL	CAL	1984	0	Shawn Green	NL	ARI	2005
0	Brett Butler	NL	LA	1991	0	Vernon Wells	AL	TOR	2005
0	Brett Butler	NL	LA	1993	0	Juan Pierre	NL	CHI	2006
0	Darren Lewis	NL	SF	1993	0	Dave Roberts	NL	SD	2006

(621) Most Assists by an Outfielder in a Season

50	Orator Shafer	NL	CHI	1879	35	Pop Corkhill	AA	BRO	1889
48	Hugh Nicol	AA	STL	1884	35	George Davis	NL	CLE	1890
45	Hardy Richardson	NL	BUF	1881	35	George Wood	PL	PHI	1890
44	Tommy McCarthy	AA	STL	1888	35	Tris Speaker	AL	BOS	1909
44	Chuck Klein	NL	PHI	1930	35	Tris Speaker	AL	BOS	1912
43	Charlie Duffee	AA	STL	1889	34	John Cahill	NL	STL	1886
43	Jimmy Bannon	NL	BOS	1894	34	Dick Johnston	NL	BOS	1887
42	Jim Fogarty	NL	PHI	1889	34	Jimmy Ryan	NL	CHI	1888
41	Orator Shafer	NL	BUF	1883	34	Hugh Duffy	PL	CHI	1890
41	Jim Lillie	NL	BUF	1884	34	Charlie Duffee	NL	WAS	1892
39	Jim Fogarty	NL	PHI	1887	34	Emmet Heidrick	NL	STL	1899
39	Tom Brown	NL	LOU	1893	34	Harry Niles	AL	STL	1906
39	Mike Mitchell	NL	CIN	1907	34	Danny Murphy	AL	PHI	1911
38	King Kelly	CHI	NL	1883	34	Gavy Cravath	NL	PHI	1914
38	Tommy McCarthy	AA	STL	1889	34	Chet Chadbourne	FL	KC	1914
38	Harry Stovey	AA	PHI	1889	34	Chief Wilson	NL	STL	1914
37	Jack Manning	NL	PHI	1883	33	Jimmy Ryan	NL	CHI	1887
37	Tom Brown	NL	LOU	1892	33	Mike Griffin	PL	PHI	1890
36	Lon Knight	AA	PHI	1884	33	Charlie Duffee	AA	COL	1891
36	Jimmy Ryan	NL	CHI	1889	33	Farmer Weaver	AA	LOU	1891
36	Jack McGeachy	NL	IND	1889	33	Hugh Nicol	AA	STL	1895
36	Jimmy Sheckard	NL	BRO	1903	33	Jimmy Sheckard	NL	BAL	1899
35	Orator Shafer	NL	CLE	1880	33	Clyde Milan	AL	WAS	1911
35	Pop Corkhill	AA	CIN	1885					

(622) Most Putouts by an Outfielder in a Season

547	Taylor Douthit	NL	STL	1928		471	Rick Manning	AL	CLE-MIL	1983
538	Richie Ashburn	NL	PHI	1951				CLE (146); MIL (325)		
514	Richie Ashburn	NL	PHI	1949		469	Lenny Dykstra	NL	PHI	1993
512	Chet Lemon	AL	CHI	1977		468	Johnny Lindell	AL	NY	1944
507	Dwayne Murphy	AL	OAK	1980		466	Rick Bosetti	AL	TOR	1979
503	Dom DiMaggio	AL	BOS	1948		465	Ruppert Jones	AL	SEA	1977
503	Richie Ashburn	NL	PHI	1956		465	Kirby Puckett	AL	MIN	1985
502	Richie Ashburn	NL	PHI	1957		462	Ken Henderson	AL	CHI	1974
496	Richie Ashburn	NL	PHI	1953		462	Gary Pettis	AL	CAL	1986
495	Richie Ashburn	NL	PHI	1958		461	Andruw Jones	NL	ATL	2001
493	Andruw Jones	NL	ATL	1999		460	George D. Wright	AL	TEX	1983
491	Jim Busby	AL	WAS	1954		460	Torii Hunter	AL	MIN	2001
490	Omar Moreno	NL	PIT	1979		458	Wally Berger	NL	BOS	1935
488	Baby Doll Jacobson	AL	STL	1924		457	Wally Berger	NL	BOS	1931
488	Bobby Thomson	NL	NY	1949		457	Vince DiMaggio	NL	PIT	1943
488	Al Bumbry	AL	BAL	1980		455	Jim Piersall	AL	BOS	1956
485	Mike Cameron	AL	SEA	2003		455	Gorman Thomas	AL	MIL	1980
484	Lloyd Waner	NL	PIT	1931		454	Sam Rice	AL	WAS	1920
483	Richie Ashburn	NL	PHI	1954		453	Ruppert Jones	AL	SEA	1979
482	Jim Busby	AL	WAS	1953		452	Dwayne Murphy	AL	OAK	1982
482	Willie Wilson	AL	KC	1980		452	Darin Erstad	AL	ANA	2002
479	Omar Moreno	NL	PIT	1980		451	Carden Gillenwater	NL	BOS	1945
477	Tom Oliver	AL	BOS	1930		450	Max Carey	NL	PIT	1923
474	Dwayne Murphy	AL	OAK	1984		450	Lloyd Waner	NL	PIT	1929
473	Lloyd Moseby	AL	TOR	1984		450	Sam West	AL	WAS	1932
472	Jim Busby	AL	CHI-WAS	1952		450	Sam Chapman	AL	PHI	1949
		CHI (42); WAS (430)				450	Kirby Puckett	AL	MIN	1988

Joe Tinker

(623) Most Double Plays by an Outfielder in a Season

15	Happy Felsch	AL	CHI	1919
14	Jimmy Sheckard	NL	BAL	1899
13	Tom Brown	NL	LOU	1893
12	Tom Brown	AA	PIT	1886
12	Tommy McCarthy	AA	STL	1888
12	Jimmy Bannon	NL	BOS	1894
12	Mike Griffin	NL	BRO	1895
12	Danny Green	NL	CHI	1899
12	Cy Seymour	NL	CIN	1905
12	Ty Cobb	AL	DET	1907
12	Ginger Beaumont	NL	BOS	1907
12	Tris Speaker	AL	BOS	1909
12	Jimmy Sheckard	NL	CHI	1911
12	Tris Speaker	AL	BOS	1914

12	Mel Ott	NL	NY	1929
11	Sam Thompson	NL	DET	1886
11	Tommy McCarthy	AA	STL	1889
11	Billy Sunday	NL	PIT-PHI	1890
			PIT (9); PHI (2)	
11	Sam Thompson	NL	PHI	1896
11	Bill Lange	NL	CHI	1899
11	Fielder Jones	AL	CHI	1902
11	Jimmy Sebring	NL	PIT	1903
11	Phil Geier	NL	BOS	1904
11	Ben Koehler	AL	STL	1905
11	Burt Shotton	AL	STL	1913
11	Chief Wilson	NL	STL	1914

(624) Teams with Three Outfielders, each Having 25 or More Assists in a Season

Sam Thompson (28)	Billy Hamilton (26)	Ed Delahanty (25)	NL	PHI	1892
Jimmy Bannon (43)	Tommy McCarthy (28)	Hugh Duffy (27)	NL	BOS	1894
Duffy Lewis (27)	Harry Hooper (27)	Tris Speaker (26)	AL	BOS	1911
Tris Speaker (30)	Duffy Lewis (29)	Harry Hooper (25)	AL	BOS	1913

NATIONAL BASEBALL HALL OF FAME LIBRARY

Mickey Cochrane

(625) Best Fielding Average by a Catcher in a Season (min. 125 G)

1.0000	Mike Matheny	NL	STL	2003		.9975	Brad Ausmus	AL	DET	1999
.9987	Tom Pagnozzi	NL	STL	1992		.9973	Tony Pena	NL	STL	1989
.9985	Wes Westrum	NL	NY	1950		.9972	Brad Ausmus	NL	HOU	2003
.9980	Elston Howard	AL	NY	1964		.9972	Glenn Borgmann	AL	MIN	1974
.9980	Brad Ausmus	NL	HOU	2006		.9972	Johnny Bench	NL	CIN	1976
.9979	Jason Varitek	AL	BOS	2004		.9970	Brad Ausmus	NL	HOU	2002
.9977	Brian Schneider	NL	MON	2004		.9970	Brad Ausmus	NL	HOU	2001
.9975	Kirt Manwaring	NL	SF	1993		.9970	A.J. Pierzynski	AL	CHI	2006

(626) Worst Fielding Average by a Catcher in a Season, since 1946 (min. 125 G)

.9719	Thurman Munson	AL	NY	1975		.9783	Ray Lamanno	NL	CIN	1948
.9738	Thurman Munson	AL	NY	1974		.9785	Butch Wynegar	AL	MIN	1976
.9746	Benito Santiago	NL	SD	1989		.9786	Barry Foote	NL	CHI	1979
.9758	Dave Duncan	AL	CLE	1974		.9787	Bob Boone	NL	PHI	1980
.9761	Benito Santiago	NL	SD	1987		.9792	Walker Cooper	NL	NY	1947
.9762	Bob Boone	NL	PHI	1974		.9793	Sammy White	AL	BOS	1954
.9766	Rich Gedman	AL	BOS	1984		.9797	Jason Kendall	NL	PIT	1996
.9771	Fran Healy	AL	KC	1974		.9797	Rick Cerone	AL	TOR	1979
.9773	Thurman Munson	AL	NY	1972		.9798	Carlton Fisk	AL	BOS	1978

(627) Most Errors by a Catcher in a Season, since 1946

23	John Bateman	NL	HOU	1963		20	Benito Santiago	NL	SD	1989
23	Thurman Munson	AL	NY	1975		19	Clay Dalrymple	NL	PHI	1963
22	Andy Seminick	NL	PHI	1948		18	Steve Yeager	NL	LA	1977
22	Thurman Munson	AL	NY	1974		18	Gary Alexander	AL	CLE	1979
22	Bob Boone	NL	PHI	1974		18	Bob Boone	NL	PHI	1980
22	Benito Santiago	NL	SD	1987		18	Rich Gedman	AL	BOS	1984
20	Terry Kennedy	NL	SD	1981		18	Tony Pena	NL	PIT	1986
20	Andy Allanson	AL	CLE	1986		18	Jason Kendall	NL	PIT	1996

(628) Fewest Errors by a Catcher in a Season (min. 125 G)

0	Mike Matheny	NL	STL	2003		3	Jim Sundberg	AL	TEX	1978
1	Wes Westrum	NL	NY	1950		3	Brad Ausmus	NL	HOU	2003
1	Tom Pagnozzi	NL	STL	1992		3	Mike Lieberthal	NL	PHI	1999
2	Elston Howard	AL	NY	1964		3	Tom Haller	NL	SF	1967
2	Tony Pena	NL	STL	1989		3	Rick Wilkins	NL	CHI	1993
2	Brian Schneider	NL	MON	2004		3	Tim McCarver	NL	STL	1967
2	Jason Varitek	AL	BOS	2004		3	Brad Ausmus	NL	HOU	2002
2	Kirt Manwaring	NL	SF	1993		3	Gabby Hartnett	NL	CHI	1934
2	Glenn Borgmann	AL	MIN	1974		3	Mickey Owen	NL	BRO	1941
2	Johnny Bench	NL	CIN	1976		3	Brad Ausmus	NL	HOU	2001
2	Rick Dempsey	AL	BAL	1983		3	Bill Dickey	AL	NY	1931
2	Brad Ausmus	AL	DET	1999		3	A.J. Pierzynski	AL	CHI	2006
2	Brad Ausmus	NL	HOU	2006						

(629) Most Assists by a Catcher in a Season

238	Bill Rariden	FL	IND	1915		183	Ray Schalk	AL	CHI	1914
215	Bill Rariden	FL	NEW	1914		181	Chief Zimmer	NL	CLE	1891
214	Pat Moran	NL	BOS	1903		180	Ed Sweeney	AL	NY	1913
212	Oscar Stanage	AL	DET	1911		179	Deacon McGuire	NL	WAS	1895
212	Art Wilson	FL	CHI	1914		179	Cy Perkins	AL	PHI	1920
210	Gabby Street	AL	WAS	1909		175	Steve O'Neill	AL	CLE	1915
204	Frank Snyder	NL	STL	1915		173	Ted Easterly	FL	KC	1914
203	George Gibson	NL	PIT	1910		170	Sam Agnew	AL	STL	1913
202	Bill Bergen	NL	BRO	1909		170	Ivey Wingo	NL	CIN	1916
202	Claude Berry	FL	PIT	1914		168	Oscar Stanage	AL	DET	1912
199	Red Dooin	NL	PHI	1909		167	Gabby Street	AL	WAS	1908
194	Walter Blair	FL	BUF	1914		167	Ed Sweeney	AL	NY	1912
192	George Gibson	NL	PIT	1909		167	Fred Jacklitsch	FL	BUF	1914
191	Red Dooin	NL	PHI	1908		166	Bill Killefer	NL	PHI	1913
190	Oscar Stanage	AL	DET	1914		166	Ray Schalk	AL	CHI	1916
189	Johnny Kling	NL	CHI	1903		165	Kid Baldwin	AA	CIN	1887
188	Chief Zimmer	NL	CLE	1890		163	Sam Agnew	AL	STL	1914
184	Boss Schmidt	AL	DET	1908						

(630) Most Putouts by a Catcher in a Season

1135	Johnny Edwards	NL	HOU	1969		965	Jorge Posada	AL	NY	2002
1055	Mike Piazza	NL	LA	1996		959	Einar Diaz	AL	CLE	2001
1050	Dan Wilson	AL	SEA	1997		956	Gary Carter	NL	NY	1985
1045	Mike Piazza	NL	LA	1997		954	Gary Carter	NL	MON	1982
1035	Michael Barrett	NL	CHI	2004		953	Mike Piazza	NL	NY	1999
1015	Jason Kendall	NL	PIT	1998		952	Jason Kendall	NL	PIT	1997
1014	Paul Lo Duca	NL	LA	2003		950	Bill Freehan	AL	DET	1967
1008	Johnny Edwards	NL	CIN	1963		949	Brad Ausmus	NL	HOU	2001
998	Jason Kendall	NL	PIT	2004		942	Johnny Bench	NL	CIN	1968
996	Jorge Posada	AL	NY	2001		942	Brad Ausmus	NL	HOU	2002
993	Javy Lopez	NL	ATL	1996		940	Damian Miller	NL	CHI	2003
990	Jason Kendall	NL	PIT	2000		939	Elston Howard	AL	NY	1964
986	Jason Kendall	AL	OAK	2005		933	Mike Lieberthal	NL	PHI	1997
984	Mike Piazza	NL	LA-FLA-NY	1998		933	Jorge Posada	AL	NY	2003
	LA (277); FLA (27); NY (680)					929	Brad Ausmus	NL	HOU	2006
982	Brad Ausmus	NL	HOU	2003		925	Tim McCarver	NL	STL	1969
981	Darren Daulton	NL	PHI	1993		925	Mike Scioscia	NL	LA	1987
978	Randy Hundley	NL	CHI	1969		925	Joe Oliver	NL	CIN	1992
978	Javy Lopez	NL	ATL	1998		924	Jason Kendall	AL	OAK	2006
976	Tony Pena	NL	PIT	1983		923	Bill Freehan	AL	DET	1964
972	Jason Varitek	AL	BOS	1999		922	Tony Pena	NL	PIT	1985
971	Bill Freehan	AL	DET	1968		920	Mike Piazza	NL	NY	2001
966	Damian Miller	NL	ARI	2001		920	Brad Ausmus	NL	HOU	2004
965	Paul Lo Duca	NL	LA	2002						

(631) Most Double Plays by a Catcher in a Season

36	Steve O'Neill	AL	CLE	1916		22	Steve O'Neill	AL	CLE	1914
29	Frankie Hayes	AL	PHI-CLE	1945		22	Bob O'Farrell	NL	CHI	1922
			PHI (6); CLE (23)			21	Gabby Hartnett	NL	CHI	1927
25	Ray Schalk	AL	CHI	1916		21	Wes Westrum	NL	NY	1950
25	Yogi Berra	AL	NY	1951		20	Johnny Kling	NL	BOS	1912
23	Jack Lapp	AL	PHI	1915		20	Ray Schalk	AL	CHI	1914
23	Muddy Ruel	AL	WAS	1924		20	Ray Schalk	AL	CHI	1923
23	Tom Haller	NL	LA	1968		20	Jason Kendall	NL	PIT	1997

(632) Most Games Caught in a Season

160	Randy Hundley	NL	CHI	1968		151	Randy Hundley	NL	CHI	1969
155	Frankie Hayes	AL	PHI	1944		151	Johnny Edwards	NL	HOU	1969
155	Ray Mueller	NL	CIN	1944		151	Manny Sanguillen	NL	PIT	1974
155	Jim Sundberg	AL	TEX	1975		151	Carlton Fisk	AL	BOS	1977
154	Johnny Bench	NL	CIN	1968		151	Jim Sundberg	AL	TEX	1980
154	Ted Simmons	NL	STL	1975		151	Benito Santiago	NL	SD	1991
154	Carlton Fisk	AL	BOS	1978		150	George Gibson	NL	PIT	1909
153	Ted Simmons	NL	STL	1973		150	Mike Tresh	AL	CHI	1945
153	Gary Carter	NL	MON	1982		150	Buck Rodgers	AL	LA	1962
152	Jim Hegan	AL	CLE	1949		150	Jim Sundberg	AL	TEX	1979
152	Randy Hundley	NL	CHI	1967		150	Jody Davis	NL	CHI	1983
152	Gary Carter	NL	MON	1978		150	Todd Hundley	NL	NY	1996
151	Ray Schalk	AL	CHI	1920		150	Brad Ausmus	AL	DET	2000
151	Frankie Hayes	AL	PHI-CLE	1945						
			PHI (32); CLE (119)							

(633) Most Passed Balls in a Season, since 1893

38	Marty Bergen	NL	BOS	1898		27	Marty Bergen	NL	BOS	1896
35	Geno Petralli	AL	TEX	1987		27	Klondike Douglass	NL	PHI	1900
34	Duke Farrell	NL	NY	1894		27	Bob Uecker	NL	PHI-ATL	1967
33	J.C. Martin	AL	CHI	1965					PHI (2); ATL (25)	
32	Bill G. Wilson	NL	LOU	1897		27	Bob Didier	NL	ATL	1969
32	Ed McFarland	NL	PHI	1899		26	Wilbert Robinson	NL	BAL	1893
28	John Grim	NL	LOU	1893		26	Bill Merritt	NL	CIN-PIT	1895
28	Farmer Vaughn	NL	CIN	1893					CIN (6); PIT (20)	
28	Deacon McGuire	NL	WAS	1895		26	Frank Bowerman	NL	NY	1900
28	John Warner	NL	NY	1898		26	Mike Macfarlane	AL	BOS	1995
28	Gus Triandos	AL	BAL	1959		25	Ed McFarland	NL	PHI	1900
28	Earl Williams	NL	ATL	1972		25	Nig Clarke	AL	CLE	1907
28	Ted Simmons	NL	STL	1975		25	John P. Henry	AL	WAS	1911
27	Heinie Peitz	NL	STL	1893		25	Dick Dietz	NL	SF	1970
27	Deacon McGuire	NL	WAS	1894		25	Ted Simmons	NL	STL	1973
27	Jack Ryan	NL	BOS	1895		25	Jason Varitek	AL	BOS	1999

(634) Best Fielding Average by a Pitcher in a Season (min. 275 IP)

					IP	
1.0000	Kid Nichols	NL	BOS	1896	372.1	
1.0000	Walter Johnson	AL	WAS	1913	346.0	
1.0000	Gaylord Perry	AL	CLE	1973	344.0	
1.0000	Jim Whitney	NL	BOS	1884	336.0	
1.0000	Sandy Koufax	NL	LA	1965	335.2	
1.0000	Phil Niekro	NL	ATL	1977	330.1	
1.0000	Walter Johnson	AL	WAS	1917	326.0	
1.0000	Gaylord Perry	NL	SF	1969	325.1	
1.0000	Randy Jones	NL	SD	1976	315.1	
1.0000	Frank Owen	AL	CHI	1904	315.0	
1.0000	Jim Colborn	AL	MIL	1973	314.1	
1.0000	Hal Newhouser	AL	DET	1945	313.1	
1.0000	Mordecai Brown	NL	CHI	1908	312.1	
1.0000	Vida Blue	AL	OAK	1971	312.0	
1.0000	Ferguson Jenkins	NL	CHI	1968	308.0	
1.0000	Grover Alexander	NL	PHI	1913	306.1	
1.0000	Steve Carlton	NL	PHI	1980	304.0	
1.0000	Phil Niekro	NL	ATL	1974	302.1	
1.0000	Alvin Crowder	AL	WAS	1933	299.1	
1.0000	Sal Maglie	NL	NY	1951	298.0	
1.0000	Larry Jackson	NL	CHI	1964	297.2	
1.0000	Bert Blyleven	AL	MIN-TEX	1976	297.2	MIN (95.1 IP); TEX (202.1 IP)
1.0000	Mel Parnell	AL	BOS	1949	295.1	
1.0000	Wilbur Cooper	NL	PIT	1922	294.2	
1.0000	Bert Blyleven	AL	CLE-MIN	1985	293.2	CLE (179.2 IP); MIN (114.0 IP)
1.0000	Mike Caldwell	AL	MIL	1978	293.1	
1.0000	Lon Warneke	NL	CHI	1934	291.1	
1.0000	Rube Walberg	AL	PHI	1931	291.0	
1.0000	Frank Meinke	NL	DET	1884	289.0	
1.0000	Lefty Grove	AL	PHI	1931	288.2	
1.0000	Lon Warneke	NL	CHI	1933	287.1	
1.0000	Herb Pennock	AL	NY	1924	286.1	
1.0000	Bucky Walters	NL	CIN	1944	285.0	
1.0000	Larry Gura	AL	KC	1980	283.1	
1.0000	Babe Adams	NL	PIT	1914	283.0	
1.0000	Roger Clemens	AL	BOS	1987	281.2	
1.0000	Eppa Rixey	NL	PHI	1917	281.1	
1.0000	Johnny Rigney	AL	CHI	1940	280.2	
1.0000	Dazzy Vance	NL	BRO	1928	280.1	
1.0000	Walter Johnson	AL	WAS	1922	280.0	
1.0000	Bobby Shantz	AL	PHI	1952	279.2	
1.0000	Mel Stottlemyre	AL	NY	1968	278.2	
1.0000	Claude Passeau	NL	CHI	1942	278.1	
1.0000	Walter Johnson	AL	WAS	1924	277.2	
1.0000	Buttons Briggs	NL	CHI	1904	277.0	
1.0000	Don Sutton	NL	LA	1974	276.0	
1.0000	Phil Niekro	NL	ATL	1975	275.2	

(635) Most Errors by a Pitcher in a Season, since 1946

10	Clay Kirby	NL	CIN	1974		8	Steve Busby	AL	KC	1974
10	J.R. Richard	NL	HOU	1976		8	Tom Griffin	NL	HOU	1974
10	Melido Perez	AL	NY	1992		8	Bill F. Lee	AL	BOS	1974
10	Joe Kennedy	AL	TB	2002		8	Jesse Jefferson	AL	TOR	1977
9	Don Drysdale	NL	LA	1965		8	Nolan Ryan	AL	CAL	1977
9	Andy Messersmith	NL	LA	1974		8	Joaquin Andujar	NL	HOU	1977
9	Matt Young	AL	SEA	1990		8	Larry Christenson	NL	PHI	1977
9	Randy Johnson	AL-NL	SEA-HOU	1998		8	Dick Ruthven	NL	ATL-PHI	1978
			SEA (8); HOU (1)						ATL (7); PHI (1)	
8	Warren Spahn	NL	BOS	1950		8	Nolan Ryan	AL	CAL	1978
8	Roger Craig	NL	NY	1963		8	John Denny	NL	PHI	1983
8	Tony Cloninger	NL	ATL	1966		8	Kevin Brown	AL	TEX	1992
8	Jim Kaat	AL	MIN	1969		8	Danny Jackson	NL	CHI-PIT	1992
8	Ray Culp	AL	BOS	1969					CHI (6); PIT (2)	
8	Tommy John	AL	CHI	1970						

(636) Fewest Errors by a Pitcher in a Season (min. 275 IP)

					IP						IP
0	Kid Nichols	NL	BOS	1896	372.1		0	Bert Blyleven	AL	CLE-MIN	1985	293.2
0	Walter Johnson	AL	WAS	1913	346.0					CLE (0); MIN (0)	
0	Gaylord Perry	AL	CLE	1973	344.0		0	Mike Caldwell	AL	MIL	1978	293.1
0	Jim Whitney	NL	BOS	1884	336.0		0	Lon Warneke	NL	CHI	1934	291.1
0	Sandy Koufax	NL	LA	1965	335.2		0	Rube Walberg	AL	PHI	1931	291.0
0	Phil Niekro	NL	ATL	1977	330.1		0	Frank Meinke	NL	DET	1884	289.0
0	Walter Johnson	AL	WAS	1917	326.0		0	Lefty Grove	AL	PHI	1931	288.2
0	Gaylord Perry	NL	SF	1969	325.1		0	Lon Warneke	NL	CHI	1933	287.1
0	Randy Jones	NL	SD	1976	315.1		0	Herb Pennock	AL	NY	1924	286.1
0	Frank Owen	AL	CHI	1904	315.0		0	Bucky Walters	NL	CIN	1944	285.0
0	Jim Colborn	AL	MIL	1973	314.1		0	Larry Gura	AL	KC	1980	283.1
0	Hal Newhouser	AL	DET	1945	313.1		0	Babe Adams	NL	PIT	1914	283.0
0	Mordecai Brown	NL	CHI	1908	312.1		0	Roger Clemens	AL	BOS	1987	281.2
0	Vida Blue	AL	OAK	1971	312.0		0	Eppa Rixey	NL	PHI	1917	281.1
0	Ferguson Jenkins	NL	CHI	1968	308.0		0	Johnny Rigney	AL	CHI	1940	280.2
0	Grover Alexander	NL	PHI	1913	306.1		0	Dazzy Vance	NL	BRO	1928	280.1
0	Steve Carlton	NL	PHI	1980	304.0		0	Walter Johnson	AL	WAS	1922	280.0
0	Phil Niekro	NL	ATL	1974	302.1		0	Bobby Shantz	AL	PHI	1952	279.2
0	Alvin Crowder	AL	WAS	1933	299.1		0	Mel Stottlemyre	AL	NY	1968	278.2
0	Sal Maglie	NL	NY	1951	298.0		0	Claude Passeau	NL	CHI	1942	278.1
0	Larry Jackson	NL	CHI	1964	297.2		0	Walter Johnson	AL	WAS	1924	277.2
0	Bert Blyleven	AL	MIN-TEX	1976	297.2		0	Buttons Briggs	NL	CHI	1904	277.0
			MIN (0); TEX (0)				0	Don Sutton	NL	LA	1974	276.0
0	Mel Parnell	AL	BOS	1949	295.1		0	Phil Niekro	NL	ATL	1975	275.2
0	Wilbur Cooper	NL	PIT	1922	294.2						

(637) Most Assists by a Pitcher in a Season

227	Ed Walsh	AL	CHI	1907		143	Tony Mullane	AA	TOL	1884
223	Will White	AA	CIN	1882		143	Harry Howell	AL	STL	1904
190	Ed Walsh	AL	CHI	1908		143	Addie Joss	AL	CLE	1907
178	Harry Howell	AL	STL	1905		142	Tim Keefe	AA	NY	1883
177	Tony Mullane	AA	LOU	1882		141	Jim Galvin	NL	BUF	1879
174	John Clarkson	NL	CHI	1885		141	Tommy Bond	NL	BOS	1880
172	John Clarkson	NL	BOS	1889		141	Sadie McMahon	AA	BAL	1891
166	Jack Chesbro	AL	NY	1904		141	Christy Mathewson	NL	NY	1908
163	George Mullin	AL	DET	1904		140	Ed Walsh	AL	CHI	1912
159	Ed Walsh	AL	CHI	1911		139	Charley Radbourn	NL	PRO	1883
157	Matt Kilroy	AA	BAL	1887		139	Mark Baldwin	PL	CHI	1890
156	Bill Hutchison	NL	CHI	1892		139	Silver King	PL	CHI	1890
154	Jim Galvin	NL	BUF	1884		139	Sadie McMahon	AA	PHI-BAL	1890
154	Frank E. Smith	AL	CHI	1909				PHI (112); BAL (27)		
154	Ed Walsh	AL	CHI	1910		138	Amos Rusie	NL	NY	1892
145	Guy Hecker	AA	LOU	1884		137	Claude Hendrix	FL	CHI	1914
145	Cy Young	NL	CLE	1896		137	Hooks Dauss	AL	DET	1915
144	Tommy Bond	NL	BOS	1879		135	Jim McCormick	NL	CLE	1880
144	Jack B. Taylor	NL	STL	1898						

GEORGE BRACE

Hughie Jennings

(638) Most Putouts by a Pitcher in a Season

57	Dave Foutz	AA	STL	1886		42	Ted Breitenstein	NL	STL	1893
54	Tony Mullane	AA	LOU	1882		42	Ted Breitenstein	NL	STL	1894
50	George Bradley	NL	STL	1876		42	Harry Howell	AL	STL	1907
50	Guy Hecker	AA	LOU	1884		42	Oil Can Boyd	AL	BOS	1985
49	Mike Boddicker	AL	BAL	1984		41	Bobby Mathews	NL	NY	1876
47	Larry Corcoran	NL	CHI	1884		41	Tony Mullane	AA	TOL	1884
45	Al Spalding	NL	CHI	1876		41	Ed Walsh	AL	CHI	1908
45	Ted Breitenstein	NL	STL	1895		41	Joe Wood	AL	BOS	1912
44	Jim Devlin	NL	LOU	1876		41	Kevin Brown	NL	LA	1999
44	Dave Foutz	AA	STL	1887		40	Guy Hecker	AA	LOU	1883
44	Bill Hutchison	NL	CHI	1890		40	Charlie Buffinton	NL	BOS	1884
43	John Ward	NL	PRO	1880		40	Tony Mullane	AA	CIN	1886
43	Jim McCormick	NL	CLE	1882		40	Bob Caruthers	AA	STL	1887
43	Nick Altrock	AL	CHI	1904		40	Phil Knell	AA	COL	1891
42	Nat Hudson	AA	STL	1888		40	Kevin Brown	AL	BAL	1995
42	Kid Gleason	NL	STL	1892						

(639) Most Double Plays by a Pitcher in a Season

15	Bob Lemon	AL	CLE	1953		10	Carl Mays	NL	CIN	1926
12	Eddie Rommel	AL	PHI	1924		10	Willis Hudlin	AL	CLE	1931
12	Curt Davis	NL	PHI	1934		10	Freddie Fitzsimmons	NL	NY	1932
12	Randy Jones	NL	SD	1976		10	Freddie Fitzsimmons	NL	NY	1934
11	Scott Perry	AL	PHI	1919		10	Bucky Walters	NL	CIN	1939
11	Tom Rogers	AL	STL-PHI	1919		10	Dave Ferriss	AL	BOS	1945
			All with PHI			10	Bob Hooper	AL	PHI	1950
11	Art Nehf	NL	NY	1920		10	Don Drysdale	NL	LA	1958
11	Burleigh Grimes	NL	BRO	1925		10	Dan Petry	AL	DET	1983
11	Gene Bearden	AL	CLE	1948		10	Javier Vazquez	NL	MON	2001
11	Kirk Rueter	NL	SF	2001		10	Livan Hernandez	NL	MON	2004
10	Nick Altrock	AL	CHI	1905		10	Jon Garland	AL	CHI	2006

BASE RUNNING RECORDS

Base Running Records

(640) Most Career Stolen Bases

1406	Rickey Henderson	596	Dummy Hoy	506	Luis Aparicio
938	Lou Brock	586	Maury Wills	504	Paul Molitor
914	Billy Hamilton	583	George Van Haltren	495	Willie Keeler
897	Ty Cobb	580	Ozzie Smith	495	Clyde Milan
808	Tim Raines	574	Hugh Duffy	487	Omar Moreno
752	Vince Coleman	568	Bid McPhee	474	Roberto Alomar
742	Arlie Latham	558	Brett Butler	473	Mike Griffin
741	Eddie Collins	557	Davey Lopes	468	Tommy McCarthy
738	Max Carey	550	Cesar Cedeno	465	Jimmy Sheckard
723	Honus Wagner	548	Bill Dahlen	465	Eric Young
689	Joe Morgan	540	John Ward	463	Delino DeShields
668	Willie Wilson	537	Herman Long	461	Bobby Bonds
657	Tom Brown	518	Patsy Donovan	455	Ed Delahanty
649	Bert Campaneris	518	Jack Doyle	455	Ron LeFlore
620	Otis Nixon	509	Harry Stovey	453	Curt Welch
619	George Davis	509	Fred Clarke		
599	Kenny Lofton	509	Barry Bonds		

(641) Highest Career Stolen Base Percentage (min. 100 steals)

87.6	Carlos Beltran	80.6	Andy Van Slyke	78.6	Mike Cameron
84.7	Pokey Reese	80.6	Orlando Cabrera	78.6	Amos Otis
84.7	Tim Raines	80.5	Dave Roberts	78.5	Kirk Gibson
84.1	Eric Davis	80.4	Corey Patterson	78.4	Aaron Boone
83.3	Henry Cotto	80.2	Ichiro Suzuki	78.3	Johnny Damon
83.3	Willie Wilson	80.1	Alex Rodriguez	78.3	Barry Bonds
83.1	Tony Womack	80.1	Mickey Mantle	78.1	Alan Wiggins
83.1	Barry Larkin	80.1	Derek Jeter	77.9	Devon White
83.0	Davey Lopes	79.9	Jimmy Rollins	77.9	Tommy Harper
82.8	Stan Javier	79.8	Lenny Dykstra	77.9	Miguel Cairo
82.8	Carl Crawford	79.7	Ozzie Smith	77.8	Alfonso Soriano
82.4	Doug Glanville	79.7	Kenny Lofton	77.8	Rudy Law
81.5	Julio Cruz	79.6	Enzo Hernandez	77.8	Joe Carter
81.0	Brian L. Hunter	79.5	Gary Redus	77.8	Mike Felder
81.0	Joe Morgan	79.4	Paul Molitor	77.7	Chuck Knoblauch
80.9	Vince Coleman	79.0	R. J. Reynolds	77.6	Bob Dernier
80.8	Rickey Henderson	78.8	Luis Aparicio		
80.6	Roberto Alomar	78.7	Marquis Grissom		

(642) Most Career Steals of Home

54	Ty Cobb	20	George Sisler	17	Eddie Collins
33	Max Carey	19	Frankie Frisch	17	Larry Doyle
28	George J. Burns	19	Jackie Robinson	16	Tommy Leach
27	Honus Wagner	18	Jimmy Sheckard	15	Ben Chapman
23	Sherry Magee	18	Tris Speaker	15	Fred Clarke
23	Frank Schulte	18	Joe Tinker	15	Lou Gehrig
21	Johnny Evers	17	Rod Carew		

(643) Most Stolen Bases in a Game, since 1900

6	Eddie Collins	AL	PHI	Sep 11, 1912	5	Bert Campaneris	AL	OAK	Apr 24, 1976
				3 in 7th inn.	5	Lonnie Smith	NL	STL	Sep 4, 1982
6	Eddie Collins	AL	PHI	Sep 22, 1912	5	Alan Wiggins	NL	SD	May 17, 1984
				1G	5	Tony Gwynn	NL	SD	Sep 20, 1986
6	Otis Nixon	NL	ATL	Jun 16, 1991	5	Rickey Henderson	AL	OAK	Jul 29, 1989
6	Eric Young	NL	COL	Jun 30, 1996	5	Alex Cole	AL	CLE	Aug 1, 1990
5	Dan McGann	NL	NY	May 27, 1904	5	Alex Cole	AL	CLE	May 3, 1992
5	Clyde Milan	AL	WAS	Jun 14, 1912	5	Damian Jackson	NL	SD	Jun 28, 1999
5	Johnny Neun	AL	DET	Jul 9, 1927	5	Kenny Lofton	AL	CLE	Sep 3, 2000
5	Amos Otis	AL	KC	Sep 7, 1971					13 inn.
5	Davey Lopes	NL	LA	Aug 24, 1974	5	Ryan Freel	NL	CIN	Jul 27, 2005
	Thrown out in 6th attempt								

(644) Players who Stole Home Twice in a Game

Honus Wagner	NL	PIT	Jun 20, 1901	Eddie Collins	AL	PHI	Sep 6, 1913
Ed Konetchy	NL	STL	Sep 30, 1907	Bill Barrett	AL	CHI	May 1, 1924
Joe Tinker	NL	CHI	Jun 28, 1910	Doc Gautreau	NL	BOS	Sep 3, 1927
Larry Doyle	NL	NY	Sep 18, 1911				1G
Joe Jackson	AL	CLE	Aug 11, 1912	Vic Power	AL	CLE	Aug 14, 1958
Guy Zinn	AL	NY	Aug 15, 1912				10 inn.

Ty Cobb

(645) Pitchers who Stole Home, since 1900

Win Mercer	AL	WAS	PHI	Aug 10, 1901	
Jock Menefee	NL	CHI	BRO	Jul 15, 1902	
Joe McGinnity	NL	NY	BRO	Aug 8, 1903	2G; McGinnity pitches and wins both games. His steal of home comes as Brooklyn is arguing whether he was out at 3rd.
Henry Schmidt	NL	BRO	STL	Aug 15, 1903	2G
Joe McGinnity	NL	NY	BOS	Apr 29, 1904	
Frank Owen	AL	CHI	WAS	Aug 2, 1904	
Frank Owen	AL	CHI	WAS	Jun 13, 1905	
Bill Donovan	AL	DET	CLE	Sep 14, 1905	
Bill Donovan	AL	DET	CLE	May 7, 1906	Steals 2B, 3B and home in 5th
Frank Owen	AL	CHI	STL	Apr 27, 1908	
Ed Walsh	AL	CHI	NY	Jun 13, 1908	
Ed Walsh	AL	CHI	STL	Jul 2, 1909	
Eddie Plank	AL	PHI	CHI	Aug 30, 1909	
Jack Warhop	AL	NY	CHI	Aug 27, 1910	1G
Christy Mathewson	NL	NY	BOS	Sep 12, 1911	2G
Red Ames	NL	NY	BRO	May 27, 1912	
Christy Mathewson	NL	NY	BOS	Jun 28, 1912	1G
Jack Warhop	AL	NY	STL	Jul 12, 1912	
Ray Caldwell	AL	NY	CLE	Jul 20, 1912	1G; pinch runner
Slim Sallee	NL	NY	STL	Jul 22, 1913	
Ray Fisher	AL	NY	PHI	May 3, 1915	
Red Faber	AL	CHI	PHI	Jul 14, 1915	
Sherry Smith	NL	BRO	NY	Apr 19, 1916	
Ray Fisher	AL	NY	STL	May 22, 1916	
Tom Seaton	NL	CHI	CIN	Jun 23, 1916	
Reb Russell	AL	CHI	BOS	Aug 7, 1916	
Jim Bagby Sr.	AL	CLE	PHI	May 20, 1917	
Bob Steele	NL	NY	STL	Jul 26, 1918	
Babe Ruth	AL	BOS	STL	Aug 24, 1918	
Hippo Vaughn	NL	CHI	NY	Aug 9, 1919	
Dutch Ruether	NL	CIN	CHI	Sep 3, 1919	
Jesse Barnes	NL	NY	STL	Jul 27, 1920	Front end double steal
Dutch Ruether	NL	CIN	NY	May 4, 1921	
Dickie Kerr	AL	CHI	NY	Jul 8, 1921	Front end double steal
Red Faber	AL	CHI	STL	Apr 23, 1923	
George Mogridge	AL	WAS	CHI	Aug 15, 1923	
Johnny Vander Meer	NL	CIN	NY	Sep 23, 1943	2G; only career steal
Joe Haynes	AL	CHI	STL	Sep 17, 1944	2G
Bucky Walters	NL	CIN	PIT	Apr 20, 1946	
Fred Hutchinson	AL	DET	STL	Aug 29, 1947	Steals home after triple
Harry Dorish	AL	STL	WAS	Jun 2, 1950	2G
Don Newcombe	NL	BRO	PIT	May 26, 1955	Steals home after triple
Curt Simmons	NL	STL	PHI	Sep 1, 1963	Botched squeeze play
Pascual Perez	NL	ATL	SF	Sep 7, 1984	Only career steal
Rick Sutcliffe	NL	CHI	PHI	Jul 29, 1988	
Darren Dreifort	NL	LA	TEX (AL)	Jun 12, 2001	Front end of double steal

(646) Game-ending Steals of Home, since 1900

			OPP.	OPP. PITCHER		
Harry Arndt	NL	STL	PIT	Deacon Phillippe	Sep 12, 1905	
Frank Chance	NL	CHI	CIN	Jake Weimer	April 28, 1906	
Eddie Grant	NL	PHI	PIT	Fred Beebe	July 15, 1909	2G; 14 inn.
Bobby Byrne	NL	PIT	BRO	George G. Bell	Aug 25, 1910	12 inn.; steals 3B before home
Wilbur Good	NL	CHI	PIT	Howie Camnitz	April 15, 1913	Pinch runner; 10 inn.
Heinie Zimmerman	NL	CHI	STL	Bill Doak	Jun 24, 1915	
Mike Gonzalez	NL	STL	PHI	Joe Oeschger	Jun 11, 1917	15 inn.
Merlin Kopp	AL	PHI	DET	Hooks Dauss	May 20, 1918	14 inn.
Jim Thorpe	NL	NY	PIT	Wilbur Cooper	June 5, 1918	
Pat McNulty	AL	CLE	BOS	George Murray	Jun 14, 1924	11 inn.
Cliff Heathcote	NL	CHI	PHI	Bill Hubbell	Jul 17, 1924	
Ossie Bluege	AL	WAS	STL	Chad Kimsey	Jun 4, 1929	
Oscar Melillo	AL	STL	CHI	Red Faber	May 31, 1930	
Danny Taylor	NL	CHI	NY	Joe Heving	Aug 24, 1930	
Tony Lazzeri	AL	NY	DET	Elon Hogsett	Sep 13, 1931	1G; 12 inn.
Al Lopez	NL	BRO	CHI	Charley Root	Jul 2, 1933	2G
Zeke Bonura	AL	CHI	NY	Jimmy DeShong	Aug 26, 1935	1G; 15 inn.
Billy Werber	AL	PHI	WAS	Bill Phebus	Apr 29, 1938	
Gene Moore	NL	BRO	CHI	Charley Root	Jun 1, 1939	14 inn.
Wally Moses	AL	PHI	CHI	Thornton Lee	Aug 20, 1940	2G; 10 inn.
Jeff Heath	AL	CLE	STL	Jack Kramer	Jul 4, 1941	1G
Huck Geary	NL	PIT	BOS	Al Javery	Jun 1, 1943	14 inn.
Wally Moses	AL	CHI	BOS	Mace Brown	Jul 7, 1943	14 inn.
Dee Fondy	NL	CHI	CIN	Bob Kelly	Sep 6, 1953	1G
Earl Torgeson	AL	DET	NY	Bob Turley	Jul 17, 1955	10 inn.
Jim Gilliam	NL	BRO	STL	Lindy McDaniel	Jun 14, 1957	10 inn.
Vic Power	AL	CLE	DET	Frank Lary	Aug 14, 1958	10 inn.; 2 steals of home in game
Ed Charles	AL	KC	MIN	Ray Moore	Aug 8, 1962	
Willie Davis	NL	LA	PHI	Morrie Steevens	Sep 19, 1964	16 inn.
Tommie Agee	NL	NY	LA	Jim Brewer	Jul 24, 1970	10 inn.
Rod Carew	AL	MIN	CLE	Steve Mingori	Sep 1, 1972	10 inn.
George Brett	AL	KC	CLE	Dave LaRoche	Aug 17, 1976	10 inn.
Eddie Murray	AL	BAL	CHI	Guy Hoffman	Aug 15, 1979	12 inn.
Glenn Brummer	NL	STL	SF	Gary Lavelle	Aug 22, 1982	12 inn.
Marquis Grissom	AL	CLE	BAL	Randy Myers	Oct 11, 1997	ALCS; 12 inn.

(647) Most Stolen Bases in a Season, 1886-1897

138	Hugh Nicol	AA	CIN	1887		106	Tom Brown	AA	BOS	1891
129	Arlie Latham	AA	STL	1887		103	Pete Browning	AA	LOU	1887
117	Charlie Comiskey	AA	STL	1887		103	Hugh Nicol	AA	CIN	1888
111	John Ward	NL	NY	1887		102	Jim Fogarty	NL	PHI	1887
111	Billy Hamilton	AA	KC	1889		102	Billy Hamilton	NL	PHI	1890
111	Billy Hamilton	NL	PHI	1891		100	Billy Hamilton	NL	PHI	1894
109	Arlie Latham	AA	STL	1888					

Stolen bases were not tabulated before 1885. Between 1886-1897, stolen bases often were awarded for taking an extra base on a hit.

(648) Most Stolen Bases in a Season, since 1898

130	Rickey Henderson	AL	OAK	1982		81	Eddie Collins	AL	PHI	1910
118	Lou Brock	NL	STL	1974		81	Bob Bescher	NL	CIN	1911
110	Vince Coleman	NL	STL	1985		81	Vince Coleman	NL	STL	1988
109	Vince Coleman	NL	STL	1987		80	Rickey Henderson	AL	NY	1985
108	Rickey Henderson	AL	OAK	1983		80	Eric Davis	NL	CIN	1986
107	Vince Coleman	NL	STL	1986		79	Dave Collins	NL	CIN	1980
104	Maury Wills	NL	LA	1962		79	Willie Wilson	AL	KC	1980
100	Rickey Henderson	AL	OAK	1980		78	Ron LeFlore	AL	DET	1979
97	Ron LeFlore	NL	MON	1980		78	Tim Raines	NL	MON	1982
96	Ty Cobb	AL	DET	1915		78	Marquis Grissom	NL	MON	1992
96	Omar Moreno	NL	PIT	1980		77	Jimmy Sheckard	NL	BAL	1899
94	Maury Wills	NL	LA	1965		77	Davey Lopes	NL	LA	1975
93	Rickey Henderson	AL	NY	1988		77	Omar Moreno	NL	PIT	1979
90	Tim Raines	NL	MON	1983		77	Rudy Law	AL	CHI	1983
88	Clyde Milan	AL	WAS	1912		77	Rickey Henderson	AL	NY-OAK	1989
87	Rickey Henderson	AL	NY	1986					NY (25); OAK (52)	
83	Ty Cobb	AL	DET	1911		77	Vince Coleman	NL	STL	1990
83	Willie Wilson	AL	KC	1979						

NATIONAL BASEBALL HALL OF FAME LIBRARY

Johnny Evers

(649) Highest Stolen Base Percentage in a Season, since 1951 (min. 20 SB)

					SB	CS	
100.0	Kevin McReynolds	NL	NY	1988	21	0	
100.0	Paul Molitor	AL	TOR	1994	20	0	
96.9	Brady Anderson	AL	BAL	1994	31	1	
96.9	Carlos Beltran	AL	KC	2001	31	1	
96.3	Chris Duffy	NL	PIT	2006	26	1	
96.2	Max Carey	NL	PIT	1922	51	2	Only pre-1951 player to rank so high
95.8	Ken Griffey Sr.	NL	CIN	1980	23	1	
95.7	Ichiro Suzuki	AL	SEA	2006	45	2	
95.5	Jason Bay	NL	PIT	2005	21	1	
95.2	Stan Javier	AL	OAK	1988	20	1	
94.4	Doug Glanville	NL	PHI	1999	34	2	
94.3	Amos Otis	AL	KC	1970	33	2	
93.9	Jack Perconte	AL	SEA	1985	31	2	
93.8	Alfonso Soriano	AL	TEX	2005	30	2	
93.3	Carlos Beltran	AL-NL	KC-HOU	2004	42	3	KC (14 SB, 3 CS); HOU (28 SB, 0 CS)
93.1	Miguel Dilone	NL	MON	1984	27	2	
93.1	Bob Dernier	NL	CHI	1986	27	2	
92.9	Kirk Gibson	NL	LA	1990	26	2	
92.9	Barry Larkin	NL	CIN	1994	26	2	
92.7	Dave Roberts	NL-AL	LA-BOS	2004	38	3	LA (33 SB, 1 CS); BOS (5 SB, 2 CS)
92.6	Rafael Furcal	NL	ATL	2003	25	2	
92.6	Brandon Phillips	NL	CIN	2006	25	2	
92.3	Don Baylor	AL	BAL	1972	24	2	
92.3	Oddibe McDowell	AL	TEX	1987	24	2	
92.3	Orlando Cabrera	NL	MON	2003	24	2	
92.2	Davey Lopes	NL	CHI	1985	47	4	
92.1	Eric Davis	NL	CIN	1988	35	3	
92.0	Cesar Cedeno	NL	HOU	1978	23	2	
92.0	Henry Cotto	AL	SEA	1992	23	2	
92.0	Mike Cameron	AL	CHI	1997	23	2	
92.0	Delino DeShields	AL-NL	BAL-CHI	2001	23	2	BAL (11 SB, 1 CS); CHI (12 SB, 1 CS)

Caught stealing data is incomplete before 1951.

COURTESY OF GEORGE MICHAEL

Stan Musial

(650) Lowest Stolen Base Percentage in a Season, since 1951 (min. 10 caught stealing)

						SB	CS
0	Pete Runnels	AL	WAS	1952		0	10
8.3	Eddie Yost	AL	WAS	1957		1	11
8.3	Jose Vizcaino	NL	NY	1994		1	11
14.3	Jerry Morales	NL	CHI	1974		2	12
14.3	Curt Flood	NL	STL	1958		2	12
15.4	Elliott Maddox	NL	NY	1978		2	11
16.7	Luis Gomez	AL	TOR	1978		2	10
16.7	Johnny Groth	AL	DET	1952		2	10
16.7	Charlie Moore	AL	MIL	1982		2	10
16.7	Todd Cruz	AL	SEA	1982		2	10
18.8	Rick Miller	AL	CAL	1978		3	13
18.8	Tony Johnson	AL	TOR	1982		3	13
22.7	Will Clark	NL	SF	1987		5	17
23.1	Max Alvis	AL	CLE	1967		3	10
23.1	Mike A. Marshall	NL	LA	1985		3	10
26.7	George Scott	AL	BOS	1970		4	11
27.8	Dave Parker	NL	CIN	1985		5	13
27.8	Bill Virdon	NL	PIT	1962		5	13
28.6	Willie Tasby	AL	WAS	1961		4	10
28.6	Pete Rose	NL	CIN	1964		4	10
28.6	Bobby Adams	NL	CIN	1951		4	10
29.4	Rick Monday	NL	CHI	1973		5	12

Caught stealing data is incomplete before 1951.

(651) Most Stolen Bases by a Team in a Season, 1886-1897

581	STL	AA	1887		447	BOS	AA	1891		389	BRO	AA	1889
545	BAL	AA	1887		441	BAL	NL	1896		382	CHI	NL	1887
527	CIN	AA	1887		434	PHI	AA	1888		373	BOS	NL	1887
476	PHI	AA	1887		421	TOL	AA	1890		355	PHI	NL	1887
472	KC	AA	1889		415	NY	NL	1887		355	CLE	AA	1887
469	CIN	AA	1888		412	BOS	PL	1890		353	CLE	AA	1888
468	STL	AA	1888		409	BRO	AA	1887		353	COL	AA	1890
466	LOU	AA	1887		409	BRO	NL	1892		350	IND	NL	1888
462	CIN	AA	1889		401	BAL	NL	1897		350	CIN	NL	1896

Stolen bases were not tabulated before 1885. Between 1886-1897, stolen bases often were awarded for taking an extra base on a hit.

(652) Most Stolen Bases by a Team in a Season, since 1898

364	BAL	NL	1899	283	CHI	NL	1906	267	CHI	NL	1905
347	NY	NL	1911	282	NY	NL	1910	265	CHI	AL	1902
341	OAK	AL	1976	280	CHI	AL	1901	264	NY	NL	1903
319	NY	NL	1912	280	DET	AL	1909	264	PIT	NL	1907
314	STL	NL	1985	280	CIN	NL	1909	262	STL	NL	1986
310	CIN	NL	1910	276	DET	AL	1911	260	PIT	NL	1977
296	NY	NL	1913	274	BRO	NL	1900	259	CHI	NL	1903
291	NY	NL	1905	274	WAS	AL	1912	258	PHI	AL	1912
290	CIN	NL	1911	273	BRO	NL	1903	256	MIL	AL	1992
288	NY	NL	1906	273	IND	FL	1914	251	NY	AL	1914
288	NY	AL	1910	271	BRO	NL	1899	250	BAL	NL	1898
287	WAS	AL	1913	270	DET	AL	1912				
283	NY	NL	1904	269	NY	AL	1911				

TRANSCENDENTAL GRAPHICS

Rickey Henderson

(653) Fewest Stolen Bases by a Team in a Season, since 1886

13	WAS	AL	1957	21	PIT	NL	1954	24	CIN	NL	1931
16	KC	AL	1960	22	CHI	NL	1947	24	STL	NL	1948
17	STL	NL	1949	22	DET	AL	1948	24	NY	AL	1948
17	STL	AL	1953	22	PIT	NL	1955	24	PIT	NL	1956
17	DET	AL	1972	22	KC	AL	1955	25	PHI	AL	1931
18	STL	NL	1953	22	WAS	AL	1958	25	BOS	NL	1933
18	BOS	AL	1964	22	KC	AL	1958	25	PHI	NL	1940
19	NY	NL	1934	22	SF	NL	1967	25	STL	AL	1945
19	CIN	NL	1938	23	BOS	NL	1936	25	PHI	AL	1945
19	CLE	AL	1945	23	STL	AL	1946	25	CIN	NL	1953
19	CHI	AL	1950	23	STL	NL	1950	25	WAS	AL	1955
20	BOS	NL	1935	23	DET	AL	1950	25	CLE	AL	1970
20	BOS	AL	1951	23	PIT	NL	1973	25	NY	NL	1994

(654) Best Stolen Base Duos in a Season, 1886-1897 (min. 30 SB each)

246	STL	AA	1887	Arlie Latham	129	Charlie Comiskey	117
233	CIN	AA	1887	Hugh Nicol	138	Bid McPhee	95
202	STL	AA	1888	Arlie Latham	109	Tommy McCarthy	93
200	KC	AA	1889	Billy Hamilton	111	Herman Long	89
191	BOS	AA	1891	Tom Brown	106	Hugh Duffy	85
185	CIN	AA	1888	Hugh Nicol	103	John Reilly	82
182	BAL	AA	1887	Mike Griffin	94	Blondie Purcell	88
182	PHI	AA	1888	Curt Welch	95	Harry Stovey	87
176	BOS	PL	1890	Harry Stovey	97	Tom Brown	79
174	LOU	AA	1887	Pete Browning	103	Hub Collins	71
172	PHI	AA	1887	Tom Poorman	88	Chippy McGarr	84
162	CLE	AA	1887	Cub Stricker	86	Ed McKean	76
160	BAL	NL	1896	Joe Kelley	87	Jack Doyle	73
159	PHI	NL	1887	Jim Fogarty	102	Ed Andrews	57
157	NY	NL	1887	John Ward	111	Jim O'Rourke	46
156	BRO	AA	1889	William "Darby" O'Brien	91	Hub Collins	65
146	PHI	NL	1890	Billy Hamilton	102	Al Myers	44
145	BRO	NL	1892	John Ward	88	William "Darby" O'Brien	57
143	CIN	AA	1889	Hugh Nicol	80	Bid McPhee	63
143	STL	AA	1890	Tommy McCarthy	83	Shorty Fuller	60
143	PHI	NL	1895	Billy Hamilton	97	Ed Delahanty	46
139	CHI	NL	1894	Walt Wilmot	74	Bill Lange	65
136	BRO	AA	1887	Bill McClellan	70	Jim McTamany	66
136	BOS	NL	1887	King Kelly	84	Dick Johnston	52
135	CHI	NL	1896	Bill Lange	84	Bill Dahlen	51
134	STL	AA	1889	Arlie Latham	69	Charlie Comiskey	65
134	PHI	NL	1894	Billy Hamilton	98	Bill Hallman	36
133	BAL	NL	1897	Jake Stenzel	69	Willie Keeler	64
132	TOL	AA	1890	Bill Van Dyke	73	Perry Werden	59
132	ROC	AA	1890	Ted Scheffler	77	Jimmy Knowles	55
132	BRO	NL	1890	Hub Collins	85	George Pinkney	47
131	BOS	NL	1889	King Kelly	68	Tom Brown	63

Stolen bases were not tabulated before 1885. Between 1886-1897, stolen bases often were awarded for taking an extra base on a hit.

(655) Best Stolen Base Duos in a Season, since 1898 (min. 30 SB each)

166	STL	NL	1985	Vince Coleman	110	Willie McGee	56
160	MON	NL	1980	Ron LeFlore	97	Rodney Scott	63
152	STL	NL	1987	Vince Coleman	109	Ozzie Smith	43
150	BAL	NL	1899	Jimmy Sheckard	77	John McGraw	73
148	STL	NL	1974	Lou Brock	118	Bake McBride	30
140	OAK	AL	1983	Rickey Henderson	108	Mike Davis	32
138	STL	NL	1986	Vince Coleman	107	Ozzie Smith	31
138	STL	NL	1988	Vince Coleman	81	Ozzie Smith	57
137	WAS	AL	1913	Clyde Milan	75	Danny Moeller	62
136	LA	NL	1962	Maury Wills	104	Willie Davis	32
132	MON	NL	1991	Marquis Grissom	76	Delino DeShields	56
131	DET	AL	1915	Ty Cobb	96	Donie Bush	35
129	DET	AL	1909	Ty Cobb	76	Donie Bush	53
129	OAK	AL	1976	Billy North	75	Bert Campaneris	54
128	PIT	NL	1980	Omar Moreno	96	Phil Garner	32
124	MON	NL	1992	Marquis Grissom	78	Delino DeShields	46
123	DET	AL	1911	Ty Cobb	83	Donie Bush	40
123	PIT	NL	1977	Frank Taveras	70	Omar Moreno	53
122	IND	FL	1914	Benny Kauff	75	Bill McKechnie	47
121	CIN	NL	1910	Bob Bescher	70	Dode Paskert	51
120	PHI	NL	1984	Juan Samuel	72	Von Hayes	48
118	CIN	NL	1911	Bob Bescher	81	Dick Egan	37
118	WAS	AL	1912	Clyde Milan	88	Danny Moeller	30
118	SD	NL	1980	Gene Richards	61	Ozzie Smith	57
117	PIT	NL	1978	Omar Moreno	71	Frank Taveras	46
117	MON	NL	1982	Tim Raines	78	Andre Dawson	39
114	DET	AL	1910	Ty Cobb	65	Donie Bush	49
113	BRO	NL	1903	Jimmy Sheckard	67	Sammy Strang	46
113	KC	AL	1979	Willie Wilson	83	Amos Otis	30
112	NY	NL	1911	Josh Devore	61	Fred Snodgrass	51
112	NY	AL	1914	Fritz Maisel	74	Roger Peckinpaugh	38
111	NY	NL	1905	Art Devlin	59	Sam Mertes	52
110	CLE	AL	1996	Kenny Lofton	75	Omar Vizquel	35

ROOKIE RECORDS

Rookie Records

- From 1876-1970, a batter is considered a rookie if he did not have 90 previous major league at-bats.
  From 1971-2006, a batter is considered a rookie if he did not have 130 previous major league at-bats.

- From 1876-1970, a pitcher is considered a rookie if he did not have 45 previous major league innings-pitched.
  From 1971-2006, a pitcher is considered a rookie if he did not have 50 previous major league innings-pitched.

- For these lists, all players are considered rookies in 1876, whether or not they played in the National Association.

(656) Most Plate Appearances in a Season by a Rookie

738	Chuck Schilling	AL	BOS	1961
738	Ichiro Suzuki	AL	SEA	2001
737	Juan Samuel	NL	PHI	1984
734	Nomar Garciaparra	AL	BOS	1997
731	Harvey Kuenn	AL	DET	1953
731	Jake Wood	AL	DET	1961
725	Kevin Seitzer	AL	KC	1987
723	Carlos Beltran	AL	KC	1999
721	Rich Rollins	AL	MIN	1962
720	Jimmy Rollins	NL	PHI	2001
719	Dick Howser	AL	KC	1961
718	Tony Oliva	AL	MIN	1964
716	Wally Moon	NL	STL	1954
715	Ken Hubbs	NL	CHI	1962
713	Carl Lind	AL	CLE	1928
713	Roy Johnson	AL	DET	1929
712	Tom Tresh	AL	NY	1962
711	Frank Baumholtz	NL	CIN	1947
710	Jim Gilliam	NL	BRO	1953
709	Lu Blue	AL	DET	1921
709	Dick Allen	NL	PHI	1964
708	Joe Morgan	NL	HOU	1965
703	Johnny Ray	NL	PIT	1982
702	Roy Thomas	NL	PHI	1899
701	Jackie Robinson	NL	BRO	1947
701	Chili Davis	NL	SF	1982
700	Dale Alexander	AL	DET	1929
700	Tom Oliver	AL	BOS	1930
700	Hanley Ramirez	NL	FLA	2006

(657) Most At-bats in a Season by a Rookie

701	Juan Samuel	NL	PHI	1984
692	Ichiro Suzuki	AL	SEA	2001
684	Nomar Garciaparra	AL	BOS	1997
679	Harvey Kuenn	AL	DET	1953
672	Tony Oliva	AL	MIN	1964
663	Jake Wood	AL	DET	1961
663	Carlos Beltran	AL	KCA	1999
661	Ken Hubbs	NL	CHI	1962
656	Jimmy Rollins	NL	PHI	2001
650	Carl Lind	AL	CLE	1928
647	Johnny Ray	NL	PIT	1982
646	Tom Oliver	AL	BOS	1930
646	Chuck Schilling	AL	BOS	1961
643	Frank Baumholtz	NL	CIN	1947
641	Kevin Seitzer	AL	KC	1987
641	Chili Davis	NL	SF	1982
641	Tony Womack	NL	PIT	1997
640	Roy Johnson	AL	DET	1929

(658) Most Walks in a Season by a Rookie

123	Bill Joyce	PL	BRO	1890
115	Roy Thomas	NL	PHI	1899
107	Ted Williams	AL	BOS	1939
106	Les Fleming	AL	CLE	1942
103	Lu Blue	AL	DET	1921
100	Al Rosen	AL	CLE	1950
100	Jim Gilliam	NL	BRO	1953
97	Joe Morgan	NL	HOU	1965
97	Alvin Davis	AL	SEA	1984
96	Jack Crooks	AA	COL	1890
95	Ferris Fain	AL	PHI	1947
95	Billy Grabarkewitz	NL	LA	1970
94	Bernie Carbo	NL	CIN	1970
92	Eddie Stanky	NL	CHI	1943
92	Dick Howser	AL	KC	1961
91	Joe Foy	AL	BOS	1966
90	Don Lenhardt	AL	STL	1950

(659) Most Hit by Pitch in a Season by a Rookie

22	Charlie Babb	NL	NY	1903		17	Keith Ginter	NL	MIL	2003
21	Bucky Harris	AL	WAS	1920		16	Bill Keister	NL	BAL	1899
21	David Eckstein	AL	ANA	2001		16	Bert Daniels	AL	NY	1910
20	Frank Robinson	NL	CIN	1956		16	Minnie Minoso	AL	CLE-CHI	1951
20	Reed Johnson	AL	TOR	2003					CLE (2); CHI (14)	
18	Angel Berroa	AL	KC	2003		15	Elmer Flick	NL	PHI	1898
17	Roy Thomas	NL	PHI	1899		15	Jason Kendall	NL	PIT	1996
17	Heinie Manush	AL	DET	1923		15	Olmedo Saenz	AL	OAK	1999

(660) Most Hits in a Season by a Rookie

242	Ichiro Suzuki	AL	SEA	2001		207	Kevin Seitzer	AL	KC	1987
223	Lloyd Waner	NL	PIT	1927		206	Johnny Frederick	NL	BRO	1929
219	Jimmy Williams	NL	PIT	1899		206	Hal Trosky	AL	CLE	1934
219	Ralph Garr	NL	ATL	1971		206	Joe DiMaggio	AL	NY	1936
217	Tony Oliva	AL	MIN	1964		205	Johnny Pesky	AL	BOS	1942
215	Dale Alexander	AL	DET	1929		203	Earle Combs	AL	NY	1925
211	Benny Kauff	FL	IND	1914		201	Roy Johnson	AL	DET	1929
209	Harvey Kuenn	AL	DET	1953		201	Dick Allen	NL	PHI	1964
209	Nomar Garciaparra	AL	BOS	1997		200	Dick Wakefield	AL	DET	1943

(661) Most Doubles in a Season by a Rookie

52	Johnny Frederick	NL	BRO	1929		44	Brad Fullmer	NL	MON	1998
47	Fred Lynn	AL	BOS	1975		43	Dale Alexander	AL	DET	1929
47	Albert Pujols	NL	STL	2001		43	Earl Averill	AL	CLE	1929
47	Ryan Zimmerman	NL	WAS	2006		43	Tony Oliva	AL	MIN	1964
46	Hanley Ramirez	NL	FLA	2006		42	Carl Lind	AL	CLE	1928
45	Roy Johnson	AL	DET	1929		42	Hideki Matsui	AL	NY	2003
45	Hal Trosky	AL	CLE	1934		41	Warren Cromartie	NL	MON	1977
44	Benny Kauff	FL	IND	1914		41	Ben Grieve	AL	OAK	1998
44	Bob L. Johnson	AL	PHI	1933		40	Bill Kenworthy	FL	KC	1914
44	Joe DiMaggio	AL	NY	1936		40	Bob Meusel	AL	NY	1920
44	Ted Williams	AL	BOS	1939		40	Johnny Bench	NL	CIN	1968
44	Nomar Garciaparra	AL	BOS	1997		40	Chris Sabo	NL	CIN	1988

(662) Most Triples in a Season by a Rookie

28	Jimmy Williams	NL	PIT	1899		17	George Treadway	NL	BAL	1893
25	Tom Long	NL	STL	1915		17	Kip Selbach	NL	WAS	1894
22	Paul Waner	NL	PIT	1926		17	Bill Hassamaer	NL	WAS	1894
20	Perry Werden	AA	TOL	1890		17	Jim Kelly	FL	PIT	1915
19	Joe Cassidy	AL	WAS	1904		17	Charlie Gehringer	AL	DET	1926
19	Frank Baker	AL	PHI	1909		17	Russ Scarritt	AL	BOS	1929
19	Juan Samuel	NL	PHI	1984		17	Jim Gilliam	NL	BRO	1953
18	Bill Joyce	PL	BRO	1890		16	Marty Sullivan	NL	CHI	1887
18	Jim Canavan	AA	CIN-MIL	1891		16	Harry Davis	NL	NY-PIT	1896
			CIN (14); MIL (4)						NY (10); PIT (6)	
18	Harry Lumley	NL	BRO	1904		16	Bill Keister	NL	BAL	1899
18	Glenn Wright	NL	PIT	1924		16	Kitty Bransfield	NL	PIT	1901
18	Ival Goodman	NL	CIN	1935		16	Sam Bohne	NL	CIN	1921
17	John Peltz	AA	IND	1884		16	Kiki Cuyler	NL	PIT	1924

(663) Most Home Runs in a Season by a Rookie

49	Mark McGwire	AL	OAK	1987		33	Earl Williams	NL	ATL	1971
38	Wally Berger	NL	BOS	1930		33	Jose Canseco	AL	OAK	1986
38	Frank Robinson	NL	CIN	1956		32	Tony Oliva	AL	MIN	1964
37	Al Rosen	AL	CLE	1950		32	Matt Nokes	AL	DET	1987
37	Albert Pujols	NL	STL	2001		31	Ted Williams	AL	BOS	1939
35	Hal Trosky	AL	CLE	1934		31	Jim Ray Hart	NL	SF	1964
35	Rudy York	AL	DET	1937		31	Tim Salmon	AL	CAL	1993
35	Ron Kittle	AL	CHI	1983		30	Bob Allison	AL	WAS	1959
35	Mike Piazza	NL	LA	1993		30	Pete Incaviglia	AL	TEX	1986
34	Walt Dropo	AL	BOS	1950		30	Willie Montanez	NL	PHI	1971
33	Jimmie Hall	AL	MIN	1963		30	Nomar Garciaparra	AL	BOS	1997

(664) Most Extra-base Hits in a Season by a Rookie

89	Hal Trosky	AL	CLE	1934		80	Dick Allen	NL	PHI	1964
88	Joe DiMaggio	AL	NY	1936		79	Wally Berger	NL	BOS	1930
88	Albert Pujols	NL	STL	2001		75	Fred Lynn	AL	BOS	1975
86	Ted Williams	AL	BOS	1939		74	Earl Averill	AL	CLE	1929
85	Nomar Garciaparra	AL	BOS	1997		74	Hanley Ramirez	NL	FLA	2006
84	Tony Oliva	AL	MIN	1964		71	Frank Robinson	NL	CIN	1956
83	Dale Alexander	AL	DET	1929		70	Walt Dropo	AL	BOS	1950
82	Johnny Frederick	NL	BRO	1929		70	Juan Samuel	NL	PHI	1984
81	Mark McGwire	AL	OAK	1987		70	Ryan Zimmerman	NL	WAS	2006

(665) Most Runs in a Season by a Rookie, before 1893

142	Mike Griffin	AA	BAL	1887
137	Herman Long	AA	KC	1889
126	Ross Barnes	NL	CHI	1876
121	Bill Joyce	PL	BRO	1890
115	Emmett Seery	UA	BAL-KC	1884
			BAL (113); KC (2)	
115	Harry L. Taylor	AA	LOU	1890
114	Tommy Tucker	AA	BAL	1887
114	Jimmy Cooney Sr.	NL	CHI	1890
114	Bill Dahlen	NL	CHI	1891
113	Perry Werden	AA	TOL	1890
110	Lefty Marr	AA	COL	1889
109	Cupid Childs	AA	SYR	1890
107	Bug Holliday	AA	CIN	1889
107	Jim Canavan	AA	CIN-MIL	1891
			CIN (74); MIL 33)	
103	Jim Burns	AA	KC	1889
102	Eddie Burke	NL	PHI-PIT	1890
			PHI (85); PIT (17)	
101	Yank Robinson	UA	BAL	1884

(666) Most Runs in a Season by a Rookie, since 1893

137	Roy Thomas	NL	PHI	1899
133	Lloyd Waner	NL	PIT	1927
132	Joe DiMaggio	AL	NY	1936
131	Ted Williams	AL	BOS	1939
129	Bill Everitt	NL	CHI	1895
128	Roy Johnson	AL	DET	1929
127	Johnny Frederick	NL	BRO	1929
127	Ichiro Suzuki	AL	SEA	2001
126	Jimmy Williams	NL	PIT	1899
125	Jackie Robinson	NL	BRO	1947
125	Jim Gilliam	NL	BRO	1953
125	Dick Allen	NL	PHI	1964
122	Frank Robinson	NL	CIN	1956
122	Nomar Garciaparra	AL	BOS	1997
120	Benny Kauff	FL	IND	1914
120	Barney McCosky	AL	DET	1939
119	Hanley Ramirez	NL	FLA	2006
117	Earle Combs	AL	NY	1925
117	Hal Trosky	AL	CLE	1934
114	Donie Bush	AL	DET	1909
112	Chick Stahl	NL	BOS	1897
112	Minnie Minoso	AL	CLE-CHI	1951
			CLE (3); CHI (109)	
112	Carlos Beltran	AL	KC	1999
112	Albert Pujols	NL	STL	2001
110	Earl Averill	AL	CLE	1929
110	Dale Alexander	AL	DET	1929
109	Emmet Heidrick	NL	STL	1899
109	Tony Oliva	AL	MIN	1964
108	Dick Howser	AL	KC	1961
107	Vince Coleman	NL	STL	1985
106	Bill Hassamaer	NL	WAS	1894
106	Wally Moon	NL	STL	1954
105	Ike Davis	AL	CHI	1925
105	Johnny Pesky	AL	BOS	1942
105	Bobby Thomson	NL	NY	1947
105	Juan Samuel	NL	PHI	1984
105	Kevin Seitzer	AL	KC	1987
105	Dan Uggla	NL	FLA	2006
104	Harlond Clift	AL	STL	1934
104	Derek Jeter	AL	NY	1996
104	Terrence Long	AL	OAK	2000
103	Lu Blue	AL	DET	1921
103	Bob L. Johnson	AL	PHI	1933
103	Fred Lynn	AL	BOS	1975
103	Ryne Sandberg	NL	CHI	1982
103	Devon White	AL	CAL	1987
102	Irv Waldron	AL	MIL-WAS	1901
			MIL (48); WAS (54)	
102	Carl Lind	AL	CLE	1928
102	Hershel Martin	NL	PHI	1937
101	Joe Sewell	AL	CLE	1921
101	Paul Waner	NL	PIT	1926
101	Walt Dropo	AL	BOS	1950
101	Pete Rose	NL	CIN	1963
101	Ralph Garr	NL	ATL	1971
100	John Farrell	AL	WAS	1901
100	Evar Swanson	NL	CIN	1929
100	Kiddo Davis	NL	PHI	1932
100	Buddy Lewis	AL	WAS	1936
100	Al Rosen	AL	CLE	1950
100	Sam Jethroe	NL	BOS	1950
100	Joe Morgan	NL	HOU	1965
100	Scott Podsednik	NL	MIL	2003

(667) Most RBI in a Season by a Rookie

145	Ted Williams	AL	BOS	1939
144	Walt Dropo	AL	BOS	1950
142	Hal Trosky	AL	CLE	1934
137	Dale Alexander	AL	DET	1929
130	Albert Pujols	NL	STL	2001
125	Joe DiMaggio	AL	NY	1936
119	Wally Berger	NL	BOS	1930
118	Mark McGwire	AL	OAK	1987
117	Joe Vosmik	AL	CLE	1931
117	Jose Canseco	AL	OAK	1986
116	Jimmy Williams	NL	PIT	1899
116	Al Rosen	AL	CLE	1950
116	Alvin Davis	AL	SEA	1984
114	Tony Lazzeri	AL	NY	1926
114	Smead Jolley	AL	CHI	1930
113	Ken Keltner	AL	CLE	1938
112	Dave Orr	AA	NY	1884
112	Ray Jablonski	NL	STL	1953
112	Mike Piazza	NL	LA	1993
111	Glenn Wright	NL	PIT	1924
111	Johnny Rizzo	NL	PIT	1938

110	Zeke Bonura	AL	CHI	1934
110	Ryan Zimmerman	NL	WAS	2006
108	Carlos Beltran	AL	KC	1999
107	Gus Suhr	NL	PIT	1930
107	Luke Easter	AL	CLE	1950
106	Del Bissonette	NL	BRO	1928
106	Hideki Matsui	AL	NY	2003
105	Fred Lynn	AL	BOS	1975
104	Bug Holliday	AA	CIN	1889
104	Willie Horton	AL	DET	1965
103	Pinky Whitney	NL	PHI	1928
103	Rudy York	AL	DET	1937
102	Al Simmons	AL	PHI	1924
102	Bill Brubaker	NL	PIT	1936
102	Jim Rice	AL	BOS	1975
101	Ray Pepper	AL	STL	1934
101	Babe Young	NL	NY	1940
100	Jim Greengrass	NL	CIN	1953
100	Ron Kittle	AL	CHI	1983
100	Wally Joyner	AL	CAL	1986

GEORGE BRACE

Ted Williams

347

(668) Highest Batting Average in a Season by a Rookie
(min. 3.1 PA per scheduled game)

.370	Benny Kauff	FL	IND	1914		.329	Dick Cox	NL	BRO	1925
.358	Bill Everitt	NL	CHI	1895		.329	Johnny Mize	NL	STL	1936
.355	Jimmy Williams	NL	PIT	1899		.329	Albert Pujols	NL	STL	2001
.355	Lloyd Waner	NL	PIT	1927		.328	Emmet Heidrick	NL	STL	1899
.354	Dave Orr	AA	NY	1884		.328	Bob Meusel	AL	NY	1920
.354	Chick Stahl	NL	BOS	1897		.328	Homer Summa	AL	CLE	1923
.354	Kiki Cuyler	NL	PIT	1924		.328	Johnny Frederick	NL	BRO	1929
.352	Ginger Beaumont	NL	PIT	1899		.328	Mike Greenwell	AL	BOS	1987
.352	Hack Miller	NL	CHI	1922		.327	Ted Williams	AL	BOS	1939
.350	Ichiro Suzuki	AL	SEA	2001		.326	Minnie Minoso	AL	CLE-CHI	1951
.345	Cupid Childs	AA	SYR	1890			CLE (.429 in 8 G); CHI (.324 in 138 G)			
.343	Gene DeMontreville	NL	WAS	1896		.325	Roy Thomas	NL	PHI	1899
.343	Dale Alexander	AL	DET	1929		.324	Bill Dickey	AL	NY	1929
.343	Ralph Garr	NL	ATL	1971		.323	Joe DiMaggio	AL	NY	1936
.342	Patsy Dougherty	AL	BOS	1902		.323	Tony Oliva	AL	MIN	1964
.342	Earle Combs	AL	NY	1925		.323	Mike Hargrove	AL	TEX	1974
.337	Ike Boone	AL	BOS	1924		.323	Kevin Seitzer	AL	KC	1987
.336	Harry Moore	UA	WAS	1884		.322	Bill Hassamaer	NL	WAS	1894
.336	Paul Waner	NL	PIT	1926		.322	Hughie Critz	NL	CIN	1924
.334	Socks Seybold	AL	PHI	1901		.322	Alvin Dark	NL	BOS	1948
.333	Richie Ashburn	NL	PHI	1948		.322	Walt Dropo	AL	BOS	1950
.332	Earl Averill	AL	CLE	1929		.321	Bug Holliday	AA	CIN	1889
.331	Mickey Cochrane	AL	PHI	1925		.321	Ray Grimes	NL	CHI	1921
.331	Johnny Pesky	AL	BOS	1942		.321	Dusty Baker	NL	ATL	1972
.331	Fred Lynn	AL	BOS	1975		.321	Dave Stapleton	AL	BOS	1980
.330	Hal Trosky	AL	CLE	1934		.320	Del Bissonette	NL	BRO	1928
.330	Rico Carty	NL	MIL	1964		.320	Joe Vosmik	AL	CLE	1931
.329	Bill Keister	NL	BAL	1899		.320	Homer Bush	AL	TOR	1999

This list contains only those players who appeared in at least 100 games.

Richie Ashburn

(669) Highest On-base Percentage in a Season by a Rookie
(min. 3.1 PA per scheduled game)

.457	Roy Thomas	NL	PHI	1899		.412	Joe Sewell	AL	CLE	1921
.447	Benny Kauff	FL	IND	1914		.411	Earle Combs	AL	NY	1925
.436	Ted Williams	AL	BOS	1939		.410	Richie Ashburn	NL	PHI	1948
.434	Cupid Childs	AA	SYR	1890		.407	Patsy Dougherty	AL	BOS	1902
.430	Elmer Flick	NL	PHI	1898		.407	Lefty Marr	AA	COL	1889
.422	Minnie Minoso	AL	CLE-CHI	1951		.406	Ray Grimes	NL	CHI	1921
	CLE (.529); CHI (.419)					.406	Chick Stahl	NL	BOS	1897
.417	Jimmy Williams	NL	PIT	1899		.405	Al Rosen	AL	CLE	1950
.416	Ginger Beaumont	NL	PIT	1899		.405	Mitchell Page	AL	OAK	1977
.416	Lu Blue	AL	DET	1921		.404	Perry Werden	AA	TOL	1890
.414	Billy Goodman	AL	BOS	1948		.404	Ike Boone	AL	BOS	1924
.414	Ferris Fain	AL	PHI	1947		.403	Albert Pujols	NL	STL	2001
.413	Bill Joyce	PL	BRO	1890		.402	Johnny Mize	NL	STL	1936
.413	Paul Waner	NL	PIT	1926		.402	Kiki Cuyler	NL	PIT	1924
.412	Les Fleming	AL	CLE	1942		.401	Fred Lynn	AL	BOS	1975

This list contains only those players who appeared in at least 100 games.

(670) Highest Slugging Average in a Season by a Rookie
(min. 3.1 PA per scheduled game)

.618	Mark McGwire	AL	OAK	1987		.570	Mike Greenwell	AL	BOS	1987
.614	Wally Berger	NL	BOS	1930		.566	Fred Lynn	AL	BOS	1975
.610	Albert Pujols	NL	STL	2001		.561	Mike Piazza	NL	LA	1993
.609	Ted Williams	AL	BOS	1939		.558	Frank Robinson	NL	CIN	1956
.598	Hal Trosky	AL	CLE	1934		.557	Dick Allen	NL	PHI	1964
.583	Walt Dropo	AL	BOS	1950		.557	Tony Oliva	AL	MIN	1964
.580	Dale Alexander	AL	DET	1929		.554	Rico Carty	NL	MIL	1964
.577	Johnny Mize	NL	STL	1936		.550	Jason Bay	NL	PIT	2004
.576	Joe DiMaggio	AL	NY	1936						

This list contains only those players who appeared in at least 100 games.

(671) Most Total Bases in a Season by a Rookie

374	Hal Trosky	AL	CLE	1934		319	Del Bissonette	NL	BRO	1928
374	Tony Oliva	AL	MIN	1964		319	Frank Robinson	NL	CIN	1956
367	Joe DiMaggio	AL	NY	1936		316	Ichiro Suzuki	AL	SEA	2001
365	Nomar Garciaparra	AL	BOS	1997		310	Juan Samuel	NL	PHI	1984
363	Dale Alexander	AL	DET	1929		309	Orlando Cepeda	NL	SF	1958
360	Albert Pujols	NL	STL	2001		307	Mike Piazza	NL	LA	1993
352	Dick Allen	NL	PHI	1964		305	Benny Kauff	FL	IND	1914
344	Ted Williams	AL	BOS	1939		304	Roy Johnson	AL	DET	1929
344	Mark McGwire	AL	OAK	1987		304	Hanley Ramirez	NL	FLA	2006
342	Johnny Frederick	NL	BRO	1929		303	Smead Jolley	AL	CHI	1930
341	Wally Berger	NL	BOS	1930		301	Al Rosen	AL	CLE	1950
328	Jimmy Williams	NL	PIT	1899		301	Kevin Seitzer	AL	KC	1987
326	Walt Dropo	AL	BOS	1950		301	Carlos Beltran	AL	KC	1999
321	Earl Averill	AL	CLE	1929						

(672) A .300 Batting Average in Rookie Season only (min. 3.1 PA per scheduled game)

.336	Harry Moore	UA	WAS	1884
.329	Dick Cox	NL	BRO	1925
.322	Hughie Critz	NL	CIN	1924
.322	Walt Dropo	AL	BOS	1950
.322	Bill Hassamaer	NL	WAS	1894
.321	Dave Stapleton	AL	BOS	1980
.320	Homer Bush	AL	TOR	1999
.317	Bill Kenworthy	FL	KC	1914
.317	Jim Viox	NL	PIT	1913
.317	Alex Cintron	NL	ARI	2003
.316	Dick Wakefield	AL	DET	1943
.314	Ralph Hodgin	AL	CHI	1943
.314	Greg Gross	NL	HOU	1974
.314	Don Padgett	NL	STL	1937
.314	Scott Podsednik	NL	MIL	2003
.313	Les Scarsella	NL	CIN	1936
.313	Buzz Arlett	NL	PHI	1931
.313	Dutch Zwilling	FL	CHI	1914
.312	Jake Powell	AL	WAS	1935
.312	Joe Knight	NL	CIN	1890
.311	Irv Waldron	AL	MIL-WAS	1901
			MIL (.297); WAS (.322)	
.310	Bob Bailor	AL	TOR	1977
.309	Kiddo Davis	NL	PHI	1932
.309	Al Lopez	NL	BRO	1930
.308	Jumbo Schoeneck	UA	CP-BAL	1884
			CHI/PIT (.317); BAL (.250)	
.307	Mitchell Page	AL	OAK	1977
.307	Sandy Griffin	AA	ROC	1890
.306	Mike Caruso	AL	CHI	1998
.306	Lefty Marr	AA	COL	1889
.306	Sam Barkley	AA	TOL	1884
.306	Harry L. Taylor	AA	LOU	1890
.305	Red Barnes	AL	WAS	1928
.305	Bama Rowell	NL	BOS	1940
.304	Josh Devore	NL	NY	1910
.304	Benny Meyer	FL	BAL	1914
.304	Jim Burns	AA	KC	1889
.304	Eddie Waitkus	NL	CHI	1946
.304	Lou Chiozza	NL	PHI	1934
.303	Marty Barrett	AL	BOS	1984
.303	Marlon Byrd	NL	PHI	2003
.302	Algie McBride	NL	CIN	1898
.302	Sam Mele	AL	BOS	1947
.302	Jim Bucher	NL	BRO	1935
.302	Simon Nicholls	AL	PHI	1907
.302	Jim Finigan	AL	PHI	1954
.302	Roberto Kelly	AL	NY	1989
.301	Johnny Rizzo	NL	PIT	1938
.301	William "Darby" O'Brien	AA	NY	1887
.301	Richie Hebner	NL	PIT	1969
.301	Manny Jimenez	AL	KC	1962
.300	Chris Singleton	AL	CHI	1999
.300	Bucky Harris	AL	WAS	1920
.300	Benito Santiago	NL	SD	1987
.300	George Barclay	NL	STL	1902

(673) Longest Consecutive-games Hit Streak by a Rookie

34	Benito Santiago	NL	SD	1987
30	Jerome Walton	NL	CHI	1989
30	Nomar Garciaparra	AL	BOS	1997
27	Jimmy Williams	NL	PIT	1899
26	Jimmy Williams	NL	PIT	1899
26	Guy Curtright	AL	CHI	1943
25	Joe McEwing	NL	STL	1999
24	Chico Carrasquel	AL	CHI	1950
23	Goldie Rapp	NL	PHI	1921
23	Richie Ashburn	NL	PHI	1948
23	Alvin Dark	NL	BOS	1948
23	Mike Vail	NL	NY	1975
23	Kent Hrbek	AL	MIN	1982
23	Ichiro Suzuki	AL	SEA	2001
22	Johnny Mize	NL	STL	1936
22	Dale Mitchell	AL	CLE	1947
22	Willie McCovey	NL	SF	1959
22	Ralph Garr	NL	ATL	1971
22	Edgar Renteria	NL	FLA	1996
21	Taft Wright	AL	WAS	1938
21	Danny Litwhiler	NL	PHI	1940
21	Lou Klein	NL	STL	1943
21	Dick Wakefield	AL	DET	1943
21	Jackie Robinson	NL	BRO	1947
21	Ichiro Suzuki	AL	SEA	2001
21	Robb Quinlan	AL	ANA	2004
20	Al Libke	NL	CIN	1945
20	Pancho Herrera	NL	PHI	1960
20	Fred Lynn	AL	BOS	1975

(674) Most Grounded into Double Plays in a Season by a Rookie

28	George Kell	AL	PHI	1944		21	Al Kaline	AL	DET	1954
27	Billy Johnson	AL	NY	1943		21	Chico Fernandez	NL	PHI	1957
27	Al Rosen	AL	CLE	1950		21	Julio Franco	AL	CLE	1983
26	Sid Gordon	NL	NY	1943		21	Albert Pujols	NL	STL	2001
25	Nippy Jones	NL	STL	1948		21	Jason Phillips	NL	NY	2003
25	George Scott	AL	BOS	1966		20	Johnny Hudson	NL	BRO	1938
25	Hideki Matsui	AL	NY	2003		20	Gil Torres	AL	WAS	1944
24	Gene Green	NL	STL	1958		20	Ed Busch	AL	PHI	1944
24	Bobby Darwin	AL	MIN	1972		20	Ken Hubbs	NL	CHI	1962
24	Joe Charboneau	AL	CLE	1980		20	Mike Hershberger	AL	CHI	1962
23	Pete Suder	AL	PHI	1941		20	George Foster	NL	SF-CIN	1971
23	Dick Wakefield	AL	DET	1943					SF (4); CIN (16)	
23	George Vico	AL	DET	1948		20	Doug Ault	AL	TOR	1977
22	Bob Allison	AL	WAS	1959		20	Bobby Crosby	AL	OAK	2004
22	Eddie Murray	AL	BAL	1977						

(675) Most Games by a Rookie Pitcher

90	Wayne Granger	NL	CIN	1969		78	Tim Burke	NL	MON	1985
88	Sean Runyan	AL	DET	1998		78	Ricky Stone	NL	HOU	2002
86	Oscar Villarreal	NL	ARI	2003		78	Brad Lidge	NL	HOU	2003
85	Matt Capps	NL	PIT	2006		77	Butch Metzger	NL	SD	1976
83	Mike Myers	AL	DET	1996		77	Mike Perez	NL	STL	1992
83	Kelly Wunsch	AL	CHI	2000		76	Larry Hardy	NL	SD	1974
82	Ray King	NL	MIL	2001		75	Dan Quisenberry	AL	KC	1980
80	Mitch Williams	AL	TEX	1986		75	Kerry Ligtenberg	NL	ATL	1998
78	Ed Vande Berg	AL	SEA	1982		75	Brian Fuentes	NL	COL	2003

(676) Highest Winning Percentage by a Rookie Pitcher, since 1893 (min. 15 wins)

.842	Emil Yde	NL	PIT	1924	16-3		.767	Vean Gregg	AL	CLE	1911	23-7
.838	Bill Hoffer	NL	BAL	1895	31-6		.742	Noodles Hahn	NL	CIN	1899	23-8
.833	King Cole	NL	CHI	1910	20-4		.741	Gene Bearden	AL	CLE	1948	20-7
.833	Hoyt Wilhelm	NL	NY	1952	15-3		.731	Wilcy Moore	AL	NY	1927	19-7
.826	Elmer Riddle	NL	CIN	1941	19-4		.727	Dick Hughes	NL	STL	1967	16-6
.813	Russ Ford	AL	NY	1910	26-6		.722	Larry Cheney	NL	CHI	1912	26-10
.810	Johnny Allen	AL	NY	1932	17-4		.714	Jake Weimer	NL	CHI	1903	20-8
.810	Ted Wilks	NL	STL	1944	17-4		.714	Jack Pfiester	NL	CHI	1906	20-8
.808	Larry Jansen	NL	NY	1947	21-5		.714	Joe Bush	AL	PHI	1913	15-6
.792	Wally Bunker	AL	BAL	1964	19-5		.714	Slick Castleman	NL	NY	1935	15-6
.789	Hank Borowy	AL	NY	1942	15-4		.714	Brooks Lawrence	NL	STL	1954	15-6
.789	Joe Black	NL	BRO	1952	15-4		.708	Jeff Tesreau	NL	NY	1912	17-7
.778	Johnny Beazley	NL	STL	1942	21-6		.708	Joe Boehling	AL	WAS	1913	17-7
.773	C.C. Sabathia	AL	CLE	2001	17-5		.708	Ernie White	NL	STL	1941	17-7
.769	Jerry Nops	NL	BAL	1897	20-6		.704	Jack Sanford	NL	PHI	1957	19-8
.769	Bob Grim	AL	NY	1954	20-6		.704	Gary Peters	AL	CHI	1963	19-8

(677) Most Wins in a Season by a Rookie Pitcher, before 1893

47	Al Spalding	NL	CHI	1876		29	George Derby	NL	DET	1881
45	George Bradley	NL	STL	1876		29	Matt Kilroy	AA	BAL	1886
43	Larry Corcoran	NL	CHI	1880		28	Billy Rhines	NL	CIN	1890
34	Mickey Welch	NL	TRO	1880		28	Nig Cuppy	NL	COL	1892
34	Ed Morris	AA	COL	1884		27	Lee Viau	AA	CIN	1888
32	Lee Richmond	NL	WOR	1880		27	Kid Nichols	NL	BOS	1890
32	Silver King	AA	STL	1887		26	Ed Daily	NL	PHI	1885
32	Jesse Duryea	AA	CIN	1889		26	Gus Weyhing	AA	PHI	1887
31	Tommy Bond	NL	HAR	1876		25	Charley Radbourn	NL	PRO	1881
31	Jim Whitney	NL	BOS	1881		25	Jumbo McGinnis	AA	STL	1882
30	Jim Devlin	NL	LOU	1876		25	Charlie Buffinton	NL	BOS	1883
30	Will White	NL	CIN	1878		25	Ed Seward	AA	PHI	1887
30	Tony Mullane	AA	LOU	1882		25	Gus Krock	NL	CHI	1888
29	Terry Larkin	NL	HAR	1877		25	Mickey Hughes	AA	BRO	1888

(678) Most Losses in a Season by a Rookie Pitcher, before 1893

48	John Coleman	NL	PHI	1883		31	Billy Crowell	AA	CLE	1887
41	Larry McKeon	AA	IND	1884		30	Mickey Welch	NL	TRO	1880
37	Kid Carsey	AA	WAS	1891		29	Doc Landis	AA	PHI-BAL	1882
37	George Cobb	NL	BAL	1892					PHI (1); BAL (28)	
35	Jim Devlin	NL	LOU	1876		29	Bert Cunningham	AA	BAL	1888
35	Adonis Terry	AA	BRO	1884		28	Hank O'Day	AA	TOL	1884
35	Fleury Sullivan	AA	PIT	1884		28	Gus Weyhing	AA	PHI	1887
34	Bobby Mathews	NL	NY	1876		27	Park Swartzel	AA	KC	1889
34	Matt Kilroy	AA	BAL	1886		26	Dory Dean	NL	CIN	1876
33	Harry McCormick	NL	SYR	1879		26	George Derby	NL	DET	1881
33	Jim Whitney	NL	BOS	1881		26	Al Atkinson	AA-UA-UA	PHI-CP-BAL	1884
33	Hardie Henderson	NL-AA	PHI-BAL	1883					PHI (11); CP (10); BAL (5)	
			PHI (1); BAL (32)			25	Terry Larkin	NL	HAR	1877
32	Lee Richmond	NL	WOR	1880		25	Charlie Ferguson	NL	PHI	1884
32	John Harkins	NL	CLE	1884		25	Mike Morrison	AA	CLE	1887
31	Sam Weaver	NL	MIL	1878		25	Ed Seward	AA	PHI	1887

(679) Most Games Started by a Rookie Pitcher, before 1893

68	Jim Devlin	NL	LOU	1876		55	George Derby	NL	DET	1881
68	Matt Kilroy	AA	BAL	1886		55	Tony Mullane	AA	LOU	1882
66	Lee Richmond	NL	WOR	1880		55	Adonis Terry	AA	BRO	1884
64	George Bradley	NL	STL	1876		55	Gus Weyhing	AA	PHI	1887
64	Mickey Welch	NL	TRO	1880		54	Harry McCormick	NL	SYR	1879
63	Jim Whitney	NL	BOS	1881		53	Kid Carsey	AA	WAS	1891
61	John Coleman	NL	PHI	1883		52	Will White	NL	CIN	1878
60	Al Spalding	NL	CHI	1876		52	Ed Morris	AA	COL	1884
60	Larry Corcoran	NL	CHI	1880		52	Ed Seward	AA	PHI	1887
60	Larry McKeon	AA	IND	1884		51	Fleury Sullivan	AA	PIT	1884
56	Bobby Mathews	NL	NY	1876		51	Bert Cunningham	AA	BAL	1888
56	Terry Larkin	NL	HAR	1877		50	Ed Daily	NL	PHI	1885

(680) Most Complete Games by a Rookie Pitcher, before 1893

66	Jim Devlin	NL	LOU	1876	
66	Matt Kilroy	AA	BAL	1886	
64	Mickey Welch	NL	TRO	1880	
63	George Bradley	NL	STL	1876	
59	John Coleman	NL	PHI	1883	
59	Larry McKeon	AA	IND	1884	
57	Lee Richmond	NL	WOR	1880	
57	Larry Corcoran	NL	CHI	1880	
57	Jim Whitney	NL	BOS	1881	
55	Bobby Mathews	NL	NY	1876	
55	Terry Larkin	NL	HAR	1877	
55	George Derby	NL	DET	1881	
54	Adonis Terry	AA	BRO	1884	
53	Al Spalding	NL	CHI	1876	
53	Gus Weyhing	AA	PHI	1887	
52	Will White	NL	CIN	1878	
52	Ed Seward	AA	PHI	1887	
51	Tony Mullane	AA	LOU	1882	
51	Fleury Sullivan	AA	PIT	1884	
50	Bert Cunningham	AA	BAL	1888	

(681) Most Shutouts by a Rookie Pitcher, before 1893

16	George Bradley	NL	STL	1876	
9	George Derby	NL	DET	1881	
8	Al Spalding	NL	CHI	1876	
8	Ben Sanders	NL	PHI	1888	
7	Kid Nichols	NL	BOS	1890	
6	Tommy Bond	NL	HAR	1876	
6	John Ward	NL	PRO	1878	
6	Jim Whitney	NL	BOS	1881	
6	Billy Rhines	NL	CIN	1890	
5	Jim Devlin	NL	LOU	1876	
5	Candy Cummings	NL	HAR	1876	
5	Will White	NL	CIN	1878	
5	Harry McCormick	NL	SYR	1879	
5	Lee Richmond	NL	WOR	1880	
5	Tony Mullane	AA	LOU	1882	
5	Matt Kilroy	AA	BAL	1886	

Ichiro Suzuki

353

(682) Most Innings Pitched by a Rookie Pitcher, before 1893

622.0	Jim Devlin	NL	LOU	1876	
590.2	Lee Richmond	NL	WOR	1880	
583.0	Matt Kilroy	AA	BAL	1886	
574.0	Mickey Welch	NL	TRO	1880	
573.0	George Bradley	NL	STL	1876	
552.1	Jim Whitney	NL	BOS	1881	
538.1	John Coleman	NL	PHI	1883	
536.1	Larry Corcoran	NL	CHI	1880	
528.2	Al Spalding	NL	CHI	1876	
516.0	Bobby Mathews	NL	NY	1876	
512.0	Larry McKeon	AA	IND	1884	
501.0	Terry Larkin	NL	HAR	1877	
494.2	George Derby	NL	DET	1881	
476.0	Adonis Terry	AA	BRO	1884	
470.2	Ed Seward	AA	PHI	1887	
468.0	Will White	NL	CIN	1878	
466.1	Gus Weyhing	AA	PHI	1887	
460.1	Tony Mullane	AA	LOU	1882	
457.1	Harry McCormick	NL	SYR	1879	
453.1	Bert Cunningham	AA	BAL	1888	
441.0	Fleury Sullivan	AA	PIT	1884	
440.0	Ed Daily	NL	PHI	1885	
429.2	Ed Morris	AA	COL	1884	
424.0	Kid Nichols	NL	BOS	1890	
416.2	Charlie Ferguson	NL	PHI	1884	
415.0	Kid Carsey	AA	WAS	1891	
410.1	Park Swartzel	AA	KC	1889	
401.1	Billy Rhines	NL	CIN	1890	
401.0	Jesse Duryea	AA	CIN	1889	
408.0	Tommy Bond	NL	HAR	1876	
394.1	George Cobb	NL	BAL	1892	
393.2	Al Atkinson	AA-UA-UA	PHI-CP-BAL	1884	PHI (184.0); CP (140.0); BAL (69.2)
391.0	John Harkins	NL	CLE	1884	
390.0	Silver King	AA	STL	1887	
389.1	Billy Crowell	AA	CLE	1887	
388.1	Jumbo McGinnis	AA	STL	1882	
387.2	Lee Viau	AA	CIN	1888	
383.0	Sam Weaver	NL	MIL	1878	
382.0	Tom Vickery	NL	PHI	1890	
376.0	Nig Cuppy	NL	CLE	1892	
367.1	Hardie Henderson	NL-AA	PHI-BAL	1883	PHI (9.0); BAL (358.1)
364.1	Bill Wise	UA	WAS	1884	
363.0	Mickey Hughes	AA	BRO	1888	
361.1	Sam Kimber	AA	BRO	1884	
360.0	Doc Landis	AA	PHI-BAL	1882	PHI (17.0); BAL (343.0)
352.1	John Keefe	AA	SYR	1890	

(683) Most Strikeouts by a Rookie Pitcher, before 1893

513	Matt Kilroy	AA	BAL	1886
308	Larry McKeon	AA	IND	1884
302	Ed Morris	AA	COL	1884
268	Bill Wise	UA	WAS	1884
268	Larry Corcoran	NL	CHI	1880
255	James Burke	UA	BOS	1884
247	Al Atkinson	AA-UA-UA	PHI-CP-BAL	1884
		PHI (93); CP (104); BAL (50)		
243	Lee Richmond	NL	WOR	1880
239	Bill Stemmeyer	NL	BOS	1886
230	Adonis Terry	AA	BRO	1884
222	Kid Nichols	NL	BOS	1890
212	George Derby	NL	DET	1881

(684) Most Walks by a Rookie Pitcher, before 1893

230	Adonis Terry	AA	BRO	1884		161	Kid Carsey	AA	WAS	1891
222	Kid Nichols	NL	BOS	1890		157	Bert Cunningham	AA	BAL	1888
212	George Derby	NL	DET	1881		148	John Keefe	AA	SYR	1890
205	Mike Morrison	AA	CLE	1887		148	Ted Breitenstein	NL	STL	1892
184	Tom Vickery	NL	PHI	1890		144	Bill Stemmeyer	NL	BOS	1886
182	Matt Kilroy	AA	BAL	1886		140	Ed Seward	AA	PHI	1887
167	Gus Weyhing	AA	PHI	1887		140	George Cobb	NL	BAL	1892
166	Phil Knell	PL	PHI	1890						

(685) Most Hits Allowed by a Rookie Pitcher, before 1893

772	John Coleman	NL	PHI	1883		481	Park Swartzel	AA	KC	1889
693	Bobby Mathews	NL	NY	1876		477	Will White	NL	CIN	1878
575	Mickey Welch	NL	TRO	1880		476	Matt Kilroy	AA	BAL	1886
566	Jim Devlin	NL	LOU	1876		470	George Bradley	NL	STL	1876
548	Jim Whitney	NL	BOS	1881		465	Gus Weyhing	AA	PHI	1887
542	Al Spalding	NL	CHI	1876		445	Ed Seward	AA	PHI	1887
541	Lee Richmond	NL	WOR	1880		443	Charlie Ferguson	NL	PHI	1884
541	Billy Crowell	AA	CLE	1887		432	Doc Landis	AA	PHI-BAL	1882
517	Harry McCormick	NL	SYR	1879				PHI (16); BAL (416)		
513	Kid Carsey	AA	WAS	1891		418	Tony Mullane	AA	LOU	1882
510	Terry Larkin	NL	HAR	1877		412	Bert Cunningham	AA	BAL	1888
505	George Derby	NL	DET	1881		409	Hardie Henderson	NL-AA	PHI-BAL	1883
496	Fleury Sullivan	AA	PIT	1884				PHI (26); BAL (383)		
495	George Cobb	NL	BAL	1892		405	Tom Vickery	NL	PHI	1890
488	Larry McKeon	AA	IND	1884		404	Larry Corcoran	NL	CHI	1880
486	Adonis Terry	AA	BRO	1884		401	Silver King	AA	STL	1887

(686) Lowest ERA by a Rookie Pitcher, before 1893 (min. 1.0 IP per scheduled game)

0.86	Tim Keefe	NL	TRO	1880	1.75	Al Spalding	NL	CHI	1876
1.21	Denny Driscoll	AA	PIT	1882	1.79	Will White	NL	CIN	1878
1.23	George Bradley	NL	STL	1876	1.86	Lady Baldwin	NL	DET	1885
1.30	Guy Hecker	AA	LOU	1882	1.88	Tony Mullane	AA	LOU	1882
1.51	John Ward	NL	PRO	1878	1.90	Ben Sanders	NL	PHI	1888
1.56	Jim Devlin	NL	LOU	1876	1.95	Sam Weaver	NL	MIL	1878
1.67	Candy Cummings	NL	HAR	1876	1.95	Larry Corcoran	NL	CHI	1880
1.68	Tommy Bond	NL	HAR	1876	1.95	Charlie Getzien	NL	DET	1884
1.69	Jim McCormick	NL	IND	1878	1.95	Billy Rhines	NL	CIN	1890
1.74	Henry Boyle	UA	STL	1884	1.97	Perry Werden	UA	STL	1884

(687) Most Wins in a Season by a Rookie Pitcher, since 1893

31	Bill Hoffer	NL	BAL	1895	21	Johnny Beazley	NL	STL	1942
28	Joe McGinnity	NL	BAL	1899	21	Bill Voiselle	NL	NY	1944
28	Grover Alexander	NL	PHI	1911	21	Dave Ferriss	AL	BOS	1945
26	Russ Ford	AL	NY	1910	21	Larry Jansen	NL	NY	1947
26	Larry Cheney	NL	CHI	1912	20	Jerry Nops	NL	BAL	1897
25	Vic Willis	NL	BOS	1898	20	Roy Patterson	AL	CHI	1901
24	Wiley Piatt	NL	PHI	1898	20	Christy Mathewson	NL	NY	1901
24	Ed Summers	AL	DET	1908	20	Jake Weimer	NL	CHI	1903
23	Jay Hughes	NL	BAL	1898	20	Irv Young	NL	BOS	1905
23	Noodles Hahn	NL	CIN	1899	20	Jack Pfiester	NL	CHI	1906
23	Roscoe Miller	AL	DET	1901	20	King Cole	NL	CHI	1910
23	Jack Harper	NL	STL	1901	20	Hugh Bedient	AL	BOS	1912
23	George McQuillan	NL	PHI	1908	20	Scott Perry	AL	PHI	1918
23	Vean Gregg	AL	CLE	1911	20	Lou Fette	NL	BOS	1937
23	Jeff Pfeffer	NL	BRO	1914	20	Cliff Melton	NL	NY	1937
22	Henry Schmidt	NL	BRO	1903	20	Jim Turner	NL	BOS	1937
22	Reb Russell	AL	CHI	1913	20	Gene Bearden	AL	CLE	1948
22	Monte Weaver	AL	WAS	1932	20	Alex Kellner	AL	PHI	1949
21	Ted Lewis	NL	BOS	1897	20	Harvey Haddix	NL	STL	1953
21	Deacon Phillippe	NL	LOU	1899	20	Bob Grim	AL	NY	1954
21	Sam Leever	NL	PIT	1899	20	Tom Browning	NL	CIN	1985
21	Wes Ferrell	AL	CLE	1929					

(688) Most Losses in a Season by a Rookie Pitcher, since 1893

28	Bill Hill	NL	LOU	1896		21	Stan Yerkes	NL	STL	1902
27	Chick Fraser	NL	LOU	1896		21	Irv Young	NL	BOS	1905
27	Bill Carrick	NL	NY	1899		21	Joe Harris	AL	BOS	1906
26	Bob Groom	AL	WAS	1909		21	Al Mattern	NL	BOS	1909
25	Harry McIntire	NL	BRO	1905		21	Ed Brandt	NL	BOS	1928
24	Red Donahue	NL	STL	1896		20	Doc McJames	NL	WAS	1896
23	Win Mercer	NL	WAS	1894		20	Pete Dowling	NL	LOU	1898
23	Sam Leever	NL	PIT	1899		20	Ed Scott	NL	CIN	1900
23	Tom J. Hughes	NL	CHI	1901		20	Bill Reidy	AL	MIL	1901
23	Beany Jacobson	AL	WAS	1904		20	Henry Keupper	FL	STL	1914
23	Orval Overall	NL	CIN	1905		20	Jesse Haines	NL	STL	1920
23	Vive Lindaman	NL	BOS	1906		20	Bobo Newsom	AL	STL	1934
23	Elmer Myers	AL	PHI	1916		20	Nate Andrews	NL	BOS	1943
22	Joe Yeager	NL	BRO	1898		20	Sam Jones	NL	CHI	1955
22	Charlie Knepper	NL	CLE	1899		20	Al Jackson	NL	NY	1962
22	Joe Lake	AL	NY	1908		20	Clay Kirby	NL	SD	1969
21	Jack W. Taylor	NL	CHI	1899						

Benny Kauff

(689) Most Games Started by a Rookie Pitcher, since 1893

43	Bill Carrick	NL	NY	1899	38	Christy Mathewson	NL	NY	1901
42	Irv Young	NL	BOS	1905	38	Tom Browning	NL	CIN	1985
42	George McQuillan	NL	PHI	1908	37	Wiley Piatt	NL	PHI	1898
41	Joe McGinnity	NL	BAL	1899	37	Jack Harper	NL	STL	1901
41	Bill Voiselle	NL	NY	1944	37	Stan Yerkes	NL	STL	1902
39	Win Mercer	NL	WAS	1894	37	Grover Alexander	NL	PHI	1911
39	Bill Hill	NL	LOU	1896	37	Larry Cheney	NL	CHI	1912
39	Sam Leever	NL	PIT	1899	37	Jesse Haines	NL	STL	1920
39	Jack W. Taylor	NL	CHI	1899	37	Herman Pillette	AL	DET	1922
39	Orval Overall	NL	CIN	1905	37	Carl Morton	NL	MON	1970
38	Bill Hoffer	NL	BAL	1895	37	Steve Busby	AL	KC	1973
38	Chick Fraser	NL	LOU	1896	37	Paul Thormodsgard	AL	MIN	1977
38	Vic Willis	NL	BOS	1898	37	Roger Erickson	AL	MIN	1978
38	Deacon Phillippe	NL	LOU	1899					

(690) Most Complete Games by a Rookie Pitcher, since 1893

41	Irv Young	NL	BOS	1905	32	Orval Overall	NL	CIN	1905
40	Bill Carrick	NL	NY	1899	32	Vive Lindaman	NL	BOS	1906
39	Jack W. Taylor	NL	CHI	1899	32	George McQuillan	NL	PHI	1908
38	Joe McGinnity	NL	BAL	1899	31	Jay Hughes	NL	BAL	1898
36	Chick Fraser	NL	LOU	1896	31	Ed Scott	NL	CIN	1900
36	Christy Mathewson	NL	NY	1901	31	Oscar Jones	NL	BRO	1903
35	Sam Leever	NL	PIT	1899	31	Grover Alexander	NL	PHI	1911
35	Roscoe Miller	AL	DET	1901	31	Elmer Myers	AL	PHI	1916
33	Wiley Piatt	NL	PHI	1898	30	Win Mercer	NL	WAS	1894
33	Deacon Phillippe	NL	LOU	1899	30	Ted Lewis	NL	BOS	1897
32	Bill Hoffer	NL	BAL	1895	30	Pete Dowling	NL	LOU	1898
32	Bill Hill	NL	LOU	1896	30	Roy Patterson	AL	CHI	1901
32	Joe Yeager	NL	BRO	1898	30	Ed Siever	AL	DET	1901
32	Noodles Hahn	NL	CIN	1899	30	Fred Glade	AL	STL	1904
32	Tom J. Hughes	NL	CHI	1901	30	Scott Perry	AL	PHI	1918

(691) Most Shutouts by a Rookie Pitcher, since 1893

8	Russ Ford	AL	NY	1910	7	Grover Alexander	NL	PHI	1911
8	Reb Russell	AL	CHI	1913	7	Jerry Koosman	NL	NY	1968
8	Fernando Valenzuela	NL	LA	1981	6	Wiley Piatt	NL	PHI	1898
7	Irv Young	NL	BOS	1905	6	Fred Glade	AL	STL	1904
7	George McQuillan	NL	PHI	1908	6	Gene Bearden	AL	CLE	1948
7	Harry Krause	AL	PHI	1909	6	Harvey Haddix	NL	STL	1953

(692) Most Innings Pitched by a Rookie Pitcher, since 1893

379.0	Sam Leever	NL	PIT	1899		315.0	Jeff Pfeffer	NL	BRO	1914
378.0	Irv Young	NL	BOS	1905		315.0	Elmer Myers	AL	PHI	1916
367.0	Grover Alexander	NL	PHI	1911		314.0	Bill Hoffer	NL	BAL	1895
366.1	Joe McGinnity	NL	BAL	1899		312.2	Bill Voiselle	NL	NY	1944
361.2	Bill Carrick	NL	NY	1899		312.1	Roy Patterson	AL	CHI	1901
359.2	George McQuillan	NL	PHI	1908		311.0	Vic Willis	NL	BOS	1898
354.2	Jack W. Taylor	NL	CHI	1899		309.0	Noodles Hahn	NL	CIN	1899
349.1	Chick Fraser	NL	LOU	1896		308.2	Jack Harper	NL	STL	1901
336.1	Win Mercer	NL	WAS	1894		308.2	Harry McIntire	NL	BRO	1905
336.0	Christy Mathewson	NL	NY	1901		308.1	Tom J. Hughes	NL	CHI	1901
332.1	Scott Perry	AL	PHI	1918		307.1	Vive Lindaman	NL	BOS	1906
332.0	Roscoe Miller	AL	DET	1901		306.0	Wiley Piatt	NL	PHI	1898
324.1	Oscar Jones	NL	BRO	1903		303.1	Larry Cheney	NL	CHI	1912
321.0	Deacon Phillippe	NL	LOU	1899		301.2	Jesse Haines	NL	STL	1920
319.2	Bill Hill	NL	LOU	1896		301.1	Bill Reidy	AL	MIL	1901
318.0	Orval Overall	NL	CIN	1905		301.0	Henry Schmidt	NL	BRO	1903
316.2	Reb Russell	AL	CHI	1913		301.0	Ed Summers	AL	DET	1908
316.1	Al Mattern	NL	BOS	1909		300.2	Jay Hughes	NL	BAL	1898
315.0	Ed Scott	NL	CIN	1900						

(693) Most Strikeouts by a Rookie Pitcher, since 1893

276	Dwight Gooden	NL	NY	1984		215	John Montefusco	NL	SF	1975
245	Herb Score	AL	CLE	1955		209	Russ Ford	AL	NY	1910
236	Hideo Nomo	NL	LA	1995		209	Don Sutton	NL	LA	1966
233	Kerry Wood	NL	CHI	1998		206	Gary Nolan	NL	CIN	1967
227	Grover Alexander	NL	PHI	1911		206	Bob D. Johnson	AL	KC	1970
225	Tom J. Hughes	NL	CHI	1901		204	Mark Langston	AL	SEA	1984
221	Christy Mathewson	NL	NY	1901		200	Tom Griffin	NL	HOU	1969

(694) Most Walks by a Rookie Pitcher, since 1893

185	Sam Jones	NL	CHI	1955		149	Bobo Newsom	AL	STL	1934
168	Elmer Myers	AL	PHI	1916		148	Vic Willis	NL	BOS	1898
166	Chick Fraser	NL	LOU	1896		147	Orval Overall	NL	CIN	1905
155	Bill Hill	NL	LOU	1896		143	Bobby Witt	AL	TEX	1986
154	Herb Score	AL	CLE	1955						

(695) Most Hits Allowed by a Rookie Pitcher, since 1893

485	Bill Carrick	NL	NY	1899	334	Ed Siever	AL	DET	1901
445	Win Mercer	NL	WAS	1894	333	Joe Yeager	NL	BRO	1898
396	Chick Fraser	NL	LOU	1896	331	Deacon Phillippe	NL	LOU	1899
380	Jack W. Taylor	NL	CHI	1899	328	Watty Lee	AL	WAS	1901
376	Red Donahue	NL	STL	1896	322	Al Mattern	NL	BOS	1909
370	Ed Scott	NL	CIN	1900	321	Henry Schmidt	NL	BRO	1903
364	Bill Reidy	AL	MIL	1901	320	Oscar Jones	NL	BRO	1903
358	Joe McGinnity	NL	BAL	1899	316	Ted Lewis	NL	BOS	1897
353	Bill Hill	NL	LOU	1896	310	Doc McJames	NL	WAS	1896
353	Sam Leever	NL	PIT	1899	309	Tom J. Hughes	NL	CHI	1901
345	Roy Patterson	AL	CHI	1901	307	Charlie Knepper	NL	CLE	1899
341	Stan Yerkes	NL	STL	1902	303	Vive Lindaman	NL	BOS	1906
340	Harry McIntire	NL	BRO	1905	303	Jesse Haines	NL	STL	1920
339	Roscoe Miller	AL	DET	1901	301	Johnny Couch	NL	CIN	1922
337	Irv Young	NL	BOS	1905	300	Charlie Chech	NL	CIN	1905

(696) Lowest ERA by a Rookie Pitcher, since 1893 (min. 1.0 IP per scheduled game)

1.39	Harry Krause	AL	PHI	1909	1.80	Vean Gregg	AL	CLE	1911
1.42	Ed Reulbach	NL	CHI	1905	1.83	Hippo Vaughn	AL	NY	1910
1.51	Jack Pfiester	NL	CHI	1906	1.90	Reb Russell	AL	CHI	1913
1.53	George McQuillan	NL	PHI	1908	1.96	Jeff Tesreau	NL	NY	1912
1.64	Ed Summers	AL	DET	1908	1.97	Carl Lundgren	NL	CHI	1902
1.65	Russ Ford	AL	NY	1910	1.97	Jeff Pfeffer	NL	BRO	1914
1.69	Bill Burns	AL	WAS	1908	1.98	Scott Perry	AL	PHI	1918
1.80	King Cole	NL	CHI	1910					

NATIONAL BASEBALL HALL OF FAME LIBRARY

Christy Mathewson

(697) Most Hit Batters in a Season by a Rookie Pitcher

37	Gus Weyhing	AA	PHI	1887		22	Mike Morrison	AA	CLE	1887
30	Vic Willis	NL	BOS	1898		22	Pete Dowling	NL	LOU	1898
28	Joe McGinnity	NL	BAL	1899		22	Jack W. Taylor	NL	CHI	1899
27	Jack Easton	AA	COL	1890		21	Henry Schmidt	NL	BRO	1903
26	Gus Shallix	AA	CIN	1884		20	Fleury Sullivan	AA	PIT	1884
26	Jack Warhop	AL	NY	1909		20	Kid Madden	NL	BOS	1887
25	Chief Bender	AL	PHI	1903		20	Billy Crowell	AA	CLE	1887
24	Ed Seward	AA	PHI	1887		20	Charlie Sprague	AA	TOL	1890
24	Frank Knauss	AA	COL	1890		20	Harry McIntire	NL	BRO	1905
23	Bill Carrick	NL	NY	1899		20	Ed Summers	AL	DET	1908
23	Frank Bates	NL	TOT	1899						

(698) Most Wild Pitches by a Rookie Pitcher, since 1893

27	Chick Fraser	NL	LOU	1896		16	Mike McDermott	NL	LOU	1895
24	Doc McJames	NL	WAS	1896		16	Tom J. Hughes	NL	CHI	1901
23	Christy Mathewson	NL	NY	1901		16	Stu Flythe	AL	PHI	1936
22	Jack Hamilton	NL	PHI	1962		16	John Wetteland	NL	LA	1989
22	Bobby Witt	AL	TEX	1986		15	Jim Bibby	NL-AL	STL-TEX	1973
19	Jack Harper	NL	STL	1901					STL (5); TEX (10)	
19	Ed Correa	AL	TEX	1986		15	Blake Stein	AL	OAK	1998
19	Hideo Nomo	NL	LA	1995		14	Bill Hogg	AL	NY	1905
18	Orval Overall	NL	CIN	1905		14	Eddie Cicotte	AL	BOS	1908
18	Larry Cheney	NL	CHI	1912		14	Gene Krapp	AL	CLE	1911
18	Ernie McAnally	NL	MON	1971		14	Phil Marchildon	AL	PHI	1941
18	Dan Reichert	AL	KC	2000						

(699) Most Stolen Bases in a Season by a Rookie, 1886-1897

94	Mike Griffin	AA	BAL	1887		62	Tom Shinnick	AA	LOU	1890
89	Herman Long	AA	KC	1889		59	Perry Werden	AA	TOL	1890
85	Tommy Tucker	AA	BAL	1887		57	Frank Scheibeck	AA	TOL	1890
82	Dummy Hoy	NL	WAS	1888		57	Jack Crooks	AA	COL	1890
76	Ed McKean	AA	CLE	1887		56	Jim Burns	AA	KC	1889
73	Bill Van Dyke	AA	TOL	1890		56	Cupid Childs	AA	SYR	1890

Stolen bases were not tabulated before 1885. Between 1886-1897, stolen bases often were awarded for taking an extra base on a hit.

(700) Most Stolen Bases in a Season by a Rookie, since 1898

110	Vince Coleman	NL	STL	1985		56	Quilvio Veras	NL	FLA	1995
75	Benny Kauff	FL	IND	1914		56	Ichiro Suzuki	AL	SEA	2001
72	Juan Samuel	NL	PHI	1984		55	Emmet Heidrick	NL	STL	1899
71	Tim Raines	NL	MON	1981		54	Pat Listach	AL	MIL	1992
66	Kenny Lofton	AL	CLE	1992		53	Donie Bush	AL	DET	1909
64	Eric Yelding	NL	HOU	1990		53	Omar Moreno	NL	PIT	1977
60	Tony Womack	NL	PIT	1997		50	Larry Lintz	NL	MON	1974
58	Chuck Carr	NL	FLA	1993		50	Miguel Dilone	AL	OAK	1978
57	Hap Myers	NL	BOS	1913		50	John Cangelosi	AL	CHI	1986
56	Gene Richards	NL	SD	1977		50	Tom Goodwin	AL	KC	1995

MISCELLANEOUS RECORDS

Miscellaneous Records

(701) Oldest Players to Appear in a Major League Game

	YEARS	MONTHS	DAYS		YEARS	MONTHS	DAYS
Satchel Paige	59	2	18	Nolan Ryan	46	7	22
Nick Altrock	57	0	16	Charlie Hough	46	6	21
Jim O'Rourke	54	0	21	Sam Thompson	46	6	5
Charley O'Leary	51	11	15	Jesse Orosco	46	5	6
Minnie Minoso	51	10	6	Dan Brouthers	46	4	26
Jack Quinn	50	0	2	Grover Hartley	46	2	28
Hoyt Wilhelm	49	11	14	Bobo Newsom	46	1	6
Jimmy Austin	49	9	28	Tommy John	46	0	3
Arlie Latham	49	6	15	Kid Gleason	45	10	1
Hughie Jennings	49	5	0	Carlton Fisk	45	5	28
Gabby Street	48	11	21	Cap Anson	45	5	16
Deacon McGuire	48	6	0	Ted Lyons	45	4	21
Phil Niekro	48	5	26	Pete Rose	45	4	3
Johnny Evers	48	2	15	Fred Johnson	45	2	0
Julio Franco	48	1	8	Red Faber	45	0	14
Kaiser Wilhelm	47	7	0	Gaylord Perry	45	0	6
Hod Lisenbee	46	11	15				

(702) Players who Played in at least 10 Seasons for Two Different Teams

Eddie Collins	AL	PHI	1906-14, 27-30	AL	CHI	1915-26
Charlie Hough	NL	LA	1970-80	AL	TEX	1980-90
Carlton Fisk	AL	BOS	1969, 71-80	AL	CHI	1981-93

(703) Most Years Spent with One Franchise

23	Brooks Robinson	AL	BAL	Entire career	21	Ted Lyons	AL	CHI	Entire career
23	Carl Yastrzemski	AL	BOS	Entire career	21	Walter Johnson	AL	WAS	Entire career
22	Al Kaline	AL	DET	Entire career	21	Willie Mays	NL	NY-SF	
22	Cap Anson	NL	CHI	Entire career	21	Willie Stargell	NL	PIT	Entire career
22	Mel Ott	NL	NY	Entire career	20	Alan Trammell	AL	DET	Entire career
22	Stan Musial	NL	STL	Entire career	20	Luke Appling	AL	CHI	Entire career
22	Ty Cobb	AL	DET		20	Mel Harder	AL	CLE	Entire career
21	Cal Ripken	AL	BAL	Entire career	20	Phil Cavarretta	NL	CHI	
21	George Brett	AL	KC	Entire career	20	Red Faber	AL	CHI	Entire career
21	Hank Aaron	NL	MIL-ATL		20	Robin Yount	AL	MIL	Entire career
21	Harmon Killebrew	AL	WAS-MIN		20	Tony Gwynn	NL	SD	Entire career
21	Phil Niekro	NL	MIL-ATL		20	Warren Spahn	NL	BOS-MIL	

(704) Career Spent with One Team (min. 15 years)

23	Brooks Robinson	AL	BAL	1955-77
23	Carl Yastrzemski	AL	BOS	1961-83
22	Cap Anson	NL	CHI	1876-97
22	Mel Ott	NL	NY	1926-47
22	Stan Musial	NL	STL	1941-44; 1946-63
22	Al Kaline	AL	DET	1953-74
21	Walter Johnson	AL	WAS	1907-27
21	Ted Lyons	AL	CHI	1923-42; 1946
21	Willie Stargell	NL	PIT	1962-82
21	George Brett	AL	KC	1973-93
21	Cal Ripken	AL	BAL	1981-2001
20	Red Faber	AL	CHI	1914-33
20	Mel Harder	AL	CLE	1928-47
20	Luke Appling	AL	CHI	1930-43; 1945-50
20	Robin Yount	AL	MIL	1974-93
20	Alan Trammell	AL	DET	1977-96
20	Tony Gwynn	NL	SD	1982-2001
19	Charlie Gehringer	AL	DET	1924-42
19	Ted Williams	AL	BOS	1939-42; 1946-60
19	Ernie Banks	NL	CHI	1953-71
19	Jim Palmer	AL	BAL	1965-67; 1969-84
19	Dave Concepcion	NL	CIN	1970-88
19	Lou Whitaker	AL	DET	1977-95
19	Barry Larkin	NL	CIN	1986-2004
19	Craig Biggio	NL	HOU	1988-2006
18	Bid McPhee	AA-NL	CIN	1882-99
18	Ossie Bluege	AL	WAS	1922-39
18	Bob Feller	AL	CLE	1936-41; 1945-56
18	Mickey Mantle	AL	NY	1951-68
18	Roberto Clemente	NL	PIT	1955-72
18	Ed Kranepool	NL	NY	1962-79
18	Bill Russell	NL	LA	1969-86
18	Mike Schmidt	NL	PHI	1972-89

18	Frank White	AL	KC	1973-90
18	Edgar Martinez	AL	SEA	1987-2004
18	John Smoltz	NL	ATL	1988-99; 2001-06
17	Pie Traynor	NL	PIT	1920-35; 37
17	Lou Gehrig	AL	NY	1923-39
17	Bill Dickey	AL	NY	1928-43; 47
17	Frankie Crosetti	AL	NY	1932-48
17	Bill Mazeroski	NL	PIT	1956-72
17	Bob Gibson	NL	STL	1959-75
17	Johnny Bench	NL	CIN	1967-83
17	Jim Gantner	AL	MIL	1976-92
16	Clyde Milan	AL	WAS	1907-22
16	Carl Hubbell	NL	NY	1928-43
16	Tommy Bridges	AL	DET	1930-43; 1945-46
16	Stan Hack	NL	CHI	1932-47
16	Pee Wee Reese	NL	BRO-LA	1940-42; 1946-58
16	Whitey Ford	AL	NY	1950; 1953-67
16	Vern Law	NL	PIT	1950-51; 1954-67
16	Jim Rice	AL	BOS	1974-89
16	Bernie Williams	AL	NY	1991-2006
15	Hooks Dauss	AL	DET	1912-26
15	Travis Jackson	NL	NY	1922-36
15	Bob Lemon	AL	CLE	1941-42; 1946-58
15	Carl Furillo	NL	BRO-LA	1946-60
15	Bill Freehan	AL	DET	1961; 1963-76
15	Tony Oliva	AL	MIN	1962-76
15	Mickey Stanley	AL	DET	1964-78
15	John Hiller	AL	DET	1965-70; 1972-80
15	Roy White	AL	NY	1965-79
15	Paul Splittorff	AL	KC	1970-84
15	Jeff Bagwell	NL	HOU	1991-2005

(705) Most Times Ejected from a Major League Game as a Player or a Manager

131	John McGraw		73	Tony La Russa	52	Casey Stengel
124	Leo Durocher		71	Lou Piniella	52	Johnny Evers
123	Bobby Cox	All as manager	68	Clark Griffith	51	Billy Martin
97	Earl Weaver	All as manager	66	Joe Torre	50	Al Lopez
86	Frankie Frisch		65	Bill Dahlen		
80	Paul Richards		58	Bill Rigney		

(706) Most Times Ejected from a Major League Game as a Manager

123	Bobby Cox	80	Paul Richards	52	Bill Rigney
117	John McGraw	73	Tony La Russa	47	Sparky Anderson
97	Earl Weaver	62	Clark Griffith	46	Mike Hargrove
95	Leo Durocher	58	Joe Torre	46	Billy Martin
82	Frankie Frisch	57	Lou Piniella	45	Ralph Houk

(707) Umpires who Have Ejected the Most Players and Managers

239	Bill Klem	128	Bob Emslie	103	Bob Davidson
185	Cy Rigler	127	Tommy Connolly	101	Joe West
174	Hank O'Day	119	Ernie Quigley	100	Frank Dascoli
150	Jim Johnstone	106	Bill Byron		
144	Silk O'Loughlin	104	Jocko Conlan		

John McGraw

(708) Most Years Together for Two Teammates

19	Alan Trammell, Lou Whitaker	AL	DET	1977-95
18	Fred Clarke, Honus Wagner	NL	LOU	1897-99
		NL	PIT	1900-11, 13-15
18	Joe Judge, Sam Rice	AL	WAS	1915-32
18	George Brett, Frank White	AL	KC	1973-90
17	Roberto Clemente, Bill Mazeroski	NL	PIT	1956-72
17	Tony Perez, Pete Rose	NL	CIN	1964-76
		NL	PHI	1983
		NL	CIN	1984-86
17	Jim Gantner, Robin Yount	AL	MIL	1976-92
16	Walter Johnson, Clyde Milan	AL	WAS	1907-22
16	Babe Adams, Max Carey	NL	PIT	1910-16,18-26
16	Lloyd Waner, Paul Waner	NL	PIT	1927-40
		NL	BOS	1941
		NL	BRO	1944
16	Carl Hubbell, Mel Ott	NL	NY	1928-43
16	Gil Hodges, Duke Snider	NL	BRO	1947-57
		NL	LA	1958-61
		NL	NY	1963
16	Mark Belanger, Jim Palmer	AL	BAL	1965-67, 69-81
16	Dwight Evans, Jim Rice	AL	BOS	1974-89
15	Jeff Bagwell, Craig Biggio	NL	HOU	1991-2005

(709) Most Years Together for Three Teammates

15	George Brett, Hal McRae, Frank White	AL	KC	1973-87
15	George Brett, Frank White, Willie Wilson	AL	KC	1976-90
15	Jim Gantner, Paul Molitor, Robin Yount	AL	MIL	1978-92
14	Fred Clarke, Tommy Leach, Honus Wagner	NL	LOU	1898-99
		NL	PIT	1900-11
14	Carl Furillo, Gil Hodges, Duke Snider	NL	BRO	1947-57
		NL	LA	1958-60
14	Norm Cash, Al Kaline, Dick McAuliffe	AL	DET	1960-73
14	Jack Morris, Alan Trammell, Lou Whitaker	AL	DET	1977-90

(710) Most Years Together for Four Teammates

13	Fred Clarke, Tommy Leach, Deacon Phillippe, Honus Wagner	NL	LOU	1899
		NL	PIT	1900-11
13	Gates Brown, Bill Freehan, Willie Horton, Mickey Lolich	AL	DET	1963-75

(711) Most Years Together for Five Teammates

12	Gates Brown, Bill Freehan, Willie Horton, Mickey Lolich, Mickey Stanley	AL	DET	1964-75

(712) Most Years Together for Six Teammates

| 12 | Gates Brown, Bill Freehan, Willie Horton, Mickey Lolich, Al Kaline, Norm Cash | AL | DET | 1963-74 |

(713) Most Years Together for Seven Teammates

| 11 | Gates Brown, Bill Freehan, Willie Horton, Mickey Lolich, Al Kaline, Norm Cash, Dick McAuliffe | AL | DET | 1963-73 |

(714) Most Years Together for Eight Teammates

| 11 | Gates Brown, Bill Freehan, Willie Horton, Mickey Lolich, Al Kaline, Norm Cash, Jim Northrup, Mickey Stanley | AL | DET | 1964-74 |

(715) Most Years Together for Nine Teammates

| 10 | Gates Brown, Bill Freehan, Willie Horton, Mickey Lolich, Al Kaline, Norm Cash, Dick McAuliffe, Jim Northrup, Mickey Stanley | AL | DET | 1964-73 |

(716) Firsts by Foreign-born Players

20-game Winner, before 1893	Tommy Bond	NL	HAR	1876	Ireland
20-game Winner, since 1893	Dolf Luque	NL	CIN	1923	Cuba
Batting Champion	Bobby Avila	AL	CLE	1954	Mexico
Cy Young Award	Mike Cuellar	AL	BAL	1969	Cuba
Rookie of the Year	Luis Aparicio	AL	CHI	1956	Venezuela
Most Valuable Player	Zoilo Versalles	AL	MIN	1965	Cuba
Hall of Famer	Roberto Clemente	NL	PIT	1973	Puerto Rico

(717) Last Active Player for Teams that Moved

			LAST TEAM	LG	LAST YEAR
Milwaukee Brewers (1901)	AL	George McBride	WAS	AL	1920
Baltimore Orioles (1901-1902)	AL	Roger Bresnahan	CHI	NL	1915
Boston Braves (1876-1952)	NL	Eddie Mathews	DET	AL	1968
St. Louis Browns (1902-1953)	AL	Don Larsen	CHI	NL	1967
Philadelphia A's (1901-1954)	AL	Vic Power	CAL	AL	1965
Brooklyn Dodgers (1890-1957)	NL	Bob Aspromonte	NY	NL	1971
		Aspromonte had one at bat for Brooklyn in 1956			
New York Giants (1883-1957)	NL	Willie Mays	NY	NL	1973
Washington Senators I (1901-1960)	AL	Jim Kaat	STL	NL	1983
Milwaukee Braves (1953-1965)	NL	Phil Niekro	ATL	NL	1987
		Niekro also played for Cleveland and Toronto in 1987			
Kansas City A's (1955-1967)	AL	Reggie Jackson	OAK	AL	1987
Seattle Pilots (1969)	AL	Fred Stanley	OAK	AL	1982
Washington Senators II (1961-1972)	AL	Toby Harrah	TEX	AL	1986

(718) Last Active Player for Various Defunct Leagues

LEAGUE			LAST TEAM		YEAR	
National Association (1871-1875)	NA	Cap Anson	CHI	NL	1897	
Union Association (1884)	UA	Joe Quinn	WAS	AL	1901	
Players League (1890)	PL	Arlie Latham	NY	NL	1909	First appearance since 1899
American Association (1882-1891)	AA	Hughie Jennings	DET	AL	1918	First appearance since 1912
Federal League (1914-1915)	FL	Grover Hartley	STL	AL	1934	First appearance since 1930
Negro Leagues (1920-1960)	XX	Minnie Minoso	CHI	AL	1980	First appearance since 1976

(719) Most Consecutive Wins by a Team in a Season

WINS					HOME	ROAD	
26	NL	NY	1916	Sep 7-Sep 30 (1G)	26	0	1 tie
21	NL	CHI	1880	Jun 2-Jul 8	11	10	1 tie
21	NL	CHI	1935	Sep 4-Sep 27 (2G)	18	3	
20	UA	STL	1884	Apr 20-May 22	16	4	From start of season
20	NL	PRO	1884	Aug 7-Sep 6	16	4	
20	AL	OAK	2002	Aug 13-Sep 4	10	10	
19	AL	CHI	1906	Aug 2-Aug 23	11	8	1 tie
19	AL	NY	1947	Jun 29 (2G)-Jul 17 (2G)	6	13	
18	NL	CHI	1885	Jun 1-Jun 24	14	4	
18	NL	BOS	1891	Sep 16-Oct 2	16	2	1 tie
18	NL	BAL	1894	Aug 24-Sep 16 (1G)	13	5	
18	NL	NY	1904	Jun 16-Jul 4 (2G)	13	5	
18	AL	NY	1953	May 27-Jun 14 (2G)	3	15	
17	AA	STL	1885	May 5-Jun 1	14	3	
17	NL	BOS	1897	May 31-Jun 21	16	1	
17	NL	NY	1907	Apr 25-May18	14	3	
17	AL	WAS	1912	May 30 (2G)-Jun 18	1	16	
17	NL	NY	1916	May 9-May 29	0	17	
17	AL	PHI	1931	May 5-May 25 (2G)	5	12	
17	AL	BAL	1970	Sep 20-Oct 13	10	7	
16	UA	BAL	1884	Jul 14-Aug 8	7	9	
16	NL	PHI	1887	Sep 15-Oct 8	5	11	To end of season; 1 tie
16	NL	PHI	1890	Jul 8-Jul 26	14	2	
16	NL	PHI	1892	Jun 10-Jun 28	11	5	
16	NL	PIT	1909	Sep 9-Sep 27 (1G)	12	4	
16	NL	NY	1912	Jun 19-Jul 3 (2G)	11	5	
16	AL	NY	1926	May 10-May 26	12	4	
16	NL	NY	1951	Aug 12 (1G)- Aug 27 (2G)	13	3	
16	AL	BAL	1971	Sep 19-Oct 11	7	9	
16	AL	KC	1977	Aug 31-Sep 15 (2G)	9	7	
15	NL	DET	1886	May 8-May 29	12	3	
15	AA	STL	1887	Apr 24-May 18	15	0	
15	NL	PIT	1903	Jun 2-Jun 25 (1G)	11	4	
15	AL	NY	1906	Aug 29-Sep 8	12	3	
15	AL	PHI	1913	May 27 (1G)-Jun 10	13	2	
15	FL	IND	1914	Jun 11 (1G)-Jun 24	15	0	
15	NL	BRO	1924	Aug 25-Sep 6 (1G)	3	12	

(719) *(continued)*

WINS					HOME	ROAD	
15	NL	CHI	1936	Jun 4-Jun 21 (1G)	11	4	
15	NL	NY	1936	Aug 11-Aug 28	7	8	
15	AL	BOS	1946	Apr 25-May 10	11	4	
15	AL	NY	1960	Sep 16-Oct 2	9	6	To end of season
15	AL	MIN	1991	Jun 1-Jun 16	10	5	
15	NL	ATL	2000	Apr 16-May 2	9	6	
15	AL	SEA	2001	May 23-Jun 8	10	5	
14	NL	CHI	1886	Aug 23-Sep 8 (2G)	13	1	
14	AA	PHI	1889	May 29-Jun 14	13	1	1 tie
14	NL	BAL	1895	Aug 9 (2G)-Aug 24	13	1	
14	NL	CIN	1899	Jul 26 (2G)- Aug 12 (2G)	10	4	
14	NL	PIT	1903	Aug 22 (1G)-Sep 6	7	7	1 tie
14	NL	CHI	1906	Aug 20-Sep 1	14	0	
14	NL	PIT	1909	May 30 (1G)-Jun 15	12	2	
14	AL	DET	1909	Aug 19-Sep 2	14	0	
14	NL	NY	1913	Jun 26 (1G)-Jul 9	6	8	
14	AL	STL	1916	Jul 23-Aug 4	13	1	
14	NL	CHI	1932	Aug 20-Sep 3 (1G)	14	0	
14	AL	DET	1934	Jul 31 (2G)- Aug 14 (2G)	9	5	
14	NL	STL	1935	Jul 2-Jul 18	12	2	
14	AL	NY	1941	Jun 28-Jul 13 (2G)	6	8	
14	AL	CHI	1951	May 15-May 30 (2G)	3	11	
14	NL	SF	1965	Sep 4-Sep 16	6	8	
14	AL	BAL	1973	Aug 12-Aug 27	10	4	
14	AL	OAK	1988	Apr 23-May 9	5	9	
14	AL	TEX	1991	May 12-May 27	7	7	
14	AL	KC	1994	Jul 23-Aug 5	12	2	
14	NL	SD	1999	Jun 18-Jul 2	10	4	

Joe and Phil Niekro

TRANSCENDENTAL GRAPHICS

(720) Most Consecutive Losses by a Team in a Season

					HOME	ROAD	
26	AA	LOU	1889	May 22-Jun 22 (2G)	5	21	
24	NL	CLE	1899	Aug 26-Sep 16	5	19	
23	NL	PIT	1890	Aug 12-Sep 2	1	22	
23	NL	PHI	1961	Jul 29-Aug 20 (1G)	6	17	
22	AA	PHI	1890	Sep 16-Oct 12	6	16	To end of season
21	AL	BAL	1988	Apr 4-Apr 28	8	13	From start of season
20	NL	LOU	1894	May 28 (1G)-Jun 18 (2G)	0	20	
20	AL	BOS	1906	May 1-May 24	19	1	
20	AL	PHI	1916	Jul 1-Aug 8	1	19	
20	AL	PHI	1943	Aug 7-Aug 24 (1G)	3	17	
20	NL	MON	1969	May 13-Jun 7	12	8	
19	NL	BOS	1906	May 17-Jun 8	3	16	
19	NL	CIN	1914	Sep 5-Sep 23 (1G)	6	13	
19	AL	DET	1975	Jul 29-Aug 15	9	10	
19	AL	KC	2005	Jul 28-Aug 19	8	11	
18	NL	CIN	1876	Jul 11-Aug 22	9	9	
18	NL	LOU	1894	Aug 15-Sep 5	0	18	
18	NL	STL	1897	Sep 3-Sep 26 (2G)	4	14	
18	AL	PHI	1920	Jun 8-Jun 27	0	18	
18	AL	WAS	1948	Sep 3 (1G)-Sep 18	8	10	
18	AL	WAS	1959	Jul 19 (2G)-Aug 5 (1G)	3	15	
17	NL	WAS	1894	May 3-May 28	4	13	
17	AL	BOS	1926	Aug 20-Sep 7	14	3	
17	NL	NY	1962	May 21-Jun 6 (2G)	7	10	
17	NL	ATL	1977	Apr 23-May 11	8	9	
16	NL	TRO	1882	Aug 17-Sep 18	5	11	1 tie
16	NL	BUF	1885	Sep 16-Oct 10	12	4	To end of season
16	NL	DET	1888	Jul 28-Aug 21	5	11	
16	NL	CLE	1899	Sep 18 (2G)- Oct 15 (2G)	0	16	To end of season
16	NL	BOS	1907	Aug 2-Aug 17	5	11	
16	AL	BOS	1907	Sep 12-Oct 2	9	7	2 ties
16	NL	BOS	1911	Jul 17 (1G)-Aug 1	8	8	
16	NL	BRO	1944	Jun 28 (1G)-Jul 16 (1G)	0	16	
16	NL	PHI	1945	May 29-Jun 13 (1G)	4	12	
15	AA	BAL	1882	Jun 6-Jul 4	0	15	
15	AA	WAS	1884	Jun 29-Jul 19	0	15	
15	UA	KC	1884	Aug 25- Sep 20	3	12	1 tie
15	AA	LOU	1891	Jul 7-Jul 25	0	15	
15	NL	LOU	1895	May 12-Jun 1	10	5	
15	NL	BOS	1909	Aug 3-Aug 15 (2G)	0	15	
15	NL	STL	1909	Sep 6 (1G)-Sep 24	11	4	
15	NL	BOS	1927	Sep 5 (2G)-Sep 17 (2G)	0	15	
15	AL	BOS	1927	Jun 21 (1G)-Jul 4 (1G)	10	5	
15	NL	BOS	1935	Jul 6 (2G)-Jul 21	0	15	
15	AL	PHI	1937	Jun 27 (2G)-Jul 14	10	5	1 tie
15	NL	NY	1963	Jun 28-Jul 14	8	7	
15	AL	TEX	1972	Sep 13-Sep 30	5	10	
15	NL	NY	1982	Aug 15 (2G)- Aug 31	6	9	
14	NL	MIL	1878	Jun 20-Jul 23	9	5	
14	NL	WOR	1882	Jun 16-Jul 11	2	12	
14	NL	PHI	1883	Aug 11-Sep 1	4	10	

(720) *(continued)*

					HOME	ROAD	
14	UA	KC	1884	Jun 28-Jul 19	0	14	
14	AA	LOU	1889	Aug 7-Aug 20	14	0	
14	NL	STL	1896	Jun 25-Jul 8	9	5	1 tie
14	NL	WAS	1898	Aug 27-Sep 11	3	11	
14	NL	CLE	1899	Jul 1 (2G)-Jul 15 (2G)	1	13	
14	NL	STL	1905	Jun 21-Jul 6	9	5	
14	NL	BOS	1911	May 9-May 24	14	0	
14	AL	STL	1911	Jun 10-Jun 28	6	8	
14	NL	STL	1916	Sep 16-Oct 1	0	14	To end of season
14	NL	PHI	1927	Sep 7 (2G)-Sep 24	1	13	
14	AL	BOS	1930	May 17-May 31	3	11	
14	NL	BOS	1935	Aug 28 (2G)-Sep 13	4	10	
14	NL	PHI	1936	Aug 21 (1G)-Aug 16	10	4	
14	NL	BRO	1937	Sep 16 (2G)-Sep 30 (2G)	0	14	
14	NL	CIN	1937	Sep 21 (2G)-Oct 3 (2G)	10	4	To end of season
14	AL	STL	1940	Jul 3-Jul 18	0	14	
14	AL	PHI	1945	Jun 19 (1G)-Jul 3	0	14	
14	AL	STL	1953	Jun 3-Jun 14 (2G)	14	0	
14	AL	STL	1954	Aug 11-Aug 25	7	7	
14	AL	WAS	1961	Aug 18-Sep 1 (1G)	11	3	
14	AL	WAS	1970	Sep 19 (1G)- Oct 1	4	10	To end of season
14	AL	OAK	1977	Jul 29-Aug 12	9	5	
14	AL	MIN	1982	May 19-Jun 2	6	8	
14	AL	SEA	1992	Sep 2-Sep 18	4	10	
14	AL	MIL	1994	May 11-May 25	6	8	
14	NL	CHI	1997	Apr 1-Apr 20	6	8	From start of season
14	NL	ARI	2004	Jul 9-Jul 25	3	11	

Jesus, Matty, and Felipe Alou

(721) Most Consecutive Home Wins by a Team in a Season

27	AA	STL	1885			18	AL	NY	1942	
26	NL	NY	1916	No road games during this streak		18	AL	CLE	1994	
						17	NL	PRO	1884	
24	NL	PIT	1978			17	AA	NY	1884	1 tie
24	AL	BOS	1988			17	PL	BRO	1890	1 tie
22	NL	BRO	1899			17	NL	NY	1893	1 tie
22	AL	PHI	1931			17	NL	CIN	1896	
21	NL	CHI	1880	From start of season		17	AL	CLE	1902	
21	AL	BOS	1949	To end of season		17	AL	DET	1909	
19	AA	PHI	1889	1 tie		17	AL	CHI	1983	
19	NL	HOU	2004			17	AL	OAK	2001	To end of season
18	NL	NY	1885	To end of season		16	UA	STL	1884	Start of season
18	NL	DET	1886	From start of season		16	AA	LOU	1890	
18	NL	CHI	1886			16	NL	BOS	1891	End of season; no road games during this streak
18	NL	BOS	1897							
18	NL	STL	1935			16	NL	NY	1904	
18	NL	CHI	1935	To end of season; no road games during this streak		16	AL	NY	1938	
						16	AL	NY	1941	
						16	AL	WAS	1943	
						16	AL	CLE	1951	

SPALDING

Joe Medwick

(722) Most Consecutive Home Losses by a Team in a Season

20	AL	STL	1953		13	AL	PHI	1920	
19	AL	BOS	1906	No road game during this streak	13	NL	PHI	1944	
					13	NL	NY	1979	
17	AL	NY	1913	1 tie; from start of season	12	NL	DET	1884	
					12	NL	BUF	1885	To end of season
17	AL	DET	1996	To end of season	12	NL	STL	1897	
15	AL	SEA	1969						1 tie
15	AL	CAL	1974						
15	NL	NY	2002		12	AL	STL	1910	
14	AA	LOU	1899	No road games during this streak					1 tie
					12	AL	PHI	1916	
14	NL	BOS	1911	No road games during this streak	12	NL	PHI	1928	No road games during this streak
14	AL	BOS	1926	No road games during this streak; to end of season	12	NL	PHI	1936	
					12	AL	PHI	1937	
					12	AL	PHI	1942	
					12	AL	STL	1949	
14	AL	DET	1956	1 tie	12	AL	DET	1953	1 tie
13	NL	PHI	1883	From start of season	12	NL	NY	1962	
13	NL	WAS	1886	No road games during this streak	12	NL	MON	1969	
					12	NL	SD	1972	
13	NL	LOU	1895		12	AL	OAK	1977	
13	NL	BOS	1909	No road games during this streak	12	NL	CHI	1994	Start of season
					12	AL	BOS	1994	

(723) Most Consecutive Road Wins by a Team in a Season

17	NL	NY	1916	No home games during this streak	13	NL	PHI	1976	
					13	AL	SEA	2003	
17	AL	DET	1984	From start of season	12	NL	NY	1912	1 tie
16	AL	WAS	1912	No home games during this streak	12	AL	CLE	1922	No home games during this streak
15	NL	NY	1912		12	NL	BRO	1924	
15	AL	BOS	1939		12	AL	WAS	1933	
15	AL	CHI	1951		12	NL	STL	1941	From start of season
15	AL	NY	1953		12	NL	STL	1944	2 ties
15	NL	CIN	1957		12	NL	CHI	1945	
14	NL	CHI	1906		12	AL	DET	1950	
14	NL	NY	1911		12	AL	OAK	1971	
14	AL	PHI	1931		12	AL	CHI	2000	
13	AL	NY	1947						

(724) Most Consecutive Road Losses by a Team in a Season

41	NL	PIT	1890		15	AA	BAL	1882	No home games during this streak
24	AA	LOU	1889						
22	NL	CLE	1899		15	AA	COL	1883	
22	AL	PHI	1943		15	AA	LOU	1891	No home games during this streak
22	NL	NY	1963						
21	NL	CIN	1876		15	NL	NY	1899	
21	NL	WAS	1894	From start of season	15	NL	BOS	1927	No home games during this streak
20	AA	KC	1889						
20	NL	LOU	1894	No home games during this streak	15	NL	PHI	1928	
					15	NL	BOS	1935	No home games during this streak
20	AL	PHI	1916						
19	AA	WAS	1884	To end of season	15	AL	WAS	1959	No home games during this streak
19	NL	CIN	1933						
19	AL	PHI	1945		15	AL	KC	1959	
19	NL	PIT	1985		15	AL	OAK	1986	
18	NL	LOU	1894	No home games during this streak	15	AL	SEA	2004	
					14	NL	DET	1883	
18	NL	CIN	1914	1 tie	14	AA	BAL	1883	
18	AL	PHI	1920	No home games during this streak	14	UA	KC	1884	
					14	NL	STL	1895	1 tie
18	AL	BOS	1932		14	NL	STL	1897	To end of season; no home games during this streak
18	AL	WAS	1949						
17	NL	CIN	1877						
17	AA	PHI	1890	To end of season	14	NL	STL	1916	To end of season; no home games during this streak
17	NL	BRO	1944						
17	NL	PHI	1961						
17	AL	MIL	1970		14	AL	CHI	1924	
16	NL	CLE	1899	To end of season; no home games during this streak	14	AL	WAS	1927	1 tie
					14	AL	BOS	1929	
					14	NL	BRO	1937	To end of season; no home games during this streak
16	NL	BOS	1906	No home games during this streak					
16	NL	BRO	1909		14	AL	PHI	1938	
16	NL	BOS	1909		14	AL	STL	1940	No home games during this streak
16	NL	PIT	1914						
16	NL	BOS	1922		14	NL	PHI	1942	
16	NL	CIN	1930		14	AL	MIN	1961	
16	AL	WAS	1948		14	AL	CAL	1969	
16	AL	WAS	1961		14	AL	SEA	1988	
					14	NL	PHI	1996	

(725) Most Consecutive Wins in a Season for a Team that Finished Last

11	AL	CLE	1982	AL East; tied for last	8	NL	WOR	1881	
11	NL	PIT	1996	NL Central	8	FL	STL	1914	
10	AL	CHI	1976	AL West	8	NL	SD	1980	NL West
10	NL	MIL	2003	NL Central	8	AL	CAL	1987	AL West
9	NL	STL	1907		8	AL	CHI	1989	AL West
9	AL	WAS	1949		8	NL	CHI	1994	NL Central
9	AL	DET	1975	AL East	8	AL	TEX	2002	AL West
9	NL	HOU	1991	NL West	8	AL	TEX	2003	AL West
9	NL	PIT	1998	NL Central; 1 tie					

(726) Most Consecutive Losses in a Season for a Team that Finished First

11	NL	NY	1951		8	NL	CIN	1990	NL West
11	NL	ATL	1982	NL West	8	NL	PIT	1991	NL East
9	AL	NY	1953		8	NL	SD	1996	NL West
9	AL	MIN	1970	AL West	8	NL	SF	2000	NL West
8	NL	BOS	1883		8	NL	HOU	2001	NL Central
8	NL	BRO	1899		8	AL	MIN	2003	AL Central
8	AL	NY	1922		8	NL	LA	2004	NL West
8	NL	CIN	1961		8	NL	SD	2005	NL West
8	NL	PHI	1976	NL East	8	NL	STL	2006	NL Central
8	AL	KC	1980	AL West					(Jun 20-Jun 27)
8	AL	OAK	1981	AL West	8	NL	STL	2006	NL Central
8	AL	CAL	1982	AL West					(Jul 27-Aug 4)

Ed Reulbach

(727) Most Wins by a Team in a Season

116	NL	CHI	1906		107	AL	PHI	1931
116	AL	SEA	2001		107	AL	NY	1932
114	AL	NY	1998		106	NL	NY	1904
111	AL	CLE	1954		106	AL	NY	1939
110	NL	PIT	1909		106	NL	STL	1942
110	AL	NY	1927		106	NL	ATL	1998
109	AL	NY	1961		105	NL	NY	1905
109	AL	BAL	1969		105	AL	BOS	1912
108	AL	BAL	1970		105	NL	STL	1943
108	NL	CIN	1975		105	NL	STL	1944
108	NL	NY	1986		105	NL	BRO	1953
107	NL	CHI	1907		105	NL	STL	2004

(728) Most Losses by a Team in a Season

134	NL	CLE	1899		111	NL	PHI	1941
120	NL	NY	1962		111	NL	NY	1963
119	AL	DET	2003		111	NL	ARI	2004
117	AL	PHI	1916		110	AL	WAS	1909
115	NL	BOS	1935		110	NL	MON	1969
113	AA	PIT	1890		110	NL	SD	1969
113	AL	WAS	1904		109	AL	PHI	1915
112	NL	PIT	1952		109	NL	PHI	1928
112	NL	NY	1965		109	NL	PHI	1942
111	AA	LOU	1889		109	NL	NY	1964
111	NL	STL	1898		109	AL	TOR	1979
111	AL	BOS	1932		109	AL	DET	1996
111	AL	STL	1939					

NATIONAL BASEBALL HALL OF FAME LIBRARY

*Joe DiMaggio, Charlie Keller,
Hank Bauer, and Tommy Henrich*

(729) Opening Day Record (current franchises)

			WON	LOST	TIED	
.622	NL	NY	28	17	0	
.581	AL	NY	61	44	1	(BAL 1-1 NY 60-43-1)
.581	AL	BAL	61	44	1	(MIL 0-1 STL 27-24-1 BAL 34-19)
.571	NL	COL	8	6	0	
.568	NL	MIL	21	16	1	NL 5-3-1; AL 16-13 (SEA 1-0 MIL 15-13)
.566	NL	CHI	73	56	2	
.561	NL	SF	69	54	1	(NY 38-36-1 SF 31-18)
.556	AL	TB	5	4	0	
.525	NL	PIT	63	57	0	
.522	AL	LA	24	22	0	
.519	AL	CHI	55	51	0	
.519	AL	CLE	55	51	0	
.517	NL	LA	60	56	1	(BRO 36-31-1 LA 24-25)
.511	NL	HOU	23	22	0	
.509	AL	MIN	54	52	0	(WAS 32-28 MIN 22-24)
.500	AL	SEA	15	15	0	
.500	AL	TOR	15	15	0	
.500	NL	FLA	7	7	0	
.491	AL	OAK	52	54	0	(PHI 25-29 KC 7-6 OAK 20-19)
.488	NL	ATL	63	66	2	(BOS 39-36-2 MIL 7-6 ATL 17-24)
.486	AL	BOS	51	54	1	
.483	NL	CIN	56	60	1	
.478	NL	STL	54	59	2	
.476	AL	DET	50	55	1	
.474	NL	WAS	18	20	0	(MON 18-18 WAS 0-2)
.451	NL	PHI	55	67	2	
.447	NL	SD	17	21	0	
.413	AL	TEX	19	27	0	(WAS 2-9 TEX 17-18)
.342	AL	KC	13	25	0	
.333	NL	ARI	3	6	0	

(730A) Batting Firsts at Various Major League Parks

PARK	CITY	OPENED	BATTER	HIT	HOME RUN
South Side Park III	Chicago, IL	Apr 24, 1901	Ollie Pickering	Jack McCarthy	Erve Beck
Bennett Park	Detroit, MI	Apr 25, 1901	Irv Waldron	Billy Gilbert	Sam Mertes
Oriole Park IV	Baltimore, MD	Apr 26, 1901	Tommy Dowd	John McGraw	Mike Donlin
Columbia Park	Philadelphia, PA	Apr 26, 1901	John Farrell	Jack O'Brien	Billy Clingman
Burns Park (Sundays only)	Detroit, MI	Apr 28, 1901	Irv Waldron	Irv Waldron	Wid Conroy
American League Park I	Washington, DC	Apr 29, 1901	John McGraw	Jimmy Williams	Frank Foutz
Lloyd Street Grounds	Milwaukee, WI	May 3, 1901	Dummy Hoy	Frank Shugart	Wid Conroy
Huntington Avenue Grounds	Boston, MA	May 8, 1901	Jack Hayden	Dave Fultz	Buck Freeman
Palace of the Fans	Cincinnati, OH	Apr 17, 1902	Jimmy Slagle	Jake Beckley	Erve Beck
Hilltop Park	New York, NY	Apr 30, 1903	Rabbit Robinson	Rabbit Robinson	Buck Freeman
American League Park II	Washington, DC	Apr 14, 1904	Topsy Hartsel	Bill Coughlin	Lew Drill
Shibe Park	Philadelphia, PA	Apr 12, 1909	Amby McConnell	Simon Nicholls	Frank Baker
Sportsman's Park III	St. Louis, MO	Apr 14, 1909	Josh Clarke	Tom Jones	Danny Hoffman
Forbes Field	Pittsburgh, PA	Jun 30, 1909	Johnny Evers	Frank Chance	Mike Mitchell
League Park II	Cleveland, OH	Apr 21, 1910	Matty McIntyre	Nig Clarke	Roy Hartzell
Comiskey Park I	Chicago, IL	July 1, 1910	George Stone	George Stone	Lee Tannehill
Griffith Stadium	Washington, DC	Apr 12, 1911	Larry Gardner	Tom Madden	Eddie Collins
Polo Grounds V	New York, NY	Jun 28, 1911	Bill John Sweeney	Bill John Sweeney	Larry Doyle
Crosley Field	Cincinnati, OH	Apr 11, 1912	Johnny Evers	Jimmy Sheckard	Jimmy Esmond
Fenway Park	Boston, MA	Apr 20, 1912	Guy Zinn	Harry Wolter	Hugh Bradley
Navin Field	Detroit, MI	Apr 20, 1912	Jack Graney	Ossie Vitt	Del Pratt
Ebbets Field	Brooklyn, NY	Apr 9, 1913	Dode Paskert	Dode Paskert	Casey Stengel
Oriole Park V	Baltimore, MD	Apr 13, 1914	Charlie Hanford	Charlie Hanford	Jimmy Walsh
Gordon and Koppel Field	Kansas City, MO	Apr 16, 1914	Max Flack	George Stovall	George Perring
Handlan's Park	St. Louis, MO	Apr 16, 1914	Benny Kauff	Everett Booe	Fred Kommers
Weeghman Park	Chicago, IL	Apr 23, 1914	Chet Chadbourne	John Potts	Art Wilson
Greenlawn Park	Indianapolis, IN	Apr 23, 1914	Al Bridwell	Ward Miller	Vin Campbell
Federal League Park	Buffalo, NY	May 11, 1914	Benny Meyer	Hack Simmons	Charlie Hanford
Harrison Field	Harrison, NJ	Apr 16, 1915	Benny Meyer	Vern Duncan	Al Wickland
Braves Field	Boston, MA	Aug 18, 1915	Miller Huggins	Art Butler	Doc Johnston
Yankee Stadium	Bronx, NY	Apr 18, 1923	Chick Fewster	George H. Burns	Babe Ruth
Cleveland Municipal Stadium	Cleveland, OH	July 31, 1932	Max Bishop	Max Bishop	Johnny Burnett
County Stadium	Milwaukee, WI	Apr 14, 1953	Solly Hemus	Joe Adcock	Billy Bruton
Memorial Stadium	Baltimore, MD	Apr 15, 1954	Chico Carrasquel	Chico Carrasquel	Clint Courtney
Municipal Stadium	Kansas City, MO	Apr 12, 1955	Harvey Kuenn	Fred Hatfield	Red Wilson
Seals Stadium	San Francisco, CA	Apr 15, 1958	Gino Cimoli	Charlie Neal	Daryl Spencer
LA Memorial Coliseum	Los Angeles, CA	Apr 18, 1958	Jim Davenport	Jim Davenport	Hank Sauer
Candlestick Park	San Francisco, CA	Apr 12, 1960	Joe Cunningham	Bill White	Leon Wagner
Metropolitan Stadium	Bloomington, MN	Apr 21, 1961	Marty Keough	Marty Keough	Dale Long
Wrigley Field	Los Angeles, CA	Apr 27, 1961	Zoilo Versalles	Lenny Green	Earl Averill Jr.
D. C. Stadium	Washington, DC	Apr 9, 1962	Jake Wood	Jake Wood	Bob W. Johnson
Colt Stadium	Houston, TX	Apr 10, 1962	Lou Brock	Billy Williams	Roman Mejias
Dodger Stadium	Los Angeles, CA	Apr 10, 1962	Eddie Kasko	Eddie Kasko	Wally Post
Shea Stadium	Flushing, NY	Apr 17, 1964	Dick Schofield	Willie Stargell	Willie Stargell
The Astrodome	Houston, TX	Apr 12, 1965	Tony Taylor	Tony Taylor	Dick Allen
Atlanta Stadium	Atlanta, GA	Apr 12, 1966	Matty Alou	Gene Alley	Joe Torre

(730A) *(continued)*

PARK	CITY	OPENED	BATTER	HIT	HOME RUN
Anaheim Stadium	Anaheim, CA	Apr 19, 1966	Tommie Agee	Jim Fregosi	Rick Reichardt
Busch Stadium	St. Louis, MO	May 12, 1966	Felipe Alou	Gary Geiger	Felipe Alou
Oakland-Alameda County Stadium	Oakland, CA	Apr 17, 1968	Curt Blefary	Boog Powell	Boog Powell
San Diego Stadium	San Diego, CA	Apr 8, 1969	Jesus Alou	Jesus Alou	Ed Spiezio
Sick's Stadium	Seattle, WA	Apr 11, 1969	Luis Aparicio	Tommy Harper	Don Mincher
Jarry Park	Montreal, Canada	Apr 14, 1969	Lou Brock	Curt Flood	Mack Jones
Riverfront Stadium	Cincinnati, OH	Jun 30, 1970	Sonny Jackson	Felix Millan	Hank Aaron
Three Rivers Stadium	Pittsburgh, PA	July 16, 1970	Ty Cline	Richie Hebner	Tony Perez
Veterans Stadium	Philadelphia, PA	Apr 10, 1971	Boots Day	Larry Bowa	Don Money
Arlington Stadium	Arlington, TX	Apr 21, 1972	Sandy Alomar Sr.	Frank Howard	Frank Howard
Royals Stadium	Kansas City, MO	Apr 10, 1973	Dave Nelson	Amos Otis	John Mayberry
The Kingdome	Seattle, WA	Apr 6, 1977	Jerry Remy	Don Baylor	Joe Rudi
Exhibiton Stadium	Toronto, Canada	Apr 7, 1977	Ralph Garr	Richie Zisk	Richie Zisk
Olympic Stadium	Montreal, Canada	Apr 15, 1977	Jay Johnstone	Dave Cash	Ellis Valentine
Hubert H. Humphrey Metrodome	Minneapolis, MN	Apr 6, 1982	Julio Cruz	Dave Engle	Dave Engle
The SkyDome	Toronto, Canada	Jun 5, 1989	Paul Molitor	Paul Molitor	Fred McGriff
Comiskey Park II	Chicago, IL	Apr 18, 1991	Tony Phillips	Alan Trammell	Cecil Fielder
Oriole Park at Camden Yards	Baltimore, MD	Apr 6, 1992	Kenny Lofton	Paul Sorrento	Paul Sorrento
Joe Robbie Stadium	Miami, FL	Apr 5, 1993	Jose Offerman	Bret Barberie	Tim Wallach
Mile High Stadium	Denver, CO	Apr 9, 1993	Mike Lansing	Marquis Grissom	Eric Young
Jacobs Field	Cleveland, OH	Apr 4, 1994	Rich Amaral	Eric Anthony	Eric Anthony
The Ballpark in Arlington	Arlington, TX	Apr 11, 1994	Pat Listach	David Hulse	Dave Nilsson
Coors Field	Denver, CO	Apr 26, 1995	Brett Butler	Brett Butler	Rico Brogna
Turner Field	Atlanta, GA	Apr 4, 1997	Brian McRae	Chipper Jones	Michael Tucker
Bank One Ballpark	Phoenix. AZ	Mar 31, 1998	Mike Lansing	Mike Lansing	Vinny Castilla
Tropicana Field	St. Petersburg, FL	Mar 31, 1998	Brian L. Hunter	Tony Clark	Luis Gonzalez
Safeco Field	Seattle, WA	July 15, 1999	Quilvio Veras	Eric Owens	Russ Davis
Enron Field	Houston, TX	Apr 7, 2000	Doug Glanville	Doug Glanville	Scott Rolen
Pacific Bell Park	San Francisco, CA	Apr 11, 2000	Devon White	Devon White	Kevin Elster
Comerica Park	Detroit, MI	Apr 11, 2000	Mark McLemore	John Olerud	Juan Gonzalez
Miller Park	Milwaukee, WI	Apr 6, 2001	Barry Larkin	Sean Casey	Michael Tucker
PNC Park	Pittsburgh, PA	Apr 9, 2001	Barry Larkin	Sean Casey	Sean Casey
Great American Ball Park	Cincinnati, OH	Mar 31, 2003	Kenny Lofton	Ken Griffey Jr.	Reggie Sanders
Petco Park	San Diego, CA	Apr 8, 2004	Ray Durham	Brian Giles	Marquis Grissom
Citizens Bank Park	Philadelphia, PA	Apr 12, 2004	D'Angelo Jimenez	D'Angelo Jimenez	Bobby Abreu
New Busch Stadium	St. Louis, MO	Apr 10, 2006	Brady Clark	Carlos Lee	Bill Hall

(730B) Batting Firsts at Various Major League Parks

PARK	CITY	OPENED	GRAND SLAM	CYCLE
South Side Park III	Chicago, IL	Apr 24, 1901	Herm McFarland	None
Bennett Park	Detroit, MI	Apr 25, 1901	Ty Cobb	None
Oriole Park IV	Baltimore, MD	Apr 26, 1901	Jimmy Williams	None
Columbia Park	Philadelphia, PA	Apr 26, 1901	Herm McFarland	None
Burns Park (Sundays only)	Detroit, MI	Apr 28, 1901	Deacon McGuire	None
American League Park I	Washington, DC	Apr 29, 1901	Ducky Holmes	Bill Bradley
Lloyd Street Grounds	Milwaukee, WI	May 3, 1901	None	None
Huntington Avenue Grounds	Boston, MA	May 8, 1901	Harry Davis	Harry Davis
Palace of the Fans	Cincinnati, OH	Apr 17, 1902	Miller Huggins	Chief Wilson
Hilltop Park	New York, NY	Apr 30, 1903	Freddy Parent	Otis Clymer
American League Park II	Washington, DC	Apr 14, 1904	Joe Stanley	None
Shibe Park	Philadelphia, PA	Apr 12, 1909	Duffy Lewis	Danny Murphy
Sportsman's Park III	St. Louis, MO	Apr 14, 1909	Joe Jackson	Tris Speaker
Forbes Field	Pittsburgh, PA	Jun 30, 1909	Tommy Leach	Honus Wagner
League Park II	Cleveland, OH	Apr 21, 1910	Ivy Olson	Oscar Melillo
Comiskey Park I	Chicago, IL	July 1, 1910	Lee Tannehill	Baby Doll Jacobson
Griffith Stadium	Washington, DC	Apr 12, 1911	Doc Gessler	Bob Meusel
Polo Grounds V	New York, NY	Jun 28, 1911	Chief Meyers	Mike Mitchell
Crosley Field	Cincinnati, OH	Apr 11, 1912	Edd Roush	Joe Medwick
Fenway Park	Boston, MA	Apr 20, 1912	Rabbit Maranville	Moose Solters
Navin Field	Detroit, MI	Apr 20, 1912	Roger Peckinpaugh	Bobby Veach
Ebbets Field	Brooklyn, NY	Apr 9, 1913	Ed Konetchy	Dave Robertson
Oriole Park V	Baltimore, MD	Apr 13, 1914	Jimmy Walsh	None
Gordon and Koppel Field	Kansas City, MO	Apr 16, 1914	Bill Kenworthy	Ed Lennox
Handlan's Park	St. Louis, MO	Apr 16, 1914	Steve Evans	None
Weeghman Park	Chicago, IL	Apr 23, 1914	Rollie Zeider	Hack Wilson
Greenlawn Park	Indianapolis, IN	Apr 23, 1914	Frank LaPorte	None
Federal League Park	Buffalo, NY	May 11, 1914	Hal Chase	None
Harrison Field	Harrison, NJ	Apr 16, 1915	None	None
Braves Field	Boston, MA	Aug 18, 1915	Red Smith	Ross Youngs
Yankee Stadium	Bronx, NY	Apr 18, 1923	Tris Speaker	Goose Goslin
Cleveland Municipal Stadium	Cleveland, OH	July 31, 1932	Willie Kamm	Leon Culberson
County Stadium	Milwaukee, WI	Apr 14, 1953	Eddie Mathews	Gary Ward
Memorial Stadium	Baltimore, MD	Apr 15, 1954	Cass Michaels	Tony Horton
Municipal Stadium	Kansas City, MO	Apr 12, 1955	Jim Hegan	Lou Clinton
Seals Stadium	San Francisco, CA	Apr 15, 1958	Frank J. Thomas	None
LA Memorial Coliseum	Los Angeles, CA	Apr 18, 1958	Willie Mays	None
Candlestick Park	San Francisco, CA	Apr 12, 1960	Ernie Banks	Richie Zisk
Metropolitan Stadium	Bloomington, MN	Apr 21, 1961	Mickey Mantle	Freddie Patek
Wrigley Field	Los Angeles, CA	Apr 27, 1961	Carroll Hardy	None
D. C. Stadium	Washington, DC	Apr 9, 1962	Clete Boyer	None
Colt Stadium	Houston, TX	Apr 10, 1962	Don Buddin	Ken Boyer
Dodger Stadium	Los Angeles, CA	Apr 10, 1962	Brooks Robinson	Jim Fregosi
Shea Stadium	Flushing, NY	Apr 17, 1964	Jim Hickman	Wes Parker
The Astrodome	Houston, TX	Apr 12, 1965	Bob Aspromonte	Dave Kingman
Atlanta Stadium	Atlanta, GA	Apr 12, 1966	Hank Aaron	Jim Ray Hart
Anaheim Stadium	Anaheim, CA	Apr 19, 1966	Curt Blefary	Jim Fregosi
Busch Stadium	St. Louis, MO	May 12, 1966	Curt Flood	Billy Williams

(730B) *(continued)*

PARK	CITY	OPENED	GRAND SLAM	CYCLE
Oakland-Alameda County Stadium	Oakland, CA	Apr 17, 1968	Sal Bando	Eric Chavez
San Diego Stadium	San Diego, CA	Apr 8, 1969	Al Oliver	John Olerud
Sick's Stadium	Seattle, WA	Apr 11, 1969	Rich Rollins	None
Jarry Park	Montreal, Canada	Apr 14, 1969	Dal Maxvill	None
Riverfront Stadium	Cincinnati, OH	Jun 30, 1970	Tony Perez	Mike Easler
Three Rivers Stadium	Pittsburgh, PA	July 16, 1970	John Bateman	Joe Torre
Veterans Stadium	Philadelphia, PA	Apr 10, 1971	Roger Freed	Gregg Jefferies
Arlington Stadium	Arlington, TX	Apr 21, 1972	Carlos May	Cal Ripken
Royals Stadium	Kansas City, MO	Apr 10, 1973	Dave May	John Mayberry
The Kingdome	Seattle, WA	Apr 6, 1977	Joe Rudi	Jack Brohamer
Exhibiton Stadium	Toronto, Canada	Apr 7, 1977	Hector Torres	Kelly Gruber
Olympic Stadium	Montreal, Canada	Apr 15, 1977	Mike Ivie	Chris Speier
Hubert H. Humphrey Metrodome	Minneapolis, MN	Apr 6, 1982	Gary Ward	Kirby Puckett
The Skydome	Toronto, Canada	Jun 5, 1989	Terry Steinbach	George Brett
Comiskey Park II	Chicago, IL	Apr 18, 1991	Kevin Romine	Mike Blowers
Oriole Park at Camden Yards	Baltimore, MD	Apr 6, 1992	Randy Milligan	None
Joe Robbie Stadium	Miami, FL	Apr 5, 1993	Jeff Conine	None
Mile High Stadium	Denver, CO	Apr 9, 1993	Junior Felix	None
Jacobs Field	Cleveland, OH	Apr 4, 1994	Paul Sorrento	None
The Ballpark in Arlington	Arlington, TX	Apr 11, 1994	Bernie Williams	Mark Teixeira
Coors Field	Denver, CO	Apr 26, 1995	Todd Hundley	John Mabry
Turner Field	Atlanta, GA	Apr 4, 1997	Javy Lopez	None
Bank One Ballpark	Phoenix. AZ	Mar 31, 1998	Cecil Fielder	None
Tropicana Field	St. Petersburg, FL	Mar 31, 1998	Johnny Damon	Carlos Guillen
Safeco Field	Seattle, WA	July 15, 1999	Raul Ibanez	Miguel Tejada
Enron Field	Houston, TX	Apr 7, 2000	Thomas Howard	Luis Gonzalez
Pacific Bell Park	San Francisco, CA	Apr 11, 2000	Bobby Estalella	Eric Byrnes
Comerica Park	Detroit, MI	Apr 11, 2000	Trot Nixon	Damion Easley
Miller Park	Milwaukee, WI	Apr 6, 2001	Jose Hernandez	Chad Moeller
PNC Park	Pittsburgh, PA	Apr 9, 2001	Sammy Sosa	None
Great American Ball Park	Cincinnati, OH	Mar 31, 2003	Russ Branyan	Randy Winn
Petco Park	San Diego, CA	Apr 8, 2004	Adam Dunn	None
Citizens Bank Park	Philadelphia, PA	Apr 12, 2004	Andruw Jones	David Bell
New Busch Stadium	St. Louis, MO	Apr 10, 2006	Aramis Ramirez	None

(731A) Pitching Firsts at Various Major League Parks

PARK	CITY	OPENED	FIRST PITCH	WIN	LOSS
South Side Park III	Chicago, IL	Apr 24, 1901	Roy Patterson	Roy Patterson	Bill Hoffer
Bennett Park	Detroit, MI	Apr 25, 1901	Roscoe Miller	Emil Frisk	Bert Husting
Oriole Park IV	Baltimore, MD	Apr 26, 1901	Joe McGinnity	Joe McGinnity	Win Kellum
Columbia Park	Philadelphia, PA	Apr 26, 1901	Chick Fraser	Bill Carrick	Chick Fraser
Burns Park (Sundays only)	Detroit, MI	Apr 28, 1901	Ed Siever	Jack Cronin	Pete Dowling
American League Park I	Washington, DC	Apr 29, 1901	Bill Carrick	Bill Carrick	Joe McGinnity
Lloyd Street Grounds	Milwaukee, WI	May 3, 1901	Pink Hawley	John Skopec	Pink Hawley
Huntington Avenue Grounds	Boston, MA	May 8, 1901	Cy Young	Cy Young	Bill Bernhard
Palace of the Fans	Cincinnati, OH	Apr 17, 1902	Len Swormstedt	Jack W. Taylor	Len Swormstedt
Hilltop Park	New York, NY	Apr 30, 1903	Jack Chesbro	Jack Chesbro	Happy Townsend
American League Park II	Washington, DC	Apr 14, 1904	Highball Wilson	Eddie Plank	Highball Wilson
Shibe Park	Philadelphia, PA	Apr 12, 1909	Eddie Plank	Eddie Plank	Frank Arellanes
Sportsman's Park III	St. Louis, MO	Apr 14, 1909	Jack Powell	Addie Joss	Jack Powell
Forbes Field	Pittsburgh, PA	Jun 30, 1909	Vic Willis	Ed Reulbach	Vic Willis
League Park II	Cleveland, OH	Apr 21, 1910	Cy Young	Ed Willett	Cy Young
Comiskey Park I	Chicago, IL	July 1, 1910	Ed Walsh	Barney Pelty	Ed Walsh
Griffith Stadium	Washington, DC	Apr 12, 1911	Dolly Gray	Dolly Gray	Joe Wood
Polo Grounds V	New York, NY	Jun 28, 1911	Christy Mathewson	Christy Mathewson	Al Mattern
Crosley Field	Cincinnati, OH	Apr 11, 1912	Frank E. Smith	Bert Humphries	King Cole
Fenway Park	Boston, MA	Apr 20, 1912	Buck O'Brien	Charles Hall	Hippo Vaughn
Navin Field	Detroit, MI	Apr 20, 1912	George Mullin	George Mullin	Vean Gregg
Ebbets Field	Brooklyn, NY	Apr 9, 1913	Nap Rucker	Tom Seaton	Nap Rucker
Oriole Park V	Baltimore, MD	Apr 13, 1914	Jack Quinn	Jack Quinn	Earl Moore
Gordon and Koppel Field	Kansas City, MO	Apr 16, 1914	Gene Packard	Claude Hendrix	Gene Packard
Handlan's Park	St. Louis, MO	Apr 16, 1914	Bob Groom	Cy Falkenberg	Bob Groom
Weeghman Park	Chicago, IL	Apr 23, 1914	Claude Hendrix	Claude Hendrix	Chief Johnson
Greenlawn Park	Indianapolis, IN	Apr 23, 1914	Cy Falkenberg	Henry Keupper	Cy Falkenberg
Federal League Park	Buffalo, NY	May 11, 1914	Bob Smith	Kaiser Wilhelm	Gene Krapp
Harrison Field	Harrison, NJ	Apr 16, 1915	Cy Falkenberg	Bill Bailey	Cy Falkenberg
Braves Field	Boston, MA	Aug 18, 1915	Dick Rudolph	Dick Rudolph	Slim Sallee
Yankee Stadium	Bronx, NY	Apr 18, 1923	Bob Shawkey	Bob Shawkey	Howard Ehmke
Cleveland Municipal Stadium	Cleveland, OH	July 31, 1932	Mel Harder	Lefty Grove	Mel Harder
County Stadium	Milwaukee, WI	Apr 14, 1953	Warren Spahn	Warren Spahn	Gerry Staley
Memorial Stadium	Baltimore, MD	Apr 15, 1954	Bob Turley	Bob Turley	Virgil Trucks
Municipal Stadium	Kansas City, MO	Apr 12, 1955	Alex Kellner	Alex Kellner	Ned Garver
Seals Stadium	San Francisco, CA	Apr 15, 1958	Ruben Gomez	Ruben Gomez	Don Drysdale
LA Memorial Coliseum	Los Angeles, CA	Apr 18, 1958	Carl Erskine	Carl Erskine	Al Worthington
Candlestick Park	San Francisco, CA	Apr 12, 1960	Sam Jones	Sam Jones	Larry Jackson
Metropolitan Stadium	Bloomington, MN	Apr 21, 1961	Camilo Pascual	Joe McLain	Ray Moore
Wrigley Field	Los Angeles, CA	Apr 27, 1961	Eli Grba	Camilo Pascual	Eli Grba
D. C. Stadium	Washington, DC	Apr 9, 1962	Bennie Daniels	Bennie Daniels	Don Mossi
Colt Stadium	Houston, TX	Apr 10, 1962	Bobby Shantz	Bobby Shantz	Don Cardwell
Dodger Stadium	Los Angeles, CA	Apr 10, 1962	Johnny Podres	Bob Purkey	Johnny Podres
Shea Stadium	Flushing, NY	Apr 17, 1964	Jack Fisher	Bob Friend	Ed Bauta
The Astrodome	Houston, TX	Apr 12, 1965	Bob Bruce	Chris Short	Bob Bruce
Atlanta Stadium	Atlanta, GA	Apr 12, 1966	Tony Cloninger	Don Schwall	Tony Cloninger

(731A) (continued)

PARK	CITY	OPENED	FIRST PITCH	WIN	LOSS
Anaheim Stadium	Anaheim, CA	Apr 19, 1966	Marcelino Lopez	Tommy John	Marcelino Lopez
Busch Stadium	St. Louis, MO	May 12, 1966	Ray Washburn	Don Dennis	Phil Niekro
Oakland-Alameda County Stadium	Oakland, CA	Apr 17, 1968	Lew Krausse Jr.	Dave McNally	Lew Krausse Jr.
San Diego Stadium	San Diego, CA	Apr 8, 1969	Dick Selma	Dick Selma	Don Wilson
Sick's Stadium	Seattle, WA	Apr 11, 1969	Gary Bell	Gary Bell	Joe Horlen
Jarry Park	Montreal, Canada	Apr 14	1969, Larry Jaster	Dan McGinn	Gary Waslewski
Riverfront Stadium	Cincinnati, OH	Jun 30	1970, Jim McGlothlin		Pat Jarvis Jim McGlothlin
Three Rivers Stadium	Pittsburgh, PA	July 16, 1970	Dock Ellis	Clay Carroll	Dock Ellis
Veterans Stadium	Philadelphia, PA	Apr 10, 1971	Jim Bunning	Jim Bunning	Bill Stoneman
Arlington Stadium	Arlington, TX	Apr 21, 1972	Dick Bosman	Dick Bosman	Clyde Wright
Royals Stadium	Kansas City, MO	Apr 10, 1973	Paul Splittorff	Paul Splittorff	Pete Broberg
The Kingdome	Seattle, WA	Apr 6, 1977	Diego Segui	Frank Tanana	Diego Segui
Exhibition Stadium	Toronto, Canada	Apr 7, 1977	Bill Singer	Jerry Johnson	Ken Brett
Olympic Stadium	Montreal, Canada	Apr 15, 1977	Don Stanhouse	Steve Carlton	Don Stanhouse
Hubert H. Humphrey Metrodome	Minneapolis, MN	Apr 6, 1982	Pete Redfern	Floyd Bannister	Pete Redfern
The Skydome	Toronto, Canada	Jun 5, 1989	Jimmy Key	Don August	Jimmy Key
Comiskey Park II	Chicago, IL	Apr 18, 1991	Jack McDowell	Frank Tanana	Jack McDowell
Oriole Park at Camden Yards	Baltimore, MD	Apr 6, 1992	Rick Sutcliffe	Rick Sutcliffe	Charles Nagy
Joe Robbie Stadium	Miami, FL	Apr 5, 1993	Charlie Hough	Charlie Hough	Orel Hershiser
Mile High Stadium	Denver, CO	Apr 9, 1993	Bryn Smith	Bryn Smith	Kent Bottenfield
Jacobs Field	Cleveland, OH	Apr 4, 1994	Dennis Martinez	Eric Plunk	Kevin King
The Ballpark in Arlington	Arlington, TX	Apr 11, 1994	Kenny Rogers	Jaime Navarro	Kenny Rogers
Coors Field	Denver, CO	Apr 26, 1995	Bill Swift	Mark Thompson	Mike Remlinger
Turner Field	Atlanta, GA	Apr 4, 1997	Denny Neagle	Brad Clontz	Terry Adams
Bank One Ballpark	Phoenix. AZ	Mar 31, 1998	Andy Benes	Darryl Kile	Andy Benes
Tropicana Field	St. Petersburg, FL	Mar 31, 1998	Wilson Alvarez	Justin Thompson	Wilson Alvarez
Safeco Field	Seattle, WA	July 15, 1999	Jamie Moyer	Will Cunnane	Jose Mesa
Enron Field	Houston, TX	Apr 7, 2000	Octavio Dotel	Randy Wolf	Octavio Dotel
Pacific Bell Park	San Francisco, CA	Apr 11, 2000	Kirk Rueter	Chan Ho Park	Kirk Rueter
Comerica Park	Detroit, MI	Apr 11, 2000	Brian Moehler	Brian Moehler	Freddy Garcia
Miller Park	Milwaukee, WI	Apr 6, 2001	Jeff D'Amico	David Weathers	Dennys Reyes
PNC Park	Pittsburgh, PA	Apr 9, 2001	Todd Ritchie	Chris Reitsma	Todd Ritchie
Great American Ball Park	Cincinnati, OH	Mar 31, 2003	Jimmy Haynes	Kris Benson	Jimmy Haynes
Petco Park	San Diego, CA	Apr 8, 2004	David Wells	Eddie Oropesa	Matt Herges
Citizens Bank Park	Philadelphia, PA	Apr 12, 2004	Randy Wolf	Paul Wilson	Randy Wolf
New Busch Stadium	St. Louis, MO	Apr 10, 2006	Mark Mulder	Mark Mulder	Tomo Ohka

(731B) Pitching Firsts at Various Major League Parks

PARK	CITY	OPENED	SHUTOUT	NO-HITTER
South Side Park III	Chicago, IL	Apr 24, 1901	Clark Griffith	Nixey Callahan
Bennett Park	Detroit, MI	Apr 25, 1901	Roscoe Miller	Frank E. Smith
Oriole Park IV	Baltimore, MD	Apr 26, 1901	Roy Patterson	None
Columbia Park	Philadelphia, PA	Apr 26, 1901	Eddie Plank	None
Burns Park (Sundays only)	Detroit, MI	Apr 28, 1901	Joe Yeager	None
American League Park I	Washington, DC	Apr 29, 1901	Earl Moore	None
Lloyd Street Grounds	Milwaukee, WI	May 3, 1901	Dale Gear	None
Huntington Avenue Grounds	Boston, MA	May 8, 1901	Watty Lee	Cy Young
Palace of the Fans	Cincinnati, OH	Apr 17, 1902	Noodles Hahn	None
Hilltop Park	New York, NY	Apr 30, 1903	Bill Dinneen	Cy Young
American League Park II	Washington, DC	Apr 14, 1904	Jack Chesbro	None
Shibe Park	Philadelphia, PA	Apr 12, 1909	Lew Brockett	Chief Bender
Sportsman's Park III	St. Louis, MO	Apr 14, 1909	Addie Joss	Eddie Cicotte
Forbes Field	Pittsburgh, PA	Jun 30, 1909	Mordecai Brown	None
League Park II	Cleveland, OH	Apr 21, 1910	Ed Willett	Wes Ferrell
Comiskey Park I	Chicago, IL	July 1, 1910	Barney Pelty	Ed Walsh
Griffith Stadium	Washington, DC	Apr 12, 1911	Tom J. Hughes	Bobby Burke
Polo Grounds V	New York, NY	Jun 28, 1911	Christy Mathewson	Rube Marquard
Crosley Field	Cincinnati, OH	Apr 11, 1912	Rube Marquard	Hod Eller
Fenway Park	Boston, MA	Apr 20, 1912	Joe Wood	George "Iron" Davis
Navin Field	Detroit, MI	Apr 20, 1912	George Kahler	George Mullin
Ebbets Field	Brooklyn, NY	Apr 9, 1913	Tom Seaton	Dazzy Vance
Oriole Park V	Baltimore, MD	Apr 13, 1914	George Suggs	None
Gordon and Koppel Field	Kansas City, MO	Apr 16, 1914	Tom Seaton	None
Handlan's Park	St. Louis, MO	Apr 16, 1914	Jack Quinn	Frank Allen
Weeghman Park	Chicago, IL	Apr 23, 1914	Mike Prendergast, Doc Watson	Fred Toney
Greenlawn Park	Indianapolis, IN	Apr 23, 1914	Hank Keupper	None
Federal League Park	Buffalo, NY	May 11, 1914	Claude Hendrix	Alex Main
Harrison Field	Harrison, NJ	Apr 16, 1915	Harry Moran	None
Braves Field	Boston, MA	Aug 18, 1915	Tom L. Hughes	Tom L. Hughes
Yankee Stadium	Bronx, NY	Apr 18, 1923	Sam P. Jones	Monte Pearson
Cleveland Municipal Stadium	Cleveland, OH	July 31, 1932	Lefty Grove	Don Black
County Stadium	Milwaukee, WI	Apr 14, 1953	Johnny Antonelli	Jim Wilson
Memorial Stadium	Baltimore, MD	Apr 15, 1954	Ned Garver	Hoyt Wilhelm
Municipal Stadium	Kansas City, MO	Apr 12, 1955	Alex Kellner	None
Seals Stadium	San Francisco, CA	Apr 15, 1958	Ruben Gomez	None
LA Memorial Coliseum	Los Angeles, CA	Apr 18, 1958	Johnny Podres	None
Candlestick Park	San Francisco, CA	Apr 12, 1960	Johnny Podres, Ed Roebuck	Juan Marichal
Metropolitan Stadium	Bloomington, MN	Apr 21, 1961	Jack Kralick	Jack Kralick
Wrigley Field	Los Angeles, CA	Apr 27, 1961	Ken McBride	None
D. C. Stadium	Washington, DC	Apr 9, 1962	Art Quirk, Wes Stock	None
Colt Stadium	Houston, TX	Apr 10, 1962	Hal Woodeshick, Dick Farrell	Don Nottebart
Dodger Stadium	Los Angeles, CA	Apr 10, 1962	Jim Kaat	Bo Belinsky
Shea Stadium	Flushing, NY	Apr 17, 1964	Al Jackson	Jim Bunning
The Astrodome	Houston, TX	Apr 12, 1965	Chris Short	Don Wilson
Atlanta Stadium	Atlanta, GA	Apr 12, 1966	Vern Law	Phil Niekro

(731B) *(continued)*

PARK	CITY	OPENED	SHUTOUT	NO-HITTER
Anaheim Stadium	Anaheim, CA	Apr 19, 1966	Fred Newman, Bob Lee	Clyde Wright
Busch Stadium	St. Louis, MO	May 12, 1966	Al Jackson	Bob Forsch
Oakland-Alameda County Stadium	Oakland, CA	Apr 17, 1968	Joe Coleman Jr.	Catfish Hunter
San Diego Stadium	San Diego, CA	Apr 8, 1969	Johnny Podres, Tommie Sisk	Dock Ellis
Sick's Stadium	Seattle, WA	Apr 11, 1969	Gary Bell	None
Jarry Park	Montreal, Canada	Apr 14, 1969	Jerry Koosman, Nolan Ryan	Bill Stoneman
Riverfront Stadium	Cincinnati, OH	Jun 30, 1970	Gary Nolan	Ken Holtzman
Three Rivers Stadium	Pittsburgh, PA	July 16, 1970	Dock Ellis	Bob Gibson
Veterans Stadium	Philadelphia, PA	Apr 10, 1971	Ferguson Jenkins	Terry Mulholland
Arlington Stadium	Arlington, TX	Apr 21, 1972	Pete Broberg	Mike Witt
Royals Stadium	Kansas City, MO	Apr 10, 1973	Dick Bosman	Nolan Ryan
The Kingdome	Seattle, WA	Apr 6, 1977	Frank Tanana	Randy Johnson
Exhibition Stadium	Toronto, Canada	Apr 7, 1977	Ferguson Jenkins	None
Olympic Stadium	Montreal, Canada	Apr 15, 1977	Don Stanhouse	Charlie Lea
Hubert H. Humphrey Metrodome	Minneapolis, MN	Apr 6, 1982	Lary Sorensen	Scott Erickson
The Skydome	Toronto, Canada	Jun 5, 1989	Dave Stieb, David Wells	Dave Stewart
Comiskey Park II	Chicago, IL	Apr 18, 1991	Frank Tanana	None
Oriole Park at Camden Yards	Baltimore, MD	Apr 6, 1992	Rick Sutcliffe	Hideo Nomo
Joe Robbie Stadium	Miami, FL	Apr 5, 1993	Tommy Greene	Al Leiter
Mile High Stadium	Denver, CO	Apr 9, 1993	Terry Mulholland	None
Jacobs Field	Cleveland, OH	Apr 4, 1994	Mark Clark	None
The Ballpark in Arlington	Arlington, TX	Apr 11, 1994	Kevin Brown, Tom Henke	Kenny Rogers
Coors Field	Denver, CO	Apr 26, 1995	Tom Glavine	Hideo Nomo
Turner Field	Atlanta, GA	Apr 4, 1997	Greg Maddux, Mark Wohlers	Randy Johnson
Bank One Ballpark	Phoenix. AZ	Mar 31, 1998	John Thomson, Chuck McElroy	Jose Jimenez
Tropicana Field	St. Petersburg, FL	Mar 31, 1998	Wilson Alvarez, Esteban Yan, Jim Mecir	None
Safeco Field	Seattle, WA	July 15, 1999	Randy Johnson	None
Enron Field	Houston, TX	Apr 7, 2000	Joe Mays, Travis Miller, La Troy Hawkins, Eddie Guardado	None
Pacific Bell Park	San Francisco, CA	Apr 11, 2000	Joe Nathan, John Johnstone, Alan Embree	None
Comerica Park	Detroit, MI	Apr 11, 2000	Aaron Sele	None
Miller Park	Milwaukee, WI	Apr 6, 2001	Jose Lima, Billy Wagner	None
PNC Park	Pittsburgh, PA	Apr 9, 2001	Jimmy Anderson, Scott Sauerbeck, Mike Williams	None
Great American Ball Park	Cincinnati, OH	Mar 31, 2003	Chris Reitsma, Scott Williamson	None
Petco Park	San Diego, CA	Apr 8, 2004	Randy Johnson	None
Citizens Bank Park	Philadelphia, PA	Apr 12, 2004	Randy Wolf, Rheal Cormier	None
New Busch Stadium	St. Louis, MO	Apr 10, 2006	Aaron Harang, Kent Mercker, Todd Coffey, David Weathers	None

(732) Most Lopsided Wins

DIFFERENCE				OPP.			
31	NL	CHI	35	CLE	4	Jul 24, 1882	
29	NL	CHI	36	LOU	7	Jun 29, 1897	
28	NL	PRO	28	PHI	0	Aug 21, 1883	
28	NL	NY	29	PHI	1	Jun 15, 1887	
27	AA	MIL	30	WAS	3	Sep 10, 1891	
25	NL	HAR	28	NY	3	May 13, 1876	
25	NL	BOS	29	PHI	4	Jun 20, 1883	
25	NL	PHI	29	LOU	4	Aug 17, 1894	
25	AL	BOS	29	STL	4	Jun 8, 1950	
24	NL	CHI	31	BUF	7	Jul 3, 1883	
24	NL	NY	24	BUF	0	May 27, 1885	
24	AA	BRO	25	BAL	1	Jun 24, 1886	
24	NL	NY	26	WAS	2	Jun 11, 1887	
24	NL	PHI	24	IND	0	Jun 28, 1887	
24	AL	CLE	27	BOS	3	Jul 7, 1923	1G
23	NL	CHI	30	LOU	7	Jul 22, 1876	
23	NL	CHI	24	TRO	1	Sep 9, 1882	
23	AA	CIN	23	BAL	0	Jul 6, 1883	
23	NL	CHI	28	BRO	5	Aug 25, 1891	
23	NL	PIT	25	STL	2	Aug 1, 1893	1G
23	NL	CIN	26	BOS	3	Jun 4, 1911	
23	AL	NY	25	PHI	2	May 24, 1936	2G
23	AL	CLE	26	STL	3	Aug 12, 1948	
23	AL	CHI	29	KC	6	Apr 23, 1955	

(733) Most Lopsided Shutouts

			OPP.		
28-0	NL	PRO	PHI	Aug 21, 1883	
24-0	NL	PHI	IND	Jun 28, 1887	
24-0	NL	NY	BUF	May 27, 1885	
23-0	AA	CIN	BAL	Jul 6, 1883	
22-0	NL	PIT	CHI	Sep 16, 1975	
22-0	AL	CLE	NY	Aug 31, 2004	
21-0	AA	STL	COL	May 7, 1889	
21-0	AL	DET	CLE	Sep 15, 1901	
21-0	AL	NY	PHI	Aug 13, 1939	2G
20-0	NL	CHI	WAS	May 28, 1886	
20-0	AA	CIN	BAL	Aug 10, 1889	

(734) Oldest Batteries

TOTAL YEARS & DAYS	PITCHER	YEARS, MONTHS, DAYS	CATCHER	YEARS, MONTHS, DAYS			
88-276	Clark Griffith	43-10-14	Jack Ryan	44-10-22	AL	WAS	Oct 4, 1913
87-227	Jack Quinn	46-10-17	Wally Schang	40-9-0	AL	PHI	May 22, 1930 2G
87-204	Joe McGinnity	33-6-3	Jim O'Rourke	54-0-21	NL	NY	Sep 22, 1904 1G
86-181	Jack Quinn	49-10-28	Clyde Manion	36-7-3	NL	CIN	Jun 3, 1933
86-56	Phil Niekro	48-3-19	Rick Dempsey	37-10-7	AL	CLE	Jul 20, 1987
86-9	Satchel Paige	59-2-18	Billy Bryan	26-9-21	AL	KC	Sep 25, 1965
85-73	Curt Davis	41-8-18	Clyde Sukeforth	43-5-25	NL	BRO	May 25, 1945
85-37	Jack Quinn	49-1-20	Val Picinich	35-11-17	NL	BRO	Aug 25, 1932
84-322	Jamie Moyer	42-8-9	Pat Borders	42-2-13	AL	SEA	Jul 27, 2005
84-273	Terry Leach	39-3-8	Carlton Fisk	45-5-25	AL	CHI	Jun 21, 1993
84-51	Hoyt Wilhelm	49-11-14	Chris Cannizzaro	34-2-07	NL	LA	Jul 10, 1972 2G
83-295	Mike Flanagan	40-9-11	Rick Dempsey	43-0-14	AL	BAL	Sep 27, 1992
83-292	Fritz Ostermueller	40-11-5	Johnny Riddle	42-10-17	NL	PIT	Aug 20, 1948
83-135	Jesse Orosco	45-4-10	Chad Kreuter	38-0-5	NL	LA	Sep 1, 2002
83-135	Hoyt Wilhelm	49-1-21	Tom Haller	34-2-24	NL	LA	Sep 17, 1971
83-40	John Franco	44-0-16	Todd Zeile	39-0-24	NL	NY	Oct 3, 2004
83-30	Ellis Kinder	41-9-06	Walker Cooper	41-3-24	NL	STL	May 2, 1956
82-123	Don Sutton	42-5-25	Bob Boone	39-10-8	AL	CAL	Sep 27, 1987
82-93	Don Sutton	43-4-7	Rick Dempsey	38-10-26	NL	LA	Aug 9, 1988
82-58	Jesse Orosco	46-3-29	John Flaherty	35-9-29	AL	NY	Aug 20, 2003
82-51	Johnny Niggeling	42-2-11	Rick Ferrell	39-11-9	AL	WAS	Sep 21, 1945
81-339	Bobo Newsom	46-0-20	Ray Murray	35-10-19	AL	PHI	Aug 31, 1953
81-281	Danny Darwin	41-8-10	Tony Pena	40-1-1	AL	CHI	Jul 5, 1997
81-243	Jerry Reuss	40-1-5	Carlton Fisk	41-6-28	AL	CHI	Jul 24, 1989
81-229	Bobo Newsom	39-10-25	Rick Ferrell	41-8-24	AL	WAS	Jul 6, 1947 1G
81-220	Roger Clemens	44-1-25	Brad Ausmus	37-5-15	NL	HOU	Sep 29, 2006
81-208	Hoyt Wilhelm	48-1-13	Bob Tillman	33-5-15	NL	ATL	Sep 9, 1970
81-198	Lou Polli	42-11-22	Gus Mancuso	38-6-26	NL	NY	Jul 1, 1944
81-108	Jack Quinn	46-11-20	Cy Perkins	34-3-28	AL	PHI	Jun 25, 1930 2G
81-74	Pete Appleton	41-3-18	Rick Ferrell	39-10-26	AL	WAS	Sep 8, 1945
81-60	Dave Stieb	35-9-7	Carlton Fisk	45-4-3	AL	CHI	Apr 29, 1993
81-21	Emil "Dutch" Leonard	44-6-0	Clyde McCullough	36-6-21	NL	CHI	Sep 25, 1953
81-15	Charley Root	41-4-24	Gabby Hartnett	39-7-21	NL	CHI	Aug 11, 1940 1G
81-14	Jim Konstanty	39-5-10	Walker Cooper	41-7-04	NL	STL	Aug 12, 1956
81-12	Cy Young	44-5-19	Johnny Kling	36-6-23	NL	BOS	Sep 18, 1911 2G
81-1	John Franco	44-9-14	Brad Ausmus	36-2-17	NL	HOU	Jul 1, 2005

(735) Most Winning Games Played in, 1957-2006

1972	Pete Rose	1406	Rafael Palmeiro
1718	Carl Yastrzemski	1396	Dwight Evans
1623	Brooks Robinson	1391	Harold Baines
1601	Eddie Murray	1390	Paul Molitor
1585	Rickey Henderson	1382	Graig Nettles
1579	Reggie Jackson	1349	Dave Concepcion
1552	Barry Bonds	1333	Darrell Evans
1503	Tony Perez	1325	Steve Finley
1501	Cal Ripken	1320	Dave Parker
1494	Dave Winfield	1317	Willie Davis
1489	Hank Aaron	1313	Rusty Staub
1452	George Brett	1312	Lou Brock
1433	Robin Yount	1307	Willie McCovey
1422	Frank Robinson	1303	Tim Raines
1414	Craig Biggio	1301	Carlton Fisk
1412	Joe Morgan		

GEORGE BRACE

Mickey Mantle

(736) Most Losing Games Played in, 1957-2006

1633	Rusty Staub	1305	Barry Bonds
1589	Carl Yastrzemski	1300	Lou Brock
1583	Pete Rose	1294	Craig Biggio
1497	Cal Ripken	1294	Ted Simmons
1496	Rickey Henderson	1292	Paul Molitor
1478	Dave Winfield	1282	Bill Buckner
1437	Harold Baines	1282	Billy Williams
1424	Eddie Murray	1277	Willie McCovey
1423	Rafael Palmeiro	1275	Ozzie Smith
1422	Robin Yount	1270	Tony Perez
1374	Hank Aaron	1257	Buddy Bell
1350	Darrell Evans	1254	George Brett
1329	Andre Dawson	1248	Brooks Robinson
1318	Graig Nettles	1248	Tony Gwynn
1314	Gary Gaetti	1240	Reggie Jackson

(737) Highest Winning Percentage for Games in which They Appeared, 1957-2006 (min. 200 wins)

	WINS	LOSSES	PCT.		WINS	LOSSES	PCT.
Charles Gipson	261	112	.700	Mike Squires	462	314	.595
Frank Quilici	263	141	.651	Andruw Jones	953	653	.593
Sam Mejias	213	120	.640	Aaron Rowand	408	280	.593
So Taguchi	284	164	.634	Mark Ellis	294	204	.590
Paul Blair	1207	740	.620	Gil McDougald	308	215	.589
Tony Muser	409	252	.619	Rafael Furcal	574	401	.589
Jerry Zimmerman	294	186	.612	Jim Busby	270	189	.588
Sammy Esposito	288	184	.610	Frank Torre	352	250	.585
Hideki Matsui	326	211	.607	Jorge Posada	753	535	.585
Bill Plummer	222	145	.605	Bernie Williams	1211	862	.584
Derek Jeter	1014	663	.605	Mark Lemke	624	445	.584
Dick Tracewski	367	241	.604	Gerald Williams	677	489	.581
Cesar Geronimo	916	604	.603	Eric Chavez	678	488	.581
Tony Kubek	654	435	.601	Albert Pujols	541	392	.580
Lynn Jones	316	211	.600	Bobby Richardson	805	584	.580
Chipper Jones	1056	704	.600	David Justice	933	675	.580
Mark Belanger	1203	813	.597				

(738) Lowest Winning Percentage for Games in which They Appeared, 1957-2006 (min. 200 losses)

	WINS	LOSSES	PCT.		WINS	LOSSES	PCT.
Hawk Taylor	100	291	.256	Joe Christopher	208	425	.329
Elmer Valo	98	248	.283	Chip Hale	111	222	.333
Lou Klimchock	91	227	.286	Roger Freed	115	229	.334
Faye Throneberry	100	239	.295	Larry Stahl	245	484	.336
Neil Chrisley	89	211	.297	Manny Jimenez	143	283	.336
Winston Llenas	89	211	.297	Ron Brand	191	376	.337
John Stephenson	135	314	.301	Irv Noren	110	215	.338
Gene Locklear	88	204	.301	Mike de la Hoz	168	326	.340
Rod Kanehl	103	235	.305	Dave Philley	162	315	.340
Billy Bryan	115	258	.308	Eric Munson	106	204	.342
Bob Will	125	280	.309	Ron Stone	133	255	.343
Jesse Gonder	123	271	.312	Leron Lee	211	403	.344
Cito Gaston	326	700	.318	Don Mason	116	219	.346
Bobo Osborne	115	244	.320	Ivan Murrell	196	367	.348
Ray Jablonski	96	203	.321	Wallace Johnson	149	279	.348
Julio Becquer	154	319	.326	Jim Fairey	139	259	.349
Ray Webster	125	255	.329	Jim Beauchamp	137	256	.349

Cy Young

(739) Most Career Game-ending Outs, 1957-2006

150	Pete Rose	116	Darrell Evans	108	Todd Zeile
146	Ted Simmons	116	Gary Gaetti	108	Joe Carter
140	Rusty Staub	116	Julio Franco	107	Eddie Murray
139	Dave Winfield	115	Robin Yount	107	Reggie Jackson
137	Brooks Robinson	115	Chili Davis	107	Shawon Dunston
130	Carl Yastrzemski	114	Ernie Banks	107	Tony Perez
128	Graig Nettles	114	Larry Parrish	107	Dave Kingman
126	Cal Ripken	114	Buddy Bell	106	Al Oliver
126	B.J. Surhoff	113	Ruben Sierra	106	Hank Aaron
120	Rafael Palmeiro	112	Andre Dawson	106	Tim Wallach
120	Bill Mazeroski	111	Ron Fairly	106	Billy Williams
120	Paul Molitor	111	Rickey Henderson	106	George Brett
119	Tim Raines	110	Ozzie Smith	105	Jeff Burroughs
119	Harold Baines	109	Tony Phillips	105	Bill Buckner
117	Craig Biggio	109	Barry Bonds		
116	Lou Brock	108	Tony Taylor		

(740) Families with Three or More Brothers who Played in the Major Leagues

5	Delahanty	Ed, Frank Jim, Joe, Tom	3	Edwards	Dave, Marshall, Mike
4	O'Neill	Jim, Jack, Mike, Steve	3	High	Andy, Charlie, Hugh
3	Allen	Dick, Hank, Ron	3	Mansell	John, Mike, Tom
3	Alou	Felipe, Matty, Jesus	3	Molina	Bengie, Jose, Yadier
3	Boyer	Ken, Clete, Cloyd	3	Paciorek	Jim, John, Tom
3	Clarkson	Dad, John, Walter	3	Perez	Melido, Pascual, Carlos
3	Cross	Amos, Frank, Lave	3	Sadowski	Ed, Bob, Ted
3	Cruz	Tommy, Hector, Jose Sr.	3	Sewell	Luke, Joe, Tom
3	DiMaggio	Joe, Dom, Vince	3	Sowders	John, Len, Bill
3	Drew	J.D., Stephen, Tim	3	Wright	George, Harry, Sam

LIST INDEX

List Index

Pitching Records

Fielding Records

Miscellaneous Records

PLAYER INDEX

Player Index

A

Aaron, Hank, 001, 002, 004, 006, 008, 010, 012, 015, 017, 018, 020, 022, 024, 032, 038, 040, 042, 044, 050, 052, 054, 056, 058, 060, 062, 064, 071, 076, 079, 081, 083, 086, 087, 088, 089, 090, 093, 097, 099, 110, 115, 118, 119, 120, 122, 127, 128, 129, 135, 136, 137, 138, 156, 191, 221, 239, 241, 244, 246, 286, 288, 290, 323, 328, 329, 330, 331, 332, 339, 341, 367, 369, 569, 571, 703, 730, 730, 735, 736, 739

Aaron, Tommie, 156, 339

Abbaticchio, Ed, 615

Abbott, Kyle, 521

Abernathy, Ted, 420, 446, 447, 487, 489

Abreu, Bobby, 034, 035, 039, 042, 043, 075, 080, 092, 094, 200, 256, 263, 282, 286, 730

Acker, Tom, 532

Adair, Jerry, 596, 599

Adams, Babe, 393, 395, 396, 424, 440, 444, 499, 504, 505, 634, 636, 708

Adams, Bobby, 154, 650

Adams, Buster, 067, 263

Adams, Sparky, 072, 196, 293, 600

Adams, Terry, 167, 532, 731

Adcock, Joe, 040, 071, 099, 101, 104, 115, 158, 164, 172, 331, 533, 549, 550, 730

Agbayani, Benny, 174

Agee, Tommie, 146, 172, 646, 730

Agnew, Sam, 046, 629

Agosto, Juan, 446, 448

Aguayo, Luis, 533

Aguilera, Rick, 371, 372, 398, 399, 419

Aguirre, Hank, 049

Aikens, Willie, 168

Ainsmith, Eddie, 576, 578, 581

Alexander, Dale, 191, 267, 357, 656, 660, 661, 664, 666, 667, 668, 670, 671

Alexander, Doyle, 375, 416, 436, 583

Alexander, Gary, 251, 627

Alexander, Grover, 159, 374, 375, 377, 378, 380, 381, 383, 384, 386, 387, 389, 390, 392, 393, 395, 396, 406, 407, 412, 413, 414, 415, 416, 424, 430, 431, 432, 433, 434, 440, 444, 450, 451, 457, 458, 461, 462, 471, 472, 475, 476, 483, 499, 504, 505, 510, 520, 522, 529, 530, 582, 585, 586, 634, 636, 687, 689, 690, 691, 692, 693

Alexander, Matt, 014

Alfonseca, Antonio, 478, 479

Alfonzo, Edgardo, 164, 172, 599

Alicea, Luis, 172, 597

Allanson, Andy, 627

Allen, Dick, 038, 040, 042, 044, 074, 076, 083, 099, 117, 155, 306, 339, 604, 605, 656, 660, 664, 666, 670, 671, 730, 740

Allen, Frank, 731

Allen, Hank, 339, 740

Allen, Johnny, 389, 390, 429, 469, 523, 676

Allen, Neil, 147

Allen, Ron, 339, 740

Alley, Gene, 616, 730

Allison, Bob, 115, 344, 663, 674

Almada, Mel, 172, 283

Almanzar, Carlos, 343

Almon, Bill, 612

Alomar Jr., Sandy, 161, 280, 281, 339, 575, 577, 579

Alomar Sr., Sandy, 131, 179, 182, 187, 359, 730

Alomar, Roberto, 005, 009, 013, 021, 022, 025, 029, 033, 037, 041, 045, 053, 057, 061, 065, 077, 082, 090, 094, 100, 105, 123, 154, 202, 212, 227, 232, 237, 242, 247, 339, 356, 551, 552, 553, 555, 556, 596, 598, 599, 640, 641

Alou, Felipe, 124, 156, 165, 181, 191, 279, 294, 337, 339, 730, 740

Alou, Jesus, 156, 339, 730, 740

Alou, Matty, 156, 179, 180, 184, 185, 189, 190, 194, 195, 305, 339, 730, 740

Alou, Moises, 040, 044, 129, 306, 337, 358

Altizer, Dave, 172

Bottomley, Jim, 023, 027, 031, 039, 051, 059, 130, 162, 163, 189, 190, 239, 240, 260, 358, 367, 545, 547, 548, 550, 587, 594

Bouchee, Ed, 146

Boudreau, Lou, 036, 066, 094, 161, 358, 565, 567, 568, 616

Bouton, Jim, 167

Bowa, Larry, 005, 009, 013, 021, 029, 065, 182, 197, 293, 563, 564, 565, 567, 568, 610, 613, 614

Bowerman, Frank, 576, 578, 580, 581, 633

Bowman, Bob, 366

Boyd, Oil Can, 638

Boyer, Clete, 048, 156, 339, 557, 558, 559, 561, 562, 607, 609, 730, 740

Boyer, Cloyd, 740

Boyer, Ken, 106, 126, 156, 302, 339, 369, 557, 558, 559, 560, 562, 605, 609, 730, 740

Boyle, Ed, 085

Boyle, Henry, 148, 405, 440, 470, 502, 686

Boyle, Jack, 160, 361

Bradley, Bill, 162, 172, 204, 206, 533, 558, 559, 560, 730

Bradley, George, 392, 393, 405, 437, 440, 445, 449, 456, 460, 464, 470, 474, 502, 527, 584, 638, 677, 679, 680, 681, 682, 685, 686

Bradley, Hugh, 730

Bradley, Phil, 147

Brain, Dave, 162

Branca, Ralph, 146

Brand, Ron, 738

Brandt, Ed, 388, 423, 467, 688

Bransfield, Kitty, 292, 548, 662

Brantley, Jeff, 343, 399, 478, 479

Branyan, Russ, 730

Braun, Steve, 363

Braxton, Garland, 488

Brazle, Al, 532

Bream, Sid, 365, 366, 593

Brecheen, Harry, 147, 391, 394, 443, 477, 511, 532, 585

Breeden, Hal, 308

Breitenstein, Ted, 377, 379, 382, 388, 404, 450, 452, 454, 457, 459, 463, 465, 467, 491, 493, 513, 517, 583, 638, 684

Bresnahan, Roger, 036, 576, 578, 581, 717

Brett, George, 001, 002, 003, 006, 007, 010, 011, 015, 018, 019, 022, 023, 050, 051, 054, 055, 058, 059, 062, 063, 070, 071, 080, 083, 086, 089, 094, 098, 129, 130, 138, 155, 209, 210, 220, 225, 259, 260, 264, 280, 281, 283, 331, 332, 339, 557, 558, 560, 562, 605, 607, 646, 703, 704, 708, 709, 730, 735, 736, 739

Brett, Ken, 339, 731

Brewer, Jim, 400, 418, 435, 532, 646

Brewer, Tom, 146

Bridges, Tommy, 402, 403, 543, 704

Bridwell, Al, 566, 730

Briggs, Button, 634, 636

Briggs, John, 148

Briley, Greg, 148, 155

Brinkman, Ed, 047, 048, 361, 563, 564, 567, 568, 610, 613, 614

Britton, Gil, 085

Broaca, Johnny, 049

Broberg, Pete, 731

Brock, Lou, 001, 002, 003, 006, 007, 010, 011, 015, 018, 019, 023, 027, 054, 055, 063, 074, 075, 089, 090, 091, 093, 124, 172, 179, 180, 185, 287, 305, 369, 569, 571, 572, 618, 619, 640, 648, 655, 730, 735, 736, 739

Brockett, Lew, 731

Brodie, Steve, 078, 178, 194, 195, 264, 574

Broglio, Ernie, 532

Brogna, Rico, 589, 592, 593, 730

Brohamer, Jack, 730

Brosius, Scott, 146

Brosnan, Jim, 147

Brouthers, Dan, 023, 026, 027, 030, 031, 034, 035, 039, 042, 043, 051, 055, 078, 086, 095, 096, 127, 164, 172, 183, 188, 193, 198, 203, 204, 205, 208, 213, 218, 223, 228, 233, 235, 238, 243, 254, 264, 335, 545, 547, 548, 701

Brower, Jim, 446, 447, 487

Brown, Buster, 466

Brown, Carroll, 535

Brown, Eddie, 131, 196

Brown, Gates, 101, 167, 363, 366, 710, 711, 712, 713, 714, 715

Brown, Jimmy, 197

Brown, Kevin, 375, 406, 407, 410, 415, 416, 428, 438, 583, 635, 638, 731

Clarkson, Walter, 740

Clayton, Royce, 563, 564, 565, 567, 568, 613

Clear, Mark, 418, 485, 486

Clemens, Roger, 374, 375, 380, 381, 383, 384, 389, 390, 395, 396, 402, 403, 406, 407, 409, 410, 413, 414, 415, 416, 424, 425, 426, 428, 429, 432, 433, 434, 436, 437, 438, 439, 441, 442, 468, 469, 495, 496, 500, 510, 511, 516, 523, 530, 536, 538, 583, 634, 636, 734

Clement, Matt, 049, 507

Clemente, Roberto, 001, 002, 004, 008, 010, 012, 015, 018, 020, 024, 026, 028, 032, 052, 056, 060, 062, 064, 070, 071, 083, 086, 089, 090, 091, 130, 147, 155, 162, 259, 569, 570, 571, 704, 708, 716

Clements, Jack, 576, 578

Clendenon, Donn, 126, 307, 590, 591, 595

Cleveland, Reggie, 148

Clift, Harlond, 036, 081, 092, 234, 236, 557, 558, 559, 560, 562, 607, 609, 666

Cline, Monk, 171

Cline, Ty, 730

Clingman, Billy, 730

Clinton, Lou, 730

Cloninger, Tony, 150, 163, 507, 635, 731

Clontz, Brad, 447, 731

Clymer, Bill, 085

Clymer, Otis, 730

Coan, Gil, 173

Coates, Jim, 532

Cobb, George, 464, 678, 682, 684, 685

Cobb, Ty, 001, 002, 003, 006, 007, 010, 011, 015, 016, 017, 018, 019, 022, 023, 026, 027, 030, 031, 034, 035, 039, 042, 043, 050, 051, 054, 055, 058, 059, 062, 063, 079, 080, 086, 087, 089, 090, 091, 093, 094, 095, 096, 125, 138, 164, 172, 189, 190, 195, 204, 205, 209, 210, 214, 215, 234, 235, 265, 266, 267, 269, 272, 273, 274, 275, 279, 280, 281, 283, 309, 332, 358, 569, 570, 571, 572, 574, 623, 640, 642, 648, 655, 703, 730

Cochrane, Mickey, 030, 031, 034, 035, 043, 277, 575, 580, 668

Coffey, Todd, 447, 731

Colavito, Rocky, 040, 081, 099, 110, 114, 118, 142, 151, 158, 164, 172, 321, 323, 328, 329, 330, 617, 620

Colbert, Nate, 073, 114

Colborn, Jim, 634, 636

Colbrun, Greg, 365

Colcolough, Tom, 512

Cole, Alex, 643

Cole, King, 468, 469, 676, 687, 696, 731

Coleman Jr., Joe, 492, 731

Coleman, Dave, 085

Coleman, Ed, 364

Coleman, Jerry, 602

Coleman, John, 445, 464, 678, 679, 680, 682, 685

Coleman, Vince, 029, 197, 237, 283, 293, 640, 641, 648, 655, 666, 700

Collins, Dave, 172, 207, 648

Collins, Eddie, 001, 002, 003, 006, 007, 010, 011, 015, 018, 019, 026, 027, 030, 031, 034, 035, 051, 054, 055, 063, 068, 070, 079, 080, 086, 089, 090, 093, 095, 190, 194, 195, 357, 551, 552, 553, 554, 556, 601, 640, 642, 643, 644, 648, 702, 730

Collins, Hub, 233, 236, 654

Collins, Jimmy, 557, 558, 559, 560, 607, 608, 608

Collins, Ray, 473

Collins, Rip, 015

Collins, Ripper, 172, 192, 202, 212, 222, 227, 232, 237, 242, 247, 277, 314

Collins, Shano, 028

Colon, Bartolo, 390, 409, 410, 514, 518

Coluccio, Bob, 155

Combs, Earle, 027, 030, 031, 034, 035, 096, 162, 172, 189, 190, 204, 205, 235, 660, 666, 668, 669

Comiskey, Charlie, 188, 193, 233, 236, 548, 647, 654

Comorosky, Adam, 204, 206

Concepcion, Dave, 001, 004, 008, 020, 068, 071, 563, 564, 565, 567, 568, 704, 735

Conde, Ramon, 085

Cone, David, 403, 406, 407, 409, 410, 437, 439, 441, 442, 468, 469, 496, 500, 536

Conigliaro, Billy, 156

Conigliaro, Tony, 156, 340

Conine, Jeff, 730

Conlan, Jocko, 707

Conley, Gene, 166

Connally, Sarge, 147

Connaughton, Frank, 172

Gettman, Jake, 279

Getzien, Charlie, 401, 405, 527, 529, 686

Giambi, Jason, 034, 035, 038, 039, 042, 043, 075, 078, 092, 098, 128, 147, 156, 172, 214, 215, 220, 225, 240, 255, 256, 300, 307, 328, 329, 339

Giambi, Jeremy, 156, 339

Gibson, Bob, 102, 146, 362, 375, 380, 381, 383, 384, 395, 396, 402, 403, 406, 407, 409, 410, 413, 414, 415, 426, 432, 439, 441, 442, 444, 471, 472, 475, 476, 482, 483, 496, 504, 505, 511, 522, 523, 530, 583, 586, 704, 731

Gibson, George, 576, 578, 580, 581, 629, 632

Gibson, Kirk, 075, 144, 299, 641, 649

Gilbert, Billy, 554, 730

Gilbert, Pete, 248, 253

Giles, Brian, 034, 035, 038, 039, 042, 043, 147, 172, 255, 256, 339, 730

Giles, Marcus, 161, 201, 279, 339

Gilkey, Bernard, 152, 172

Gill, George, 521

Gillenwater, Carden, 622

Gilliam, Jim, 021, 037, 057, 065, 082, 207, 237, 646, 656, 658, 662, 666

Gilligan, Barney, 046

Ginter, Keith, 659

Gipson, Charles, 014, 737

Girardi, Joe, 577, 579

Gladden, Dan, 152, 165, 168

Glade, Fred, 465, 466, 690, 691

Glanville, Doug, 152, 179, 181, 186, 573, 641, 649, 730

Glasscock, Jack, 188, 193, 198, 243, 263, 563, 564, 566

Glaus, Troy, 073, 106, 302, 319, 356, 605

Glavine , Tom, 373, 374, 376, 380, 382, 383, 385, 388, 391, 402, 404, 406, 408, 413, 414, 415, 416, 436, 583, 585, 586, 731

Gleason, Bill, 178, 193, 233, 566

Gleason, Kid, 021, 029, 057, 197, 401, 405, 450, 451, 457, 458, 491, 492, 513, 551, 552, 553, 554, 638, 701

Glockson, Norm, 085

Gochnaur, John, 361

Goldsmith, Fred, 176, 389, 390, 393, 440, 470, 524

Gomez, Chris, 343, 567

Gomez, Lefty, 379, 385, 389, 391, 404, 427, 443, 463, 468, 469, 510

Gomez, Luis, 046, 650

Gomez, Ruben, 731

Gonder, Jesse, 738

Gonzalez, Alex, 146

Gonzalez, Alex S., 107, 302, 567, 616

Gonzalez, Juan, 038, 040, 042, 044, 052, 060, 088, 097, 099, 111, 122, 128, 134, 142, 201, 221, 229, 231, 239, 241, 246, 264, 291, 321, 328, 329, 330, 356, 730

Gonzalez, Luis, 022, 023, 051, 058, 059, 063, 070, 075, 078, 080, 083, 094, 098, 108, 154, 185, 199, 200, 220, 225, 230, 239, 240, 244, 245, 271, 280, 281, 303, 304, 311, 312, 321, 327, 331, 356, 569, 617, 620, 730

Gonzalez, Mike, 646

Gonzalez, Tony, 573

Good, Wilbur, 646

Gooden, Dwight, 389, 390, 406, 407, 409, 410, 426, 433, 468, 469, 471, 472, 495, 496, 500, 510, 523, 693

Goodman, Billy, 669

Goodman, Ival, 139, 662

Goodwin, Tom, 154, 573, 700

Gordon, Joe, 105, 318, 356, 551, 552, 553, 554, 556

Gordon, Sid, 175, 300, 307, 368, 674

Gordon, Tom, 371, 372, 399, 409, 410, 447, 478, 479

Gore, George, 055, 160, 208, 233, 235, 254, 570, 572, 574

Gorman, Tom, 343

Gosger, Jim, 155

Goslin, Goose, 003, 007, 011, 019, 022, 023, 026, 027, 031, 039, 043, 050, 051, 055, 058, 059, 062, 063, 086, 088, 090, 108, 130, 142, 151, 263, 267, 280, 281, 299, 307, 356, 569, 570, 571, 572, 574, 730

Gossage, Goose, 371, 372, 398, 399, 409, 410, 416, 417, 418, 419, 420, 439, 441, 442, 485, 486, 488, 489

Gowdy, Hank, 576

Grabarkewitz, Billy, 172, 658

Grace, Mark, 022, 023, 068, 080, 143, 199, 200, 545, 546, 547, 549, 550, 589, 593

Grady, Mike, 581

Graham, Jack, 590

Granderson, Curtis, 249, 250

Graney, Jack, 730

Granger, Wayne, 146, 446, 447, 487, 488, 489, 675

Grant, Eddie, 646

Grant, Mudcat, 146, 447, 489

Grantham, George, 035, 172, 554

Graves, Danny, 398, 399

Gray, Dolly, 731

Gray, Sam, 465, 466

Grba, Eli, 731

Green, Danny, 623

Green, Dick, 555

Green, Gene, 674

Green, Lenny, 154, 730

Green, Shawn, 039, 075, 098, 110, 158, 164, 172, 200, 240, 245, 283, 286, 295, 312, 323, 328, 617, 620

Greenberg, Hank, 032, 034, 036, 038, 040, 042, 044, 052, 094, 099, 128, 129, 151, 172, 199, 201, 221, 226, 229, 231, 236, 239, 241, 244, 246, 264, 267, 282, 288, 291, 304, 306, 311, 313, 317, 321, 327, 328, 356, 357, 367

Greene, Tommy, 731

Greengrass, Jim, 067, 161, 667

Greenwell, Mike, 163, 668, 670

Greer, Rusty, 154, 356

Gregg, Hal, 498

Gregg, Tommy, 308

Gregg, Vean, 473, 676, 687, 696, 731

Gremminger, Ed, 608

Grich, Bobby, 081, 105, 126, 146, 318, 551, 552, 553, 555, 556, 596, 599, 601, 602

Grieve, Ben, 250, 368, 661

Griffey Jr., Ken, 038, 039, 042, 043, 050, 051, 055, 058, 059, 062, 063, 074, 075, 080, 083, 088, 097, 098, 109, 115, 120, 122, 133, 134, 151, 157, 168, 172, 220, 229, 230, 239, 240, 244, 245, 259, 264, 284, 290, 297, 304, 311, 312, 322, 327, 328, 329, 330, 331, 337, 340, 356, 367, 569, 571, 730

Griffey Sr., Ken, 157, 332, 337, 649

Griffin, Alfredo, 021, 029, 048, 182, 207, 563, 564, 565, 568, 616

Griffin, Ivy, 268

Griffin, Mike, 055, 087, 152, 172, 198, 233, 235, 254, 276, 283, 570, 572, 574, 621, 623, 640, 654, 665, 699

Griffin, Sandy, 672

Griffin, Tom, 635, 693

Griffith, Bert, 338

Griffith, Clark, 362, 377, 378, 384, 390, 413, 428, 509, 513, 582, 705, 706, 731, 734

Grim, Bob, 159, 676, 687

Grim, John, 581, 633

Grimes , Ray, 271, 277, 668, 669

Grimes, Burleigh, 362, 375, 377, 378, 380, 381, 383, 384, 386, 387, 402, 403, 413, 414, 415, 416, 455, 540, 542, 582, 584, 586, 639

Grimm, Charlie, 068, 281, 292, 545, 546, 547, 548, 549, 550

Grissom, Marquis, 004, 068, 109, 181, 569, 571, 573, 641, 646, 648, 655, 730

Groat, Dick, 071, 179, 181, 196, 357, 563, 564, 565, 566, 568, 612, 616

Groh, Heinie, 148, 559, 561, 562, 603, 606

Groom, Bob, 465, 466, 688, 731

Groom, Buddy, 371, 373, 417, 448

Gross, Greg, 283, 363, 672

Gross, Wayne, 342, 343

Grote, Jerry, 146, 575, 577, 579

Groth, Johnny, 573, 650

Grove, Lefty, 102, 376, 377, 379, 380, 382, 383, 385, 388, 389, 391, 394, 397, 402, 404, 406, 408, 413, 414, 415, 429, 461, 463, 468, 469, 493, 510, 520, 523, 528, 529, 634, 636, 731

Grubb, Johnny, 146

Gruber, Henry, 401, 490, 534

Gruber, Kelly, 730

Grudzielanek, Mark, 154, 199, 201, 596, 599

Guante, Cecilio, 147

Guardado, Eddie, 371, 373, 398, 400, 417, 446, 448, 478, 480, 731

Guerrero, Pedro, 044, 605

Guerrero, Vladimir, 030, 032, 036, 038, 040, 042, 044, 083, 088, 091, 099, 110, 118, 128, 129, 156, 163, 221, 246, 259, 280, 281, 286, 304, 323, 329, 339, 618, 619

Guerrero, Wilton, 156, 339

Guidry, Ron, 385, 389, 391, 408, 411, 443, 463, 468, 469, 473, 475, 477, 484, 504, 506, 511, 536, 585

Guillen, Carlos, 123, 202, 730

Guillen, Jose, 294, 307

Guillen, Ozzie, 563, 564, 567, 568, 614

Gulan, Mike, 085

Gullett, Don, 146, 389, 391

Gullickson, Bill, 514, 536

Gulliver, Glenn, 084

Hooper, Bob, 639

Hooper, Harry, 003, 007, 019, 026, 027, 055, 080, 112, 148, 152, 165, 172, 569, 570, 574, 624

Hopkins, Marty, 084

Horlen, Joe, 483, 505, 731

Horner, Bob, 158, 164, 294, 306

Hornsby, Rogers, 010, 012, 017, 020, 022, 024, 026, 028, 030, 032, 034, 036, 038, 040, 042, 044, 050, 052, 054, 056, 058, 060, 062, 064, 081, 086, 090, 091, 094, 105, 118, 125, 129, 130, 172, 174, 189, 191, 206, 209, 211, 214, 216, 219, 221, 224, 226, 229, 231, 234, 236, 239, 241, 244, 246, 264, 266, 267, 269, 270, 271, 272, 273, 274, 275, 276, 279, 280, 281, 282, 288, 318, 332, 356, 358, 551, 552, 553, 554, 556, 600

Hornung, Joe, 160, 173, 248, 572

Horton, Tony, 146, 299, 730

Horton, Willie, 066, 111, 126, 331, 667, 710, 711, 712, 713, 714, 715

Hotaling, Pete, 572

Houck, Byron, 498

Houck, Sadie, 162

Hough, Charlie, 146, 371, 372, 380, 381, 386, 387, 402, 403, 406, 407, 416, 424, 428, 436, 437, 439, 441, 442, 486, 488, 489, 701, 702, 731

Houk, Ralph, 706

Howard, Elston, 307, 334, 342, 343, 579, 625, 628, 630

Howard, Frank, 040, 044, 074, 076, 083, 097, 099, 126, 134, 255, 257, 259, 284, 299, 328, 342, 343, 368, 730

Howard, Ryan, 220, 229, 230, 245, 249, 250, 259, 299, 311, 312, 317, 327

Howard, Thomas, 154, 730

Howell, Harry, 393, 423, 582, 637, 638

Howell, Jack, 299, 308

Howell, Jay, 399

Howell, Ken, 486, 507

Howell, Roy, 163

Howry, Bob, 446, 447, 487

Howser, Dick, 186, 612, 656, 658, 666

Hoy, Dummy, 055, 078, 080, 087, 172, 183, 193, 233, 254, 570, 572, 574, 640, 699, 730

Hoyt, La Marr, 499

Hoyt, Waite, 381, 384, 387, 416

Hrabosky, Al, 418, 485

Hrbek, Kent, 545, 546, 549, 550, 673

Hubbard, Glenn, 552, 555, 556, 600

Hubbard, Trenidad, 152

Hubbell, Bill, 646

Hubbell, Carl, 376, 379, 382, 383, 385, 388, 389, 391, 394, 397, 408, 413, 415, 429, 463, 468, 473, 475, 477, 506, 511, 522, 523, 586, 704, 708

Hubbs, Ken, 656, 657, 674

Hudler, Rex, 154, 165

Hudlin, Willis, 586, 639

Hudson, Charles, 049

Hudson, Johnny, 674

Hudson, Nat, 638

Hudson, Orlando, 172

Hudson, Tim, 389, 390

Huggins, Miller, 021, 037, 082, 162, 172, 217, 237, 258, 551, 552, 553, 554, 600, 730

Hughes, Dick, 676

Hughes, Jay, 461, 462, 468, 528, 531, 687, 690, 692

Hughes, Mickey, 524, 677, 682

Hughes, Roy, 172, 293

Hughes, Tom J., 466, 528, 688, 690, 692, 693, 695, 698, 731

Hughes, Tom L., 469, 731

Hughey, Jim, 465, 466, 509

Hulse, David, 730

Hume, Tom, 488, 489

Humphries, Bert, 731

Humphries, Johnny, 146

Hundley, Randy, 337, 579, 630, 632

Hundley, Todd, 073, 100, 103, 123, 174, 222, 232, 242, 252, 314, 316, 337, 577, 579, 632, 730

Hunt, Ron, 078, 172, 253

Hunter, Brian L., 165, 186, 641, 730

Hunter, Catfish, 362, 375, 384, 395, 396, 407, 413, 436, 439, 440, 441, 442, 455, 483, 504, 505, 514, 528, 731

Hunter, Torii, 573, 622

Hunter, Willard, 532

Hurst, Bruce, 376, 408, 411

Hurst, Don, 230, 356

Huskey, Butch, 342, 343

Husting, Bert, 731

Lee, Manuel, 613

Lee, Thornton, 379, 455, 646

Lee, Travis, 166, 549, 589, 592

Lee, Watty, 695, 731

Leever, Sam, 389, 390, 392, 393, 396, 444, 457, 458, 466, 687, 688, 689, 690, 692, 695

Lefebvre, Bill, 149

Lefebvre, Joe, 299

Lefferts, Craig, 159, 373, 400, 419, 446, 448

LeFlore, Ron, 181, 186, 280, 281, 640, 648, 655

Lehane, Mike, 248

Leiber, Hank, 175, 357

Leibrandt, Charlie, 148

Leifield, Lefty, 392, 394, 397, 443, 444, 473, 477, 544

Leiter, Al, 049, 376, 402, 404, 408, 409, 411, 428, 443, 731

Lemanczyk, Dave, 507

Lemaster, Denny, 411, 507

LeMaster, Johnnie, 047

Lemke, Mark, 737

Lemon, Bob, 102, 315, 390, 402, 403, 413, 414, 475, 476, 528, 583, 586, 639, 704

Lemon, Chet, 078, 571, 622

Lemon, Jim, 175

Lenhardt, Don, 658

Lennox, Ed, 730

Leonard, Emil Dutch, 387, 416, 532, 734

Leonard, Hubert "Dutch", 379, 394, 397, 443, 444, 471, 473, 477, 482, 484, 504, 506, 515

Lerchen, Dutch, 085

Leslie, Sam, 067, 364

Leverenz, Walt, 521

Lewis, Allan, 014

Lewis, Buddy, 016, 180, 185, 666

Lewis, Darren, 148, 172, 573, 617, 620

Lewis, Duffy, 292, 570, 624, 730

Lewis, Ed, 528

Lewis, Jack, 162

Lewis, Ted, 687, 690, 695

Libke, Al, 673

Lidge, Brad, 447, 675

Lieber, Jon, 499, 503

Lieberthal, Mike, 316, 577, 579, 628, 630

Ligtenberg, Kerry, 675

Lillie, Jim, 248, 361, 621

Lima, Jose, 503, 512, 731, 514

Lind, Carl, 656, 657, 661, 666

Lind, Jose, 555, 596, 599

Lindaman, Vive, 466, 688, 689, 690, 692, 695

Lindblad, Paul, 373, 418, 420

Lindell, Johnny, 161, 498, 622

Lindstrom, Freddie, 016, 032, 172, 189, 191, 196, 211

Lintz, Larry, 700

Linzy, Frank, 418, 419, 485, 486

Lipon, Johnny, 176, 616

Lisenbee, Hod, 539, 541, 701

Listach, Pat, 154, 700, 730

Littleton, Larry, 085, 359

Litton, Greg, 174

Litwhiler, Danny, 617, 620, 673

Llenas, Winston, 738

Lloyd, Graeme, 343, 446, 448, 487

Lo Duca, Paul, 146, 630

Loaiza, Esteban, 167

Lock, Don, 738

Lockhart, Keith, 342, 343

Locklear, Gene, 738

Lockman, Whitey, 154, 165

Lockwood, Skip, 486

Lofton, Kenny, 055, 124, 165, 172, 180, 185, 276, 335, 571, 617, 620, 640, 641, 643, 655, 700, 730

Lolich, Mickey, 376, 379, 382, 385, 388, 395, 397, 404, 406, 408, 409, 411, 426, 433, 436, 438, 443, 450, 452, 455, 457, 459, 463, 467, 495, 497, 514, 710, 711, 712, 713, 714, 715

Lolich, Ron, 147

Lollar, Sherm, 078, 575, 577, 579

Lombardi, Ernie, 032, 068, 071, 103, 161, 308, 368, 575, 578, 580, 581

Loney, James, 163

Long, Dale, 284, 590, 591, 730

Manning, Jack, 572, 621

Manning, Rick, 622

Mansell, John, 740

Mansell, Mike, 740

Mansell, Tom, 740

Mantilla, Felix, 139

Mantle, Mickey, 001, 005, 009, 013, 021, 033, 034, 037, 038, 041, 042, 045, 050, 053, 054, 057, 058, 061, 062, 065, 074, 077, 079, 082, 087, 092, 097, 100, 109, 115, 117, 119, 122, 123, 135, 137, 212, 214, 217, 219, 222, 224, 227, 232, 237, 242, 247, 255, 258, 262, 266, 290, 302, 304, 311, 314, 322, 327, 328, 329, 330, 331, 333, 334, 340, 358, 569, 571, 641, 704, 730

Manush, Heinie, 011, 019, 023, 026, 027, 030, 031, 086, 091, 094, 180, 189, 190, 200, 267, 280, 281, 358, 659

Manwaring, Kirt, 625, 628

Maranville, Rabbit, 001, 002, 004, 006, 008, 012, 018, 020, 026, 028, 056, 172, 181, 184, 186, 206, 293, 563, 564, 565, 566, 568, 600, 614, 615, 730

Marberry, Firpo, 389, 390

Marchildon, Phil, 698

Marcum, Johnny, 531

Marichal, Juan, 146, 159, 381, 383, 384, 389, 390, 395, 396, 406, 407, 413, 432, 433, 436, 438, 440, 455, 475, 476, 503, 504, 505, 511, 530, 538, 583, 731

Marion, Marty, 565, 568

Maris, Roger, 114, 115, 132, 141, 154, 230, 261, 284, 297, 311, 312, 323, 325, 326, 327, 333, 334

Maroth, Mike, 467

Marquard, Rube, 376, 379, 382, 385, 388, 394, 397, 404, 408, 429, 463, 467, 471, 473, 523, 528, 529, 731

Marr, Lefty, 665, 669, 672

Marrero, Connie, 424

Marshall, Mike A., 650

Marshall, Mike G., 372, 398, 399, 417, 418, 419, 420, 446, 447, 485, 486, 487, 488, 489

Marshall, Willard, 617, 620

Martin, Al, 172

Martin, Billy, 705, 706

Martin, Hershel, 666

Martin, J. C., 511, 581, 633

Martin, Russell, 146

Martin, Tom, 448

Martinez, Buck, 047, 113

Martinez, Dave, 335

Martinez, Dennis, 374, 375, 380, 381, 383, 384, 387, 402, 403, 406, 407, 415, 416, 428, 432, 436, 583, 586, 731

Martinez, Edgar, 022, 024, 032, 034, 036, 040, 042, 044, 060, 064, 079, 081, 086, 094, 111, 115, 129, 151, 172, 199, 201, 214, 216, 226, 231, 257, 300, 324, 356, 704

Martinez, Pedro, 049, 389, 390, 406, 407, 409, 410, 426, 428, 438, 439, 440, 441, 442, 468, 469, 482, 483, 495, 496, 500, 503, 504, 505, 510, 538

Martinez, Ramon, 155

Martinez, Ramon J., 410, 536

Martinez, Tino, 051, 075, 098, 104, 172, 230, 317, 356, 545, 546, 547, 549, 550, 592

Martinez, Tippy, 400

Mason, Jim, 046, 161

Mason, Roger, 486

Matheny, Mike, 577, 579, 625, 628

Mathews, Bobby, 377, 378, 412, 440, 464, 502, 584, 638, 678, 679, 680, 682, 685, 405

Mathews, Eddie, 007, 039, 043, 051, 055, 058, 059, 062, 063, 070, 074, 075, 079, 080, 097, 098, 106, 115, 122, 134, 135, 136, 146, 240, 312, 319, 328, 329, 330, 331, 557, 558, 559, 560, 561, 562, 605, 717, 730

Mathews, Mike, 448

Mathewson, Christy, 374, 375, 377, 378, 380, 381, 383, 384, 387, 389, 390, 392, 393, 395, 396, 406, 407, 412, 413, 414, 415, 430, 434, 438, 440, 444, 450, 451, 457, 458, 461, 462, 471, 472, 475, 476, 496, 499, 503, 504, 505, 507, 510, 522, 528, 529, 530, 582, 583, 637, 645, 687, 689, 690, 692, 693, 698, 731

Mathewson, Henry, 535

Matlack, Jon, 015, 394, 397, 408, 477

Matranga, Dave, 167

Matsu, Hideki, 172, 661, 667, 674, 737

Matsui, Kaz, 148, 149, 165

Mattern, Al, 688, 692, 695, 731

Matthews Jr., Gary, 202, 337

Matthews Sr., Gary, 068, 337

Mattimore, Mike, 529

Mattingly, Don, 083, 094, 172, 179, 180, 185, 189, 190, 199, 200, 230, 240, 245, 284, 291, 300, 545, 546, 547, 549, 550, 589, 592

Maul, Al, 501, 528

McGinnis, Jumbo, 440, 508, 677, 682

McGinnity, Joe, 377, 378, 383, 384, 389, 390, 392, 393, 412, 413, 414, 422, 428, 450, 451, 454, 457, 458, 461, 462, 468, 472, 475, 476, 509, 518, 520, 523, 528, 582, 584, 645, 687, 689, 690, 692, 695, 697, 731, 734

McGlothlin, Jim, 731

McGlynn, Stoney, 465, 466

McGraw, John, 078, 209, 210, 214, 215, 234, 235, 560, 655, 705, 706, 730

McGraw, Tug, 371, 373, 394, 398, 400, 411, 416, 417, 418, 419, 420, 435, 441, 443

McGregor, Scott, 585

McGriff, Fred, 001, 003, 007, 039, 043, 050, 051, 055, 058, 059, 062, 063, 069, 070, 071, 074, 075, 079, 080, 083, 088, 097, 098, 104, 122, 135, 137, 145, 151, 168, 259, 263, 296, 329, 330, 331, 545, 546, 547, 548, 550, 730

McGuire, Deacon, 575, 576, 577, 578, 580, 581, 629, 633, 701, 730

McGwire, Mark, 036, 038, 040, 042, 044, 052, 060, 073, 074, 076, 079, 081, 083, 097, 099, 104, 115, 119, 120, 122, 132, 133, 134, 135, 142, 172, 175, 216, 219, 221, 224, 226, 229, 231, 241, 246, 255, 257, 259, 262, 263, 296, 297, 298, 302, 303, 304, 311, 313, 317, 325, 326, 327, 328, 329, 330, 333, 336, 545, 546, 547, 549, 550, 663, 664, 667, 670, 671

McHale, Marty, 015

McHenry, Austin, 067

McInnis, Stuffy, 012, 020, 032, 086, 196, 545, 546, 547, 548, 549, 550, 589, 592, 594

McIntire, Harry, 465, 466, 509, 688, 692, 695, 697

McIntyre, Matty, 730

McJames, Doc, 454, 458, 466, 507, 509, 528, 688, 695, 698

McKean, Ed, 028, 095, 178, 183, 204, 206, 264, 292, 566, 654, 699

McKechnie, Bill, 655

McKeon, Larry, 464, 494, 678, 679, 680, 682, 683, 685

McLain, Denny, 439, 440, 441, 442, 461, 462, 468, 469, 475, 476, 495, 496, 504, 505, 514, 538

McLain, Joe, 731

McLean, Larry, 580

McLemore, Mark, 021, 037, 082, 154, 555, 730

McMahon, Don, 371, 372, 399, 417, 418, 419, 420, 532

McMahon, Sadie, 378, 401, 405, 412, 492, 508, 518, 584, 637

McManus, Marty, 356, 601

McMillan, Roy, 048, 563, 564, 565, 567, 568, 616

McMullen, Ken, 048, 101, 533, 561, 562

McNabb, Edgar, 501

McNally, Dave, 015, 376, 385, 391, 394, 397, 408, 429, 443, 452, 463, 482, 484, 504, 506, 523, 526, 528, 731

McNulty, Pat, 646

McPhee, Bid, 004, 020, 026, 028, 054, 056, 081, 087, 095, 160, 162, 183, 203, 206, 233, 236, 551, 552, 553, 554, 587, 601, 640, 654, 704

McPherson, John, 521

McQuillan, George, 392, 393, 442, 471, 472, 531, 687, 689, 690, 691, 692, 696

McQuinn, George, 280, 281, 546, 550

McRae, Brian, 337, 573, 730

McRae, Hal, 024, 111, 199, 201, 241, 337, 709

McReynolds, Kevin, 573, 649

McTamany, Jim, 154, 233, 236, 248, 254, 654

McVey, Cal, 208, 280, 281

Meadows, Lee, 387, 466, 582

Mecir, Jim, 146, 731

Medwick, Joe, 012, 017, 022, 024, 030, 032, 040, 044, 052, 060, 064, 086, 091, 094, 130, 161, 172, 189, 191, 199, 201, 211, 221, 229, 231, 239, 241, 244, 246, 266, 279, 291, 367, 730

Meeker, Roy, 148

Meekin, Jouett, 102, 159, 162, 450, 451, 454, 457, 458, 461, 462, 491, 492, 507, 517, 528

Meinke, Frank, 248, 634, 636

Mejias, Roman, 618, 730

Mejias, Sam, 737

Mele, Sam, 672

Melendez, Luis, 533

Melillo, Oscar, 172, 646, 730, 552, 553, 556, 600

Melton, Bill, 607

Melton, Cliff, 687

Mench, Kevin, 172, 284

Mendoza, Mario, 046

Menefee, Jock, 465, 466, 645

Menke, Denis, 165, 344

Merced, Orlando, 101, 126, 308

Mercer, Win, 362, 428, 450, 451, 466, 509, 517, 525, 584, 645, 688, 689, 690, 692, 695

Murray, Eddie, 001, 002, 005, 006, 009, 010, 013, 015, 018, 021, 022, 025, 033, 037, 041, 045, 050, 053, 054, 057, 058, 061, 062, 065, 066, 071, 074, 077, 079, 082, 083, 089, 090, 093, 097, 100, 104, 120, 123, 137, 138, 142, 145, 163, 212, 232, 237, 242, 247, 258, 259, 302, 314, 330, 331, 332, 339, 367, 545, 546, 547, 548, 549, 550, 593, 646, 674, 735, 736, 739

Murray, George, 646

Murray, Ray, 734

Murray, Red, 206

Murray, Rich, 339

Murrell, Ivan, 738

Murton, Matt, 161

Muser, Tony, 737

Musial , Stan, 001, 002, 003, 006, 007, 010, 011, 015, 018, 019, 022, 023, 026, 027, 030, 031, 034, 035, 038, 039, 042, 043, 050, 051, 054, 055, 058, 059, 062, 063, 071, 079, 080, 086, 087, 088, 089, 090, 091, 093, 094, 096, 097, 098, 114, 117, 118, 119, 121, 128, 129, 130, 131, 137, 145, 172, 189, 190, 199, 200, 219, 220, 224, 225, 239, 240, 244, 245, 259, 265, 267, 271, 280, 281, 283, 291, 331, 332, 341, 369, 703, 704

Mussina, Mike, 375, 384, 389, 390, 406, 407, 409, 410, 414, 415, 436, 438, 511, 543, 585

Myer, Buddy, 552, 553, 556, 601, 602

Myers, Al, 554, 654

Myers, Elmer, 015, 466, 491, 492, 688, 690, 692, 694

Myers, Hap, 700

Myers, Hy, 196, 204, 206

Myers, Mike, 371, 373, 417, 446, 448, 487, 675

Myers, Randy, 373, 398, 400, 417, 419, 478, 480, 646

N

Nabors, Jack, 521

Naehring, Tim, 151, 172

Nagy, Charles, 731

Nash, Billy, 557, 558, 559, 560, 562, 608

Nathan, Joe, 478, 479, 731

Navarro, Jaime, 731

Naylor, Rollie, 466

Neagle, Denny, 391, 411, 731

Neal, Charlie, 730

Neal, Offa, 085

Nealon, Jim, 261

Needham, Tom, 046

Nehf, Art, 379, 385, 391, 394, 522, 528, 586, 639

Nelson, Dave, 730

Nelson, Jeff, 371, 372, 417

Nelson, Roger, 504, 505

Nen, Robb, 398, 399, 478, 479

Nettles, Graig, 001, 003, 007, 048, 051, 070, 075, 080, 097, 098, 101, 106, 114, 119, 137, 138, 145, 154, 156, 284, 319, 330, 331, 332, 339, 341, 557, 558, 559, 560, 561, 562, 607, 609, 735, 736, 739

Nettles, Jim, 156, 339

Neun, Johnny, 588, 643

Nevin, Phil, 300, 319, 342, 343

Newcombe, Don, 102, 315, 362, 389, 390, 522, 645

Newhouser, Hal, 376, 379, 382, 385, 388, 391, 394, 397, 402, 404, 408, 443, 455, 461, 463, 473, 477, 493, 495, 497, 498, 510, 511, 529, 634, 636

Newman, Fred, 731

Newsom, Bobo, 375, 381, 386, 387, 402, 403, 407, 415, 455, 491, 492, 513, 518, 533, 688, 694, 701, 734

Newton, Doc, 509

Nicholls, Simon, 672, 730

Nichols, Kid, 146, 374, 375, 377, 378, 380, 381, 383, 384, 386, 387, 389, 390, 395, 396, 405, 412, 413, 414, 415, 428, 430, 433, 434, 437, 450, 451, 454, 457, 458, 461, 462, 474, 513, 517, 524, 525, 527, 528, 529, 582, 583, 634, 636, 677, 681, 682, 683, 684

Nichols, Tricky, 521

Nicholson, Bill, 114

Nicholson, Dave, 046, 249, 251

Nicol, Hugh, 570, 621, 647, 654

Niekro, Joe, 372, 374, 375, 381, 384, 386, 387, 402, 403, 416, 424, 437, 507, 511, 583

Niekro, Phil, 371, 372, 374, 375, 380, 381, 383, 384, 386, 387, 395, 396, 402, 403, 406, 407, 414, 415, 416, 424, 428, 432, 434, 436, 437, 450, 451, 491, 492, 496, 511, 514, 516, 520, 582, 583, 586, 634, 636, 701, 703, 717, 731, 734

Nieman, Butch, 308

Nieves , Melvin, 252

Niggeling, Johnny, 734

Niles, Harry, 621

Nilsson, Dave, 175, 730

Nixon, Otis, 197, 573, 640, 643

Nixon, Trot, 730

S

Schmidt, Mike, 001, 004, 008, 036, 038, 040, 042, 044, 050, 052, 056, 058, 060, 062, 064, 074, 076, 079, 081, 083, 088, 092, 097, 099, 106, 117, 122, 135, 136, 142, 158, 164, 221, 226, 249, 251, 257, 259, 319, 328, 329, 330, 331, 557, 558, 559, 560, 561, 562, 607, 609, 704

Schmidt, Willard, 147, 177

Schmitz, Johnny, 146, 167

Schneider, Brian, 625, 628

Schneider, Pete, 535

Schoendienst, Red, 005, 009, 013, 021, 025, 029, 033, 057, 065, 072, 182, 192, 197, 202, 212, 293, 364, 365, 551, 552, 553, 555, 556, 602

Schoeneck, Jumbo, 672

Schoeneweis, Scott, 448

Schofield, Dick, 047, 730

Schofield Jr., Dick, 147, 567, 568, 613, 616

Schreckengost, Ossee, 578

Schriver, Pop, 578

Schulte, Frank, 205, 260, 300, 642

Schulz, Al, 493

Schumacher, Hal, 102, 315

Schupp, Ferdie, 159

Schwall, Don, 731

Scioscia, Mike, 575, 577, 579, 630

Score, Herb, 482, 484, 493, 497, 498, 528, 693, 694

Scott, Deacon, 131

Scott, Ed, 688, 690, 692, 695

Scott, Everett, 563, 564, 565, 615

Scott, George, 071, 071, 076, 271, 545, 546, 547, 548, 550, 590, 591, 650, 674

Scott, Jack, 423

Scott, Jim, 392, 393, 441, 442, 444, 515

Scott, Mike, 482, 483, 495, 496, 504, 505

Scott, Rodney, 655

Seaton, Tom, 645, 731

Seaver, Tom, 374, 375, 380, 381, 383, 384, 386, 387, 395, 396, 402, 403, 406, 407, 410, 413, 414, 415, 416, 426, 429, 431, 432, 433, 434, 436, 437, 438, 439, 440, 441, 442, 495, 496, 505, 511, 518, 530, 536, 538, 583, 586

Sebring, Jimmy, 623

Secory, Frank, 174

Seerey, Pat, 114, 158, 164

Seery, Emmett, 248, 572, 665

Segui, David, 037, 041, 045, 202, 212, 263, 549, 589, 592

Segui, Diego, 731

Seitzer, Kevin, 656, 657, 660, 666, 668, 671

Selbach, Kip, 028, 172, 204, 206, 572, 574, 662

Sele, Aaron, 731

Selkirk, George, 155, 356

Selma, Dick, 146, 731

Seminick, Andy, 175, 627

Severeid, Hank, 072, 576

Seward, Ed, 401, 481, 508, 511, 524, 529, 677, 678, 679, 680, 682, 684, 685, 697

Sewell, Joe, 031, 035, 072, 094, 131, 200, 615, 666, 669, 740

Sewell, Luke, 575, 576, 578, 580, 740

Sewell, Rip, 015

Sewell, Tom, 740

Sexson, Richie, 073, 120, 151, 249, 251, 298, 300, 317, 356

Seybold, Socks, 668

Seymour, Cy, 172, 205, 267, 427, 452, 459, 463, 491, 493, 509, 528, 535, 572, 574, 623

Shafer, Orator, 198, 208, 271, 570, 572, 621

Shallix, Gus, 508, 697

Shamsky, Art, 169, 302

Shanks, Howard, 608

Shantz, Bobby, 443, 463, 586, 634, 636, 731

Shaute, Joe, 362

Shaw, Al, 162

Shaw, Dupee, 379, 394, 405, 440, 445, 449, 464, 494, 518, 529, 536

Shaw, Jeff, 398, 399, 478, 479

Shawkey, Bob, 731

Sheckard, Jimmy, 080, 162, 168, 172, 255, 256, 340, 569, 570, 572, 574, 621, 623, 640, 642, 648, 655, 730

Sheehan, Tom, 521

Sheely, Earl, 036, 172, 594

Sheets, Ben, 049, 496, 503, 536

Sheets, Larry, 139, 342, 343, 344

Sheffield, Gary, 008, 034, 036, 038, 040, 042, 044, 050, 052, 056, 060, 064, 070, 078, 079, 081, 088, 097, 099, 113, 118, 121, 126, 128, 146, 151, 153, 175, 216, 221, 226, 255, 257, 283, 321, 323, 329, 330, 331, 332, 356, 604, 605

Virtue, Jake, 203, 207

Visner, Joe, 203, 205

Vitt, Ossie, 607, 730

Vizcaino, Jose, 279, 650

Vizquel, Omar, 001, 005, 009, 013, 021, 057, 065, 082, 154, 212, 563, 564, 565, 567, 568, 610, 613, 655

Voiselle, Bill, 532, 687, 689, 692

Vollmer, Clyde, 149, 155, 160

Vosmik, Joe, 032, 191, 206, 667, 668

W

Waddell, Rube, 379, 382, 385, 388, 391, 392, 394, 395, 397, 406, 408, 409, 411, 426, 428, 438, 439, 440, 441, 443, 444, 450, 452, 457, 459, 463, 471, 473, 477, 495, 497, 510, 515, 522, 530, 532, 584

Wadsworth, Jack, 512, 539, 541

Wagner, Billy, 147, 373, 398, 400, 448, 478, 480, 731

Wagner, Heinie, 566, 614, 615

Wagner, Honus, 001, 002, 004, 006, 008, 010, 012, 015, 018, 020, 022, 024, 026, 028, 030, 032, 036, 044, 050, 052, 054, 056, 058, 060, 062, 064, 078, 081, 086, 088, 089, 090, 093, 095, 096, 125, 138, 204, 206, 211, 267, 332, 358, 563, 564, 565, 566, 640, 642, 644, 708, 709, 710, 730

Wagner, Leon, 307, 730

Wainhouse, Dave, 343

Wainright, Adam, 149

Waitkus, Eddie, 279, 549, 672

Wakefield, Dick, 660, 672, 673, 674

Wakefield, Tim, 428, 436, 514

Walberg, Rube, 388, 404, 528, 634, 636

Waldron, Irv, 666, 672, 730

Walker, Chico, 366

Walker, Curt, 172, 173, 574

Walker, Dixie, 086, 172

Walker, Gee, 146, 199, 201, 357

Walker, Harry, 271

Walker, Jamie, 448

Walker, Larry, 023, 031, 034, 035, 038, 039, 042, 043, 051, 055, 058, 059, 063, 070, 075, 078, 094, 097, 098, 110, 128, 129, 142, 172, 219, 220, 224, 225, 235, 239, 240, 244, 245, 271, 286, 288, 295, 304, 312, 323, 331, 356, 358

Walker, Tilly, 570

Walker, Todd, 279

Walkup, Jim, 521

Wallace, Bobby, 004, 008, 020, 028, 206, 563, 564, 565, 566, 614, 615

Wallach, Tim, 024, 106, 144, 557, 558, 559, 561, 562, 607, 730, 739

Walling, Denny, 148, 363

Walsh, Ed, 392, 393, 395, 396, 430, 431, 439, 440, 441, 442, 444, 450, 451, 454, 457, 458, 461, 462, 471, 472, 475, 476, 482, 483, 496, 504, 505, 517, 520, 522, 528, 529, 530, 582, 637, 638, 645, 731

Walsh, Jimmy, 172, 730

Walters, Bucky, 362, 395, 396, 403, 455, 510, 586, 634, 636, 639, 645

Walton, Jerome, 280, 281, 673

Wambsganss, Bill, 172, 293, 554, 588, 601

Waner, Lloyd, 018, 019, 031, 072, 091, 156, 172, 179, 180, 189, 190, 194, 195, 571, 622, 660, 666, 668, 708

Waner, Paul, 001, 002, 003, 006, 007, 010, 011, 015, 018, 019, 022, 023, 026, 027, 030, 031, 034, 035, 043, 051, 054, 055, 058, 059, 062, 063, 072, 080, 086, 087, 090, 091, 093, 094, 095, 156, 161, 189, 190, 194, 195, 199, 200, 204, 205, 210, 235, 277, 282, 358, 369, 569, 570, 571, 574, 662, 666, 668, 669, 708

Ward, Daryle, 308, 364

Ward, Duane, 447, 478, 479

Ward, Gary, 730

Ward, John, 019, 055, 159, 178, 183, 188, 193, 233, 292, 390, 392, 393, 405, 412, 437, 439, 440, 445, 449, 456, 460, 470, 474, 502, 566, 638, 640, 647, 654, 681, 686

Ward, Pete, 604, 605

Ward, Piggy, 160, 217

Warhop, Jack, 509, 645, 697

Warneke, Lon, 167, 390, 433, 585, 634, 636

Warner, John, 576, 578, 581, 633

Warstler, Rabbit, 154

Washburn, Ray, 731

Washington, Claudell, 075, 143, 155

Washington, Herb, 014

Waslewski, Gary, 731

Watkins, George, 172

Watson, Doc, 731

Watson, Milt, 540

Weathers, David, 371, 372, 447, 731

Weaver, Buck, 192, 196, 212, 357, 615

Weaver, Earl, 705, 706

Weaver, Farmer, 621

Weaver, Monte, 687

Weaver, Sam, 524, 678, 682, 686

Webb, Earl, 067, 199, 200

Webster, Ray, 738

Wegener, Mike, 015

Wehmeier, Herm, 055

Weidman, Stump, 146, 401, 405, 421, 464, 584

Weik, Dick, 427, 535

Weilman, Carl, 392, 394, 443

Weimer, Jake, 444, 509, 515, 528, 646, 676, 687

Weintraub, Phil, 163, 172

Weiss, Walt, 037, 172, 567

Welch, Bob, 146, 375, 407, 468, 583

Welch, Curt, 078, 152, 198, 233, 253, 572, 574, 640, 654

Welch, Mickey, 374, 375, 377, 378, 380, 381, 383, 384, 386, 387, 393, 395, 396, 401, 405, 412, 413, 414, 429, 434, 437, 445, 449, 456, 460, 470, 474, 494, 523, 524, 530, 538, 584, 677, 678, 679, 680, 682, 685

Wells, David, 376, 382, 385, 388, 391, 408, 414, 415, 416, 424, 436, 438, 499, 503, 532, 731

Wells, Vernon, 179, 181, 186, 191, 201, 241, 617, 620

Wendell, Turk, 447

Werber, Billy, 161, 172, 646

Werden, Perry, 096, 178, 183, 203, 204, 206, 548, 654, 662, 665, 669, 686, 699

Wert, Don, 561

Wertz, Vic, 146, 161, 172

West, Joe, 707

West, Max, 307

West, Sam, 571, 622

Westrum, Wes, 151, 164, 172, 625, 628, 631

Wetteland, John, 398, 399, 698

Weyhing, Gus, 374, 375, 377, 378, 380, 381, 383, 384, 386, 387, 401, 405, 412, 413, 414, 421, 428, 437, 465, 466, 490, 508, 509, 513, 524, 530, 584, 677, 678, 679, 680, 682, 684, 685, 697

Wheat, Zack, 001, 003, 007, 010, 011, 018, 019, 023, 026, 027, 031, 051, 063, 086, 089, 093, 095, 190, 271, 358, 569, 570, 571, 572, 574

Wheeler, Harry, 173

Whitaker, Lou, 007, 055, 068, 075, 080, 105, 124, 154, 165, 172, 283, 318, 551, 552, 553, 555, 556, 596, 599, 704, 708, 709

White, Bill, 180, 357, 730

White, Deacon, 072, 208, 209, 210, 218, 223, 560

White, Devon, 021, 045, 057, 061, 065, 074, 077, 100, 123, 124, 152, 154, 202, 237, 252, 571, 641, 666, 730

White, Doc, 376, 379, 382, 385, 388, 392, 394, 395, 397, 428, 430, 431, 443, 444, 463, 467, 471, 473, 477, 504, 506, 522, 528, 529, 533, 582

White, Ernie, 676

White, Frank, 105, 551, 552, 553, 555, 556, 596, 599, 704, 708, 709

White, Hal, 531

White, Rondell, 172

White, Roy, 021, 037, 045, 065, 082, 123, 187, 573, 617, 620, 704

White, Sammy, 176, 626

White, Will, 377, 378, 381, 384, 392, 393, 396, 401, 405, 412, 413, 437, 440, 445, 449, 453, 456, 460, 464, 470, 474, 508, 524, 584, 637, 677, 679, 680, 681, 682, 685, 686

Whitehead, Burgess, 600, 601

Whitehill, Earl, 376, 379, 382, 385, 388, 402, 404, 415

Whiten, Mark, 114, 158, 163, 164

Whiteside, Matt, 146

Whitfield, Fred, 101

Whiting, Ed, 359

Whitney, Art, 047, 560

Whitney, Jim, 160, 171, 362, 377, 378, 386, 387, 401, 405, 412, 413, 421, 437, 440, 445, 456, 464, 494, 502, 524, 537, 584, 634, 636, 677, 678, 679, 680, 681, 682, 685

Whitney, Pinky, 356, 356, 357, 559, 561, 603, 606, 667

Whitt, Ernie, 579

Whitted, Possum, 533

Wicker, Bob, 518, 528

Wickersham, Dave, 049

Wickland, Al, 730

Wickman, Bob, 147, 166, 167, 343, 371, 372, 398, 399, 417, 478, 479

Z

SOCIETY FOR AMERICAN BASEBALL RESEARCH

Since August 1971, when sixteen "statistorians" gathered in Cooperstown to form the Society for American Baseball Research, SABR has been committed to helping people produce and publish baseball research.

Today, SABR has more than 7,000 members worldwide. They come from all walks of life, but the one thing they all have in common is a love for the game and its history.

Members receive the latest editions of SABR's research annuals, including the *Baseball Research Journal* and *The National Pastime.* Also included is a subscription to *The SABR Bulletin,* access to online newsgroups and research forums, and other special books and publications.

SABR membership is open to everyone who is interested in baseball and its history. Annual dues are $60 US and $75 for overseas memberships. Student and senior discounts are also available. For details about the benefits of SABR membership, call **(800) 969-SABR** or visit **www.sabr.org** today!

Society for American Baseball Research
Dept BBREC
812 Huron Rd E #719
Cleveland OH 44115

(800) 969-7227
www.sabr.org